SCHOOL OF
ORIENTAL AND AFRICAN STUDIES
UNIVERSITY OF LONDON

EARLY SOUTH EAST ASIA

EARLY SOUTH EAST ASIA

ESSAYS IN ARCHAEOLOGY, HISTORY AND HISTORICAL GEOGRAPHY

EDITED BY

R. B. SMITH

Reader in the History of South East Asia in the
University of London

AND

W. WATSON

Professor of Chinese Art and Archaeology in the
University of London

OXFORD UNIVERSITY PRESS
NEW YORK   KUALA LUMPUR
1979

Oxford University Press, Walton Street, Oxford OX2 6DP

OXFORD LONDON GLASGOW NEW YORK
TORONTO MELBOURNE WELLINGTON CAPE TOWN
IBADAN NAIROBI DAR ES SALAAM LUSAKA ADDIS ABABA
KUALA LUMPUR SINGAPORE JAKARTA HONG KONG TOKYO
DELHI BOMBAY CALCUTTA MADRAS KARACHI

ISBN 0 19 713587 0

© SCHOOL OF ORIENTAL AND AFRICAN STUDIES 1979

Typeset by
Gloucester Typesetting Services Ltd.,
Printed in Great Britain
by Pitman Press, Bath

PREFACE

In the past fifteen years the study of the archaeology of South East Asia has made great strides. By comparison with the situation that existed in the 1950s, it is now possible to discern the beginnings of a new framework of chronology and cultural development within which it will eventually be possible to arrive at a complete re-assessment of the early development of the whole region. Many of the papers in the present volume insist that the subject is still in its infancy, that a great deal of research remains to be done. Nevertheless, enough progress has been made by now to justify a new survey of the later prehistory and early history of the region, in terms which will at least remove old mis-understandings and suggest new starting-points. It is not to undervalue the work of such major scholars as Coedès, Heine-Geldern or Van Heekeren, to suggest that there is need to re-examine their pioneer interpretations—many of which were avowedly speculative but which have subsequently become accepted as 'established'. It is a measure of the significance of the new research that practically all the accounts of early South East Asia appearing in the introductory chapters of textbooks on the region are now hopelessly out of date.

It is the object of the present volume to remedy this deficiency by collecting together a series of papers on major aspects of the subject which have been affected by recent research, and to present the conclusions that have so far emerged from the excavations of new sites and the pursuit of new lines of enquiry. It is in the nature of the subject that there should be contributions from a wide range of authors. In the present state of knowledge, no one specialist could claim sufficient direct experience of all the research involved to be able to produce an up-to-date synthesis on his own. The papers are, for the most part, those submitted to a Colloquy on Early South East Asia held at the School of Oriental and African Studies, London, in September 1973. The object of the Colloquy was to bring together specialists in the field in order to discuss the results of recent research and to try to reconcile some of the differences of opinion to which the interpretation of that research has given rise. It would be going too far to claim that the discussions resulted in a final settlement of the many points of controversy which have been raised during the past decade. But all agreed that a new perspective is required. From the collection of papers as a whole, it is believed that a new perspective does in fact emerge.

South East Asia is a region which has tended in the past to be treated as merely a meeting-point of cultural influences derived from neighbouring parts of the world: as a southward extension of East Asia or as an eastward extension of 'India'. This tendency has been especially marked in relation to periods before about 1000 A.D. for which the principal written source materials are in Chinese, in Sanskrit, or at least in scripts derived from ancient India. It has been reinforced by the fact that such materials are accessible only to scholars proficient in either Chinese or Sanskrit, many of whom have been primarily specialists on the countries to which those languages belong. The importance of Indian cultural influence in the region as a whole, and of Chinese influence in certain areas, is not to be denied. But there is room now for an interpretation which will place rather less emphasis on that influence, and rather more on the continuity of cultural development within South East Asia itself. It would be possible, after all, to insist that Western Europe too, in a comparable period of its early development, experienced profound cultural influences from Egypt and Mesopotamia, as well as from the Greek region: but no one pretends that Western Europe should for that reason be regarded as no more than a field for the reception of cultures derived from elsewhere. Why then should we not treat South East Asia as an equally autonomous region whose archaeological development can be seen in terms of its own prehistory, followed by the growth of its own distinctive civilization? Like Western Europe, South East Asia has its own character (which allows nevertheless for considerably cultural diversity within the region), and the time has come when its prehistory and early history can be presented in such a way as to allow the region a perspective of its own. Within this new perspective it is possible to see South East Asian civilization not as an alien implantation coming from India or from China, but as something which grew out of developed prehistoric cultures whose origins go back at least to the third millennium B.C. Some scholars, though not all, are of the opinion that South East Asia developed bronze metallurgy at an even earlier date than its first known occurrence in either India or China. Certainly the beginnings of ceramics and metallurgy in the lowland areas of the region must be traced back far beyond the period when, in the early centuries A.D. recognizably Indian or Chinese cultural influences began to appear there.

In this respect it might be said that the London Colloquy attempted to create a new balance in the study of early South East Asia, by bringing to bear the results of recent prehistoric research on the problems which have for so long been discussed by historians, historical geographers and epigraphists. The initial intention was to examine the periods of the first millennium B.C. and the first millennium A.D. and to explore the question of cultural continuity between the two. In order to consider the question how far the region—or certain parts of it—had progressed technologically and materially by 1000 B.C. it became necessary also to take into account evidence from certain sites whose early levels may well go back beyond 2000 B.C. For without necessarily reaching final decisions on the most controversial aspects of their chronology, the Colloquy established beyond doubt that the results from excavations at those sites have already transformed our ideas about the picture of the region as it was during the first millennium B.C. The recognition of this fact was our principal starting-point. It would be a mistake however, to suppose that the only revisions of old interpretations are to be sought in the prehistoric field. It is evident that new research on the epigraphy, art history and Chinese documentation concerning the first millennium A.D. will require a reassessment of that period too. The need to look at South East Asia in its own terms means that we must abandon old assumptions about the nature of states and other institutions in the earliest period of South East Asian history (or proto-history), and ask new questions about the origins of cities, states and other forms of organization and identity in the region. Whilst some of the papers in the later part of the book are concerned with re-examining the historical evidence, others attempt a more theoretical approach to these questions. Taken as a whole, the collection of papers will, it is hoped, open up new possibilities in the spheres of both research and interpretation.

During the 1950s and early 1960s, the initiative in these different areas of excavation was taken mainly by European and American archaeologists. In the past ten years, however, there has been a great upsurge in the development of archaeological work, including excavation, by South East Asian scholars. It was with great pleasure that the London Colloquy welcomed a number of these scholars, and contributions by them appear in the present volume. They represent a small part of the growing body of work by South East Asian archaeologists, some of whose results will appear from the bibliography, whilst others still await publication. It will be recognized that, as has long been the case with China and Japan, keeping pace with archaeological discovery in South East Asia will in future require that European and American specialists be familiar with the principal languages of the region.

The volume is divided into two parts, each with its own Introduction. Part I deals, in principle, with the later prehistory of South East Asia; Part II with the early history of the region, in the first millennium A.D. But inevitably there is some measure of overlap between them. Appendices at the end include a check-list of published Carbon-14 datings from South East Asia, and a list of bronze drums of Heger's Type I.

Some inconsistency in the spelling of place names will be noticed between one paper and another, since in some cases we have not challenged the variants preferred by our authors.

We express our gratitude to the school of Oriental and African Studies for meeting the cost of publication of this volume.

Although complete standardisation has not been possible throughout the book, the editors have made every effort to ensure that papers are printed as submitted. However, owing to circumstances beyond their control, it is particularly regretted that it has not been possible to reproduce the Vietnamese national script correctly in Mr. Jeremy Davidson's papers.

R. B. SMITH
W. WATSON

CONTENTS

PART I
THE LATER PREHISTORY OF SOUTH EAST ASIA

PART II
SOUTH EAST ASIA IN THE FIRST MILLENNIUM A.D.

LIST OF MAPS

LIST OF FIGURES

LIST OF PLATES

(between pp. 268–9)

CONTRIBUTORS

(*Members of Organizing Committee for the London Colloquy)

D. T. BAYARD	Senior Lecturer in Prehistory, University of Otago, Dunedin.
BOECHARI	Deputy Dean for Academic Affairs, Faculty of Letters, University of Indonesia, Jakarta.
B. BRONSON	Assistant Curator for Asian Archaeology and Ethnology, Field Museum of Natural History, Chicago.
J. P. CARBONNEL	Laboratoire de Géologie Dynamique, Université de Paris VI.
*A. H. CHRISTIE	Lecturer in South East Asian Archaeology, School of Oriental and African Studies, London.
*J. H. G. S. DAVIDSON	Lecturer in Vietnamese, School of Oriental and African Studies, London.
J. G. DE CASPARIS	Reader in the History of South and South East Asia, School of Oriental and African Studies, London.
MAGDALENE VON DEWALL	Südasien-Institut der Universität Heidelberg. (Seminar für Ethnologie).
R. B. FOX	Presidential Assistant on Anthropology, Pambansang Museo, Manila.
*I. C. GLOVER	Lecturer in Archaeology, Institute of Archaeology, University of London.
JUDITH M. JACOB	Lecturer in Cambodian, School of Oriental and African Studies, London.
C. JACQUES	Directeur des Études, Ecole Pratique des Hautes Études, University of Paris.
H. H. E. LOOFS	Reader in Asian Civilizations, Australian National University, Canberra.
ELIZABETH LYONS	Project Specialist in Art and Archaeology, Ford Foundation, Bangkok.
R. C. Y. NG.	Lecturer in Geography with reference to South East Asia, School of Oriental and African Studies, London.

Contributors

NIKOM SUTHIRAGSA	*National Museum, Bangkok.*
B. A. V. PEACOCK	*Lecturer in History, University of Malaya, Kuala Lumpur.*
MICHÈLE PIRAZZOLI-T'SERSTEVENS	*Musée Guimet, Paris.*
I. R. SELIMKHANOV	*Institute for History, Baku, USSR.*
*R. B. SMITH	*Reader in the History of South East Asia, School of Oriental and African Studies, London.*
SOEKMONO	*National Archaeological Institute of Indonesia, Jakarta.*
W. G. SOLHEIM II	*Professor of Anthropology, University of Hawaii, Honolulu.*
P. SØRENSEN	*Scandinavian Institute of Asian Studies, Lampang, Thailand.*
M. C. SUBHADRADIS DISKUL	*Dean of the Faculty of Archaeology, Silpakorn University, Bangkok.*
VEERAPAN MALEIPAN	*Lecturer in Archaeology, Silpakorn University, Bangkok.*
*W. WATSON	*Professor of Chinese Art and Archaeology, and Head of the Percival David Foundation, School of Oriental and African Studies, London.*
P. WHEATLEY	*Professor of Geography and of Social Thought, University of Chicago.*
O. W. WOLTERS	*Professor of History, Cornell University.*

PART I

THE LATER PREHISTORY OF SOUTH EAST ASIA

Introduction

THE initial intention of the organizers of the London Colloquy was to consider principally the first millennium B.C. and the first millennium A.D., in the belief that a span of two thousand years would be sufficiently great to serve as a context for studying the problem of continuity between the prehistoric and early historic societies of the region. However, it is clear from the results of recent research in Thailand and elsewhere that no such chronological neatness is permissible in the present state of our knowledge. The Colloquy was to some extent successful in reducing the degree of controversy which has surrounded several of the excavations at South East Asian sites, but it cannot be denied that there are some questions which must remain open at the present time. The question whether rice was first domesticated in South East Asia need not be raised here: there seems little doubt now that rice was being cultivated in both South East Asia and China well before 2000 B.C. Nor is it possible to settle finally the chronology of the first development of bronze metallurgy in the region. It is claimed, on the evidence of an increasing number of radiocarbon tests, that bronze was first cast in the north of Thailand at a hitherto unsuspected early date: possibly before 2000 B.C., with greater probability before 1000 B.C. This conclusion rests chiefly on the intensive study of a single site (that of Non Nok Tha—see the paper by Bayard) and is involved in complex problems of stratigraphy. Many will look to the similar study of comparable sites, the establishment of the evidence *in extenso*, before giving their assent to this revolutionary conclusion on the course of technological progress in an area once regarded as remote from the main highways of progress in Asia. But whatever conclusion the controversy may reach, and whatever precise dates may be established, the old view that the introduction of advanced bronze-working was in any sense an aspect of the Hinduisation of South East Asia, or took place only shortly before that process began, is now shown to be wholly mistaken. It is very likely that there were prehistoric contacts between India and the western parts of South East Asia, and between China and the eastern parts of the area, before the influence of Indian colonization and religion began to be felt. Even iron would appear to have been first used in the region, perhaps having spread there from India, several hundred years before we find the first evidence of Hinduism or Buddhism.

II

In the development of research into South East Asian prehistory, as in other parts of the world, it is possible to distinguish between two different approaches or tendencies each producing its own kind of contribution to the overall picture. One approach is centred upon the collection and analysis of individual finds, their types and distribution, whilst the other concentrates upon the sequences of cultures suggested by the excavation of specific sites. Both approaches are necessary, but either of them on its own must suffer from severe limitations. It is important to recognize that during the first half of the twentieth century, the picture of South East Asia which was presented by prehistorians was to a very large extent based upon only the first approach. It is true that there were a number of excavations during the 1920s and 1930s, but the majority of them were unskilled, undertaken by archaeologists more interested in recording finds than in establishing stratigraphy. Moreover a great many of the finds which entered into the work of comparative analysis were studied in museums, and their original provenance was often only very approximately known. With the development of more scientific excavation in South East Asia since the mid-1950s, some of the theories that were based only on the study of finds have come to be challenged.

At least three major ideas in the growth of South East Asian prehistory (down to the 1950s) can be seen to stem almost entirely from typological study of artefacts and their distribution:

(1) Heine-Geldern and others attached great importance to distinctions between three types of stone adze or axe: the 'round', the 'shouldered', and the 'quadrangular', whose distribution on the map must certainly have some significance for the overall pattern of neolithic cultures throughout East and South East Asia. But the time-scale involved would now seem to be much longer than was once thought, and the assumptions of the *Kulturkreis* philosophy of Heine-Geldern and his contemporaries of the German and Austrian Schools, whereby culture-movement is established from the distribution of a discrete set of important artefacts, are no longer acceptable to the majority of archaeologists and prehistorians. In this case especially, the notion that axe-types may be related to ethno-linguistic groups must be discarded, as a primary proposition. Heine-Geldern sought to use this distinction between axe-types to create a basic framework for the prehistory of the region: it is now clear that such an approach is far too simple, and those of his conclusions which depended upon it must be viewed with great scepticism. Likewise his attempt to distinguish between 'older' and 'younger' megalithic traditions finds no support in recent interpretations.

(2) The same generation of scholars produced a picture of the South East Asian Bronze Age which stemmed very largely from the study of bronze

drums, whose shape and decorative styles were first systematically analysed by F. Heger in 1902. He inclined to the view that the earlier type of drum was diffused widely over South East Asia, the Malayan archipelago and Java, from a centre of invention situated in the Yünnan-Kweichow region of south-west China. Drums of Heger's type I were found at Dong-son in the Thanh-hoa province of north Viet-Nam in 1924, when Pajot excavated a group of graves containing these and other distinctive southern bronzes alongside material emanating from the pure Chinese tradition and possibly imported from the north. As to the date of this eponymous site of what has come to be called the Dong-son culture—used broadly to denote the whole phenomenon of bronze-age culture in South East Asia and the islands—Goloubew favoured the first century A.D., and Karlgren afterwards argued more convincingly for the first century B.C. Karlgren (1942) further associated the artistic component of the Dong-son culture with his Huai tradition of metropolitan China, and therefore looked for the foundation of the South East Asian tradition as early as the fifth century B.C. Recent work has tended to confirm the late second or first century B.C. date for the early drums and the Dong-son graves, while Karlgren's thesis on the early constitution of the Dong-son artistic tradition remains questionable, since his argument on this point rested on minor elements of decoration (circles, triangles, spirals and the like). These were certainly widely employed in south China from an early date, but cannot prove such ancient ancestry for the characteristic complex designs and plastic motifs of Dong-son—that is, for the very features by which the drums and other bronzes are brought into a single tradition. Nevertheless it is acknowledged that to explain the dispersal of Heger's type I drums, it may be necessary to postulate an undiscovered prototype (undiscovered perhaps because it was manufactured out of perishable material) which must be of greater age.

The concept of Dong-son culture once established, controversy raged about its possible date and origins, with a sharp conflict between those who believed that it could be traced back to early 'Western' influences in the region, and those who saw it as emanating from 'China'. But it is now clear that the drums are evidence of travel, and possibly of trade, rather than of cultural diffusion; that they could be associated with diverse cultural contexts, and are not in themselves evidence of a period of wholesale uniformity at a certain stage of cultural evolution in South East Asia. The South East Asian Bronze Age must now be seen as much more complicated than was once imagined. In the light of evidence which makes it possible to relate drums and other finds to archaeological contexts as well as to one another, and especially in the light of new evidence from excavations in northern Viet-Nam, some see the 'drum' culture of

Dongson and other places as the culmination of a long cultural evolution stretching back into the second millennium B.C.

(3) A third idea which has grown out of the study of finds is that of the pottery tradition. The classification of techniques and decorative principles have developed side by side with the expansion of excavation, so that it is possible to relate a growing quantity of South East Asian prehistoric pottery to specific sites and their stratigraphies. The pioneer in this field was W. G. Solheim II, who in the 1950s identified a pottery tradition linking material from Kalanay (in the Philippines) with that from Sa-huynh (central Viet-Nam), which was clearly of the greatest importance for the later prehistory of those areas. Since then, other distinctive pottery traditions have emerged from excavations in different regions, and it is clear once again that South East Asian prehistory must be recognized as much more complex and diversified than was once supposed.

III

The transformation of the subject began with the arrival on the scene of a new generation of archaeologists in the 1950s, and a complete revision of the old theories became necessary as a result of subsequent work during the 1960s. The application of increasingly strict principles of stratigraphy, combined with the growing use of scientific dating methods, made it possible to establish cultural sequences for certain sites. A new chronological dimension was thus introduced, on the basis of which it was possible to challenge the assumptions of those who had worked mainly with typological and distributional evidence.

The years 1954–7 marked a turning-point in certain areas. It was then that R. B. Fox and A. Evangelista began working in the Philippines, with excavations of the Bato Caves and the caves of Cagraray Island. Fox followed up that work with the very important excavations of the Tabon and related caves on Palawan Island in the 1960s. A little farther south, in Borneo, T. and B. Harrisson in 1957 began an exploration of the Niah Cave complex which was to last for ten years. Other caves were excavated in western Malaysia: Gua Cha (Kelantan) by G. de G. Sieveking in 1954, and Gua Kechil (Pahang) by F. L. Dunn in 1963. Also during the 1950s, work on pottery was being undertaken by W. G. Solheim II and by B. A. V. Peacock, in relation to the Philippines, Viet-Nam and Malaysia.

During the 1960s excavation became more widespread, though it would be foolish to pretend that there is not still a great deal to be done. In Indonesia, important work was undertaken by Indonesian archaeologists, notably R. P. Soejono (whose excavation at Gilimanuk, Bali, forms the subject of a paper in the present volume). There was also work by an Australian-Indonesian group, which included I. C. Glover, in southern Sulawesi; whilst Glover also excavated some cave sites in Portuguese Timor. The developing picture of archaeology in these maritime areas of South East Asia is covered in the present volume by contributions from Glover, Peacock and Fox; whilst a note on Sumatra is added by B. Bronson, based on fieldwork there in 1972.

In the countries of mainland South East Asia, important work has been undertaken in Viet-Nam and Thailand, and to a lesser extent in Cambodia. The work of the Vietnamese archaeologists since 1954, hitherto accessible only to those who read Vietnamese, can be seen from a paper by J. H. C. S. Davidson to be of crucial importance for our understanding of the later prehistory of that area, and of the origins of the Dong-son culture. Davidson has also summarized the results of work by French archaeologists, notably E. Saurin and P. Fontaine, in south Viet-Nam during the 1960s; and a short paper by J. P. Carbonnel indicates the work done by R. and C. Mourer and others in Cambodia during the same period. But it is in Thailand that excavation has produced the most startling challenges to old images of South East Asian prehistory, and no apology is necessary for the fact that a disproportionate amount of space in the present volume is given to that area.

In central Thailand, the Thai-Danish archaeological expedition of 1960–2, led by P. Sørensen, was responsible for important excavations at two sites in Kanchanaburi province: Ban Kao and the Ongbah Cave. A few years later, a Thai-British team led by W. Watson and H. H. E. Loofs was responsible for excavating the sites of Kok Charoen (Lopburi province) and Tha Muang (U Thong), the latter an important site in relation to the protohistoric period to be covered in Part II. The Ban Kao excavation has been reported upon in great detail by Sørensen; in the present volume he discusses the bronze drums found at Ongbah Cave. W. Watson considers the significance of the Kok Charoen site in relation to the general picture of the later prehistory of the area. A number of other important sites were found in north-east Thailand, where in 1964 W. G. Solheim II took the initiative in organizing a field survey of localities about to be flooded by the reservoirs of the Mekong Development Project. It was this survey which led to the identification of the now famous site at Non Nok Tha, where in 1966 and 1968 Solheim and D. T. Bayard found a cultural sequence which seemed to indicate that bronze was being worked at a remarkably early date. Other evidence pointing towards a similar conclusion, that the South East Asian Bronze Age began long before anyone had supposed, came from a nearby site at Non Nong Chik, excavated by R. H. Parker and C. F. Higham in 1970, and from another famous site at Ban Chieng, near Udorn. In the present volume, Bayard discusses the significance of his results from Non Nok Tha, while Nikhom Suthiragsa presents a summary of his findings during the 1972 excavations at Ban Chieng. The latter site is well known as the source of large quantities of red-painted pottery, mostly dug by collectors or by local farmers, which has acquired a significant market value during the past few years—to the detriment of archaeological knowledge.

In the context of all this excavation, it is possible for the analysis of artifacts, of pottery, and of decorative metalwork, to be seen in a new light. W. G. Solheim II and M. Ayres present a paper dealing with pottery from northeast Thailand, with special reference to the blackware found at the late prehistoric site of Phimai. Other aspects of the comparative study of pottery from the Thai area are covered by papers dealing with the sites already mentioned. It is now possible to use pottery comparisons as a means of relating one site to another; but it must be admitted that so far no general sequence of pottery styles or types can be discerned, such as has been established in India during the past two or three decades. Until a quite late period, one is impressed much more by the great local diversity of pottery traditions, especially in South East Asia, especially in mainland areas.

Likewise several papers cover aspects of the problem of bronze drums, but in a different spirit from that which pervaded earlier work on the 'Dong-son civilization'. Sørensen and Peacock both deal with drums which have been excavated from recorded archaeological contexts, and not merely collected. M. Pirazzoli-t'Serstevens considers the possible social and ritual significance of the drums found at the Yünnan site of Shi-zhai-shan, and Davidson also considers this aspect of the drums from Tongking and Thanh-hoa. An appendix attempts to list as many as possible of the Heger type I drums found throughout South East Asia. The importance of the drums is still apparent, but their significance must now be considered in different ways. The same may be said of the notorious 'megaliths', which are discussed in a paper by A. H. Christie. The elaborate theories of Heine-Geldern must certainly be abandoned, but the term does nevertheless indicate the presence of a number of actual remains whose importance should not be overlooked, and which had ritual significance. In another paper relating to the analysis of finds, M. von Dewall applies a method of analysis of decorative styles to indicate a number of distinctions between different regions, which suggests yet another dimension of what must now be recognized as a highly complex South East Asian Bronze Age.

IV

While many questions cannot yet be answered with precision, it becomes clear from the papers that several areas of South East Asia were experiencing important changes during the second millennium B.C.: changes which had their origins before 2000 B.C. The picture cannot be drawn with full confidence, either chronologically or geographically, for the amount of relevant excavation has so far been limited to certain areas. In particular, we must leave Burma out of account at the present time, although it may well have been an area of key importance in relations between Central South East Asia and the Indian sub-continent even in prehistoric times

In the central part of mainland South East Asia, the area of present-day Thailand, there is evidence of settled life at a number of lowland sites well before 1000 B.C.: at Non Nok Tha, Non Nong Chik and Ban Chieng in north east Thailand, and at Kok Charoen and Ban Kao farther west. A burial which may be comparable in date to those found at Kok Charoen was excavated by Veerapan Maleipan at Sab Champa, and is described briefly in his paper in Part II below. Whilst controversy still surrounds some of the dates reported from these sites, on the basis of radiocarbon and thermoluminescence tests, the overall impact of the evidence is difficult to deny. Between them these sites have produced at least fourteen radiocarbon dates and several thermo-luminescence dates which fall within the second millennium B.C. It is impossible to reject the conclusion that a settled social life existed in these lowland places by that time. It was characterized by a diversity of pottery traditions, and by inhumation burials in which pottery vessels and stone (and eventually bronze) tools were buried with the corpse; although it has been suggested that some of the burials at Ban Kao belong to a period somewhat later than 1000 B.C. In due course it will be possible to build up a much more detailed picture of the material culture of these settlements; for the time being we must be content to recognize their existence. They represent the first step of South East Asia towards an early civilization which would appear to owe nothing at all to formal Indian influences.

Settled life continued at these sites after 1000 B.C., though all of them appear to have been abandoned by the early part of the first millennium A.D. The most important problem which can be identified in this region during the first millennium B.C. is that of the precise date of the introduction of iron. Two pieces of iron were found in burials at Ban Kao (Thailand), a discovery which led certain commentators on that excavation to place the date of the burials later than that claimed for them by the excavators. It seems unlikely, in any event, that the Ban Kao settlement of the second millennium B.C. belonged to iron-using people. On the other hand a series of thermolumines-cence datings on pottery found at several sites in Central Thailand has led B. Bronson to argue for the introduction of iron into that area well before 500 B.C.: possibly at a date comparable to its first appearance in India. The sites in question—at Chansen and near Lopburi—are on lower ground than the sites known to have been occupied several centuries earlier. But the argument for this dating is less secure than the dates which have been claimed for the first appearance of bronze. We have no *radiocarbon* evidence which can be claimed to date the first appearance of iron in either central or north-east Thailand. The earliest radiocarbon dates for South East Asian contexts containing iron come from southern Viet-Nam and from Palawan Island: the former a date of 600–300 B.C. from a jar-burial at Phu-hoa; the latter a date in the third–second century B.C. also for a jar-burial. These dates would not contradict the impression that iron technology may have spread eastwards, perhaps from India, during the centuries before 200 B.C. But an argued date of 800 B.C. for iron in central Thailand (cf. B. Bronson's paper in Part II) has yet to be substantiated. It is possible that bronze was still used for weapons long after iron had begun to be adopted for agricultural purposes, and that the decorated bronze weapons from various parts of South East Asia belong to a period when iron was already in use in certain lowland areas.

Whatever the chronology of the introduction of iron, its consequence was almost certainly the expansion of settlement into many lowland areas which had not previously been cleared. It is unfortunate that we cannot yet date with greater precision such an important landmark in the development of South East Asian civilization, but it is likely to have occurred well before the arrival of distinctively Indian religious influences. That need not however mean that there was no contact between South East Asia and India before the first appearance of Hindu-Buddhist statues and inscriptions; it seems likely that there was.

Another possible sign of cultural change, and perhaps population growth, during the later centuries of the first millennium B.C. is found at Phimai, in north-east Thailand. The date of the distinctive pottery known as 'Phimai blackware' is still not firmly established, but it would appear to belong to a 'pre-Indian' culture which flourished (perhaps around the end of the first millennium B.C.) in an area that was later to become a Hindu centre. B. Bronson, in his paper on Chansen (central Thailand) in Part II, suggests that the Phimai site and one of the early phases of the Chansen sequence (second–first centuries B.C.) may represent the same phase of development. It may be noteworthy that both sites have continuity with later periods, whereas there is no actual site continuity between Ban Kao, Kok Charoen, Non Nok Tha or Ban Chieng, and the Indianised sites of the Dvaravati period. Probably therefore we should look for a change sometime during the second half of the first millennium B.C.—possibly coinciding with the spread of iron metallurgy —which would count as the effective beginning of the continuous development of lowland civilization in this part of South East Asia.

The more northerly areas of mainland South East Asia have also yielded important evidence of prehistoric cultures during the past decade. The important work of North Vietnamese archaeologists since 1954 has shown that we must take into account another area of early lowland settlement whose origins probably go back to the second millennium B.C. The precise chronology is again still somewhat unclear, and Vietnamese writers have themselves disagreed about the interpretation of results from a number of different sites in relation to one another. But there seems little doubt, in general terms, that by the first half of the first millennium B.C. there flourished in the north Vietnamese lowlands (especially in the area above Hanoi) a culture which has become known by the name of a site at Phung-nguyen. It was to begin with a Neolithic culture, characterized by several pottery types, but in due course it too developed bronze metallurgy—at an uncertain date, but well before the introduction of Chinese culture (and perhaps also of iron) after 200 B.C. It was out of this culture that Dong-son culture developed by the end of the first millennium B.C. Davidson suggests that it was also the culture which later Vietnamese historians were dimly conscious of when they wrote about the Hung-Vuong kingdom, overthrown by the kingdom of Thuc in the mid-third century B.C., after at least several centuries of existence.

The term northern South East Asia is used here to include not only northern Viet-Nam (whose prehistory differs in certain respects, though not totally, from that of the Centre and South), but also Yünnan and the upland areas of Laos and northern Thailand. The earliest settled life in this region may well be represented by the rice-growing cave-dwellers whom C. F. Gorman has identified at two cave sites near Mae Hong Son, and which he has dated to around 6000 B.C. Archaeologically there is however a serious gap between those sites and the Bronze Age evidence from the region. The Dian culture of Yünnan was characterized by bronze drums and other material showing affinities with Northern Viet-Nam's Dong-son culture, but was almost certainly later in date. The weapons and other bronzes from these areas indicate a more developed phase of the Bronze Age than that present at Non Nok Tha or Ban Chieng, and any relationship between the bronze metallurgy of the two areas remains to be established. But in northern South East Asia the picture which now emerges is also one of a distinctive culture without precise parallels outside the region. The famous Dong-son drums, but not other elements of the bronze culture of northern South East Asia, are found scattered across South East Asia—though not in the Philippines or Borneo—and also in southern China, suggesting a connection with maritime movement, perhaps in the later centuries of the first millennium B.C. An important area for these drums is the western part of central Thailand, and P. Sørensen raises the question whether the drums from Ongbah Cave represent a distinctive centre of drum manufacture.

Turning to the maritime regions of South East Asia, we find there too signs of significant human activity in the second millennium B.C. A number of cave sites have yielded evidence of human occupation from periods several millennia earlier than that, but it is beyond the scope of the present volume to explore the evidence relating to those earlier periods. Looking at the whole of the maritime area (including the seaboard of southern Viet-Nam and Cambodia) as it must have been during the early first millennium B.C., it is possible to identify a number of centres of activity: no doubt more will be revealed by further excavations. All the sites so far attributable to this or earlier periods are caves, including some with habitation remains and others with burials. They are all without metal, and can reasonably be described as 'neolithic'. Whatever the chronology of the use of bronze and iron in the mainland areas, there is nothing yet to suggest the practice of metallurgy in maritime South East Asia before the second half of the first millennium B.C. Pottery, on the other hand, was in use by perhaps 2500 B.C.

Amongst the most important cave sites are those of eastern Indonesia, Timor, and eastern Malaysia (Borneo). In Portuguese Timor, the caves of Uai Bobo and Lie Siri have produced, in addition to several much earlier dates, four dates in the second millennium B.C. and one in the range 800–600 B.C.; Leang Burung (Sulawesi) has produced two dates within the limits of 1900–1700 B.C., both associated with stone tools and pottery. In eastern Malaysia three caves at Niah have produced radiocarbon dates from the second millennium, and it would seem that the Great Cave was occupied for at least some of the time during the first half of the first millennium B.C., with a number of both extended and jar burials apparently belonging to that period. Farther north, on Palawan Island (Philippines), the Manunggul Cave was also occupied during the latter period and two neolithic jar burials found there are dated to the period 970–630 B.C. Crossing to the western side of the South China Sea, early cave sites have been found in Cambodia and Malaya (as well as in some upland areas of the mainland). A series of radiocarbon dates from Loang Spean (Battambang), indicates a probable continuity of occupation from well before 2000 B.C. until the latter half of the first millennium A.D. Two caves excavated in western Malaysia have yielded radiocarbon dates: one from Gua Kechil, in the third millennium B.C. or earlier, the other from Gua Harimau in the mid-second millennium B.C.

The later centuries of the first millennium B.C. clearly saw important changes in maritime as in mainland South East Asia. The chronological relationship between bronze metallurgy and the introduction of iron-using has yet to be worked out, and it is possible that we shall still need to talk about the 'Bronze-Iron age' in eastern maritime South East Asia. With the possible exception of Leuwilliang (West Java), which is as yet an unreported excavation, no site has produced stratigraphic evidence of a separate period in which bronze was used but not iron. However, it is clear that both were present in the maritime area by the end of the first millennium B.C.: a copper ornament at Uai Bobo Cave (Timor) is dated by radiocarbon tests to the period 350–150 B.C., while the earliest datable iron in the maritime region occurs in a jar-burial at Manunggal Cave (Palawan) in the period 300–100 B.C. Several other cave sites, including Niah, were still occupied during the early metal period, and some (like the Painted Cave, Niah) well into the first millennium A.D. But also during the 'Bronze-Iron age' there appear also considerable numbers of lowland settlements. Whilst a good deal of the evidence from this period consists of chance finds, ranging from bronze axes and ornaments to Dong-son drums, a number of sites have been excavated. An important site at Gilimanuk (Bali) combines evidence of habitation with a number of burials, including both extended burials, secondary burials, and jar burials. A number of places in Java were settled in this period, notably perhaps Leuwilliang, and also sites in Sumatra and western Malaysia. On the mainland seaboard, an important group of early iron age sites was excavated in the vicinity of Sa-huynh (Central Viet-Nam) by Colani, and the type-site has given its name to a pottery tradition whose affinities with the Kalanay pottery tradition of the Philippines are well known. More recently, a number of sites have been excavated in the area east and north of Saigon, notably that at Hang-gon, where jar-burials with affinities to the Sa-huynh culture are dated by radiocarbon to the period 500–1 B.C.

Comparing the maritime region with mainland South East Asia, it is clear that there were certain differences in their respective development in the later prehistoric period: for example in the likelihood that the central and northern parts of mainland South East Asia had bronze metallurgy much earlier than the eastern part of the maritime region. There would seem also to have been at least one significant difference in burial practices, for the jar burials which are such a common feature of the maritime region (including the Indochinese seaboard) are not found in most of the mainland. The people of Ban Kao, Kok Charoen, Non Nok Tha and Ban Chieng would appear to have been burying their dead in extended posture, in individual graves, at the same period when the cave-dwellers of Manunggal and Niah were using jars. Other types of grave which are commonly found in the maritime region, at least by the time that iron was being used, are the cist-grave, the slab-grave and the sarcophagus. The significance of this contrast in burial customs was discussed during the course of the London Colloquy, but a full study of the subject has yet to be undertaken.

In conclusion, it can be seen from the evidence collected in the papers that even by the end of the first millennium B.C. South East Asia had begun to take on something of the pattern of diversity which has characterized the whole of its history. It might not be going too far to suggest that already by that time we can distinguish two principal contrasts in its cultural make-up. First, the beginnings of contrast between upland and lowland areas, which would become more and more marked as the lowland societies began to develop both a greater capacity for production and the potentiality for increasingly sophisticated political structures. This contrast was especially marked in the valleys of mainland South East Asia, but the growth of lowland societies is also observable in Java and Sumatra in due course. Perhaps the most important starting-point for this development was the spread of iron technology, which was so important in the transformation of India during the first millennium B.C. The process had probably begun long before the first signs of what is usually termed the Indianization of lowland South East Asia, supposedly from about the third century A.D. onwards. Perhaps an initial stage of the development, foreshadowing the later temple-builders of Java and Cambodia, is indicated by some of the 'megalithic' structures of the region, although their date is by no means securely established.

The second contrast is that between maritime and hinterland societies, which applies to the mainland seaboard as well as to maritime South East Asia. In looking at the latter area, Glover concludes that the distinction was already present by the first millennium B.C. It is characteristic of the whole subsequent history of the region, culminating in modern times in the arrival of Europeans and Americans, as well as many settlers from China. The coastal societies were not—until relatively recent times—capable of sustaining major political growth. Yet they played a key part in the growth of trade and in the relations between this region and those to the east and the west. It is in this context that we must place the eventual arrival of Indian and Chinese influences in South East Asia. During the centuries before about 200 A.D., what mattered more was the gradual evolution of trade and cultural relationships between different parts of the region itself. This growing cohesion is indicated by the bronze drums, whose cultural origins are in northern South East Asia, but which are found scattered through a large area (not the whole) of the maritime region by perhaps the last centuries B.C. It is in this context too that we must see the relationship between pottery traditions on both the eastern (Kalanay) and western (Sa-huynh) coasts of the South China Sea. There can be no doubt that well before the coming of Indian religions and writing-systems, well before the arrival of envoys from the Chinese empire, South East Asia already had a flourishing pattern of societies and communications whose roots are to be sought in the region's own prehistory. With the gradual development of modern archaeological investigation, that pattern is beginning to emerge.

The Chronology of Prehistoric Metallurgy in North-east Thailand: *Silabhumi* or *Samrddhabhumi?**

D. T. BAYARD

Introduction

THIS paper represents an attempt to investigate in some detail the evidence currently available for the dating of bronze metallurgy in a portion of that area known to the Indians in early historic times as *Suvarṇabhūmi*, 'the Land of Gold'. The principal question I am concerned with is the technology of the area prior to its becoming *Suvarṇabhūmi*; is mainland South East Asia during the last two millennia B.C. better viewed as *Śilābhūmi* or as *Samṛddhabhūmi*—a 'Land of Stone' or a 'Land of Bronze'?[1] As many readers will recognize, this question is but part of a larger one concerned with the course of prehistory in the area for the past 15,000 years or more. Prior to 1967, the role of South East Asia in world prehistory was universally viewed as a very minor one; the region was isolated, backward, and primitive. Plagued by swamps and jungles, it was slow to accept the cultural developments impinging on it from progressive centres in India and China.

> In south-eastern Asia, the environment is extremely humid, presenting the difficulties of rain forests and also requiring large drainage projects. And in both areas (south-east Asia and Yucatàn), the civilizations appear to have been later than, and in part derived from, those of the irrigation areas (Steward 1955: 199).

> It is interesting to note that even in prehistoric times the autochthonous peoples of Indochina seem to have been lacking in creative genius and showed little aptitude for making progress without stimulus from outside (Coedès 1966: 13).

> One of the main reasons why the mainland of south-east Asia merits study is that it forms a kind of funnel through which people have spread over Indonesia, Melanesia, and farther afield. Another is its intermediate position between the two main foci of culture in India and China respectively. Claims that it was in itself the cradle of an early civilization

* See Plate I.

based on the cultivation of rice are not substantiated by the archaeological evidence (Clark 1965: 201).

At the time Clark wrote his comprehensive outline, the concluding remarks above were of course quite correct; there was in fact little firm archaeological evidence to substantiate anything about South East Asian prehistory. In fact, the first extensive and well-reported excavation in the Thailand region to be carried out shortly thereafter, the Thai-Danish excavation at Ban Kao (Sørensen 1964, Sørensen and Hatting 1967), also seemed to support the traditionally late arrival (*c.* 1800–2000 B.C.) of agriculture from China and the introduction of bronze and iron only shortly before the beginning of the present era (Sørensen 1972). However, since 1965 evidence has begun to accumulate in favour of a radically different view of the prehistory of mainland South East Asia: possible cultivation of legumes and other crops by 10,000 B.C. (Gorman 1969, 1971); the cultivation of rice prior to 3500 B.C. (Bayard 1970, 1971; Solheim 1970); and domesticated bovines and possibly domestic pig at the same date (Higham and Leach 1971; Bayard 1971: 32). In addition to this startling reversal in our opinion of prehistoric economic developments in the area, doubt has also been cast on South East Asia's technological backwardness: pottery is present in northern Thailand at a secure date of 6800 B.C. (Gorman 1969, 1971), and may well have been recovered in a still earlier context at the date of this writing (May 1973); true tin bronze seemingly appears at about 2700 B.C. (Bayard 1970, 1971, 1972); and most surprisingly sites containing iron tools have been thermoluminescene dated as early as 1224 and 1340 B.C. (Bronson and Han 1972).[2]

Reactions to these admittedly radical claims, with their implications for world prehistory as a whole, have been varied. The botanical evidence suggesting plant cultivation some twelve millennia ago has been viewed both critically (Ho 1969: 32–3; Harlan 1971, Harlan and de Wet 1973: 52) and quite favourably (Harris 1972a, 1972b). Similarly, views on the validity of a date in the middle or early third millennium for bronze in mainland South East Asia have ranged from cautious reservation of opinion (Chang 1968: 413) to more or less uncritical acceptance (Treistman 1972: 130; Clarke 1973: 11). To date, there has been little comment on the startling possibility of the presence of iron in central Thailand at a date when it was unknown in India and still largely a monopoly of the Hittite Empire (Allchin and Allchin 1968: 205, 327). Obviously, many more dates will be required before even tentative conclusions can be reached; however, on the evidence of one of these sites, Chan Sen (Bronson 1972), iron was almost certainly present in the area prior to the onset of any marked influences from India and China. Indications from the site of Ban Chieng also support the presence of iron prior to Indianization. The later four to six of the eleven thermoluminescence dates tentatively

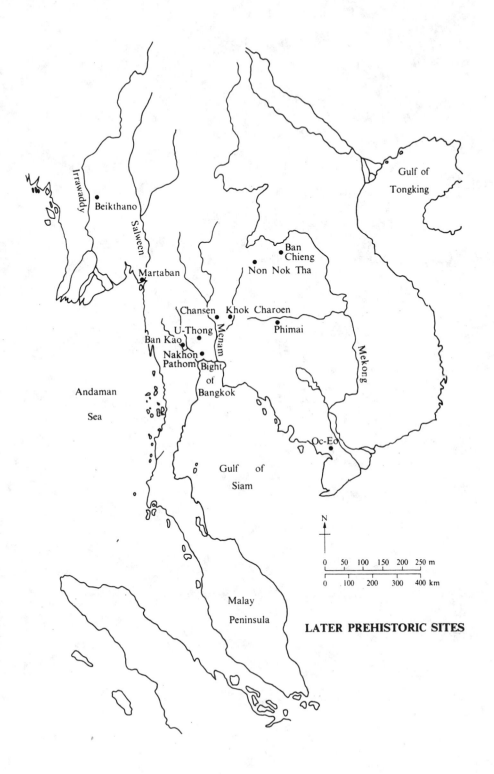

Irrawaddy

Beikthano

Salween

Gulf of
Tongking

Ban
Chieng
Non Nok Tha

Martaban

Chansen Khok Charoen
U-Thong   Phimai
Ban Kao
Nakhon
Pathom Bight
        of
        Bangkok

Mekong

Andaman

Sea

Oc-Eo

Gulf   of

Siam

N

0   50 100 150 200 250 m

0   100   200   300   400 km

Malay

Peninsula

LATER PREHISTORIC SITES

provenanced to the 'metal age', ranging from 1300–1000 B.C. to 500–400 B.C., may prove on further investigation to be in association with the iron tools recovered from the site (see Nikhom paper, this volume). Moreover, the fact that all iron tools found there so far are designed for socketed rather than tanged hafting (as are almost all of the earlier bronze tools at Ban Chieng, Non Nok Tha, and other sites) could conceivably be used to support an argument for the indigenous development of an iron technology in the region directly out of the earlier bronze techniques. However, I would prefer to reserve judgement on this issue until considerably more evidence is available. Nonetheless, iron may well prove to have a surprising antiquity in mainland South East Asia (Bronson and Han 1972: 325).

At present, I feel that our chronology does not really justify complete and totally uncritical acceptance of any of these early developments—few events in prehistory do! However, I do believe that we have sufficient evidence to argue strongly against a traditionally late and more or less simultaneous entry of both bronze and iron into mainland South East Asia. I feel we can now modify with a high degree of confidence statements such as the one retained by Clark in his 1969 revision of *World Prehistory*:

> Neither south-east Asia, Indonesia nor the Philippines experienced a phase of technology fully comparable with the Bronze Age in certain parts of the world. Yet, while stone tools continued in general use into the Christian era, a certain number of bronze artifacts . . . found their way over these territories during the latter half of the first millennium B.C. and in the richer graves of Annam these were sometimes accompanied by objects made of iron (Clark 1969: 238).

This paper will thus be devoted to a survey of recent data relevant to the question of the age of bronze metallurgy in north-eastern Thailand as it relates to the rest of mainland South East Asia and to the traditionally earlier metallurgy in surrounding areas; some comments on metal technology will also be included, in a report by Professor I. R. Selimkhanov.

The Evidence from Non Nok Tha

The site which has to date produced the largest amount of evidence for a distinctive bronze-period technology lacking iron is also one of the most thoroughly dated in South East Asia; unfortunately, the dates are by no means wholly consistent. The mound of Non Nok Tha (Phu Wiang district, Khon Kaen province), like most other open sites in Thailand, is characterized by an exceedingly complex and hard-to-interpret stratigraphy (Bayard 1971: 5–6) which is further complicated by the dense concentration of burials (205 recovered in the 1966 and 1968 excavations) and other cultural disturbance.

As a result of this and other factors such as possible contamination, the absolute dates from the site do not form a single tidy sequence, but rather may be interpreted in terms of several sequences. While this is regrettable from the standpoint of the area's chronology, it at least provides us with an example of the problems still to be encountered with absolute dating, not to mention excavation by natural stratigraphy on the refractory soils of open sites in mainland South East Asia.

At the time of writing we have some thirty-two radiocarbon dates and four thermoluminescence dates from the site (Table 1). I have discussed the problem of the chronology in detail on two previous occasions: when our total of dates stood at twenty-five (1970: 130–4), and in the light of four thermoluminescence and one radiocarbon date received subsequently (1971: 26–31). The six additional radiocarbon dates received in early 1973 will require still further discussion in view of their lack of agreement with almost all of the earlier dates.

TABLE I: Non Nok Tha Radiocarbon and Thermoluminescence Dates

Sample No.	Provenance		B.P. Date	Corrected to 5730 half-life	2 Sigma Range
			1966 Dates		
GaK– 908	Layer 9	LP2	710±90	1220±90 A.D.	1020–1420 A.D.
GaK– 956	Layer 19	MP3	4120±90	2290±90 B.C.	2490–2090 B.C.
GaK– 957	Layer 13	MP8	1720±80	180±80 A.D.	20 B.C.–380 A.D.
GaK– 958	Layer 9	LP2	2220±110	340±110 B.C.	560–120 B.C.
GaK– 959	Layer 21	EP2	1860±140	30±140 A.D.	250 B.C.–310 A.D.
GaK–1027	Layer 9	LP2	2480±80	600±80 B.C.	800–400 B.C.
GaK–1028	Layer 11	LP1	2560±100	690±100 B.C.	890–490 B.C.
GaK–1029	Layer 17 or '17–18' B. 48	MP4 or 5	2830±100	960±100 B.C.	1160–760 B.C.
GaK–1030	Layer 18	MP3	Less than 250 B.P.		1700–1950 A.D.
GaK–1031	Layer 18	MP3	2530±120	660±120 B.C.	900–420 B.C.
GaK–1032	Layer 20 B. 69	MP2	8100±250	6390±250 B.C.	6890–5890 B.C.
GaK–1033	Layer 17 B. 10 or '17–18' B. 9?	MP4 or 5	2990±110	1130±110 B.C.	1350–910 B.C.
GaK–1034	Layer 21 B. 26	EP3	5370±320	3590±320 B.C.	4230–2950 B.C.
TF – 651	Layer 19	MP3	4275±200	2325±200 B.C.	2720–1920 B.C.
Y –1851	Layer '17–18' B. 78?	MP4	3170±200	1310±200 B.C.	1710–910 B.C.
			1968 Dates		
FSU– 339	Level VIII pit	LP3	Modern plus 0·07 counts per min. per gram.		
FSU– 340	Level O (Layer II)	EP1	4435±130	2620±130 B.C.	2880–2360 B.C.

TABLE I—continued

Sample No.	Provenance		B.P. Date	Corrected to 5730 half-life	2 Sigma Range
			1968 Dates		
FSU– 341	Level IV	MP1	2470±140	590±140 B.C.	870–310 B.C.
FSU– 342	Level III	EP3	3055±130	1200±130 B.C.	1460–940 B.C.
FSU– 343	Level IX kiln	LP4	Modern plus 0·2 CPM/g		
FSU– 345	Level I B. 125	EP1	3560±130	1720±130 B.C.	1980–1460 B.C.
GX –1609	Level VIII pit	LP3	500±85	1430±85 A.D.	1230–1630 A.D.
GX –1611	Level V B. 15	MP4	3685±110	1840±110 B.C.	2060–1620 B.C.
GX –1612	Level I pit	EP1	2750±130	880±130 B.C.	1140–630 B.C.
I –5324	Level III B. 90 bone	EP3	2595±95	720±95 B.C.	920–520 B.C.
N –1324	Level I B. 8 bone	EP1	1010±85	910±90 A.D.	710–1110 A.D.
N –1325	Level I B. 14 bone	EP1	2160±195	280±200 B.C.	680 B.C.–120 A.D.
N –1326	Level III B. 52 bone	EP3	1580±115	320±115 B.C.	550–90 B.C.
N –1327	Level II B. 78 bone	EP2	2440±125	560±130 B.C.	820–300 B.C.
N –1328	Level II B. 88 bone	EP2	2420±75	540±80 B.C.	740–340 B.C.
N –1362	Level III B. 90 bone	EP3	1820±220	70±230 A.D.	390 B.C.–530 A.D.
Y –2485	Level VI B. 95	MP5	3090±120	1230±120 B.C.	1470±990 B.C.
			Thermoluminescence		
PT – 276	Level III B. 90	EP3	4370±200	2420±200 B.C.	2620–2220 B.C.
PT – 277	Level I B. 14	EP1	4945±320	2995±320 B.C.	3315–2675 B.C.
PT – 278	Level IV B. 73	MP1	4485±200	2535±200 B.C.	2735±2335 B.C.
PT – 279	Level IV B. 73	MP1	4300±150	2350±150 B.C.	2500–2200 B.C.

Given the distribution of the thirty-six dates as it stands at present (Fig. 1), an imaginative person could construct at least four quite distinct sequences: (1) a 'latest' sequence, with the earliest pre-metal habitation at the site beginning about 500 B.C.[3] and the entry of bronze at the beginning of the present era; (2) a 'traditional' sequence with first occupation at *c.* 900 B.C. and bronze at 700 B.C.; (3) an 'intermediate' or compromise sequence largely based on four of the six FSU dates which we suspect resulted from contamination (the remaining two samples contained more C14 than modern standards), with pre-metal and bronze periods beginning at 1800 B.C. and 1200 B.C.

respectively; and (4) the 'early' sequence, with first occupation of the site occurring prior to 3500 B.C. (based on the GaK-1034 date for an Early Period level 3 (EP 3) burial) and bronze appearing about 2700 B.C. A thermoluminescence date of 3090±520 BP on two crucible fragments from Middle Period Level 5 was obtained by the MASCA Laboratory of the University of Pennsylvania in early 1974. Although the standard deviation is large, the date adds further support to the 'early' sequence. All these sequences would presumably terminate with the GaK-957 date for Middle Period level 8 (MP 8) and the beginning of the gap between bronze and iron-using periods at the site; this date of 180 A.D. would quite likely be acceptable to both radical and conservative workers in the field.

Absolute Dates from Non Nok Tha :

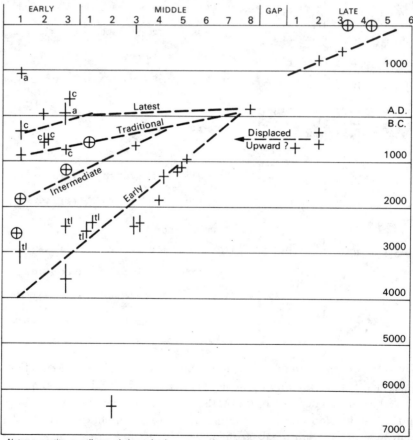

Notes: a–apatite, c–collagen, tl–thermoluminescence, others charcoal. Circled dates are those thought to have been affected by modern contamination. Range shown is one standard deviation.

Obviously such a situation is irreconcilable on the basis of the dates *per se*; we must examine several more general questions in order to arrive at the most probable chronology for the site. These are:

(a) the nature and reliability of the different dating techniques—charcoal collagen, and apatite radiocarbon versus thermoluminescence dating of potsherds;

(b) the internal consistency exhibited by artefacts and burial typology at the site;

(c) the presence or absence of a period of whatever duration during which bronze was in use but iron was entirely lacking;

(d) the amount of change in artefact and burial attributes which occurred during the first two periods of occupation, and the length of time over which these changes plausibly may have taken place; and finally

(e) external evidence, both from adjacent sites and from those more distant but still possibly related. Obviously thorough treatment of all these questions is beyond the scope of this paper, and I have dealt with most of them in some detail in the publications referred to above. However, a brief coverage of each area would be of help in attempting to resolve the chronology of the site, which would in turn be of considerable aid in settling the question of the date of appearance of bronze metallurgy in the Indochinese Peninsula.

Since I am very far indeed from being an expert on dating techniques, my comments on this aspect of the problem are mainly in the form of questions. I have already mentioned the probability of contamination of the six FSU dates; the subsequent date of 500 BP (GX-1609) on charcoal from the same firepit which produced one of the two FSU 'modern' dates (FSU-339) would support this probability. If we eliminate these dates, we are left with seven bone dates and three on charcoal which would compress the Early and Middle Periods at the site into the first millennium B.C., although no consistent sequence is apparent. On the other hand, eight dates on charcoal and four thermoluminescence dates form a fairly plausible early sequence.

Since this early sequence is better supported by dates on charcoal than on bone, the question of the accuracy of provenance of the charcoal samples is one of considerable importance, and one which received fairly lengthy discussion at the Colloquy. I feel quite certain that the accuracy of provenance to the layers and burials indicated is high; no samples from layer interfaces or the upper and middle portions of grave fills were submitted. Sample weights varied from 2 to 39 g., with most of them closer to the lower part of this range, as charcoal was scarce in the site. However, the heaviest sample came from a very secure context under one scapula of MP 5 Burial 95, and yielded a date supporting the early sequence. Given the rarity of charcoal at the site, several samples were submitted which consisted of scatters of small fragments present at the same depth in the layer rather than single large pieces. These were not collected over an area greater than 3 m², however, and samples combining fragments from different squares or even different portions of squares were never used. Some anomalous dates could well be explained by upward or downward displacement; e.g. the three early dates on the Late Period very probably resulted from the redeposition of Middle Period charcoal due to the 'mining' of burial pots which apparently took place during the Late Period (Bayard 1971: 22).

While I thus feel that the provenance of the sample is secure in almost all cases, there remains the question of the origin of the charcoal dated. It is certainly conceivable that some of the charcoal could have been the result of non-human action, such as forest fires, which occurred prior to the occupation of the site and the subsequent redeposition of the resultant charcoal in the cultural layers. On the other hand, I find it very hard to envisage a series of fires corresponding to the early sequence dates producing charcoal which is then neatly and sequentially redeposited in the proper order during a period of human use corresponding to the traditionally accepted dates. This is simply asking too much of coincidence. Moreover, the distribution of the submitted charcoal samples is rather interesting. Only five samples of charcoal sufficient for dating (plus one thought to be possibly pre-occupation in date) were recovered from the three Early Period levels present in both 1966 and 1968 areas of the site. However, twelve samples were submitted from the eight Middle Period levels, only three of which were present in both areas (Bayard 1971: 13). Ten were submitted to date the six Late Period levels, of which five occurred in both areas. It would thus appear by this rough index that charcoal is relatively more common in the Middle Period levels and burials than it is in the other two periods. One possible explanation for this which occurred to me following the Colloquy is that it is during the Middle Period that we find evidence for bronze casting *on the site* in the form of numerous fragments of bronze which according to all expert opinion are definitely casting spillage (Selimkhanov, this volume; Pittioni in Solheim 1970: 158; N. Barnard, C. S. Smith, pers. comm.). At least some of the Middle Period charcoal (e.g. the two MP 3 dates) may well be derived from melting and casting operations, and hence certainly contemporaneous with them. Admittedly, there should have been more charcoal present if intensive casting operations were being carried out; however, bronze-working at the site appears to have been on quite a small scale. In any event, I feel it is fair to state that the provenance and derivation of the Non Nok Tha charcoal samples are as secure as those from any stratigraphically excavated open site in the region, and considerably more so than dates from sites excavated by the unit-level method with no attention to stratification.

A second crucial question involves the accuracy of the late dates on bone material. Five of the seven dates were on bone collagen, while the remaining two were on the apatite fraction of bone carbonate. I have been informed by one of the laboratories in question (Rikagaku Kenkyūsho) that the reliability of apatite dating is still an open question, although in at least one experiment on fossil bone apatite dating yielded results much closer to the true age than did collagen dates on the same specimen (Haynes 1968). On the other hand, a more recent article states that, while collagen is more accurate than any of the carbonate fractions, the majority of collagen dates are still 'falsely young' (Tamers 1972: 21). This would appear to be the case with collagen dates which are apparently too recent from the Thai site of Kok Charoen (H. H. E. Loofs, personal comm.). The issue is further complicated by the fact that the skeletal material from Non Nok Tha is apparently very low in collagen. A brochure received from Geochron Laboratories in 1969 states that collagen can be as low as 1–2% in bone 10,000 years old, but all of the samples dated by this method by Rikagaku Kenkyūsho (all but N–1324 and N–1362 which contained almost no collagen) contained less than 0·8% collagen. One of these four (N–1325) was particularly collagen-poor, and may well have yielded an even younger date than usual. We may safely rule out the N–1324 and N–1325 dates on EP 1: the former, at A.D. 910, would put the earliest level at the site well into the Khmer period; also both the burials dated are stratified directly beneath undisturbed Middle Period burials. The remainder are still within the realm of possibility, although I believe this credibility is much reduced by such contradictions as the failure of overlap, even at the two-sigma range of the two dates on EP 3 Burial 90. In addition to the apatite date of A.D. 70 mentioned above, Teledyne Isotopes produced a date of 720 B.C. on bone from the same skeleton. As this latter date was on collagen, and the material apparently contained 'almost no collagen' (T. Hamada, pers. comm. to W. G. Solheim II), it could well be inaccurate. On the other hand, a recent letter from Teledyne Isotopes states that bone with 1–2% collagen may well be much younger than the 10,000 year age implied by the Geochron Laboratories statement above. In addition, the sample of bone submitted to Teledyne Isotopes contained 'approximately one per cent collagen,' which would appear to be at variance with the statement of the Rikagaku Kenkyusho laboratory. Given this discrepancy, I can only agree with the representative of Teledyne Isotopes when he states that 'I personally would put more confidence in a charcoal date than bone or apatite dates' (J. Buckley, pers. comm.), particularly since pottery associated very securely with this same burial has been dated to 2420 B.C. (PT–276).

One final question remains to be asked here: how valid are our four thermoluminescence dates *vis-à-vis* the eight radiocarbon dates on charcoal which appear to support the early sequence? A sequence of twenty-two dates from Non Nok Tha and other Thai sites has been shown to present a considerable degree of internal consistency (Bronson and Han 1972: 325),[4] although one should note that twelve of these dates are on sherds which are either unprovenanced or from unit-level excavations. However, given the security of provenance of the sherd samples and those carbon dates in the early sequence which derive from large samples in burials, I find it puzzling that the thermo-luminescence dates seem somewhat too young when compared with the dates on charcoal. This becomes particularly perplexing when the radiocarbon dates are adjusted for the variations in C14 content now generally accepted to have been considerable prior to 2000 B.C. (Suess 1970); e.g. dates TF–651 and GaK–956 produce a date in calendar years for MP 3 of about 2900 B.C., earlier than the three thermoluminescence dates on EP 3 and MP 1. It seems apparent that some problems remain in the correlation of the two dating techniques. However, Dr. Aitken's comments made in the course of the London Colloquy would appear to indicate that while various factors may produce an error of about 20% in thermoluminescence dates, contamination of one sort or another is more likely to produce a date that is too recent than one which is too old; perhaps this may account for some of the discrepancies.

We can deal with the other questions relative to Non Nok Tha itself with considerably more brevity. As checks on the internal consistency of the relative sequence of levels at the site, we have (a) the sequence as defined by natural stratigraphy; (b) consistency of burial posture, orientation, and grave depth among burials originating within a given level; (c) intersections of burials from adjacent levels for all pairs of levels save EP 3 and MP 1; (d) consistency in ceramic and artifactual typologies of grave goods for each level *vis-à-vis* any other; (e) consistent patterns of change in temper, surface finish, decoration and rim form of non-burial sherds from the various levels.[5] While these are obviously not completely independent of each other, in that b, d, and e were originally defined during the excavations with reference to a and c, taken as a whole they form a highly consistent body of data which clearly indicates the demarcation and relative sequence of levels as presented here.

Given the internal consistency outlined above, the presence of a clearly defined period when bronze was in use but iron apparently unknown is indicated by the distribution of the two metals through the Middle and Late Periods at the site. The span of Middle Period levels (1–6) in the 190 m² excavated in 1968 produced some nine bronze artefacts and 156 bronze fragments (mainly casting spillage); no iron was recovered.[6] The Late Period levels (levels 2–6 were present in the 1968 area) yielded twelve iron fragments and three iron artefacts, in contrast to only two pieces from bronze axes and eighty-nine bronze fragments, fifty-nine of which came from the base of the Late Period levels and may have been deposited by erosion of MP 7 and 8 in this area of the site (see Bayard 1971: 25). There is obviously a considerable period in the site's history during which bronze was in use but iron was not.

With regard to amount of change in artefact and burial attributes through the first two periods at the site, data indicating that a fairly large amount of change took place in metallurgical techniques have already been presented in an earlier paper (original version of Bayard 1974). The amount of change apparent in vessel types, kinds of grave goods, and burial arrangement and orientation can be seen by referring to the burials and grave goods recovered in 1968 (Bayard 1971: 14–26, 43–64). Evidence relating to overall change in ceramic attributes will appear in the references given in footnote 5. The general point to be emphasized is that I feel it would be quite difficult to postulate that the changes apparent in the sequence from EP 1 through to MP 8 could have taken place in the 700 or 1,100 years allowed them by the 'latest' or 'traditional' sequences presented above. This might be the case were the changes concentrated in one particular level or group of levels; but although there is a marked peak of change between the Early and Middle Periods (Bayard 1971: 18–19), differences in all of the attributes mentioned above are clearly apparent from one level to the next. Such differences indicate a gradual development within a single tradition rather than a series of sharp breaks or replacement by distinct traditions.

Our final area of inquiry, that of the support afforded the Non Nok Tha sequence by evidence from other sites, is better dealt with in the following section. In summing up the internal evidence, I think it fair to state that while it is not entirely conclusive it does convincingly support the presence of distinct bronze and iron periods rather than a single 'Metal Period' in at least one area of mainland South East Asia, as well as the first appearance of bronze there prior to 2000 B.C. Conclusive proof will come only with sequences of large numbers of dates from stratigraphical excavations of large areas of sites related to Non Nok Tha. As one who has been involved with the chronology of this site for the past six years, I can only hope that such proof, whether of 'early bronze' or 'late bronze', will appear in the very near future! The detailed discussion above does at least serve as a cautionary tale warning us about the pitfalls of accepting one or even a half-dozen dates from a site as 'conclusive'.

Other Evidence: Pro and Con

If we accept the cautions implicit in the above outline of Non Nok Tha chronological problems, the number of adequately dated sites in the region available for comparison is nil. However, there are a number of sites with obvious ties (and some less obvious) to Non Nok Tha during the Middle Period, and of these some seven have sequences supported by one to ten absolute dates.

The sites most clearly related by Non Nok Tha are Non Nong Chik and Don Sawan, located some seven and fourteen kilometres to the south inside the mountain ringwall of Phu Wiang. Both sites were the subject of test excavations by the University of Otago in 1970 (Higham and Parker 1970), and subsequent analysis of the pottery recovered showed the expected close ties to the later Middle Period and early Late Period at Non Nok Tha, as well as filling the gap between the two periods at the latter site (Buchan n.d.; Bayard n.d.b.). The stratigraphy of the two test excavations proved as refractory as that at Non Nok Tha; despite this, four of the six dates from Non Nong Chik (Don Sawan is still undated) agree closely with the postulated early sequence at Non Nok Tha. These are as follows: layer 7 (equals Non Nok Tha MP 6 or somewhat earlier?), 3580±95 BP (R–2931/3); layer 7 (MP 6 or somewhat later?), 2830±105 BP (R–2809/4); top of layer 6 (MP 7), 2340±76 BP (R–2931/4); layer 5 (early MP 8?), 2120±75 BP (R–2089/3). The remaining two dates (post-layer 3 burial, 2900±120 BP (R–2809/9) and layer 3 or 4, 2160±270 BP (R–2931/5)) remain unexplained, but may be the result of upward displacement of the charcoal dated. Bronze fragments were present at Non Nok Chik almost to the bottom of the site, but no iron was recovered below layer 4. This site thus offers further support for a distinctive bronze period in the area.

Relationships are less clear but still quite apparent between Non Nok Tha and the site of Ban Chieng in eastern Udorn Province. This site has been the subject of several excavations by the Thai Fine Arts Department. A summary of the 1972 excavations (in Thai) may be found in Nikhom (1972: in Thai) and in the same author's paper in this volume, so that there is no need to discuss the site in detail here. It is sufficient to say that ties to Non Nok Tha are evident between the distinctive (and beautiful) red-on-white pottery found in abundance at Ban Chieng and similar but cruder vessels which occur sporadically in burials of EP 3 and MP 1–2 age at Non Nok Tha. Ties are equally apparent in a number of stone, metal, and clay artefacts; the bronze and even the iron tools recovered from Ban Chieng resemble the bronze tools from Non Nok Tha in their use of socketed rather than tanged hafting.

The five cultural layers present at Ban Chieng are described by the excavator as (1) Humus, (2) Late Metal Age, (3) Early Metal Age, (4) Late Neolithic, and (5) Neolithic (Nikhom 1972: 42); the presence of a metal bracelet in the fourth layer (as shown in a section drawing on p. 43 of the same publication) may indicate that small quantities of metal were present during this Late Neolithic period, or perhaps the artefact lay in a later disturbance. The Early Metal Age layer contained only bronze tools, while metal finds in the Late Metal Age layer were exclusively iron (p. 52). Although the distinctive painted pottery begins in the fourth layer, it is concentrated mainly in the second and third layers. The pottery is stylistically different in the two layers: mainly large and round-bottomed with crowded triangular and curvilinear designs in the bronze-period layer; and smaller and ring-footed with more open spiral designs in the iron-period layer above (p. 55). Oddly enough the related vessels at Non Nok Tha are of the latter type; however, a large sample of vessels from Ban Chieng and adjacent sites will be required before a detailed typology is available.

Three painted sherds from the site have been thermoluminescence-dated at 4630 B.C. (surface find), 3570 B.C. (70–80 cm. level; in layer 3, according to Nikhom 1972: 57), and 3590 B.C. (130 cm. level; layer 5?; in layer 4 burial?). The chronology of the site is thus far from settled, but the association of bronze and painted pottery is certain, and would imply an early date for the former. The presence of both bronze and iron in association with variants of this distinctive ware would imply a long tradition of its manufacture in the area. Research to be undertaken in the very near future should tell us much more about this important site and its relations with other sites in north-eastern Thailand. At present all we can conclude is that it appears to support the thesis of a very early appearance of bronze in the area.

Turning our attention to much more distantly related sites outside the north-eastern Thai area, there are two to the east which have single dates related to our area of inquiry. Hàng Gòn, near Saigon, has produced sandstone axe moulds quite similar to those at Non Nok Tha (Saurin 1963: pls. 26, 27; 1968: pls. 2, 7) radiocarbon-dated to 2120±250 B.C. (Saurin 1968: 3).[7] On the other hand, there is a date of 1380±120 B.C. from the well-known Cambodian site of Samrong Sen in an apparently Neolithic context (Carbonnel and Delibrias 1968). Although the bronze objects reported from the site by Mansuy (1902, 1923 and others) have long been recognized to be of very dubious provenance (Worman 1949), I believe that the 'pure Neolithic' status of the site is not yet settled. In any event, since the date presented is on shells collected from two different points and at two different depths (1 and 1·5 m. below present surface), both of which are at the top of the zone affected by annual flooding (Mansuy 1902: 3), I do not feel the date is an overly reliable one.

Looking to the west of our area of interest, we find sites with apparently closer connections to those in the north-east. The excavations at Kok Charoen (Loofs and Watson 1970; Loofs 1970) have yielded numbers of burials containing pottery with general but obvious relationships to the funerary pottery of Non Nok Tha Middle Period levels 1–5 (e.g. most of Loofs and Watson's Class II pedestalled vessels subdivided into eight types: vessels with pedestals or high ringfeet do not occur in the Non Nok Tha Early Period). The two thermoluminescence dates of 1180±300 B.C. and 1080±300 B.C. (Loofs 1970: 180) seem rather too recent, and as mentioned above the collagen dates in the second half of the first millennium B.C. seem much too late. Although the excavations at Kok Charoen were extensive, no metal of any sort has been recovered from the burial levels. If the pattern of somewhat young thermoluminescence dates and much too young collagen dates holds true for this site in the way that I believe it might for Non Nok Tha, Kok Charoen may possibly date from the mid-second millennium B.C. or there-abouts. The absence of bronze is thus rather strange but may be due to a lack of established trade connections across the Phetchabun Range to the north-east. Hopefully further dates will be forthcoming.

If the excavator's interpretation is correct, the major site of Ban Kao (Sørensen and Hatting 1967), in western central Thailand, provides considerable evidence for the traditionally late date of appearance of bronze and iron in the region. The site is interpreted as a Neolithic occupation area with later Neolithic burials, save for two burials with iron tools which supposedly derive from a later iron period. Using the copious data provided by the excavator, this view of the site has been criticized elsewhere (Parker 1968; Solheim 1969b), and I agree with the revised interpretations of the sequence presented there. The site would appear to be a second millennium occupation area later used as a cemetery; a thermoluminescence date of 290±255 B.C. on burial pottery (Bronson and Han 1972) may possibly indicate that at least some of the site's burials are iron-period in origin. However, the London Colloquy was in general agreement that the doubtful provenance of the dated sherd necessitated the ruling out of the date as adequate evidence. Given the apparently long span of the Ban Kao site, the date is certainly far more dubious than the controversial Hàng Gòn 1 date discussed above.

Arguing from different evidence, the relative sparseness of the Ban Kao burials (only 44 in 400 m² of area; *cf.* some 205 in 340 m² at Non Nok Tha) and the absence of any marked disturbance of earlier burials by later ones also tend to indicate that the site was used as a cemetery for a relatively shorter period. One should note as well that the absence of metal in a series of burials does not make them 'Neolithic': only ten of the 205 Non Nok Tha burials contained bronze artefacts, a proportion quite close to the two out of forty-four burials at Ban Kao which contained iron.

Given this revised interpretation, the eight radiocarbon dates available from Ban Kao (*Radiocarbon*, xv, i, 1973: 109–10) indicate a span for occupational use of the site from 1800–1300 B.C. It should be noted that the excavator believes these dates also date the burials found there, in that the samples were stratified above them, but since the site was excavated by unit levels rather than by natural stratigraphy, and since in no cases were grave outlines detected (Sørensen and Hatting, 1967: 65), this belief cannot be supported. Even if the charcoal dated could be shown to have been in the fill of the graves concerned, it could still have originated in the habitation layers into which the graves were dug. A ninth date from the adjacent Lu site (Sørensen and Hatting, op. cit.) of 2550±100 B.C. provides some evidence of earlier occupation in the Ban Kao area; the date is on what the excavator considered a pointed house post base, although he later suggested it was in fact unrelated to the cultural deposit at the site (Tauber 1973: 110). In the light of such a firm initial interpretation, the subsequent revision seems unlikely.

Taking into consideration the possible dates of iron prior to 1000 B.C. at the relatively close sites of Lop Buri and Chan Sen, I can only agree with Parker when he states that the absence of bronze 'remains the site's most puzzling feature' (1968: 312). The excavator does mention 'some almost disintegrated tiny fragments of bronze . . . in the uppermost layers' (Sørensen and Hatting 1967: 15), but these are not further discussed. Since at least one burial at the site (B. 44) apparently lies only some 35 cm. below surface, the 'uppermost layers' may in some areas predate the burials.

Further evidence for the antiquity of bronze in this area comes in the form of two radiocarbon dates on charcoal from the cave site of Tham Ongbah to the north-west of Ban Kao. The site is apparently an earlier Hoabinhian one overlaid by Early Metal Age layers with burials (Sørensen 1962). The Hoabinhian dates give the expected age range from about 7500 to 9500 B.C., but two of the three Metal Age dates are 'older than expected' by the excavator (*Radiocarbon* 1973: 110–14); these are 2420±100 B.C. for a layer with 'burials of late Metal Age', and 2130±100 B.C. from a layer which 'contained traces of bronze' (Tauber 1973: 111). The excavator comments that the 'apparently undisturbed layers in Hall 4 were mixed'; however, previously he described the deposits as 'stratified'. If clear stratigraphy was in fact present, it would imply that the traces of bronze and charcoal were in association, whether in a layer of primary deposition or in a part of a layer redeposited in reverse order due to later gravedigging. According to the interpretation presented here, a third date of 300±100 B.C. on a wooden coffin in the same cave, would represent a use of the cave subsequent to the earlier bronze-period layers. In any event it is difficult to reach firm conclusions until further data on the site are published.

To conclude our survey of the evidence for early bronze in other parts of mainland South East Asia, we should take a brief look northward to south-west China and the handful of absolute dates for China as a whole which have been published recently. Of major interest here is a date of 1150±90 B.C. from the site of Hai Men Kou[8] in Jianchuan, northern Yünnan. The site has been described as 'chalcolithic' (von Dewall 1967: 10) and 'essentially Neolithic' (Chang 1968: 427). However, some fourteen copper artefacts were found, including cast axes and hammered knives, chisels, fishhooks, and other small artefacts (Chang, loc. cit.). From the brief description available to me, the metallurgy would appear to be as foreign to that we have been considering here as it seems to be to the contemporary sophisticated Yin technology of the Zhongyuan. As I have said elsewhere (Bayard 1974), a scatter of absolute dates in China gives us little reliable information to work from. However, the presence of metal in Yünnan at a date considerably earlier than the warring States estimate given by Chang (1968: 444) and Barnard (1967: 192) is now somewhat more likely than it was previously. Equally interesting is the presence of a large 'percentage of striking Lungshanoid types' (Chang 1968:

427) at Hai Men Kou and the apparent absence of any sign of Shang influence accompanying the metal objects. This would imply (a) that metal was not a direct importation into the area from the Zhongyuan; and (b) that in at least one part of China the Lungshanoid lingered on quite late. We can say (or better speculate) little more until a much larger number of dates are available; those from Late Neolithic and Early Bronze period sites in Guangxi and Guangdong, as well as Yünnan and Sichuan, should be of particular interest.

Conclusions

In summary, the evidence supporting the appearance of a distinctive bronze metallurgy in mainland South East Asia at present can be divided into two categories, the second of which is to some extent dependent on the first. We have the Non Nok Tha sequence, secure in relative terms both internally and through its close ties to other sites in the Phu Wiang area; this regional sequence can in turn be connected to a significant degree to other sites in north-eastern and central Thailand (Bayard 1971: 35–9), and even to a lesser extent to the more distant sites of Samrong Sen and Hàng Gòn.

Secondly, we have the thirty-six absolute dates from Non Nok Tha, making it to the best of my knowledge the most thoroughly dated site in mainland South East Asia. We also have some twenty-odd absolute dates from the more or less related sites discussed above. This relatively large sample of dates would appear to be distributed as follows: those supporting a pre-1000 B.C. appearance of bronze, 21; post-1000 B.C. dates indicating a much earlier appearance of bronze, 7; dates prior to 1000 B.C. from comparable sites which apparently do not exhibit the expected presence of bronze, 12; and finally, dates which would definitely support an appearance of bronze in the first millennium B.C., 12–15 (the number of collagen dates from Kok Charoen has not been published). Hence the balance on the question of early bronze metallurgy at present would seem to be pro, 28; con, 12–15; and neutral (no bronze recovered to date) 12. Further investigations at the sites producing neutral dates might prove them to have been bronze-using as well; at present all we can say is that the absence of bronze is balanced by the presence of artefacts stylistically similar to sites definitely containing metal.

Thus the case for *Samṛddhabhūmi* is still not conclusively proven. But I feel we can safely say that the burden of proof no longer rests with those of us supporting the early presence of bronze in the area. The defence must now shift to those supporting the traditional view of mainland South East Asia as a late, technologically retarded *Śilābhūmi*, a defence which I believe will become increasingly more difficult as more data come to light on the early development of technological and economic sophistication in this 'Fortunate Land' of *Samṛddhabhūmi*.

NOTES

1. In the early Sanskrit of the *Rg Veda*, *ayas* rather than *samrddha* would be the more proper term. However, as Sanskrit and Thai scholars will recognize, the former term subsequently came to mean 'iron' (Basham 1959: 37), and the terms were later borrowed into Thai with the meanings 'iron' and 'bronze' respectively. In addition, *Samrddha*, in the sense of 'successful' or 'fortunate', serves to emphasize the essentially progressive nature of South East Asian prehistory which I am supporting here.

2. General summaries of these recent developments have been made by Solheim (1969*a*, 1970, 1972) for mainland South East Asia as a whole, and by Higham (1972) for northern and north-eastern Thailand in particular.

3. A.D.–B.C. dates are here presented with half-life corrected to 5730 years; B.P. dates use standard 5568 half-life.

4. Note that date PT–227 is provenanced in this report as 'Level ?'; this should read 'Level I'—i.e. EP1.

5. Data for (a), (b), and (c) plus a summary of (d) can be found in Bayard 1971; full details on (d) and (e) for the 1968 excavation are in Bayard n.d.a. and n.d.b., and data for both excavations at the site will appear in Solheim, Parker, Bayard, and Higham n.d.

6. It is possible that iron first arrived in the area during MP 8 times (see Bayard n.d.b.); however, none was recovered from this level in the 1966 excavation.

7. In a recent number of *Antiquity* (48: 58–62), Loofs has rejected this date on the grounds of its uncertain provenance and the early date it would imply for a 'megalithic civilization' in South East Asia. With regard to the provenance of the organic-tempered sherd dated, I can only accept the excavator's interpretation of the site as a short, single-phase one. As far as its association with a 'megalithic civilization' (the nearest 'megalith' to the site is 3 km. distant), I refer the reader to Glover's comments on South East Asian 'megaliths' in this volume. I continue to view the Hàng Gòn l date as admissible evidence, although obviously not of the highest quality.

8. Pinyin romanization.

ADDITIONAL REFERENCES

(for South East Asian references, see *Bibliography*)

Clarke, D. L. 1973. Archaeology: The Loss of Innocence. *Antiquity*, xlvii (185), 6–18.

Harlan, J. R. 1971. Agricultural Origins: Centers and Non-centers. *Science*, 1974: 568–73.

Harlan, J. R. and de Wet, J. M. J. 1973. On the Quality of Evidence for the Origin and Dispersal of Cultivated Plants. *Current Anthropology*, xiv (1), in press.

Harris, D. A. 1972*a*. The Origins of Agriculture in the Tropics. *American Scientist*, x (2), 180–93.

Harris, D. A. 1972*b*. Swidden Systems and Settlement. In *Man, Settlement and Urbanisation*, P. J. Ucko, R. Tringham and G. W. Dimbleby, eds., pp. 245–62. Duckworth, London.

Haynes, V. 1968. Radiocarbon: Analysis of Inorganic Carbon of Fossil Bone and Enamel. *Science*, 161: 687–8.

Ho, P. T. 1969. The Loess and the Origin of Chinese Agriculture. *American Historical Review*, 75: 1–36.

Nikom Suthiragsa. 1972. Raingan Kankhutkhom Thang Borankhadi Konprawatisat thi Ban Chieng, Tambon Ban Chieng, Amphoe Nong Han, Changwat Udon Thani, Kumphaphan–Minakhom P.S. 2515 (Report on prehistoric archaeological excavations at Ban Chieng, Ban Chieng township, Nong Han district, Udon Thani province, Feb.–Mar. 1972). *Silapakon*, xvi (3), 36–57.

Steward, J. H. 1955. *The Theory of Culture Change: The Methodology of Multilinear Evolution.* Urbana, Illinois.

Suess, H. 1970. Bristlecone Pine Calibration of the Radiocarbon Timescale 5200 B.C. to the Present. In *Nobel Symposium 12: Radiocarbon Variation and Absolute Chronology*, I. U. Olsson, ed., pp. 303–11. Uppsala.

Tamers, M. A. 1972. Radiocarbon Dating of Kill Sites. *Archaeometry*, 14 (1), 21–7.

The Chemical Characteristics of some Metal Finds from Non Nok Tha

I. R. SELIMKHANOV

Introduction

THE research Laboratory for Archaeological Technology at the Institute of History for the Azerbaijan Academy of Sciences (U.S.S.R.) has carried out spectroanalytical investigations of some metal finds from the mound of Non Nok Tha in north-eastern Thailand. This site was the subject of two fairly large excavations carried out by the teams of the Universities of Hawaii and Otago, of New Zealand (Bayard 1972). The results obtained in this investigation are of great importance in solving many problems connected with ancient metallurgy and especially the problem of the provenance of tin in antiquity for making bronze in regions where local sources were absent. Earlier we have expressed our opinion that no tin deposits ever existed in the Caucasus, and the possibility that tin was imported during the Bronze Age from South East Asia (Kashkai, Selimkhanov 1954).

Our present paper deals with the results of quantitative spectral analysis of twenty-seven metal pieces found in the successive levels of the mound Non Nok Tha.[1] Unfortunately, none of the metal pieces sent to us were complete objects. Only some of them might be parts of small objects (beads, wire or nails, flat pieces, etc.); the rest are certainly merely lumps of metal spilled during casting while in the molten stage. All the pieces described below were in completely oxidized condition, without metallic core.

Results of Analyses: A. Table.

Samples with catalogue number prefixed 'NP' originate from the 1966 excavations, while those prefixed 'NNT' come from the 1968 excavations.[2] All figures are per cent.

B. Notes

I. Catalogue No. NNT–523. Only one piece from level EP 3, of an approximate age of 2700 B.C. was analysed. The data obtained suggest that it is bronze with a high proportion of tin and very little admixture of other metals.

A. *Table*

	Number	Weight	cu	Sn	Ag	Bi	Ni	Fe	Mo	Pb	Zn	As	Sb	Au	Co	P
I.	NNT–523	1·00 gr.	Base	14·2	0·051	0·004	0·003	0·05	0·002	—	—	—	—	—	—	—
II.	NNT–402	0·2 gr.	Base	16·0	0·06	—	0·002	0·043	0·001	0·006	—	—	—	—	—	—
III.	NNT–318															
	(1)	0·2 gr.	Base	9·0	0·001	0·007	0·008	0·008	—	0·03	—	—	—	—	—	—
	(2)	0·15 gr.	Base	9·3	0·065	0·06	0·002	0·001	—	0·03	—	—	—	—	—	—
	(3)	0·15 gr.	Base	16·0	0·084	—	0·004	—	—	—	—	—	—	—	—	—
	(4)	0·15 gr.	Base	16·0	0·001	0·002	0·002	—	—	—	—	—	—	—	—	—
IV.	NP–390															
	(1)	0·3 gr.	Base	9·3	0·075	0·006	—	—	—	0·002	—	—	—	—	—	0·1
	(2)	0·6 gr.	Base	9·6	0·06	—	0·003	3·1	—	0·007	—	—	—	—	—	0·75
	(3)	0·32 gr.	Base	8·0	0·001	0·003	0·001	—	—	—	—	—	—	—	—	0·1
	(4)	0·05 gr.	Base	9·8	0·03	—	0·001	3·1	—	0·005	—	—	—	—	—	1·5
V.	NP–241															
	(1)	0·25 gr.	Base	15·0	0·072	—	0·002	0·004	—	—	—	—	—	—	—	0·4
	(2)	0·25 gr.	Base	10·4	0·25	—	0·002	0·18	—	—	—	—	—	—	—	1·0
VI.	NNT–263															
	(1)	0·35 gr.	Base	10·6	0·065	0·007	0·003	0·1	—	0·04	—	—	—	—	—	0·75
	(2)	0·35 gr.	Base	9·6	0·034	0·006	0·003	0·02	—	0·002	—	—	—	—	—	0·35
	(3)	0·2 gr.	Base	12·9	0·039	0·009	0·003	0·006	—	—	—	—	0·2	—	—	1·0
	(4)	0·85 gr.	Base	8·8	0·091	0·05	0·002	0·07	—	0·03	—	—	—	—	—	2·0
	(5)	0·8 gr.	Base	6·6	0·037	0·001	0·001	—	—	0·001	—	—	—	—	—	—

A. *Table—continued*

Number	Weight	cu	Sn	Ag	Bi	Ni	Fe	Mo	Pb	Zn	As	Sb	Au	Co	P
VII. NNT-299	0·2 gr.	Base	20·0	—	—	0·0008	—	—	—	—	—	—	—	—	0·85
VIII. NP-291	0·8 gr.	Base	16·6	0·001	0·003	0·002	—	—	0·02	—	—	—	—	—	—
IX. NP-279															
(1)	0·42 gr.	Base	8·0	0·005	0·002	0·002	0·05	0·0005	0·02	—	—	—	—	—	0·9
(2)	0·07 gr.	Base	15·1	0·08	0·3	0·003	0·03	0·0004	—	—	—	—	—	—	3·0
(3)	0·02 gr.	Base	26·0	0·122	0·02	0·003	0·01	—	0·03	—	—	—	—	—	1·0
X. NP-303															
(1)	0·3 gr.	Base	19·6	0·052	0·06	0·003	—	0·0003	0·02	—	—	—	—	—	2·5
(2)	0·3 gr.	Base	11·1	0·014	0·003	0·005	0·005	0·0005	—	—	—	—	—	—	1·0
(3)	0·35 gr.	Base	12·4	0·002	0·004	0·003	0·001	0·0005	0·02	—	—	—	—	—	0·5
(4)	0·4 gr.	Base	16·4	0·005	—	0·002	3·1	0·0005	—	—	—	—	—	—	0·9
(5)	0·1 gr.	Base	15·8	0·005	0·06	0·005	0·05	—	0·004	—	0·05	—	0·001	—	5·0
XI. NNT-209	0·7 gr.	Base	15·7	0·001	0·002	0·002	0·1	0·0004	0·02	—	0·02	0·008	—	—	0·8

II. Cat. No. NNT–402. One piece from level MP 1, of approximate age of 2400 B.C., was analysed. The composition of this tin bronze is very nearly similar to the sample above. Very small admixtures of lead and the absence of bismuth in this case could be explained by irregularities of their content in ancient bronzes.

III. Cat. No. NNT–318. Four pieces from levels MP 1–4, of an uncertain age between 2400 B.C. and 1800 B.C. The piece '3' can be described as tin bronze of an exceptionally high purity.

IV. Cat. No. NP–390. Four pieces from level MP 3 or 4. The age is within the range 2000–1800 B.C. All pieces are of different shape and weight. The data obtained clearly show the difference in the composition. Pieces '2' and '3' are found to contain a high proportion of iron (3·1%). Apparently they are from another level or levels and represent metal smelted from sulphide ores. But the high proportion of iron can be explained by imperfect smelting of sulphide ores.

V. Cat. No. NP–241. Two pieces from levels MP 3–6. The uncertain age is considered to be within the limits 2000–1100 B.C. The composition of these pieces is quite similar. Some irregularity in the proportion of tin and silver can be explained by corrosion of metal.

VI. Cat. No. NNT–263, level MP 5, of an approximate age of 1800 B.C. From this level five metal pieces have been analysed, all of different weight and shape. The piece '3' in this group has been found to contain antimony (0·2%). This is the first specimen to contain antimony, being absent in other samples, and suggests the use of ores from other sources for smelting.

VII. Cat. No. NNT–299. There are two pieces from level MP 6, dated at 1100 B.C. But for the present time only one piece has been analysed: it can be described as tin bronze of exceptionally high purity. The high proportion of phosphorous could be explained by its migration into the oxidized layer of the metal from the soil environment.[3] Because of the very high tin proportion the piece is from an ingot for further casting.

VIII. Cat. No. NP–291. One piece from level MP 6 approximately 1100 B.C., has been analysed. The high proportion of tin, as well as the presence of very small admixtures of lead, silver, bismuth, and nickel, is remarkable.

IX. Cat. No. NP–279. Three pieces from level MP 7, dated at 500 B.C., of different shape and weight. The high proportion of tin and silver is remarkable, but the small weight of piece '3' should be taken into account.

X. Cat. No. NP–303. Five pieces from level MP 8, dated at 200 A.D., have been analysed. The similarity in composition of piece '4' with two pieces of group 'IV' in their equal proportion of iron (3·1%) is evident. It follows that all three pieces belong to the same level, but from which?[4] Unfortunately it is not yet established.

XI. Cat. No. NNT–209. Five metal pieces from uncertain level, either MP 5–6 or LP 2. Accordingly the age of pieces is within the wide limits 1800 B.C. and 1200 A.D. Only one piece allotted to this time, weighing 0·7g., has been analysed. The use of sulphide ores is evident.

Conclusions

Our scientific conclusions, based on the results of spectral analysis of metal finds from Non Nok Tha, are limited because of their bad condition—all are without metallic core. Nevertheless, the results obtained are of interest:

(1) All the metal pieces are bronzes with a high tin proportion, but there are two types of bronzes: (a) tin bronze only, with very little admixture of other metals. (b) tin bronzes with a high proportion of iron, other metals as traces.

(2) No regularity in the content of tin in pieces found in different levels exists. The most ancient bronze sample, dated 2700 B.C., contains 14·2%, and those dated 200 A.D. 19·1% and also 11·1%.

(3) The discovery of very ancient bronze with a high proportion of tin suggests that the existence of more ancient samples of bronzes in Thailand is not excluded. Further archaeological explorations are necessary.

(4) All bronzes from Non Nok Tha are of uncomplex composition, mostly alloyed with tin, except in three cases when iron also is present (3·1%). Other metals are present as very small admixtures. They differ from the composition of ancient bronzes from other regions, for example, from ancient bronzes found in the Near East, Europe, and the Caucasus, which are often alloyed with arsenic, antimony, nickel, zinc, etc. This could be explained by the abundance of local tin in South East Asia but its absence in most other countries. That is the reason why ancient smelters in these other areas always tried to substitute other metals for the expensive tin.

(5) Among bronzes investigated by Professor Pittioni in Vienna, a few are from Non Nok Tha (Pittioni 1969). They are tin bronzes with lead added. It is possible that in some cases the ancient smelter added lead to improve the fluidity of the alloy. But in our bronzes lead is present only in traces.

(6) The establishment of ore sources by means of correlation of impurities is a very complicated task. Each of the two metals introduced its own impurities and one cannot make any orientation based upon 'impurities pattern'. But some facts attract attention: (a) in all samples cobalt and

zinc are completely absent, which means the use of ores without these impurities; (b) arsenic and antimony are present only in two samples. It seems that ancient smelters used ores from the same sources and it could be oxidized ores or, if bronzes contain sulphur, also sulphide ores. Unfortunately determination of sulphur in our samples was not possible, they were without metallic core.

(7) The use of tin bronzes during the first half of the third millennium B.C. in the territory of Thailand maintains our opinion about importation of tin to the Near East and Caucasus from South East Asia.

(8) Extensive examinations for copper and tin ores used in ancient times in South East Asia should be carried out. The development of international scientific co-operation in this field would help to solve many problems of history, ancient metallurgy, and especially the problem of tin supply during the Bronze Age, which up to now remains a mystery.

NOTES

1. This investigation was carried out in co-operation with the University of Otago.

ADDITIONAL NOTES

(by D. T. Bayard)

2. Specimens assigned to two or more levels come from layer interfaces and could not be securely provenanced to a single level.

3. The analysis of P in the soils at the site would confirm this explanation and perhaps explains the high P content of group VI specimens as well. The P content of layer 6 in the eastern portion of the 1968 excavation is ·817% by weight, compared with ·365% and ·450% for layers 5 and 7 respectively. Unfortunately figures are not available from the 1966 excavation.

4. An alternative possibility is the use of ores from different sources (or perhaps specialized alloys) throughout the Middle Period.

A Comment on the Non Nok Tha Dates

R. B. SMITH

IT is always somewhat risky for one who has not been directly involved in an excavation to suggest an interpretation of its results, especially when the final report of the site has not yet been published. The following comment is intended as no more than a question, which those directly concerned with the excavation of Non Nok Tha may be able to answer. It is based on a reading of Dr. Bayard's publication of preliminary data concerning levels and periods at Non Nok Tha, and his list of C14 and TL dates.

Dr. Bayard suggests in his paper that 'an imaginative person could construct four distinct sequences' for the thirty-six dates from Non Nok Tha. Is it necessary, however, to think only in terms of 'sequences' which embrace at one fell swoop all phases of the evidence? Dr. Bayard also presents a comprehensive table showing the relationship between the stratigraphy of his own excavation of 1968 and that of Professor Solheim at the same site in 1966. He divides the Early and Middle Periods into eleven sub-phases: EP 1–3 and MP 1–8. The later period is not involved in the present comment, although it needs to be stressed that its date is at present quite unclear. But if we take the eleven sub-phases of the first two periods, it is possible to suggest, on the face of things, a division into four periods—each with its own problems of dating: EP 1–3; MP 1–3; MP 4–6, and MP 7–8. If these phases or periods are examined separately, it is possible to suggest an interpretation of the evidence which may prove to be less controversial, although inevitably it will leave some important questions unanswered. It will be helpful to work backwards in time, from MP 8; and to take into account the evidence from Non Nong Chik which Dr. Bayard has also presented.

MP 7–8: Non Nok Tha has yielded only one date for these sub-phases: that of A.D. 180±80 (GaK–957). But Dr. Bayard suggests that two dates from layers 5 and 6 at Non Nong Chik belong to a cultural context similar to MP 7–8 at Non Nok Tha: they are 170±75 B.C., and 390±76 B.C. These three dates suggest a phase at these two sites which belongs to the same period as, for example, the jar-burials at Hàng-Gòn or the early iron burial at Manunggal Cave, Palawan.

MP 4–6: This phase is crucial for the dating of Non Nok Tha, and the important point of the present comment is that it involves no serious problems. There seems to be no doubt that it was a period in which bronze was present at the site, and was presumably being worked here and not merely imported. We have five C14 dates for MP 4–5:

$$1840 \pm 110 \text{ B.C. } \quad \text{(GX–1611)}$$
$$1310 \pm 200 \text{ B.C. } \quad \text{(Y–1851)}$$
$$1230 \pm 120 \text{ B.C. } \quad \text{(Y–2485)}$$
$$1130 \pm 110 \text{ B.C. } \quad \text{(GaK–1033)}$$
$$960 \pm 100 \text{ B.C. } \quad \text{(GaK–1029)}$$

This suggests a very coherent sequence indeed, which would make this period correspond roughly to that of the habitation period at Ban Kao and to the burial period at Kok Charoen. Moreover, Dr. Bayard again produces corroborative data from Non Nong Chik, where he sees layer 7 as corresponding roughly to Non Nok Tha's MP 6 (for which there are in fact no dates). That layer produced dates of 1630 ± 95 B.C. and 880 ± 105 B.C.; and it contained some trace of bronze. If this were all the evidence we had, there would be no doubt whatsoever that a bronze-using culture flourished in this part of mainland South East Asia by at the latest the second half of the second millennium B.C. The problem which has still to be resolved is that of its origins, and that cannot be settled merely on the basis of the evidence from Non Nok Tha.

MP 1–3: The period immediately before this very clear one is slightly less clearly dated; but it too is a bronze-using period, and it is possible that we should place its beginning around 2300 B.C. or earlier. There are in fact seven dates from these three sub-phases. One can be dismissed out of hand: a date of 6390 B.C. from MP 2, which fits in with nothing else at all. Two others seem to be ruled out by what has already been demonstrated about MP 4–6: namely 660 ± 120 B.C. (GaK–1031) and 590 ± 140 B.C. (FSU–341) for MP 3, and MP 1 respectively. The one possible explanation for them is that burials were made at this depth during a period between MP 6 and MP 7: a possibility which seems to be ruled out by the excavation report. The other four dates are remarkably consistent in suggesting that in fact MP 1–3 belongs to the period around 2300 B.C. They are:

$$2535 \pm 200 \text{ B.C. } \quad \text{(TL date: PT–278)}$$
$$2350 \pm 150 \text{ B.C. } \quad \text{(TL date: PT–279)}$$
$$2325 \pm 200 \text{ B.C. } \quad \text{(TF–651)}$$
$$2290 \pm 90 \text{ B.C. } \quad \text{(Gak–956)}$$

It has to be admitted, however, that none of these dates is shown in any of the published evidence to prove conclusively the date of the bronze found in these layers.

EP 1–3: It is only when we get back to the Early Period that the evidence becomes totally confusing. It is easy to accept Dr. Bayard's suggestion that all the bone datings from these levels are suspect: they could only be taken seriously if it could be demonstrated that the burials of these deepest layers were made at a date later than the end of MP 6. The excavation reports seem to indicate that that could not have been the case: it would have involved disturbing the burials at higher levels, which does not appear to have occurred. Three other dates fall in the range which we have already related to MP 4–6: these are FSU–345 (1720 B.C.), FSU–342 (1200 B.C.) and GX–1612 (880 B.C.). Finally, there are four dates which takes us back beyond the date of *c.* 2300 B.C., which seems to be appropriate for MP 1–3. Two are TL dates:

2995±320 B.C.   (PT–277): from EP 1
2420±200 B.C.   (PT–276): from EP 3.

Another is a date of 2620±30 B.C. (FSU–340), from the layer below the earliest occupation of the site. In view of the problems surrounding the other FSU dates, this could well be too late. But there seems at least a prima facie case for believing that the site was occupied by an essentially 'Neolithic' culture during the first half of the third millennium B.C. In this context, the final date of 3590±320 B.C. (Gak–1034) for EP 3 must for the time being be regarded as an outlier, possibly unreliable, certainly isolated. Even so, the likeliest dates for EP 1–3 would make Non Nok Tha the earliest dated lowland site in South East Asia, except for the still controversial Ban Chieng. This early phase was contemporary with the occupation of certain cave sites, notably Duyong Cave (Palawan), Gua Kechil (Pahang), and Phnom Laang (Kampot, Cambodia).

If this interpretation were to prove acceptable, it might help to make Non Nok Tha seem a less controversial site and to establish its importance as the earliest known bronze site in South East Asia so far.

The Ban Chieng Culture*

NIKOM SUTHIRAGSA

Ban Chieng and its Recent History

BAN CHIENG is situated in the *tambol* (sub-district) of Ban Chieng in the *amphoe* (district) of Nong Han, Udorn Thani Province, north-east Thailand. If one travels by road to Udorn Thani Province, one must take the Udorn Thani–Sakonnakorn highway to about 50 km. outside Udorn Thani. There is a road on the left going to Ban Chieng, which is about 4–5 km. distant. It is a large village, with a population of 4,476. The village is set on a high egg-shaped mound above flood level, about one square kilometre in area. The surface of the area surrounding it, used for growing rice and other crops, is hilly for the most part. West of the village, there is a reservoir which can be used all year round, and which is the heart of Ban Chieng, in that all life there depends on it. It is used for household consumption, and is called Bueng Na Kam. To the north there is a small creek called Huay Na Kam, which connects with Huay Ban south of the Ban Chieng. On the eastern part of the mound which is the present-day Ban Chieng village, the people have used the wide surface to build wooden houses which for the most part have high spaces beneath them. They are built closely crowded together, most of them without fences. There are old style houses, some with their wooden roofs still remaining, and also there are several shops. The people have a very close-knit relationship with each other, for it is difficult for an outsider to settle there and make a living. Therefore most of the people of Ban Chieng are related by blood.

The territory called Ban Chieng has a history that has been passed down through the years. Briefly, the story goes that during the Ratanakosin period about A.D. 1827, there was a group of people called 'Thai Puan' who migrated from Chieng Kwang in southern Laos. They settled down as permanent residents on a large mound called 'Dong Paeng' and built wooden houses. This village grew larger, as new groups of Thai Puan came down. Then they changed the name of the place to a more auspicious one—'Ban Chieng'. The people of Ban Chieng stayed on to make their living and to prosper. Their descendents continued the line and entered the modern civilization of today. We have said that the history of Ban Chieng began in the Ratanakosin period; According, however, to the evidence that has appeared on the Ban Chieng

* See Plate II.

mound, it had actually begun in the Neolithic Period, six or seven thousand years previously. This evidence will be described below.

The Discovery of Painted Pottery

For a long time the people of Ban Chieng themselves have been finding broken remnants of painted earthenware which have risen to the surface of the ground. No one was interested nor wondered about the peculiar shape and ornament before, because they had been seeing these remnants of earthenware since they were small children. Due to the eroding action of the rain, the sherds had been rising naturally to the surface. Then in the year 1957 Mr. Banloo Montripitaksa, a citizen of Ban Chieng, discovered a painted earthenware pot in perfect condition. He showed it to the teacher, Prommee Srisunakrua, who at that time was the headmaster of the Ban Chieng school. Seeing that it was a beautiful thing and in perfect condition, he kept it and also collected potsherds for visitors to Ban Chieng school to admire.

In 1960, Mr. Charoen Poltecha, who at that time held the position of Head of Fine Arts Unit No. 7, went to inspect archaeological matters in the unit's area of supervision. He discovered the painted pottery at the Ban Chieng school and on Ban Chieng mound. This counts as the first discovery by a Government official. In the year 1963, Mr. Prommee Srisunakrua had a sample of the painted potsherds sent to Mr. Charoen Poltecha to ask for it to be sent for laboratory study to the Fine Arts Department. In 1966 Mr. Stephen Young, son of the then American Ambassador to Thailand, travelled to Ban Chieng. During his anthropological studies he came upon painted potsherds on Ban Chieng mound, collected some, and sent them to Princess Chumphot for safe-keeping at the museum of Suan Pakkad Palace. Princess Chumphot sent them to the Fine Arts Department for examination.

In 1967 the Fine Arts Department sent Mr. Vithya Intakosai, an archaeologist of the Archaeological Division, to perform a technical excavation. (This was the first excavation by the Government.) In one pit was found a human skeleton and a large amount of painted pottery, bronze and iron bracelets and glass beads. Early in January 1972, the Deputy Director of the Fine Arts Department, Mr. Noom Yoonaidharma, and the Head of the Archaeological Division, Mr. Banchob Thiemthat, with Mr. Nikom Suthiragsa, went to inspect the government Fine Arts Units No. 6 in Pimai and No. 7 at Khon Kaen. They went in quietly to investigate the ancient site at Ban Chieng, and discovered that there were many tourists buying painted potsherds. The residents of Ban Chieng themselves had seen that there was profit in it and had become interested in excavating for coloured pots to sell indiscriminately. The Deputy Director advised the National Executive Council that if they let this go on, archaeological evidence important to the nation would be totally destroyed. Within a very short time he went to consult the abbot of Wat Posrinai (a wat located on top of Ban Chieng mound) in order to ask him to allow scientific excavations within his wat; for by this time the villagers were guarding their own property very closely, so as to dig up and sell coloured pots themselves. This was making the seeking of an excavation site difficult. Therefore the Deputy Director and the committee worked together to explain to the people the importance of the national treasures in their land. They explained that this was something that would bring much progress and fame to Ban Chieng. The Abbot was then glad to co-operate and to permit the excavations.

After that, the Deputy Director ordered the authorities to draw up urgent plans for scientific excavation. Then he sent Mr. Pote Kueakun, Assistant Curator of Fine Arts Unit No. 6 (Pimai) and Mr. Wipak Sornthat, Assistant Curator of Fine Arts Unit No. 7 (Khon Kaen), to join in this excavation. Both of them opened sites in the compound of Wat Posrinai.[1] Later, in February 1972, the Fine Arts Department sent Mr. Nikom Suthiragsa, archaeologist of the Fine Arts Department, with Mr. Pote Dhamsut as driver and assistant, to excavate scientifically and to obtain specimens, on the 'Montripitak' site. This lies on land belonging to Mr. Pote Montripitak, citizen of Ban Chieng, who was willing to co-operate by offering his land for excavation without charge or any consideration of return.

Excavation of the 'Montripitak' Site and the Test Pit[2]

A series of 4 × 4 m. squares was opened in the south-eastern quarter of the village, on an area covering about 65 sq. m. (including the removal of intermediate balks and an outlying square). In addition a single test pit of 2 × 2 sq. m. was excavated, some 100 m. west of the Wat Posrinai area. All areas investigated in 1972 were excavated in spits of 10 cm. from the surface to the bottom of cultural deposits. Finds encountered in each spit were kept separate for later study and investigation. Although excavation was carried out using this unit-level method, stratigraphic drawings of the balks were prepared following completion of the excavations.

A. *Stratigraphy*

(i) Square MP 1A

There is a humus layer present in the first 10 cm. over both sides of the northern portion of the square; this tapers off toward the southern part. Pot-sherds recovered included both painted and unpainted, cord-marked wares. Also found were iron spear blades; clay ornaments of a round or oval shape pierced through the long axis and covered with deeply impressed designs (these are interpreted as cloth-decorating tools); and green glass beads.

10–20 cm. layer: The colour of the soil changes to a dark grey, with a dense concentration of painted potsherds and only a small number of cord-marked sherds. This dark grey layer extends to a slight extent over the southern part of the square, while in the centre of the square it extends downward to a level 50 cm. below ground surface. This layer is believed to represent the latest of two living floors in the deposit.

Layer 3 is of a greyish-yellow colour, and is a continuation of the grey layer above (layer 2) down to the 70 cm. level. In this layer both painted and cord-marked styles of pottery were mixed together, but the total number of painted sherds exceeded the cord-marked ones. This would indicate that this layer represents a transition between the period when painted pottery was in use and an earlier period characterized by cord-marked pottery.

Layer 4 is a very dark grey layer featuring concentrations of pottery extending to a level of 90 cm. below surface; the majority of pottery was cord-marked, with only a slight amount of painted ware mixed in. In addition, fragments of bone, pieces of stone bracelets, and several styles of stone adzes were recovered. This is believed to be the earlier of the two living floors.

Layer 5 is again of a greyish-yellow colour, with a decreasing amount of artefacts; only cord-marked pottery was recovered. This layer extended to an absolute depth of 110 cm., and no painted sherds at all were found.

Layer 6 is yellow, and no potsherds or artefacts were apparent down to the level of bedrock aside from a burial (Burial 4) encountered in this space. The grave featured a complete skeleton, accompanied by cord-marked vessels at the feet and an additional two vessels placed on both sides of the skeleton.

(ii) Test Pit Site

Cultural evidence was obtained from this pit in the form of pottery and pottery designs which differed from each other in many ways, but the natural stratigraphy was the same as that encountered at the Montripitak site. This is as follows:

Layer 1 is a very thin layer of humus, of 6 cm. thickness.

Layer 2 was on the average 65 cm. thick, and was a living floor of Late Metal Age people. A burial from this level was similar to Burial 1 (also from layer 2) at the Montripitak site.

Layer 3 dates from the Early Metal Age; painted earthenware vessels are for the most part of a round-bottomed style without ring-feet or pedestals and are of a large size. Tools and ornaments are of bronze, and are not the same as those of layer 2, where there are only iron tools, and small earthenware vessels with ring-feet which resemble vases.

Layer 4 is of the Neolithic period, and is on the average about 65 cm. thick.

Layer 5 is also the same as the Montripitak site. Earthenware was found there in a burial dug deeply into layer 6; this had designs stranger than any encountered before at Ban Chieng. The designs were deeply incised and the ware was black in colour. The designs consisted of curved incised lines with the areas between them filled with impressed punctations; the pattern resembled a snake. In a burial encountered in layers 5 and 6 were found portions of a deer skull, bones, and clusters of two types of snail shells; earthenware with overall cord-marking was also recovered. Layer 5 lay 200 cm. below the surface; beneath it was layer 6, yellow in colour, from which no artefacts were recovered.

B. *Burials*

Eight burials were found at this site. Each period has its distinctive types. In the Neolithic age the bodies were buried full-length, face up, with tools and ornaments of stone placed around the body. Pottery of the cord-marked and deeply-etched types was placed in the area near the feet. As for the graves of the Bronze and Iron Ages, the custom was to place the cord and painted pottery in the area near the head and the chest as well as the feet, along with tools and ornaments.

Pottery and other Finds

Six main types of earthenware pottery have been found at Ban Chieng:
(1) Black surface, incised with spiral designs.
(2) Grey surface, cord-marked.
(3) Creamy white surface, etched with spiral designs and painted with red.
(4) Creamy white surface, incised and painted with red.
(5) Creamy white surface, painted with red, usually on the outside only.
(6) Pink surface, painted with red.

The painted pottery from Ban Chieng is of a very high quality. There are all kinds of shapes and characteristics, the colour used being red-paint all over the pot. The pottery was for the most part buried in the Ban Chieng mound; but some has been found in other places in the vicinity not very far from Ban Chieng. The type of earthenware pottery that is painted all over is characteristic of one period. Ban Chieng traditionally-made painted pottery is different from that in other places in Thailand, so far as is known. The special characteristic of painted pottery with red all over the pots suggests a distinctive culture which might be called 'Ban Chieng culture'.

Amongst other finds belonging to the Ban Chieng culture may be mentioned:

(a) *Utensils*
  1. Rounded tools used for shaping pots from inside.
  2. Spindle whorls.
  3. Earthenware spoons.
  4. Earthenware crucibles.
  5. Earthenware rollers used in making printed designs on cloth.
  6. Earthenware bullets.
(b) *Ornaments*
  1. Glass beads, some long narrow shapes like 'magic beads' and some little round shapes like stone beads.
  2. Bronze bracelets, some with bells and some without bells.
  3. Bronze rings.
  4. Bronze ornaments with four knobs on under side.
  5. Glass or jade, some circular, with a hole in the middle.
(c) *Tools and metal weapons*
  1. Iron tools of various shapes.
  2. Bronze spear heads.
  3. Bronze fish hooks.
  4. Moulds for casting bronze weapons.
(d) *Moulded and carved figures*
  1. Earthenware cows.
  2. Animal bones carved into figures resembling male sexual organs.

The various pieces of evidence that have come from the excavations described here enable us to make a number of observations about the prehistory of Ban Chieng.

(1) There were people living here as early as the Neolithic period.
(2) By the Late Neolithic Age, there were a greater number of people who knew how to apply paint to earthenware pots of the cord-marked type and other types of the Neolithic Age.
(3) In the Bronze Age, a much greater number of people were making various types of pottery, including earthenware pots of a large, round-bottomed type; and they painted designs of various kinds in red. The population increased and spread out into various places; for example, to the areas of Ban Ornkaew, Ban Dong Yen, Ban Tung Fon, Ban Ya, Ban That, Ban Nong Sara Pla, Ban Dung in Udorn Thani Province, and even as far as Sakon Nakon Province.
(4) The Iron Age is characterized by earthenware pottery of a type that had a pedestal and was painted with spiral designs. Tools were made of iron for the most part.
(5) Later, man moved from Ban Chieng, perhaps to seek a more fertile place. Then, about 200 years ago, the Thai Puan migrated and settled here, to stay until the present time.

The 1973 Excavations

In 1973 the Department of Fine Arts undertook a further archaeological excavation at Ban Chieng in addition to those already carried out.[3] I surveyed the vicinity of the village with a view to an excavation to determine the cultural relationship between the Montripitak site (M.P.) and the Wat Posrinai site (W.P.). On completion of the survey, I laid out a grid for a pit of 8×3 m., on the road running through Ban Chieng which lay directly between the Montripitak site and the Wat Posrinai site (see the diagram of the site position), and allotted it the reference-name of B.Ch.1/73 (i.e. Ban Chieng 1 of 1973). The excavation went down in levels of 10 cm. at a time and turned up potsherds and a whole variety of objects relating to human habitation, which have been subjected to scrutiny, together with their soil-levels.

During the survey of the Ban Chieng cultural area, surveying was extended as far as Ban Na-Yia, about 10 km. away from Ban Chieng. It was found that in the vicinity of Ban Na-Yia there was a high mound, standing above any floodwater as at Ban Chieng, and that the local people had dug up a variety of moulded pottery, beads, stone axes, and metal tools, all mixed together. I checked the soil levels and the objects that had been recovered, and found that in the pits that were still left the natural soil-levels were narrower and shallower than at Ban Chieng. Most of the pottery finds were of black ware with incised patterns, mixed with some cord-marked ware. There was very little painted pottery, and such as there was, was found in the topsoil. This indicates that the area had been in use for habitation ever since the time when black cord-marked ware or black incised ware was used (or preferred, as against any preference for painted ware); which implies that the people who settled this area go back in time to the Neolithic period. They must have moved southwards in order to find new land and to expand their population. Thus they had come to mix with the original owners of the land at Ban Chieng, about 10 km. to the south, at about the beginning of the Metal Age; but leaving a remnant of the Ban Na-Yia people to live on and to develop at their original home.

From the B.Ch.1/73 excavation it was found that there had been burials at 350 cm., with some moulded, black, cord-marked pottery with incised pattern (not a trace of any painted ware at all); and with the placing of large stones, which can be interpreted as soul-retaining stones or as grave-markers. The most important fact about the burials is that the human skeletons, quite complete, lay at the deepest level, next to the sterile level, in which not even any fragments of pottery are found. At this deepest level, altogether eight bronze bracelets were found on the bodies' left wrists, which indicates that the people who came to settle in Ban Chieng in the time of the deepest soil-level (namely, the very first period of settlement) already knew the use of metals sufficiently to make artefacts; and they themselves developed this skill further in later times. We could say, indeed, that the group of people who formerly lived to the north had moved down from the Neolithic and had set up a permanent establishment at Ban Chieng at the beginning of the Bronze Age, by mixing in with the original inhabitants both racially, culturally, and occupationally.

The lowest soil level of the B.Ch.1/73 pit had a width of about 1 m. on average; the soil was pale grey. It corresponds to an Early Metal Age and went down to a depth of 350 cm. below the surface. The Early Metal Age finds are as follows:

(1) Incised-pattern and cord-marked black pottery.
(2) Bronze bracelets on skeletons buried at 350 cm. depth.
(3) No consistent direction for orientation of burials.
(4) Post-holes of 23 cm. diameter on average.
(5) There were ash-heaps, charcoal, and impressed traces in the earth of a coarse material of woven texture found at a depth of 280 cm. together with a quantity of cooked rice too.
(6) A variety of sizes of stones placed in all the burials.

The next layer up from this was a different soil; it corresponds to the Middle Bronze Age. From the objects found there, it can be seen that the people who used to live on the Ban Chieng mound had developed from the rudimentary stage of their ancestors and had adapted their technology so as to produce more beautiful artefacts. That is to say, the people of this period knew how to get colour from what we know today as haematite, and to mix it with resin and paint it in between the incisions on their pottery vessels, which had originally used only linear or cord-marked decoration. This pottery painting between incised lines or cord-marked patterns constituted a major step forward in beautiful decorative work. The shapes of the vessels became more varied too: that is, there were some with footrim stands and some with round bottoms. In addition, at about 220 cm. depth in B.Ch.1/73, some silk was discovered spread for a burial beneath the skeleton. The evidence of this silk shows that the people of the Middle Bronze Age already knew how to make silk cloth, and this is probably the earliest date for it known to present-day archaeology. Moreover, in the same soil level were found green glass beads and also a heap of cooked rice in the neighbourhood of a burial.

To sum up, the important facts to emerge from the layer of the Middle Bronze Age are:

(1) Dark-grey soil colour.
(2) Painted pottery, with the colour painted between incised lines or cord-marks.
(3) Bronze bangles, consisting of strands of round cross-section interwoven together as one piece, found on both arms and legs.
(4) Burials, again with no consistent direction for orientation.
(5) Post-holes of 35 cm. diameter on average.

(6) Silk, spread under the hips of a skeleton in one burial at 220 cm. depth.

(7) Green glass beads in a burial at 220 cm. depth, and pottery rollers too.

(8) Charcoal and cooked rice near to each other at a depth of 260 cm.

(9) Stones placed with some of the burials.

(10) Fragments of iron tools at a depth of 220 cm.

In the next level above this, there appears yet another soil-type, with a width of 70 cm.; this is the Late Metal Age level. There are many pottery shapes, most of them resembling those of the painted pottery, of different sizes and with different patterns. These are the pots for which the archaeological evidence is so abundant. The indications, therefore, are that the people of this layer had a culture developed from that of their forefathers, who lived in the Ban Chieng area in the previous layers, and that they knew how to adapt tools, artefacts, and decoration to give them a high degree of beauty and fine suitability for their purpose. A summary of the important finds of the Late Metal Age follows:

(1) Creamy-coloured soil.

(2) Assorted types and sizes of painted pottery vessels.

(3) Assorted types of bronze bangles, both ornamented and unornamented.

(4) Burials, more than at other levels, but again without any consistent orientation.

(5) Green glass beads in burials at 160 cm. depth.

(6) Widespread charcoal residue.

(7) Most noticeable was the whorl or spiral decoration on a bronze bangle, identical with those found in Dvāravati-period archaeological sites, thus encouraging the idea that the people at Ban Chieng in the Late Metal Age survived to become eventually contemporaries of the Early Dvāravati period; and thenceforth were overtaken by cultural changes arising from a Buddhist civilization whose intrusive influence on the peoples of South East Asia brought about changes in, and even the ultimate disappearance of, the original cultures.

The new archaeological evidence that has been revealed by the 1973 excavation is thus as follows. (a) We now know that the area around Ban Chieng was first settled at the time of the Early Metal Age by people moving in from the north who had progressed from a Neolithic culture, a small minority of the representatives of which constituted the original population there. (b) These people themselves achieved development by learning how to use metal for tools and ornaments and, in particular, by making pottery, originally marked by incisions or by cord-marking; but later also coloured, between the incised lines or cord-marking. (c) With the Middle Metal Age came the ability to make glass beads, silk, and an assortment of pottery vessel-types. (d) With the Late Metal Age came the use of colour without any linear boundaries, and a great variety of patterns, the noticeable basis of all of them being a whorl or a spiral turned back upon itself. (e) From the decoration on bronzeware it can be seen that there is a connection with Dvāravatī culture, meaning that it is possible for the people of Ban Chieng to have progressed so far as to have attained, and become the possessors of, a Dvāravatī culture in later times.

NOTES

1. See additional note by Dr. D. T. Bayard, below. He has calculated that if one includes the 1967 as well as the 1972 excavations, the total excavated area by the end of 1972 was about 130 sq. m.

2. For a full account of this excavation (in Thai) see the report by Nikom Suthiragsa in *Silapakorn*, xvi, no. 3 (1973), pp. 36–63.

3. The team consisted of myself, Miss Pacharee Komolthitti who helped by keeping the daily work-in-progress reports at the site, Miss Suphawadee Bhaktibutra, who recorded the finds, Mr. Chert Chandrakhong in charge of the labour force, and Mr. Phot Dharmasuddhi, our driver.

ADDITIONAL NOTES

1. *The Wat Posrinai Site—a note by D. T. Bayard*

Some 56 sq. m. were excavated within the compound of Wat Posrinai, at the eastern extremity of the village, after the Abbot of the *wat* had granted permission. This excavation was under the direction of Mr. Pote Kueakoon and Mr. Wipak Sornthat, of Fine Arts Department Units 6 and 7 (Phimai and Khon Kaen). I am told by Mr. Pote that the division into five cultural layers found in the Montripitak and test pit areas is also characteristic of the Wat Posrinai area. (Mr. Pote's report on the Wat Posrinai area should be forthcoming in the near future.) However, it should be noted that the depth of these layers is far from uniform in the different areas. Sterile soil is reached at a depth of about 100 cm. in the Montripitak area, but cultural deposits extend to 200 cm. or more below surface in the vicinity of the test pit and Wat Posrinai excavations. Thus there is no correlation between the absolute depth of a particular 10-cm. spit and the cultural level with which it is associated from one area to another. Nor is there a high degree of correlation within the stratigraphy recorded for the Montripitak site; thus the layer 2/layer 3 boundary varies from 10 to 60 cm. below the surface, while the 3/4 boundary occurs at depths of between 25 and 90 cm. Such variation in deposition is almost certainly responsible for the broad range and considerable overlap in the recently announced series of sixteen thermoluminescence dates, provenanced to absolute level only, which were derived from the Wat Posrinai excavations.

2. *The Thermoluminescence Dates—a note by the Editors*

No radiocarbon dates have so far been obtained from Ban Chieng, but two series of dates have been published based on tests of the thermoluminescence of some of the pottery.

A. *Three samples tested at the Museum of Applied Science Centre for Archaeology, University of Pennsylvania, Philadelphia*

The first sample (no. 104) said to have been a surface find, produced a date of 4630 B.C. (+520). This date cannot, on its own, be accepted as of any significance in relation to any part of the stratigraphy of the site. The two other samples (nos. 271, 273) were taken from specific levels:

70–80 cm. no. 271: 3570 B.C. (±480)
130 cm. no. 273: 3590 B.C. (±275)

(Bronson and Han 1972: 322–6).

B. *Report of Professors Y. Ichikawa and K. Nakagawa, of the Nara University of Education, to the Thai Fine Arts Department, March 1973*

This sequence of dates, apparently based on material from the 1972 excavations, was published by Pisit Charoenwangsa (1973: 27–8):

Level	Specimens	Range of dates
50–60 cm.	1: 1 to 5	1640–570 B.C.
80–90 cm.	2: 1 to 5	2830–400 B.C.
110–120 cm.	3: 1 and 4	2860–2460 B.C.
190–200 cm.	4: 1 to 4	4420–3400 B.C.

It is noted that specimen no. 3:1, dated to 2860 B.C. is the oldest piece of *painted* pottery so far dated from this site.

The Nara sequence suggests that the Pennsylvania dates might well be too early, if the levels from which they came are at all comparable stratigraphically to those represented by the Nara samples. Nevertheless, it would appear that we now have prima facie evidence for treating Ban Chieng as a more ancient site than Non Nok Tha, and for suggesting that its earliest phases *might* date back to the fourth millennium B.C.

Kok Charoen and the Early Metal Age of Central Thailand*

W. WATSON

IN recent writing the traditional model of pre-metallic culture has been all but discarded in discussing Thai prehistory. The boundary between food-gatherers and food-producers loses its old revolutionary meaning as these two economies are shown, or postulated, to be less exclusive in sparsely inhabited regions than was supposed hitherto. On the other hand, archaeologists working in Thailand have made much of the introduction of bronze metallurgy, in the apparent unshaken belief that the appearance of this technique even at isolated points in a given region betokens a fundamental and widespread change in economic and social life, as it certainly did in the densely populated centres of Asian bronze-age civilization. If the adoption of bronze in Thailand occurred at anything like the early date now proposed, it is remarkable that a thousand years later sites in the same fairly limited area should betray no contact, or only dubious and remote contact, with metal users. The following observations from the study of excavations at Kok Charoen may contribute to the understanding of a mode of progress peculiar to Thailand, in circumstances probably not untypical of South East Asia as a whole (Watson 1968; Watson and Loofs 1967; Loofs 1970).

The site of Kok Charoen is situated in north central Thailand in a region of low limestone hills on the eastern edge of the Menam plain 13·5 km. from Chaibadan on the west side of the road to Petchabun. A few hundred metres to the east of it begin the foothills of the mountain chain which separates the Menam from the Khorat Plateau. The surroundings and climate would correspond more closely to Bayard's 'Piedmont area' than to the Khorat Plateau or the territories of the north-east. The site is on a tongue of land bounded by two small streams and reaching to their junction. In the wet season the streams carry abundant water. Around the site a shallow rolling topography suggest powerful water action at various times, perhaps in excess of what is experienced today. The Menam itself is some 15 km. distant at the most accessible point. Nearly adjacent to the site on the south is a stretch of fairly flat country, extending for a kilometre or more. As it appears today it seems that the site was chosen to be near water, and more likely for the sake of wet cultivable land than for the small streams themselves. Since the occupation and burials

* See Plate III.

at Kok Charoen will be shown to centre around the date of 1000 B.C., the site appears to fall outside the model proposed by Higham, which limits wet rice agriculture to the period A.D. 0–900 (Higham 1972). Had livelihood depended on dry rice farming and cattle herding, there seems little advantage in clearing this difficult terrain in preference to the slightly higher land of the vicinity, which might be less heavily wooded and would certainly be better drained. The excavated material has not, however, produced direct evidence of grain cultivation.

The area in which burials and evidence of habitation are found extends north and south for about 200 m., and for at least half that distance east and west. Excavation was carried out in three places. Kok Charoen 1 is at the point of a triangle, near the junction of the streams, which at this place run in deep gulleys. Kok Charoen 2 and 3 are about 200 m. to the south and fairly close together, but though contiguous they record different dates and activity. The bed-rock is limestone at most a metre below the surface, and exposed at places. The soils over it consist of limy gravels passing irregularly into humus. The lines of junction between one soil formation and another, though they do not leap to the eye, are nevertheless clearly traceable in texture, in one case distinctly by colour, and by the difference of constituents which reveals itself by fissures in drying. All three divisions of the site that have been explored show the distinction of an upper and a lower soil separated by a discontinuity. A similar phenomenon was noted at Non Nok Tha, where a radical change in soil was invariably associated with a prolonged gap in the occupational sequence (Bayard 1971). Such disconformity of deposition was not, however, recorded at Ban Kao (Sørensen 1972a).

The problem of interpretation presented by this sequence of soils is one familiar to excavators of tropical sites. It is arguable that the phenomena described here are all the result of chemical action, the equivalent, in tropical conditions of rain, temperature, and abundant vegetation, of the podsols of temperate Asia and Europe. Thus far the examination of soil samples taken from Kok Charoen has not demonstrated a sequence of leaching and precipitation such as would be looked for in a podsol cycle; although it must be conceded that the reason for this in the vicinity of Kok Charoen may be the relative shallowness of soil of any kind, and the excessive and generalized drenching which this soil has received annually, without renewal of humus, ever since the primaeval vegetational cover was removed by man. But the possibility that the observed banding and grading of the Kok Charoen deposits may have been largely or even wholly caused by bacterial and chemical action does not dispense from the need to examine the data under the alternative hypothesis, that of differential deposition and mechanical degrading caused by natural agencies other than chemical assault. This paper considers the archaeological inference ensuing from provisional acceptance of the mechanical theory. Its conclusions, insofar as they depend on this theory, are advanced in the belief that archaeological argument is as necessary for soil history as the pedological analysis, since chemical change may have obliterated horizons of deposition.

It cannot yet be said whether the cause of the disconformity observed at Kok Charoen was a general climatic one—an increase in precipitation which reversed local soil accretion to erosion for an unascertainable period; or the result of local interference, such as forest and scrub clearance, which set off a phase of local erosion lasting until the natural balance was restrored. One could not be certain in either case whether the break marks a short or long passage of time, but the evidence from Kok Charoen suggests that it may have at least been long enough to show a cultural change before and after. Only close dating, not available at Kok Charoen, can resolve this problem. Meantime observation of stratigraphy at other sites should make it possible to co-ordinate an important climatic datum, which itself would contribute to the interpretation of radiocarbon dates, or demonstrate a regular feature of the traces of human activity in the Piedmont area.

On the evidence of thermoluminescence dating available for burials at Kok Charoen 2 and 3, which appear to lie respectively after and before the erosion line, the change in the soil regime falls around 1000±300 B.C. At Kok Charoen 1 the burials were too fragmentary and too much disturbed to allow a dependable conclusion, though the absence of incised-and-pricked pottery (see below) points to the post-erosion group as deduced elsewhere, and none of the burial pots is of the earliest kind found on the site. At Kok Charoen 2 only one burial was rather dubiously referred to the top pre-erosion soil, the remaining forty-one burials lying in pits cut from the surface of, or within, the first post-erosion soil. At Kok Charoen 3 these conditions were reversed: the eight burials of this portion of the site belong to the top pre-erosion soil. The thermo-luminescence dates for the two grave groups, Kok Charoen 2 and 3, were respectively 980±450 B.C. and 1180±300/1080±300 B.C. The tentative nature of the following interpretation should be plain. It is offered as a point of departure for comparison with similar phenomena at other sites. The Soil(s) A are the later, subsequent to the disconformity, the arrow marking the direction of time. The occupation levels which are indicated are inferred either from the solution of continuity in the deposition, or from the presence in the level of a large amount of small and rubbed fragments of pottery.

Kok Charoen 1

↑ Soil A: Layer I   — Burials with red pedestal bowls, etc.,
OCCUPATION

Disconformity ———————————————————————————

Soil B: Layer II   — Pit with cylindrical pot decorated in incised-and-pricked style, buried singly, no inhumation. The soil filling the pit and otherwise seen only on a small area surrounding it was extremely fine, cafe-au-lait and more plastic than the gravelly soil above (in which the pits of the burials had been dug). Its appearance corresponded closely to Layer IV of Kok Charoen 2, both having the character of a leached soil. It seems clear that the same erosion as deduced for Kok Charoen 2 was responsible at Kok Charoen 1 for removing the habitation surface from which the pit of the 'vessel deposit' was dug. Two exploitations of this part of the site must be assumed: the pre-erosion occupation, presumably habitation, when the vessel deposit pit was dug through the top soil lower humus 'soil 4'; and its post-erosion use as a cemetry.

———————————————————————————

Kok Charoen 2

↑ Soils A:

    1. Layer I   — Recent disturbance in currently forming humic soil.
OCCUPATION

    2. Layer II   — Gravelly soil resembling a 'hill-wash', probably contemporary with OCCUPATION at some part of the site.

    3. Layer III   — Limy gravelly soil from which all but one of the graves were dug. Burials with red pedestal bowls, etc. Sherds outside graves small and rolled.
OCCUPATION

Disconformity ─────────────────────────────────
Soils B:

    4.   Layer IV — Light brown fine soil.
                        Sherds lime-encrusted, not rolled.
                             OCCUPATION on the surface over this soil, which has been eroded away. Vessel deposit pit cut from this soil.

    5.   Layer V   — Coarse whitish gravelly soil.
    6.   Layer VI — Natural.

Kok Charoen 3

↑ Soils A:

    1.   Layer I   — Recent disturbance in currently forming humic soil.
                           OCCUPATION

    2.   Layer II   — Heavy black soil.
                           OCCUPATION Post-holes

    3.   Layers III, IV — Dark soil, splitting on drying.
                           OCCUPATION Post-holes

Disconformity ─────────────────────────────────
Soils B:

    4.   Layer V   — Fine gravelly soil.
                           Burials with red pedestal bowls, etc., and incised-and-pricked bowls.

        Layer VI — Fine gravelly soil.
                             Burials with red pedestal bowls, etc., but no bowls with incised-and-pricked ornament.

    5.   Layer VII — Sterile
    6.   Layer VIII — Natural

It is clear that the Kok Charoen community lived the neolithic life. The size of their burial grounds, the uniformity of their burial practices, the excellence of their superior ceramic, as well as the siting of their settlement (assuming that this was not far removed from the cemeteries) all indicate comparatively long sojourn in one place, or in a restricted region. These circumstances would appear to be incompatible with the itinerant agriculture of slash-and-burn, or with the roving pastoralism attributed by Ssu-ma Ch'ien to the Yünnanese in the second–first centuries B.C. The only hint to be found at Kok Charoen of the influence of metal-users comes from the stone tools.

Stray finds of stone pillow-shaped axes, *walzenbeile*, point to a stage of lithic industry once present in central Thailand which can only have corresponded to an earlier neolithic phase. But like the stone adzes reported from Bang Kao, the stone implements of Kok Charoen are small, sub-rectangular in outline and section, with flat ground sides, sometimes the slightest shouldering, and exactly ground edges placed centrally as in an axe, or to one side as in an adze. The broad analogy is with the stone axes of the South-Chinese neolithic which fall within the period of bronze-using culture farther north. On all parts of Kok Charoen the small stone axes were found accompanying burials or in the vicinity of burials; and freely scattered in the site. The burial pieces were nearly all small, and of limestone already softened by the action of rain water. These presumably had been made especially for burial. Other pieces were made of good greenstone, and not included in graves. Some moreover were unfinished, or abandoned after breakage probably caused in manufacture, a circumstance which disproves the suggestion that the stone axes had been collected by the Kok Charoenians for superstitious reasons, as is done today by the country people of Thailand. Stone was in use, but it is likely that the small size of the axes and their oblong cross-section with flat-ground sides, reflect an influence of the users of bronze axes, possibly at a great distance. Had metal been available to them, even if they could not afford to acquire it for tools, these comparatively well-to-do farmers might be expected to procure at least bronze ornaments; but the bracelets and earrings placed with the dead were of shell. In China it can be shown that small adzes with neatly-squared shoulders and tang were made in an early phase of the south Chinese bronze-age, being confined to the south and south-east provinces. Just such a piece was found on the surface at Kok Charoen where it probably relates to an occupation posterior to that approximately coinciding with the post-erosion burials. In south China such shouldered axes are to be dated after 1000 B.C., and more probably to the middle of the first millennium B.C. at the earliest (Watson 1971). The implication for Kok Charoen, the shouldered axe evidently being present in the region but totally absent from the burials, is that the occupation to which the burials relate ceased at some time between 1000 and 500 B.C.

Kok Charoen pottery falls into two sharply divided classes. A red ware, with burnished surface often enhanced by a haematite dressing, supplied the pedestal bowls which were the chief part of the grave vessels. Pots decorated more or less elaborately with incised lines and cording-filled figures belong also to the red ware, but their fabric is better levigated and the surface usually smoothed without the burnishing by pebble or narrow spatula which is characteristic of the pedestal bowls. The contrasting ware is covered over the greater part of the outer surface with true cord impressions, or (in a minority) with striations closely simulating the cording. The dominant shape is a subpherical bowl with restricted mouth and everted rim. In comparison with pottery found at Non Nok Tha further north, and at Ban Kao lying to the south-west, and accepting provisionally the dating proposed for these sites, one is obliged to accept an extraordinarily long survival of pottery types in central Thailand. This is true both of the coarser corded ware and the more elaborate types. For example, the red pedestal bowls are represented at Non Nok Tha only by pieces from layer 20 (Level II) for which a radiocarbon date in the mid-third millennium B.C. is claimed. At the biggest stretch of the Kok Charoen dates, a gap of a thousand years or more separates the appearance of the comparable potteries at the two sites, although the distance between them is only some 200 km.

The comparison of Ban Kao pottery with that of Kok Charoen raises chronological problems no less fundamental. The pedestal bowls from the former site (Ban Kao, type 2 var. A) are substantially different from the Kok Charoen type. A singleton from Kok Charoen 1 (where it may belong to the pre-erosion phase, though this was not stratigraphically established) comes nearer to the Ban Kao shape, and so suggests the possibility of equating the 'Early Neolithic Sub-phase' at Ban Kao (to which type 2 belongs on Sørensen's chronology) with the pre-erosion phase at Kok Charoen. Another resemblance in favour of this correlation is of the 'deposit pot' from Kok Charoen 1 (cylindrical body with incised and pricked meanders of varied shape) with Sørensen's pedestal bowl from B44 for the ornament, and his type 10 as represented by Plate 102*d* for the shape (Sørensen 1967, p. 102). Both of these Ban Kao pieces are put in the early phase. The bowl makes the most telling comparison, for the ornament is quite like that of Kok Charoen and there is a moulding at the join of pedestal and bowl which occurs on the earlier-looking pieces at this site. Since it is argued from Kok Charoen 3 that the incised-and-pricked ware belongs to the later pre-erosion burials, the correlation is at a date c. 1100 B.C. (Kok Charoen dating) as far as the shape is concerned, with the possibility arising from the ornament that the correlation ante-dates any of the Kok Charoen burials. Kok Charoen does not, however, give any support for Sørensen's placing the pedestal bowl from his Burial 44 at the *beginning* of the Early Neolithic Sub-phase, and c. 1800 B.C. If the erosion level postulated at the Kok Charoen sites even approximates in date to 1100 B.C., the effect of these comparisons is to support Hamilton Parker's argument for reducing all the dates proposed for Ban Kao, so as to place them largely within the first millennium B.C., with only pots from the earliest graves coinciding significantly with Kok Charoen. A parallel not previously made is of Sørensen's pot type 8 with a bronze drum body, now in the British Museum (cf. Gray 1949–50), which came either from the Tien necropolis at Shih-chai-shan, or a closely allied site in the same region. Here too is either a case of the millennary survival of a characteristic type, or a correlation indicating a much later date than the one proposed for the Early Neolithic Sub-phase at Ban Kao.

Before proposing some tentative conclusions to be drawn from this brief analysis of the finds made at Kok Charoen it is well to consider the scheme of neolithic culture proposed on the evidence of the more abundant and varied material yielded by excavations at Ban Kao (Sørensen 1972). The affinities of this site according to Sørensen lead to the south, rather than into central or north Thailand, and then only within discrete boundaries: 'As the archaeological evidence of the Ban Kao culture from the earliest to very late phases is concentrated in North Malaysia, it is very difficult to assess its influence further southwards. Some pottery types are however common both to North Malaysia and to some of the burial pottery from the Niah caves in Borneo; on the other hand it is uncertain whether the culture extends further into Borneo or may simply have made contact without settlement'. The conclusion is that the Ban Kao culture intrudes into the region as an integrated complex, and Dr. Sørensen propounds the thesis that it marks a far-travelled migration from a Chinese zone of transitional Lung-shan (or 'Lungshanoid') character. (Such a view conforms to K. C. Chang's diffusionist model of Lung-shan expansion, but fits less well with the views of those who have questioned the formal basis of the current Chinese argument for a unitary neolithic tradition, with Lung-shan as wholly the issue and successor of Yang-shao neolithic). Radiocarbon dating is claimed to allow that this migrating culture reached Ban Kao about 1800 B.C.; the transition from the Early to the Late Sub-phase is estimated at *c.* 1500 B.C., while the Late Sub-phase is agreed to flourish until *c.* 1300 B.C. and perhaps for a couple of centuries longer.

Sørensen places a corded ware culture in contrast to the Ban Kao complex. He supposes that a *neolithicised Bacsonian* dates from the early centuries of the second millennium and carries a corded and incised ware at its ceramic diagnostic. The earlier phase, lasting until *c.* 1100 B.C., is associated with 'quadrangular adzes', and to these, in the succeeding phase, shouldered adzes are added. The neolithicised Bacsonian is referred in a general way to the neolithic of south China, that is, the neolithic lying beyond the pale of the Yang-shao and Lung-shan cultures. In this case the question of migration is not raised.

Despite the series of similar pottery shapes which can be found in the Ban Kao and the transitional Lung-shan ware, Sørensen's thesis has yet to receive the support of students of the Chinese neolithic. The fabric of his vessels is different, and no other definite feature of his Ban Kao culture can be said to link significantly with Lung-shan, whether transitional or classical. In the counter-argument the dating of such sites as those at Kok Charoen may prove crucial, for here smooth-surfaced ware analogous technically to Ban Kao ware, and paralleling it in some shapes, occurs intimately combined with corded vessels, which certainly issue from the broad tradition descending from the neolithicised Bacsonian. Kok Charoen both throws doubt on the possibility of separating a Ban Kao-like ceramic from corded ware in the cultural classification, and by indicating a possibly later date for the Early Sub-phase at Ban Kao reduces any plausibility the attribution to Lung-shan may appear to have. In making these comparisons due weight must be allowed to the technical individuality of the Thai potteries. The thin potting, sharp carination, and burnished black of classical Lung-shan nowhere appear, and the standard of both shape and fabric is superior at Ban Kao and Kok Charoen to the pieces now referred to as transitional Lung-shan. Moreover, while the corded ware represents the Thai aspect of a very widely diffused tradition, it is nevertheless distinct. The firing is higher and the corded surfaces (at Kok Charoen there are seven distinct varieties of cording) remain to a degree *sui generis*, distinct from those of the south Chinese neolithic and recognizably South East Asian.

Although some ceramic types are of long duration, and must be regarded as extraordinarily long-lived if the dates claimed by their excavators for Non Nok Tha and Ban Kao are substantiated, it does not follow that all ceramic types are equally persistent. The pedestal bowls are forms which might be expected to have a more specific and shorter history than less characteristic shapes. The sub-spherical corded pots with reverted rim, ubiquitous at Kok Charoen and numbered with the earliest vessels at Ban Kao, lasted well into the Early Metal Age, and their readily recognizable descendants figure in the Bangkok flower-market at the present day. It is worth noting that at a cave site near Fang, Tham Nguang Chang, crude versions of this ceramic type occurred with burials which were accompanied by iron axes. Over one of the burials, but not demonstrably included in a grave, was found a bronze socketed axe resembling a poor cousin of the axe made by the Non Nok Tha mould. Since the iron can hardly date before 500 B.C., more than 2,000 years must intervene between the bronze axes of Tham Nguang Chang and the Non Nok Tha specimens (accepting their proposed early date). The former corresponds approximately to examples of the same tool found in the boat graves of Szechwan, for which a date around 350 B.C. appears probable.

It thus appears that the close combination of smooth-surfaced and corded potteries encountered in central Thailand, while it occurs in such varying degrees as to preclude the idea of cultural migration *de toutes pièces*, nevertheless indicates the contact of two ceramic traditions which appear separated in their farther extensions into south China and north Malaysia. This further suggests variety rather than uniformity in the prehistoric settlement, and consequently a varying response to the possibility of acquiring bronze metallurgy when this became available anywhere in the region. The variety of ceramic practice, in Thailand as elsewhere in Asia, is likely to reflect the economic differences which determined acceptance of metal. The Chinese Central Plain gives an analogy: there bronze metallurgy was first established in the comparatively restricted zone where the Yang-shao and Lung-shan traditions had overlapped geographically; and, while at a few centres the new industry advanced rapidly, its impact on the neolithic population at large was scarcely perceptible for many centuries.

The tentative conclusions from the stratigraphy of the Kok Charoen sites indicate that towards the end of the second millennium B.C. bronze metallurgy was not present close enough to this part of Lopburi province to leave much mark on a culture which evidently had not direct access to the metal. The relationship of the Kok Charoen culture to bronze-users settled at some distance might be compared to that of various branches of the European Neolithic to the Mediterranean Bronze Age. It must be emphasized, however, that the impression, somewhat subjective, of the influence of bronze-using culture at Kok Charoen (chiefly the form of stone axes and adzes), might be accounted for in terms of bronze-founding much farther away than Non Nok Tha. At Kok Charoen some clear tokens of neolithic tradition are the stone bracelets and shell bracelets and earrings. If the remoteness from bronze of even a community of some substance such as that of Kok Charoen should prove general in central Thailand, it follows that more than rare bronze artefacts and radiocarbon datings will be necessary for a satisfactorily broad study of economic and social development. Conclusions on this subject may depend in the last resort on the collation of a statistically significant number of sites, and not on the rich material and stratigraphic clarity of a single site. If either of the two possible ranges of dates is substantiated for Non Nok Tha, Ban Kao and Kok Charoen are put into the category of retarded, post-bronze neolithic. The greatest promise for making the correlations necessary for a regional and social study of our, thus far, too isolated data, lies in exhaustive ceramic typology, on the lines initiated by Sørensen's Ban Kao report, and in rigorous stratigraphic and pedological study. Meanwhile the hints to be found in the Kok Charoen excavation tell against rather than in favour of the existence of advanced bronze metallurgy in any near-lying locality.

NOTE

The views on the stratigraphy of the Kok Charoen deposits are the result of observations by all three members of the excavation—H. Loofs, H. Parker, and the author of this paper. The author wishes to thank Mr. Parker for his assistance specially regarding the excavations at Kok Charoen 3. The thermoluminescent dates are quoted by courtesy of the Oxford Laboratory for Archaeology and the History of Art.

The Late Prehistoric and Early Historic Pottery of the Khorat Plateau, with Special Reference to Phimai*

WILHELM G. SOLHEIM II *and* MARTI AYRES

Introduction

SYSTEMATIC archaeological exploration for and excavation of prehistoric sites began in north-eastern Thailand in 1963 with the beginning of the archaeological salvage programme of the Fine Arts Department—University of Hawaii Expedition (Solheim and Gorman 1966; Solheim 1966a). This expedition under my direction (senior author), discovered a total of twenty-one archaeological sites the first year, of which we felt two sites in the Lam Pla Plerng reservoir area, south-west of Korat, and two to four sites in the Nam Pong area north-west of Khon Kaen were prehistoric (Solheim and Gorman 1966: 179). During the second year of this programme one or two more sites were found not far from those found the first year. With the exception of one of the sites in the Nam Pong area, excavations were made in all of the prehistoric sites, found the first year, during the second and third year of the programme. Headquarters for the expedition were maintained in the Fine Arts Department compound in Phimai. During the 1965–6 field season we found that there was a pre-Khmer occupation evident beneath the famous ruins in Phimai. At the end of the season we made a small test excavation of this culture (Solheim 1965).

Ban Chieng was first noted as an area with painted pottery in 1960 but no action followed. In 1966 the area was rediscovered and painted pottery brought to the National Museum in Bangkok (Intakosai 1972). Much local digging of this pottery developed for its sale as antiquities. The National Museum conducted excavations in 1967 and 1972 (Suthirak 1972). There are no doubt several sites included in the digging that has been done.

The University of Otago in New Zealand and the National Museum of Thailand, with the co-operation of the University of Hawaii, in 1969–70 made exploratory surveys in the Roi Et provinces of north-eastern Thailand and in Phu Wiang, an unusual geological feature west of Khon Kaen. Test excavations were made in three Roi Et sites out of eight sites located, revealing that all of them had prehistoric levels. In Phu Wiang eighteen sites were located

* See Plates IV, V.

and four of these tested. All sites tested had prehistoric levels (Higham and Parker, n.d.).

I have knowledge of about fifty sites on the Korat Plateau, not counting fully historic sites located by the National Museum, and of these at least twenty have prehistoric levels about which we have some information.

Data on the pottery from the known archaeological sites is variable. In no case has a final report yet been completed, let alone published. The only prehistoric pottery on which I have relatively good data is that from Phimai and Non Nok Tha, with less data but still some details on the Phu Wiang pottery. From the other sites there is very little data. What can be done with the data we have?

The primary purpose of this paper is to put on record a more detailed but still somewhat preliminary report on the *Phimai black pottery*. The available data on pottery from the other sites on the Khorat plateau of roughly comparable dating to that of Phimai is summarized by way of comparative background.

The Phu Wiang Sites and Non Nok Tha

There are hundreds of restored or partly restored vessels from the Non Nok Tha burials but while most of these have been described, measured, and pictured, and the data put on punch cards, the final analysis of the material has not yet been run. The 1966 excavation layers which would correspond in time to the Phimai black period are about 17 through 13. Much of this period was missing in the 1968 excavations. Level VII of the 1968 excavation is probably at the early end of this period. Probably from this level came two animal effigy vessels; one we felt to be an elephant, the other a frog (Bayard 1970: pl. IVa).

One of the most striking observations of the Non Nok Tha pottery is that over the more than 5,000 year intermittent use of the site, the pottery of the final occupation resembles the common pottery of the first occupation; it is one pottery tradition from beginning to end, with numerous changes but with continuity, particularly of the cord-marked pottery, from start to finish. The pottery is not similar in appearance to the pottery made in north-eastern Thailand today. There were changes taking place during the time of the Phimai black sequence but they were changes of detail. It is more meaningful to summarize the changes from the first pottery to the first millennium A.D. gap in the Non Nok Tha sequence, than to deal only with the late prehistoric pottery.

The very neatly done incised and impressed decoration of large vessels (Plate IVa) was found only in the deepest level, associated with burials. A number of these vessels have been illustrated (Solheim 1966b: pl. IIIc; 1967a: pl. IVc–d; 1967b: fig. 5, 1970a: pl. Id). At times associated with the incised and impressed pottery are somewhat smaller cord-marked jars with two to four incised, more or less parallel lines around the circumference, over the cord-marking (Solheim 1970a: pl. 1f). While the well done incising and impressing is found only in the bottom level, these poorly incised jars are found in three or four levels above as well.

Low ring feet on small, cord-marked pots first show up in Level II (Solheim 1970a: pl. IId, 1972: fig. 9c). From Levels III and IV four painted jars, all with low ring feet and perforations through the ring foot and rim (Plate IVb), were found (Solheim 1967a: pl. IVe, 1970a: pl. Ie, 1970b: pl. II: 1972: fig. 9d). From Level IV, and several latter levels, were found large round-bottomed jars with cord-marked bodies and well-smoothed shoulders, often red-slipped (Solheim 1970a: pl. IIe, 1972: fig. 9b). Beginning in this level were the two most common funerary vessels of all later levels, a globular or ovoid, ring-footed vessel with short vertical or slightly everted rim (Solheim 1967a: pl. IIIf, 1970a: pl. IIb–c, 1972: fig. 4), and a shallow, footed goblet with a sharply angled shoulder (Solheim 1967a: pl. IIIb, 1972: fig. 9a). There is much more variation in pottery form than here indicated but this is not the place to go into this detail. Some of this variation can be seen in the illustrations in other papers. (For further details of the above see Bayard 1968 and n.d.)

The pottery from the Phu Wiang sites matches nicely with Non Nok Tha and should furnish a good test of the Non Nok Tha sequence. The C14 dates also fit quite well with the early Non Nok Tha sequence. Very few whole pots were recovered in these sites so the analysis that has been made was based on the temper and surface finish. The most noticeable change through time of this pottery is a decline in sand and prepared clay temper and cord-marking and the correlated increase in fibre (rice chaff primarily) temper and plain body finish (Buchan 1973: 104).

The few illustrated whole or restored vessels are very similar to Non Nok Tha pottery except for one large pot from Non Nong Chik (pot 6, NNC–12, Buchan 1973: 159 and 165). This is much like the Phimai, black, large globular pot with rows of slightly raised bands at the base of the shoulder (p. 72 and Plate IVa). The rim form is not a common form in Non Nok Tha but is a common Phimai black rim form. There is a simple design of parallel red lines high on the shoulder. This pot was with Burial 1, from Layer 5. A C14 date of 2120±75 B.C. comes from this layer (Buchan 1973: 54), but dates both above and below this layer are somewhat earlier.

Ban Chieng

The Ban Chieng sites and pottery are covered by another paper, so I will make only a few general remarks. The earlier incised and impressed decoration followed by the painted pottery at Ban Chieng matches the incised and impressed pottery of the bottom level at Non Nok Tha and the painted pottery at levels 3 and 4. None of the large, early variety of painted pottery found at Ban Chieng (Nikom Suthiragsa 1972: 55) was found at Non Nok Tha. The Non Nok Tha painted pottery is distinct from that at Ban Chieng but is more similar to the middle, pedestalled jars than the early large non-pedestalled jars. This would suggest that there may have been a considerable time range between the first and third levels at Non Nok Tha. The three thermo-luminescence dates from Ban Chieng (Bronson and Han 1972), fit reasonably well with the early sequence of dates for Non Nok Tha and three of the four thermoluminescence dates for Non Nok Tha. The date for pottery from the lowest Non Nok Tha level would appear to be too recent.

Lam Pla Plerng Pottery

The Lam Pla Plerng sites were excavated in late 1964 and early 1965 by Ernestine Green. Unfortunately the collection from these excavations has been only partially analyzed so the data on the pottery of these sites comes from the test pots excavated the year the sites were found (Solheim and Gorman 1966: 116–17, 120–21).

No sherds were found that were large enough to tell anything about form of the pottery. A total of 169 sherds were recovered from the two sites tested. Classifying by temper there were three different kinds of pottery. The most common had a sand temper. The sherds of this variety averaged less than 2 gm./sherd. While most sherds were plain, two cord-marked sherds and several carved paddle impressed sherds were recovered (Solheim and Gorman 1966: pl. IV*b*), as well as two with an applique bridge into the surface of which lenticular surfaces had been pinched (Solheim 1966*b*: pl. I). The second ware had a fibre temper and the sherds were larger, averaging 3·7 gm./sherd; all were plain. The third ware had a fired-clay temper. Only one sherd of this was found, a cord-marked sherd from the deepest layer from which pottery was recovered.

One C14 date from a middle level of one of the three sites excavated in 1964 (one additional site was found in the second year) was 1450±100 B.P. (Gak–653): i.e. fifth and sixth centuries A.D.

The Pre-Khmer Pottery of Phimai[1]

In May 1966, R. H. Parker directed the excavation of a small mound near the ancient town wall of Phimai, Nakornratsima, north-east Thailand, to obtain a large sample of what was called 'Phimai black ware'. The Phimai black is a new kind of earthenware pottery, first reported on by Prof. W. G. Solheim II (1965: 249–63). This report concerns the analysis made of the pottery collected during the 1966 excavations; the analysis was made during the 1972–3 academic year at the University of Hawaii by Marti Ayres and two undergraduate student helpers.

As the bags from the excavations were unpacked, it became obvious that we were dealing with a large number of sherds that could not be pieced together into whole vessels. It was decided that the most efficient way of handling such a vast quantity of sherds would be to code the designated attributes on IBM cards and do most of the analysis by computer. In order to avoid producing as many cases or IBM cards as there were sherds, the pottery was handled according to square and layer, rather than by individual bag number. The bags from each square within each layer were combined, and the pottery sorted into mutually exclusive categories defined by the attributes used in the IBM code. This IBM code was written specifically for the Phimai pottery, and was designed to record most of the attributes in such a way as to be amenable to recombination, comparison, and other methods of statistical analysis. Thus, all sherds having the same defining attributes were counted together as a single case, and the number of such sherds in a particular case was also coded on the IBM card.

The excavations at Phimai consisted of four pits on the mound, two pits at the exposed face of the mound, and two pits located off the mound. Eight soil layers were distinguished, although not all eight were present within each square. Approximately half of the boxes containing Phimai material which was shipped to Hawaii were found to have undergone such rough treatment that most of the bags were split and the sherds from all layers and squares mixed together. The largest provenienced sample that could be salvaged came from the four squares on the mound (which happened to yield the largest sample of material), with only a few bags from the other pits surviving the trip.

Solheim's 1965 report described the black pottery that was collected in 1964 from beneath the foundation of the central tower of the Khmer sanctuary in Phimai and several whole pieces from the mound which was later excavated. He gave it the name 'Phimai black'. The surface treatment of the Phimai blackware was described as polished lines standing out against a dull un-polished background, with many designs such as spirals, horizontal and verti-cal lines, and possibly even geometric patterns. Four vessel forms were presented: small bowls with concave bases, round-bottomed pots, shallow bowls with ring stands, and a single extremely thick shallow bowl with a flat bottom that may have been used as a crucible.

After working with the material for a while, it became obvious that there are five different kinds of pottery represented: Phimai black earthenware, thick fibre-tempered earthenware, sand-tempered high-fired earthenware, stoneware, and porcelain. This classification should be regarded as composed of groupings established for convenience in presenting an analysis of a large amount of previously unknown pottery obtained from a test excavation; it is not a theoretically oriented typology directed toward the solution of a particular problem. It should be noted that in the following description the individual wares from all layers are treated together, as there is little change through time within each particular ware. The vessel forms can be determined from the few reconstructed vessels, and photographs of whole vessels that were taken by Solheim in Thailand.

Three charcoal samples were dated from the Phimai black pottery site and two of these dated more recent than 280 years. The third, from square M7, Layer 6, dated 1930±100 B.P. (Gak–991; half life 5,568 years): i.e. first century B.C. to first century A.D.

(i) *Phimai Black Ware*

This is the largest category of pottery, consisting of many different vessel forms and colours. Solheim's description of the paste is still applicable: 'The paste has a coarse texture with a great deal of fibre temper . . . The sherds have a horizontally textured appearance like a flaky pastry, probably from the great quantity of temper used. This apparently did not affect the strength of the walls as the breakage is primarily vertical through the walls with very little layering. Small holes are evident in the surfaces and in the breaks.' (1965: 250).

The fibre used for temper is rice chaff. A less common temper is rice chaff mixed with a very small amount of sand; quite rare is the addition of some laterite. Much of the black ware appears to also contain some mica in the paste. The colour of the paste is usually black and sometimes grey. The rice chaff itself is also usually black, with checkerboard impressions (see also Bayard 1970: pl. IV; Solheim 1970a: pl. I). Sometimes—though not always—the chaff will be pure white when the clay has been slightly oxidized red, grey or tan. The colour of the chaff may therefore vary within a single sherd, from white where the sherd has been slightly oxidized on the outside, to black inside, where the paste remains black. In a grey sherd with grey paste, the chaff may be white throughout the piece. It therefore appears that the firing atmosphere determines the colour of the fibre temper.

When working with the pottery one imagines it to be mostly black in colour, but actually various shades of grey, tan, red, and brown are quite common. Fire-clouds are also common; because the pottery was fired under reduced conditions, a fire-cloud occurs where more oxygen had seeped through to the vessel. The colour of the fire-cloud is therefore red, tan, or grey instead of black, as in other pottery complexes in Thailand.[2] Some of these fire-clouds are quite a brilliant colour, and, especially if the vessel has also been polished, they may resemble a slip.

Because of this tendency to produce such brilliant fire-clouds, it is unlikely that differences in the composition of the clay could account for the variation in colour. There does not appear to be any correlation between a certain colour and a particular body form.

An interesting observation on the colouring of this ware is that when the outside colour is black, the inside colour will most likely be black also (80–85% of the time). But if the outside is grey, tan, red, or brown, there will be a greater likelihood of that particular colour or other oxidized colour on the inside, even though there will still be a high percentage of black. Sometimes the fire-cloud extends right through the pot to the inside, but more often the fire-cloud is only on the outer surface. It thus appears as though the firing was more controlled on the inside of the vessel than on the outside. Many bowls have a sharp line on the tip of their lip between the inner black and the outer red or tan, and it may indicate some bowls were fired open end downward. Also, some bowls, and especially the few available whole pots, show their fire-clouding on the bottom part of the vessel. There is a consistently higher percentage of rims with the same colour inside as outside (whether black or oxidized), indicating conditions of more even firing.

In general the pottery is not very thick, averaging 3–7 mm. There are a few base sherds with concentric striations which might indicate they were made on a slow wheel, but most of the pottery appears to have been hand-made. The mouths of the bowls are often more or less lopsided.

Two basic vessel forms are bowls and pots, distinguished by the ratio of height to mouth diameter. A bowl has quite a wide mouth compared to the body height; in fact, usually the mouth will be much wider than the vessel will stand high. A pot has a narrower mouth width in comparison with its deep body height. For most vessels this distinction presents no problem, but there are a few vessels which are questionable, and unfortunately are not well represented in the collection.

A. *Bowls*

(1) Small shallow bowls with straight sides (Solheim 1965: pl. 1*a–b*)

The average height of these bowls is 4·5–5·5 cm., and the rim diameter 11–15 cm. Lips may be rounded or flat, and sometimes is curved inward at the lip. There may be a small 'step' below the lip, but this feature is not to be confused with the prominent angle change characteristic of the angled bowls, as this small step does not alter the basic shape of the body. However, there may turn out to be a gradation in form between a small step and an angle, since prominent steps appear almost as angles. The walls of the bowl vary in the degree to which they flare; some have sides which are quite vertical, others have wider flaring sides. In all, however, they are straight.

The base is concave, 5–6·5 cm. in diameter. There does not appear to be any correlation between height of bowl or degree of flaring of sides and the diameter of the base. Some of the bowls have extremely low ring feet, which are actually nothing more than ridges around at the base. The breakage pattern of the bases is uniform: around the joint between the body sides and the base.

(2) Small shallow bowls with curved sides

These bowls are approximately 3·5 cm. high and have rim diameters of approximately 9 cm. Although it seems to be a much smaller kind of vessel, these figures are only approximate since this form is not as common as the straight-sided bowl or the angled bowl. It appears as though the lip may be most often rounded. The curved sides do not form an abrupt angle as they do with the angle bowls. The base is gently rounded, but the only whole vessel available is well-proportioned and stands up despite the rounded base.

(3) Angled bowls (Solheim 1965: pl. 1c)

The height averages 5–7·5 cm. and the rim diameter 14–18 cm. with one specimen as large as 28 cm. These figures may be more accurate in the lower range: there are many vessels which appear to be quite large, yet because of their fragmentary nature it is impossible to obtain accurate measurements.

There are several varieties of these angled bowls, but the distinctive feature is the angle between the upper rim and the bowl proper. In the first variety the rim itself is straight vertical in orientation, and the bowl body begins with the abrupt change in orientation following the angle (pl. va). The lip is either rounded, flat, or flat slanting outward. Here the rim may be quite plain and the angle simple, or the rim may be more elaborate with many small channels or grooves on one or both sides. The second variety has a straight inverted rim, usually with small grooves on the outside, and a rounded lip. Like the straight-sided bowls, there is some variation in the degree to which the sides of the body of both these varieties flare out.

There may be a third variety of angled bowl, characterized by a short, straight everted rim and large channels on both sides immediately below, extending to the body or bottom. There are many sherds of this type but no partial pots.

All the complete angled bowls have concave bases exactly like the base from the straight-sided bowls. In the photographs from Thailand there are also angled bowls with round bottoms (Solheim 1965: pl. 11a) and angled bowls with ring feet (Solheim 1965: fig. 2, pl. 111a). The several ring feet from the excavations cannot be attached to the vessel bodies. Unlike the low, bulging ring feet on some of the straight-sided bowls, these are higher and more like those from Non Nok Tha in Thailand. Breakage is at the juncture of the bowl side and the top of the ring foot. The ring feet average 7·5 cm. in diameter and 1·5–2 cm. in height; concave bases are from 6–8 cm. in diameter, and may be even larger. At this point it is impossible to correlate a particular base form with any angled bowl variety.

(4) Wide shallow bowls (Solheim 1965: pl. 111*b–d*)

This type of bowl has already been described by Solheim (1965: 252–4). That particular vessel still remains the only definite vessel of its kind, and thus substantiates his original opinion that it was a rare form of Phimai blackware. It is extremely thick and heavy, with several signs of wear scratching. The rim diameter is between 38 and 40 cm. and the flat bottom is 13 cm. in diameter. He has suggested that it may be a crucible.

(5) Large deep bowls

Since this form is not well represented, it may turn out to be a larger version of the straight-sided bowl. The only whole vessel of this kind is in a photograph from Thailand. It has a gently rounded rim tapering down to what appears to be a flat or concave base. There are other shapes in the 1966 collection, but they are only fragments. The rims which indicate this type of vessel are the same as a small straight-sided bowl in form, but are considerably larger, both in rim diameter and minimum height of vessel. One such piece is already 13 cm. (with no base) and must be at least 28 cm. in diameter. Another piece which may be from the same vessel, has a low bulging ring foot like those of the small straight-sided bowls. There is one giant concave base with a low bulging ring foot which may go with a large bowl; its rim diameter is 14 cm.

The decoration used most often on all bowls is that of streak-polishing, made by pressing and drawing a small blunt object like a pebble, hard seed, or nut, and forming line decorations, leaving the background a dull matt. Other decoration forms include polishing—a uniform high gloss made either by wiping or by streak-polishing so close together there was no matt area left —and streak-polishing on top of polishing. This last kind is very rare.

For all the bowl types the outside is most often either left undecorated or has only a few horizontal streak-polishing lines running around the bowl just below the lip. Less common is polishing, regular close-together horizontal streak-polishing, or wide-apart streak-polishing (approximately 1 cm. or greater apart). It is the insides of the bowls which contain the most variety in decoration. In the straight-sided bowls the inside may be either regular streak-polished or complex streak-polished (slanted or checkerboard pattern on rim, extending down about 2 cm. then horizontal streak-polishing continuing down to base), and less often polished. The insides of bowls are almost never undecorated.

The angle bowls and curved-sided bowls usually combine several streak-polishing decorations inside, especially horizontal streak-polishing on the rim extending down to the angle or curve, and either vertical, slanted, or complex slanted or checkerboard on the body sides.

The inside bases of all bowls have either a spiral design, a lenticular design (pl. *vb*), or less often a triangular or star design; they are never undecorated. The outside bottoms of the bases are only very rarely decorated.

B. *Globular Pots*

There are several whole and partial pots of this type, and the basic difference among them appears to be in the size of the vessel. The large globular pots are all the same: straight vertical, straight everted, or slightly curved everted rims (Solheim 1965: pl. 11*b*), 1·5–4 cm. in height, shoulders sloping down toward the body which then curves inward (forming almost a heart-shaped body), and rounded bottoms. Lips may be rounded, flat, or concave. Rim diameters average 20 cm., maximum diameter of pot is approximately 30–32 cm. and minimum height is at least 22 cm. Breakage indicates the rims were probably pre-formed, and then applied to the pot. Some rims have obviously been formed of two layers of clay. Many sherds do not indicate definite shoulders, but others show rounded shoulders. In fact, the upper part of the shoulder in some pots angles up to the rim almost like a fat neck. There are large numbers of rim and shoulder sherds from vessels of this kind, indicating that it may be more common than was originally thought.

The small globular pots have everted rims 1–1·5 cm. high, rim diameters of 10–12 cm. and minimum body height of 9 cm. (pl. v*c*). So far the body form is completely globular (Solheim 1965: fig. 1), as opposed to the more heart-shaped form of the larger vessels.

There is more variety in the decorations made on pots than there is on the bowls. The large globular pots all appear to have more or less the same decoration format. Rims are usually polished inside, the polishing extending down on the inside of the body to the shoulder, sometimes they may be horizontally streak-polished or matte. The outside rims are either undecorated or horizontally streak-polished.

There is quite a bit of variation in the decoration on the outside shoulder. The predominant decoration is a row of impressed hollow connecting circles running around the pot, perhaps made by a bird bone or a piece of bamboo. There are many variations of this: a single row of large circles about 5 mm. in diameter or of small circles about 2 mm. in diameter, two or more rows of large or small circles with raised bands between the rows (pl. v*d*), two rows of large circles without the raised bands, or one row of widely spaced large circles. The most common are single rows of connecting circles and several rows of small circles with raised bands. There is no correlation between size of circle and size of pot.

The other common outside shoulder decoration is several rows of slightly raised bands perhaps made by heavily pressing the blunt tool end, forming a wide incised line and slightly raised band simultaneously. The outside shoulder may also be polished or horizontal streak-polished. Sometimes there will be a raised band with vertical incised lines on it at the juncture of rim and shoulder.

What little is known about the outside body decoration indicates it is usually regular horizontal streak-polishing, wide apart streak-polishing, or undecorated. Sometimes the streak-polishing is fanned, haphazard, mixed close together and wide apart, or herringbone, and one sherd shows a series of arcs of circles forming a geometric pattern. The inside body is undecorated.

The few small globular pots available show regular horizontal streak-polishing over the entire body from the rim down; others are completely undecorated or have horizontal streak-polishing on the shoulder only (Solheim 1965: fig. 1).

(ii) *Thick Fibre-tempered Earthenware*

This kind of pottery comprises approximately 15% of all the Phimai pottery of 1966 but the collection is entirely of either large pieces of body sherds or parts of the rim. There are not even any partial pots, and there is only one complete rim. It is included as a separate kind of pottery because, although it has several features characteristic of the Phimai blackware, many important distinguishing features indicate it may not be the same kind of ware.

In temper it is like the black pottery, mostly fibre or fibre and some sand; the only difference is in the quantity of sand used, as sometimes there will be more sand in this thick pottery. The correlation between degree of oxidation and chaff colour is also true of some pieces of this pottery. The paste is usually black, although there are many sherds with a dark brown paste. In texture it is very rough, and it crumbles rather than cleanly snaps when broken. This pottery is usually between 1 and 1·5 cm. thick, and many rims are considerably thicker, up to 5 cm.

It is colour, form, and surface treatment with distinguishes this pottery most from the blackware. Approximately half of the sherds are red or tan on one or both sides; grey is the next most common colour, and black is the least common. The consistently black or brown paste indicates that the firing atmosphere would still be reducing, even though much of the thick pottery is evenly oxidized on both sides. Fire-clouds are rare, a further indication of even firing, although some of the colours will grade from a red to a tan on a single large sherd. The black colour of the thick sherds is usually not as solid or intense a black as it is in the blackware.

None of the forms characterizing the blackware seem to be present in this thick pottery. Most of the rims are straight everted, 4–5 cm. high, with a bevelled or triangular profile. A common feature is an internal mid-flange, with grooves continuing all around the inside of the rim from the flange to the body juncture. The lip is usually round, sometimes it is concave. A less common rim form, found mostly in the lowest layers, is an everted angled rim with a concave lip and internal flange at the angle point. This rim type is either black, grey, or tan, often has small raised bands inside or outside, and may have a series of slanted impressed lines along the outer edge of the rim. This type of rim also seems to be formed of two layers of clay.

The rim types and flat body sherds suggest that the vessel form is a large pot or jar, and the flanges might indicate the use of lids. One body sherd measures 29 × 21 cm. and shows very little curvature. No bases that appear to go with this pottery have been found, and it may be that the bottoms are rounded.

The surface treatment of this pottery also differs from the blackware. The surface has not been wiped smooth or polished, consequently it is very rough.

None of the decorations used in the blackware, with the possible exception of raised bands and channels, are found on this thick pottery. The only decoration found is cord-marking and it is quite common. Much of it is uni-directional cord-marking, but there is some cross-hatch cord-marking. Many thick sherds show the cord-marking giving way to an abrupt smooth shoulder.

In rim type, body form, and surface treatment this thick pottery does not resemble the blackware. But many thick black sherds could be considered blackware, except for their texture and thickness, and there are some sherds which are definitely streak-polished blackware, but which are also quite thick. This may indicate that this thick pottery will eventually be considered a variety of Phimai blackware.

(iii) *Sand-tempered Earthenware*

This is quite a different kind of pottery from the two wares just discussed. The temper is almost always either sand or sand and laterite; there are some pieces which have white rice chaff temper, but they could never be confused with the fibre-tempered blackware. This ware is highly fired in an oxidizing atmosphere. The texture is fine and uniform, and when snapped it breaks cleanly and evenly; when dropped the ware has a musical ring to it. The pottery shows evidence for having been manufactured on a wheel. Most pieces are uniform 5–7 mm. thick.

The colour is usually a solid red, orange, tan buff, or steel grey throughout, although sometimes the inside paste will be a light grey or tan. Some sherds are so light they are virtually white, others are the dark steel grey. This dark grey may be the result of use associated with fire, or it may be a fire-cloud; if it is fire-clouding, there is a difference from the black pottery in that this is a gentle gradation of colour rather than a well-defined cloud. The dark grey occurs inside as well as outside, but is most common outside.

Rim form is always curved everted, with a rounded or curled lip and some-times a lip bulb at the tip. There are a few sherds which may have grooves around the upper surface of the rim; several have internal flanges.

From the appearance of the rims, body sherds, and one partial pot, it appears that the only body form present is globular, as opposed to the more heart-shaped form of the large black pots. These are smaller in size, 26–28 cm. rim diameter, 30 cm. maximum body diameter and approximately 20 cm. high. There are a few rims with shoulders which probably came from larger pots than this, but most are small. The bottoms appear to be round.

The surface of this pottery may be undecorated, wiped smooth (producing a smooth but not glossy finish), or decorated. Rims may be undecorated or wiped smooth on either or both sides, the inside of the body is undecorated. The decorations on the outer body occur in the shoulder area and may consist of a variety of forms, of which wide incised lines with raised bands are the most common. This decoration is very similar to the same decoration on the blackware. Also present are rows of incised zigzags with raised bands, rows of impressed dotted stamp with raised bands, and other combinations of incised scrolls, u's, wavy lines, and rouletting with raised bands.

(iv) *Stoneware*

There may be several different kinds of stoneware, but altogether the collection is not large enough for a good analysis. The most common stoneware is very thick, 1–1·5 cm. and sand-tempered a highly vitrified grey or brown. The outside is sometimes matt brown, but usually has a multicoloured drip glaze composed of various combinations of brown, black, blue-grey, gold, and greenish gold. The inside is matte. The only decorations are wide-apart incised lines, raised bands and one sherd with rouletting and incised lines. There is another kind of stoneware, which is not common, that has a dull solid red-brown glaze on both sides.

The few partial rims are short curved or straight everted with many raised bands on the outside. The rims are small in comparison with the thickness of the pieces and in relation to other kinds of pottery. The rims indicate one vessel form might be globular, and the red-brown stoneware has a base which is flat with low bulging foot, similar to the large blackware bowls. The only other base is flat, perhaps part of a thick bowl.

The third kind of stoneware is thick, 3–5 mm. and is represented by only a few sherds. Some are solid brown on both sides, some are solid black, and one sherd has the same blue-grey drip glaze outside as the thick stoneware does. This piece probably comes from a bowl.

(v) *Other Wares*

There are some sherds which are not from any of the five wares just discussed. Several sherds from layers 2 and 3 are fibre-tempered earthenware with black paste and solid tan inside and outside; the other with connecting square spirals. There are also a few thin tan cord-marked sherds which may be Phimai blackware. In layers 6b and 7 appear a few fibre-tempered earthen-ware sherds which are painted: thin and wide brown lines on cream, wide red lines on red, and wide light grey lines on dark grey. The use of slips was not mentioned, but it is possible that there are some red-slipped earthenware sherds, and also rims and sherds with a white or light buff slip. It is also a possibility that some of the blackware had a black slip applied to it.

According to the computer analysis so far, there does not appear to be any significant change through time in the style of these five different wares. There is, however, a general change in the pottery within the site as a whole. The most obvious is the decrease in the Phimai blackware (from 99·6% in layer 8 to 58% in layer 2), and the marked increase in sand-tempered ware (from 3% in layer 8 to 37% in layer 2). Stoneware increases along with the sand-tempered ware (from 1% in layer 7 to 4·5% in layer 2). There is also a decrease in the variety of blackware, as in the upper layers there are few angled bowls, few channelled sherds, few globular pots, and no large bowls. This general change is especially pronounced from layer 4 or 5 upward, which corresponds to the layers which Parker described as garden soil, showing evidence for much constant disturbance. Many pieces from different layers within these five were found to fit together, also indicating movement.

Pottery from the Roi Et Provinces

These excavations have been made at three sites in the Roi Et provinces— Bo Phan Khan, Don Tha Pan, and Non Düa. All three sites were salt-producing sites, going back about 2,000 years or a bit more according to the C14 dates available (Buchan 1973: 44–5). Very little detail is presented on the pottery recovered but red, tan, and black wares were found (a thick, soft, black-ware from the bottom), decoration included, painting, incising and spatula-impressed. There was cord-marked pottery and some fine sherds with a high burnish (Higham and Parker, n.d.: 9–10). It is logical that large salt-producing communities, as these were, were producing salt for trade and were, therefore, in contact directly or indirectly with a wide area. The variety of pottery sug-gested by the little data point to at least some of the pottery found being trade ware, at least having been brought in from outside. Going any further than this would be stretching the data too far.

Conclusions

I have seen none of the Roi Et pottery but I was told in conversation that it was distinct from the Ban Chieng, Non Nok Tha, and Phimai pottery. If this is so this further extends the primary observation that we can make about the three latter pottery complexes. While rare contacts can be seen among these pottery complexes, there was extremely little diffusion among them. There must have been considerable trade involving metals from sometime around 3000 B.C.[3] and possibly somewhat later in salt, yet this led to little if any change in the pottery. This further suggests a peaceful life without movement of women (potters at least) through either slavery or warfare. Even in the historic levels there is little indication of importation of Chinese or Siamese porcelains so the area may have been somewhat isolated, at least in early historic times.

ADDENDUM

There is more information available on the dating of the Phimai black pottery by May 1974. First, by making use of the Bristlecone pine calibration of radiocarbon dates (Ralph, Michael, and Han 1973) the C14 sample from Layer 6 of square M7 gives a date of A.D. 60 ± 100. A sherd of Phimai black pottery gave a thermoluminesence date of 330 ± 250 B.C. for Layer 6b (lower portion of the layer) in square L7 (Carriveau 1974). The circle-impressed jar pictured in Plate v*d* is from Layer 7. It is this jar which was similar to the large pot from Non Nong Chik, from the burial in Layer 5 which layer had a C14 date of about 200 B.C. Finally, a piece of iron slag excavated at Phimai which lost its provenence through destruction of its container, has a thermoluminesence date of 870 ± 420 B.C. (Carriveau 1974: dates from the Museum Applied Science Center for Archaeology at the University of Pennsylvania, with thanks). This would suggest that iron smelting at Phimai, and probably the manufacture of Phimai black pottery, goes back beyond 500 B.C., and possibly quite a way beyond.

NOTES

1. The Phimai portion of this by Marti Ayres.
2. Since most of the data comes from sherds and not whole pots, it is impossible to determine whether an oxidized sherd is part of a larger fire-cloud, or whether it represents the colour of the whole vessel. From what we now have, it appears that there are quite few whole red, tan, or brown vessels, and that coloured sherds come from fire-clouds.
3. Accepting the 'early' dating of Non Nok Tha. *Editors.*

ADDITIONAL REFERENCES

Vidya Intakosai. 1972. Painted pottery at Ban-Chiang, north-east Thailand. Paper presented at the Seminar on South East Asian prehistory and archaeology, Manila, proceedings being edited by Eric S. Casino.

Ralph, E. K., Michael, H. N. and Han, M. C. 1973. Radiocarbon Dates and Reality. *MASCA Newsletter,* 9 (1).

Carriveau, Gary W. 1974. Personal communication.

The Ongbah Cave and Its Fifth Drum

P. SORENSEN

The Ongbah Cave and its Deposit

THE Ongbah Cave, might have been as challenging and informative to archaeologists as the Niah caves of Borneo, had it been undisturbed. However, its fate was that of many South East Asian caves, at first to have its top soil dug away by local farmers collecting bats' excrement, in the course of which some prehistoric finds may have been uncovered, and following this on several subsequent occasions between 1957 and 1965 to suffer ransacking by treasure hunters.

The cave was visited by Mr. Chin You-di of the National Museum, Bangkok, in 1957, and by the members of the Thai-Danish Prehistoric Expedition 1960–62, on which occasion fragments of four bronze kettledrums were saved together with various other surface finds. Finally in 1965–6 the members of the 2nd Thai-Danish Prehistoric Expedition undertook extensive excavations in the cave, during which much useful material was saved by controlled excavation, important observations made, and most valuable supplementary information gathered. A detailed find history of the cave has already been given elsewhere (Sørensen 1973a), for which reason only the aspects of it pertinent to this paper will be repeated briefly here.

The cave is located in the hills between Menam Kwae Yai and Menam Kwae Noi in Kanchanaburi, Amphoe Sri Sawat (long. 98°57′E., lat. 14°41′N.) approximately 10 km. to the west of the boat-landing of Sri Sawat. Access to it is from the track connecting the Muang Rae Bo Yai lead mines with the boat-landing of Sri Sawat. From the track one has to walk through rushwood and elephant grass for about 700 m. and then climb the hill for another 300 m., thus reaching the north entrance to the cave. The 98 m. long cave has four halls, two of which are inside the low crescent-shaped north entrance, the two others with a separate opening towards the south-west. A narrower passage—called 'The Gallery' because of its beautiful stalactite formations—connects the two pairs of halls.

As a result of the diggings and ransacking most of the original deposit was spoiled almost all over in the cave. Only just inside the two entrances were minor areas intact, as well as along parts of the walls, particularly in Hall 4 inside the south-west entrance. The deposit of the cave was resting upon the floor of calcareous substance the upper part of which was very soft. The floor was penetrated in Hall 3 by the treasure hunters, but soil samples from right underneath the floor, at about one metre down and from the bottom of the 'crater' were analyzed but showed no evidence of human occupation.[1]

The deposit consisted of three main strata:

(A) A 10–15 cm. thick layer of reddish sandy soil, sterile of finds except for what might have been pressed down from the above horizon. This layer extended all through the cave, resting directly on the floor. It was overlain by:

(B) A grey sandy soil 2 m. or more in thickness, right inside the north entrance, but not exceeding 1 m. at the rear of Hall 2. It continued through the 'Gallery' and into Halls 3 and 4, but was there only 10–15 cm. thick. In Hall 1 this layer could be subdivided into three main horizons, all of which contained a Hoabinhian-like tool assemblage with animal bones, a few charred shells of nuts (*Canarium*),[2] and lots of charcoal. Otherwise no evidence of collected or cultivated plants were ascertained from the layer. It is the only evidence of human settlement from the cave. A series of C14 dates on the charcoal date the deposit between 11180±180 B.P. and 9350±140 B.P. (9230 and 7400 B.C.).

(C) After a considerable chronological gap this phase was followed by a series of interments, related to the Ban Kao culture (Sørensen 1967 and 1972), but clearly representing a phase later than the Late Sub-phase of the Bang site at Ban Kao, being closer to the Lue site I of Ban Kao, and the Nong Chae Sao site of Ratburi, in absolute chronological terms estimated at 1300 B.C. to 1100 B.C.

As shown elsewhere (Sørensen, n.d., A.P.) another chronological gap separates these burials from the second interment phase, verified for the Ongbah Cave: that of the Early Metal Ages, comprising (1) simple interments, and (2) elaborate inhumations in boat-shaped wooden coffins with rich grave furnitures including (as inferred below) the three pairs of bronze kettledrums. Both of these latter groups, as well as that of the Ban Kao related burials were in the top deposit of the cave[3] a layer generally 75 cm. to 1 m. thick, of hard-consolidated brown soil, which through numerous thin white lines, the result of intensified periodical drippings from the ceiling, and by ashy layers, probably from ritual surface fires, can be further divided into a different number of sub-strata. From this clear stratigraphy it was generally easy to see from which part of the then surface interments had been cut. But because there were so many interments—the number of wooden coffin burials alone came to about ninety—the layers have been contaminated repeatedly with earlier and later material. This was in fact proved by the charcoal samples submitted for C14 dating; layer 2, counted from the top of the deposit, turned out to be older than layer 5. These dates accordingly had to be discarded.

Description of the Ongbah Finds[4]

Of the finds from the top deposit of the Ongbah Cave, those related to the Ban Kao culture can be left out of consideration in this account, as no evidence has been found to prove their contemporaneity with the Early Metal Age finds (Sørensen, n.d., *A.P.*) as proposed for their prototypes from Ban Kao (Solheim 1971: 127; Bayard 1970: 109).

The finds of bronze and iron were either collected from the spoil heaps of the treasure hunters, or found left in wooden coffins; or excavated. As evidence from the excavation clearly shows, these finds could have had one of three possible origins: (*a*) stray in the deposit, but not associated with a burial; (*b*) from the simple interments; or (*c*) from the boat-shaped wooden coffins.

(*a*) Except for a few bronze nodules from an ashy pocket in the deposit along the south wall of Hall 4, no bronzes were originally stray in the deposit. The bronzes collected consist of fragments of four of kettledrums, spiral arm-rings, bracelets with T-section and preserved casting core, simple bracelets with U-section, and a small bronze cup. Except for the kettledrums, all the bronzes were confirmed by informers who had participated in the ransacking, to originate from the wooden coffins, together with certain iron implements and lots of beads—the primary object of the treasure hunters. The beads were said 'to be lying in long strings, extending from the neck, or slung around the waist of the skeleton'. From the excavation two main types of beads were verified: (1) long, cylindrical, green beads, and (2) hexagonal, double conical red beads, both of which are extremely common types in Early Metal Age contexts.

Strictly speaking, the kettledrums were originally 'stray in the deposit'. However, all information gathered from informants, and the observations made during the excavation, point to their having been *closely associated with the wooden coffin burials*. They are accordingly more logically to be dealt with under point (*c*).

There were however, stray in the deposit, several iron implements, mainly to be classified as carpeters' tools (Sørensen, n.d., *A.P.*). Similar tools were associated with some of the simple interments, but some were also found in semi-intact wooden coffins.[5] No other types of iron artefacts were excavated 'stray in the deposit'.

(*b*) Simple interments were found in the intact deposits both inside the north entrance, and particularly inside the south-west entrance to the cave. The skeletons, all except one supine, were associated with from one to seven iron tools, mainly knives and carpenters' tools. Doubtless a lot of the iron artefacts otherwise collected in the cave originate from similar simple inter-ments. Some kind of surface marking of the simple interments—as well as of the coffin burials—may have existed, as post-holes observed in the deposit near the burials seem to indicate. Further support of this is seen in the fact that Early Metal Age burials apparently did not disturb each other, although they were placed very close to each other. Thus at the north entrance a semi-intact coffin burial was excavated, at a distance of less than 1 m. from a simple interment which was intact. A nearby post-hole may have held the surface marking.

(c) One of the most fascinating find groups from the Ongbah Cave are the about ninety fragmentary or complete boat-shaped wooden coffins. Being in fact nothing but simple dugouts made from trunks of a local hardwood (one of the abundant *Dahlbergia* sp.), they were in every state of preservation from extremely good, even bearing recognizable tool marks, to a state of almost complete decomposition. In most cases simple boards were used as a lid; but from the feather-and-tongue carvings along the rim of some coffins, it appears as if in certain cases one boat served as a lid for another.

Coffin burials had been placed all over the cave, but from the spoil heaps and other evidence it seems as if they were mainly concentrated in Halls 2 and 4 and 'The Gallery', i.e. the darkest parts of the cave. With delicately carved stylized animal heads at both ends, the horns of which may have acted as handles, their full length measured 3–3·5 m., and had an interior dugout chamber about 2 m. long and 40–45 cm. wide, just large enough to keep a body with some small-sized grave furniture. The grave furniture of the coffin burials consisted—as mentioned above—of bronzes, beads, and iron tools. Most likely also the iron weapons found stray originated from them. Besides this, some miniature clay vessels may have been associated (Sørensen 1962: 35).

The similarity between the iron artefacts of the coffin burials and those of the simple interments point to a relative chronological contemporaneity. The iron artefacts have almost no external relationships. Those which can be established are at a very general level and insufficient to indicate any external derivation, either from Thailand, or from neighbouring countries or areas. This points to a local development and production, their prototypes not unexpectedly being easily recognized among artefacts of stone, bone, and shell in the Ban Kao culture (Sørensen, n.d., *A.P.*).

The three pairs of kettledrums were too large to have been in the coffins. Two of the drums were in Hall 2, in a cluster of coffin burials; another two in 'The Gallery', in extreme proximity to a coffin which had been burned already during prehistoric times (and which accordingly could be C14 dated, yielding the date 2180±100 B.P. or 230 B.C.); and the last pair were in the darkest corner of Hall 3, alongside a coffin left *in situ* but otherwise emptied. These locations are strong evidence for their association with the coffin burials. The relationship between boat and drum gets further support from the numerous boat pictures on drums; even one of the Ongbah drums has such pictures. But

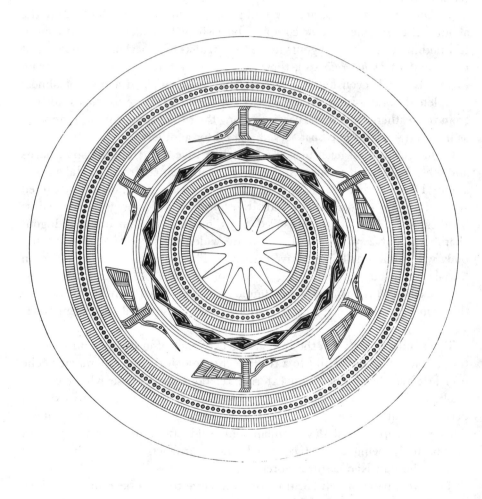

The drum O.B.G.D. from Ong Bah Cave, Kachanaburi Province, Thailand
(View from top)

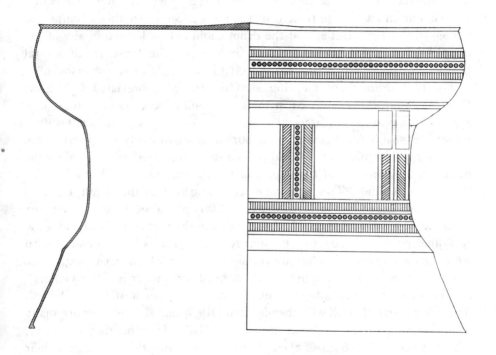

The drum O.B.G.D. from Ong Bah Cave, Kachanaburi Province, Thailand
(View from side)

probably they are nowhere better illustrated than on the Ngoc-lu drum, where one boat depicted on the drum is clearly shown to carry a drum (Goloubew 1929: pl. xxviia).

Before the members of the Thai-Danish Prehistoric Expedition 1960–62 first visited the Ongbah Cave, and saved the fragments of the four drums of Heger Type I, two drums had already been removed from the cave. They were reputedly in the best state of preservation. One of these drums disappeared while under transportation to Bangkok, and has never been rediscovered. The other was given to the Governor of Kanchanaburi, in whose office the members of the expedition saw it. The governor later gave it to a temple, but an attempt to trace it in 1966 was in vain. Another attempt was made early in 1973, but at first the drum could not be located in any of the temples in or near Kanchanaburi. However, with the assistance of several persons, the drum was finally rediscovered in a temple in Kanchanaburi.[6]

The fifth drum from the Ongbah Cave (to be abbreviated G.D.; i.e. Governor's Drum) reappeared in the same good state of preservation, as it appears in a photograph from 1960 (see fig.). All four pairs of handles were missing, probably from before it was buried, and two fractures appear in the bulging upper section of the mantle: from their size, obviously caused by the hacks used by farmers or by helpers of the treasure hunters; but otherwise the drum was intact. This to some extent confirms that this drum, together with the one which disappeared, was most likely placed in the shallowest part of the deposit, which can only have been that of the rear end of Hall 3. Of the two other pairs of drums, the stylistically related drums OB. 86 and OB. 89 were the most damaged. They are certainly the ones which, according to one of our workers, 'were found upside down, filled with stones in "The Gallery" and because of the little light available were very damaged by the hacks'. This fits in perfectly well with the idea that OB. 87 and OB. 88 were originally in the deep deposit in the cluster of coffins in Hall 2. Here hacking was easier, with the result that both of them lost the upper mantle section and their tympanon. A description of the drums will be found in the appendix to this paper.

Chronology and Significance of the Ongbah Finds

On the assumption that a constant decline in the decoration of bronze artefacts in general, and kettledrums in particular, took place; which approach is generally accepted and also applied to the Dian finds by E. Bunker (Bunker 1972: 317), it should be possible to establish the following relative chronology for the Ongbah drums:

(1) OB. 89, with its decoration of feathered figures, boats, and still unconventionalized arrangement of patterns in the decoration of the tympanon, is doubtless the oldest.

(2) Close to it is OB. 86. The arrangement of the decoration on the tympanon and the conventionalizing of the decoration of the mantle indicates its later age, but the feathered figures, the stylized but not completely stereotype birds, the house pictures etc., would all place it chronologically in the proximity of OB. 89.

(3) Unfortunately the essential parts of OB. 87 and OB. 88 are missing. From their size they are closely related to the two former, and the resemblances in the horizontal bands of decoration on the lower part of the middle section would place OB. 87 not too far from OB. 86; but the fact that the 'ladder' motif of the vertical frames of OB. 86 is replaced on both OB. 87 and OB. 88 by a kind of chevron pattern, distances the two drums from OB. 86, and links them together.

(4) By its size OB. G.D. stands out from the four other drums. The tympanon decoration has now reached the stage of complete conventionalizing, with (a) a band of zones of geometrical patterns, (b) a zone of highly stylized flying birds, and (c) a repetition of (a). This corresponds to the description given by Loewenstein for his group Ic of the Heger I drums (Loewenstein 1962: 30). Undoubtedly it is the youngest of the drums from the Ongbah Cave, but it is clearly linked with the earliest through the presence of the solid centre meander pattern of zone 4.

This author is of the opinion that the drums were generally old when they were buried. This view is largely supported by the evidence from the Ongbah finds, where at the utmost a couple of centuries can have separated the earliest drum from the latest. Conditions for preservation were similar, and accordingly it must also to some extent have been factors other than age and soil conditions that caused the present differences in the state of preservation of the decoration; from being almost obliterated on OB. 89 and 86, to being well preserved at OB. 87, 88, and G.D. One factor which might have caused this difference is wear, due to extensive use prior to the burying of the drum. Further support for this theory comes from the Ban Gaw drum (Sørensen 1973b), which was in a perfect state of preservation, but where almost all decoration of the main zone of the tympanon (a bird zone?) was absolutely unrecognizable, obviously due to wear, while some of the decoration closer to the central star zone was visible. The decorative frame near the rim of the tympanon was almost intact. The theory is also supported by information on the more recent use and function of drums. It will suffice here to recall U. Guehler's information about the history of one of the drums in his possession (1944: 25), as well as the information compiled by Heine-Geldern (1932: 531).

With this in mind an investigation into the problem of the absolute age of the drums will be undertaken. Only the single C14 date mentioned above is available, showing 230 ± 100 B.C., from a wooden coffin near OB. 86 and

OB. 89. Since these two drums were apparently buried as a pair, and as furthermore OB. 86 is the younger of the two, the date is applicable to OB. 86 rather
than to OB. 89. However, as Bunker correctly states (1972: 326) the value and
interpretation of a single C14 date should not be over-emphasized. Using
Sigma 2 the total time span covered by this date is from 430 B.C. to 30 B.C.
Further, allowing at least one generation of age for OB. 86 prior to its being
buried, it can be dated at 460 B.C. or 0, or anywhere in between. The former
date fits well with one of the dates published by Peacock for the two new
drums from Malaysia (Peacock 1965: 3), which is 485±95 B.C., while the low
date for OB. 86 fits in very well indeed with the chronological frame proposed
by Bunker (1972: 317) based on her interpretation of the evidence from the
Dian find.[7]

One of these two chronological systems must be wrong, or else applicable
only to local conditions; so it becomes imperative to investigate whether other
means of dating exist. In this connection some attention should be given to
the boat-coffin burials. Coffin burials are known from Szechwan (Feng 1960:
1–167), the Niah caves in Borneo (Harrison 1958: 199) and from Kuruswanan
Ledge, Palawan Island, the Philippines (Fox 1970: 173). The boats differ in
shape and presumably represent local types. Of the boat-coffin burials the
Szechwanese seem to owe their origin to the wooden chamber graves of the
Ch'u state and thus could hardly be earlier than the sixth century B.C., while
the latest of them are dated by Pan Liang coins, first issued after the unification of China under Ch'in in 221 B.C. One C14 date is available for the boat-
coffin burials from Niah yielding 2695±65 B.P. or 745 B.C.; allowing Sigma 2,
between 875 B.C. and 615 B.C. (*Radiocarbon* 1964: 359); whilst the Philippine
coffin burial was dated by Chinese trade pottery to the twelfth century A.D.

It may be argued that the dates are related to the coffin burials more than
to the drums. The evidence from Malaysia and Ongbah clearly points to a
relationship between the coffin burials and the drums, which cannot be
explained away. In other words it is evident that the date for the production
of OB. 86 can hardly be much later than about 250–260 B.C., and that of
OB. 89, considering its relative chronological distance from the former, cannot have been made much later than between 300 B.C. and 275 B.C.; this is
based on the assumption that they are separated by one generation only, and
that OB. 86 was at least twenty-five to thirty years old when buried. It is
impossible to estimate how much younger than these OB. 87–88 are, but
obviously a considerable gap in the degree of stylization of the birds exist
between OB. G.D. and Heger's drum No. 11, now in the Victoria and Albert
Museum, which by an inscription is dated to A.D. 199 (Loewenstein 1962: 34),
unless that is, the inscription was carved on to the drum much later.

The dates established above for OB. 86 and OB. 89 are in concordance with
the dates of the early Dong-son culture, proposed by Karlgren (Karlgren

1942: 25). His group of earliest drums, to which should be added the drum from Hoang-ha (Goloubew 1942: 383–409), includes the Saleier drum, but Karlgren makes it absolutely clear that this drum does not belong exclusively to the group of earliest drums, as it has got frogs along the rim of the tympanon. On the other hand the feathered figures on the drum are stylistically 'far from so strongly corrupted . . . as in the later drums of Type I' (Karlgren 1942: 2).

An examination by Karlgren of pattern after pattern clearly indicate their Chinese origin, which in turn allows their dating to be put at the third to fourth century B.C. As noticed in the summary description of OB. 89 (cf. Appendix), the latter is extremely close to the Saleier drum; the main difference being the lack of the 'saw-tooth motif' on OB. 89. This motif is ubiquitous on the early drums, as well as on the drums from Shi-zhai shan (Report 1959; Bunker 1972; von Dewall 1972). Except for the Laos drum, the Kuala Trengganu drums (Peacock 1966: 198–201, 1967: 27–30), the 'Frog' drum from Kampong Sungai Lang (Peacock 1965: 1, 1964: 248–53), and the Saleier drum, the 'saw-tooth motif' has not (as far as the investigations of this author have allowed) been found outside a very limited area comprising Tongking and Thanh-hoa in north Vietnam and Yunnan. It may therefore very well be considered a very local decorative element, the relative chronological significance of which may be matched by other patterns outside the outlined area of its distribution, pre-supposing the Laos, the Kuala Trengganu, the Sungai Lang, and the Saleier drums to have been exported from this area. We may therefore assume that the Tongking–Thanh-hoa–Yunnan area represents one stylistic and thus production centre (perhaps even that it is the earliest), without this totally excluding the possibility that other centres or 'art-schools' existed in other areas contemporaneously with this or beginning slightly later.

The Chronology and Significance of the Dian Find

In the light of the above evidence, all pointing to a beginning of the 'drum phase' of the so-called Dong-son culture no later than the late fourth century B.C., it should be asked whether the very short chronology, and very late dating of bronze drums, proposed by Bunker (1972: 317, 321) can be maintained. However, before discussing the Dian chronology and the evidence of the Shi-zhai shan find, this author feels it necessary to emphasize a point of some importance which hitherto has been given insufficient consideration. The fact is that the Shi-zhai shan find reflects the economic and political possibilities, the wealth, and power, of its society or at least of its ruling classes. Compared with Dian, the courts of other local South East Asian princes—or maybe vassals of Dian—including that of the Dong-son site itself, can only have been of second rank, and thus, 'provincial', in exactly the same way as Dian presumably would have appeared to any visitor from the court of Ch'u, had such a possibility ever existed.

The wealth accumulated by the prince and his court is on full display in the grave furniture. It shows that its artists had the opportunity to do their very best, to show their craftmanship, to create and invent. But this does not necessarily mean that everything was first created and invented at Dian, nor in Yünnan. On the contrary the craftsmen must have brought their knowledge along from somewhere else. Besides that, the economic basis had to be established prior to the place becoming the playground of extremely skilled artists and craftsmen. So the Dian find does not necessarily represent the cradle of Dong-sonian art. It shows, in the opinion of this author, merely the Dong-sonian art in full blossom, at its peak when the economic and political background was strong enough to allow it to develop. It shows what it could probably have developed into at other places or centres in South East Asia, if conditions had been equally favourable. Especially in its depiction of aspects of daily life, the Dian find provides a marvellous and unequalled insight in the local society and its culture; but this picture does not seem much different from that which appears from the study of other South East Asian cultures, e.g. as described in the *Man Shu*.

In contradistinction to Watson, who does not believe the Dian drums were of great age when they were deposited in the graves (Watson 1960: 65), the present writer sees them as old specimens. These drums most certainly were 'very powerful' drums, since they were in so many cases 'killed' before being deposited in the graves. Evidence of the 'killing' is seen in the holes cut in the centre of the tympanon, cutting out the central star (sun, moon, eye, or whatever may have been the concept of this, the most important area of the drum, the area beaten to produce the sound); not to forget the more common instances where apparently the whole tympanon has been removed and replaced by a disc with other decoration. The practical purpose of this may of course be claimed to be that of converting the drum into a cowrie-container, but in order to make it serve that purpose it might have been easier just to turn it upside down. The use of drums as cowrie-containers is, as was correctly pointed out by Watson, unparalleled elsewhere (Watson 1970: 56). One might almost believe that the idea behind the drum had been forgotten at the court of Dian, were it not for the several other cases where the use of drums in the Dian community was shown, e.g. the disc showing a house in which are placed nine drums. U. Guehler's information about the history of the drum in his possession is once more brought into focus (Guehler 1944: 25).

Two types of 'cowrie-containers' exist, one resembling the mid section of 'ordinary drums' (Bunker 1972: 293), the other being Heger Type I drums,[8] the more distinctive lower mantle sections of which presumably are to be regarded as a local feature. Also their 'squatness' (Bunker 1972: 308) does not indicate anything pre-Heger, as the same is characteristic of most Heger IV drums, the so-called 'Chinese type' (Heger 1902: 16). As another local feature, this author sees the extensive use of the 'sawtooth-circle—sawtooth' pattern, used to frame both the rim and often also the central star area of the tympanon, as well as to frame the decoration on the upper mantle section and to serve as a lower frame at the mid-mantle section. As such, this pattern combination not only represents a continuation of a local pattern. (As mentioned above it is ubiquitous on the group of early drums as separated out by Goloubew and Karlgren.) It also seems to undergo a pattern evolution similar to that which can be followed outside this area, that of 'short radial lines—circles (single, double, pointed, tangent-connected, etc.)—short radial lines', which is well exemplified on the Ongbah drums OB. 86–89. It is furthermore common on the majority of drums of Loewenstein's group Ic (Loewenstein 1962: 30), distributed from the South East Asian mainland through Indonesia and well into New Guinea (Elmberg 1959: 70), and of which OB. G.D. is another good example.

In other words, there are good reasons to believe that at least two different developments in the decoration of drums existed more or less contemporaneously; with Dian being the place of amalgamation, since evidence of both decorative styles exists there without the evidence being the result of trade. The point of coincidence and contemporaneity is exemplified by the drum in the 'non-Dian Style', carrying also a picture of a (?)Dian nobleman. (Watson 1970: 63). Accordingly the relative chronology for the Heger I drums proposed by Bunker (1972: 317) is not accepted by this author; and this of course influences the concept of the absolute chronology.[9]

The finds from Dian which are dateable consist of coins, mirrors, and a royal seal (Bunker 1972: 321). The coins range from 175 B.C. to 32 B.C., while the mirrors are (a) one of Chan-kuo, i.e. before 221 B.C.; (b) one of Ch'u, i.e. before 221 B.C., for both of which some age probably must be allowed prior to their deposition in the graves; and (c) the majority dating from the second half of Western Han, i.e. first century B.C. The seal dates from 109 B.C. onwards. The total time span covered by the find can thus be put at between *c*. 175 B.C. and *c*. 25 B.C., with a majority of finds centering around 125 B.C. and 75 B.C. So it seems relevant to date the two burials with Chan-kuo mirrors (3 and 10) at or slightly before 175 B.C.; the richly furnished burials 12 and 13 at about 100 B.C. or slightly later; and the graves with Wu-shu coins (5 and 8), both of which lack drums, according to their latest coins, i.e. after 32 B.C. but (on the negative evidence of the absence of Wang-mang coins) before A.D. 9.

Whether or not the datings proposed above can be accepted, it is obvious that the use of the drums in Dian must have come to an end between 80 B.C. and approximately 25 B.C. It is therefore impossible in the opinion of this author to place the same importance on the Dian find as do Watson and

Bunker, regardless of the fact that its value as an individual find can hardly be exaggerated. It remains a find of a rather restricted value, without significant bearing on the development of the rest of South East Asia. Not only the chronological factors contradict this, but further analysis shows that several elements, claimed by Watson and Bunker to be significant for Dian and from there dispersed into the rest of South East Asia, might equally be the result of a common heritage, indigenous to South East Asia. Thus shamanism evidence of which was correctly pointed out by Watson to be present in the Dian find need not necessarily have come to Dian with other influences directly from central Asia—or transmitted through the Li-Fan finds as suggested by Chang Kwang-chih (Chang 1968: 437). Evidence of shamanism seems to be present in the Ban Kao culture between 1500 B.C. and 1300 B.C. (Sørensen 1965: 303). The same applies to the importance of the snake, which Watson (1970: 65, 68) links with the Yüeh tribes of central and east China. Early evidence of snakes is known from South East Asia itself. Thus snake pictures appear on painted vessels from the Ban Chieng find from north-east Thailand;[10] and on the two sole decorated earthenware pots from the Early Sub-phase of the Ban Kao culture at Bang site, Ban Kao (Sørensen 1967: pls. 62*i* and 63). One shows a snake (cobra?) following or pursuing a boat with two persons (or drums?).[11] The boat is quite similar to the small boats with only four persons shown on some Tien drums (Dewall 1972: 337). However, the picture is otherwise too simple to allow any far reaching conclusions, yet clear enough to prove an early indigenous origin of the motif, and thus probably for the belief behind it.

That the Dian finds together give evidence of a centre is obvious. The presence of a king, regardless of his relationship to the Chinese emperor, would naturally have created some economic background for artistic and other activities, the king supposedly having been surrounded by a court of noble-men, administrators, and military officers; the former perhaps holding the two latter positions. However, all groups requested various kinds of commodities, services, etc. So Dian represents one kind of centre, the production centres of which may have been elsewhere, inside or outside Yünnan. Given the rather short lifespan of the Dian kingdom itself, it is a question of how much external influence it was actually able to exercise, culturally or economically, for example as exporter of drums. To this author it appears to be extremely limited, or non-existent.

The Ongbah finds: do they provide evidence for the presence of a centre?

The Ongbah finds are different from those of Dian, as the above description will have shown. The coffin burials and the simple interments clearly indicate the presence of two different social levels of a community whose settlement yet remains to be discovered. That the settlement would have been located far from the burial place is unlikely.

The community probably comprised several social levels, of which only two were allowed to use the cave for burial purposes. These probably were the ruling classes and their relatives, whatever their titles or ranks may have been. They were buried in wooden coffins, the most wealthy of the rulers being further associated with their kettledrums. Judging from the composition and the function of the iron implements associated with the simple interments, these burials belong to a class of skilled craftsmen whose crafts may have been particularly esteemed in order to raise them to this social status, particularly when compared with China where craftsmen were usually not even allowed inside the town walls; although the vivid description of the reputation of certain master smiths does suggest some recognition even from the royalty.[12]

If a certain social stratification, as reflected by the burials, can be accepted, and if a settlement in the proximity of the Ongbah Cave existed, then it is necessary also to assume an economic background to support a society. Two factors may have been of major importance:

(a) The location of the Ongbah Cave, with a nearby settlement, between the rivers of Mae Kwae Noi and Kwae Yai, meant a certain possibility of controlling the trade and traffic on both rivers; and the proximity to the Three Pagoda Pass, would mean some control also of the trade between both sides of the mountain ranges separating the present kingdom of Thailand from Burma.

(b) Although no definite proof exists so far of the use of the neighbouring lead mines during prehistoric times,[13] the owner of the mines once told this author that the workers on opening one of the mines many years ago had found some tools and what may have been crucibles, but that these finds were lost. The possibility cannot be excluded that some mining may have taken place, and that this could account for part of the subsistence of a community in these remote hills. Considering the amounts of lead often found in East Asian bronzes, and the increased demand for certain commodities of bronze during the latter half of the first millennium B.C. arising from the spread of bronze-iron technology into South East Asia,[14] the market for metals like lead and tin (to judge from the Heger I drums alone) must have been quite substantial, and so the advanced hypothesis gets into the realm of plausibility. However, this should not be regarded as anything more than a working hypothesis.

The kind of centre which may be assumed to have existed in the upper Kwae valley was basically different from that of Dian, being based on trade and perhaps on mining. Originating from the Ban Kao culture, evidence of which is seen in its iron implements, it probably developed slowly into the society reflected in the Ongbah burials. From the single C14 date and the external evidence discussed above, it can be estimated to have been fully developed about the beginning of third century B.C.; but exactly when it started and when it came to an end is indeterminable from the present evidence.

The many connections established through the study of the drums have shown their dependence, in origin, on a group of early drums. Later similarities, as with OB. 86, point more to a relationship with the drums from Indonesia in general, in particular, noteworthy resemblances are found with the drum of the farthest islands like Roti, Sangeang, and Kai. It is worth noticing too that Marschall, upon examining certain finds from Indonesia, particularly fragments of moulds, states that none of the Indonesian drums can possibly have been made in Indonesia (Marschall 1968: 51), but that they are rather to be regarded as imports from the South East Asian mainland. The distribution of drums in Indonesia (Marschall 1968: Map I) is in favour of a route from the mainland along the coast of Peninsular Thailand and Malaysia. This gains support from the Kuala Trengganu drums from the east coast of western Malaysia, and brings the Ongbah finds (and the possible centre) into focus as a transmitter. But that Ongbah should have been the producer of the drums is unlikely.

Largely the same route as that of the drums passing by way of Ongbah is indicated by the boat-shaped coffin burials. The local types of boats exhibited in the different finds point to their local manufacture, it is the idea that moved. But from where to where? C14 dates point to an origin in Borneo, but the metallurgical knowledge which presumably accompanied the idea would place their origin in Szechwan. In the light of this, we may recall Chang's statement 'that the Li-Fan and Kantzu group of Szechwan civilizations, however, certainly provided the immediate sources for any Asian elements in the Dong-son culture' (Chang 1968: 437). This is extremely important and it should be asked whether an early centre could have existed in Szechwan, as the ultimate source of the different centres in Yunnan and the rest of South East Asia. However, that question lies outside the scope of the present paper.

That centres other than Dian and the probable Ongbah centre, may have existed is more than likely. A mapping of the earliest and early Heger I drums from the Mainland and the Archipelago suggests the presence of a centre somewhere around Pakse in Laos, from which area come both the Laos drum, the Nelson drum, and the Ubon drum in the National Museum in Bangkok. Another centre, perhaps similar to the Ongbah one, may have existed near Uttaradit in north Thailand, where four kettledrums showing a stylistic development similar to that observed on the Ongbah drums come from a cave which also contained iron implements (Parmentier 32: 171). That one or two centres existed at Java also seems obvious, and the concentration of drums on the small island of Gunung Api (the Sangeang drums: van Heekeren 1958: 24) points to the presence of another centre. Further area studies including elements other than kettledrums are likely to accentuate the presence of these centres and perhaps provide sufficient evidence for identifying other centres. With the increased material now at the disposal of archaeologists, this might prove very fruitful.

Appendix: Description of the Ongbah Drums

OB. 86 to 89 are already described and discussed elsewhere (Sørensen 1973); only their main data and decorative elements will be repeated here. These are:

OB. 86. Total height: 53·5 cm. Diameter of tympanon: 66·5–67 cm. Tympanon: central twelve-rayed star with close resemblances to the Laos and Roti drums. The interray decoration is rather similar to that of the Roti and Saleier drums. It is surrounded by eight concentric zones of decoration, which numbered from the star are characterized by:

Zone 1: Angular meander with solid centre. This is close to OB. 89, the Yunnan (Gillet I), Hoang-ha, Ngoc-lu, and Muong drums.[15]

Zone 2: Tangent-connected pointed circles.

Zone 3: Nine stylized birds, one of which has circlets at the end of the tail, probably indicating a peacock. The birds are shown partly in front-view, partly in side-view, in counterclockwise arrangement. Apparently unmatched elsewhere, though the present working conditions of the author have not permitted a full search for comparative elements.

Zone 4: Ten stylized feathered figures, clearly recognizable as human beings. Divided into two groups, separated from each other by two identical houses of 'Indonesian' Quang-xu'ong style houses (Heine-Geldern 1932: 525 and 1947: 167; Goloubew 1941: 410, fig. 11).

Zone 5: Eight stylized long-beaked flying birds (White Herons) in counterclockwise arrangement, fairly ordinary, but a detailed study clearly shows individual features. They differ in details from most 'flying birds', having their closest parallels among the birds of the Quang-xuong and Roti drums.

Zone 6–8: A typical frame zone of radial short lines, double band of tangent-connected pointed circles and short radial lines.

The decoration of the mantle is largely a repetition of the Tympanon zone 6–8 pattern, used horizontally on the upper mantle section and horizontally and vertically at the mid-mantle section, however, all over framed by a narrow chevron pattern.

OB. 87. Preserved height: 35·4 cm. Estimated total height about 50 cm. Estimated diameter of Tympanon about 60 cm. Decoration only preserved at the mid-section of the mantle. Being purely geometrical, it resembles that of OB. 86 very much, but appears still simpler as the 'short radial lines' in 'ladder' pattern, in the vertical section are substituted by a chevron pattern.

OB. 88. Preserved height 40·3 cm. Estimated total height about 50 cm. Estimated diameter of tympanon about 58 cm. The decoration of the mantle is intact on the mid-section and to a minor extent preserved on the lower part of the upper section. Being purely geometrical it resembles that of OB. 87, but has the tangent-connected double spiral pattern reduced to a single row of pointed circles.

OB. 89. Total height about 59·5 cm. Diameter of tympanon about 74 cm. Tympanon: twelve-rayed central star, slightly convex-sided rays, resembling those of the Battambang drum but the convexity is less than on the latter (Loewenstein 1962: 22). The interray decoration of equilateral triangles in a chevron pattern resembles that of the tympanon from the Dieng plateau in Indonesia.

The central star zone is surrounded by nine concentric zones of decoration, the tenth zone, along the rim of the tympanon having had four sculptured frogs. They are:

Zone 1: A meandroid pattern with solid rectangular almost parallellogram-shaped centre, rather similar to that of OB. 86, so having the same set of references as this.

Zone 2: Ordinary pointed double circles.

Zone 3: Short radial lines.

Zone 4: Meandroid pattern with solid triangular centre. Rather similar to that of the Roti drum, with further resemblances to the Muong, Saleier, Semarang (Java No. 1830), Sangeang, and Kai drums.

Zone 5: Dissoluted feathered figures in a dense arrangement, hardly recognizable as human being, yet still more so than their closest parallel, which are on the Roti drum.

Zone 6: Two times eleven flying birds, separated by a running animal in one place, and diagonally to this by two peacocks, facing each other. These 'separations' are —interestingly enough—on top of the casting ridges on the mantle. The stylized White Herons are of two kinds, one with an angular chin, the other with a rounded chin. The flying birds may in general be said to be quite similar from one drum to the other. However, detailed studies reveal quite a number of dissimilarities among them when they are compared. So the tails of these birds resemble mostly the birds tails of the Dieng drum, while the drawing of the wings is more similar to those on the drum from Banjumening. No exact parallels to 'the separating' birds are known. However, some similarity might be found between the two peacocks facing each other and the picture of the two birds, also facing each other, sitting on the roof of a house, shown in zone 6 on the Hoang-ha drum (Goloubew 1941: 399, fig. 7, a–b). The other animal, perhaps a cervid, is too obliterated for determination, but still bears some resemblance to or could at least have been derived from walking deers depicted on the Ngoc-lu drum.

Zone 7: Another meander-like pattern, best described as broad and low Z-figures in two rows on top of each other and so that the top line of one lower row Z forms the base line of a top row Z. Although slightly different, the closest and best parallels are once again seen on the Saleier and Roti drums.

Zone 8: Pointed double circles.

Zone 9: Decoration completely obliterated. To judge from other drums it may have been short radial lines.

The decoration of the mantle is very interesting. The upper section has a horizontal frame of short vertical lines, pointed double circles and short vertical lines. This pattern of geometrical elements is also used as a frame at the lower part of the mid-section of the mantle, and in a vertical position at the mid-mantle section to frame the panels. The horizontal lower framing of the upper mantle section and the upper horizontal framing of the mid-mantle section consist of meanders with solid centre, similar to those of the tympanon zone 4.

Between the upper and lower frames on the upper mantle section are fragments of four boat pictures. The boats are long with raised stern and prow, filled with feathered figures, dissoluted to the same extent as those on the tympanon zone 5. As distinct from other boat pictures (Goloubew 1941: 404; van Heekeren 1958: fig. 12; Sørensen 1972: 13) these are not provided with a steering oar, but has a device under the stern, which can hardly be interpreted as anything but a fixed rudder. Each boat is guided by or followed by birds, more naturalistically drawn than those of the tympanon, and very similar to some birds depicted around one of the houses on the tympanon of OB. 86. However, the best similarity is again with the Saleier drum (Heger 1902: XXXIV. 1).

The panels of the mid-mantle section are filled with dissoluted feathered human figures, resembling those of the tympanon and those manning the boats.

OB. G.D. This drum, which has not previously been dealt with, shall be described here in a way similar to that used for OB. 86–89 and another drum recently published by this author (Sørensen 1973b), in order to facilitate comparisons between them.

As mentioned above the drum is in a good state of preservation, having apparently lost its handles already in prehistoric times, and with only two minor damages at the upper bulging section of the mantle. The decoration is clear with the exception of the interray pattern only. It obviously has had such one, but this was too obliterated to determine with any certainty. However, it seems as if it has been a kind of chevron pattern.

The measurements given below are for the mantle taken along the casting ridges, for the tympanon diagonally across it between the casting ridges of the mantle. They are:

Total height: 44·3 cm.
Height of mantle, upper section: 15·3 cm.
Height of mantle, middle section: 18·5 cm.
Height of mantle, lower section: 11·5 cm.
Thickness of mantle: 0·2 cm. at upper section.
Diameter of tympanon: 62·4 cm.
Thickness of tympanon: 0·5 cm.
Greatest width of mantle, upper section: 64·0 cm.
Bottom diameter: 64·5 cm.
Width of handles (lacking, but place and width clearly seen): 4·6 cm.
Shortest distance between two pair of handles: 14·7 cm.

The rim of the tympanon protrudes slightly over the side of the mantle at the point of junction. It is plain except for the 0·5 cm. raised central star, which is surrounded by eight concentric zones of decoration.

The mantle is divided into three parts, a convex bulging upper section, an almost cylindrical, slightly concave-sided middle section, both having geometrical decoration, and a truncated conical lower section, which is plain. Its rim has an interior triangular thickening.

The four pair of handles are missing. Traces of where they were attached to the lower side of the upper mantle section and to the middle section of the mantle, are clearly visible, but it is impossible to determine with sufficient accuracy, whether they consisted of one strap only, a strap with cut-outs like at OB. 87 or two separate straps. Each two pair of handles were spaced regularly, but the distance between them and the casting ridges differ slightly.

The tympanon is cast in one piece and joined to the mantle, which was cast in two pieces and joined. Means of separating the mantle core from the mould mantle during the casting were numerous square bronze nails, 0·6–0·8 cm., placed in horizontal rows spaced 4·5 cm. horizontally and vertically.

The decoration of the tympanon was as above-mentioned well preserved. It consists of a twelve-rayed central star in low relief framed by a concentric low and flat list 0·5 cm. wide, the total zone being 15·2 cm. in diameter. The interray decoration could not be determined.

The surrounding eight zones of decoration are separated from each other by 0·4 cm. wide, low grooves. The numbering of the zones begin from the central star zone. They are:

Zone 1: 1·2 cm. wide band of short radial lines.
Zone 2: 1·2 cm. wide band of point circles.
Zone 3: 1·2 cm. wide band of short radial lines.
Zone 4: eighteen points meander, parallelogram-shaped with solid centre, 2·5 cm. wide. Rather similar to that of OB. 89 zone 4, and accordingly with the same set of references.
Zone 5: a 4·8 cm. wide band with six counterclockwise flying stylized birds, like on other drums probably White Herons. They differ slightly, as the nostrils are not quite similar and the interior throat line on some is closed towards the head, on others it is open. Stylistically they have some resemblances to the birds on the drums from Banjumening (Heger 1902: XXXVIII, 14–14a) but differ in the drawing

of the chin and the hackles. Other resemblances can faintly be seen to the drums from Battambang and Dong-son (Loewenstein 1962: 36), as the tails to some extent parallels the Battambang ones, while the wings are closer to those of the Dong-son drum.

Zone 6–8 are exact repetitions of zones 1–3, the total width of them amounting to 5·0 cm.

The zone 6–8 pattern is used to decorate the mantle, placed horizontally in a band around its upper section at the point of greatest width, and at the lower part of the middle section. Basically it is also this pattern, which is used vertically to frame the plain panels of the mid-section, the only difference being that the short straight lines (the 'ladder' motif) are replaced by lines sloping in alternate directions, so producing a kind of chevron pattern. This is similar to OB. 88, the Banjumas and Semarang drums from Java (van Heekeren 1958: fig. 8, b–c), and partly also to the Klang drum (Loewenstein 1962: 18) and the Ban Gaw drum from Chiang Mai, Thailand (Sørensen 1973*b*), and the drum from the 'Indonesian tomb 2' at Dong-son (Janse 1958: 38).

NOTES

1. I am most grateful to Dr. M. M. Shouls, formerly of Chiang Mai University, for having analyzed the three sub-floor samples from Tam Ongbah.

2. Determination by Dr. Bertel Hansen (of the Botanical Museum, University of Copenhagen) is gratefully acknowledged.

3. In Hall 3 and Hall 4, where the distance between the floor of the cave and the bottom of the topsoil rarely exceeded 20–30 cm., several interments were placed on the floor of the cave.

4. A fuller description and discussion of the individual finds has been given in Sørensen (1973*a*: and n.d., *A.P.*).

5. No coffins were found completely intact, but four were found upon investigation to have been emptied prior to the more recent ransacking of the cave, as they were covered by later and intact depositions of the brown topsoil, their excavation gave very valuable additional information. The information obtained by cross-questioning of some of our workers, who had previously been employed by the treasure hunters, was confirmed.

6. Without the assistance of Professor Emeritus, Dr. Sood Sangvichien, Mahidol University, and Dr. Kasem, medical doctor to the Kanchanaburi paper factory, and an official from the Governor's office in Kanchanaburi, and the tireless efforts of Mallika and Maliwan Angsuthornrangsi, secretary and draughtsman respectively of the S.I.A.S. at Lampang, the rediscovery of this drum would not have been possible. I am most grateful to all of them for the assistance rendered.

It was possible to identify the drum from an old photograph taken in 1960 by Dr. H. R. van Heekeren, then a member of the expedition. Nobody in the temple in Kanchanaburi, where the drum was kept, was aware who had donated it, nor from where it originated. I am most grateful to the abbot of the temple, The Hon. Phra Visuthirungsi, for all help and assistance rendered, for his warm welcome and for his written permit to publish the drum.

7. The Tien (Dian) drums were buried between *ca* 150 and 80 B.C. *Editors*.

8. Bunker's definition (1972: 308) of the so-called pre-Heger I drums is rather obscure. The interpretation of a picture of such a drum (von Dewall 1972: 347, 5b) is erroneous. Upon re-examination of the original illustration the drum depicted is not found to differ from those otherwise found at Dian. Bunker's SCS IIa drums are perhaps better omitted from her listing of types until illustrations of the profiles of the drums are provided, allowing a more accurate classification and discussion.

9. Bunker (1972: 321–2) discards the Chinese excavators' dating of 220–175 B.C., of the graves 14–17, because they 'contain material which is related to the contents of

Tombs 12 and 13', which she considers the earliest; further arguing that 'they also contain the two very stylized SCS IIIb drums, which are obviously of a later date than the gong found in Tomb 12'. However, in the typological discussion of the drums (1972: 310), the said gong is stated to be belonging to SCS IV, 'due to its decoration'. Finally Tombs 3, 10, 12, 13, and 21 are linked because of the presence of lacquer coffins. But Tombs 3 and 10 contain the two third-century mirrors, while Tomb 13 has coins not minted before 175 B.C., and an early first-century mirror. The latter example gives a clear indication of the lifespan of antiquities prior to their deposition in the burials. The coins may very well have been fifty to one hundred years old when buried. However, the typology and the interpretation of the relative and the absolute chronology, as presented by Bunker, appears conflicting.

10. Good examples of this are in the Sood Sangvichien Museum, Siriraj Hospital, Bangkok.

11. The contents of the boat—simple as it is—executed in single lines filled with comb impression, actually bears some resemblances to the drum shown in a boat depicted on the Ngoc-lu drum (Goloubew 1941: 404, 15B).

12. The many vivid descriptions of early iron manufacturing in China, given by Needham (Needham 1964), point to this concept.

13. It is hoped that lead isotope determinations, to be made on fragments of the Ongbah drums and samples of recent lead from the mines, will give some information on the problem whether or not the mines had been in use during this period. However, even if negative evidence of a relation between the drums and the mines is obtained from the test, it still does not exclude the possibility of mining, as the drums may have been exported from other places.

14. The finds of early bronzes from north-east Thailand (Solheim 1968: 59; Bayard 1970: 109) are not considered in this context. A discussion of these finds, and of those from Ban Chieng, is outside the scope and aims of this paper.

15. In this survey of comparative motifs an attempt was made to incorporate also the motifs from the two pairs of drums from Malaysia, recently published by Peacock. However, the illustrations do not allow any such detailed analysis.

It appears, however, to this author that the 'Frog' drum from Sungai Lang has a decor very similar to that of OB. 89, and that the smaller drum from the same find resembles the Ban Gaw drum. Of the two drums from Kuala Trengganu the smaller one may be older than the bigger, which is very close to OB. 89, also in certain details, although the arrangement of the decorative bands differs slightly.

ADDITIONAL REFERENCES

Anonymous. 1959. *Yün-nan Chin-ning Shih-chai-shan ku-mu-chün fa-chüeh pao-kao.* Peking.

Feng, Han-chi et. al. 1960. *Szechwan Ch'uan-kuan Tsang Fa-chüeh Pao-kao.* Peking, Wen-Wu Press.

Archaeology in Northern Viet-Nam since 1954

JEREMY H. C. S. DAVIDSON

Introduction

ARCHAEOLOGICAL activity in Viêt-Nam falls conveniently into two periods: (1) the French period, to 1954; and (2) the post-French Independence period, since 1954. The purpose of this paper is to deal with the second period, to survey the archaeological work undertaken since the virtual cessation of the French presence there and, where possible, to comment upon it. Pre-1954 discoveries will be referred to only when relevant to more recent activities. Unfortunately, this survey is not exhaustive, since not all works known to me were available for inclusion.[1] Regarding the period of French control, only a few cursory comments need be made here.

French archaeological enterprise, which began in the closing decades of the nineteenth century, was largely 'overground'; concerning itself primarily with the study and preservation of monuments, of their statuary, and of inscriptions. Most French scholars in Indochina were either Sinologists who looked to China for inspiration and consequently regarded Viêt-Nam as an extension of Chinese culture, or they were Indologists concerned with the study of the Hinduization process, devoting their labours to Khmer and Cham remains and further, to the 'Indonesian' world. Thus Viêt-Nam, overshadowed by both India and China, received little attention in her own right. French interests were either documentary (inscriptions and other written records) or art-historical (monuments and statuary). This latter attitude in particular prevailed and continues to prevail in French studies of the material culture of Viêt-Nam from the Bronze Age to modern times. The predominant French view, expressed frequently by Bezacier (1953: 73-4; 1954: 178; 1958: 516; 1972: 226) is that *Vietnamese* archaeology begins in the seventh century A.D. with Đại-la thành, and deals in the main with monuments, their remains, and inscriptions. Sites and artefacts of earlier date, in no way connected with this Vietnamese archaeology, are funerary, being either Chinese or 'Indonesian' (Đông-so'n) in provenance, and are Vietnamese only by virtue of their geographical siting on Vietnamese soil (ibid.).

Three major discoveries were made during the French period: the Hòa-bình-Bắc-so'n lithic cultures, Đông-so'n, and the Óc-eo site. Generally speaking, however, the 'excavations' were haphazard, technically inadequate

(Hà 1963: 43–5, i.a.), displayed a lack of knowledge of the area and of the use of corroborative literary documentation (Lan 1963: 17–18 and 31), were mainly concerned with speculative interpretations of the religious and ritual significance of artefacts and art motifs (ibid., 22), and showed an insufficient attentiveness paid to details (e.g. Ngọc 1965: 63–4; also Bezacier 1972: 289, Nota), all of which often resulted in inaccurate dating, wild associations (Vu'ọ'ng 1966a: 49) and other mistakes. The predominant Western views of early Viêt-Nam remain: either, that Viêt-Nam had a primitive level of culture at the time that it was successfully annexed by China (first century A.D.); or, that it was basically a loan culture, learning metal working and other important activities from outside sources (Linh 1964: 30; Vu'ọ'ng 1966b: 48).

It is sincerely to be hoped that knowledge of recent and continuing work in Viêt-Nam will serve to rectify some of these errors and misconceptions. A few surveys of this period, relating principally to North Viêt-Nam, have been attempted. Two summarize previous data, the first (Tôt 1969) from the art-historical, the second (Bezacier 1972) from a more archaeological, point of view. Both are based, where relevant to this paper, on Lan (1963), which is itself a preliminary though invaluable study of the Bronze Age in North Viêt-Nam. In comparison, Chikamori's (1965) brief note is too general to be of value, and the Regional Reports published in *Asian Perspectives* tantalizing in their lack of specific information.

Since 1954 archaeologists and historians in the Democratic Republic of Viêt-Nam have been very active and certain of the archaeological discoveries made will alter views held by earlier or as yet uninformed researchers into the beginnings and continuity of civilization in Viêt-Nam. The attitudes of North Vietnamese archaeologists, naturally falling within the Marxist-Leninist framework of history, may be summarized as follows: archaeology is a branch of history, hence it is a study of society and its job is to flesh the skeleton of history in simple language, to make the past live (Vu'ọ'ng 1966b: 43, 46). To achieve this necessitates a rigorous precision in archaeological method which is essential to the subsequent and accurate interpretation of the finds (ibid., 45), and it also requires the substantiated criticism and rejections of old, incorrect and invalid views and interpretations of archaeology (ibid., 44). One may, therefore, define the subject as archaeological sociology.

The Phùng-nguyên Culture Complex

The most startling discovery in North Viêt-Nam made in 1959 at Phùng-nguyên, in Phú-thọ province. Subsequent excavations in the area—Phú-thọ, Hà-tây, and Vĩnh-phú provinces—have revealed the existence of an extensive culture, today encompassing more than twenty sites,[2] which ranges from Late Neolithic to Bronze (*KCH* 1969: 68) in objects and date.

The study of this Phùng-nguyên culture complex, so called after the type-site of that name, has had far-reaching effects, throwing new light on the continuity of traditions in decoration, pottery, bronze, and stone goods in North Vietnamese sites from Phùng-nguyên to Đông-so'n, and it has also demonstrated the further extension of Phùng-nguyên culture complex links into the Centre, especially Sa-huỳnh, the South, particularly at Long-khánh sites, and into maritime South East Asia.

The discovery of the Phùng-nguyên complex, intimately linked with the Hùng-vu'o'ng[3] and their kingdom of Văn-lang, of necessity rearranges the chronology of bronze in Viêt-Nam and enables one to restate, for the first time with solid material evidence, the pre-third century B.C., that is pre-Nam-Viêt (207–111 B.C.), history of the region.

Admittedly the complex still requires much detailed study (Kinh 1969: 56); its full extent[4] and the analyses of sites and finds remain to be established. The actual geographical location of the centre of the culture is still in dispute,[5] but investigation of the finds has brought to a head a disagreement over what artefacts should be used for dating purpose. Chinh (1966: 173 ff.) uses stone goods, thereby attributing the culture at Phùng-nguyên and Gò Bông (Thu'ọ'ng-nung, Vĩnh-phú) squarely to the neolithic, while other scholars use pottery (Tân 1968: 57–8; Kinh 1969: 54–5), believing lithic materials to be imprecise chronological indicators, a very reasonable standpoint in view of the inescapable reality of paralithic[6] culture in the territory.

It is generally agreed that the complex spans three chronological levels:

    I. Late Neolithic;

    II. Copper—Bronze; or Early Bronze;

    III. Bronze (*KCH* 1969: 68; Kinh 1969: 58)

but the dates of type-sites—Phùng-nguyên, Lũng-hòa, and Gò Mun respectively—or of other sites representative of the major stages in the evolution of the culture, are hotly disputed, and the classification of sites into this three-fold periodization indicates a wide divergence of opinions. The cautiously conservative datings for the three levels at their type-sites give:

I.	Late Neolithic	Phùng-nguyên	2000–1500 B.C.
II.	Copper—Bronze	Lũng-hòa	c. 1000 B.C.
III.	Bronze	Gò Mun	1000–500 B.C.

Phùng-nguyên is held to be Late Neolithic by Khải (1960: 6 ff.), Chinh (1966: 173 ff.), Linh (1968b: 29), and Tân (1968: 54), yet Boriskovsky (1966: 193) believes its inhabitants knew the use of metals. Indeed, finds here of opal string-beads and of 'tubes' of semi-precious stone, for necklaces, the holes in which were perhaps bored with a bronze drill (Tân, ibid.; Kinh 1969: 57),[7] lend weight to that suggestion.

At Gò Bông, the pottery factory for the early stages of the complex, which is dated as contemporary with the type-site by Lan (1969: 57), similar apparel

Table : *Summary of opinions of Vietnamese archaeologists concerning the date of four[a] major sites*

	Phùng-nguyên	Đông-dậu	Gò Mun	Đông-so'n	Hùng-vu'o'ng	Văn-lang
1. Diệp đình Hoa	2800–2300 / Gò Bông: 2300–1800	1800–1300	1300–800	800 B.C.–A.D. 300	2800–200	2800–200
2. Nguyễn duy Tỳ	2500–1400	1500–1100	1200–700	700 B.C.–A.D. 100	2500–200	2500–200
3. Hà văn Tấn	2300–1700	1700–1200	1200–800	800 B.C.–A.D. 100	1700–200	—
4. Trân quốc Vu'ọ'ng	2100–1500	1500–1250	1200–900	900 B.C.–A.D. 100	700–200	700–200
5. Nguyễn Linh	2000–1500	1500–700[b]	700–200	700 B.C.–A.D. 200	2000–200	700–200
6. Phạm văn Kinh	2000–1500	1500 onwards[c]		third century B.C.–first century B.C.		
7. Lê văn Lan	2000–1000	—	—[d]	1000 B.C.–A.D. 100	2000 B.C.	700–200
8. Hoàng xuân Chinh	2000–1000	1000	1000–200	200–100	1000–200	1000–200

a. The Hung-vuong and their kingdom of Van-lang are associated with these four sites.
b. This date includes sites such as Lũng-hòa and Gò Bông.
c. Dates coincide more or less with conventional dates.
d. 1500–700?

All dates are B.C.

as well as metal dross (*cục* 'lumps') which when analysed showed up as an alloy of copper, tin, and silver (Tân 1968: 54), place the site firmly in Level II. Such data suggested a transitional neolithic to chalcolithic periodization for Phùng-nguyên, Gò Bông, An-đạo, also in Vĩnh-phú province, and for Dậu-du'o'ng (Gò Chè) in Phú-thọ to Linh (1968a: 21); while close similarities revealed in a comparison of artefacts from Gò Bông and Dậu-du'o'ng led Tân (ibid., 53) to associate the two sites very closely (cf. Kinh 1968: 56 ff.) and class them as Early Bronze Age factories. Similarly, both Kinh (1968: 57) and Nghĩa (1960: 33) incline towards an Early Bronze Age dating for Phùng-nguyên and Gò Bông.

Lũng-hòa (Chinh 1966: 173 ff. and 1968; Lan 1969: 57) and its associated site of Văn-điên (Dung 1966: 64; Chinh 1966: 173 ff.) are also considered by many scholars to be Late Neolithic, although somewhat younger than Phùng-nguyên. However, dross and a stone mould from Lũng-hòa (Linh 1968b: 30) suggest bronze-casting there; while in Boriskovsky's (1966: 193) opinion Văn-điên was a community with a knowledge of metal-working. One should here keep in mind the significance of C14 dates for samples from Đông-đậu[8] in Vĩnh-phú province, a site particularly rich in stone moulds for labour-tools and weapons (Lan 1968: 43), hence undeniably Bronze Age and, from all indications, later in date than Lũng-hòa. Results of the tests give a date of 1378 ± 100 B.C., which necessitates a revision of the new conventional dates for the beginnings of bronze working in the North by some three centuries and of the traditional datings by about a millennium.

Gò Mun (= Viêt-tiên, Phú-thọ: Linh 1964: 39–40, 1968a: 21; Tu' 1966: 231–8; Tân 1968: 55; Lan 1969: 58–9), an indisputably Bronze Age site,[9] represents the last stages of the Phùng-nguyên culture and the first stages of the Đông-so'n (I) culture.[10] Gò Mun-related Bronze Age sites[11] developed into Đông-so'n (II) culture sites proper, various phases of which are represented by places like Viêt-trì in Hà-đông, Viêt-khê in Hải-phòng, Đào-thinh in Yên-bái, and Thiêu-du'o'ng in Thanh-hóa province.[12]

This brief exposition of the Phùng-nguyên culture complex, itself the preparatory and early stages of Đông-so'n culture, highlights the need for further exploration and the vast amount of research that has yet to be done. Meanwhile, the astounding implication remains that a knowledge of bronze-casting existed in Viêt-Nam in the early second or late third millennium B.C.

Stone

Despite their sometimes harsh, sometimes bromidic language (e.g. Vu'ọ'ng 1966b: 48), North Vietnamese criticisms of previous archaeological activity and of previous or current interpretations of the finds are well-substantiated and, by and large, justifiable. One example, from Hoà-binh, will suffice.

In 1960–1, the nine Hoà-bình sites studied by Colani were reinvestigated and a marked carelessness in excavational method and the omission of numerous objects from consideration on her part (Hà 1963: 43)[13] was revealed. Her assessments of the sites were based more on the styles of implements than on the archaeological levels at which they were found and which she failed to record properly (Hà 1963: 45). This has led to a continuing dating controversy over Hoà-bình Levels I–III. Is it Paleolithic as Colani believed? or Mesolithic?[14] Following from this, to what Neolithic level then does Bắc-so'n belong? Boriskovsky (1966: 1) and Vu'ọ'ng (1962: 45 ff.) believe Bắc-so'n, and Quỳnh-văn in Nghê-an province, are Early and Middle Neolithic continua respectively (Kinh 1971: 50; Tâm 1969: 29, chart) and that the Hoà-bình-Bắc-so'n cultures are a continuous development; an idea that Kinh (1971: 51), among others, does not accept. So the controversy continues with Hoà-bình dated most generally between 8000–4000 B.C. (Lan 1969: 55) and only one site, Núi Đọ, Thanh-hóa, escapes safely into the Paleolithic (Boriskovsky 1966: 4; Tâm 1969: 29 ff.; Kinh 1971: 48).

A further suggestion to explain the notable scarcity of Paleolithic sites in the area was advanced by the geologist Nguyễn Đú'c Tâm (1969). He believes that the recession of the sea and consequent land-formation processes during the Late Pleistocene were not completed during the Paleolithic. Hence sites dating from that period are only to be found on high ground such as mountains, whence Núi Đọ, and islands, which excludes most of the known culture sites in Viêt-Nam, dating as they do from more recent archaeological periods.

Three new cave sites in the Hoà-Bình area—Hang Muôi, Hang Tùng, and Sao-đông II—were also studied in 1960–1. Finds of snail shells, common at Hoà-bình and Bắc-so'n stations, were made; other artefacts of stone and clay suggest a Bắc-so'n culture (Hà 1963: 43 ff.) as at Quỳnh-văn (Boriskovsky 1966: 1) and possibly at Soi-nhụ (Quảng-ninh: Ninh 1968: 61).

An engraving of a plough on a Bắc-so'n schist axe from Lạng-so'n (1925; Colani 1929: 278; Bezacier 1966–7: 551, fig. 1) has been shown by Bezacier (ibid., 555) to date from about the first century B.C., although the date of the axe is genuine. Well-made polished stone, basalt, adze-axes (*riù*), *bôn*, and a bracelet (*vòng*) came to light in the Tây-bắc bản Mu'ò'ng-giang in 1969 (Hà 1969: 62–3). Dated provisionally as Late Neolithic, these finds are therefore roughly contemporary with the stone factory of Đông-khôi, Thanh-hóa province (Kinh 1971: 51), which is associated with the earliest levels of the Phùng-nguyên complex. Belonging to that complex and showing a higher level of culture than Đông-khôi (*VSH* 1961: 9–15; Boriskovsky 1966: 122–5; Tân 1968: 53; Kinh 1968: 56; 1969: 56) is the stone factory of Dậu-du'ọ'ng (= Gò Chè), Phú-thọ province. The implements and shavings from this last site show a highly developed aesthetic sense as well as a high level of technical skill and all interestingly, are made from non-local stone of unknown provenance.[15] Other stone factories in the North have been known since the 1920s[16] and some must also have existed in the Centre and South of Viêt-Nam.

Also assigned to the Late Neolithic, *c.* 1000 + B.C. (Liễn 1963 : 64) is a series of finds made in 1961–2, at various sites in neighbouring districts of Yên-bái province, of different types of stone adze-axe and *bôn⁻* square (*tú' giác* or *hình can xu'ng*) and shouldered (*riù có vai*), within which are several sub-classes plus chisels, bracelets, some of which are of blue-green flint, and decorative beads. Made of a variety of stones such as takhilit, diabase, basalt, flint, some axes bear marks that suggest the use of a stone-saw (ibid., 63). Associations once again are with Phùng-nguyên.[17]

A characteristic feature of Vietnamese sites is the stone shouldered axe. Although most finds have been made in the North, the type is widespread and also present in the Centre and South (Lan 1962*a*: 19, map),[18] and develops 'heeling' (e.g. Phùng-nguyên, Phú-hậu, An-đạo: Lan 1962*a*: fig. 1. 5–6),[19] perhaps through a reworking of the original shouldered form. The origin of these shouldered axes—contrary to the belief of Heine-Geldern (1945 : 134 ff.) that they were borrowed from the West, or of Janse that they are Chinese, since they are found at Lạch-tru'ò'ng, Thanh-hóa—can first be seen in Hoà-bình, Bắc-so'n and other somewhat later Neolithic sites like Bâu-tró in Quảng-bình, and Cù-lao Rùa in Biên-hoà province (Lan 1962*a*: 19). And from the finds made, it appears that the Indochinese Peninsula[20] is the focal (perhaps innovation?) centre for the form, with a limited extension in area to include parts of south China, and maritime South East Asia. Of particular note is the development of these stone shouldered to heeled axes into the bronze 'paring-knife' (*riù hình dao xén*) or pediform (*hình lu'õ'i xéo*) axe common in Bronze Age sites in North Viêt-Nam (Lan 1962*a*: 15 ff; 1963 : pl. III. 1–9, or pl. IV. 1–3).[21] The method of attachment of blade to handle, still seen today in highland regions (Lan 1962*a*: 25, fig. 3), is the insertion of a haft into the socket of the blade, the haft in turn fitting through a hole in the handle (ibid., 26, fig. 4), giving an exact experimental reconstruction of the representations seen on bronze drums.

Paralithic culture is yet another characteristic feature of Vietnamese sites which cannot escape notice. The use of stone implements from earlier periods is known (Văn Tân 1962*b*; Liễn 1963 : 64; Bezacier 1966–7: esp. 555) and the continued use of stone as a material for all sorts of items during the Bronze Age (e.g. Nuí Voi: Lan 1963 : 93–4; 1964*b*:. 63; Gò Mun: Tu' 1966: 231 ff.; Đại-áng: Hu'ng 1968: 48 ff.) and down into the Iron and modern periods has been observed by several scholars (Lan 1963 : 252; Liễn 1963 : 64; Chinh 1962: 45). In fact, one cannot discuss Vietnamese sites without constant reference to, and awareness of, the stone artefacts found alongside metal ones, paralleling them, copying them (Kinh 1969: 57), and sometimes providing the inspiration for them (Lan 1962*a*).

Apart from the many square and shouldered axes and *bôn* found at various sites (e.g. Gò Chè: Tân 1968: 53; Đại-áng: Hu'ng 1968: 49–50; Văn-điên: Lan 1963: 248; Gò Mun: Linh 1964: 36–7; Thiêu-du'o'ng: Lan 1963: pl. xxxiv. 2–3), there are also stone *polissoirs*, bracelets (Viêt-tiên: Lan 1963: pl. xxxv. 1–2), net weights, pestles, chisels, beads, and arrows which have been excavated (Linh 1964; Lan 1963: 250–60). The excavations at Lũng-hòa unearthed a stone *qua* (*ge*: Chinh 1968: 53; Kinh 1969: 57)[22] which, although not necessarily an imported piece, is certainly Chinese in inspiration (Lan 1963: 165). Beads of semi-precious stone,[23] including nephrite, are known (Lũng-hoà: Chinh 1968: 25–9 and 101–3, pls. xliii. 12 and xlv. 3; cf. Phú-hoà: Fontaine 1972: 436 ff.), as are ear-rings and bracelets of nephrite (Làng Vạc, Nghê-an: Tỳ 1973: 64) and bracelets of nephrite and of jasper from Tràng Kênh,[24] Hải-phòng. Round or square rings and ear-rings found at Phùng-nguyên sites are common to Đông-so'n (Janse 1958: vol. iii, 76–8, figs. 32–3, pls. xlviii–l) and recall forms found on Cham statuary.[25]

Văn-điên provides an interesting red-brown quartz statuette of a male figure (Dung 1966: 64), the first from a Vietnamese site, and certainly rare in other parts of the Far East. It appears to have come from a burial and perhaps served as a fertility symbol (Lan 1970*a*: 39).

Stone moulds have been known since 1926, and more recently shouldered axe-moulds (Lan 1963: pl. ii. 1) have been found at Núi Voi, Công-vị (Hà-nôi), and Chu'o'ng-my (Hà-đông) (ibid., 115). Weapon and labour-tool moulds have also been discovered at Đông-đậu (Lan 1968: 43), as well as a heeled-axe mould (q.v. Lan 1963: pl. iv: 1) from Vĩnh-linh (Quảng-bình: Ngọc 1965: 63–4), and an axe-mould from Làng Vạc, Nghê-an (Tỳ 1973: 64). An interesting one comes from Lạng-so'n (Lan 1963: 158–61, pls. xiv. 3–4 and xv. 5), a dagger cast in one piece—blade and handle.[26]

The Vĩnh-linh mould has been the object of scientific study, and Ngọc (1965: 64), while noting metallic residue in it and in Colani's 1926 mould, concludes that the stone, as at Long-khánh sites, could not possibly have withstood the temperatures of molten bronze (700°–900°) or copper (1050°–1330°); it would have split. The stone mould was therefore the positive into which metals of lower melting point such as lead, or possibly tin, were poured and from the facsimile in this softer metal a disposable, fired earth (*dat nung*) mould was made to take the bronze cast. The argument is convincing since kiln-fired sherds from Phùng-nguyên culture sites[27] were fired at *c.* 800°–900° (Gò Mun: Linh 1964: 34; Lan 1963: 238; Thiêu-du'o'ng, *c.* 600°–700°: ibid.) and could easily withstand the temperature of molten bronze. It would also explain the absence of moulds for larger bronze objects like the drums, *thap*, and *thô*; the earthen mould would be chipped off after the metal had set. Exactly this method was still in use in Hà-đông some twenty years ago (Durand 1953: 397–8). Finally, the amount of time a skilled craftsman would require to produce a stone mould of good quality, a task demonstrated experimentally by Ngọc (1965: 64, n. 1), coupled with the very small number that have turned up, argues that these stone moulds were the first stage of casting, for facsimiles.[28]

Pottery

Vietnamese pottery (Lan 1963: 230–50) may be classified:

(1) by the method of its decoration (stamped, incised, etc.);
(2) by its colour: (i) the Đông-sơn range, red through light brown to grey, found in Quảng-bình, Hà-tĩnh, Nghê-an, Thanh-hóa (Bắc Trung-bô);
        (ii) the light yellow or light grey ware of more northerly and inland sites (Bắc-bô); or
(3) by its most common decorative patterns.

Common to the Neolithic are such general designs as toothcomb, basket-weave, etc., which are continued into later periods. A general comment on degree and positioning of patterns, is that Bắc-bô ware is more highly decorated, and the decoration more often found on the neck, than in Bắc Trung-bô pottery. The distribution of patterns also suggests that there were three metropolitan pottery centres: Gò Bông and Gò Mun representing the early and late phases of the Phùng-nguyên complex; and their successor Thiêu-du'o'ng, representing a developed stage of Đông-sơn culture (Lan 1963: pl. XXXIII); the former through the latter, exerting demonstrable influence on the more distant production centre of Sa-huỳnh (Linh 1964: 39–40; Tân 1968: 55 ff.; Kinh 1969: 60).[29]

Đông-sơn pottery inclusive of Thiêu-du'o'ng ware (Lan 1963: pls. XXVII–XXX), not found at any Chinese sites (Bezacier 1972: 226–7)[30], is characterized: by a red to light brown to grey colour range perhaps because of the use of lateritic and podzolic soils;[31] by the presence of *nôi* ('cooking pots': full-bellied, with wide mouth and small foot: Lan 1963: pl. XXVII) and *chac* (*chan-gio*: ' "pig's foot" pot' = 'vase tronconique': ibid., pl. XXX) and tends to be coarse in material.[32] The characteristic Đông-sơn *noi* is not found at Shízhàishān, but it and the *chac* show a distinct resemblance to Bâu-tró and Sa-huỳnh ware (Bezacier 1972: 227 and pls. X–XI; cf. Malleret 1961: pls. VI–VII; Long-khánh ware: Fontaine 1972: 423 ff.).

However, these characteristics of Đông-sơn pottery are all found in the Phùng-nguyên culture complex at most of whose sites sherds are found and where, as already observed at other discoveries,[33] pottery occurs associated with other materials. The pottery is wheel-made (Tân 1968: 53; Kinh 1969: 58, i a.), the material is coarse, and *nôi* and *chac* abound.

Gò Bông ware has the same types, *nôi*, *chac* etc., and geometric designs as the pottery of Gò Mun (Linh 1964: 33; Lan 1969: 60); the latter site shows unmistakable affinities with Phùng-nguyên in stone and pottery, and with Đông-so'n in pottery and bronze (Tu' 1966: 231–8; Kinh 1969: 60). The similarities in form and design between Viêt-tiên and Thiêu-du'o'ng, and Sa-huỳnh, wares are noted (Kinh, ibid.; Linh 1964: 39–40; Tân 1968; Bezacier 1972: 227), and all Vietnamese archaeologists agree that Viêt-tiên is transitional between Phùng-nguyên and Đông-so'n (Linh, loc. cit.; Lan 1963: 248, i.a.); all forming a cultural continuum.

Of interest in this respect is the similarity of Gò Mun clay statuary (Linh 1964: 33–5, esp. 35, fig. 9) and of the geometric designs found on Gò Mun ware to Đào-thịnh bronze statuettes and to linear representations found on Đào-thịnh bronzes (Tỳ 1962: 61–2; Lan 1963: pls. x and xxvi), identical as the latter are with Đông-so'n forms (Linh 1964: 38; Tân 1968: 55 ff.).

In Đông-so'n, pottery is fairly crude, while the decoration of bronzes is excellent. The geometric patterns and designs found on Đông-so'n bronze-ware and used as dating evidence for the beginnings of bronze working in Viêt-Nam (Karlgren 1942, Huái style: fourth–third centuries B.C.) are all astoundingly found on Phùng-nguyên and Gò Bông pottery (Tân 1968: 56, fig. 1, esp. 59, fig. 2; cf. Viêt-tiên–Thiêu-du'o'ng ware, Lan 1963: pls. xxxii–xxxiii). If the dates for Phùng-nguyên and Gò Bông (*c.* 2000–1500) are correct, and there now seems little reason to doubt them, given the C14 dates from Đông-đậu, or they are conservatively lowered to agree with the dates proposed for the beginnings of the Gò Bông continuation, Gò Mun (*c.* 1000 B.C.), they still push the date for the beginning of bronze working back several centuries, and show either creation or independent discovery of decorative motifs which when found previously at Đông-so'n were educed as demonstrating affinity with, and influence from, Huai culture (Karlgren 1942: 8, 13–14, 24). While the reverse of Phùng-nguyên influence on Huai culture is not proven, the affinity undoubtedly exists and, at least, suggests a minimal origin date for Phùng-nguyên of about the early seventh century B.C. (*Viet su' lu'o'c, c.* 1377: q.1/1.3–4) the beginning of the Huái style.

A further interesting site which belongs to the Phùng-nguyên complex, the stone factory of Dậu-du'o'ng (Kinh 1968: 56 ff.; Tân 1968: 53 ff.) has very few sherds but they seem to display evidence of an independent pottery culture.[34] One possible explanation is that the pottery we associate with the culture centres Viêt-tiên, Đông-so'n, Sa-huỳnh, etc. was produced for the élite, and that Dậu-du'o'ng demonstrates ware used by the artisans and peasants, a people's pottery.

Bronze

The Bronze Age of Viêt-Nam has, since its discovery, captured the imagination of researchers, and hence it is the period on which most work has been done. Certainly a wealth of information about the society of the time can be gleaned from artefacts of this era, and in keeping with the new historiography, DRV scholars argue that a slave society was required to produce the richness of this culture (Lan 1963: 13, i.a.).

Drums: Drums are the most obvious feature of this so-called Đông-so'n culture, whose beginnings are determined largely by the study of the décor of its drums. Since 1954 some twenty-six bronze drums[35] have been discovered, Bezacier (1972: 290–6) gives a list of the fifty-four Heger I type drums[36] known in Viêt-Nam to 1963, the end of Lan's survey, when over thirty of the total number came from the Đông-so'n area (Chinh 1962: 44): his discussion of the Bronze Age in the context of the drum culture[37] is a competent account of the established views, modified somewhat by recent discoveries from Yúnnán.

(1) *Origin:* The two traditional proposals for the prototype-origin are:

(a) Goloubew's theory (1932: 137–44) that they were based on drums of skin drawn tightly over perishable cane or wood frames, thus echoing in part Hirth's (1890) idea. Bezacier (ibid., 217) agrees, illustrating the idea with reference to the *trông dò'n* placed on a wicker stand (ibid., 214, fig. 118). Since *trông dò'n* are of Chinese origin, this proposal fits in with Goloubew's (1938: 8) belief that Đông-so'n drums too, are of Chinese origin, a view rejected by Lan (1962c: 37).

(b) Levy's theory (1948: 19) that they are modelled after bronze *nôi* (Bezacier 1972: 216, fig. 120g), with which he compares them; the drums being achieved by stretching a skin tympanum over the mouth.[38]

There are several flaws in these suggestions, however attractive they may seem. They are based on shapes that might well be later in origin than the bronze drum instead of its prototype; on the drum's decoration (Lan 1962c: 30) which admittedly is closely connected with its functions (ibid., 32); imply that the drums were beaten *à la chinoise* in an almost vertical position; ignore the fact that there are no bronze *nôi* belonging to the early period of the drum culture; the bronze *nôi* is a Dōng Hàn period object at the earliest (ibid., 32); and disregard a feature of primary importance in the manufacture of the bronze drums, and intimately connected with drumming technique, that they are hollow with a foot as a resonance outlet.

The shape of the drums may possibly have been suggested by a clay *nôi* (Lan 1963: pl. XXVII 4; cf. Zhōu 1178: j.7/74) turned upside down and given a flattened bottom, but to understand their origin one must take cognizance of how they were drummed. Many sources tell us that the drums were suspended (*Guǎngzhōujì*, quoted in Tắc, *c.* 1339: q.1/31–32 =. 48; also *Cíhǎi* 1378: 6; Lo 1967: 110–14: *Súishū*),[39] beaten with hairpins, and that the ground was hollowed out *underneath* the suspended drum (Fàn 1175: j.1/18a7–b1). This last preparation would be pointless if *nôi* or Chinese drums, beaten in the Chinese manner, were the origin. One must therefore, look elsewhere. Very pertinent are the observations made by Lan (1962c) among the Mu'ờ'ng of Xã Mang-so'n and Lai-đông, Phú-thọ. A Heger II drum discovered in 1962 was prepared for drumming. The drum, with its tympanum horizontal, was hung off the ground by its handles on rattan straps from a cross-bar supported at each end by crossed-sticks lashed together (ibid., **34).** It was hung above a circular hole dug in the ground for resonance; a minimum of six drummers including a drum-major stood in a circle around it and beat it with long poles, exactly as if they were pounding grain in a mortar (*côi*) (ibid., 32–5). The drum-major beat out different rhythms on different parts of the face to the drone set up by the others on the outer rim, the resulting sound being very like pestles pounding into mortars.[40] The shape of the drum —sometimes very like an inverted mortar (Shízhàishān drum: Tôt 1969: pl. XIII)[41] sometimes modified, perhaps under the influence of the uniquely Đông-so'n *nôi?*—the methods of suspension, of beating, of pounding pestle into mortar are all represented on the drums themselves as well as on other bronze implements. Given all these points discussed above, the mortar, inverted, as the origin of the drum is more probable than any previous suggestion (Lan 1962c: 36); and the idea of a Chinese origin and beating methods is to be discarded.

(2) *Socio-religious use:* This aspect of drum culture has been discussed at length elsewhere (e.g. Bezacier 1972: 192 ff.). One need only add the following points of information: the Muong beat drums and empty mortars in the same way at Têt, rice rituals, marriage and funeral ceremonies all of which are fertility situations, and to venerate their ancestors (Lan 1962c: 33–5). The Lao do so at times of illness (*Sòng huìyàogao*: 198–5/74a9); the Nán Mán (*Mánshū* j.10/30b7 = 160) beat drums at lunar New Year, funerals[41a] (as do the Jeh who accompany funerals with animal sacrifice and wine at the graveside), and at water festivals. At water festivals the custom of beating drums is found also among the Javanese (Huáng 1520: j.1/9a4); Javanese (ibid.) and Chams beat drums at marriages (ibid., 2b2), Chams also indulge in the practice at royal ceremonies (ibid., 2a4).

The use of bronze drums as inhumation receptacles, apparently found at Shízhàishān,[42] is not common in the Vietnamese area (Lan 1970b: 80), where large 'vases' (*thap*) and '*situle*' (*thô*) were used instead. Drums were, nonetheless, buried. Zhōu Qùfēi (ibid.) notes that the Vietnamese travel to Guăngxī to buy drums and on their return bury them in the mountains. Cuisinier's (1948: 450–85) Mu'ờ'ng tradition that drums function as funerary objects is, as can be seen, only one aspect of drum culture among them.

(3) *Types, decoration, interpretation:* Information on drum types can be found in Lan (1963: 188–207) and Bezacier (1972: 185–92); small drums were probably used as grave goods (Lan 1962c: 31).

Two early competent descriptions of shape and decoration are given by the Sòng writers Zhōu Qùfēi and Fàn Chéngdà (loc. cit.). Discussions of the decorative motifs will undoubtedly continue, yet one controversy, that over the identification of the mysterious bird that occurs on the tympana of drums and certain other bronze objects[43] should diminish since the weight of literary evidence, tradition, and occurrence comes down strongly on the side of the crane-egret. In fact drums and drum-tunes were named after the *hè* and *lù*, whose symbolism is well documented.

It is perhaps worth remarking here that the 'frog' of almost all writings on drum décor is actually a toad (*Bufo vulgaris: chánchú*) according to Chinese sources. The star on drums, *thap* lids, and *chau*,[44] has been regarded as evidence of a sun-cult (Colani 1940; Ling 1955). However, since the dualism of symbols is well-established and the rain-invoking potency of drums without question, one need only state the obvious, that for good crops both sunshine and rain are needed. The geometrical construction of the star shape could have been executed with the aid of a compass, and the rays themselves may have served as spatial indicators for the execution of the outer rings of decoration.[45] Twelve-rayed stars are the most common; all Laos drums have twelve rays, though the number of rays may differ on objects from the same area. With the exception of the seven-rayed *chau*, rays go up by twos from 8 to 22, with 18 missing,[46] but what significance, if any, can we attach to that omission remains undetermined. Can the numerical variations be used for purpose of dating or provenance?

From a study of décor, it seems that the Hũ'u-chung drum is a transitional form (Lan 1962b: 63–4), and the Chu'o'ng-my example may be the original type for Class II (Lan 1963: 200), but such classifications are tentative, highlighting how much more detailed study remains to be done.[47]

Thap, etc.: Most important of the other finds are the *thap* (jars) and the *thô* ('situle'), both of which come in large, utensil, and small, grave-good size. The *thap* (Lan 1963: 139–46), a uniquely Đông-so'n culture form (Hu'ng 1962: 57–61), occurs in two classes: with, or without, lid. In decoration comparable to the drums (Lan 1963: pls. IX–X), they have been found at Đào-thịnh, Yên-bái, where a small *thap* was found inside the large one; Đông-so'n and Thiêu-du'o'ng; at Làng Vạc (Nghê-an: Tỳ 1973:64); Viêt-khê and Thuy-du'o'ng (Hải-phòng: Băng 1970: 63–4), Viêt-trì and Nam-chính in Hà-đông province and at Vạn-thắng (Phú-thọ: Lụ'u 1963: 39–40). Discovered at burial sites, it is they not the drums that serve as burial urns (Lan 1970b: 74–5 and 80). Two types of funerary use are found: cremation (Đào-thịnh,

Vạn-thắng); and as receptacles for human heads (Thiêu-du'o'ng), giving evidence of decapitation (Lan 1963: 284).[48] Copulating human figures perhaps suggesting rebirth, are found on the lids of some *thap* (ibid., pls. x and xxvi. 2ab). Attention should be drawn to the object, represented as carried in boats and seen on the bodies of drums (Ngọc-lũ drum, Đào-thỉnh *thap*). Previously interpreted as a drum, it is in fact much more like a *thap* which, given the latter's proven function as a burial urn, would fit in with the suggested interpretation of the pirogues as boats of the dead.

The *thô*, possibly bronze mortars hence symbolic of fertility and rebirth (Lan 1963: 136–9), which are found in abundance at Đông-so'n, Việt-khê, Thiêu-du'o'ng (ibid., pl. vIII) and other sites, are also burial receptacles, notably for decapitated heads, which would help disprove Goloubew's (1929: 20, n. 2) statement that the small versions served as currency.

Several other types of burial are known from Việt-Nam. Large clay *nôi*, placed mouth to mouth, were used for the inhumation of children (Hoằng-lý, Thanh-hóa). Smaller *nôi* are often found placed on or around skeletons in rectangular graves in the ground (Núi Nấp, Thanh-hóa). Brick tombs from the Chinese period are common (Ngọc-so'n, Tú-kỳ, Hải-du'o'ng: Lan 1964*b*: 63; Hoàng-mai, Hà-nôi: Lang 1963: 63–4). Special are the bamboo-section tomb, or coffin, burials of Aí-quôc (Hu'ng-yên: Lan 1964*b*: 63) and the hollowed-out log (?canoe) burials from the important site of Việt-khê (Lan 1963: 95–9 and 271; also Nam-sách: Lan 1964*b*: 63).[49]

Most Bronze Age finds have associated stone utensils and pottery.[50] Modelled on stone forms are the variety of bronze axes (Lan 1963: pls. II–IV; 1964*a*: 63–4: square, splayed, shouldered, heeled; some special forms are decorated), military weapons (ibid., pls. xI–xX: spears, javelins, fighting axes, daggers, arrows, shields or breast-plates, swords), various specialized utensils (ibid., pl. v: awls, chisels, needles, fishhooks, scrapers), rings and bracelets (ibid., pl. xxv) and assorted agricultural implements (ibid., pl. 1; 1964*a*: 63). Socketed spades and the 'duck's foot' ploughshare (Vu'o'ng 1960: 133; Chi 1964: esp. 35, fig. 1; Lan 1963: pl. 1. 3–5) are also represented at Shízhaìshān (von Dewall 1967: figs. 3–4). The 'duck's-foot' ploughshare is probably a hoe, but an implement classed as a special axe (Lan 1963: pl. III. 12) could well be a grave-good representation of a ploughshare—the holes could have been used for guy-ropes, and a handle of some sort inserted into the socket (cf. Bezacier 1966–7: 551 ff.: Hàn period). According to historical tradition Cu'u-chân was introduced to the buffalo-drawn plough during the Wáng Mǎng-Dōng Hàn period. The buffalo may, however, have already been domesticated and used as a draught animal some centuries earlier.[51]

Of Chinese origin but copied locally in stone or bronze were the short swords (Lan 1963: pl. xvi), *qua* (ibid., pl. xvII: most are decorated), *bình* (ibid., pl. vi: cf. a wooden *bình* found at Việt-khê), and *chậu* (pl. vII).

A number of bronze sculptures of birds and other figures has been discovered, apparently copied from pottery figurines (Lan 1963: 249; Linh 1964:
33; Hu'ng 1962: 59; Tỳ 1962: 61–4). Interpretations of the function of the
birds differ—they are held by Tỳ (ibid.) to be toys, by Lan (1963: 293) to be
evidence of bird-worship, a possibility considering the many birds represented
on bronzes (Hu'ng 1962: 61).

Finally, of the multitude of Chinese objects discovered, Chinese mirrors
from Thiêu-du'o'ng have been the subject of a study by Hu'ng (1961–2).
Based on the different styles that occur, they have been dated from early
Xī-Hàn to early Dōng-Hàn.

Iron

Iron is generally associated with the Chinese annexation of Giao-chi by
Hàn Wudì in 111 B.C.,[52] although documentary evidence suggests iron in
Nam-Việt about a century earlier (*Cu'o'ng-muc*, 1884: Tb 1/22 =. 66),
while some Vietnamese scholars even believe iron working had already begun
by the mid third century B.C. (Châu 1969: 33). In North Việt-Nam it is
initially always associated with Hàn Chinese tombs which suggests the interment of Chinese or sinicized local notables and equally argues against a local
origin. The use of iron was, however, widespread during the first century
B.C.–A.D., as is shown by its occurrence in the Centre and South; production
techniques, whether originally local or imported perhaps from indianized
states, may have improved with Chinese influence. At Đông-so'n (1961–2)
iron swords, hoes, spears, and axes, modelled on their stone or bronze counterparts, are associated as grave-goods with stone and bronze objects, including
small drums (Lan 1963: 261–4 and pl. XXXVI). Their manufacture may be
fairly crude, but unfortunately their rusted state prevents decisive assessment.
As iron culture took hold in the north (first century A.D.), the artistry in other
metals apparently declined, the decoration of bronze goods for instance
becomes extremely simplified or non-existent (Chinh 1962: 45).

Apart from iron, finds from Việt-khê tell of the use of wood—for spear-
handles, oars, coffins, even a wooden *bình*—and hide, painted and appliqued
with silver. Paint pigments were black, brown, red, blue-grey, sometimes with
a gold trim. The richness and variety of the finds is astounding, and results of
studies are eagerly awaited, for Việt-khê is indeed exciting.

Historical Considerations

The major arguments over the dates and origins (Bezacier 1972: 228 ff.) of
the Đông-so'n culture, a term now justifiable only on the grounds that bronzes
were first found there, will be familiar to all. Karlgren's (1942) dating (fourth-
third century B.C.),[53] the most widely accepted, must now be reviewed in the

light of the Phùng-nguyên culture, the preparatory and early stages of Đông-so'n. Similarly the proposed origins or community of culture[54] are to be reviewed in the same context. Karlgren's masterly article demolished the Hallstatt theory, and the geometric motifs found in common between Đông-so'n, Huái, and Shízhaìshān may now find their origin in Phùng-nguyên rather than Central Asian stimuli. The marked Central Asian presence in the civilization of Diān in the second-first centuries B.C. (e.g. von Dewall 1967: 12, fig. 3.8) may be explained by contacts exclusive of North Vietnamese culture, since Diān is demonstrably later in date than the early stages of Đông-so'n civilization as we now know it. The discovery of the Phùng-nguyên culture and its development into what is usually called Đông-so'n (traditionally fourth-third B.C.) also argues strongly against Heine-Geldern's supposition that Yúnnán was the cradle of the civilization and that the Vietnamese manifestations were its last phase.

Phùng-nguyên culture, whose extensive influence reached to Sa-huỳnh, Long-khánh and beyond to maritime South East Asia[55] is thus of paramount importance for large tracts of South East Asia and for the early history of Viêt-Nam.

The existence of the kingdom of Văn-lang (Maspero 1919), of the Hông-bàng dynasty and of the Hùng-vu'o'ng (Viêt: ?–258 B.C.) has long been known as a cherished Vietnamese tradition and has generally been considered unreliable historically, given the extravagant antiquity attributed to it by many Vietnamese historical sources. The historical period has, therefore, been considered to date at the earliest from the Bā-Shu control of the area, the Âu-lạc Kingdom (258–208) of Thục Phán, overthrown by the Chinese general Zhào Túo (Triêu Đà) who set up the kingdom of Nam-Viêt (207–111) in its place and which in its turn was finally submitted to Chinese suzerainty under Hàn Wudì (Aurousseau 1923). The Chinese colonies of the Xī-Hàn and Xīn retained a degree of independence that was brought to an abrupt end by Mǎ Yuán's (A.D. 43) suppression of the unsuccessful rebellion of the Hai Bà Tru'ng. That date saw the end of Đông-so'n culture and the inclusion of the colonies as provinces of the Dōng-Hàn empire.

Phùng-nguyên culture (?2000– B.C.), dated most conservatively as beginning in the early seventh century B.C., furnishes us with a completely new framework for the historical validity of Văn-lang and the Hùng Kings. The anonymous *Viêt su' lu'o'c* (c. 1377: q.1/1. 3–4) notes that the kings[56] and their state were first known of during the reign of Zhōu Zhuāngwáng (696–682).

Historical documentation locates Văn-lang and its territory, Phong-châu, in the Phú-thọ, Vĩnh-phú, Hà-tây area of the North, and it is this very area that constitutes the heartland of the Phùng-nguyên culture complex (Linh 1968: 21–3; Lan 1968: 34; 1969: 58; 1970b: 76). The *locus originalis* of the capital was at Bạch-hạc ('white crane') in the centre of what was traditionally

Phong-châu (Trãi 1435: 23; Chú 1820: vol. 1, 97; Linh and Lan, loc. cit.).

Since the equation Phùng-nguyên–Văn-lang/Hùng-vu'o'ng seems probable on archaeological and documentary evidence (Linh 1968: ab; Châu 1967: 35 ff., i.a.), and a later stage of this culture, Gò Mun (*c.* 1000–500), has close and incontestable connections with Đông-so'n, we may suggest that the origins of Văn-lang and the Hùng-vu'o'ng are to be dated at least from the early seventh century B.C. phases of the Phùng-nguyên culture, perhaps developing from neolithic settlements in the same area and that the continuation of the Hông-bàng dynasty (Gò Mun/Đông-so'n 1), should be dated from some time during the sixth century B.C. It has also been suggested that Phong-châu was the ruling centre of a loosely knit confederation of tribes of different ethnic composition (Linh 1968a: 18)[57] the Bǎi-Yuè. While a study of the histories, traditions and archaeology relating to the period may well confirm this proposition, one sees from the distribution of Bronze Age sites three distinct centres:

(1) the area around the confluence of the Hông River (Phùng-nguyên = Viêt);

(2) a shift to the more southerly Thanh-hoá region (Đông-so'n = Viêt); and

(2a) a series of Bronze Age sites, sparse and dwindling as they move inland— very few drums have been found in this inland and border region— mounting up the Hông to:

(3) the Yúnnán area (Diān). (Lan 1963: 101 and 103 maps.)

Given this distribution, the conservative dates advocated for Phùng-nguyên and the Hông-bàng dynasty, the dates and the finds of old bronzes, especially Heger I drums, in Yúnnán, one may propose that the Diān area was a part of, and secondary to, the Văn-lang hegemony (Lan 1963: 304) in the early period, a recipient of Phùng-nguyên–Đông-so'n (I–II) culture. Then in the third century B.C. this outpost of the confederation increased in importance, rose up against the Hùng leadership of the confederation, overthrew it and replaced it with the short-lived Thục kingdom of Âu-lạc, centred on the territory of the capital of the now vanquished Hùng-vu'o'ng (Linh 1968a: 21–2, i.a.).[58] Archaeological evidence from North Vietnamese sites of this period show that certain axes (Lan 1970b: 80; q.v. 1963: pl. II. 11) and 'ploughshares', etc. (Lu'u 1963: 40, fig. 3; Chi 1964: 38 ff.; cf. von Dewall 1967: esp. 12–13, figs.), quite unlike those usually found in the Vietnamese culture settlements, are common to Shízhàishān.[59] Vietnamese traditions native to the area (Phú-thọ, Vĩnh-phú, Hà-tây) and relating to the struggle between the Hùng-vu'o'ng and Thục regard the Thục as the adversary (Châu 1967: 35 ff.; Linh 1969: 33 ff.). In 208 B.C., Triêu Đà[60] overthrew the Thục. The vacuum that the Ailao-Thục had left in their Yúnnán homeland during their brief supremacy in the Vietnamese delta (258–208) permitted some other group of the confederation (their vassals?) to gain control and to develop what we now know as the rich Bronze Age civilization of Diān (second-first century B.C.).

Triêu Đà's Nam-Viêt, governed with the aid of local tribal leaders and the Âu-lạc (Lan 1968: 35 ff.), brought with it the first direct Chinese influence, the first phase so to speak of 'sinicising Đông-so'n', and this Chinese influence was strengthened during the second annexation (111 B.C.–) by the Xi-Hàn. Finally the Ailao-Thục,[61] we know, assisted Mǎ Yuán in putting down the Tru'ng rebellion (A.D. 43), an attempted Viêt resurgence whose failure saw the end of Đông-so'n and the inclusion of the area as Chinese provinces of the Đōng-Hàn, under strict Chinese control.

Conclusion

Over a hundred sites, many of which await investigation, have been discovered since Independence, and large tracts of the country are still regarded as virgin territory awaiting excavation. Vietnamese archaeologists admit that their studies are preliminary, with a multitude of problems remaining to be solved.

The information that the finds provide on the society and culture of the time is fascinating but regrettably not within the scope of this survey. The ethnic mix of the area is still under question (Bezacier 1972: 278–9; Duy 1966; Genet-Varcin 1958–9; Patte 1965; Lan 1963: 306–16),[62] yet Đông-so'n culture has sometimes been called proto-Cham, hence 'Indonesian'. Although undeniably Cham styles do occur,[63] associations are still too tenuous to warrant the ascription.

There is a marked conservatism in the shape of everyday utensils from Stone Age through Bronze Age to the Modern Period, in which counterparts can be found (Linh 1964: 35) as well as in decorative apparel (Trinh 1968: 57) and funerary objects. Undecorated bronze goods were probably used by the wealthier members of the society, tools of stone being generally used (cf. Chinh 1962: 45). There is a continuity and development of styles within a given class of objects (Lan 1962*ab*), the function of the highly decorated bronzes being most likely ritualistic but, although shape might vary there exists a remarkable homogeneity in the decorative forms represented on them and throughout different types of bronze object.

Certain lines of enquiry perhaps merit consideration.

(1) The participation of geologists, mineralogists, and metallurgists is essential to our further understanding of this culture. Where, for instance, did the stone for Côn-so'n and Dậu-du'o'ng come from? Is any particular type of stone used for objects with specific (?ritual) functions?

From historical sources relating to more recent periods we know of mining areas for various metals (e.g. Chú 1820: vol. III, 77–8), but not which sites were worked in earlier times. Copper was probably extracted from malachite, and tin is scarce in the country (Malleret 1960: vol. II, 193, 253, 267). Chemical analyses of some bronzes have been conducted (Lan 1963: 218 ff.; Bezacier 1972: 281–9) and it was remarked, to Goloubew's (1929: 46) surprise that Vietnamese bronzes had a very high lead content (cf. *Yúnnán*, 1959: 135; Chinh 1962: 42), so most utensils are not particularly hard, with the exception of Thiêu-du'o'ng agricultural implements. Further analyses might tell us of the development of metal casting techniques, and perhaps throw light on dating. Where musical instruments are concerned, copper-zinc alloys are traditionally regarded as of low quality for sonority (Durand 1954: 397), so analyses of drums, etc., might reveal two classes of high and low copper content which could determine function more precisely, or help us date the instruments.

(2) In pottery, is it possible that a particular colour is associated with certain patterns only and linked to a specific function, or ethnic group? For example, black pottery is not common in Viêt-Nam, but is found scattered throughout the country at widely separated sites. Its presence raises several questions about provenance, materials, and so forth.

(3) A study of Vietnamese place names could perhaps reveal the existence of several sites worth investigating, as witnessed by the discoveries of Phật-tích (Bezacier 1954: 135 ff.), and the use of documentary sources is obviously essential to corroborate material evidence.[64]

(4) Finally, the study of emblems could be a very fruitful line of enquiry, throwing light on dating and the development of styles, among other things, despite the fact that totemic animals have diminished greatly in importance among various peoples. The toad is uncle of Heaven (Chu'o'ng 1971: 28–44), and a common rain-associated symbol in the region, so that it and the fish, the deer (a possible Indonesian element?), and various birds abounding on bronzes, cannot here be too suggestively linked with particular peoples. The crocodile might be a martial emblem, since it is equally feared by Vietnamese and Cham alike, while the tiger (Lan 1963: pl. XVII.4) was an important beast to the Vietnamese, and could possibly be connected with them emblematically. The crane is unquestionably linked with the Hùng-vu'o'ng, but what relationship could be determined for the pelican (with fish) is uncertain. It occurs at Shízhaìshān (Rudolph 1960: 43, fig. 1e), perhaps imported from Văn-lang. The elephant (Lan 1963: pl. XVII.6) is frequently mentioned with regard to Champa: one should note in this context that the founder-chief of the Ailao— a dragon totem person—married an elephant totem woman (Cham element?), and their peoples were tatooed[65] with elephant and dragon totems (YNBZZ j.1/37b4ff.). By comparison, the Nánchao were *Lóngwei* ('dragon-tail') and

Tuòhè ('entrusted of the crane'?), possible totemic groupings (*Xīn Tángshū*, j. 222A/1a1).

More solid is the association of the snail with the Thục. Their capital, Cô-loa or Loa-thành, was built in spiral form resembling a snail. The snail spiral is noted on various bronzes (Lan 1963: pl. XIV.4: dagger; pl. VIII.1–2: *thô*) and in pottery, and the geometric stylized representation of the snail pattern could perhaps have been an artistic motif, an Ailao ethnic design, that spread throughout the confederation, but the plastic representation of a snail on a Thieu-duong *thô*[66] suggests its manufacture during the period of the Thục supremacy. Intriguing problems abound.

NOTES

1. Notably the various *báo cáo* of the Đôi khao cô and the journal *Khao cô hoc*, all of which are publications of the Democratic Republic of Viêt-Nam. Data for South Viêt-Nam comes from divers sources, some of which may have been missed.

2. Major sites are: Phùng-nguyên, Phú-hâu, Dâu-du'o'ng, and Gò Mun in Phú-thọ province; An-đạo, Yên-tàng, Gò Chùa, Lũng-hòa, Văn-điên, Gò Bông, Đông-dâu, and Đôn-nhân in Vĩnh-phú province; An-thu'ọ'ng, Gò Vu'ò'n Chuôi, and Gò Chiên Vây in Hà-tây. See also n. 11.

3. Some C14 dates have been calculated at the Centralinstitut für Alte Geschichte und Archäologie in the DDR from samples taken from Phùng-nguyên culture sites associated with the Hùng-vu'o'ng. These are:

Vinh Quang, Hà-tây: trench 1   1m80   3046 ±120 years
(*KCH* 2 (9–1969), 70).
Gò Vu'ò'n Chuôi, Hà-tây,   0m80   3070 ±100 years
Gò Chiên Vây, Hà-tây   0m65   2350 ±100 years
(*KCH* 7/8 (12–1970), 40).
All readings are calculated from 1950.

4. The inclusion of certain sites such as Đông-khôi is controversial, while others originally included have now been excluded. Illustrative of this is Phù-lu'u, first considered part of the complex by Chinh (1966: 173 ff.) who later rejected his own original ascription (Kinh 1969: 55 ff.). Whether the decision to exclude sites like Phù-lu'u implies a reclassification of the periodisation of those sites or the existence of a second culture, or perhaps sub-culture, is not yet clear.

5. Phú-thọ or Vĩnh-phú? cf. Chinh (1966: 173–80); Tân (1968: 51 ff.); Linh (1968b: 19 ff.); Lan (1969: 56 ff.); Kinh (1969: 56).

6. The *Paralithic* (age, period, culture, etc.) is defined as that lithic age which succeeds the Neolithic and which parallels the established metal-working ages— chalco-lithic, copper, and especially bronze and iron ages. It is applied to cultures of those various periods in which the use of stone for a variety of purposes and implements continues side by side with the use of metals. Viêt-Nam is a prime example of such a culture. (JD).

7. Both writers rejected flint as unsuited to the task of boring these particular holes.

8. Carbonised wood collected in April 1969 was the sample material for analysis by the DDR Centralinstitut to give C14 date results, taking the readings from 1950, of:
Đông-dâu, Vĩnh-phú   *c.* 4m00   3328 ±100 years
(*KCH* 2 (9–1969), 70).

9. Đại-ang, Hà-tây, which remained a settlement area down to the fourteenth century A.D., is also probably of the same date as Gò Mun (Hu'ng 1968: 49 ff.).

10. Tân (*KCH* 1 (6–1969), 90) noted that there are many similarities between Gò Mun and Non Nok Tha 20, for which dates of *c.* 2500 B.C. have been suggested. This led him to propose Phùng-nguyên 3500–2500; Gò Mun 2500–1500; Đông-so'n begining in the first half of the first millenium B.C. as revised dates for the cultural continuum. cf. n. 6 above.

11. Representative of these are: Thụy-vân, Hoằng-ngô A, Đại-áng, Thanh-đình, Nghĩa-lu'ng, Tù'-so'n, and Đông-lâm.

12. C14 dates for some of these sites are known to exist but precise details are not yet available.

13. cf. Boriskovsky (1961: 27 ff.; 1962: 25) who commends Colani but is himself criticised for incompleteness and for inconsistency of technical detail in his own work on Hoà-bình sites (Vu'ọ'ng 1963a: 1–5; Hà 1963: 45 ff.).

14. Saurin (1957: 587); Vu'ọ'ng (1963b: 46); and Boriskovsky (1961: 31) who considers it to be mesolithic but who notes that certain associated sites are neolithic. Vu'ọ'ng (1962: 44) observes that there are no characteristic mesolithic microliths, a fact that has been widely discussed. Phong (1970: 45; cf. Kinh 1971: 49) has postulated the reason why only macroliths are found to be because Hòa-bình was a bamboo culture area, an explanation refuted by most DRV archaeologists and historians. Vu'ọ'ng (1962: 45–6), Phong (1970), and Kinh (1971: 48) think Hòa-bình might be transitional mesolithic to neolithic, while several others think all (Tân 1965: 56) or some (Boriskovsky 1966: Hoà-bình 111) of the levels are neolithic. For Patte (1936: 287 ff.) it is early neolithic; Hà (1963: 40 ff.) and Văn Tân (1962a and 1962b: 22–30) are less specific, classing all three levels as neolithic.

15. cf. Long-khánh basalt ware (Saurin 1968: 8 ff.; and 1971: 49 ff.); note Côn-so'n material (Saurin 1964: 11) and Long-khánh imported sandstone.

16. e.g. Mansuy 1925: 25.

17. Bezacier's (1972: 276–7) list of neolithic sites does not go beyond 1954 for the DRV.

18. Lan (ibid.) lists sites in Quang-trị, Thù'a-thiên, Kontum, Biên-hòa, Tây-ninh; Lafont (1956: pl. X) illustrates Plei-ku finds, and Saurin (1968: pls. 1. 3*ab* and 5*ab*) provides examples from Hàng-gòn and Bình-lọ'i.

19. 'Heeling' is also observed at Plei-ku (Lafont 1956: pl. X.11) and at Bình-lọ'i (Saurin 1968: pl. 1. 3ab).

20. Liễn (1963: 64) believes the centre of origin for the form to be Yên-bái.

21. See also representations of such axes on the Đao-thịnh *thạp* (Lan 1963: pl. X), and on the Hoàng-hạ and Ngọc-lũ drums (ibid., pl. XXII).

22. cf. bronze *qua* (=*gē*) found at Shízhàishān (Rudolph 1960: 43, fig. 1a), at Hénán and So'n-tây (Karlgren 1942: pl. 20. 2–3), and at other DRV sites (Hòa-bình, Phú-thọ, Thanh-hoá: Lan 1963: pl. XVII).

23. They are distributed widely throughout Viêt-Nam sites like Văn-điên (Chinh 1968: 127) and Yên-bái (Lien 1963: 64) in the North, as well as at Sa-huỳnh in Central, and Long-khánh in Southern, Viêt-Nam.

24. C14 dates established at the DDR Centralinstitut for carbon samples give readings, calculated from 1950, of:
Tràng Kênh, Hai-phòng　　　*c.* 1m90–2m10　　　3405 ±100 years
(*KCH* 7/8 (12–1970), 40).

25. Especially My-so'n statuary. See also the figures on the bronze dagger and short sword (Lan 1963: pls. XV.9 and XVI.1) and note, too, the similarity between the necklet (ibid., pl. XVI.1) and the *pendeloque-affûtoir* from Hàng-gòn 3 and 4 (Saurin 1968: pls. 1. 4ab, 11. 1ab).

26. Interestingly, this is the method of manufacture of a *kris*, and it seems more likely that the *kris* is related to the *dao găm* 'dagger' (Lan 1963: pl. XIV. 2 and 4) than that it has its origin in the *qua* (=*gē*), a belief held by Janse (1931: 99–139).

27. At Phùng-nguyên itself, sherds were fired at 500°–600° C., according to Kinh (1971: 52).

28. Note Marschall's (1968: 51) conclusion, from a study of mould fragments, that Indonesian drums were not local products but imports from the Mainland. Also, the high lead content of Vietnamese bronze would lower its melting point temperature and permit casting in Thiêu-du'o'ng, and perhaps in Phùng-nguyên, kiln-fired earth (clay) moulds.

29. For somewhat more detailed discussion, see below, pp. 218–9.

30. Chinese sherds and tiles are, of course, abundant at late levels of many sites.

31. Some Gò Mun ware is grey-white and unglazed (Linh 1964: 34) and one finds grey ware at Soi-nhụ (Ninh 1968: 60). Pure black pottery seems rare and worthy of note. (qv. Dâu-du'o'ng: Kinh 1968: 56 ff.).

32. All the pottery is considered coarse. A possible explanation might be that firing temperatures were not high enough to fuse the various oxidic constituents.

33. Although it is a Đông-so'n II culture site, hence later than Gò Mun, a notable exception is Viêt-khê, Hai-phòng. No pottery has yet been discovered at this richly accoutred burial site of probable mid-seventh century B.C. date.

34. Dâu-du'o'ng pottery is wheel-made and kiln-fired. The sherds are noticeably thin and are grey, black, or light brown in colour.

35. Four small drums (grave-goods?) were unearthed in 1959 at Gia-hôi, Thanh-nga, and núi Bú-dò'n, Nghê-an (Lan 1963: 37), but no further details are available.
In addition, three new Heger I type drums were found in 1970:
Provenance: Nghê-an, Làng Mun, xã Tam-so'n, huyên Quỳ-họ'p.
Characteristics: I. large: diam. 50 cm.; height 40 cm.; 4 toads on tympanum
                     II. —
                     III. small: diam. 40 cm.; height 30 cm.; 3 toads on tympanum
Reference: Đan 1970: 120. No further details are available.
Further, several large fragments of another Heger I type drum came to light in 1971:
Provenance: Thanh-hoá, xã Hoằng-vinh, huyên Hoằng-hóa.
Characteristics: A study of the decorations on the pieces has led to its classification with the Quang-xu'o'ng II type (Lan 1963: 197).
Reference: Kinh 1973: 63–4.
Finally, two small drums and two Heger I type drums were discovered in graves of the cemetery complex at Làng Vạc, in 1973:
Provenance: Nghê-an, Làng Vạc, xã Nghiã-hoà, huyên Nghiã-dàn.
Characteristics: Minimal descriptive details are given for one of the large drums: diam. 55 cm.; height 50 cm.
Reference: Tỳ 1973: 64.

36. The Miêu-môn and the Thu'ọ'ng-lâm drums in fact may be one and the same. (Lan 1963: 190, n. 5).

37. Bezacier's exposition is resumed and restated by Mme. Pirazzoli-t'Serstevens' paper to this colloquy. (See pp. 125–36.)

38. cf. E. Porée-Maspero's (1964: vol. II, 418, n. 1, fig. 16, etc.) proposals, illustrated in Bezacier (1972: 216, fig. 119), and P. Sørensen's paper to this colloquy, pp. 78–97.

39. Decorations on the tympana of the Hoàng-hạ, Sông-đà, and Ngọc-lũ drums (q.v. esp. Karlgren 1942: pl. 2.1) show this suspension.

40. One should note that both Mu'ò'ng *chàm* 'to beat' and Vietnamese *dâm* 'id' are used for 'to beat (a drum)', and 'to pound (a pestle in a mortar)'.

41. See also: tympanum of the Ngọc-lũ drum (Karlgren 1942: pls. 1.2, 2.1., 3.1–2, 4.3) and compare the bronze *thô* from Thiêu-du'o'ng and Viêt-khê (Lan 1963: pl. VIII).

41a. Luce's (1961: 102) translation: 'to express their grief' is incorrect. The text reads: 'to lead (*dào* = *dǎo*) the mourning ululations'.

42. Mme. Pirazzoli-t'Serstevens claims that drums were not so used at Shízhàishān.

43. q.v. Lan (1963: pl. XXI.4). Karlgren (1942: 16 ff.) believes the bird to be a crane as does Khai (1961*a*: 54; cf. Hu'ng 1962: esp. 60–1), whereas Bezacier (1972: 169 ff.) favours the identification of a rufous hornbill (*Buceros hydrocorax*).

44. For illustrations, see: Lan (1963: pl. x) for a *thạp* lid; Parmentier's (1918: 17 and pl. I BC) Ngọc-lũ 'gong' is actually a *thạp* lid. Lan (1963: pl. VII.I) shows a *chậu* with 7-rayed star reminiscent of the Hũ'u-chung drum; and (ibid., pl. VII.2) one with 8 rays which is reminiscent of the Quang-xu'o'ng 11 drum.

45. cf. Zhōu 1178: j.7/74.

46. 6-rayed stars are found on roof-tiles from Cô-loa.

47. cf. Lowenstein 1962.

48. cf. Shízhaìshan headhunting.

49. See also the large Bronze Age cemetery at Làng Vạc, Nghê-an (Tỳ 1973: 64).

50. The Đông-khô site in Thanh-hoa is no exception. However, certain features have led Chinh (1962: 38–45) to consider that it was a local centre in a tributary relationship to, but somewhat independent of, the aristocratic Đông-so'n hegemony.

51. Evidence in support of this is the finds of bones at many sites, among which are both Núi Nap and Đông-so'n in Thanh-hoá (Lan 1963: 56–9 and 317–18), plus Soi-nhụ in Quang-ninh (Ninh 1968: 57 ff.).

52. cf. Duy (1965: 2) and Trinh (1966: 53–4) who differ markedly on the date of La-dôi, Hai-phòng. Note also the considerably earlier date advanced for iron-working in Nam-kỳ (below, pp. 220–1.).

53. cf. Maspero (1919: 9); Aurousseau (1923: 233); Goloubew (1932: 139); Stein-Callenfels (1937: 150 ff.); Heine-Geldern (1937: 191–4); note also, Peacock's (1965: 1–3) C14 dates for the Sungai Lang bronze drum.

54. Opinions are: Goloubew 1932: Chinese; Heine-Geldern 1937: Hallstatt influencing Huái, Yúnnán, and North Viêt-Nam; cf. Heger 1902: 90; Karlgren 1942: Huái; Chang 1968: Sìchuān cultures as transmitters of Asian elements in Đông-so'n.

55. Did Sa-huỳnh function as the intermediary between Red River, and Mekong, Delta sites, or was there more direct contact between the two? The culturally developed sites in the Hai-phòng region point to the second as a distinct possibility, although to accept both first-hand and transmitted contact is, at this moment, certainly the wiser approach.

56. Of interest is the scribal error *duì* 'to pound in a mortar' for *xióng* (Sino-Viet.: *hùng*).

57. Chinh believes that the Phùng-nguyên sites were peopled by members of the same tribe, of the same ethnic group (Kinh 1969: 55).

58. The Thục, interestingly, are equated with the Āiláo (Lan 1970*b*: 80; Linh 1969: 50). *láo* may be used as a loan character for *lǎo/liáo* 'animal sacrifice; burnt offering sacrifice'.

59. Of particular importance is the large cache of bronze arrowheads whose very high copper content is analogous with that of the manufacturing proportions found at Shízhaìshàn.

60. Note the numerous Chinese artefacts, including iron (Lan 1969: 58; cf. p. 112 ff. above), discovered at the Thục capital of Cô-loa, which later became a Hàn dynasty settlement.

61. On the Ailao = Thục, the following remarks are of interest. Nánchāo, a traditional adversary of Viêt-Nam, was originally Āiláo ethnically (*Xīn Tángshū*, j. 222A/1a1) and may well have built on Thục and usurpatory Diān traditions and culture on regaining the control of the homeland. In the 860s the Nóng, a Thai group of substantiable Vietnamese connections, assisted the Chinese in conquering Nánchāo and assumed control over it, with a consequent change in name to Dà-Lǐ (Thai?). These points serve to show the importance of the Viêt-Nam—Yúnnán link by the Hông river, a link as yet little studied.

62. Lan, loc. cit., thinks that the 'Indonesian' predominance during the Neolithic

gave way to another racial strain during the Bronze Age, basing his argument on skeletal remains from Thiêu-du'o'ng.

63. For instance, Lan (1963: pl. XXVI.1) shows a figure playing a *khèn* which is identical with the Cham *ra-kle*. Goloubew's (1929: 42, fig. 21) geometric patterns found among the Batak and Dayak must now be seen in the light of their relationship to Phùng-nguyên culture.

64. An example is of bricks inscribed *Jiāngxījūn* found together with tiles of Lý and Trân dynasty date, i.e. eleventh to fourteenth centuries A.D., and therefore dated by association as of that date. They actually belong to the period *c.* A.D. 860–863 (Vu'o'ng 1966a: 49 ff.).

65. n.b. Văn-lang = 'country of the tatooed'.

66. q.v. Lan (1963: pl. VIII.2). One should recall that *thô* are burial urns for decapitated heads, yet another possible link of the Ailao-Thục with Yúnnán-Diān civilization.

Additional Bibliography

Bằng, Nguyễn duyên, 1970. So' bô nghiên cú'u vê môt sô hiên vât dô dông tìm thây ó' xã Thuy-du'o'ng, huyên Thuy-nguyên thành phô Hai-phòng. *NCLS* 131 (3/4–1970), 62–4.

Boriskovsky, P. I. 1961. Môt sô vân dê nghiên cú'u thò'i dại dô dá o Việt-nam. *NCLS* 24 (3–1961), 25–31.

Châu, Tru'o'ng hoàng, 1967. Nên văn hoa khao cô học duy nhât trong thò'i dại dông thau Việt-nam và vân dê nu'o'c Văn-lang cua Hùng-vu'o'ng. *NCLS* 105 (12–1967), 35–41.

— 1969. Chung quanh vân dê tòa thành dât cô trên dât Cô-loa. *NCLS* 129 (12–1969), 26–41.

Chi, Nguyên dông, 1964. Vê môt loại nông cụ bằng dông thau tìm thây trong các địa điêm khao cô Dông-so'n và Thiêu-du'o'ng. *NCLS* 61 (4–1964), 35–41.

Chikamori Tadashi, 1965. Trends in the Archaeology of South East Asia: 1965 *Archaeologica Japonica: Annual Report of the Japanese Archaeologists Association,* 18, 1 (11), 27–31. (in Japanese).

Chinh, Hoàng xuân, 1962. Nhân dọc bài 'Mây y kiên vê nên văn hóa Dông-so'n'. *NCLS* 44 (11–1962), 42–51.

— 1966. Vài ý kiên vê các giai đoạn phát triên cua thò'i dại dô dá mó'i o' Việt-nam. *Môt sô báo cao vê khao cô học Việt-nam.* Hànôi, Dôi khao cô, 173–80.

— 1968. *Báo cao khai-quât do't I di chi Lũng Hòa.* Hànôi, Dôi khao cô, 201 p.+30 plates.

Chú, Phan huy, 1820. *Lịch triêu hiên chu'o'ng loại chí.* Hànôi, NXB Su' học, 1960–1, 4 vols.

Chu'o'ng, Nguyên ngọc, 1971. Thu' tìm hiêu vê môt sô hoa văn trên trông dông Ngọc-lũ. *NCLS* 141 (11/12–1971), 28–44.

Cu'o'ng-mục. 1884. Quôc su' quán, *Việt su' thông giám cu'o'ng mục. Tiên biên.* Tâp I. Tô biên dịch Ban nghiên cú'u văn su' địa biên dịch và chú giai. Hànôi, NXB Văn su' địa, 1957–.

Dung, Ngọc, 1966. Tin tú'c khoa học lịch su': Môt pho tu'ọ'ng dá mó'i tìm thây trong môt di chi dô dá. *NCLS* 87 (6–1966), 64.

Duy, Nguyên, 1965. Tìm thây di tích nhũ'ng ngu'ò'i cô sông trong thò'i dại dô dông thau. *Nhân dân* 4153 (17-8-1965), 2, col. 7.

Duy, Nguyên, 1966. (and Nguyên quang Quyên). Yùenán beǐfāng Yìānshěng Qióngwén (= Nghê-an tinh Quỳnh-văn) di zǎoqǐ xīnshíqì shídài réntóugǔ. *Gujizhūi dòngwù yú guréntóu* 10 (2–1966), 47–57 and plates and diagrams.

Đan, Ngô thọ, 1970. Tin tú'c hoạt đông su' học: Nhiêu trông đông tìm thây o' Nghê-an. *NCLS* 132 (5/6–1970), 120.

Fàn Chéngdà. *c.* 1175. *Gūihǎi yúhéngzhì.* Gǔjìn shūohaǐ ed., of Jīajìng 23 (A.D. 1544), Dàoguāng re-edition, 1821.

Hà, Nguyên, 1963. Xung quanh vân đê văn hóa Hòa-Bình. (Góp ý kiên vói ông Trân-quôc-Vu'ọ'ng). *NCLS* 53 (8–1963), 40–7.

Hà, Lê đình, et. al. 1969. Tin tú'c khoa học lịch su': Môt di tích khao cô o' Thuân-châu. *NCLS* 128 (11–1969), 62–3.

Huang Shěngzēng, 1520. *Xīyáng cháogòng diǎnlù.* běn 21, Yǐngyìn zhǐhaǐ ed., Sho-ǔshāngé text of Daoguāng 21 (A.D. 1841).

Hu'ng, Hoàng, 1961/2. Thu' tìm hiêu niên đại nhũ'ng chiêc gu'o'ng đông thau Thiêu-du'o'ng, Thanh-hóa. *NCLS* 33 (12–1961), 17–25; 34 (1–1962), 45–52.

— 1962. Y kiên trao đôi: Vê bài 'Vài ý kiên vê chiêc thạp đông Đào-thịnh và văn hóa đông thau' cua ông Đào-tu'-Khai. *NCLS* 40 (7–1962), 53–61.

Hu'ng, Hoàng and Nguyên minh Chu'o'ng. 1968. Vài ý kiên bu'ó'c đâu vê địa điêm khao cô học Đại-áng, Thu'ò'ng-tín (Hà-tây). *NCLS* 113 (8–1968), 48–51 and 64.

KCH. 1969–. *Khao cô hoc.*; esp. *KCH* 1969. Vê niên đại các di tích Hùng-vu'o'ng. *KCH* 1 (6–1969), 64 ff–.

Kinh, Phạm văn and Lê văn Lan. 1968. Xu'o'ng chê tạo đô đá o' Dâu-du'o'ng (Tam-nông, Phú-thọ). *NCLS* 109 (4–1968), 55–60.

Kinh, Phạm văn, 1969. Vài ý kiên vê môt nhóm di tích khao cô mó'i phát hiên đu'ọ'c o' miên Bắc Viêt-nam. *NCLS* 120 (3–1969), 53–60.

— 1971. Vài ý kiên vê môt sô vân đê khao cô học trong quyên 'Kinh tê thò'i nguyên thuy o' Viêt-nam'. *NCLS* 136 (1/2–1971), 45–52 and 64.

— 1973. Tin tú'c hoạt đông su' học: Chiêc trông đông mó'i tìm thây o' xã Hoằng-vinh (Thanh-hóa). *NCLS* 148 (1/2–1973), 63–4.

Khai, Đào tu', 1960. Vài ý kiên góp vê vân đê di chi đô đá Cô-nhuê. *NCLS* 12 (3–1960), 5 ff.

— 1961*ab.* Vài ý kiên vê chiêc thạp đông Đào-thịnh và văn hoá đông thau. *NCLS* 27 (6–1961), 46–56; 29 (8–1961), 45–54.

Lan, Lê văn, 1962*a.* Môt ít tài liêu vê nhũ'ng chiêc rìu cô cua ta. *NCLS* 36 (3–1962), 15–27.

— 1962*b.* Tin tú'c khoa học lịch su': Phát hiên trông đông o' Hũ'u-chung (Hai-du'o'ng). *NCLS* 37 (4–1962), 61–4.

— 1962*c.* Tìm hiêu nguôn gôc cua nhũ'ng chiêc trông đông cô. *NCLS* 42 (9–1962), 30–8.

— 1963. (and Phạm văn Kinh, Nguyên Linh, 1963). *Nhũ'ng vet tích dâu tiên cua thò'i dai đô đông thau o' Viêt-nam.* Hànôi, NXB Khoa học, 328 pp.

— 1964*a.* Tin tú'c khoa học lịch su': Tìm đu'ọ'c no'i cât giâu di vât cua thò'i đại đô đông thau o' núi Mai-đô (Nam-định). *NCLS* 61 (4–1964), 63–4.

— 1964*b.* Tin tú'c khoa học lịch su': Nhũ'ng phát hiên khao cô học mó'i o miên đông bằng ven biên Bắc-bô. *NCLS* 69 (12–1964), 63.

Lan, Lê văn and Phạm văn Kinh. 1968. Di tích khao cô trên đât Phong-châu địa bàn gôc cua các vua Hùng. *NCLS* 107 (2–1968), 34–46.

Lan, Lê văn, 1969. Tài liêu khao cô học và viêc nghiên cú'u thò'i đại vua Hùng. *NCLS* 124 (7–1969), 52–60.

— 1970*a.* Vê môt hình thú'c sinh hoạt văn hóa tinh thân o' thò'i đại các vua Hùng. *NCLS* 130 (1/2–1970), 35–44.

— 1970*b.* Vê tục hoa táng o' thò'i đại các vua Hùng. *NCLS* 132 (5/6–1970), 74–80.

Lang, Văn, 1963. Tin tú'c khoa học lịch su': Phát hiên mô cô o' Hoàng-mai (Hànôi). *NCLS* 51 (6–1963), 63–4.

Liên, Nguyên and Lê văn Lan. 1963. Tin tú'c khoa học lịch su': Nhũ'ng đô đá mó'i tìm đu'ọ'c o' Yên-bái. *NCLS* 57 (12–1963), 63–4.

Linh, Nguyên, 1964. Di chi Gò Mun và vân đê thò'i đại đô đông thau o' Viêt-nam. *NCLS* 58 (1–1964), 29–40.

Linh, Nguyên and Hoàng Hu'ng. 1968a. Vân đê Hùng-vu'o'ng và khao co học. *NCLS* 108 (3–1968), 18–23.

Linh, Nguyên, 1968b. Su' thât lịch su' trong truyên thuyêt Hông Bàng: Vê sụ' tôn tại cua nu'ó'c Văn-lang. *NCLS* 112 (7–1968), 19–32.

— 1969. Bàn vê nu'ó'c Thục cua Thục Phán. *NCLS* 124 (7–1969), 33–51.

Lụ'u, Đô and Đoan thê Khai. 1963. Hai chiêc thạp đông mó'i đu'ọ'c phát hiên o' Phú-thọ. *NCLS* 47 (2–1963), –6o.

Mánshū by Fán Chuò, late ninth century. Edition in *YNBZZ* 1910, vol. 1, j. 2.

Ninh, Đô văn, 1968. Khai quât hang Soi-nhụ, Quang-ninh. *NCLS* 117 (12–1968), 57–61.

Nghĩa, Nguyên văn, 1960. Báo cáo vê công tác phát hiên và tham dò: Di chi tân thạch khí Cô-nhuê (Lâm-Thao, Phú-thọ). *NCLS* 11 (1960), 27–34.

Ngọc, Huyên, 1965. Tin tú'c khoa học lịch su': Phát hiên đu'ọ'c khuôn rìu hình dao xén bằng đá. *NCLS* 72 (3–1965), 63–4.

Phong, Đăng, 1970. *Kinh tê thò'i nguyên thuy o' Viêt-nam*. Hànôi, NXB Khoa học xã hôi.

Sòng hùiyàogaǒ, compiled by Xú Song.

Tac, Le., c. 1399. *An-nam chi-luoc*. Vien Daihoc Hue: Uy-ban phien-dich su-lien Viet-Nam, Hue, 1961.

Tâm, Nguyên đúc, 1969. Mây giai đoạn lịch su' liên quan vó'i hoạt đông cua ky Đê tú' và đăc điêm qui luât khao cô học o' Viêt-nam và Đông Nam A. *NCLS* 122 (5–1969), 28–46.

Tân, Hà văn, 1968. Môt số vân đê vê văn hóa Phùng-nguyên. *NCLS* 112 (7–1968), 51–9.

Tân, Chu' văn, 1965. Tro' lại vân đê văn hóa Hòa-bình—Bắc-so'n. *NCLS* 71 (2–1965), 45–58 and 72.

Trãi, Nguyên, 1435. *Du' dia chí*. Hànôi, NXB Su' học, 1960.

Trinh, Trân khoa, 1966. Y kiên trao đôi: Vài ý kiên góp vó'i ông Nguyên Duy trong bài: 'Tìm thây di tích nhũ'ng ngu'ò'i cô sông trong thò'i đại đô đông thau'. *NCLS* 82 (1–1966), 53–4.

— 1968. Phát hiên tiên vàng, cúc vàng, gôi bạc cô trong thành nhà Mạc, tại Câm-pha, tinh Quang-ninh. *NCLS* 108 (3–1968), 55–7 and 64.

Tu', Trân văn, 1966. Đào khao cô Gò Mun lân thú' hai. *Môt sô báo cáo vê khao cô học Viêt-nam*. Hànôi, Đôi khao cô, 231–8.

Ty, Nguyên duy, 1962. Tin tú'c hoạt đông su' học: Lại phát hiên nhũ'ng đô đông mó'i o' Đào-thịnh (Yên-bái). *NCLS* 44 (11–1962), 60–4.

— 1973. Tin tú'c hoạt đông su' học: Cuôc khai quât khao cô làng Vạc (Nghê-an). *NCLS* 150 (5/6–1973), 64.

Văn Tân, 1962a. Y kiên trao đôi: Phê bình quyên *'Lịch su' chê đô công san nguyên thuy o'Viêt-nam'* cua ông Trân quôc Vu'o'ng và ông Hà văn Tân. *NCLS* 35 (2–1962), 35–46.

— 1962b. Y kiên trao đôi: Tra lò'i ông Trân-quôc-Vu'ọ'ng và ông Hà-văn-Tân. *NCLS* 38 (5–1962), 22–30.

Viêt su' lu'o'c. c. 1377. Cõngshū jìchéng ed., Shànghǎi, Commercial Press, 1936.

VSH 1961. Viên su' học. Tiêu ban nghiên cu'u khao cô học (ed.), *Dâu vêt xu'a cua ngu'ò'i nguyên thuy trên dât Viêt-nam*. Hànôi, NXB Su' học.

Vu'ọ'ng, Trân quôc and Hà văn Tân. 1960. *Lịch su' chê đô công san nguyên thuy o' Viêt-nam*. Hànôi, NXB Giáo-dục.

Vu'ọ'ng, Trân quoc and Hà văn Tân. 1962. Y kiên trao đôi: Vê quyên Lịch su' chê đô công san nguyên thuy o' Viêt-nam (tra lò'i ông Văn-Tân). *NCLS* 37 (4–1962), 43–8 and 64; 39 (6–1962), 55–64.

Vu'ọ'ng, Trân quôc, 1963a. Môt bu'ó'c mó'i trong viêc nghiên cú'u nên văn hóa Hòa-bình. *Tin tú'c hoat dong khoa hoc* 5 (5–1963), 1–5.

— 1963b. Y kiên trao đôi: Đôi điêm chung quanh vân đê văn hóa Hòa Bình. *NCLS* 55 (10–1963), 45–6.

— 1966a. Vài nhân xêt nho vê nhũ'ng viên gạch 'Giang-tây quân'. *NCLS* 83 (2–1966), 49 and 64.

— 1966b. Vài ý kiên vê vân đê quân triêt nguyên tắc tính Đang trong công tác nghiên cú'u khao cô học. *NCLS* 91 (10–1966), 43–9.

Xin Tángshu. Bónàběn ed.

YNBZZ 1910. *Yúnnán bèizhēngzhì*, by Wang Song. 2 vols., nos. 45–6 of *Zhōngguó fǎngzhì cōngshū* facsimile ed., Taíběi, Chéngwén chūbǎnshè, 1967.

Yúnnán 1959. *Yúnnán Jìnníng Shízhàishān gǔmù qínfājúe bàogào*. Peking.

Zhoū Qùfēi, 1178. *Lingwài daìdá*. Cōngshū jìchéng ed., Shànghǎi, Commercial Press, 1936.

POSTSCRIPT

Knowledge of the Vietnamese archaeological record and its cultural manifestations is a year-to-year affair. Since this paper, the complementary survey for Southern Viet-Nam, and the discussion of urban genesis based on archaeological evidence from sites in North Viet-Nam, were submitted for publication, new discoveries have been reported which not only expand our sample of artifacts but also introduce a new dimension into our considerations. The unearthing of the Middle Palaeolithic Son-vi Culture of Vinh-phu, for example, does both. Such discoveries may even significantly alter what has been said previously. That will be revealed by further studies of which, as yet, none has become available to me. Meanwhile, two more recent surveys of archaeological activity in Viet-Nam are:

Nguyen phuc Long. 1975. Les nouvelles recherches archéologiques au Vietnam. (Complément au *Vietnam* de Lois Bezacier). *Arts Asiatiques*, Numéro Special, EFEO XXXI; and, Jeremy H.C.S. Davidson. 1976. Recent Archaeological Activity in Viet-Nam. *Journal of the Hong Kong Archaeological Society* VI, 80–99.

The Bronze Drums of Shizhai shan, their Social and Ritual Significance*

MICHELE PIRAZZOLI-T'SERSTEVENS

The Civilization of the Kingdom of Dian[1]

BETWEEN 1955 and 1960, some fifty tombs were discovered at Shizhai shan, Jinning, in Yunnan province. This far-distant region, known as the kingdom of Dian during the Western Han period (206 B.C.–A.D. 9), was thus shown to have possessed a Bronze Age culture hitherto entirely unknown to archaeologists and historians of Han China. The richness, originality, and complexity of the artistic vocabulary shown by this culture, which flourished during the second and third centuries B.C., has led us, from the moment of its discovery, to take a new look not only at Chinese archaeological knowledge of the period, but also at some of the traditional views on East Asian history.

Since 1955, other excavations in Yunnan have helped to complete and corroborate the extraordinary findings of Shizhai shan. A Bronze Age sepulture anterior to the Shizhai shan tombs was excavated in the village of Dapona, south-east of Dali, in 1964. Within a radius of 40 km. of Jinning, two other sites of the same period as the Shizhai shan site, and also appertaining to the kingdom of Dian, have been brought to light: Taiji shan in 1964, and Lijia shan in 1972.

Immediate verification and completion of the scanty information left to us by the contemporary Han historians, writing about this 'barbarian' region just before and at the beginning of the Chinese occupation, has been made possible by the Shizhai shan discoveries. In view of this relatively sparse textual evidence, the tombs discovered round the Lake of Dian form a particularly precious source of information. The Dian civilization, such as it appears in the light of the archaeological findings, historical sources, and some ethnological comparisons, is characterized by a specific group of material goods and cultural features: the importance of livestock (horses and cattle), the form and the decoration of the habitat, the dress, the war customs, some survivals of 'droit maternel', headhunting, some human sacrifice, the use of the bronze drum, an aristocratic taste for adornment, an entire animal repertory both symbolic and decorative, as well as a feeling for particular combinations of geometric patterns.

The twenty rich tombs of Shizhai shan must have been those of the king of

* See Plate VI.

Dian and his clan. The burial customs, together with the style and technique of the find in these graves, indicate a chronologically short evolution. We may therefore date this royal cemetery to a time within the Western Han period, between 150–120 B.C., which were the years of illegal trade with China using the merchants of Sichuan as intermediaries, and 86 B.C., the year of the first of the series of revolts and heavy repressions which followed colonization. As a result of these upheavals, the former kingdom of Dian, conquered in 109 B.C., disappeared completely and became part of Chinese territory.

We do not yet know the origin or the pre-mature stage of this culture. A study of its art shows elements borrowed from Zhou China and from the animal style of the Steppes. But in Shizhai shan these elements appear to be perfectly assimilated and freely recombined, which leads to the supposition that there are several previous sequences which remain to be discovered.

In the same way, the ethnic composition of this population of farmer–stock-breeders is not known. It was most probably already very complex. Elements of Chinese, or sinicized, origin are difficult to identify at Dian in fields other than art. Agricultural and metalworking techniques, and also the burial customs, seem to have been influenced by indirect contacts with the Chinese world, passing through the Chu kingdom and Sichuan province. Here again, our knowledge in the field of Chinese archaeology is still fragmentary, particularly where central and southern China are concerned.

The influence from the Steppes (the form and decoration of some of the weapons, representations of animal combats, geometrical associations), the importance of stock-breeding and the proximity of itinerant tribes, all raise the problem of a nomadic origin for at least a part of the population of Dian. These steppic influences also raise the problem of penetration from the north-west towards the south-western cultural centres. The route, which is well known, corresponds grosso modo to that taken by Mongol troops in the thirteenth century and, in the opposite direction, to that of the Long March. Although part of the archaeological evidence is still missing, the very important Western Han period discoveries made in recent years at Wuwei, Gansu province, show an art of western China which was extremely original and refined.

The exact spread of the Dian civilization remains difficult to delimit with accuracy. The contacts between Yunnan, south-east China and North Viet-Nam, in the Shizhai shan period, make us think that there existed at the end of the first millennium B.C. a sort of cultural confederation comprising at least three centres: Yue (south-east China), Dông-son (North Viet-Nam), and Shizhai shan. Each of these centres presents its own characteristics and local colouring visible even in manifestations common to the three groups. It is likely, from this point of view, that Dian served as a link between the animal style of the Steppes and the Dông-son civilization.

At their apogee, at the end of the Bronze Age, these cultures found themselves subject to the pressure of the Chinese Iron Age civilization. Once caught in this grip, part of their populations may have emigrated, prolonging former contacts in South East Asia and as far as the Pacific, and increasing the dispersion of certain features particular to this confederation (the bronze drums for example).

Systematic excavations in regions bordering on Yunnan would shed light on the extension of the Dian civilization. Ethnological parallels are, as we shall see, most often established with Tibeto-Burmese groups, particularly from northern Burma and northern Assam. These ethnological parallels seem to indicate that these populations have inherited certain ways of thinking and certain customs which existed in Dian nearly 2,000 years ago. These survivals confirm Luce's opinion whereby most of the Tibeto-Burmese populations of Burma and Assam came down from the north between the fourth and eighth centuries A.D. We even think that the Chinese colonization of Yunnan could well have entailed population movements before the fourth century.

A cultural crossroads of crucial importance, the civilization of Dian was also placed at a turning point in history, when a large Bronze Age confederation lost its independence before breaking up under the impact of a more strongly structured civilization, that of Han China.

The Bronze Drums

This paper will try to show, with the help of historical and ethnological evidence, what can be found out from the bronze drums about the Dian mentality in the socio-religious field. The bronze drums appear at Shizhai shan in different contexts:

(a) in scenes of sacrifice (M12: 26, M20: 1):[2] they are either lined up or piled up. The scene M20: 1 also shows a figure beating a drum with a mallet (Plate vi*a, c*).

(b) on ornaments showing houses (M3: 64, M6: 22, M13: 259): figures beat a drum, next to dancers. A drum is placed either on the veranda or else on the lower floor of the house (Plate vi*d, e*).

(c) some of the bronze drums in the Shizhai shan graves were upturned and filled with cowrie shells.

(d) several shaft-finials show an animal or a female figure on a drum.

Thus the bronze drums seem to have embodied several uses and several virtues. Musical instruments used during feasts, religious ceremonies, and gatherings, they are also marks of prestige and of power reserved for the chiefs. What is more, the presence, on their striking surface, of frogs (ex. M10: 3), birds, and feather-crested men, links them with themes for invoking rain.

A. *The drum as musical instrument and sign of power*

These two uses are witnessed from very earliest times by Chinese texts, and are confirmed by ethnological evidence. Since the historical references are often quoted, we shall mention only those which appear significant in the context of Shizhai shan:

(i) The treaty on geography of the *Sui shu* (Lo 1967: 110–14) mentions that 'throughout the twenty districts to the south of the Nan shan, the different Lao tribes make bronze drums. When a new drum is made, it is suspended in the courtyard of its owner, who gets in a supply of wine and invites his relations and friends. These throng in, and the rich guests bring big gold or silver hairpins to beat the drum. The pins are made especially for this use, and after the ceremony they are given to the host as a souvenir . . . Before going off to war, the chief summons the warriors of the tribe by beating the drum. The tribesmen take an oath of allegiance to these chiefs, who are called Dulao.'

(ii) The *Man shu* (Luce 1961: 102), quoting the *Kuicheng tu jing*, says that the southern barbarians (Man) worship spirits (*gui*). When they are in mourning they beat war drums, as they do at each feast.

(iii) The *Xin Tang shu* (*Nan Man zhuan*) (Lo 1957: 106) mentions that the Dongxie barbarians who live 300 *li* to the west of Qianzhou use bronze drums, bullocks, and horses as rewards. During gatherings they beat the drums and blow horns. On the subject of the same people, W. Eberhard (1942: 135, n⁰ 28) adds that their chief in the eighth century payed his visit of homage, and brought as tribute a fur headdress of black bearskin, boots, and woollen clothing. These Dongxie dressed their hair in a hammer-shaped knot, round which they tied a cord which hung down behind. Weddings were celebrated with alcohol and beef. During the festivities, the horn was played, the bronze drums were beaten and there was dancing.

(iv) The Po-yi, according to the *Yunnan tongzhi* (1894: k. 299, 5–13), beat on a bronze drum at times of mourning. At this signal, all the relatives arrive. The same text (k. 202, 1–2) notes that the Miao ren, at festivities, beat the bronze drums, blow horns, and make a procession to greet the spirits.

(v) The *Dushao xian zhigao* (He 1965: 31–9) mentions that the Hei Miao of Guizhou, during funerals, beat the bronze drums and play the khene (*sheng*). These observations are completed by modern ethnological evidence (Beauclair 1956: 20–35) which states that the Miao from middle and east of Guizhou use the bronze drums for keeping grain, or for preparing sweet wine made with glutinous rice. The drums are beaten at the New Year and for weddings.

(vi) The use of bronze drums by the Zhongjia of the west of Guizhou, mentioned in the *Guiyang fuzhi* and in the *Guizhou tongzhi* (He 1965: 31–9) is confirmed by I. de Beauclair who notes that the drum, among the Zhongjia people, is suspended with special ceremonies and kept in the upper part of the house of the village elder, covered with a woman's garment to prevent it escaping. It is beaten during the New Year feast and in the case of death, while the corpse is in the house.

(vii) Among the Woni in southern Yunnan (Soulié 1908: 353), during funerals, those who come to pay their respects to the dead man beat drums and tam-tams and shake hand-bells. They stick pheasant tails on their heads and dance. They are called 'those who disperse spirits'.

(viii) In North Viet-Nam, among the Mu'o'ng (Cuisinier 1946: 450–85), the death of a chief is generally announced by the bronze drum. The officiants, in the funeral rite, wear among other attributes a sliced-off cone made of basket work to which are attached banners and peacock feathers. During the period of mourning between the death and burial, twice a day a food tray is brought to the dead man and the bronze drum beaten to tell him that the meal is served. Some drums were buried with the body of the person at whose funeral they had served. According to the Muong tradition, the drums were given to the chiefs as a sign of investiture and were used for funerals.

(ix) In Assam, among the Naga tribes, the wooden war drum plays an important rôle in village ceremonies. Among the Ao, it is even considered as to be a village god, and when a new drum is made pigs and chickens are sacrificed on it.

(x) Among the Garos (Playfair 1909: 103–10), when a chief dies, his body is laid out on rows of drums, and one of his own drums is consecrated, by having a hole pierced in it, which makes it unusable.

(xi) In Upper Burma, among the Kachins, at funeral rites a bullock is often sacrificed and a drum beaten (Scott 1900: 1:410). Drums, like buffalo (Scott speaks of cattle), moreover form part of the objects of wealth (*hpaga*) used in ritual exchanges among the Kachins (Leach 1972: 173, 176).

(xii) In each Wa village, a house of spirits contains the village drum which is made of wood. This drum is beaten with wooden mallets for every important event in the life of the community, and above all when captured heads are brought back, or when sacrifices are offered (Scott 1900: 1:501).

(xiii) But it is the Karens of Burma who have conserved the richest and most significant traditions concerning the drums. The Karens (Marshall 1922: 118–19) distinguish between 'hot' drums, used for funeral ceremonies or in case of calamity, and 'cold' drums, used for secular purposes, such as feasts. In the Pegu mountains, the hot drums are only decorated with simple frogs on the striking surface; the cold drums have superimposed frogs on the tympanum, and elephants and snails on the sides. On the other hand, in certain districts this distinction does not exist and either kind of drum is used indifferently for feasts or for funerals.

U. Guehler (1944: 17–71) tells the story of the drum he acquired in 1929 in a village near Loikaw, in the Karen States. The owner, a tribal chief, told him that his grandfather, while alive, had filled the drum with silver coins and had then buried it. He ordered his sons to dig up the drum and the silver at the moment of his death, and to have the drum beaten at his burial and to use the money to pay for the funeral ceremonies. In addition the old chief left instructions that an elephant be torn off the drum and buried with him, and this was done. Marshall also has noted this custom of detaching a bit off the drum when its owner dies so that he may take with him into the hereafter the drum's essence. It is possible that originally, when numerous new drums were still being made, the whole drum accompanied the dead man, as is the case at Dian.

To own a bronze drum, for the Karens, was a sign of wealth. The man who did not have one was not thought rich, whatever other goods he may have had. A drum often formed the ransom of a village, the dowry of a girl. It was a sign of nobility among the tribal chiefs and the elders. The drum was beaten when a village was abandoned and a new site looked for, during gatherings in case of war, at rainmaking invocations, and at feasts. In isolated districts, offerings were still being made to the drums at the beginning of the twentieth century; to neglect these oblations would have brought sickness and ill luck on the drum's owner.

The Karens say that their ancestors have venerated the drums since immemorial times, and certain traditions link the drums with a legendary figure, Pü Maw Taw. This man was working in the fields when he saw a troop of monkeys arrive; he kept still. The monkeys sent for their drums to carry out their funeral ceremonies. The first drum was of silver, the second was of gold, and the third was white. The last drum fell into a pond and was lost. Pü Maw Taw suddenly interrupted the funeral rites, and the monkeys fled, leaving the other two drums behind them on the ground. The old man took them home, and from then on they became the most precious possessions of his people who each year consecrated them with great pomp. In this legend the link between the drum and funeral rites should be noted, as should the fact that the first owner of the drum is an old man, thus already an elder. All the old Karens think that the bronze drums link their people to a distant past.

Originating in Yunnan, the Karens seem to have descended into the Burmese plains in the seventh or eighth centuries A.D. (Luce 1959: 1–18) or even earlier. It is a fact that there are numerous links between Karen customs and non-Chinese Yunnan traditions: survivals among the Karens of themes noted at Shizhai shan deserve to be noted. They refer not only to religious practices but also to the place of the woman in society.

These texts and ethnological comparisons, relative to the use of bronze drums among the populations in southern China and northern Indochina at different periods confirm:

(a) the rôle of bronze drums as a sign of wealth and of power, as the chiefs' apanage. These 'palladia' were often offered at the time of submission to China or brought as tribute (ex. *Song shi, Man Yi zhuan* for the year 966: He 1965: 31–9), when they were not confiscated by the Chinese generals during victories over the 'Man' chiefs (*Ming shi, Liu Xian zhuan:* He 1965: 31–9). The story of Guehler's drum appears very enlightening when it is compared with the recipients and drums containing cowrie shells at Shizhai shan.

(b) the importance of the drums in funeral ceremonies on the one hand, and in rejoicing (feasts, weddings) on the other. It is a musical instrument, but also a ritual and symbolic object which must be consecrated and to which sacrifices are made.

(c) the important part played by the drums in the day-to-day life of the community: going off to war, gatherings, a change of site, etc.

B. *Themes associated with the drums: frogs, birds, feathered men, and boats*

One of the drums of Shizhai shan (M10: 3) shows, on its striking surface, frogs (or toads). Rolf Stein (1942: 135–8), following Marcel Granet, has shown that frogs are supposed to provoke rain and that for this reason they are modelled on the bronze drums. Concerning this point, he recalls an interesting anecdote from the *Ling biao lu yi* (written between 889 and 904 by Liu Xun): A shepherd meets a croaking frog and follows it. He sees it enter a hole. He digs there, and discovers the tomb of a Man chief, but the frog has disappeared. In the hole, in its place, he finds a bronze drum patinated and rusty; tree frogs and ordinary frogs are carved on its striking surface. The frog followed by the shepherd was doubtless the 'essence' of the drum. Rolf Stein notes that the frog is qualified by the epithet *ming* 'which croaks, which cries'; however *ming gu* means 'to make a drum resound'.

As Max Kaltenmark mentioned (1948: 1–113), the bronze drums decorated with frogs are constantly linked with water, and more especially with the deities of tumultuous waters stirred up by a storm. A drum represents thunder for it makes the same sound and stimulates its energy. Pledge of prosperity for the land and its inhabitants, it embodies the voice and the energy of a deity who presides over the fruitfulness of Nature. The Man, when burying their drums, wish to bring the thunder into contact with the underground waters and to ensure that this quickening water, animated by the thunder, remains in their earth. The drums 'sont aussi en rapport avec les troubles militaires: quand ils résonnent, c'est un présage de guerre. Quelquefois ils présagent au contraire une bonne récolte, toujours en vertu de ce double aspect du tonnerre qui peut être le signal du déclenchement de la justice céleste ou du réveil printanier' (Kaltenmark 1948: 27).

According to Chinese tradition, Ma Yuan and Zhuge Liang invented the bronze drums. 'Ces deux héros cachaient des tambours de bronze dans les torrents et dans les cascades de sorte que l'eau en les frappant produisait un bruit effrayant qui terrorisait les Man' (Kaltenmark 1948: 23). The worship of Zhuge Liang flourished among the Man tribes in Yunnan, in Guizhou, and in Guangxi. The *Ming shi* adds that, according to the tradition, Zhuge Liang overcame the Man tribes by means of his drums and the loss of the drums meant for the Barbarians the meeting of their fate. There is also a legend which tells that the drums were buried by Ma Yuan and Zhuge Liang to subdue these same Man tribes.

The *Xu Yunnan tongzhi gao* (Kaltenmark 1948: 25) tells that in Ninger (Yunnan), a sacred tam-tam, a souvenir of Zhuge Liang, is kept in a cave. The aborigines go and fetch it at the time of spring ploughing to make sacrifices to it, after which they take it back to the cave. This rite is repeated in the autumn; they thus hope to reap an abundant harvest.

This attribution to Ma Yuan and to Zhuge Liang of the bronze drums is explained by M. Kaltenmark as follows:

> L'administration chinoise avait intérêt à faire remonter l'invention des tambours de bronze à Ma Yuan et à Zhuge Liang. Elle pouvait ainsi considérer que ces palladia avaient été conférés par l'empereur aux barbares: étant tout à la fois les symboles de la domination chinoise et de l'autorité temporelle et religieuse des chefs, concédée a titre précaire, les tambours pouvaient théoriquement être retirés à tout moment, en même temps que prenait fin l'autonomie des aborigènes (Kaltenmark 1948: 78).

For the Han, the problem was to subdue the barbarian deities of the territories coming under their sway; these deities were most probably the dragons of the underground waters to which the southern barbarians are assimilated. The bronze drums 'govern' the barbarian land by giving it life; it is therefore necessary to take them over, to civilize them by assimilating them, just as it is necessary to domesticate the gods of a territory that one wishes to dominate, above all the gods of its waters, source of life. The Chinese seem to have wanted to turn the local mythology to their own advantage by sinicizing it. Their soldiers became thunder, representing Heavenly Justice. The tamer of the Barbarians became a tamer of dragons and thus the protector of the autochthons against the devils of their own lands. These dragons of the underground waters correspond, in the language of the Han, to the snake which plays an essential rôle in the artistic vocabulary of Dian.

In view of this interpretation, the evidence from Shizhai shan is of primary importance. The major themes attributed to Ma Yuan—drums, boats, oxen, and bronze pillars—the ways and means of domination—are here found in a 'barbarian' context dating from before Ma Yuan:

(a) the bronze drums associated with frogs,
(b) bronze oxen,

(c) the boats portrayed on the drums,

(d) the bronze pillars (sacrifices to a pillar).

What is more, the *Han shu* (1601) and the *Hua yang guo zhi* (k.4: 8r⁰) reveal the existence at Dian of an altar to black water. Thus at Dian, at the period of the Western Han and in the context of a non-Chinese State, are found the majority of the themes of Ma Yuan and Zhuge Liang.

We consider that the Chinese gave themselves the credit of inventing the bronze drums to further the submission of populations who made, used, and venerated these drums. 'Palladia' of the Barbarian chiefs, they had to pass into the keeping of the Han for the colonization to be complete and the transfer of power to be carried out. It was thus an act of appropriation of magic power and prestige by the Han, an appropriation and transfer of power which was embodied in Ma Yuan and Zhuge Liang.

On the other hand, the association of the themes drum–thunder–underground waters—beneficial rain sheds light on certain scenes of sacrifice to the bronze drums shown at Shizhai shan. These scenes can be interpreted as showing ceremonies linked to the fertility of the earth and to agricultural labour.

This barbarian origin of the association between drums, thunder, and the water deity who assures fertility, is confirmed by the legends of the flood among the Miao people: when the flood arrives, a brother and sister, carrying seeds with them, take refuge in a wooden drum which bears them off and saves them. After the flood, a huge eagle lands near the drum and takes up the brother and sister on its wings and sets them down on high ground where the land is dry. Since the eagle can find no food, the brother and sister, to show their gratitude, feed it with their own flesh; then they start to dig the land and to sow the seeds that they have brought with them (Savina 1930: 245).

The drum appears here as the protector, the means and the conserver of fertility. The rôle played by the eagle in the Miao legend brings us back to the question of the feathered headdress worn at Shizhai shan by the figures carved on the drums as well as by the spectators of three cattle fights (bronze ornaments M3: 140, M6: 41, M7: 33). Some figures here wear, stuck in their hair, a sort of tail of hair or of feathers, with a sharp end which points upwards. The same kind of headdress is found on bronze drums of the Dông-son culture. Now these elaborate headdresses are still found among numerous ethnic minorities in the south of China and in South East Asia. Cock feathers are stuck in their headknots by Miao boys and girls during gatherings. This decoration has also been found among the Woni of southern Yunnan, the Muji, the Yeren, and the Lisu.

The Lhota Naga warriors of Assam wear bearskin wigs in which are stuck different feathers according to the warrior's exploits (Mills 1922: 12). Among the Garos, cock feathers, worn as a headdress in certain dances, also play an important rôle in the bronze drum consecration ceremonies, in cure-seeking sacrifices and during funeral rites. In the latter case, cock feathers are planted on the memorial post of the dead man's house, so that at the time of reincarnation he may find his home (Playfair 1909: 25–45, 103–10).

Among the Kachins, the Jaïwa, narrator of legends and keeper of traditions wears, as ceremonial dress, a long robe and a helmet decorated with wild boar's tusks and long birds' feathers (Gilhodes 1909: 713). Headdresses decorated with feathers are also frequently found among the Chins (Scott 1900: 1, 461) of Upper Burma and the Angami Nagas of the hills of the southern Brahmaputra. The men of the Angami group deck themselves for ceremonies with a headdress in the form of a wheel of hornbill feathers. Only warriors who have captured a head during a head-hunting expedition have the right to wear hornbill feathers. Veteran warriors wear a pair of buffalo horns and a shield which is decorated at the top with pheasant, cock, or parrot feathers. A particularly interesting association of themes in the field of funeral rites has been witnessed by Mills (1922: 156–8): in certain villages of the northern Lhota Nagas, rich men were placed in wooden coffins called 'boats' hewn out of single logs of wood with the head and tail of a hornbill carved at the head and feet respectively. This custom recalls the boats decorated at the bows and the stern shown on the Yunnan and Dông-son bronze drums.

According to Rolf Stein (1947: 265) the birds, feathers, feathered men, fishes, and frogs form a set of themes linked, like the pair of opposites bird and snake, to the deities which bring the rain. We think that they are also linked consequently to the themes of fecundity and perenniality. This last idea would explain China's borrowing of the barbarian theme of feathered garments and its application to Han taoism. To bury a drum decorated with such symbols is thus not only equivalent to returning its potential of vital power to the underground world but also assures perenniality; this significance is further increased when the drum is filled with the cowrie shells, emblems of the wealth of its owner.

C. *Other associated themes: pillars, sacrifices, cattle fights*

Certain cowrie containers at Shizhai shan (M12: 26; M6: 30) show scenes of human or animal sacrifices to a pillar round which is coiled a serpent. Ma Duanlin, in his description of the Songwaizhuman, remarks that, in the region going westwards from Yelang and the lake of Dian, all the aborigines consider themselves to be descendents of Zhuang Qiao: 'They walk barefooted, travel by boat and never use vehicles . . . Acts of highway robbery are punished by death. The guilty man is judged by the whole tribe gathered round a long pole stuck in the ground, summoned by the sound of the drum. They sacrifice oxen and horses and then hold a great feast to which relatives and kinsmen are invited'. This description brings out certain themes—those of the pole, the drum, the sacrifices of cattle and horses—which tally with those of the cowrie container M12: 26 (human sacrifice to a pillar).

The offering of human sacrifices was once widespread among the majority of the tribes of Assam. The Nagas made sacrifices to appease deities, to make certain of good harvests, to settle conflicts between villages, or at the death of chiefs. The victims were always decapitated (Gait 1898: 60–5). The Garos also carried out human sacrifices on certain occasions, at the death of a chief, for example (Playfair 1909: 76). These Garos set up memorial posts in front of the dead man's house. Among the Angami Nagas, commemorative posts, dedicated to dead warriors, are placed all round the village and are often topped with effigies celebrating the warriors' achievements. The Kachins attach to their sacrificial pillars (*wudang*) the heads of buffalo offered in sacrifice. Certain *wudang*, decorated with symbols of wealth, are set up near the sacred spot where sacrifices to the spirits of heaven take place (Leach 1972: 146–7). Finally, the Mossos of north-west Yunnan place posts covered with drawings at the entrance to their villages in order to keep away evil spirits (Cordier 1908: 663–88).

The association between pillar and snake on the receptacle M12: 26 is clear. This pillar, as were later on the metal columns of Zhuge Liang and Ma Yuan (deified in fact under the form of column or serpent), seems to be linked to the underground powers. It may have served as an intermediary between the underground depths, Heaven, and those who offered the sacrifice. Post, pillar, or column thus forms the link between the different levels of the world. Their presence in funeral rites accords with this interpretation.

What is more, as A. W. Macdonald (1953: 75–6) noted concerning the Tibetan megaliths:

> les mégalithes sont liés au retour périodique de la fertilité dans le monde. Dans l'Asie des moussons, cette fertilité est considérée un peu partout, et avec beaucoup de raison, comme le résultat de l'interaction de la pluie et du sol, c'est-à-dire des relations équilibrées entre le ciel, la terre et le monde souterrain, entre les morts et les vivants, entre les eaux célestes et les eaux terrestres.

Like the Tibetan megalith, like the Chinese stele, the pillar and piled-up drums of Dian express the idea of a cosmic axis which sanctifies, and round which is organized the 'territory', the living space.

We should like to quote two final associated themes: that of cattle sacrifices, which were apparently carried out at Dian, and that of cattle fights (the Shizhai shan ornaments M3: 140, M6: 41, M7: 33). Buffalo fighting is known among the Miao of eastern and central Guizhou, where it is considered as a sport not necessarily followed by sacrifice (Beauclair 1956: 20–35). However, spectacular processions precede buffalo fights before the great sacrifice to the ancestors which takes place every seven or thirteen years among the white Miao. The buffaloes of different villages, preceded by musicians, are escorted by the village elders carrying parasols. The day after the fight, the sacrifice is offered. During the night ceremonies take place to invite the ancestors, and drums are beaten. A new wooden pillar with a square top has been set up near the house, next in line to similar pillars, memorials of former sacrifices. The next morning, the buffalo is attached to the pillar and immolated. It is then cut up and distributed. Until the evening, its head is placed on the top of the pillar. Its horns are kept in the house or on the veranda with those from earlier sacrifices. Here we find several associated themes, linked to ancestor sacrifices: buffalo immolation, the drum, the pillar to which a buffalo is sacrificed, the preservation of the victim's horns.

Conclusion

The culture of Dian, in its socio-religious manifestations, can be defined as a bronze drum culture, for in fact the drum is linked to every level of social organization and mythical thought. Insignia of power and prestige reserved for the chiefs, and magically-endowed musical instrument sounding all the events of the life of the group, the bronze drum is the symbol of the fecundating power of rainwater, the preserver of fertility and of perenniality.

Around the drum, the pillar, and their associated sacrifices, the religious ceremonies shown on the bronzes of Dian do seem to be linked to agricultural labour, fruitfulness, and funeral rites. It is impossible to set up dividing lines; for these, if they ever existed, were certainly not in a form which our fragmentary knowledge of the cultural context of Dian can lead us to imagine.

NOTES

1. This paper takes up material described more fully in *La civilisation du royaume de Dian a l'époque Han*, Ecole française d'Extrême-Orient (1974); The transcription of Chinese terms is in Pinyin.

2. To avoid confusion, the objects from Shizhai shan are described by their number in the Chinese reports; e.g. M12:26 = sepulture 12 n°26.

ADDITIONAL REFERENCES

Ban Gu. *Han shu*. Shanghai 1964: Zhonghua shuju.
He, Jisheng. 1965. Lueshu Zhongguo gudai tonggu di fenbu diyu *Kaogu*, i, 31–9.
Hua yang guo zhi. Shanghai 1927–35: Si bu bei yao, Zhonghua shuju.
Lo, Siang-lin. 1957. *Bai Yue yuanliu yü wenhua* Taipei.
Yunnan tongzhi 1894.

Local Workshop Centres of the Late Bronze Age in Highland South East Asia

MAGDALENE VON DEWALL

Introduction

THE present investigation is based on a series of observations made on decorated bronze weapons and tools from Late Bronze Age sites in the region of Upper South East Asia, i.e. North Vietnam, northern Thailand, Laos, and Yünnan, reaching out into the southern Chinese provinces of Kweichou, Kwangsi, and Kwangtung. What is intended is not a survey with complete coverage of relevant finds, but the co-ordination of a number of observations which allow for the definition of distinctive *key-types*. For this purpose, the observations on individual objects and their type-distinctive features are subsumed under, and correlated between, the three categories of (a) form, (b) decor technique, and (c) decorative organization.

These three categories are to be understood here as follows:

(a) *Form* includes, beyond the mere basic type of implement in the sense of answering a definable purposive need, a certain, though flexible constancy in outline and/or proportions of its constituent parts, particularly with respect to its specific functional appurtenances (edges, handle, hafting facilities, etc.).

(b) *Decor technique* seeks to distinguish between the diverse technical modes of surface treatment in rendering, as part of the metallurgical process of production, decorative elements of a graphic nature into the quasi-plastic medium of relief decoration, thus achieving discrete ornamental effects in answer to distinctive stylistic attitudes.

(c) *Decorative organization* has been introduced as a category of stylistic analysis owing to the fact that similar types with sharply contrasting schemes of decoration have been in use side by side, while a remarkable homogeneity in decorative planning can be observed on diverse groups of functional types within the same archaeological context.

Observations of this kind, of course, need not be restricted to groups of manual implements alone. They could be meaingfully extended to include, for instance, bronze drums, situlae, ornamental armour plaques, etc.[1]

The present study is intentionally limited in scope as regards the materials included, while at the same time it encompasses a wide geographical region. Three groups of manual implements in particular, namely the basic types of *ko* dagger-axe, dagger, and socketed axe, have several points in common to recommend them jointly for this kind of study. They are types accounted for in the area in question, in addition to larger numbers in general, by a wider range of distribution and, at the same time, by an interestingly *differential distribution pattern* of individual key-types. In total, they can be localized more accurately (though not with 100 % certainty in each single case) than other classes of bronze finds in the region. Separately, the three types chosen show clearly contrasting *modes of transformation* if, for the sake of methodological conclusions, the supposition of a generic process is entertained, assuming a basic typological conformity and, consequently, envisaging each key-type as the corollary of certain processual modifications of the generic type. The extent to which such theoretical abstractions can finally help in interpreting the actual find situation is another question to be taken up below.

With the emphasis placed on the distributional aspects of the so-called key-types, the chronological significance of their find associations has not been ignored nor underrated. For the time being, the temporal horizon for the Late Bronze Age of Highland South East Asia and southern China has to be estimated rather broadly, i.e. penetrating, from the sites and finds in Yünnan and Kweichou datable into the western and eastern Han period respectively (206 B.C.–A.D. 220), backwards into the first millennium B.C. for several centuries. A much more comprehensive study would be required than could be presented here, to take care of the heterogeneous archaeological associations in which such bronze implements were recovered. In temporal reconstruction the issues discussed point to processes which could be envisaged, under morphological as well as under distributional aspects, either as intermittent series of instantaneous events, or else as gradual courses of a long-term consequential order, without impairing the validity of the interpretation pursued.

The *ko* dagger-axe, as the most uniquely distinguished of the three basic types, could not but be seen against the background of its long and well documented typological history in China proper. However, such a comparison need not, and actually cannot, imply that *ko* weapons recovered outside China, i.e. in northern Thailand or in Tongking, ultimately must be derived from central China in each case. By contrast, the short pointed sword or the dagger designed for stabbing, are types not unknown in Bronze Age China, but they never occupied there the position of a leading type in armoury and have not undergone such a distinctly articulated typological development as has the *ko* dagger-axe in its early stages (v. Dewall 1966: 17 ff.). For the dagger, typological modifications seem to have been largely dependent on local demands on autochthonous bronzesmiths, culturally speaking on the periphery of China, notably in the south-west, in Szechuan, but also in the north-west and north-east. The emergence of local initiative, rather than diffusion, is corroborated by the situation prevailing in the far south, in Tongking and particularly in Yünnan, a situation which contrasts notably with deductions made at first sight from the overall distributive pattern of the *ko* weapon. Differing again from these two patterns of transformation is the socketed axe-head. With its undecorated varieties it is an almost ubiquitous type in the Far East and South East Asia. Although decreasing in numbers in central China among the burial contents over the successive phases of Early to Late Chou finds, it has not vanished from the scene and makes its re-appearance in such more southern contexts, as for instance Ning-hsiang (Hunan Prov., *Wen Wu* 1966, 4: fig. 14: 10, 12, p. 5; figs. 21, 22, p. 6) in a number of variations, some of them even lightly decorated with a bundle of straight lines. Even when we neglect for the moment all matters of decoration, the short squatted type of the southern Chinese axe, as a rule with an oblong cross-section socket, differs markedly from corresponding forms of axes in South East Asia, which mostly feature an oval, semi-circular, or near-round socket.[2]

Seen against the background of varying interrelated sub-types of one general form, covering such a wide geographical range and a long time-span, one may not necessarily expect signs of local originality in form and decor other than perhaps as variations of standard forms. From an analysis of the more elaborately decorated axe-heads it becomes evident however that regional cores can be determined also with a view to form-specialization, and that in fact the axe-head is not so diffuse a leading type as was initially suspected. The fan-like extended blade of the symmetrical axe-head with a rather long and slender body must have been a favourite shape in central Yünnan where, nevertheless, asymmetrical blades also were experimented with, but have not formed leading types. By contrast, the prevalence of asymmetrical axe-heads further south, in northern Vietnam, led to an amalgamation of functional design and decorative principles into such extreme forms as the pediform and crescent-shaped axes. Consequently the discrete qualities of a key-type are no longer separable from each other, as artistic intention has become dominant over the requirements of form.

The summary remarks about the three basic types of Late Bronze Age manual implements suggested for closer examination have underlined the necessity to focus in particular on the *correlation of form and decor* rather than on their separate description. The fate of these types within the morphological courses, sketched very roughly, has by no means been even and uniform throughout the entire region, in terms of acceptance and rejection, or modification and elaboration, from one area to the other. In view of this situation, the thesis of a unilinear development radiating from the main centre of origin towards the periphery in waves of diffusion, and resulting in a concentric pattern of 'cultural fallout' (=*Kulturgefälle*) could no longer be reasonably argued. More illuminating clues can be expected, instead, from probing into the reasons for a significant constancy between bronze forms and decor characteristics, in order to seek an explanation for the adherence to a preferential combination of techniques with specific decor schemes at the one place, and for the avoidance between certain principles of decorative organization and details of technique at the other.

If the observation is correct that positive and negative selections of this kind have crystallized into discrete key-types constituted by a relatively constant constellation of form attributes and decor qualities, these may be ascribed to traditions of individual craftsmanship promoted in diverse local *ateliers*. If, furthermore, several sites or areas can be ascertained as the foci of distribution for a number of key-types with their range of circulation differing, it is preferable to speak of manufacturing clusters which may be held responsible jointly for the development and the dissemination of recognizable co-traditions in matters of design and technique.

The interpretative terms, 'workshop centre', with reference to the place of origin for specific manufacturing techniques, and 'workshop clusters' (=*Werkstättenkreise*) for the delineation of their regionally definable sphere of influence, have already proved valid working concepts in European prehistory. In South East Asia too, the notion of regionally operative agents, working in some respects independently from, yet manifestly in others strongly interdependent with each other, is better suited to account for the complexity of trends observable even from our purposely limited material.

With reference to the more clearly definable entity of a local production centre, or in its place a conjoined workshop cluster, the notion of commercial conditions for the dispersal of their products is evoked, and this may prove particularly helpful in explaining the dissimilar distributive patterns of types even within the same co-tradition. It will allow us eventually to disentangle the intermingled network of correspondences in the field of technical practices as well as in artistic production.

*Types A, B, C, D: the ko dagger-axe**

Of all three basic types to be discussed here, the case of the *ko* dagger-axe is probably the most perplexing. Its re-occurrence in South East Asia, with a number of a-typical if not even hybrid forms, is at this late stage rather anachronistic. As the contemporary Chinese type of the Late Chou and Han periods has developed into a standardized form of different character, there can be no question of an actual importation or of direct borrowing, i.e. of imitation, in the South.

The specimens found farthest away from China (at various find spots in northern Thailand, together with other Late Bronze Age objects), are now

---

* For the distribution of key types, see map on page 141.

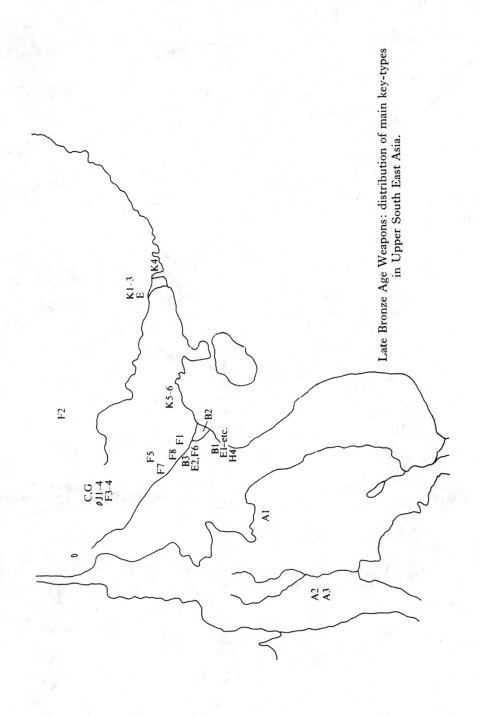

Late Bronze Age Weapons: distribution of main key-types in Upper South East Asia.

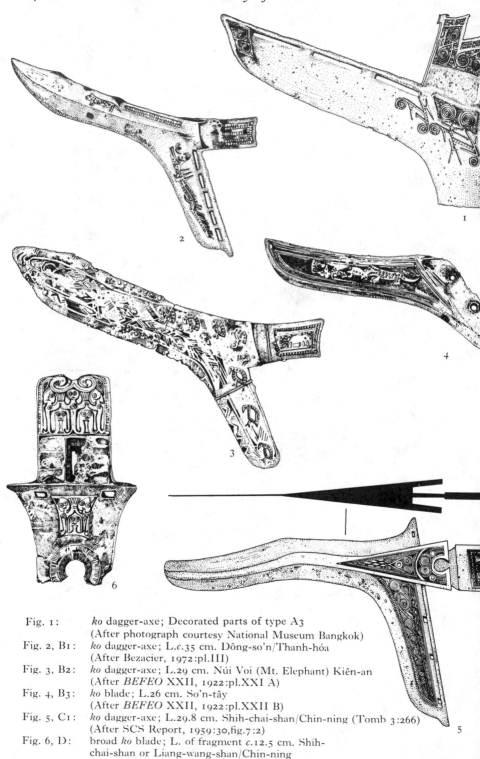

Fig. 1 :   *ko* dagger-axe; Decorated parts of type A3
               (After photograph courtesy National Museum Bangkok)
Fig. 2, B1 :   *ko* dagger-axe; L.*c*.35 cm. Dông-so'n/Thanh-hóa
               (After Bezacier, 1972:pl.III)
Fig. 3, B2 :   *ko* dagger-axe; L.29 cm. Núi Voi (Mt. Elephant) Kiên-an
               (After *BEFEO* XXII, 1922:pl.XXI A)
Fig. 4, B3 :   *ko* blade; L.26 cm. So'n-tây
               (After *BEFEO* XXII, 1922:pl.XXII B)
Fig. 5, C1 :   *ko* dagger-axe; L.29.8 cm. Shih-chai-shan/Chin-ning (Tomb 3:266)
               (After SCS Report, 1959:30,fig.7:2)
Fig. 6, D :   broad *ko* blade; L. of fragment *c*.12.5 cm. Shih-
               chai-shan or Liang-wang-shan/Chin-ning
               (After photograph courtesy British Museum, 1948.
               10–13:15)

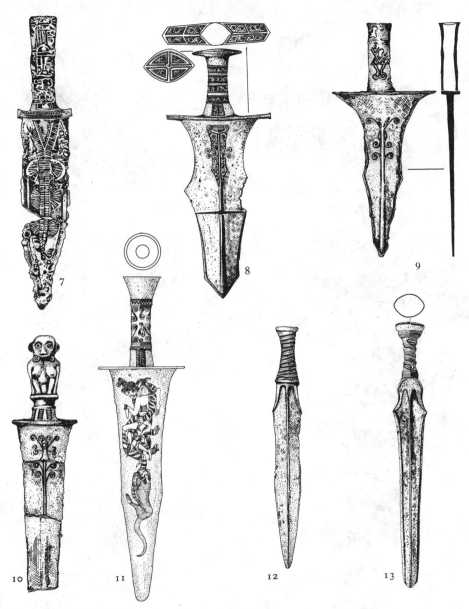

Fig. 7, E1 : dagger; L. *c.*27 cm. Dông-so'n/Thanh-hôa
(After Bezacier, 1972:pl.III)

Fig. 8, F1 : dagger; L. *c.*38 cm. Thái-nguyên
(After Lan. 1963:fig.XVI:2)

Fig. 9, F2 : dagger; L.24.5 cm. Ch'ing-chen, Kweichou
(After KKHP 1959.1:98,fig.13)

Fig. 10, F3 : dagger; L.28.2 cm. Shih-chai-shan/Chin-ning
(Tomb 6:68)
(After SCS Report, 1959:pl.28:1)

Fig. 11, F4 : dagger; L.32 cm. Shih-chai-shan/Chin-ning
(After SCS Report, 1959:44,fig.9:8)

Fig. 12, G1 : short sword; L.*c.*29 cm. Provenance unknown,
Yünnan (After Janse, 1931:pl.XV:4)

Fig. 13, G2 : short sword; L.26 cm. Ta-po-na/Tali, W. Yünnan
(After KK 1964. 12:611,fig.7:7, pl.4:1)

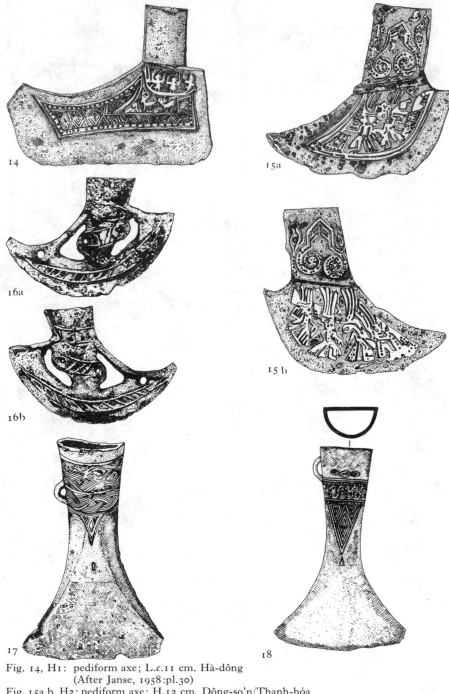

14

15a

16a

15b

16b

17

18

Fig. 14, H1:   pediform axe; L.*c*.11 cm. Hà-dông
            (After Janse, 1958:pl.30)

Fig. 15a,b, H2: pediform axe; H.12 cm. Dông-so'n/Thanh-hóa
            (After Goloubew, 1929:pl.XVI A,B)

Fig. 16a,b, H4: boatshaped axe; L.10 cm. Dông-so'n/Thanh-hóa
            (loc. 4, group 6)
            (After Janse, 1958:pl.28)

Fig. 17, J1:   symmetrical axe; L.11 cm. Shih-chai-shan
            or Liang-wang-shan/Chin-ning
            (After photograph, courtesy British Museum,
            BM 1948:10–13:9)

Fig. 18, J2:   symmetrical axes; L.14 and 13 cm. Shih-chai-

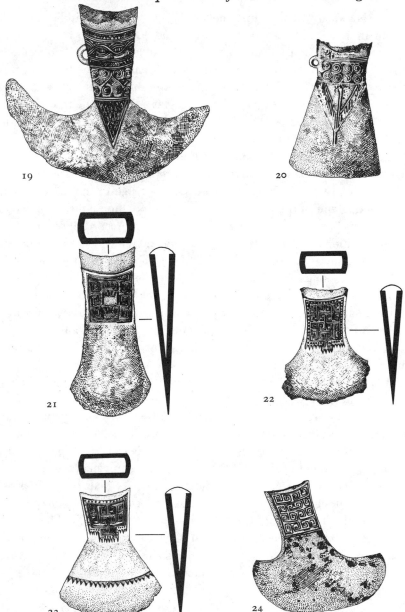

19

20

21

22

23

24

Fig. 19, J3:   shan/Chin-ning (Tomb 1)
               (After KKHP 1956.1:60,fig.18:3,2)
Fig. 20, J4:   symmetrical axe; L.11–12 cm. Li-chia-shan/
               Chiang-ch'üan, C. Yünnan
               (After WW 1972.8:pl.4:4)
Fig. 21, K1:   symmetrical axes; L.12.1, 8.6 and 9.4 cm.
Fig. 22, K2:   Ch'ing Yüan, Kwangtung
Fig. 23, K3:   After KK 1964.3:141,fig.4:2,4,3,fig.5:3,2,4–5;
               pl.9:1,2,3
Fig. 24, K5:   asymmetrical axe; H.9.8 cm. Kung Ch'eng,
               Kwangsi
               (After KK 1973.1:34,fig.7:11, pl.12:2)

kept in the National Museum in Bangkok. They were first published by T. Yamamoto in 1939, and display an outstanding combination of revival and original detail in design. The most remarkable piece (A1), from Udorn (Plate VIIa), with its large size (total length 72 cm.) and sickle-shaped outline, i.e. a curved and sharply pointed blade, still has all the essential characteristics of the Chinese *ko* weapon designed for hafting at a right angle into a wooden handle. The similarities are underlined by two more, less exorbitantly extended examples: A2 (Plate VIIb) from an unknown locality in north-west Thailand, and A3 (Plate VIIc) said to come from Nan Muong (north-west Thailand). While differing in their outline proportions (A3 with an obtuse angle formed by the axes of blade and *hu* necking or shank) and in the contour of the projecting end of the hafting plate (the *nei* in Chinese terminology), all three specimens have a clear internal affinity in form. Accordingly they retain a peculiar additional hafting device, a pair of lateral wings extending at a pointed angle sideways at the base of the blade, to which, in the case of one blade (A3), corresponds a similar lateral reinforcement at the lower end of the *hu* shank. The device of lateral wing supports for the wooden shaft was in central China an invention of the Early Chou bronzesmith and was discarded before the end of that period in the ninth century B.C. (v. Dewall 1966: 19 ff., fig. 3). Its revival is, however, not unique to northern Thailand; it has already been noted by Yamamoto on the *ko* dagger-axes discovered in Tongking (see below: B1, 2; Figs. 2, 3), and meanwhile its local re-generation can be attributed to the Tien culture in central Yünnan (Fig. 5). The lateral wings then appear as a criterion of form, interconnecting various key-types more closely than any other of their distinctive features. In particular the characteristic application of the decor on the Udorn and Nan Muong pieces, A1, 3 (Plate VIIa, c) sets them apart from their Tongking equivalents.

By contrast with its unwieldy appearance, the *ko* A1 is distinguished by a very intricately designed spiral decor on the projecting tang (=*nei*), on the wings, and on the lower end of the *hu* necking (Plate VIId, e, f). The running spirals on the tang are composed not just in bands as usual, but are graphically linked in three directions thus achieving a space-filling (=*flächendeckend*) effect, instead of merely a number of superimposed zones. The gussets in between each pair of adjacent spirals are filled with scaly triangles neatly fitted into the curvilinear pattern. A raised line and beaded edging (=*Perlmuster*) sets off the panel from its background. The rear end of the tang with its slanting border furnishes an irregular trapezoid panel, into which the spiral decor elements are elegantly adjusted by slightly altering their size and forms in the corners, without disturbing the continuous linear flow. The decoration of the lozenge-shaped panel on each wing corresponds to that on the tang in all details, except for the fact that here the connecting lines between each pair of spirals are running not obliquely but vertically and horizontally and thus give a more rigid impression. A further band of running spirals, accompanied by similar gusset fillings, is placed along the top margin of the blade. Organized again into an overall lozenge shape, but without a linear framing, the spiral decoration appears in the tip of the *hu* shank (Plate vII*f*). Resourcefully, the designer impresses the viewer by the balance struck in the oblique H-shape, with alternating combinations of pairs of spirals drawn in S- and T-form. The gussets are filled here unobtrusively with spheric triangles.

On all parts of the object the design is executed in the same manner, namely with relief lines of equal width, raised from a slightly receding background, so that the design is flush with the undecorated surface level. Since the space between any two relief lines is never allowed to be wider than they are thick, at first glance the graphic design appears as if incised, i.e. achieved by an engraving technique into the metal body. Yet clearly the graphically effective parts of the ornament are not in its negative but its positive linear elements, i.e. the even relief lines. When judged by their delicacy and by their meticulous and flawless rendering, the spiralic lines can hardly be envisaged as having been chased into the metal surface. More likely they are the result of utmost care and of masterly draughtsmanship in the graphic and technical preparation of the wax model for casting the bronze, thus yielding masterpieces comparable to those from Shang China.

The counterpart from Nan Muong A3 (Plate vIIc, Fig. 1) is similarly decorated on tang, wings, and the lower part of the *hu*, or, in this case, the additional lower pair of wings. The ornaments also consist of spiral fillings, in relief, of lozenge-shaped quadrangles, together with branch-like projections resembling brush-strokes. These, receding from the surface level and the empty spaces between and around the spirals, are filled with densely spaced small dots. The relief ornaments are set, as in the previous case A1, in recesses framed by heavy, unevenly thick partition lines which repeat, with reversed means, the brushstroke-like ornamentation on the junction of blade and necking.

In form and decor elements, but particularly in decor technique, this weapon is committed to a mixture of traditions. These commitments point in various directions, to the north, i.e. the Tien bronze craft, and to the north-east, to Tongking. The strangely distorted outline of the hafting plate is met on another undecorated *ko* weapon of a comparable type said to come from the surroundings of Hai-phong (Janse 1947: fig. 6b, p. xxvi). Furthermore, the obtuse angle formed by shank and blade is a regular feature of three decorated *ko* weapons (respectively their derivates) from Tongking. A *ko* dagger-axe recovered by Pajot in 1930 near Dong-son (*BEFEO*, xxx, 1930: 215, pl. xxvII) can serve as the key-type, *B1* (Fig. 2), to bring out the characteristics of this group and to differentiate its distinct similarities and dissimilarities with the preceding examples from Thailand.

This *ko* weapon in turn exhibits traits derived from diverse mainstreams of workmanship. A shield following closely, at *c.*1 cm. distance, the outline of the entire blade, is covered with a very fine network of tiny lozenges in raised lines. In a series of bird-like figures, loosely arranged in two groups along the necking and on the inner half of the blade, each figure consists simply of an impressed oval outline of the body, with extensions each for the head and beak, the tail, and the feet. The linear body contours, filled up with a row of small dots—which recall the beaded borders and also the interior granular body markings on a number of other types (A1, B2, B3, E2, E'', H1, H2, Plate VIId, *e*; Figs. 3, 4, 21, 15*a, b*)—are not fully congruent; hence they have not been made with one die. The inner part of the body is too badly corroded to allow for a closer examination of the conjunction between the lozenge mesh-work in relief and the intaglio execution of the bird figures. Within a double rectilinear frame surrounded at three sides by a beaded edging, the tang projection bears the figure of an elephant rendered in profile, in flat positive relief amidst a background filling of dots, reminiscent of the granular pattern of A3 (Fig. 1).

Directly corresponding in form is another *ko*, B2 (Fig. 3) found at Núi Voi (Mountain of the Elephant, Prov. Kiên-an; *BEFEO*, xxii, 1922: pl. XXIA). It combines, with a rectilinear openwork decoration on the tang and along the inner top end of the blade, two separate figurative motifs: one on the middle section of the blade, the second occupying the entire shank. Differently from the elephant executed in bas-relief on the tang of *ko* B1 (Fig. 2), here both figures—presumably a crocodile and a tiger—are impressed, flatly stamped silhouettes filled up with small dots of unequal size and in irregular spacing used to render the marking of the animals' coats.

Related to this, by its animal design more than by its form, is the *ko* blade B3 (Fig. 4) from Son-tây, where a figurative composition of two (possibly three?) animals in pursuit is set within a panel frame neatly following the contour of the blade (*BEFEO*, xxii, 1922: pl. XXII B). These three distinct peculiarities of decor: the delineation of the blade contour circumscribing a pictorial panel, the rendering of figurative motifs in impressed silhouette out-line, and the use of dotted fillings for interior marking, are features which distinguish the Tongking varieties of the *ko* dagger-axe from their counter-parts and which one would be inclined to assign to locally operative agents.

This is not the place to discuss in all necessary detail the abundant material of *ko* weapons, decorated and undecorated ones, found in the burials of the Tien culture at Shih-chai-shan (=SCS Report, 1959: pls. 15–17, table 7, pp. 32–4), at T'ai-chi-shan (KK, 1965, 9: pls. 4: 7; 6: 1, 2; fig. 7: 4, 5, p. 455) or at Li-chia-shan (WW, 1972, 8: 30).[3] Notwithstanding the internal emphasis placed on the *ko* dagger-axe as a basic type in the Tien culture, as is reflected in its manifold variant forms and rich decor schemes, not one *ko* weapon fully

characteristic of Tien forms has turned up outside its cultural sphere. Nevertheless, the Tien *ko* weapon deserves a few words of characterization, because
some of its distinct features fit suitably into the comparison between our A
and B key-types, although neither of the two can be considered its model.
Admittedly, it is a gross simplification to reduce the Tien dagger-axe, for the
present purpose, to merely one key-type C (Fig. 5), exemplified by only one
object, but it could be amply multiplied by other examples (see KKHP, 1956,
1: 60, fig. 17). Disregarding, with a view to form, the actual variations in outline and proportions, we note with interest the re-occurrence of the lateral
wings similar to key-types A and B, and, with regard to decoration, in particular the rigidly separated panels on such parts of the implement where these
panels strongly emphasize the constructive organization and functional
specialization of the total design and its constitutive parts: the tang, the wings,
and the length of the shank.

This decorative scheme has more than a casual affinity with that of the *ko*
forms from north Thailand (A1 etc., Plate VII; Fig. 1), and it contrasts sharply
with the Tongking examples (B1 etc. Figs. 2–4). A detailed comparison of all
decor elements and of the rules observed in their composition inevitably suggests that all three key-types have drawn to a large extent on a common stock,
and yet that each designer has made his own distinct choice in finding his
particular formulation. From the standpoint of stylistic consistency which
such formulations have attained, the example B3 is as instructive as the piece
A1, yet, both are surpassed by the dagger-axes C. They disclose a stylistic
unity which associates them with a considerably larger sector of decorated
bronze implements in the Tien context, a point we shall have to resume in our
discussion below.

A decorative scheme dissimilar in nearly all respects is encountered on
another type of *ko* weapon, resembling, with its broad triangular outline, the
ancient Chinese so-called *k'uei* blade. This type D (Fig. 6 represents a fragment in the British Museum; for counterparts with complete blade see
BMFEA, 14, 1942: pl. 20: 2, 3) can be formally differentiated by its evenly,
almost symmetrically widened base, normally with two slits, one above and
one below the junction with the hafting plate. No lateral wings are applied;
instead two lugs projecting symmetrically upwards and downwards from its
shoulder facilitate the hafting. Consequently, there is no *hu* necking. A large
round perforation encircled by a striated band in sunken lines usually is placed
at the upper third of the blade, limiting the decoration to the trapezoidal inner
section and to the rear end of the hafting plate. While on the key-type C each
decorative panel on the same object has been ornamented independently and
has primarily obeyed the necessities of the substructure in outline and
organization, type D examples not only have a much stronger conformity
among all representative objects known, they also disclose an immediate

pictorial parallelization in motifs and composition between both panels on one and the same object. The elements in both panels are figurative, suggesting either an anthropomorphic (Trubner 1959: 176) or, more likely, an amphibian origin (Gray 1949: 102 ff.) and are composed into an enigmatic formula: three of them on the hafting plate, two in a trapezoidal recess on the inner part of the blade, in both cases arranged symmetrically along the median axis of blade and tang.

There is no immediate need here to resolve the puzzling iconographical problems raised by this enigmatic formula, but it should be stated that the apparent stereotype has been dealt with quite liberally by the Tien designer, since it reappears 'broken down' and transfigured on many corresponding bronze implements in Tien (SCS Report, 1959: pl. 15, fig. 7, pp. 30–1). The one dagger-axe belonging to this key-type which has been recovered in Tongking (*BEFEO*, xxii, 1922: pl. XXIIA) has so far remained an isolated occurrence in North Vietnam. Yet it is true that its peculiar technique of rendering figures in broad, flat, and positive silhouette relief against a cut-away background framed as a panel is quite uncharacteristic of bronze casting and decorative techniques among Tien artisans, and thus it poses a riddle also from the technical point of view.

Types E, F, G: the dagger and shortsword

Forms of daggers or shortswords prevail so abundantly in the entire region that at first sight it seems hardly feasible to reduce such a rich variety to a few presentable key-types. The leading form (E1, etc.; see Lan 1963: fig. XIV) in the southernmost part of the region has a short lancet-shaped blade and a rather narrow hilt which grips the base of the blade tightly, and is capped by a widened, hollow top section. A find from Thiêu-duong (Prov. Thanh-hoa; Lan 1963: fig. XIV, 2), not available in photographic reproduction, is particularly interesting because of its divergent decoration on both faces. The ornament on the obverse cannot be made out in detail but appears organized in parallel zones of unequal width, set in a shield which tapers towards the tip of the blade, while on the reverse it is composed of spirals in relief raised from the surface within a shield of lancet contour. Gussets between the spirals and similar non-decorative parts seem to have been left empty. A related motif is encountered, made up of double relief lines and also contained in a tongue-like shield, on the blade of the bronze dagger (E2) from Son-tây with its rattle-shaped grip (Lan 1963: fig. XIV, 4). The decor composition evokes fewer reminiscences of the decorative organization on the *ko* A1, as could be suggested by the spiral ornament on the Thiêu-duong dagger (E1); whereas the detail of filling double contours with small dots on the Son-tây dagger places it somewhat nearer to the *ko* weapons A3 (Fig. 1) and B1 (Fig. 2), but also to the axe-head H2 (Fig. 15*a*, *b*), all featuring comparable traits.

Another variation of the same key-type, though differing totally in all decor features, is represented by several daggers with plastically shaped handles rendered as anthropomorphic figures. These have become known, in North Vietnam, from Dông-son (Lan 1963: fig. xv, 9), Hà-dông (Bezacier 1972: 115), and more recently from Núi Nua (Lan 1963: fig. xvi, 1), but also, though differing in form and execution, from Ch'ing Yüan in Kwangtung (KK 1964, 3: 141, fig. 4, 8). In Tien the anthropomorphic configuration is connected with a different type of dagger (see below, key-type F).

A rare type E' (Fig. 7) is found in a dagger also collected by Pajot in 1930 in the vicinity of Dông-son (*BEFEO*, xxx, 1930: 215). Although it cannot be matched in either form or decorative organization with any other known piece from this region, it is worth noting for its interesting combination of decorative techniques and schemes, which apparently it owed to diverse local trends. Formally, the outline of the blade resembles the E forms, but the narrow and slightly curved guard-plate is unusual. With its three horizontal rows of beading, set apart by a fine thread line, it resumes a decorative detail met on other forms in the region (*ko* B1, Fig. 2). In matters of decoration, dagger and *ko* weapon B1 also share the particularity of the lancet-shaped shield on the blade, slightly moulded on the *ko* and on the dagger in the form of a recess which bears the main decoration executed in fine and widely spaced positive filaments. The two parallel ladder-rungs, bifurcated at the top into a V-shaped section, and fitted with their pointed end into the tip of the shield and blade, give the impression of a layout well harmonized with the contour of the blade. Yet the decor remains strictly geometrical, and there is absolutely no indication of a tendency towards animation in the ornamental detail nor towards directional movement in composition. Even more static and firm than the blade decoration is that of the hilt. It consists of rectilinear motifs, and thus it contrasts with most other forms preferring curvilinear ornaments arranged horizontally or vertically on the grip.

Reference to a few more dagger fragments should be inserted at this junction, although they have remained isolated examples and cannot strictly count as key-types. Goloubew (*BEFEO*, 29, 1929: pl. xv, pp. 24–5, fig. 14) published a dagger (E'') found in Dông-son, but he does not give much additional information. In a very general way blade and hilt resemble the E forms above; E'' differs, however, with its short and narrow, straight guard-plate. Moreover, two small eyelets in the bronze are mentioned which indicate that handle and blade have been made separately. The blade is heavily encrusted, and no conclusive statement can be made about its original appearance. The decor along the guard-plate and on the handle, leaving its top section free, is made up of spirals with multiple rollings executed in a squat, somewhat uneven

delineation. While the decor panels on obverse and reverse of the handle correspond as such, the ornaments themselves differ in detail. The framework
of ladder-rungs on the reverse, carried out in thinner filaments, recalls decorative elements belonging not only to the singular dagger E', but also to the
general stock of the bronze artist in the Dông-son tradition (see also type D,
Fig. 5). On account of the spiral decor encountered similarly on a number of
other objects, Goloubew, who has been the first to pay attention to such
matters, proclaimed their common origin as attributable to one artist-author
or one 'atelier'.

It is tempting therefore to introduce in connection with this group also
another hollow dagger-hilt—its blade is missing—reported from the vicinity
of Uttaradit, now also in the Bangkok National Museum (Plate VII*g*). In contrast with the refined spiral ornaments on the *ko* weapon A1 (p. 144), the spirals
on the dagger handle are crude in execution. Their compact composition, in
groups of four on both faces, and the gusset fillings with triangles, bear however an even closer resemblance to the *ko* A1 than to either the dagger handle
illustrated by Goloubew or other correlated objects which he attributed to the
same 'atelier'. Yet the slight coincidence of some decor details between *ko*
weapon and dagger handle is by itself hardly sufficient to claim an origin from
the same workshop. It should not be ignored that a certain unevenness of the
contour line (Plate VII*g*), with three coils around the waist joined by vertical
lines, betrays a feature well attested among dagger handles and comparable
forms in Tien. Still, with its wide, flaring lower end to receive the shoulder of
the blade, thus replacing a separate guard-plate, and with the closed top section crowned by a plastic appliqué of indistinct shape, the peculiar form of the
hilt stands out against all other dagger types in the region.

The entire material of daggers and short swords recovered from Shih-chai-
shan and other sites of the Tien culture is much too complex to be presented
here extensively. Suffice to say that, among all the variegated forms, not one
type vaguely reminiscent of the E1 or E' forms has turned up in the context of
Tien. Instead of a grip tightly clutching the base of the blade, as it distinguishes the E types, the corresponding slender dagger forms in Tien either
have a rounded shoulder or else a very narrow straight guard-plate (SCS
Report, 1959: pl. 25: 1–6; fig. 9: 1–5, p. 43). But neither of the two forms
have parallels elsewhere outside the Tien sphere.

It should be noticed that with regard to the decoration of the blade, those
forms with rounded shoulder show a tendency towards compactness and strict
formalization, similar on the one hand to the E-type daggers in Tongking;
and on the other, comparable to the decor schemes dominant in Tien on the
C and D key-types of dagger-axes, but also on the socketed axe J (see below,
Figs. 17–20) and on other manual implements. The concentration on a shield
decoration of the blade is, however, by no means a dominant and typical

feature among the dagger forms of Tien. Less compact and more fluently applied to the upper section of the blade is the decor on another group of daggers in Shih-chai-shan, distinguishable as a different key-type F by their triangular blade and an extremely narrow guard-plate (SCS Report, 1959: pls. 26–8). They have, in this combination, a number of outside parallels with a rather wide distribution and significant implications.

While the most distinctive example for illustrating this decor scheme in relation to its basic form is a find, F1 (Fig. 8), not from Shih-chai-shan but from Thái-nguyên (see however, SCS Report, pl. 27: 4) a closely correspond-ing find, F2 (Fig. 9), has been made in Ch'ing-chen (Prov. Kweichou) in a burial of a somewhat later date, i.e. the Eastern Han dynasty (A.D. 8–220). Not only does the curvilinear ornamentation, symmetrically arranged along the upper section of the median rib, have its analogies among dagger forms of a similar type in Tongking (F1) and Shih-chai-shan (F3, Fig. 10), but in particular the decor pattern on the handle, although not clearly discernible from the illustration available, has to be correlated to the frequent equivalents from Shih-chai-shan (F4, Fig. 11; SCS Report, 1959: table 9, pp. 49–52) and to a number of others from Tongking and adjacent regions (Janse 1958: fig. 22, p. 52: F5, Hà-giang, cf. Lan 1963, fig. XVI: 3; Janse 1958: fig. 23, p. 52: F6, Soon-tây, cf. Bezacier 1972: figs. 41–2, p. 111; Janse 1931: pl. 16: 1: F7, Phô-lu, Upper Red River; Lan 1963: fig. XV: 6: F8, Dào-thinh).

With the exception of some daggers in Shih-chai-shan represented by the example F3, all other type F forms concur in the decorative pattern of the hilt, which is made up of a composition of horizontally arranged bands of geometrical elements, complemented at the bottom part by a rectilinear panel (F1, F2(?), F4, F5, F6, F7, F8) and occasionally amalgamated with animated organic motifs (F6). The existence of an additional pommel (F1, F5; SCS Report, pl. 27: 4) adds to the decorative scheme of the handle but does not alter it. As no photographs have been published for any of the Tongking type F daggers, and the dagger from Phô-lu (Musée des Antiquités Nationales, St. Germain-en-Laye, No. 50706) is too badly corroded to ascertain any technical details of the original decoration, their characterization has to be left open until fuller information can be drawn upon.

Notwithstanding some variation in details of form and, in decorative organization, of either blade or handle among these widely distributed repre-sentatives, the key-type F can be characterized with its essential features. They are: the narrow guard-plate of only a few millimetres in height and (seen from above), of oblong outline with pointed ends (Fig. 8); and in particular the contour line of the basically triangular blade. Normally it has a rather broad base, with the edges slightly concave in their upper half and bulging outward just above or below mid-length. These bulges may be so prominent as to form obtuse angles (F1, F2, F3, and others); they may be rounded off

(F5, F6), or else they may just result in a slight swelling (F4, F7, and several examples from Shih-chai-shan). The hilt, with the exception of the figure-shaped handles in Shih-chai-shan, is round in cross-section, hollow, and has a concave contour ending in an open, funnel-shaped top (F2, F4, F6, F7, F8), unless it bears a pommel of slightly convex form and oval outline (F1, F5, cf. Lan 1963: fig. XVI: 2, 3).

Unexpectedly, *vis-à-vis* this degree of conformity, as soon as we focus on the Tien area (and especially on the Shih-chai-shan site, since no type F examples have been recovered from the minor Tien sites, either at T'ai-chi-shan or at Li-chia-shan), the formal criteria established for this type can be convincingly employed, but in decorative and configurative matters the local designers of the relevant objects appear much more liberal than elsewhere: so much so that, paradoxically, no fully representative key-type could be chosen among the Shih-chai-shan daggers. The handle combined with the typical blade F3 (Fig. 10), which is decorated in a scheme described as open and fluent, is modelled figuratively in a manner familiar for Tien bronzes but unknown for comparable type F examples elsewhere.

In another direction, the Tien designer departed from established modes and combined with the key-type F4 handle (Fig. 11), well in keeping with other type F forms in Tongking and elsewhere, a blade decoration drawn in a completely different spirit (cf. v. Dewall 1972: fig. 6 A–D, p. 353; W. Watson 1970: fig. 23, p. 53). The figurative representations are drawn boldly over the entire space available, in complete disregard of the given substructure and its basic form. Here, balance of mass and form and the harmony among individual pictorial elements are not obtained by virtue of abstract decorative principles such as axial symmetry or tectonic and constructive necessity; they rather result directly from the dynamics of the dramatic, figurative composition. A comparable liberality in graphic figurative design has not been found on any other type of manual implements in the wider region; but when it is seen as a fruit of the ingenuity and broadmindedness of the Tien bronzemaster and his clientele, it can be matched by similar artistic attitudes in many other graphic and plastic configurations in the same cultural context.

In summary, even the most detailed observations about the correlation between coherent form and partly incoherent decoration cannot provide a definite clue about the most probable place of origin and centre of diffusion for this widely effective key-type. In compliance with the usual categories of reasoning in archaeology, those stylistically more homogeneous and therefore 'typical' forms collected in Tongking would have to be considered as proto-types which inspired local designers in Tien. If however we take into con-sideration that in actual numbers the distinct F-type daggers in Tongking represent but a small minority among other dagger forms, in part equally well defined (E1–), partly less distinct in their formal features (E'–), whilst on the other hand a total of more than 100 specimens in Shih-chai-shan can be sub-sumed under this typological category, then our argument is less readily convincing.

Probably, one should be prepared to accept an answer as complex as the problem posed. The manufacture of daggers with a figuratively sculptured handle whose principles of composition are so intricately interwoven with other three-dimensional configurations in Tien artistry (v. Dewall 1972: 352) has to be sought in the same artistic sphere; and so must the vividly drawn scenic compositions on several dagger blades. These, however, differ signi-ficantly in decorative technique from any other ornamentation discussed so far, in that they are not the direct result of the casting process itself, i.e., they have not been prepared in the wax model. Instead, they have been engraved into the finished cast, and the pictorial elements appear in fine incised, hence negative, lines. Technically, casting of the form, and drawing and incising of the image are two separate processes which, theoretically, could have taken place apart. In the light of such considerations, several undecorated examples representing the same distinct type F could claim additional interest by the range of their distribution (Janse 1938: fig. 37: Cau-công, Prov. Thanh-hóa; Janse 1958: fig. 21, p. 52, provenance unknown; Heine Geldern 1932: pl. 37: 2: Luang Prabang), although this evidence is insufficient presently to support by itself any conjectural 'trade-routes' out of Tongking into neigh-bouring or distant provinces.

With the restricted data available at present in respect of decor techniques and similar matters of metallurgical technology, it is expedient to postpone an attempt at interpretation, and only suggestions and stimuli for further enquiry can be offered in lieu of firm conclusions. We can strike a more affirmative note when we are concerned with the actual evaluation of individual forms and implements by the people who made and used them, rather than with matters of origin and production. We are left in no doubt about the pronounced popularity of the dagger in question among the occupants of the Shih-chai-shan necropolis. This is borne out not only by the elaboration of the figurative transformation of the handles (F3, Fig. 10) and by the liveliness and variety of the decor motifs on the graphically illustrated blades (Fig. 11), but also by the fact that the very same shape of dagger is drawn distinctively, in these representations, in the hands of the man defending himself against the attack-ing tiger.

With a view to the large number of closely related sub-types of key-type F daggers in Shih-chai-shan, which are now found to be shared by the out-lying villages within the same cultural sphere, another key-type of the short sword, G1, deserves noting. It is present in Shih-chai-shan in small numbers only (SCS Report 1959: pl. 27: 2), and no doubt it has its base in the western part of Yünnan, in the Tali region. Since the first example reported from

Yünnan has been published by Janse (1931: pl. xv: 4, fig. 12), many other closely corresponding in form and decor have been added in Chinese reports, at first from the Ta-po-na site (KK 1964, 12: 611, fig. 7: 7, pl. 4: 1; both pieces with bulging lower half of the blade; Fig. 13), and afterwards from other sites around Lake Erh (KK 1966, 4: 222, fig. 2: 1, 2, 3; p. 223, fig. 3: 1–4, 7). These finds serve extremely well to support an argument in favour of locally centred workshop activities, and against the unsatisfactory, simplistic concept of unilinear compact diffusion in bronze metallurgy.

The swords or daggers of the G type, considerably varying in length between 16 to over 58 cm., resemble each other in every other respect, so closely that they become almost interchangeable. This internal conformity is all the more remarkable, as its formal and decorative features set this type distinctly apart from any other group of daggers or any singular form referred to above. Its distinctive features are especially the three-pronged calyx-shaped shoulder section of the blade, continuing into angular projections at the onset of the inwardly curved and then long extended edges, and the tubular hollow hilt with a concave contour and capped by a solid cover slightly wider than the hilt at its base. The peculiar decor of the hilt is achieved either by torsion over its entire length, or, in other cases, by dissolving the surface into a granular pattern. One exceptional piece carries, on both sides of the hilt, a figurative design consisting of two entwined dragons. Another slightly modified example, with a V-shaped indentation at the junction of handle and blade and with a series of tiny annular projections instead of the calyx framing at the shoulder, constitutes the closest link not only with the Tien counterparts of type G (SCS Report 1959: fig. 9: 2, p. 44), but also with another type of short sword much in favour in Tien. This composite sword, with iron blade and bronze hilt (SCS Report: pl. 100: 1, 3), has not been found in the Tali region, nor any other daggers than those of the G-type, but an obvious resemblance between the shoulder decoration of the composite sword in Tien and one or two deviate forms from Tali must be noted (KK 1966, 4: 223, fig. 3: 5, 6), which suggests that here too imported decorative techniques most likely have been reworked into local workshop patterns.

Types H, J, K: axes

An analogous, yet in significant ways divergent, story can be told, relating to typical forms of bronze axes and their distribution over the region of South East Asia and southern China. In the introductory remarks above, the general situation has been summarized with reference to the two discretely distinguishable prototypes of the socketed axe, namely axe-heads with a symmetrical and those with an asymmetrical outline of the cutting edge. Attention is focussed here on two axes of each kind, as the contrasting modes of correlation noticeable for each pair can illuminate the conditions prevailing among the postulated workshop centres, and also the measure of their co-operation or differentiation.

The diffuse pattern of distribution for the asymmetrical axes in general has been mentioned already, while the clearly delimited occurrence of decorated key-types in the Tongking region stands out markedly against this background. After a long interval in the publication of relevant research results, new data are now available in Le Van Lan's study on the Bronze Age in North Vietnam (1963), and have been taken up to a large extent by L. Bezacier (1972) in his recent publication, with new attempts at typological differentiation. While Lan's drawings obviously pay attention to matters of decorative technique in general, they appear less reliable for the section of the asymmetrical decorated axes and have to be questioned over this issue. Bezacier's book may prove useful as a synthesis, but it is insufficient as a source of information about decoration and technique because the drawings are inadequate and the text is indifferent to the subjects central to this study.

Among many divergent forms of asymmetrical axes, the two which morphologically and stylistically differ distinctly in their extreme representatives are yet interrelated in more than one respect. Both types, the pediform axe with its heavy, near-angular heel and the foreward bent of the cutting edge (Figs. 14, 15a, b), and the boat-shaped axe with its strongly curved blade, pointed or coiled inward at both ends (Fig. 16), are subsumed here under the rubric of one key-type, on account of the correspondences between them, primarily in matters of iconography and decor system but also for typological reasons.

Postponing for a few moments the question of decorative techniques which are strikingly different on both extreme types and cause very disparate stylistic effects, the consistency in figurative details throughout the whole series is most remarkable. In its most elaborate example, on the Pediform axe H1 (Fig. 14), the pictorial decoration comprises a complete scene of dancing men in a high-prowed boat accompanied by a group of deer and other animals; and in its more abbreviated form, on the crescent-shaped type H3 (Goloubew 1929: pl. XVI), the scene is reduced to a low barge with a crew of mere line figures. Finally, on both faces of the axe H4 (Fig. 16), an unfinished piece recovered by Janse (1958: pl. 28) *in situ* in a Dông-son locality, we find it simplified even further to a streaked crescent. Differing only in detail, the decor on both faces of the blade H2 (Fig. 15a, b) also features on the obverse for, the group of dancers and musicians (?), a structural frame probably meant as a boat. The same device is repeated, this time with the obverse again showing a group of deer and a smaller animal, on the reverse face of a similar axe (H5; Goloubew 1929: pl. XV c). Men with their arms raised (a dancing gesture?) combined with deer and other small animals in vaguely boat-shaped structures or frames are found on nearly all these decorated axes in one form or other. A graphically almost dissolved version of the same pictorial content is offered in yet another case, an axe-head from Nui Nua (H6; Lan 1963: fig. III: 8), typologically connecting the two extreme modes of the pediform and crescent-shaped varieties.

What has been described pictorially as a boat is, in fact, in the majority of cases amalgamated into a border frame for the figurative scene. It always follows the contour lines of the entire blade more or less closely, and may consist of just a few parallel lines without any scenic content (Lan 1963: fig. III: 8), of a raised single or double frame (Lan 1963: fig. III: 12, IV: 3), or of a complex border decoration with geometrical ornaments as on blade H1 (Fig. 14). The connections of the beaded edging, found again on the axe H1, have been mentioned beforehand in discussing the *ko* types A1, B1, etc.; and similar correlations can be noted between the panel framed by multiple lines on H1 and 2 (Figs. 14, 15) and the *ko* form B3 (Fig. 4).

The similarities are even more immediate when the characteristic effect of the intaglio design is observed. It has been achieved on the H1 and H2 forms and a number of further counterparts by the same technique of impressed silhouettes. Doubt must be raised on the correctness of drawings in this respect, since Lan's figures III: 11 and IV: 2 seem to suggest a positive bas-relief, not a negative stamped design. As the example of the elephant figuring on the tang of *ko* B1 (Fig. 2) has shown, positive relief has actually been employed together with impressed figures on the same piece; hence its application on some axe-heads cannot be ruled out entirely. Yet it is highly unlikely that, within the strong tradition of negative silhouette figures documented so far, exactly similar motifs should have been rendered arbitrarily in either way. Parmentier's sketches are misleading (1918: pl. IX), as a comparison with analogous illustrations published by Janse (1931: pl. I: 2, 4a) can prove. Only a full photographic documentation can help to settle this problem.

That there existed nevertheless, for the decoration of the extreme boat-shaped axes (H3, 4; Fig. 16), a distinctly different technique is a significant fact. The decor effect is achieved plainly by a positive sketching with lines raised above the surface, widely spaced and of equal strength for outline and interior markings alike. The delineation appears even finer and more regularly executed for the decor of axe H6 (Lan 1963: fig. IV: 3), and shows a strong affinity to the decorative technique on drums and similar forms in the Tongking context. Both these distinctly differentiated techniques, that of silhouette stamping and that of linear drawing in positive relief, appear firmly rooted within the same base, and have exerted their influences outside rather selectively and on no grand scale (v. Dewall 1972: 351). Together they must be considered as the results of locally concentrated workshop practices whose effectiveness was counterbalanced in contiguous areas by dissimilar traditions or trends.

What is striking, when we turn to Yünnan and to the Tien area for comparison, is the total lack of any correlative objects to either the pediform or the boat-shaped H types of Tongking. The only two pediform axes found in Shih-chai-shan, within the same tomb (SCS Report 1959: pl. 31: 4), are undecorated; and all other non-symmetrical varieties of axe-heads in Tien cannot be grouped into the same category as the H types, since their blades expand, though unevenly, towards both ends (comp. also Fig. 19). In view of this absence of typical pediform axes in Shih-chai-shan, it is all the more noteworthy that it is a typical pediform axe in outline configuration which is wielded by the feather-clad warriors on the mantle decor of some bronze drum-containers recovered from Shih-chai-shan. The same motif recurs in the hands of 'feather-men' on the Dông-son drums and on a number of other objects. The explanation, under such circumstances, clearly must be that, if not the drum-container itself, the entire combination of the motif has been imported into the Tien repertory where stamped silhouette designs appear as an intrusive practice.

For the purposes of their customers the Tien bronzesmiths themselves provided a wide variety of axe forms of their own. Together with other tools usually hafted to an armlong shaft, such as the adze, the pick, also the *ko* dagger-axe and the broad battle-axe, the axe has been subjected to certain formal and functional transformations by the incorporation into the general design of a tubular socket placed at a right angle to the axis of the blade (SCS Report 1959: pls. 30, 31, 34, 35). This device of a transverse socket tube, together with its plastic accessories, dominates all these forms so strongly that it is not sensible to detach a full discussion of the axe from that of all other types.

In principle concordant tendencies in decoration are observable on the leading forms of symmetrical axe-heads in Tien. While no decorated asymmetrical blades have turned up in Tien, conversely none of the typical symmetrical axes stylistically belonging to the Tien tradition have been reported in Tongking nor anywhere else peripheral to central Yünnan. Even the symmetrical axe-heads in the Tali region in western Yünnan have a less distinct appearance and are not of the Shih-chai-shan type. Since its distribution is strictly limited to the Tien sphere, this key-type J1–4 (Figs. 17–20) can be handled more cursorily; yet it is useful as a contrasting counterpart to other types of decorated symmetrical axes known from Northern Vietnam (Lan 1963: fig. II: 3, 7, 9; Janse 1958: pl. 27: 5), with a chevron ornamentation in rough linear relief on the upper (socket) part. Formally, there is again among the J-type examples a certain variation in the normally lengthened body, with gently curved facetted sides and slightly extended and curved edge J1, 2 (Figs. 17, 18), in the forms with narrow waist and extremely curved blade distinctly set off from the socket, J3 (Fig. 19), but also in a stouter type

J4 (Fig. 20; a find from Li-chia-shan, south of Lake Tien), with short socket and straight sides.

The most obvious combining factor between these varying forms is the composition scheme of ornamentation and its arrangement with regard to the functionally determined constitutive parts of the axe. Whereas the body of the decorated asymmetrical axe, whether blade (Fig. 14) or blade and socket section (Fig. 15a, b), was potentially subject to decoration all over, with total disregard for constructive exigencies, the decoration of the symmetrical type J never comprehends the blade section. Conforming in spirit and execution, with alternately impressed and level decor delineation, and differing only in the choice and combination of individual elements, its major pattern includes a rich repertory of linear geometric motifs suited for continuously circulating drawing, such as running spirals and rows of dotted circlets (Fig. 18), plaited bands of several strands and rhombic meanders (Fig. 17), wavy ribbons and zigzag lines (Fig. 19), together with vertically joined pairs of spirals grouped unidirectionally (Fig. 20) or antithetically (Fig. 19). These ornaments are arranged in either single zones framed by narrow borders (Figs. 18, 20), or else in a series of superimposed bands of varying width, and are, except for the place of attachment for the eyelet loop, revolving horizontally. No suggestion is made towards organic form or figurative depiction within these examples, although such tendencies are traceable in other J-type axes in Tien, also distinguished by their plastic accessories (SCS Report 1959: fig. 10: 1–5, p. 53).

The horizontal section of the ornament is complemented below by an isosceles triangle placed axially, with its tip pointing towards the edge and thus emphasizing a vertical axiality in counterpoise to the circulating movement. The triangle is ornamented in diaper reticulation (Fig. 19), or with rhombic meanders, multiple lozenges, and triangles. With a pronounced emphasis on structure, the horizontal patterns are adapted to the tubular section, while the triangular complementation distinctly marks, with decorative means, the tip of the tapering socket; hence the internal functional construction.

A comparable decorative device, frequently combined with a diaper ornamentation, is found also on spearheads (KKHP 1956, 1: fig. 16: 5–8, p. 59) and on similar blades (SCS Report 1959: fig. 8: 2, 6, 7, 9, pp. 35, 36), and it has been taken up for the decoration of the lateral wings of *ko* blades (KKHP 1956, 1: fig. 17: 2, 3, 5, p. 60), although there is no socket to be marked. The composition scheme of decoration is equally concordant between all these types of manual implements in Tien; also the decor scheme of the type F dagger handles (Figs. 16, 18) so consistently uniform and, for reasons of decorative technique, as well considered characteristic for Tien metallurgy, cannot deny a certain affinity to that of the type J axes either. All these groups are cognate primarily by the considerations of structural form determining decorative articulation, secondarily by the correspondence in decor techniques, with linear designs rendered in relief flush with the body surface, and in addition by the complexity in the composition of geometrical patterns. Together these attest a rich, independent, and well-established tradition of the Tien craftsmen, and it is all the more surprising that their most characteristic products had only a restricted circulation.

Another workshop centre turning out socketed axes of the symmetrical variety catered for a more widely spaced clientele further east, centering on the Kwangtung coastal region. Several finds have been made in recent years, reaching north-westward into Kwangsi, near to the border of Hunan. No analogous finds have been reported either in the west, in Yünnan, nor in the south, in Tongking. The key-type K of the south-eastern Chinese symmetrical axe-head can best be illustrated by a set of three examples K1, 2, 3 (Figs. 21–23) recovered together with a fourth, undecorated one, from a tomb dated in the Eastern Chou period in Ch'ing Yü (Kwangtung). A fourth specimen (K4), said to come, together with a *ko* fragment and a tanged dagger decorated in a similar fashion, from a site near Hongkong, is now in the British Museum. Two more axe-heads K5, 6 (Fig. 24) of the same Eastern tradition have come to light in a chance find in Kung Ch'eng (Kwangsi) in a rather exceptional association of finds.

In more than formal respects, these representatives are held together as products of one workshop tradition by the consistency of decor organization and execution. Applied in a regular compact relief delineation to the top section of the axe, the decor is arranged axially and is organized, from the centre to the margin (Fig. 21) of each panel, separately and differently on obverse and reverse (Fig. 23). The decorative panels may be framed by a single ridge (Figs. 28, 24), or they are elaborated with beaded edgings and saw-tooth bands (Figs. 22, 23), with an additional saw-tooth line crossing the width of the blade. The saw-tooth pattern is not very familiar from other manual implements; only the beaded edgings have been found repeatedly on various groups of weapons in the southernmost region, but they have not made their way into the bronze workshops of Tien where panels and framing borders have been much more intricately designed (see Fig. 5).

Formally, type K differs markedly, with its shorter body (Figs. 22, 23), rectangular in cross-section yet with a saddleshaped mouth, from the dominant type J axes in Tien. Counterparts from workshops further south which could have furnished direct prototypes cannot easily be found. Only the two axes K5, 6 (Fig. 24) recovered farthest north play formally an interesting outside rôle, since, with their unevenly expanded fan-like edge and with lightly pointed tips, they are resuming tendencies we have noted among the Tien manufacturers. It is hardly conceivable that a similar tendency should have been fostered independently in workshops favouring otherwise straightforward forms of symmetrical axes. A casual exchange of single products and the occasional employment of borrowed designs must be reckoned with, concurrently with the intention on the side of the local bronzesmiths to fulfil the requirements of regional markets within the capacity of their own resources.

Final Comments

By way of summary, a number of theses are set forth which may serve as a basis against which the present and any new evidence expected from further field investigations may be conveniently tested.

Firstly, with a view to the conclusiveness and persuasiveness of a leading form in armoury and manual equipment, it can be stated that the more distinctive type is, in form plus decor, and the more constant in maintaining this combination formula of traits, and the more exclusive in its distributional pattern, the more directly does it stand for a distinct local tradition in bronzesmithing.

Secondly, focusing on the co-existence of leading forms within a given area or cultural context, one may deduce a strong local tradition from the dominance, numerically as well as in the degree of variation or elaboration, of several key-types concurrently, over their counterparts present only in lesser numbers and with a more diffuse character. In the extreme case, the supremacy of an indigenous leading type results in total defiance of any analogous outside equivalents and, on this particular count, in a state of apparent autarky. Conversely, it can be argued in favour of a strong, i.e. influential, local tradition also, by the wide dispersal of its distinctive types penetrating even the sphere of some other workshop cluster, where the intruders occur as a minority and yet remain unadulterated.

Finally when concentrating on the distributional pattern of recognized leading types, these may be found to be neither consistent geographically, nor necessarily congruent for any two leading forms issuing from the same centre or cluster. Their diverging range of expansion, and the incongruous coverage of each tradition, reflect market tendencies more suggestively than massive cultural diffusion.

We have to turn back now, for the illustration and verification of these theses, to the key-types as outlined above in correlating their standard features of form, decor technique, and decorative system. Within the given limitations of the three standard types, our inferences concern primarily the rôle played, in a given context, either by a single key-type individually or, in the association of correlative key-types, by any one of them, and, concurrently, the range of distribution or influence of separate key-types in their spatial correlation. Key-types, it should be kept in mind, have been construed as analytical tools. Hence it is only natural that, within the range of actual objects for which they stand, the adherence to the prototype, i.e. to its pattern of modalities, has not been equally consistent.

Veritable key-types are those which we encounter in the most conformable series and among examples least prone to compromise on any one point of either form or decor. In this strict sense, only the short sword G (Figs. 12, 13) complies completely with the criteria of having its formal and decorative features amalgamated into a genuine, i.e. thoroughly consistent key-type. Furthermore, by virtue of its concentration in the Tali region, with only a few finds straying into the sphere of Tien, this form G is, among all our key-types, the only one with the distinct qualities of a cultural 'type fossil' (=*Leitfossil*).

Despite its stereotype decor system—the most arbitrarily designed of all forms included as key-types—the broad dagger axe D (Fig. 6) cannot claim the same qualities of consistency as a key-type, since it can be demonstrated to have been subject not only formally to considerable modification in Tien, but also to disintegration of its typifying decor formulation under the impact of a different decor technique and less conformable decorative principles dominant in Tien bronze artistry. No matter where ultimately its origin would have to be localized, with regard to numbers of actual finds its major effect has been achieved in Tien, but it had been absorbed into dissimilar autochthonous artistic currents. Considering together the rôles of the three key-types J, C, and F attributable to the workshops of Tien, interesting differences come to the fore. Although the internal ramifications of key-type J have been excluded from consideration, the Tien socketed axe appears among the three types as the most genuine, consistent key-type (Figs. 17–20). There are no close formal or decorative correlations to any other type of axe-head elsewhere which could have co-determined the local design. The striking affinity of the Kung Ch'eng axes (K5, 6, Fig. 24), from the point farthest north in the entire region, with undecorated non-symmetrical axes in Tien, is only a one-sided affair of outside stimulation as far as Tien is concerned. It is an interesting instance of long-range influence from the south, whether from the undercurrents in Tien or ultimately from the mainstream in Tongking, into a region whose workshops otherwise cannot deny their still strong commitment to traditions, in form and ornamentation (e.g. the rectilinear patterning organized from the centre or axis), conditioned by a northern inheritance.

Returning to Tien and its correlative key-types, the dagger-axe C (Fig. 5), when contrasted with the *ko* weapon A (Plate VII; Fig. 1) on one side, and with type B (Figs. 2–4) on the other, bespeaks quite a different relationship. Distinguished, like type J, by the constructive emphasis of its decor system, the *ko* type C would appear, also on account of a certain affinity in handling the decor technique, as a likely prototype for the northern Thailand samples A1–3; and yet they differ in essential respects of form and decorative detail.

Consequently, two inferences are possible: either the determination of the local producer of type A has been stronger than the impact made by the Tien model, and he felt encouraged to compromise to the extent of initiating a new 'key-type'; or else both types A and C had only indirect relationships and need not be figured out as derivates of each other at all. When both types are assessed as isolated productions independently, the somewhat disharmonious appearance of A1 is largely redeemed by the sophisticated treatment of its decorative parts; indeed, such skill and refinement cannot be ascribed to the hand of inexperienced 'provincial' imitators bound to corrupting any imported models. Willingness towards experimentation and a certain assurance of a market ready to absorb its results empowered local metallurgists to play with new ideas and to engender their own style.

Judged by artistic quality alone, the *ko* weapons B1–3 (Figs. 2–4) could more readily be considered 'barbarous' distortions of foreign prototypes. There is no room for doubt that they represent local adoptions of a type which functionally was only marginal in the Tongking armoury. Yet formally they, too, were experimented with; and stylistically they were subjected, with little adjustment to their formal peculiarities but with occasional recognition to examples from outside (B1, Fig. 2, with its delicate shield decoration on the blade), to the dominant local traditions with their preference in iconography for figurative motifs, and for a technique relying mainly on sunken relief stamping. Parallels have been drawn with the axe-heads, type H (Figs. 14, 15*a*, *b*), and can be extended to other classes of bronze objects (v. Dewall 1972: 343). Despite its prominent position within the Dông-son context proper, i.e. the Tongking region, the decorative style deployed on these bronzes has been only a casual intruder in Tien, and has not noticeably influenced other workshops in contiguous provinces.

The opposite extreme to the veritable key-types is manifest, in two different ways, in the dagger key-types E and F (Fig. 7; Plate VII*g*; Figs. 8–11). The sub-types of the dagger forms E are actually so much at variance that it seems hardly justified to subsume them under the same category. There is certainly room for complementation and modification, once observations can be made by autopsy on relevant materials. Both key-types E and F are particularly interesting when we contrast their distributional aspects, together with their respective rôles as key-types. Despite their internal diffuseness with regard to form and decor, type E daggers had a limited circulation within the Tongking region. The dagger-handle E from Uttaradit (Plate VII*g*) differs considerably and does not well fit in either the Tongking or the Tien range of dagger forms. In contrast with the openness in form and decor, yet restriction in distribution for type E, type F daggers are surprising by the peculiarity of their form and by its consistency in detail (the bulging or angular edge), as also by the distinctness of decoration on either blade or handle (or both), together with the readiness to transform such decorative concepts for handle or blade, and last but not least, by their wide distribution, despite such alterations in essential parts.

In terms of distribution, key-type F must appear as an intruder into the area actually occupied by the more strictly localized E forms, and the massive concentration of F forms in Tien, where it holds a dominant position, must make it a Tien product. Yet, it may be objected against such an inference that the two distinctively different decor systems, of blade as well as handle, represent two disparate stylistic attitudes, which from previous experience with bronze artistry in prehistoric societies hardly seem compatible within the same cultural context.

The phenomenon of two diverse stylistic attitudes associated in one archaeological unit is not peculiar to Tien. In Tongking, different decorative techniques have been developed, presumably simultaneously since they were exercised side by side, on either the very same object, e.g. our example B1 (Fig. 2), or else within the range of one key-type such as H1–5 (Figs. 14–16). Here the basic decorative scheme, with the framing panel in compliance with the outline of the blade, and the iconographical figurative elements, have as a decorative formula proved stronger than the modification of the asymmetrical contour, pediform at the one extreme and crescent or boatshaped at the other. The alteration of technique, from a planar mode of rendering pictorial elements in sunken and hatched silhouettes to a more strictly graphical execution in raised linear relief, has resulted in deviant stylistic effects within the confines of near-identical sub-types; and, as we must infer from the limited distribution of these decorated asymmetrical axes, within the precincts of contiguous workshop centres.

Summarizing our fact-finding efforts, we can finally dismiss the categories set up for the observation of characteristic traits in form, decor technique and decorative system, as mere methodological props. Not one of them singly corresponds directly, with its factual content, to a particular workshop prerogative. Yet, we must duly recognize that certain standard combinations have become almost exclusively dominant in two leading areas in the Late Bronze Age metallurgy of the region: in Tongking and Tien. Their distinctiveness certainly signifies a basic difference between the two centres which deserves further attention. The potential scope for a culture-historically relevant conclusion should not be attenuated by focussing, at this stage, explicitly on the interrelation of two distinct centres only, as presently still wider applications of possible inferences are called for.

In the light of the intricate system of interaction, as generalized in our theses above, individual metallurgical workshop centres can be seen firstly as sites of production, eatering for a market of consumption. Its range need not be confined by cultural borders; the purchase of a single item manufactured outside one's own cultural area does not in itself constitute a case of 'cultural acceptance', although it may foster preferences for 'foreign' goods and, consequently, a disposition towards cultural borrowing.

Dispersal of goods to meet practical demands brought in its wake the dissemination, through a variety of conceivable channels of transmission, of non-material, i.e. intangible 'cultural elements', and with them impulses of many diverse kinds and varying degrees of strength. Persuasiveness and adaptibility on the one side, and susceptibility and fondness of innovation on the other, determined the mode of impact which any external intrusions could make, ranging between stringent imitation and total reorganization. Ultimately, as our examples illustrate, the attraction or the refusal of such forms which had a practical and also an artistic value, was not merely decided upon at the personal whim of the potential consumer; and works of art did not change hands without a mental inclination on the side of the new owner towards his acquisition.

Interaction and interdependence in matters of artistic production and in artistic expression therefore means much more, with regard to cultural exchange and cultural dynamics, than is covered by referring to the interpenetration of certain trade routes and to the overlapping of sales areas for particular groups of objects. Yet even the exchange of artistic products, and the cross-fertilization with creative designs originating from different production centres, does not necessarily attest to complete interdependence between the communities involved and is not bound to lead to total cultural homogeneity. At best, if the artistic attractivity can be postulated to stand for the popularity which some of the decorated key-types have commanded, these become indicators of artistic sensitivity channelled into a discrete stylistic attitude.

Internally, the consequences for sociocultural solidarity of the activities issuing from local workshop centres can hardly be overrated. The success, as between competitive efforts from many sides, in transplanting approved decorative combinations on to newly acquired forms, as much as the willingness to experiment freely with stimuli received from outside, and their final integration into autochthonous workshop traditions, are the denominators in the case of the Tongking traditions for evaluating the importance of an individual centre or cluster, and for measuring the strength of influences which it exerted. In the case of Tien, multifariousness of styles and non-conformity in the modes of artistic expression, combined with a vigorous assimilative power, manifest a state of artistic maturity which demands an explanation on an even more comprehensive level than is provided for by the notion of workshop centres.

Throughout the region, the acts of give and take between proclaimed clusters and their traditions were too tightly interwoven for us to consider any one metallurgical production centre, at face value only, as equivalent to a cultural nucleus. On the other hand an influential and productive bronze foundry cannot well be visualized without a socio-political agglomeration of sufficient weight to sustain it economically, and to fortify its artistic ambitions with the power of cultural integrity. In the process of cultural growth towards civilization, independent metallurgical workshops and art centres have been only one, though an important, constitutive element in the early history of South East Asia.

Remark on Matters of Documentation

The present concern with matters of decorative technique on bronze implements imposed certain restrictions on documentation which must be explained. Access to research material in the ideal form of the objects themselves was rather limited; thus personal inspection of relevant original finds was only possible in the National Museum in Bangkok, the British Museum, and the Museum of Far Eastern Antiquities in Stockholm. I gratefully acknowledge the co-operation of colleagues, staff, and authorities in all three places, and wish to express my gratitude for making photographs available and for the authorization to reproduce them and, respectively, drawings made after such photographs.

Photographic publication of relevant objects had to be relied upon in nearly all other cases where no original photographs were obtainable. As the quality of such prints would not have permitted a reproduction with sufficiently distinct results, these illustrations had to be either transposed into line drawing or else to be substituted by corresponding objects reproduced graphically. Types published in line drawing only with no photographic reproduction available for checking, therefore had to be excluded (for instance the E1-type daggers). The painstaking task of rendering, from this mess of optically inadequate data, a presentable and illuminative documentary foundation, on which the convincingness of my argumentation is totally dependent, has been undertaken with admirable dexterity and great enthusiasm by my colleague Dr. H. E. Nellissen, Köln, to whom I extend my deepest appreciation.

NOTES

1. They have in fact been tentatively carried a step further in an investigation of bronze containers and affined forms whose figurative representations and elaborate scheme of composition led to a more complex argumentation elsewhere (v. Dewall 1972).

2. For exceptions with trapezoidal cross-section see, however, Janse 1931: pls. IV, V, VIII, etc.

ADDITIONAL REFERENCES

KK 1959. Yünnan Chin-ning Shih-chai-shan ti-san-tz'u fa-chüeh chien-pao (Preliminary report on the third excavation at Shih-chai-shan, Chin-ning/Yünnan). *Kaogu*, 459–61, 490.

KK 1964. Kuangtung Ch'ing-yüan ti Tung Chou mu-tsang (Eastern Chou burials at Ch'ing Yüan/Kuangtung). *Kaogu*, 138–42, pls. VIII, IX.

KK 1964. Yünnan Hsiang-yün Ta-po-na mu-kou t'ung-kuan mu ch'ing-li pao-kao (Report on clearing a tomb with wooden chamber and bronze coffin at Ta-po-na, Hsiang-yün/Yünnan). *Kaogu*, 607–18, pls. II–V.

KK 1965. Yünnan An-ning T'ai-chi-shan ku mu ch'ing-li pao-kao (Report on clearing a group of ancient tombs at T'ai-chi-shan, An-ning, Yünnan). *Kaogu*, 451–8, pls. III–VI.

KK 1966. Yünnan Ta-li shou-chi tao i-p'i Han-tai t'ung-ch'i (Collections of bronze implements of the Han Period in the Ta-li region/Yünnan). *Kaogu*, 220–4.

KK 1973. Kuanghsi Kung-ch'eng-hsien ch'u-t'u-ti ch'ing-t'ung-ch'i (Bronzes excavated in Kung-ch'eng/Kwangsi). *Kaogu*, 30–4, pls. X–XII.

KKHP 1956. Yünnan Chin-ning Shih-chai-shan ku i-chih chi mu-tsang (The ancient site and burials at Shih-chai-shan, Chin-ning/Yünnan). *Kaoguxüehbao* (Chinese Journal of Archaeology), 48–63, pls. I–X.

KKHP 1959. Kueichou Ch'ing-chen, P'ing-pa Han mu fa-chüeh pao-kao (The excavations of the Han Tombs at P'ing-pa and Ch-ing-chen counties, Kueichou province). *Kaoguxüehbao* (Chinese Journal of Archaeology), 85–103, pls. I–VI.

Lan, Le van, Phom van Kinh, and Nguyen Linh. 1963. Nhung vet tich dau tien cua thoi dai do dong thou o Viet-Nam (Les vestiges du commencement de l'âge du bronze au Viet-Nam). Hanoi: Nha Xuat Ba'n Khom Hoc.

SCS Report 1959. *Yünnan Chin-ning Shih-chai-shan ku mu ch'ün fa-chüeh pao-kao* (Yünnan Provincial Museum: Report of excavations of a group of ancient graves at Shih-chai-shan, Chin-ning/Province Yünnan). 2 vols. Peking, Wen-Wu Press.

WW 1966. 4 Hunan sheng po-wu-kuan hsin fa-hsien-ti chi-chien t'ung-ch'i (Some newly discovered bronzes in the Hunan Provincial Museum). *Wen Wu*, 1–6.

WW 1972. 8 Yünnan Chiang-ch'uan Li-chia-shan ku mu chun fa-chüeh chien-pao (Preliminary report on the excavation of ancient tombs at Li-chia-shan, Chiang-ch'uan/Yünnan). *Wen Wu*, 7–16, pls. IV, V.

Yamamoto, T. 1939. Taikoku Unnanshō oyobi Tōkyō chihō shutto no sushū no seidoki ni tsuite (On several kinds of bronze implements unearthed in Thailand, Yünnan, and Tongking). Tōhō gakuhō (Tokyo) 10.2, 93–102, pls. I–VI.

The Late Prehistoric Period in Indonesia

I. C. GLOVER

Prehistory is a matter of a great deal of fantasy of such a degree of imagination that it sometimes appears questionable whether a sociologically and historically reliable construction of the facts can be made.

(van Leur 1967: 254)

The Problem

IN his great work, *Nusantara*, Professor Vlekke (1965: 22) pointed to the problem of the origin and evolution of early Indian-Indonesian cultural contact as, 'the crucial problem in Indonesian history'. It is a problem which some scholars had taken up before him and others wrestle with still. But a convincing framework from which even to approach the question is still quite lacking; and this, despite the considerable achievements of historians and epigraphers in refining our understanding of the extent of Indian influences in Indonesia and elsewhere in South East Asia, and outlining, roughly, the chronology of the events which brought this about. One most important element is largely unknown; the nature of pre-Indianized, Indonesian culture.

We can accept, sympathetically today, I think, van Leur's assertion that, 'the basis of Indonesian civilization was laid in the neolithic period and bronze age . . . and that it developed upon that indigenous basis' (van Leur 1967: 167). But as a prehistorian I take leave to regard with a certain scepticism his claim that this can yet be demonstrated, 'through the results of prehistorical research' (ibid.). Nevertheless, with the support of such an authority (and van Leur's insight into crucial problems and episodes in Indonesian history must be admired still today) I intend to look again at the scattered finds of trash and treasure which constitute our principle data on the Late Prehistoric period in Indonesia, to see if a useful, if not yet an 'historically reliable construction of the facts can be made'. If, in attempting this, I pillage the disciplines of ethnology, history, and geography, for ideas and data, it is a measure of my ignorance of almost all the important, and purely archaeological, aspects of the problems which ought to be considered.

Although there seems to be evidence to show that an Indianized state (Fu-nan) had developed in Cambodia by the late first or early second century A.D., there is said to be little reliable evidence to demonstrate Indian influences in Indonesia before the third century A.D. with the first inscriptions from the region appearing only in the fifth century (Coedès 1968: 16–19). This for my purposes marks the end of the Late Prehistoric period. For the opening of this period we must be flexible, given to lack of any regional, let alone Indonesia-wide, chronology which can stand on the basis of stratigraphic, typological, and radiometric observations and measurements. But I am thinking mainly of the first millennium B.C.

The process of Indianization has been the subject of academic controversy and even of national pride. Were the agents humble merchants of the *vaisya* class? Or knightly *kshatriya* warriors fleeing dynastic squabbles in India? Or Brahmin priests, magicians, and administrators, imported to give fame, authority, and organizational power to ambitious local rulers? There are important issues since they touch on the nature and complexity of the pre-Indian societies; and yet a total lack of knowledge of the primary sources has not prevented me from being convinced by the arguments of van Leur (1967: 103–4) and Bosch (1961: 3–22) that the last explanation is the most satisfying. Whatever the motivation for the Indians to travel, it was the internal needs of Indonesian societies which permitted Indian religious and political ideas to take root. It is clear, even from the fragmentary archaeological picture, that there was no massive Indian migration, no establishment of military and economic colonies, such as we find in the sixteenth and seventeenth centuries.

The Archaeological Sources

Indonesia has seen relatively little new archaeological research in the last twenty years and certainly no co-ordinated plans of survey and excavation within controlled geographical and environmental zones and involving workers from various disciplines, such as is now nearly standard procedure in Europe, western Asia, and the Americas. Furthermore, much of the slender research effort has gone into problems concerning the Pleistocene, or has not yet been published other than in a very preliminary form. It will be necessary, there-fore, to look on occasion outside Indonesia, to Malaysia, Thailand, the Philippines, Cambodia, and Vietnam, and then east to Melanesia, where recent excavations can help to place Indonesian finds within a better, although still barely adequate, chronological and distributional framework.

For the earlier work in Indonesia, van der Hoop (1940), Heine Geldern (1945), and H. R. van Heekeren have provided most valuable catalogues, sum-maries, and bibliographies of the excavations and finds recorded by scholars during the period of Dutch rule and the first few years of independence. Van Heekeren's *The Stone Age of Indonesia* (2nd ed. 1972) is largely devoted to Pleistocene material but Part II *c–d* (pp. 154–206) deals with finds attributed to a Neolithic phase of settlement, some of which concerns me here, and in the *Bronze–Iron Age of Indonesia*, van Heekeren (1958) summarizes the evidence for a post-Neolithic, pre-Indianizing cultural phase which he relates to Heine Geldern's 'Dong son Culture' of Indochina. The controversy surrounding the origins and antiquity of bronze technology in South East Asia is already well known and is discussed elsewhere in this volume (*supra*, pp. 15–31). Unfortunately, there is little new published evidence from Indonesia (but see R. P. Soejono's contribution on his excavations at Gilimauk, *infra*, pp. 185–198) to throw light on this vexed question, and we are still left with a profusion of mostly unprovenanced finds from throughout the archipelago, almost all of rather uncertain date.

In this paper I will be referring to the earlier research, for the most part, by way of the descriptions and discussion in the two books of van Heekeren, and in Heine Geldern's (1945) summary of the state of research up to 1941. Neither of these authors is exhaustive, and occasionally it is the case, as Bierling (1969: 2) has pointed out, that in comparing the original reports in Dutch with the summaries of them in the later works, 'much has been omitted which would be of vital importance in an analysis of South-east Asian prehistory'. Nevertheless, for the purposes of a synthetic and interpretive paper, the briefer and more accessible accounts are generally adequate.

Following van Heekeren's departure from Indonesia in 1956, and as a consequence of the economic and political problems which were then developing, archaeological research in the main islands of Indonesia slowed down. Soejono, working in Bali in the early 1960s was the only active professional fieldworker and has published preliminary reports (1962) on his work there, as well as recording the accidental finds which were reported to the National Archaeological Institute. In addition Soejono (1970) was able to document the history of the discovery of the country's archaeological remains and the varying interpretations put on them from the seventeenth century to 1950. In this important paper he revealed the many inadequacies of previous work and provided an assessment of what had been achieved.

The period after 1956, though difficult for Indonesian archaeologists, saw the intensification of field surveys and excavations in Sarawak and Sabah, under the energetic direction of Tom Harrisson. Although now forming western Malaysia, those territories must be considered together with Indonesia for the purposes of archaeology. But despite the controlled excavation of stratified deposits there, and the many preliminary publications, it is difficult to assess all the excavators' claims until proper site reports are available.

Of post-van Heekeren excavations (and Dr. van Heekeren's contributions indeed stand out as a major landmark in the field of Indonesian prehistory) there are a few which must be mentioned as providing data for the subject and period under discussion. Before the Dutch withdrew from west Irian some new finds had been made of bronze tools and ornaments in the Vogelkop and behind Humboldt Bay (Bruyn 1959, 1962; Elmberg 1959; Tichelman 1960,

1963) adding to van der Sande's (1907) earlier finds. In 1966–7 I myself undertook a series of excavations in caves in eastern (Portuguese) Timor (Glover 1969, 1971, 1972) which, though mostly concerned with earlier prehistory, yielded some evidence for the last millennium B.C. In Flores Father Th. Verhoeven recorded finds of bronze tools and petroglyphs (Verhoeven and Heine Geldern 1954; Verhoeven 1956), and continued his excavation of caves in Flores, Sumba, and Timor (Verhoeven 1968) and investigated a possible cemetery on Lomblen (Soejono 1962: 41–2; Lie Goan Liong 1965), in addition to his remarkable discoveries of extinct fauna and Pleistocene occupation (Maringer and Verhoeven 1970).

Finally, in 1969 a joint Australian-Indonesian expedition investigated cave deposits in south Sulawesi, already known from the work of van Heekeren and van Stein Callenfels. As in Timor, the results (Mulvaney and Soejono 1970*a* and *b*) relate mostly to a late Stone Age, probably pre-agricultural phase, but there is material, especially from the caves of Batu Edjaja 1, Ulu Leang 2, and Ulu Wae which is of interest here. Ulu Leang 1 and 2 were again excavated in 1973 by the present author, but no further results are available at the time of writing.

As suggested above, evidence for the late Prehistoric period in Indonesia comes, for the most part, from the very numerous, but largely unprovenanced or casually recorded, finds of ground stone axes and adzes, pottery, flaked stone projectile points, bronzes and moulds, beads and bracelets, from various types of burials, and from supposedly ceremonial stone structures and, in some regions, stone sculpture. Finds indicating village settlements are reported (Heine Geldern 1945: 134) and a few excavated; but even of these, few published accounts are available (van Heekeren 1972: 173–88). In addition, some of the sixty or so caves and ten shell middens which have been pratly investigated contain Neolithic or later material.

The lack of stratigraphic controls and independent dating has been mentioned, and this means that to organize this material we are still partly dependent on the criteria used by the archaeologists of the colonial era. Bierling (1969) has discussed this problem, but since his work is unpublished a few comments are needed. Almost all the earlier prehistoric archaeology was undertaken within the framework of ideas associated with the Vienna School of Diffusionists—who assumed that Stone Age cultures were essentially static, that innovation was rare, and that changes in archaeological material are most reasonably explained by the migration of people, or the diffusion of ideas and techniques from outside the region. Furthermore artefacts, like cultures, were arranged in a scale of technical sophistication—the cruder the older. Against a broad time perspective this may generally be true, but it is dangerously misleading when applied to individual artefacts or assemblages out of context. In addition individual traits were singled out to define the chronological and cultural status of finds. Thus material was called Palaeolithic if it was both crude in technique and associated with extinct animals. If the fauna contained only species still living, it was post-glacial; and accompanying artefacts were Mesolithic if there was no pottery, or Neolithic if pottery or polished stone tools occurred. Such procedures were reminiscent of the pioneer days of European prehistory and, in fact, procedures and assumptions were taken from the European experience with little regard for the effects of Pleistocene glaciation in tropical regions, or for the possibility that economic and technical development may have followed a rather different pattern in Asia.

Unpublished finds and as yet unreported excavations are numerous and make any assessment of the present state of knowledge difficult, especially for an archaeologist resident in London. But the compilations, summaries, and syntheses already referred to (van der Hoop 1941; Heine Geldern 1945; van Heekeren 1958, 1972; Soejono 1962, 1970), together with the preliminary publications of recent fieldwork, do provide a greater mass of material, unstructured though it is, than perhaps exists for any other country of South East Asia except North Viet-Nam. In following sections of this paper I will attempt to articulate some of this data with the aid of information available concerning the broad patterns of climate and resource distribution, and using ideas which have been developed by anthropologists concerning the principal structural types and interrelationships of Indonesian cultures.

The Geographical Setting for Indonesian Culture

There is virtually no palaeoclimatic data yet available from Indonesia for the period between 2,000–3,000 years ago,[1] and although active research has been under way in eastern New Guinea, it does not seem advisable yet to extrapolate from the results achieved there and in other parts of the world. I am assuming that winds, rainfall, seasonality, temperature, and land-sea relationships were not basically different from those of today.

Ho (1962) has summarized the meteorological data for the Indo-Australian tropics and has shown how the length of the dry season increases as one moves south and east from Sumatra towards the eastern Lesser Sunda Islands where between four and seven months may pass with less than 100 mm. of rain monthly. Although local relief is important, the rainfall is everywhere heavier in the northern winter (November–March), the pattern being determined by seasonal changes of air pressure above the continents of Asia and Australia and the movement of the Inter-tropical convergence zone. This seasonality corresponds quite well to differences in vegetation and, more roughly, to the percentages of land under forest today (Pelzer 1963: fig. 2) except in the densely settled parts of Java. Agricultural productivity is also determined by this seasonal rainfall pattern rather than by changes in temperature which are relatively small, altitude being more effective than seasonal variation. The heavy, year-round precipitation in Sumatra, Kalimantan, parts of Sulawesi and Moluku has led in many places to serious leaching and deterioration of the soil despite the productivity of the complex forests. Only where soil minerals are renewed by a continuous supply of young volcanic ejecta, as in Java, Bali, Lombok, and isolated parts of Sumatra, has dense, permanent agricultural settlement been possible (Mohr 1945; Pelzer 1963: map facing p. 12).

Thus, the interaction between seasonal variations in rainfall and soil fertility, within the complex island groups of Indoesia, has given rise to a few basically rather different settings for the development of human culture.

We can distinguish within the areas of almost year-round rainfall between, on the one hand Sumatra, Kalimantan, northern and eastern Sulawesi and Moluku as regions of low soil fertility and generally low settlement density, and Java, Bali, and Lombok with their rich volcanic soils. Then between these islands and those to the south-east where a long dry season produces a rather xerophytic vegetation and, with man's encouragement, extensive savanna grasslands (Pelzer 1963: 8; Ormeling 1955: 54–6) which themselves limit settlement with primitive technologies. Another contrast, perhaps more important archaeologically and culturally, is between coast and inland. The larger islands, naturally have more complex environments and variations in human adaptation. In the equatorial islands with leached soils the proportion of biological production open to exploitation by man is generally low as most exchange takes place in the high tree canopy and the non-human fauna is well adapted to life above the ground. Coasts, rivers, and lakes provide the best location for human settlement at whatever technological level, and expanding populations face limited choices. In Java and Bali these could be accommodated as a result of improved farming techniques, but in the equatorial islands intensification of agricultural production is traditionally very difficult, and improved technology more easily permits a better exploitation of aquatic resources with boats, nets, lines, traps, and poisons. With agriculture, greater economic diversification is possible than is commonly found in collecting societies. Coastal and river based societies can be highly mobile with the opportunity to specialize in fishing and trade in craft products, and the rare but valuable resources of the equatorial forest—resins, camphor, medicines, plumage, rattan, and canes, rare woods, pepper, spices, ivory, lac, and medicinal and poisonous plants. Inland, extensive agriculture was always possible provided a low density population permitted long fallow periods, and it appears to be both stable and efficient if measured in terms of output per man hour. Demographic change, so often ignored by archaeologists because of the inadequate and difficult data, may have been a key factor in determining patterns of cultural development in ancient Indonesia (cf. Introduction to, and various papers in, Spooner 1972).

In Sulawesi and Moluku, as in the west, coastal communities specializing in jungle products, craftwork, and fishing are well known in modern and recent historical times (Ellen and Glover, n.d.; Macknight 1973); and in Timor and Sumba, sandalwood (*Santalum album* L.) was a commodity valued and traded to the west from the time the earliest records are available (Ormeling 1955: 92–6). And in the eastern islands also, inland populations practised extensive swidden-agriculture, which limited to some extent the opportunities for the creation of states and urban centres. Clifford Geertz (1966) has shown very clearly the contrast in settlement patterns and densities within Indonesia, between the 'Inner' and 'Outer Islands' in the recent past. The other contrast I have made between inland and coastal, between maritime-oriented and agricultural societies, has also been made very explicitly by Hildred Geertz (1963: 25–32) when she postulated three broad types of Indonesian society:

(a) the strongly Hinduized inland wet rice peoples of Java and Bali.
(b) the trade-oriented, deeply Islamic coastal peoples—the 'Pasisir culture'.
(c) the mainly pagan tribal groups of the mountainous interiors of the outer islands.

It is against the background of the development of these cultural types, and the rôle of the first in effecting the Indianization of the inland societies of Java and Bali, that I want to examine the archaeological remains of the Late Prehistoric period.

Late Stone Age Cultural Development in South East Asia

By the late Stone Age in this context, I refer to the terminal or post-Pleistocene assemblages, cultures, or 'techno-complexes', which seem generally to predate the development of agriculture, partly to coexist with it, but were generally being abandoned by 2,000 years ago. In mainland South East Asia this phase is represented by what is commonly known as the Hoabinhian culture (Matthews 1964; Gorman 1971), for which uni- or bifacially flaked river pebbles form the most diagnostic artefact; and in the islands by a number of flake traditions (Glover 1973b). These we can date provisionally to *c.* 10000–5000 B.C. (but cf. Carbonnel, *infra*, pp. 223–226). Although they are generally outside the period under discussion here, one important point must be raised. The degree of differentiation within these cultural assemblages is higher in inland South East Asia than appears to be true for the Hoabinhian, confined as it is almost exclusively to the Asian continent. This may be due to the lack of discriminating typological analysis of the latter; but it is quite clear that in west and east Java, the southern Philippines, Sulawesi, Flores, Timor, and in New Guinea, localized areas have distinct typological traditions which have continuity over time within the area, but which scarcely affect neighbouring islands. Where there is reasonable stratigraphic and chronological evidence, in Palawan (Fox 1970), east Timor (Glover 1972), and Highland New Guinea (White 1972) the conservatism and continuity of artefact technology is pronounced, and is emphasized by the various excavators. Although man had been able to cross water barriers in the late Pleistocene, and to colonize Wallacea (Glover 1973*a*), New Guinea, and Australia, deep water transport can not have been very effective, for relatively closely neighbouring islands (Flores and Timor) show very different stone tool types. But as H. Geertz (1963: 25) points out, in recent Indonesian history, opposing coastal communities often have culturally more in common with each other than with the peoples of their respective hinterlands; the sea unites rather than divides. Such a pattern is not found among the late Stone Age cultures.

Early Agriculture in South East Asia

The original domestication of plants and animals in the region is not an issue here, nor the possible rôle of the Hoabinhian in effecting this. But of relevance is the abrupt appearance in layer 2 at Spirit Cave, north-western Thailand, of quadrangular adzes, cord-marked and burnished pottery, and bifacially-ground-edge slate knives. The excavator (Gorman 1971: 314–16) interprets this as the arrival of a new technological complex, marking the start of a shift in settlement from the inter-montane valleys to the lowland plains, and possibly associated with the development of rice cultivation. This is almost entirely consistent with the view long ago advanced by Heine Geldern (1945: 138–42) that the Quadrangular Adze Culture (*Vierkantbeilkultur*), an advanced Neolithic culture, expanded from the northern regions of South East Asia into the peninsulas and islands, bringing rice cultivation, domesticated buffaloes and pigs, the knowledge of bark cloth and outrigger canoes, together with the original Austronesian languages. The date suggested for this by Gorman's Spirit Cave—about 6800 B.C. (8,806±200 B.P.: Gak 1,846)—is earlier than Heine Geldern envisaged by some 4,000 years, and needs confirmation if it is to be accepted in the light of evidence from other 'neolithic' sites in Thailand, Cambodia, and Malaya. Data deriving from Ban Kao, the Bas-Plateaux sites, Gua Kechil, and Gua Harimau, are all more in harmony with Heine Geldern's estimates (cf. handlist of radiocarbon dates, *infra*, pp. 495–501). The recently published C14 dates for the Neolithic cultures of north China (Pearson 1973: 141–3) must also be considered if we think there is any validity in the theories for a Chinese origin of East Asian Neolithic cultures. They place the Yang Shao culture at Pan-p'o T'sun firmly in the first half of the fourth millennium B.C., and the Lung Shan culture in the late third and early second millennium B.C. The older dates, however, are strongly argued by the American and New Zealand excavators in Thailand (Higham

1972), and their case rests on evidence from a growing number of sites: Spirit and Ongba Caves, Non Nok Tha, Non Nong Chik, Ban Chieng, and Hàng-gòn in South Vietnam—none of which, however, is devoid of its own problems.

Whatever the absolute dates for these developments, it is clear that older cultural adaptations and artefact traditions were not replaced everywhere. The development of agriculture, animal husbandry, and permanent village settlement on the inland plains and in the river valleys of the South East Asian mainland, saw the start of a mosaic pattern with communities at different levels of social organization, with different artefact repertoires, and exploiting economically complementary environments, so typical of the region today as in the recent past. We should not be surprised if Hoabinhian culture lasted as long as it seems to have done at Laang Spean (Carbonnel, *infra*, p. 225), and in Malaya.

The Appearance of Bronze

The origin and antiquity of South East Asian bronze-casting technology is obviously important for an understanding of the late Prehistoric period, given the number of ancient bronze tools, weapons, drums, containers, and ornaments found throughout the archipelago. The evidence from Thailand is discussed by Bayard and by Smith (*supra*, pp. 15ff, 39ff), so I will make only a few comments on the present controversy. There seems to be inadequate evidence from controlled excavation of well preserved and clearly stratified sites to support unambiguously, either the new 'long' or the old 'short' chronology (Solheim 1968: 59–62). At the type site of Dong-son, as at Shi-zhai shan in Yunnan, the evidence is fairly clear that the bronze-using Dong-son or Tien culture was, in part at least, contemporary with the expanding Han empire. But impressionistically the material from these sites seems to represent the end of a long technical and aesthetic tradition; for instance, the drums at Shi-zhai shan are re-used, adapted for a different, if still ritual use, some by fixing of plates over the tympani bearing the famous tableaux (Watson 1970: 56). And both sites exhibit a greater range of artefacts, design motifs, and representational styles, than elsewhere; especially when compared with the Thai sites now claimed to be so much earlier in date. It is difficult to compress the development of such a sophisticated and complex tradition into a few centuries. But, the long chronology rests largely on the evidence from Non Nok Tha in north-east Thailand, from Ban Chieng, and from Hàng-gòn 1 (Saurin 1968: 1–3) in South Viet-Nam. The last two sites are inadequately investigated and reported, although the two lists of thermo-luminescence dates from Ban Chieng show an impressive pattern (*supra*, pp. 51–52). Non Nok Tha has been extensively excavated and published but quite contrary internal chronologies can be constructed from the growing number of C14 and TL dates (Bayard 1972). With its multiplicity of intercutting burial pits, each one disturbing and reincorporating deposit from the others, and from the thin habitation layer, Non Nok Tha is obviously not the site on which to base claims for a radical change in the accepted chronology using C14 dates derived, for the most part, from charcoal which is incorporated in the burial pits, but is of uncertain association with the burials themselves.

On balance, whereas 500–600 B.C. seems too late for the appearance of bronze-casting in South East Asia, more unambiguous evidence is needed before a time close to 3000 B.C. can be accepted.

The Evidence from Indonesia

A. *Polished Stone Axes, Adzes, and Knives*

These are by far the most numerous objects from the late Prehistoric period: many thousands must exist in public and private collections, and a considerable literature describes them. In addition to the sources quoted by van Heekeren (1972: 159) mention should be made of Duff's (1970) more recent survey of the adzes. These axes and adzes show considerable typological variation and they have traditionally been divided into two broad classes, Round and Quadrangular, with Shouldered Adzes being a subdivision of the latter. Each of these groups was thought to have been associated with the migration of distinct ethnic and racial groups from various parts of continental Asia (Heine Geldern 1945: 138–42). The 'Round Axe Culture' was believed to be the earliest and largely confined to north and eastern Indonesia— Kalimantan, north Sulawesi, Nusa Tengara Timor, Moluku, and the New Guinea lowlands. In western Indonesia adzes (with an asymmetrical longitudinal section) are more common than axes, and quadrangular forms dominate in Bali, Java, and south Sumatra. The antiquity of all these axe types in Indonesia is, of course, almost entirely unknown given the lack of recent excavated material. In Niah Great Cave, Sarawak, round axes are dated to *c.* 4000 B.C. and quadrangular adzes to *c.* 2000 B.C. according to Harrisson's 'Revised Niah Phaseology' (T. Harrisson 1967: 95); and a few quadrangular adzes survive as late as 500 B.C. or afterwards, as offerings in three of the cremation burials (B. Harrisson 1967: 198). In the 1969 excavations in south Sulawesi (Mulvaney and Soejono 1970*a* and *b*) no axes were found in any deposit excavated; and in Timor only one small lenticular-section adze of *Tridacna* shell was found at Bui Ceri Uato Cave, in a horizon difficult to date but provisionally assigned to the period 1500–500 B.C. (Glover 1972: 191). In caves in the south Philippines, ground shell adzes appear by 2500 B.C. (Fox 1970: 54). However, noting the age claimed for quadrangular adzes and ground slate knives at Spirit Cave, Thailand (*c.* 6800 B.C.), and the late

Pleistocene development of ground edge tools of the 'Round Axe' tradition in Australia, New Guinea, and perhaps in Borneo (Golson 1972: 537–49), it is clearly arguable whether many of the Indonesian 'neolithic' stone axes belong to the first millennium B.C.; such is the uncertain state of our knowledge!

Is there anything from these axes which can throw light on the nature of pre-Indianized Indonesian society? On the face of it not much beyond the fairly clear geographical divisions, and the indirect evidence for mastery of wood-carving, and high technical and aesthetic standards; for some of the largest pick and quadrangular adzes from west Java and south Sumatra are superbly finished, exploiting the natural markings of chalcedony and agate. But there are a number of sites in south Sumatra and Java, especially in the districts of Punung, Pacitan, and Wonogiri, where axe factory sites of an extraordinary richness have been recorded (van Stein Callenfels 1932: 25–9). In the former two districts, over 100 are known (ibid. pl. v) and indicate specialized manufacture and trade, from regions rich in raw materials to other parts of Java, if not outside the island, for silicious rocks are generally rare there. The factory sites seem to have concentrated on particular products, making blanks for either large or small adzes, for chisels, or for arrowheads (ibid. 26), with little overlap in types present at each location.

B. *Pottery*

Whereas polished stone tools have attracted much attention by archaeologists, and are often valued by the present-day villagers for their supposed prophylactic qualities, Neolithic pottery has been almost ignored in Indonesia because of its ultilitarian forms and simple decoration (but see Sutayasa 1972, 1973). Where sherds had been found in cave deposits attributed to 'mesolithic' cultures, in Toalian sites in Sulawesi (van Heekeren 1972: 108–16) or at Gua Lawa in Java (ibid. 93), these were thought intrusive from later times, just as were the sherds found in Hoabinhian sites in Malaya and Indochina (Tweedie 1965: 13). But again, recent excavations at Spirit Cave, at Gua Kechil (Dunn 1964), and at Laang Spean (Mourer and Mourer 1970), show that pottery has a much greater antiquity in South East Asia than previously recognized. In eastern Indonesia also, we now know that pottery was an integral part of those assemblages described as Mesolithic by van Heekeren, appearing in both Sulawesi and Timor at about 2500–3000 B.C. (Mulvaney and Soejono 1970*b*: 171–2; Glover 1969). Round-based cooking pots with everted rims seem to be the most common forms, at least in Indonesia, but the earliest material in Thailand exhibits a variety of decorative finishes: cord-marked, net-impressed, resin-coated, and burnished (Gorman 1970: 96–8).

It is difficult to discover from the many preliminary publications on the Niah Cave excavations exactly when pottery first appears in the archaeological sequence there, and its subsequent development. In the 1967 Progress Report, Harrisson (1967: 95) mentions pottery first in phase 6, the second of the two Neolithic phases, and gives a date of about 2000 B.C. In an earlier publication (Solheim, Harrisson, and Wall 1961: 167) however, pottery is said to be 'primarily associated with the cemetery, and, to the front, the pottery is mostly found in the top twelve inches with a much smaller number of sherds below that, and none below twenty-four inches'. In a yet earlier report (Harrisson 1957: 162), pottery is said to occur 'only fortuitously below 24 inches': the end of the edge-ground and beginning of the fully-ground, round-axe phase (phase 5). Golson (1972: 552), trying to interpret the Niah sequence, concluded that the earliest pottery, at the 24 in. level, might appear as long as 8,000 years ago. On the other hand, it is clear from Barbara Harrisson's analysis (1967) that the earliest of the 'neolithic' burials in the cemetery area, which includes most of the pottery, must be dated to 500 B.C. or after; and at least two of these burials contain bronze or copper tools (ibid. 188).

The Niah pottery has been divided into at least four groups on the basis of surface finish and decoration; plain, paddle decorated, polished, and painted-and-incised, and these groups are further subdivided. Painted-and-incised sherds account for only about 3% of the total and include what is termed 'Niah Three Coloured Ware' (Solheim, Harrisson, and Wall 1961: 168–9). Elements of incised decoration include meanders, scrolls, triangles, and interlocking arches, all singly or combined. Vessel forms of this ware are also varied and complex, whereas the carved and bound paddle decorated vessels are more commonly round-based, utilitarian vessels which have a wide distribution and a long life in the region. Nevertheless these, together with the Niah Three Coloured Ware, are incorporated into the Sa-huynh-Kalanay pottery tradition (Solheim 1966: 196–7) which is briefly discussed below.

The pottery reported by van Heekeren (1972: 185–90) from the site at Kalumpang on the Karama river, central Sulawesi, raises difficult questions. Plain sherds comprising 94% of the collections are assigned to the Neolithic, but all the decorated pieces are thought to be more appropriate for a later age. Solheim (1961: 182–3 and 1966: 205) has found parallels between the Kalumpang designs and those of his Sa-huynh-Kalanay complex, widespread elsewhere in South East Asia, and has pointed to the implications. Pottery of this tradition is found in purely Stone Age sites, as well as in those with bronze and iron. There are some distinctive features at each major locality, while many elements of decorative design and vessel form are shared between widely-separated communities in Viet-Nam, Thailand, Philippines, Malaya, Sarawak, and Indonesia. (See *Asian Perspectives*, 1959; and Solheim 1966.) Direct trade from a central source area can be ruled out, given the considerable differences which exist between each site or region, but quite clearly the communities making these wares were accomplished seafarers in regular communication with one another and participating in a cultural *oikoumene*. Other Indonesian sites with related pottery are said to be an urn-burial at Anyar, and at Buni, both in west Java (van Heekeren 1956*a*); the cemetery of Gilimanuk in west Bali; and an urn-cemetery at Melolo, east Sumba (van Heekeren 1956*b*). Some of the surface finds made by van der Hoop (1940: pls. 82–3) south-east of Lake Kerinci, south Sumatra, and others (unpublished) in the Rijksmuseum, Leiden, also are related; as are new finds of pottery from burial caves near Maros, south Sulawesi (Mulvaney and Soejono 1970*b*: pls. 9–12). Solheim (1961: 186–7) suggests that the Sa-huynh-Kalanay complex might be datable roughly to about 750 B.C.–A.D. 200, but obviously later finds have extended this. Within Indonesia the only dated new finds I am aware of are those from cave sites which I excavated in Timor in 1966–7 (Glover 1969, 1972: 378 pl. 10: 4). There, incised and impressed triangles, loops or semi-circles appear as exotic decorative elements in an existing pottery tradition during the period roughly 3,000–1,500 years ago. Other changes in the occu-pational debris, including the presence of goat bones, suggest that Timor came into more regular contact with the outside world at this time (Glover 1972: 368–9).

Solheim (1961: 187) also suggests that this widespread distribution of related pottery may be linked to Indonesian movement to Madagascar and East Africa, itself leading to contacts with, and a knowledge of, Indian civiliza-tion. No evidence of the settlement period in Madagascar is known to me; but the incised pottery from sites near Lake Alaotra (Fernandez 1970: 32–9), though apparently not ancient, lends some support to this through the presence in Madagascar of many quite typical Sa-huỳnh motifs.

C. *Burials*

Numerous burials have been found in Indonesia, some of which undoubtedly belong to the last millennium B.C. although few are properly dated. Apart from the occasional interments in cave deposits (e.g. at Niah Great Cave: B. Harrisson 1967) seven principal burial structures or containers can be recognized: urn-fields, stone slab or cist graves, stone-built graves, terrace graves, dolmens, rectangular stone sarcophagi, and cylindrical stone vats. Where any of these have been excavated in a relatively undisturbed condition, finds frequently include fragments of bronze, iron, gold, or glass which enabled van Heekeren (1958: 88) to conclude that they all belonged to the Bronze-Iron Age, and this seems a sound assessment on the evidence available.

Urn burials are known at Anyar in west Java; Ngrambe in east Java; Tebingtinggi in south Sumatra; Niah in Sarawak; Gilimanuk and Cekik in west Bali; Sa'bang in central Sulawesi; Salayar Island; and Melolo in Sumba

(Soejono 1969: 84–5; van Heekeren 1958: 80–9). The distribution is already quite wide but urn-fields are confined to coastal districts, except for the two grave urns from Tebingtinngi, and the urn-field at S'abang which is only 50 km. inland, and may not even have contained burials (Willems 1940: 207–8). Vessels from Tebingtinggi, Anyar, Gilimanuk, Cekik, and Melolo are are claimed to belong to the Sa-huỳnh-Kalanay tradition (Solheim 1961: 186; 1966: 205) and add support to the concept of a number of widely distributed, largely coastal communities during the South East Asian Early Metal Age, sharing many characteristics.

Cist graves are more restricted on present evidence, to the Pasemah Plateau in south Sumatra and to several localities in central Java (van Heekeren 1958: 51–2, 70–3). Stone sarcophagi are relatively common in east Java and inland Bali, and are known in Sumbawa and Sumba; and cylindrical stone vats are confined to north and central Sulawesi (Solheim, pers. comm.; van Heekeren 1958: 46–62); small stone burial jars have also been found in central Mindanao (Kinjack and Sheldon 1970). Terrace graves are described only from south Sumatra, although van Heekeren (1958: 69) notes that he has also seen them in south Sulawesi; and stone-built platform graves are common in Timor (Vroklage 1953, III, pl. XLVIII–XLIX). Within each of these types of burial structure, more than one form of interment has been reported: single and multiple complete interments, fractional burial, and perhaps even cremation (at Bada in Sulawesi). Compared with the distribution of urn-burials, the various forms of stone coffin are more commonly found in the inland districts of Sumatra, Java, Bali, Sulawesi, Mindanao, and Sumba, and show, it can be argued, rather greater regional differentiation than the urn-burial tradition. Unfortunately, neither the small finds nor the pottery from these sites are sufficiently published for detailed analysis.

D. *Stone Structures and Sculpture*

This leads to the vexed question of megaliths in Indonesia, a problem discussed elsewhere in this volume (*infra*, pp. 242–254). The sculpture so well-known from the Pasemah Plateau, Sumatra (van der Hoop 1932) most probably belongs to the same culture as the cist graves, dolmens, stone troughs, and terrace graves, found in the same area and provides valuable iconographic data for a reconstruction of dress, weapons, and ornament. Most authors agree that no Indian influence can be seen in this material, and that it represents a highly developed indigenous Bronze Age culture, and the beginning perhaps of the dynamic tradition of monumental stone sculpture which survived until recently in Samosir and the Nias Islands.

East of Sumatra prehistoric sculpture, other than on sarcophagi, is found at Pakouman in east Java and at Bada and Besoha in central Sulawesi; and dolmens, menhirs, and step-terrace structures and bathing places are common in Java, Bali, and the Lesser Sunda Islands. All this material was used by Heine Geldern (1945: 151) to develop a concept of an old and a young megalithic tradition. The former was believed to have introduced menirs, dolmens, stone seats, terraces and pyramids, and meeting places, and was associated with the Quadrangular Adze culture. The younger megalithic phase arrived with metal and introduced the cist and dolmen graves, and the various sarcophagi. There is, of course, no stratigraphic or recent independent dating evidence to support or to refute Heine Geldern's hypothesis, which stands as an imaginative attempt to wrest order from the data. However, I doubt that this is today a very useful way of interpreting the various prehistoric stone structures of Indonesia.

E. *Metal Finds*

The excavation of two important bronze period sites, Gilimanuk in west Bali and Leuwilliang (near Bogor) in west Java, is still in progress, but no results were available to me at the time of writing this paper. (But cf. Soejono, *infra*, pp. 185–198.) Almost all other pieces are largely undocumented, casual finds.

By far the most common category of metal finds are cast, socketed bronze and copper axes and agricultural tools which have been found in all the major island groups, but are most common from south Sumatra through Java and Bali to Flores and south Sulawesi (van Heekeern 1958: fig. 1). Soejono (1971) has distinguished eight main types with subdivisions, and has shown that while the simple axe is the most frequent and widely distributed, some varieties are quite restricted. A form of swallow-tail axe and a chisel type are confined to west Java, halberds are also found only in Java, heart-shaped axes and small votive forms are found only in Bali, and Roti has produced the only examples of a type of axe cast in one piece with the handle. In addition, two of the types of axes found in Irian Jaya are not found elsewhere in Indonesia. One of these, of which there are at least three recorded specimens has an extension of the splayed cutting edge to form a circle containing an open-work cross (Tichelman 1960: 34). The second local type in Irian has two cast loops for hafting near the open socket (de Bruyn 1962: 61–2); again, a form unknown in other parts of Indonesia. As with the incised and impressed pottery, common decorative traits on axes are widely distributed; but there is sufficient regional variation to refute any idea that these tools were all traded into Indonesia from sources on the mainland. In addition, moulds (or fragments of them) have been found near Bandung (Rothpletz 1951: pl. XI) and in Tapandong Cave, Sabah (Harrisson 1966: 175–6, pl. IIIb), and in Leang Buidane in the Talaud Islands (Belwood 1974: 6).

A great range of small bronze ornaments, bells, rings, figure pendants, and braclets, as well as occasional larger weapons, halberds, spearheads, and a dagger, have turned up at many places throughout the islands. Lost-wax and closed-mould casting were both practised, but as in China and on the mainland of South East Asia, no stage of simple open-mould casting has yet been recognized. Detailed technical investigation into early Indonesian metalworking has scarcely been attempted, but enough isolated analyses have been made to show that bronze alloys using both tin and lead were employed (van Heekeren 1958: 5, 22, 33, 35; Elmberg 1959: 79–80; Glover 1972, II: 32). It seems possible that lead was added to the larger and more complex castings but that tin-bronzes were preferred for cutting tools (Solheim 1964: 140–2). On the other hand, a typical socketed axe of Soejono's Type 1, found on the surface of a cave in eastern Timor consisted of 99·4% copper with only traces of tin, lead, and other elements (Glover 1972, II: 32). The lack of forging techniques is something of a mystery since later Indonesian iron-working was largely based on these. Perhaps they were developed only in response to different properties of iron, although the fact that the Timor copper axe was cold-hammered along the cutting edge to harden it (ibid. 34–5) suggests that the malleability of copper was already appreciated.[2]

Kettledrums obviously have a central place in the archaeology of pre-Indianized South East Asia and have attracted more detailed study than any other class of artefact. However, none has been found in a datable context in Indonesia, as they have in Viet-Nam and Malaya, and little can be added to the existing literature. Drums are certainly widespread in Indonesia and are most common in south Sumatra, Java, and Bali; but a surprisingly high proportion of drums, as with the axes and small bronze ornaments, have been found in the small islands of eastern Indonesia, and in Irian Jaya. In Bali, Alor, and Flores, a distinctive local form of drum (*moko*) developed which shows that these, at least, were made within that region. The others, all said to be Heger Type I drums, cannot be distinguished from the ancient drum types of the mainland.

Drums, axes, and some ornaments, share many elements of decoration, which is usually arranged in concentric or parallel bands utilizing circles, triangles, interlocking key, scroll, and meander patterns. Birds appear frequently and are usually represented in a highly stylized manner using triangles for the body, head, and wings, and with an exaggerated linear distortion. Human figures, fish, and animals in hunting scenes are rather more naturalistically portrayed; and boats, houses, and village scenes provide an important source of information for a reconstruction of daily life as well as religious iconography.

It is difficult to show that bronze and copper objects are more common in coastal than inland areas in Indonesia, as seems to be the case with the urn cemeteries when compared with the stone sarcophagi vats and ceremonial structures. But the wide distribution of finds and the surprising number from the smaller islands of Indonesia, as well as the representational emphasis on boats, all support the idea of a network of inter-regional trade throughout the archipelago, and linking Indonesia to the mainland.

Patterns in the Late Prehistoric Period

It is not easy from the inadequate sources outlined above to integrate the 'facts' of Indonesian archaeology into a framework which carries any more conviction than the purely diffusionist models of earlier generations. Although we may reject these on grounds of principle, it is difficult to show that their reconstructions are wrong, except for minor points or for alterations to their chronology which are not fundamental.

Nevertheless, I think another sort of pattern is latent in the data, which it may be more profitable to test against future fieldwork results, and which is more in keeping with the current reaction against the habit of seeking external cases and sources for change (cf. Clarke 1966).

By the end of the Pleistocene, all the major areas of Indonesia had long been colonized by man and strongly individual traditions of stone-working had been developed within each of the islands where remains have been found. We might make an analogy with the phenomenon of genetic drift exhibited by animal species newly colonizing islands.

In the mid-Recent period, expanding agricultural populations were spreading through these islands to New Guinea. Restricted intra-regional trade such as is found in the Melanesian trading cycles (Brookfield with Hart 1971: 314–34) may have started to integrate areas on the mainland and neighbouring islands and coasts into a few broad culture areas, at least in so far as these can be recognized on the basis of stone axe types.

(1) Thailand and Indochina;
(2) South China and Taiwan;
(3) The Philippines and western Malaysia;
(4) Malaya, Sumatra, Java, and Bali;
(5) The eastern Lesser Sunda Islands and Moluku.

Later, perhaps by the second millennium B.C., distinctions can be recognized between inland and coastal communities in the larger islands. In Java, Bali, and parts of south Sumatra, expanding populations could intensify their agriculture because of favourable soil and climatic conditions. Elsewhere, and especially in coastal districts and on the smaller islands, only the sea provided opportunities for expansion, and outward-looking, highly mobile communities developed, spreading common items of material culture, ideology, and artistic design throughout the region; the forerunners of the 'Pasisir cultures' of recent Indonesian history. These people had developed regular trading links between mainland South East Asia, India, Madagascar, and New Guinea by the first millennium B.C. Just as the Pasisir peoples were the first in Indonesia to be affected by Islam, so this network provided the means whereby earlier Indian religious ideas and art could spread through South East Asia to take root and be developed along indigenous lines by the more densely settled agricultural peoples of the great river valleys of the mainland and of the rich inland plains of Java. The Pasisir societies emerge in Indonesia in historical times from the inscriptions in east Kalimantan, Malaya, west Java, and Sumatra, and are finally recognizable in the maritime empire of Srivijaya.

NOTES

1. Palynological work is now in progress in the Lake Kerinci district of south Sumatra, and in central Java. In the former area a pollen column extending back to 10000 B.C. has been obtained, but other results are not yet available. (J. Flenley, personal comm. Oct. 1973.)

2. P. Sørensen suggested during the London Colloquy that the form of iron tools in South East Asia was affected more by pre-existing stone and shell tools than by the bronze axe types.

ADDITIONAL REFERENCES

Bellwood, P. 1974. Report on archaeological research in Sulawesi Utara (Minahasa, Sangihe, and Talaud Islands) prepared for LIPI and ARGC (unpub. roneo ANU Canberra).

Clark, J. D. G. 1966. The invasion hypothesis in British archaeology. *Antiquity*, 40: 172–89.

Harrisson, T. 1966. A stone and bronze tool cave in Sabah. *Asian Perspectives*, 8 (for 1964): 171–80.

Solheim, W. G. II. 1964. Philippine notes. *Asian Perspectives*, 7 (for 1963): 138-43.

The Significance of the Excavations at Gilimanuk (Bali)

R. P. SOEJONO

Introduction

EXCAVATIONS at Gilimanuk, north-western Bali, in 1963, 1964, and more recently in 1973, produced evidence of coastal settlement during late prehistoric times. The data obtained are unique for Indonesia and have provided deeper insight into the life of the people of that period, which appears to be of a complex nature. Before the Gilimanuk discovery was made, evidence of coastal habitation was limited to remains of burials, particularly of burials using earthenware jars. Stretched burials are in some cases found associated with these jar burials. Such burials seem to originate from around the beginning of the Christian era (van Heekeren 1958: 83) and have been discovered at Sclayar, south Sulawesi (Schröder 1912), Melolo, Sumba (van Heekeren 1956a), Anyer, west Java (van Heekeren 1956b), and Lewoleba, Flores (Verhoeven 1961; Soejono 1969: 6). Other important sites of coastal habitation, heavily disturbed through illicit exploration, are found in the northern areas of west Java (Soejono 1962). These sites have yielded a large number of neolithic quadrangular adzes, a fair amount of bronze and iron objects, various types of glass beads and small gold ornaments frequently found in association with burials. Neither the system of these burials nor their connection with stone or metal artefacts has been properly established. Stretched burials furnished with funeral objects, in particular earthenware vessels, seem to have been common practice.

The Gilimanuk project was started during the author's term of service as head of the branch office of the Archaeological Institute from 1960 to 1964 and has not yet been finished. Excavations were conducted as follows: in stages of one or two weeks' digging during July, August, and September 1963; in three months of continuous digging from September until December 1964; and in two weeks' digging in April 1973. The project was executed by eight staff members of the Archaeological Institute of Jakarta and Bali, assisted by ninety students from the Departments of Archaeology of the University of Indonesia (Jakarta), Gajah Mada University (Yogjakarta), and Udayana University (Denpasar). The students participated in groups of fifteen to twenty persons, each group in turn excavating for two weeks.

Excavations so far accomplished cover an area of approximately 137·5 sq. m.

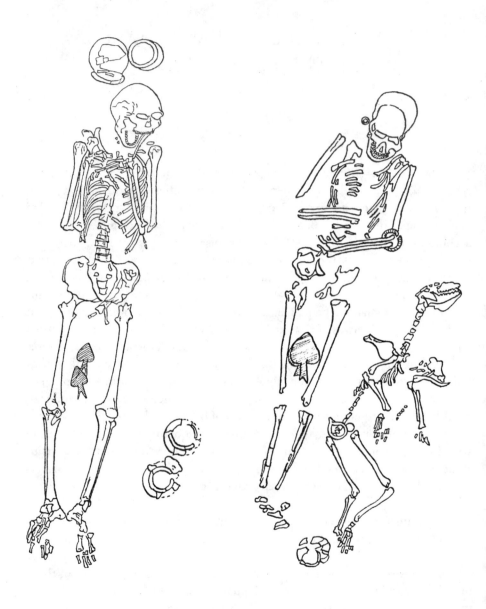

FIG. 1. Primary burial in stretched position (left)
FIG. 2. Primary burial in stretched position, accompanied by a dog (right)

and touch an average depth of 2 m. (min. approx. 1·75 m. and max. approx. 3·25 m.). The stratigraphical composition of the excavated soil indicates a considerable extension of habitation levels south and south-westwards, but occupation seems to have been most dense in the excavated area. The excavation of twenty-two pits, each measuring 2·5 × 2·5 m., produced a large amount of material which needs careful study of its different components. The greater part of the excavated material has been transported to the head office of the Archaeological Institute in Jakarta, while part is kept at the branch office at Bedulu (Bali). The human skeletons have been sent to the Anatomical Section of the Faculty of Medicine of Gajah Mada University. Up to the present, circumstances have been unfavourable for carrying out analytical work, and it is therefore only possible to set forth the most outstanding facts about the Gilimanuk finds. The Gilimanuk project has not yet achieved final results.

Systematic collection of charcoal was only started early in 1973, after contacts with foreign research institutions had been re-established. Excavations in 1963 and 1964 had to be carried out within the limits imposed by the local facilities, and therefore without the possibility of using up-to-date methods or carrying out analytical work. Further excavations will be attempted in order to gain sufficient systematized data to draw up a thorough reconstruction of the life of the people of prehistoric Gilimanuk.

Preparatory Stage: Discovery and Plan of Excavation

The author was informed in 1961 that earthenware jars and a few neolithic adzes had been found at Cekik, a hamlet situated about 6 km. south of Gilimanuk. The discovery had been made during the Japanese occupation, when construction was started on the road which connects Gilimanuk with Singaraja and which cuts through the bushy area of Cekik (Soejono 1962).

A survey at Cekik was carried out in February 1962. Trial excavations were undertaken shortly afterwards at presumably undisturbed spots alongside the southern border of the road. Numerous potsherds, scattered for several hundred metres along both sides of the road, gave some prospect of recovering jars either in complete or damaged condition at this fertile-looking site. The results of the excavation fell short of expectations. The excavated material mainly consisted of plain and decorated potsherds, besides some fragments of animal bones (cattle and fowl) and a few small grinding stones. Two varieties can be distinguished in the Cekik potsherds: namely the coarse variety, made by hand, and a less common variety of finer quality probably manufactured by means of the wheel. The common types of coarse pottery were round-bottomed jars of various sizes without distinct rim, simply having a thickening at the lip. The exterior, including the lip, is entirely decorated with a design of crossed or parallel lines, using carved paddles. Sherds of finer quality are

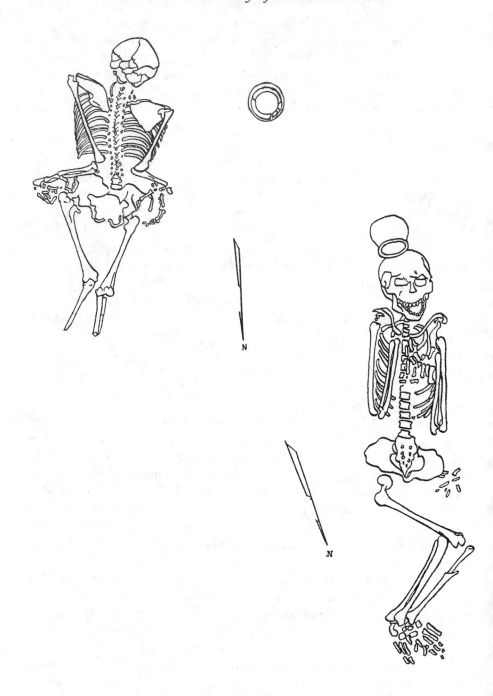

FIG. 3. Primary burial in prostrate position
FIG. 4. Primary burial in semi-flexed position

thinner and show variations of rim form. The common decoration is the impressed net-design applied with a carved paddle. Plain and polished sherds, as well as sherds bearing incised decoration, belong to this second group of pottery.

Starting from the evidence that jar fields commonly occur near seashores and that the coast of the Gilimanuk bay, being sheltered from rough sea-waves, is a suitable place for settlement, the author began his observations on the southern shore of the bay during intervals in the Cekik excavations. An east- and westward sloping elevation with an altitude of *c.* 5 m. was observed near the seashore. The section of this low plateau facing the sea was heavily eroded, since the base of the plateau lies within reach of the high tide. On the narrow bay shore along the plateau, scattered fragments of human bones, pot-sherds (ornamented and plain), broken shells, glass beads, and bronze fragments were found, which all seemed to have been washed out from the dissected part of the plateau. The potsherds found here are almost identical to the Cekik sherds. Inspection of the eroded slope, immediately after this discovery, revealed two complete round-bottomed pots with net-impressed decoration. The pots, *in situ*, were placed several centimetres inside the dilapidated wall. The smaller pot contained a pounding stone. Two more pots had previously been dug out by villagers and were reported to the author at this stage of the survey. These pots resemble in size and shape the bigger type mentioned before. A small trial pit was made on the plateau adjacent to the eroded slope to establish the composition of earthlayers. This test-digging yielded mainly decorated and undecorated potsherds, remains of edible shells, bone fragments, and an iron chopping knife. The results of the survey and of the test excavation led the author to the conclusion that the Gilimanuk plateau must have been the seat of intensive human occupation, quite probably during the Early Metal Age.

A plan was made to conduct a total excavation at this newly discovered site, to be started before improper activities could harm the as yet undisturbed condition of the site (fig. 2). Selective excavations were performed in three stages during July, August, and September 1963, in order to acquire the greatest possible insight into the structure and content of the soil before large scale excavation could be undertaken. The box system was applied as an excavation technique for the whole operation; a box measuring 2·5 × 2·5 m. could be under the control and responsibility of one small group of excavators. The use of this technique seemed appropriate in view of the physical character of the site, in open country covered for the greater part with wild grass. Baulks left between the excavated pits measured 0·50 m. in width. Selective excavation carried out in 1963 on three sectors produced encouraging results. Beside remnants of pottery and shell (which formed the main element of the whole excavated material of the Gilimanuk site) a number of burials, among

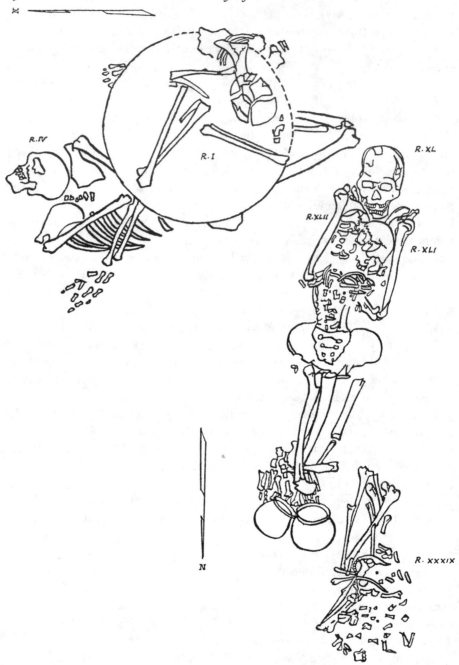

FIG. 5. Secondary burial as an urn internment, together with a primary burial in prostrate position placed beneath

FIG. 6. The combined piling-up system, with primary burial in stretched position and a double secondary burial; also a disturbed secondary burial

them a double urn burial, were recovered almost intact. Excavations in 1964 were conducted continuously for a period of three months (from September until December) on a much larger scale. In total sixteen pits (sectors) were dug during this period. Burials of approximately 100 persons (adults and children) were found, for the most part furnished with funeral gifts such as earthenware vessels, beads and other ornaments, bronze and iron objects, as well as animals (dogs and pigs). Excavation of three more sectors in April 1973 recovered two burials of children, furnished with pots and bronze objects. Charcoal particles were collected from different levels of occupation and a statistical approach was attempted for the first time, to determine the density of potsherds and waste shells from the different sectors. A trial trench was dug about 50 m. south-west of the main area of excavation. The structure of the soil here corresponded exactly with that of the excavated sectors elsewhere, although with a lower density of potsherds and shells. This proves that occupation extended further south-west, especially at the fringe area of the low plateau. Excavations should be continued to obtain more complete data of the Gilimanuk settlement.

Data from the Excavations

A. *Stratigraphy*

The plateau is built up of four layers, which appeared consistently throughout the excavated area. The third, or occupation layer, particularly varied in thickness. The structure as a whole yielded the following components (fig. 4):

Layer 1: Black humus, disturbed at several places by human action. This layer contained some waste materials from recent times. Potsherds and shells from lower levels appeared at disturbed sections. The average thickness of this humus was approx. 20 cm.

Layer 2: Yellow-grey coloured fine-grained soil. The bottom contained potsherds and shells, with indication of a gradual transition into the layer below. Skeletons of pigs were recovered in several sectors at the bottom of this layer.[1] Average thickness of the layer was approx. 15 cm.

Layer 3: Light to dark brown coloured composition of clay and sand, with cultural remnants which included a large quality of potsherds and shells, isolated vessels, pieces of ornaments, and fragments of metal objects. Other substances were skeletal fragments of pigs, fowl, and fish. Human burials only came up in some sectors. Thickness of this layer of habitation varied between about 75 cm. and 150 cm. Intercalations of sand occurred at different levels. Decrease in quantity of potsherds and shells at the bottom level indicates gradual transition into the lower sand **layer**

Layer 4: Light grey sand. Most of the human burials furnished with gifts were revealed in the upper level of this sand layer, usually down to *c.* 75 cm. below the bottom level of the previous layer. Some potsherds and shells of the type generally found at burial places imply interment immediately below the living floor. The depth of the sand layer has not been checked; sand excavated 50–100 cm. below burials proved to be sterile.

B. *Remains of Habitation*

Remains of human activity are concentrated in the third, or habitation, layer. Nearly all are found in fragmentary condition, only small numbers of isolated earthenware pottery and some small beads of glass and shell being in a good state. Funeral goods—made of bronze, iron, gold, glass, shell, and baked clay—from the sand layer are usually well preserved. The huge compound of collected artefacts, fragments as well as complete specimens, will be categorized and described in general terms only, since final results are not yet available. The total collection gives an impression of the daily life of a settlement such as this.

C. *Pottery*

The Gilimanuk pottery comprises decorated and undecorated ware. The majority of potsherds consist of undecorated, commonly burnished, fragments of various types of earthenware. Impressed net motif seems dominant, especially on globular pots (with flaring or everted rims) which are frequently found in association with burials. This motif covers the entire body of pots except for the rim portion. Other decorations shown on a number of sherds are incised straight or wavy lines and dashes, applied in various arrangements below the rim around the neck. A few potsherds show carved paddle marks of parallel and crossed lines. Scallop design on the angle is found on several sherds. Traces of red and yellow paint are visible on some earthenware pieces. The Gilimanuk earthenware pottery, as far as can be proved from complete specimens and reconstructed pieces, includes the following items: round-bottomed pots with various rims or without rims (considered to be the most typical form); dishes or plates; shallow simple bowls; carinated bowls; double rimmed vessels; vessels with angles; flat-bottomed containers; small pedestalled bowls (incense burner type); lids with a handle, and globular pots with elongated neck. Dishes, simple bowls, flat-base containers and lids are generally undecorated. Sherds of more than usual thickness are fragments of jars. Several broken specimens of this kind of pottery contained disintegrated human skeletons. This indicates that jars had a supplementary function as burial jars. The jars are round-bottomed and decorated with impressed net design all over the exterior, or are not decorated at all. The colour of the Gilimanuk earthenware varies from greyish-brown to reddish. Manufacture of the ware was evidently by hand. The Gilimanuk pottery is closely related to the pottery of Cekik, particularly to the group of finer ware, but it is more elaborate in shape and decoration. Both varieties of pottery show elements which are related to certain types of Sa-huỳnh-Kalanay pottery.

D. *Metal Objects*

Bronze objects consist mostly of funeral gifts such as the typical Balinese ceremonial axes of various dimensions, with heart-shaped and crescent-shaped blades; wristlets; foot-rings; ear-rings; and spirals. Several isolated axes, usually damaged, and fish hooks are probably discarded or lost objects. A new type of prehistoric bronze are the small pentagonal plates found under human skulls.

Iron objects are found far less frequently than the numerous bronze artefacts. Fragments of iron, beside slag, are probably pieces of unidentifiable objects. Worth mentioning are three specimens of spearheads and two specimens of daggers found connected with burials. The grip of one of the daggers is made of bronze, while remnants of a wooden shaft are traceable on both artefacts. Traces of coarse textile, seemingly wrapping material, are noticeable on the shafts.

A few human skeletons were provided with *gold* ornaments. Prominent among these were beads found near the neck and abdomen. These tiny beads were commonly shaped as irregular spheres and hollowed discs. Eleven pieces of cone-shaped ornaments were found on a human skull. Another skull had a thin foliated piece of eye-cover showing a pair of crevices in the centre. A small ring was found, not connected with any burial.

E. *Beads*

A large number of beads are found singly or in groups throughout the habitation layer. Beads belonging to burials appeared on different parts of the skeletons, namely at the neck, wrists, ankles, and pelvis. The common type of bead is made of glass, cylindrical in shape and dark blue in colour. Average diameter, as well as thickness, is approximately 0·5 cm. Other types of glass beads are smaller, sometimes even as small as a pinhead, and are red-brown, yellow, light green, and blue. The red-brown type is the so-called *Mutisala* which is found widely spread over the Indonesian archipelago and neighbouring areas. Small, flat circular beads made of shells are frequently found. Another type is the round-shaped carnelian bead, found near the ear of several skulls. Its diameter sometimes exceeds 1·5 cm.

F. *Armlets of Glass*

Skeletons were often provided with wristlets of glass, of blue, green, or brown colour. The blue and green specimens are common types, while brown wristlets are rare. The inside diameter of wristlets is about 7–8 cm. Common types are about 1 cm. thick and have either concavo-convex or semi-circular cross sections. The brown wristlets are flat with broad surface and they are all in a worn state.

G. *Armlets of Shell*

Some skeletons wear armlets made of big shells (big spider shell of *Strombidae*, big snail-like shells *Pleurotomariidae* and *Tridacna* shells). The diameter of these armlets is similar to that of the specimens made of glass. Cross sections of shell armlets vary from semi-lenticular to semi-oval. Pieces of unfinished shell armlets occurred in the habitation layer. Rare specimens are flat armlets with broad surface, these deteriorated after exposure.

H. *Objects of Stone*

Small mortars with shallow holes, small pounding stones and pestles showing abrasions on the used surfaces. Some rough stone cleavers can be included in this category of stone utensils. Neolithic adzes which are occasionally found at Early Metal Age sites on Java, do not occur here.

J. *Instruments of Shell*

Waste shells have been used for making simple instruments. Especially the very sharp edge of broken shells is suitable for cutting and scraping. Points, borers, scrapers, knives, and spoons are easily manufactured by fashioning broken pieces of shell. Scrapers and points are often made of the ventral margins of bivalve shells. Spoons and shallow cups are made of the concave walls of big cowry shells.

K. *Animal Remains*

Shellfish must have been daily food for the Gilimanuk settlers. Much sought after were cone shells, bivalve shells, mussels, snail-like shells, and sea snails. Classification of shell types collected from the excavations is not finished yet. Complete skeletons of pigs, dogs, and poultry (most probably chickens), accompanying human burials, were recovered; these animals must have been sacrificed to various deceased persons. Isolated bones, skulls, and mandibles of pigs as well as dogs, bones of small animals (probably bats and rats) and fish bones belong to the mixture of waste material in the habitation layer. This collection of animal bones and fragments has not yet been classified.

L. *Other Finds*

Also worth mentioning are all sorts of stray objects unearthed from the habitation layer. These comprise among others a perforated incisor of a dog, perforated pendants of shell, bird-like figurines of baked clay, a pedunculate stamp of baked clay bearing impressed net design on the circular surface, pieces of glass, metal, and small cowry shells.

The Burials

Most significant in the Gilimanuk discovery are the burials. The varied positions of skeletons and the wealth of funeral goods prove that the Gilimanuk settlers took good care of the deceased. Variations in skeletal deposition were such that it seems difficult to define any coherent system. Observations of burials which contained complete as well as incomplete and disturbed skeletons, however, made it possible to draw interesting conclusions as to the treatment of the deceased, and concerning the belief that the souls of the dead remain in touch with the living. Skeletons sometimes lack the skull, shin bones, both feet, or other parts of the body. Such mutilation of essential parts of dead bodies seems to have been a measure taken to prevent the deceased interfering with the life of their descendants. Skeletons of adults and children, usually not exceeding three persons, piled up or placed close together, indicate burials of nuclear families. Extraction of skeletons, observed in several cases, was obviously done to make room for subsequently interred deceased. The separated bones of the extracted skeleton were arranged as a secondary burial, on top of the subsequent burial which is normally extended. The arrangement of secondary burials followed a consistent pattern: namely the placing of ribs and smaller bones between limb bones, with the skull on the upper side. Isolated secondary burials might be skeletons re-buried a certain period after death. Gifts to the deceased, such as adornments, ceremonial objects, and domestic animals, create the impression of preparing a new life for the deceased, as a continuation of his life on earth and under similar conditions. The general orientation of burials is with the head placed more or less in the south, facing the bay of Gilimanuk which lies north of the settlement. This orientation was not strictly adhered to; a number of skeletons were deposited in diverse directions.

Four main systems could be derived from the complex variety of the burials. Primary burials (first system) and secondary burials (second system) were most frequently encountered. Variations of each system, singly or in multiples and a combination of both (third system), are numerous, indicating an almost unlimited choice of interment. Urn burials (fourth system) occurred only twice at the Gilimanuk site, but are unique because of the use of double jars as a funeral medium. Variations of the system will be briefly summarized below.

This temporary list is based on selections from the burials of approximately 100 skeletons of adults and children under various conditions.

I. *Primary burials*

These consist of a single skeleton or of two skeletons. If two skeletons, they may be in the same position or in various combinations of positions, and placed either one on top of the other (double piled up) or in counter direction. Main trends in the primary burials are:

(1) the single burial in various positions (figs. 2, 3);

(2) the double burial in piled up position (fig. 6);

(3) the double burial in counter position.

Positions of skeletons are designated as: (*a*) extended/stretched, (*b*) semi flexed (fig. 4), (*c*) squatted/crouched, (*d*) dorsal with spread knees, (*c*) kneeling, and (*f*) prostrate (fig. 3).

Arms are stretched or the fore-arms folded with the hands placed on the breast or below the chin.

II. *Secondary burials* consist of:

(1) the single burial (fig. 5);

(2) the double piled up burial;

(3) the triple piled up burial;

(4) the double side by side burial;

(5) the double linear burial.

III. *Combined burials* comprises:

(1) the primary single burial and the secondary single burial;

(2) the primary single burial and the secondary double piled up burial;

(3) the primary single burial and the secondary double linear burial;

(4) the primary double piled up burial and the secondary single burial.

A few burials have not been categorized, because of disorderly positions of bones. These burials may have been shifted from the original graves to obtain space for subsequent burials.

IV. *Double jar burials*

The custom of using double jars did not exist anywhere in Indonesia, except at Gilimanuk. The jars are joined mouth to mouth and placed vertically in the ground. The lower jar, which is bigger than the one on top, contained a secondary burial of a single person. Skeletons in the jars of Gilimanuk were not furnished with gifts. Very interesting was the discovery of evident human sacrifice in connection with jar burial here. A skeleton in prostrate position was found below a double jar. The skull squeezed backwards, the elbows pulled towards the back, and the legs folded backwards, seemed to indicate intentional killing. The placing of skeletons in jars seems to have been carried out in a few cases of deceased persons of prominent status. The sacrificed person was presumably intended to accompany the eminent deceased on his journey to the hereafter.

Some Considerations

The Gilimanuk archaeological material, though still incomplete, is sufficient to enable us to describe conditions of life which flourished towards the end of the period before the Hindu civilization entered Indonesia. It not only gives us an idea of the context of a specific settlement, but also some insight into a social situation which prevailed in the Early Metal Age. The Gilimanuk material displays a stage of local craftmanship and it also reflects economic endeavours and spiritual conceptions. An outstanding idea is the belief in the continuous relationship between the living community and the spirit world of its deceased ancestors.

That communication existed between the Gilimanuk coastal community and inland people in the mountainous areas is apparent by similarities in their material cultures and by related spiritual ideas. The custom of the double jar burial at Gilimanuk for instance[2] seems influenced by the tradition of sarcophagus burial which developed in inland Bali (Soejono 1965). Lack of volcanic stone—the material used for building sarcophagi—caused the Gilimanuk settlers to introduce double earthenware jars for the burying of prominent persons. This concept of burying also developed inland. The Gilimanuk settlers show a distinct life style adapted to the natural setting of the bay. Only thorough observation of excavated material can give us details of life in the Gilimanuk community. A superficial glance at the data shows some prevalent aspects of this life. Fishing and collecting sea shells, domestication of animals (pigs, dogs, poultry), and small game hunting (of wild boar, birds, rats, bats) are the bases of economic life. Manufacture of daily utensils, such as earthenware and simple instruments, iron objects, and some types of beads, was obviously carried out at the settlement. Trade with neighbouring inland areas in earthenware, metal objects (especially bronze and gold ware), and beads seems to have occurred. It is still premature to decide whether communications with regions outside Bali existed, although resemblances to certain of its features are found in the Archipelago. Metallurgy was not practised at Gilimanuk, as evidence of moulding is not found there; but it is evident that it had achieved a developed stage on Bali as a whole. This is proved by discoveries of bronze axes, kettledrums, and stone moulds in inland regions which are considered as specific specimens in the prehistoric bronze collection. The belief in the spirits of the ancestors, either for good or for evil, developed into complicated systems of burial practice. The manner of treatment of buried persons indicates their ranking in the community. It also points to a structure of groups in the society.

The Gilimanuk findings show us a sample of community life at that time, which was varied by diverse conditions, but was still inter-related in many ways. Later it was influenced by the Hindu civilization, and societies of greater complexity developed, especially in Sumatra, Java, Bali, and Kalimantan. The basis of those developments, however, had been formed during the preceding period.

NOTES

1. Export of pigs to Java via the harbour of Gilimanuk continues today. Pigs are stored near the harbour complex. In former times the bay area served as a place to bury pigs which died before embarkation.

2. Double jar burials are also found in the Philippines and Japan (Solheim 1960). A connection with Bali is not looked for, as the burials exist in different contexts.

The Later Prehistory of the Malay Peninsula*

B. A. V. PEACOCK

Introduction: the Physical Environment

WE have been told that 'when South-East Asia felt the earliest impact of Indian culture, it possessed a civilization of its own' (Hall 1964: 8). What was the nature of this civilization and what rôle did it play in the creation of later Indianized South East Asia? These are perhaps among the most central questions in early South East Asian history.

The present paper, concerned as it is with the later prehistory of the Malay peninsula, does not aspire to offer any general answers to such broad and far-reaching questions. It may be possible, however, to give some account of the data currently available for a limited but nonetheless important part of the region and to touch briefly on some of the outstanding problems of interpretation.

The Malay peninsula and its rather special environment have clearly played a considerable rôle in shaping the course of human history from earliest times until the present. One finds, however, that there has been a tendency to isolate two factors alone out of the many that are relevant and these, at first glance, appear to be in conflict. The first and commonest image, at least in reconstructions of prehistoric times, is of the peninsula as a 'corridor' or 'funnel' along which successive waves of population and ethnic types, Australoids, Oceanic Negroids, Proto- and Deutero-Malays, have passed. The second stresses the rôle of the peninsula as a barrier to communications, particularly as an obstacle to the sea-borne trade of the Indianized States period and later.

The almost proverbial luxuriance, variety, and extent of peninsula and South East Asian vegetation has been responsible for a widespread but erroneous belief in the miraculous fertility of their soils. The virgin forests in fact exist in a rather precarious equilibrium between the rate of humus accumulation and its reabsorbtion as plant food. This state of equilibrium is fairly easily disturbed. It has been pointed out that where soil temperature exceeds 75° the breakdown of humus by bacterial and chemical action outstrips the rate of accumulation. The felling of forest, for example by swidden cultivators, can have disastrous effects on soil fertility. The limited supply of humus disappears, and the soil, deprived of cover, is exposed to the leaching

* See Plate VIII.

effects of torrential rains and increased biochemical and chemical action brought about by rising temperatures. Under these conditions severe erosion can begin and virtually irreversible damage be done (Fisher 1964: 50). The peninsula environment offers a strictly limited potential for sedentary sub- sistence agriculture based on wet rice cultivation.

As though to compensate for its poor agricultural potential and its conse- quent low capacity to support large populations in ancient times, the penin- sula had other attractions to offer. Its hinterland is rich in a wide variety of commodities known collectively as 'jungle products', and comprising timbers, rattans and canes, palms, tanning and dye plants and woods, gums, oils and resins, fibre plants, medicinal and poisonous plants, food plants and spices, and a variety of animal products such as ivory, rhinocerous horn, hornbill casques, and lac, some of which undoubtedly figured in the earliest South East Asian trade (Dunn 1971: 217–22). It remained, however, for its mineral resources to render the attractions of the peninsula irresistible. At a time when metallurgy was developing in South East Asia, the tin and iron of the peninsula became vital commodities.

Communications along the length of the peninsula must always have been easiest by its coastal waters. River routes through the interior may often look attractive on the map, but first hand experience soon teaches the hard fact that peninsula rivers, usually shallow, fast flowing, and barred by frequent and dangerous rapids, offer fair going to bamboo raft traffic, but in one direction only—downstream. Short stretches can, it is true, be poled against the flow in specially designed, narrow, and highly unstable dugouts, moved at great expenditure of physical effort and capable of carrying three or four persons at the most with minimal baggage. Before the advent of the modern outboard engine, counter-current boat traffic was slow, exhausting, and often hazardous in the middle reaches and all but impossible in the headwaters even of the largest river systems.

For upstream movement along all or most of the river routes beloved of the historical geographers and others, the river would have to be abandoned and the traveller would be obliged to resort to his feet. Nor would the river banks facilitate his passage, for it is here, paradoxically, that the vegetation is at its densest and most impenetrable, its growth stimulated by the air and light reaching the jungle floor unimpeded by the tree canopy. Such traffic would have to depend on trackways over the less obstructed floor of the primeval forest, but it would always be arduous and unhealthy and would rely entirely on the local knowledge of the jungle dwellers. Wheatley has quoted nineteenth- century accounts of the difficulties encountered in following one of the most famous of these routes, the so-called *Penarikan*, from the west coast into the Pahang hinterland (Wheatley 1966: 167–70).

Nevertheless, a search for transpeninsula routes must always have been an attractive proposition. While the circumnavigation of the peninsula presents no special difficulties, the long coastline makes it a time-consuming business even at the present day, as the continued interest in a Kra canal bears witness. In ancient times knowledge of the narrow width of the peninsula must have greatly increased the incentive to establish suitable crossing places and associated ports. Such a need was presumably felt early in the growth of inter-regional trade.

The ridge and furrow pattern of relief further limits the choice of routes to the corridors between the mountain coulisses. Of these a series offers feasible passage in the isthmian sector where the narrowness of the peninsula confers an additional advantage. In the southern half, increasing width and the disposition of the mountain masses make the attempt at crossing distinctly less inviting. It is this factor which accounts for the Indianized entrepôt on the Bujang River in Kedah Kedah being the most southerly of such establishments on the west coast. It also accounts for the siting of two chains of major and minor entrepôts along both east and west coasts of the Isthmus with associated interior way stations and the establishment of the characteristic peninsula bi-polar settlement pattern already discernible in early historical times. It would seem perfectly reasonable to assume that the same environmental factors were operating in later prehistoric times, channeling communications and trade routes into this same isthmian segment when the search for metals and other commodities raised the peninsula to a position of economic importance.

The coastal peoples and their settlements in later prehistoric times are not likely therefore to have been truly self-sufficient, but motivated rather by reasons of trade and concerned with mineral prospecting, particularly the exploitation of the deposits of alluvial tin, South East Asia's richest, which lie mainly along the western littoral, and to a lesser extent deposits of iron and gold. Their contacts with the interior, forest adapted peoples no doubt led to the establishment and growth of trade in 'jungle products', although the initial exploitation of these natural resources could only have resulted from the specialized knowledge of the jungle dwellers and the collecting and primary distribution stages in this trade remained very largely in the latter's hands until the present day (Dunn 1971).

The Archaeological Evidence

The archaeological record relating to later prehistoric times in the Malay peninsula is sparse even when compared with the corpus of data available for still earlier times. Due no doubt in large part to the environmental factors summarized above which militated against long continued occupancy of a single site, stratigraphalic information derived from known open sites is so limited as to be virtually non-existent. For these same reasons, combined with climatic and other conditions extremely unfavourable to the survival of archaeological material, almost all the knowledge we have about the pre-historic peninsula has been gleaned from the excavation of closed sites in the fortunately numerous limestone caves of the interior. In such sites as these, deep stratified deposits are often encountered, but these are notoriously diffi-cult to interpret, a difficulty compounded by problems created by the semi-nomadic way of life followed by the peoples whose cultural remains are found contained in them.

Evidence is accumulating that by later prehistoric times a mosaic of cultures of varying types had been established on the peninsula, each co-existing in its particular ecological niche. Evidence from the rock shelter sites of Gua Cha, Gua Chawan, and Gua Tampaq, all on the Nenggiri river system of Kelantan, suggests the continued existence of a pebble tool tradition of Hoabinhian type into possibly quite late times (Peacock 1964a: 201–3; Peacock and Dunn 1968: 175). The Gua Chawan site with its clearly demarcated Hoabinhian working floor on the surface of the deposit seems to be particularly strong evidence of such a survival.

Other interior sites, and of course virtually all our knowledge has come from the excavation of rock shelters, show a by now well established pattern of secular change from the simplest Hoabinhian hunting assemblage to phases marked by the introduction of polished stone tools of the quadrangular axe/adze type, a change in burial mode from the earlier flexed type to prone extended inhumations sometimes lavishly provided with grave furniture and an increasing use of pottery of ever more sophisticated varieties.

The excavation of the rock shelter of Gua Kechil in Pahang by F. L. Dunn in 1962 was the first peninsula field study to attempt to document secular changes in culture by simple statistical analysis.

Apart from these excavations, by far the greater number of discoveries bearing on the period with which this paper is concerned were made before the Second World War. Perhaps the earliest recorded discovery was that made by the surveyor J. A. Legge in 1895 who reported the first of the series of cist (slab) graves at a place called Changkat Menteri on the Bernam River in south Perak. From the late 1920s onwards several other cist graves were investigated and reported on by I. H. N. Evans, P. V. van Stein Callenfels, H. D. Noone, P. M. de Fontaine, and H. D. Collings (Evans 1928, 1931b; Collings 1937a). In 1905, three magnificent decorated bronze bells were unearthed at Klang, near the Selangor (west) coast. These were followed in 1926 by the discovery of the tympanum of a bronze drum at Batu Pasir Garam on the Sungai Tembeling, Pahang, by fragments of a second drum from Bukit Kuda nearby towards the end of the Japanese occupation in 1944, culminating in the appearance of a pair of bronze drums at Kampong Sungai Lang on the

Selangor coast and another pair of drums at Kuala Terengganu, both in 1964.

During these same years, many scattered discoveries of iron implements, relatively the commonest category of late prehistoric artefacts, were made, either single or in hoards as well as in association with the cist graves. Five isolated socketed bronze celts were also reported from widely scattered localities.

From the above it will be seen that all the discoveries of metal antiquities and associated artefacts were made by chance and almost without exception are without systematically collected data concerning associations and context, stratigraphic or otherwise. The only two real exceptions to this are the investigations of the stone cist graves by Evans and Collings, and the excavation of the site of the discovery of the bronze drums at Kampong Sungai Lang by the writer in 1964 (Peacock 1965a, 1965b, 1966, 1967), but these were themselves, of course, basically chance discoveries all of which had suffered some degree of prior disturbance.

Most of our data then suffers from having been acquired before the introduction of modern standards of archaeological investigation. There is, however, another and perhaps more serious deficiency in our knowledge, which arises from the enormous disparity in the distribution of archaeological data over the peninsula as a whole. It will no doubt have been noticed that the items so far mentioned come entirely from provenances in the southern half of the peninsula. The isthmian sector remains almost a complete blank on the archaeological map as far as even moderately well documented discoveries and investigations are concerned. This is a particularly serious lacuna, because as has been suggested above, topographical features as well as what we know of earlier historical settlement, point to the Isthmus as being a likely focal point in the later prehistoric period as well. There are numerous archaeological indications that this was so; several very well-preserved bronze drums now in the National Museum, Bangkok, for example, come from this area and in 1968(?) two bronze drums and some magnificient bronze 'chalices' associated with iron implements, reportedly typologically similar to the southern peninsula examples, were accidentally unearthed south of Nakorn Srithammarat (Nikom Suthiragsa, personal communication). No more solid documentation is, however, at present available.

The same tantalizing lack of information exists regarding the later prehistory of the interior of the isthmian sector. This is made all the more frustrating by the knowledge that limestone caves abound in several areas, and chance discoveries of antiquities, some referable to types from better documented sites (e.g. the pottery cones recorded by Evans from Buang Bep, Surat (Evans 1931d: 207–9; Peacock 1964b: 6)), have been prolific. Unfortunately, a survey carried out by the writer in 1967 indicated that the depredations of guano diggers in the caves and rock shelters here have been, if possible, even more extensive than further south.

Considerably more data exist concerning the archaeology of the interior of the southern half of the peninsula. The documentation for this area is in fact now quite extensive, and notable advances have been made since the 1950s through such excavations as those at Gua Cha, Kelantan (Sieveking 1954–5), and at Gua Kechil, Pahang (Dunn 1964).

A general survey of this data, now somewhat outdated, exists in M. W. F. Tweedie's *Prehistoric Malaya* (1957). Fuller and more scholarly accounts, specifically of the later prehistoric material, are to be found in Prince John Loewenstein's 'The Origin of the Malayan Metal Age' (Loewenstein 1956), and in G. de G. Sieveking's 'The Iron Age Collections of Malaya' (Sieveking 1956*b*). Since both these papers contain a detailed and comprehensive treatment of virtually all the known metal antiquities and associated artefacts, omitting only the 1964 discoveries at Kampong Sungai Lang and Kuala Terengganu, it would be superfluous to repeat purely descriptive data in the present paper. The following notes are therefore intended to call attention to special features, particularly those which may have some interpretive significance.

A. *The iron implements*

Evans distinguished four and Sieveking five typological categories of iron implements (Evans 1931*e*; Sieveking 1956). These are illustrated here in Figures 3, 4, and 6. Clearly recognizable as distinct types are the following groups:
(1) Axes and adzes (Fig. 4 upper a–c; Fig. 6 E, F).
(2) Long shafted axes (Fig. 3).
(3) Knives (Fig. 4 upper d, e; Fig. 6 A, B).
(4) Sickles (Fig. 4 lower a–g).
(5) Spearheads (Fig. 6 C, D).
These typological categories are all of course based on implicit notions of function, but it must be admitted that function is often far from certain or even clear. They all possess several common features of design. One particularly noteworthy trait, one which has called for frequent comment, can only be described as their awkwardness. This is often to be seen in the peculiar disposition of the socket in relation to the blade and its cutting edge. Awkwardness is almost the essence of the long shafted axes, so much so that there has been a good deal of discussion as to whether they had a practical utility at all. Possible ritual functions or even use as currency have both on occasions been invoked.

Another common feature is that all, except a small sub-type of tanged knives with a comparatively small number of surviving examples, are equipped with hafting sockets. This is in marked contrast to the traditional Malay method of attaching handles to iron implements and weapons such as the *keris, parang*, and spearheads which is always by means of a tang. In this connection it has been pointed out that the apparently exceptional category of tanged knives in fact compares closely with its socketed counterparts in regard to the angle between the tang and blade on the one hand and the socket shaft and blade on the other (Sieveking 1956*b*: 107).

The iron implements have been found singly, in hoards and in association with other artefacts. They have been found in association with the stone cist graves, with the three bronze bells from Klang, with resin-coated pottery also at Klang and with the bronze drums from Kampong Sungai Lang and Kuala Terengganu. The distribution of the iron implements is interesting. The find spots as presently known are concentrated along the west coast of the southern half of the peninsula, with clusters in the vicinity of Klang, in Perak, and along the Sungai Tembeling and its tributaries in Pahang. The west coast localities are of course well-known as tin-producing areas, whereas the Pahang discoveries come from one of the main sources of Peninsula gold. It is almost certainly also significant that the Perak and Selangor specimens occur near deposits of haematite and limonite, both easily accessible and workable by primitive techniques.

One outlying hoard of iron implements was reported by Evans from a cave in Perlis, on the line of one of the most southerly of the Isthmian transpeninsula crossings (Evans 1931*a*: 47–8). Apart from this the only other record of iron implements believed to be typologically similar is of those found at Nakorn Srithammarat (see p. ooo above).

This group of iron artefacts with its unusual characteristics seems to be a unique product of cultures occupying the peninsula in later prehistoric times. No really convincing comparisons have so far been made with metal artefacts from other areas in South East Asia. Sieveking's attempt to show typological similarities between these peninsula artefacts and the products of mainland South East Asia in the Dong-son tradition seem to the present writer to be over-contrived.

B. *The bronze celts*

The five socketed bronze celts which have been found in the southern peninsula, here illustrated in Figures 1 and 2, are all too fragmentary to permit any but the most general typological comparisons to be drawn. One specimen (Fig. 1*c*) was found at a very isolated locality on the Sungai Jenera in the remote hinterland of Kelantan, but, significantly, in an area where minor gold workings have been carried on in recent times. The find spots of the other four clusters are in the same mineral-rich central west coast region from which most of the other metal antiquities have come.

C. *The bronze bells*

The three well-known bronze bells found at Klang on the west coast in 1905 are very closely comparable to the clapperless bronze bells from Battambang province, Cambodia, and the classic site of Dong-son itself. One of the peninsula bells has disappeared without trace or description, but the two survivors are decorated with spiral and saw-tooth motifs drawn from the typical Dong-son repertoire (see Plate IXa).

A point of some significance is that there is fairly reliable evidence that these three bells were actually recovered in association with four typical socketed iron implements (Sieveking 1956*b*: appendix 2).

D. *The bronze drums*

1. Batu Pasir Garam, Sungai Tembeling, Pahang. In 1926 widespread and severe flooding was experienced in many parts of the peninsula. These floods were instrumental in bringing to light several ancient artefacts, among them the tympanum of a bronze drum (Linehan 1928). It is indicative of the state of knowledge of prehistory at the time, that Linehan's original report of the discovery described the drumhead as 'the lid of a bronze urn used as the receptacle for the body of a chief after his death and before cremation'!

The Tembeling drumhead, illustrated in Figure 5, has purely geometric decoration made up of concentric bands of the 'ladder' pattern, circles, and highly conventionalized flying birds round a ten-pointed central star.

It is chiefly remarkable for the fact that it is technically one of the poorest examples of early South East Asian bronze casting. The decoration, composed of fine raised lines in the usual manner, has failed to register over large areas of the surface and attempts, in places extremely crude, have been made to incise the missing pattern with an engraving tool. Close inspection proves that this was an effort to remedy faulty workmanship and not to restore the effects of wear and tear. It raises an interesting problem as to how such a poor quality piece, an export reject as it were, could figure in inter-regional trade, if, as seems most likely, cast bronzes, at any rate large and elaborate ones, were not made in the peninsula in ancient times.

It may also be worth noting that the Tembeling drum was subject to some very rough usage at some stage in its career. The central star has received several deep and intentional cuts, powerfully inflicted and parts of the surface show evidence of the effects of heat sufficient to cause superficial melting.

2. Bukit Kuda, Klang, Selangor. In 1944, the tympanum and a substantial body fragment of a bronze drum was unearthed in the course of construction work on a hill near Klang called Bukit Kuda. The discovery added to the already noticeable concentration of later prehistoric antiquities on the Selangor coast adjacent to the tin fields and possible routes into Pahang with its sources of gold. The hill, Bukit Kuda, is one of several in the vicinity of the modern town of Klang, at least two of which have produced ancient metal objects. It is clear that the hills would have stood out above the dense freshwater swamp forest which must have surrounded them until modern clearance took place. They would have thus provided suitable locations for small settlements, possibly the only suitable locations for many miles in the coastal belts of mangrove and swamp forest of early times.

The Klang drum is in the geometric style and is remarkably similar to the Tembeling tympanum.

3. *Kampong Sungai Lang, Selangor* (Plates VIIIa, *b*). A few miles south of Klang on the Selangor coast, the clearance of old rubber trees in preparation for coffee planting in 1964 brought to light two bronze drums. The drums had been intentionally buried in an inverted position and the plantation work had made a thorough job of fragmenting the bodies and destroying them before the more resistant drumheads were reached. The surprise, and perhaps the superstititious fear, caused by this discovery protected the findspot from further depredations by the villagers and it was thus possible to carry out a detailed investigation of the site, the undisturbed parts being excavated.

The main features revealed by this investigation are as follows. First the two drums, one large (18 in. in diameter) and one small (14 in. in diameter), had been buried together side by side as a pair. They had been buried upside down, resting on the decorated surfaces of the drumheads. They had been placed on a rough hewn hardwood plank approximately 6 ft. 6 in. in length and showing traces of adze marks. While no positive proof is available, it is possible that this plank represents the remains of the keel of a dugout canoe, perhaps of the type with separate sewn side strakes of softer, more perishable wood.

The drums were found to have been placed roughly in the centre of a circular array of pots. None of these had survived intact, but reconstructions showed that the commonest form was a squat ovoid vessel with a very wide, sharply everted rim. Furthermore, most of the ceramics had been given an inner and outer coating of a smooth lacquer-like resinous material ranging through several shades of reddish-brown. The pottery was otherwise quite plain and undecorated. This resin-coating is presumably analagous to that reported on pottery from the peninsula cist graves and associated with iron implements at Klang. Underneath one of the pots were found large numbers of opaque terracotta red glass beads of the type known as *mutisalah*.

Perhaps the most important aspect to be established by the excavation was the fact that the drums, the dugout canoe (if that interpretation is valid) and the pottery vessels carefully arranged round them, had been buried in a circular mound about 15 ft. in diameter and originally standing to a maximum height of about 3 ft. 6 in. at the centre. Stratigraphically it was also possible to show that the mound had been erected on the mangrove mud surface, and had subsequently been wholly, or largely, buried under an accumulation of peat soil formed after the area had been colonized by freshwater swamp forest. Samples of the wooden plank have been dated by the radiocarbon method, the results of which are separately discussed below.

Among the many bronze fragments collected from the disturbed surface of the site was found the corroded socket broken from an iron implement. Its true association with the drums seems to be virtually beyond question, and it is likely that it formed the hafting socket of a spearhead.

The decoration of the drums is predominantly geometric with conventionalized flying birds. The large drum is further embellished on the outer edge of the tympanum with four frogs cast in the round, the bodies of which are covered with Dong-son geometric motifs.

Soon after the investigation of the drum site had been concluded, drainage ditch-digging operations a short distance away brought to light traces of another clay mound, from which were recovered two hemispherical bronze bowls bearing a simple linear pattern rather crudely incised on the outside, four hexagonal rock crystal beads, two crystal fragments, and several pieces of resin-coated pottery, identical to that of the drum mound. Unfortunately, the proximity of a house prevented further investigation.

4. Kuala Terengganu, Terengganu. In 1964, road improvements at Batu Burok, a short distance south of the modern town of Kuala Terengganu on the east coast of the peninsula, resulted in the discovery of another pair of bronze drums. The line of the road being constructed ran through a substantial sandbank, probably a raised beach, which runs roughly parallel with the present shoreline at a distance of just over a quarter of a mile. The drums had been buried in the sand close to the south face of a small, isolated, and greatly weathered granite outcrop, the only prominent feature in an otherwise flat landscape. The use of heavy earth-moving equipment by the road-workers caused massive damage to the drums which clearly had been intact and well-preserved before discovery. The blade of the bulldozer had shaved off the bases of both drums, reducing the bodies to fragments.

This circumstance and the testimony of eye-witnesses, whose further probing in the roadbed actually brought to light the tympanum of the smaller of the two drums, served, however, to establish beyond doubt that the drums had been buried in an inverted position after the fashion of those at Kampong Sungai Lang. It seems also certain that the drums formed a pair, one 28·5 in. in diameter and the other 21·5 in. in diameter. There is evidence that the drums had been used, at least in their final resting place, as containers. The large tympanum was found to have attached to its inner surface by corrosion products, a very fine socketed iron spearhead. Plentiful iron rust suggested the former presence of other iron objects in the drum-container, the inner patina of which had also preserved traces of woven matting.

News of the discovery did not reach Kuala Lumpur for several months, by which time the new road had been surfaced and opened to traffic, thereby precluding any further detailed examination. There were, however, eye-witness reports of the presence of great quantities of pottery sherds near the drums. Some forty of these were recovered, and these proved to be either of a light reddish brown sand-tempered earthenware, or a black earthenware tempered with carbonaceous matter. Surface decoration consisted of cord impressions, carved paddle impressions producing a diamond lozenge pattern, or fine-point impressions in the form of waves or spirals. It was not possible to reconstruct the form of any of the vessels from the evidence of the sherds.

Seven tiny glass beads were obtained from a local resident whose house bordered the road near the findspot. One of these was deep purple in colour, one yellow, and the rest pale translucent blue. Unfortunately it was not possible to verify the association of the beads with the drums, but this seems to be highly probable.

The Kuala Terengganu drums are decorated with the usual geometric motifs, but have in addition on the striking surface a broad band of an elaborate and complex design, which is difficult to interpret, but which may be based on the motif of warriors with shields and feathered headdresses. The surviving portion of the curved upper section of the smaller drum bears the representation of a boat, with its crew and what are probably sails, in a highly conventionalized form (Plate viiid).

E. *The cist (slab) graves*

The cist graves have not so far been found outside a very restricted area of the west coast, in the south of Perak and in northern Selangor, specifically along the banks of the Perak and Bernam rivers and their tributaries. The graves are constructed of relatively small, roughly prepared granite slabs, and rather puzzlingly no traces of human remains whatsoever, not even teeth, have been found in them.

The graves all seem to have been disturbed in the past, and this may account for the poor state of preservation of the associated artefacts. The pottery in particular is much fragmented and rather badly weathered. Socketed iron implements of peninsula types have been found with the cist graves and beads of glass, crystal, and carnelian are numerous.

The pottery is distinctive. Little can be learned of the shapes, but the surfaces are normally plain and it is likely that most, if not all, were given a coating of an organic resinous substance. Most characteristic of this ware is the flattening of the extreme edge of the rim, which is impressed with a variety of geometric motifs resembling closely, in some cases, the geometric designs found on South East Asian bronzes.

F. *The Kuala Selinsing settlement*

The Kuala Selinsing settlement is one of the rare open sites known to archaeology in the Malay peninsula. The settlement was of pile-dwellings, and was built on a low island just off the Perak coast not far from the modern town of Port Weld, and adjacent to the rich tin fields of Larut and Matang. The site is now surrounded by mangrove, the spread of which has been accelerated by the silting accompanying modern mining operations. The archaeological deposits consist of extensive thick layers of food debris composed mainly of shells, with some animal and fish bone, and a rich admixture of cultural material.

The chronological position of the site is obscure. Some later historical Chinese stonewares have been recorded, probably of Sung date, and even a few pieces of blue-and-white. Stratigraphical observations at Kuala Selinsing are complicated by its position in tidal mangrove mud with a fluctuating water table. The action of rising and falling tides and other hydraulic effects, indicate that Sieveking's stratigraphical discussion should be treated with some caution (Sieveking 1956a). There is, nevertheless, a good deal of evidence that the main period of occupation was contemporary with the earliest period of the establishment of the Indianized entrepôts on the peninsula, with which it was almost certainly linked commercially.

Lamb has plausibly interpreted the Kuala Selinsing settlement as a 'subsidiary entrepôt' in satellite relation to the main trading centres, and serving as a collecting base for the products of the hinterland (Lamb 1964: 108–9). The archaeological evidence seems to support this conclusion strongly. Tin ingots have been recovered from the Kuala Selinsing deposits together with numerous pieces of resin. Also significant is the presence of enormous quantities of beads of many different types and materials, and evidence, furthermore, that some types of beads were actually manufactured in the settlement. It is most likely that these beads played a rôle in some form of barter exchange, and it is also likely that some of the raw material for the glass varieties especially, was obtained from the entrepôt at Pengkalan Bujang further to the north.

Although its links to the Indianized trading posts on the peninsula seem fairly well established, the relationships of Kuala Selinsing to the other later prehistoric peninsula traditions are more problematic. The common Kuala Selinsing earthenware seems to have no affinities with the pottery associated with later prehistoric metal artefacts, but may be closer to some mainland South East Asian traditions. Boat burials reported by Evans and Sieveking from the site seem, however, to have been furnished exclusively with opaque terracotta red beads similar to those found, again exclusively, with the Kampong Sungai Lang drums.

Problems and Patterns in Later Peninsular Prehistory

In general the sequence observed at Gua Kechil is as follows: first a typical 'Hoabinhian' assemblage, including rather rough cord-impressed pottery and abundant and increasing quantities of animal bone and shell. This is followed by indications of improvements in ceramic technology and increase in its use. Finally we see the introduction of polished stone and bone tools, the appearance of a new and probably intrusive red-slipped and burnished pottery of a distinctive design, and at this point a pronounced decrease in animal bone and shell. Dunn has proposed that this decrease in animal food debris, accompanied by the appearance of new cultural types, indicates a change of subsistence mode from a basically hunting and gathering system to greater dependence on agriculture (Dunn 1964: 87–124). Although other explanations are possible, Dunn's interpretation is attractive, and the secular changes documented by the Gua Kechil excavation have received additional support from the results of other rock shelter excavations in the southern Malay peninsula (Peacock 1971).

Archaeology then, seems to have produced clear evidence of a shift towards a new subsistence mode in the later phases of prehistory in the interior. Environmental factors dictate that this new mode must have been some form of shifting cultivation, almost certainly of dry hill rice.

What evidence is there for contacts between the shifting cultivators of the hinterland and the coastal, metal-using peoples? The stray finds of iron implements along the Pahang rivers, and the isolated occurrence of a bronze celt far inside Kelantan, have already been noted. Socketed iron implements were found by Evans in a cave in Perlis, and pottery with the flattened rim, so characteristic of the cist grave ceramics, was recovered from caves in Bukit Chuping in Perlis by Evans and Collings (Evans 1931*a*; Collings 1937*b*). But these sites are not strictly in the interior jungle zone, being close to the coastal mangrove and swamp forest. Iron knives of the tanged type were reported by Evans from a rock shelter at Batu Kurau, Perak, but this again is not far from the coast and easily and directly accessible by river.

At present the only objects that clearly indicate contact between coast and interior are a single sherd of the cist grave type with flattened, decorated rim, a green glass bead, and a fragment of the rim of a bronze bowl recovered from the upper levels of deposits recently excavated at Kota Tongkat, Pahang. At another rock shelter in Pahang, Gua Orang Bertapa in Gunong Senyum only a few miles south of Kota Tongkat, recent excavations have brought to light a bronze wire ring and a single tiny glass bead associated with a prone extended burial, and certainly to be related to a late phase in the occupation of the site.

A few isolated stone implements have been reported which may possibly reflect in their design traces of the influence of metal prototypes. This is possible, for example, in the cases of three rather unusual stone spearheads from Kelantan and Pahang, described by Evans (Evans 1930: 1–3, 1931a: 65) and Sieveking (Sieveking 1956b: 123). Derivation from metal prototypes also seems possible in the case of some very beautiful, finely made stone axeheads with expanded cutting edges, found on Penang Island in 1965 (Peacock 1966: 201). Sieveking's attempt to relate a special group of stone cutting implements (reaping knives?), known in the literature as Tembeling knives, to the luxate or pediform bronze socketed axes of mainland South East Asia, seems, however, neither successful nor necessary.

In general it must be admitted that the archaeological record has so far yielded surprisingly little concrete evidence of contact between the coastal peoples and the interior. In particular it is rather puzzling that so few beads have so far been recovered in the course of excavating occupation and burial sites in the interior.

At present the most serious deficiency in our knowledge of the later prehistoric period in the Malay peninsula lies in the area of chronology. Stratified sites are available for the inland zone, but apart from the Kuala Selinsing settlement with all its unresolved problems, none is so far known along the coasts. Dating arguments based on typological comparisons using one category of artefacts or another, beads, for example, or the cast bronzes, have advanced our understanding of dating very little and in any case they are often suspiciously circular.

A handful of radiometric dates have now been provided for southern Malay peninsula sites. The first radiocarbon date was obtained for charcoal from a hearth containing cord-impressed pottery in a cave in Perak (BM43, 3450± 150 B.P.) (*Radiocarbon Suppl. Amer. Jl. Science*, Vol. 2, 1960: 29). A second radiocarbon date was obtained by Dunn for bone collagen from Gua Kechil, from a level corresponding to the change in subsistence pattern noted above (GX–0418, 4800±800 B.P.) (Dunn 1966: 352–3).

Samples from the wooden plank found underneath the pair of bronze drums, at Kampong Sungai Lang, have had the unusual distinction of being dated by the radiocarbon method by three separate laboratories. The dates obtained are as follows:

(1) GX–0280, 2435±95 B.P.

(2) GaK 684, 1850±90 B.P.
(3) ANU 27, 2145±100 B.P.

(*Radiocarbon*, Vol. 9, 1967: 15–27).

These dates are all significantly different from each other, and the dating of this important discovery must therefore remain in doubt.

More recently, attempts have been made to obtain thermoluminescence dates from ceramics, from the inland sites of Gua Orang Bertapa and Gua Kechil (Alkire n.d.). The tests were carried out by Professor Y. Ichikawa at the Nara University of Education, Japan, and the results at the time of writing are still undergoing analysis. Initial study, however, indicates that there are still considerable difficulties in the way of their satisfactory interpretation.

A. *Internal cultural relationships*

A good deal of discussion has gone on regarding the internal relationships of the later prehistoric cultures of the peninsula. In particular the question of whether there is evidence of separate Bronze and Iron Ages has commanded much attention. Linehan argued for a single Bronze-Iron culture (Linehan 1951). Loewenstein, on the other hand, considered that the bronze artefacts belonged to an earlier period separate and distinct from the period of the introduction of iron (Loewenstein 1956). In this he was supported by Sieveking who also talks of separate Bronze and Iron Ages, although the latter professed to see evidence that the Peninsula iron implement types were but derivatives of the 'Dong-son Bronze Age' (Sieveking 1956*b*).

The new evidence from Kampong Sungai Lang and Kuala Terengganu suggests that there was, in fact, much greater homogeneity in the later prehistoric cultures of the coastal zones. The same resin-coated pottery has been found with bronze drums as had earlier been found associated with cist graves and socketed iron implements. The association of cast bronzes with socketed iron implements is now established beyond question and bronze bowls, hitherto known only from the cist graves and a few isolated occurrences along Pehang rivers, are now known from a context identical with that of the Kampung Sungai Lang drums. The recent discoveries at Nakorn Srithammarat may well serve to strengthen this link between the bronze artefacts of general Dong-son type and the peninsula iron implements still further. The distribution of these metal objects and their associations is, in short, clearly concordant, and there seems little reason any longer to doubt their contemporaneity or even their use by the same, or at any rate closely similar, cultures.

It has been noticed that very little archaeological evidence has been found to illustrate the extent, and nature, of the contacts between coastal and inland cultures. There need not, of course, be any great surprise at the lack of interchange of cultural types between these two very different ecological zones.

Later historical and anthropological observations render it in the highest degree probable that there was in fact a good deal of interaction, at least of a commercial sort, between the two, and it is to this extent all the more surprising that beads, if they formed a medium of exchange, do not occur with much greater regularity in the interior sites.

B. *External cultural relationships*

The absence of copper deposits in the peninsula, the relative rarity of cast bronzes here, and the typology of the known bronzes, make it most probable that these objects were imported, and it is likely that their ultimate source was mainland South East Asia. Most of the socketed iron implements, and much of the pottery which may be associated with these bronzes are, however, distinctive and apparently indigenous to the peninsula. It is noteworthy also, that one important ancient usage of the bronze drums in the peninsula seems to differ markedly from what we know of, presumably, roughly contemporary practice in the mainland. In the peninsula the drums were buried upside down and in one instance, Kuala Terengganu, were used as containers.

These differences strongly suggest the development of a distinctive regional culture on the peninsula coasts in later prehistoric times, although these people were almost certainly in trading contact with the mainland centres.

Later Prehistoric–Early Historic Continuities

So far no direct evidence has come to light bearing on possible cultural continuities between later prehistoric cultures and the early historic settlements and entrepôts. The Kuala Selinsing settlement may, perhaps, be a partial exception to this, but interpretations of this site vary.

Recent excavations at the entrepôt site of Pengkalan Bujang have failed to show any evidence of a pre-Indianized phase of occupation. Indeed, all the indications from this work point to a rather abrupt occupation of this site, with no reliably dateable material earlier than late T'ang times.

It seems, however, a perfectly reasonable hypothesis that it was the later prehistoric coastal peoples who pioneered the Isthmian trans-peninsula crossings, the pattern of exploitation of mineral resources and other natural products, and who thus laid the foundations of the trading relationships which provided the basis for many of the most significant developments of early historical times.

Archaeology in Southern Viet-Nam
since 1954

JEREMY H. C. S. DAVIDSON

Introduction

THE political and military situation which developed following the Geneva
Accords, and the ensuing lack of security which obtained, have hampered, or
perhaps prevented, serious and extended scientific excavation in the southern
part of Viêt-Nam since 1954. Few sites have been discovered and studied,
which does not mean that they are absent, as is illustrated by the several pre-
1954 finds like Óc-eo, Sa-huỳnh and, more recently by the Long-khánh sites
(Saurin 1963ab, 1966, 1968, 1971; Fontaine 1971, 1972).

On the other hand, the centre and south of Viêt-Nam were for centuries
parts of the Cham and Khmer empires, both of which left monuments and
statuary as reminders of their presence. The obviousness of their monuments
and the need to preserve them, which has absorbed most of the efforts of
Vietnamese specialists (Lăng 1962: 270–1; Thâm 1962: 275–6; Lâm 1960:
225–70), coupled with the difficulties of conducting digs and perhaps even the
attitudes of the Vietnamese scholars involved, has resulted in, or forced, a
continuation of the French preoccupation with the 'overground'. Apart from
a brief though abortive spell of interest in excavation archaeology during the
government of Ngô Đình Diêm, because national priorities have lain elsewhere little digging has taken place and that largely by Saurin and Fontaine.

(a) Champa

The study of Champa is still in its infancy. Its inscriptions, which received
the attention of Aymonier, Bergaigne, Coedès, Finot, and Huber among
others, demand reinvestigation. Its history, certainly that of Línyì and
Huánwáng, needs to be rewritten with precision, thereby eradicating the
errors and resolving the controversies established by Pelliot (1903 and 1904),
Maspero (1928), and Stein (1947). The study of its art and architecture, which
is in no way comparable to that undertaken for Cambodia but which, since
Parmentier's major works (1909–18 and 1922) has undergone some revision
(Coral-Rémusat 1934: esp. 39; and especially Boisselier 1963), still requires
detailed attention in order to classify pieces and to define developmental
stages, styles, etc. Recently, two pieces of early tenth-century statuary have
come to light (Avalokiteśvara: Brocheux 1966: 99–104). But our knowledge

of Champa remains so fragmentary, vague, and inaccurate that the whole subject must be reworked.

(b) *'Zhēnlà-Khmer'*

'Khmer' sites in South Viêt-Nam—by which Zhēnlà and later periods are to be understood—have received sparse attention[1] and virtually none since 1954. The Śaivaite-Buddhist establishment in the Tháp-mu'ò'i region has by chance yielded a bronze Buddha and a ?Śīva image (Hu'o'ng 1970: 220–2). Some wooden Buddha-images from there (Malleret 1963: vol. IV, pl. XXI) and from Phong-my in Kiên-phong province (ibid., pl. XXVI) have been subjected to C14 dating which apparently substantiates dating suppositions already put forward. Similar tests with similar results have also been made for wooden Buddha-figures found at Đú'c-hòa in Hậu-nghiã province,[2] beyond which nothing new is known.

(c) *Óc-eo ('Fúnán')*

The Óc-eo and associated sites, enormously important discoveries, have been written about at length by Malleret (1959–63: vols. I–IV) and are well-known. Western influence there is indisputable, but suggestions that certain hellenistic forms entered Viêt-Nam there, and developed into *hát bôi, hát chèo, ca-dao* and perhaps, mediumistic rites (Janse 1961: 1666ff.; 1962: 156ff.; Smith 1961: 1793), are ludicrous and display ignorance of Vietnamese literature, music and religion.

It should go without saying that a thorough study of Hà-tiên in its historical context and in relation to Óc-eo is indispensible to the accurate understanding and interpretation of many aspects of the site,[3] a study which still remains to be done. Đá-nôi[4] near Rạch-giá (So'n Nam 1970: 175) has also produced two wooden Buddha images (Malleret 1959: vol. I, 125 ff. and pl. XCVI) for which C14 dates are available.[2] New work on the Óc-eo site or the finds does not, however, seem forthcoming.

Stone

Major discoveries after 1954 have been made in the Xuân-lôc area of Long-khánh province, known as a settlement site of longstanding since the early years of this century (Barthère 1911: 5). The Xuân-lôc megalith (Hàng-gòn 7), first discussed by Bouchot in 1927, is well publicized.

Hàng-gòn 6 (Saurin 1968: 8) has unifacial and bifacial polished adze-axes and Dâu-giây 2 (ibid., 13, and pl. Ia-c; and 1971: esp. 66), a 'limande', all acheulian, of local basalt which has been dated by Carbonnel (1969: 26–29; note Saurin 1971: 49–51). These two related sites are considered to be palaeolithic, as is the material from Nhân-gìa, Thó'i-giao (ibid., 51ff.) which includes basalt 'balls', possibly bolas (ibid., 55). Much the same type of axe occurs at Nuí Đọ, Thanh-hoá (Boriskovsky 1963) but Saurin (1971: 58) believes the forms from these two widely separated sites differ, although Nhân-gìa types and the short Hòa-bình axes probably derive from the same prototype.

At Côn-so'n, polished axes of non-local material (Saurin 1964: 11) suggest a fairly developed trade network, and imply the existence of stone-tool factories. Polished axes and adzes made from high-quality stone are common at the Plei-ku sites. Some axes are shouldered and others show the 'heeling' (Lafont 1956: pl. x, esp. x. 11) which links them closely to the Phùng-nguyên complex (Lan 1962a: 17, esp. fig. 1. 5–6) and the development of bronze heeled-axes. They are also very like the Long-khánh types (Hàng-gòn 3: Saurin 1968: pl. 5ab). Saurin (1968: 13–14 and pl. 1.3ab) noted the same reworking giving 'heeled' forms at Bình-lọ'i, a site he associates with Hàng-gòn 1 and 2 where similar forms are found (Saurin 1963a: pl. xxvi. 7–8). This type of axe, common to the whole country, was still in use during the Sòng (Janse 1941: 264 and pl. 19, 3a–d) and was noticed among the Bahnar at the beginning of this century (Verneau 1904 in Saurin 1968: 14), something which complicates the neolithic dating (Bezacier 1972: 277) generally assigned to it at Plei-ku and Long-khánh sites.[5]

Late in 1970, a sizeable find of rectangular stone adzes, provisionally dated as neolithic, was recorded following their accidental discovery at Long-bu'u (quận Thu-đú'c, Gia-định province), at a site on the bank of the Đông-nai River. Of polished sandstone, which suggests that they or the material were imported, the adzes are well-made and have a flange for the attachment of a handle. One such piece has both long edges sharpened and is shaped somewhat resembling a pointed spear-head. (*VNKCTS* 3, 201–2).

Certain stone decorative apparel is also found at Hàng-gòn 3 and 4 (Saurin 1968: pl. I. 4ab and pl. II.1) and at Phú-hòa, where stone rings, bracelets[6] and pendant ear-rings (Fontaine 1972: 436 and pl. III. 11–12) associated with semi-precious beads (ibid., 438–9), occur. This last class of object has immediate parallels with Sa-huỳnh from whence it may have been imported. A zoomorphic drop ear-ring, mentioned by Saurin (1968: 9) as found at Hàng-gòn 9, may well be similar to those from Phú-hòa (Fontaine 1972: pls. IV. 10 and IX. 18; cf. Malleret 1959: vol. 1, pl. VIIIe; Fox 1970: 129 and fig. 37a).

However, the most intriguing finds are the moulds, all of which are made of sandstone, hence probably imported. These are axe moulds from Hàng-gòn (Saurin 1963a: pls. xxvi. 12–xxvii. 1; 1968: pl. II. 7) as well as 'pin' moulds from there (Saurin 1963a: pl. xxviii; 1963b: pl. II. 3–6) and Dâu-giây (Saurin 1963a: pl. xxx. 2; 1966: 96, pl. II. 8–9; 1968: pl. II. 9ab and 10). Their very presence implies local manufacture (Saurin 1963a: 442) of copper or, more probably, bronze items (Saurin 1966: 96–7) which have possible affinities with Óc-eo.[7] Saurin believes that the smooth sandstone plate found at Dâu-giây (1966: 94, pl. II. 13) and also at Côn-so'n (1964: 11 ff.) confirms his suggestion (1963*a*: 445) that the plate, after being placed between the two smooth plates of the mould, could have served as a valve and that this could explain the univalve moulds of Đông-son (Goloubew 1929: 18).

Yet the sandstone of these moulds and 'valves' would not, it appears, withstand the temperature of molten copper or bronze, therefore a softer metal of lower melting point must, as in the North, have been used to take a first cast from which, most probably, a baked earth mould was drawn to cast the final form (Ngọc 1965: 63–4). Casting techniques remain to be confirmed.

Pottery

The most famous site is undoubtedly that of the jar-burial complex of Sa-huỳnh, Quảng-ngãi province, whose pottery was shown to relate to the Kalanay complex by Solheim in several publications (1960, 1961*abc*, 1967) and which Malleret (1961: 115 and pls. ib and VIII) maintains shows a sinicizing tendency.

The latter's belief (ibid., 113) that Sa-huỳnh was independent of northern influence is, since the discovery of the Phùng-nguyên complex, no longer tenable. Links between Phùng-nguyên and Sa-huỳnh were expressed by Tân (1968: 55–7) when he noted similarities between the former and certain maritime South East Asian pottery sites in Kalimantan, Sulawesi, and the Philippines. An extension of Phùng-nguyên connections and influence was also demonstrated to exist with Borneo (ibid.; cf. Harrisson 1965: 63–8; Goloubew 1929: 42, fig. 21) and with pottery from the Karama River site (Tân 1968: 59, esp. fig. 3; cf. Stein-Callenfels 1951: pls. xv–xviii). Phùng-nguyên influence on Sa-huỳnh (Tân 1968: 55 ff.; Kinh 1969: 60) would help explain similarities between the pottery of the Long-khánh sites, reminiscent of Sa-huỳnh in ceramics and displaying marked affinities in other artefacts, and the Viêt-tiên–Thiêu-du'o'ng ware (Lan 1963: 248 ff.; Linh 1964: 33 ff.; Tân 1968; cf. i.a. Solheim 1961*a*: figs. il, 2a and o). Admittedly the maritime region was also subject to influence from south-eastern China yet Sa-huỳnh's sinicizing tendency is perhaps initially explicable in terms of more indirect contact, through the intermediary of the northern culture complexes.

Unfortunately the pottery of other RVN sites has not received the attention it deserves, despite Fontaine's articles (1971, 1972) and Saurin's notes in various writings.

Almost all RVN sites investigated have yielded sherds. The material is usually coarse sandy clay, as in the north; the utensils hand-made; the basic décor, i.e. basket-weave, toothcomb, etc., common to the whole country.

Colour, which differs between sites, ranges from black (Hàng-gòn: Saurin 1968: 6–8; Dâu-giây: ibid., 9–13) through yellow-grey, yellow-red (Hàng-gòn 4: ibid., 6–7) yellow-brown (Dâu-giây: Saurin 1966: 90 ff.), grey-red, red-brown (Dâu-giây: Fontaine 1971: 325–6), to brown and red. It should be recalled that the red to grey to brown range is characteristic of northern sites.

Hàng-gòn 1, which C14 dates[8] established at Saclay[2] place between Laang Spean (Mourer 1970: 470–3; cf. Saurin 1963a: 452: Samrong Sen) and Đông-so'n, has provided perforated pots. Saurin (1966: 96–7) believes the perforations were made for straw-drinking purposes although the associated sites of Hàng-gòn 9 (Saurin 1968: 9)[2] and Phú-hòa (Fontaine 1972: 416) have evidence of intentionally broken pots which recalls the 'killing' of Sa-huỳnh jars (Janse 1941: 257). Hàng-gòn[9] sites tend to be interrelated (Saurin 1968: 3 and 6) and although Saurin (1966: 96) believes Hàng-gòn and Dâu-giây have fundamentally different pottery, the later Hàng-gòn sites, especially Hàng-gòn 9, are associated with Dâu-giây (Saurin 1968: 13–14),[10] and both are related to Sa-huỳnh (Saurin 1963a: 439–40; 1966: 90–4; 1968: 8–9 and 14). The shapes seen there and at Hàng-gòn (Saurin 1963a: pl. xxiii) are also very similar to those of Viêt-tiên and Thiêu-du'o'ng (Lan 1963: pls. xxvii–xxx). Dâu-giây ware (Fontaine 1971: pl. ii) also displays several patterns identical with those of Phú-hòa (Fontaine 1972: pls. ii. 5, iii. 2, viii. 5). The association of these two sites with one another (Fontaine 1971: 326 ff.; 1972: 430 ff., esp. 441–3) and with Sa-huỳnh has also been noted by Fontaine (1972: 404), who believes that, as at Sa-huỳnh, Dâu-giây and Hàng-gòn 9, the Phú-hòa jar-field was a cremation burial site (ibid., 442). C14 dates[11] for Phú-hòa (ibid., 441) make it older than Hàng-gòn 9 which is slightly earlier (Saurin 1966: 97) than Dâu-giây 1. The decoration of its pottery is much richer than elsewhere in Nam-kỳ. Fontaine (1972: 423 ff.) observes that the shapes but not the décor of Phú-hòa ware are similar to those of Sa-huỳnh, but some patterns are in fact very similar (cf. Solheim 1961a: fig. 1 k–l). A Phú-hòa–Sa-huỳnh connection where the '*lampes*' are concerned (Parmentier 1924: 325; Malleret 1961: pls. vi–vii) seems the best explanation for their appearance at Phú-hòa (Fontaine 1972: 428–9); some pottery from Dâu-giây is also strongly reminiscent of these. However, one must also remember that the '*lampes*' are characteristic of DRV Bronze Age sites (Lan 1963: pl. xxx. 1–8).

A further link with Phú-thọ–Thanh-hóa decoration might be noted. Several Phú-hòa patterns are identical with those found in the north, especially at Bronze Age sites.[12]

Much less rich in design is the pottery from the Plei-ku sites (Lafont 1956: pl. xiv) which bears certain likenesses to some Long-khánh sherds as well as to those from the northern sites already mentioned. Sa-huỳnh influence, if any, is obscure although the geographical proximity of the sites does not preclude it. Further information is needed before more definite analogies can be established.

Finally, the pottery from Côn-so'n (Saurin 1964: 9–10) apparently bears closer relationship with North Vietnamese, Nghê-an, types than with Sa-huỳnh or Nam-ky forms but adequate data is lacking to confirm the connections.

Bronze

Apart from the two bronze statuettes from Hòa-an and Thiên-my in Kiên-phong province (Hu'o'ng 1970: 221–2), very little bronze has come to light, something of a surprise considering the moulds that have been unearthed. Only the latest Hàng-gòn site has revealed evidence of bronze, a gilded bronze ear-ring (Saurin 1968: 9), for which Saurin (1963a: 446) claims an Óc-eo association.

No bronze is known from Dâu-giây, while Côn-so'n has a little, once again possibly connected with Óc-eo (Saurin 1964: 11 ff.). At Phú-hòa it is also rare (Fontaine 1972: 416 and 435); there are some bronze bracelets (ibid., 437 and pls. IV. 7; V. 6; VIII. 6–9) immediately reminiscent of Phùng-nguyên culture site finds (Chinh 1968: 127) and some little bells (*grelots*: Fontaine 1972: 435–6) which are the same as at Sa-huỳnh (Parmentier 1924: 340, fig. 17de) and at Óc-eo (Malleret 1960: vol. II, 221–7 and pl. xci. 4). Malleret (ibid., 226) believes the bells belong to:

> un cycle culturel propre à l'ensemble des pays de la Mer de Chine méridionale.

Perhaps the answer for the very small number of bronze objects lies in the scarcity of the metals required to make the alloy.

Iron, etc.

Little iron has been found at Hàng-gòn and that at Hàng-gòn 9 (scissors and a sword: Saurin 1968: 9). The same scarcity applies to Dây-giây (ibid., 10). None has been found at Plei-ku; it is from Phú-hòa that the majority of finds come. Fontaine (1972: 432 ff.) has noted that of these Phú-hòa iron objects, the 'pickaxes' (ibid., pls. IV. 9; V. 7; VII. 12) are perhaps axes and are similar to objects found at Sa-huỳnh (Parmentier 1924: 340). It is worth drawing attention here to the shorthandled axe-mattocks of the Jeh, the *chuang* and *siput*, used for log-felling, woodsplitting, and hole digging, which resemble the Phú-hòa forms closely. The sickles (Fontaine 1972: 433 and pls. II. 12–13; IV. 5, etc.) are the same as those made of bronze at other sites. The method he suggests (ibid., 434, fig. 28) of attaching the blade to the handle is possible (cf. Lan 1962a: 25, fig. 3, and 26, fig. 4) but the incision into the handle method, observable in the Jeh *mak*, is more likely. Bracelets (Fontaine 1972: 437) and rings (ibid., 435) of iron were also found, as were lumps of iron which suggests iron smelting nearby (q.v. Óc-eo: Malleret 1960: vol. II, 255). On the evidence of such stone, bronze, and iron artefacts, Fontaine (1972: 441–3) concludes that Phú-hòa and Sa-huỳnh are connected, justifiably it would seem at this juncture.

There is some evidence that gold was worked (Hàng-gòn 9: Saurin 1968: 9); glass for beads (ibid.) and bracelets (Phú-hòa: Fontaine 1972: 437–8), and semi-precious stones (ibid., 436–7) which recalls such burial associated finds at the Phùng-nguyên sites of Lũng-hòa and Văn-điên (Chinh 1968: 25–9 and 101–3, pls. XLIII. 12 and XLV. 3) have also been unearthed.

Conclusion

The lines of enquiry suggested as worth pursuing in the conclusion to the survey of North Vietnamese archaeological activity obtain for the South too. Here, conservation work, especially for Cham materials belonging to a period outside the scope of this colloquy, has been the first priority. Monuments and statuary continue to dominate the archaeological horizon; in excavational terms the South remains largely virgin territory, awaiting survey and the archaeologist's trowel. Although post-Independence finds have not been rich, the sites discovered to date in South Viêt-Nam suggest potentially more variety in material culture there than in the North.

Of immediate note are the early date of iron at the Xuân-lôc sites, predating its use in the North by several centuries, the virtual absence of bronze objects, and also that the sites predate Óc-eo by several centuries. Beyond that, the paucity of the sites and their artefacts does not provide enough information to permit us to draw new conclusions of any note; our knowledge has not notably increased since 1954.

NOTES

1. See, for example, Parmentier 1923, i.a., in which notes are made on some finds.
2. C14 dates are given in R. B. Smith's checklist in this Colloquy, Appendix 1.
3. cf. So'n Nam 1970: esp. 176–7 with Malleret 1959: vol. 1, on Rạch-gia and Đá-nôi.
4. Đa-nôi: 'stones raised up'? evidence of Megalithic culture.
5. cf. Malleret 1960: vol. 11, 19.
6. Identical bracelets are recorded at the Lũng-hòa and Văn-điên sites (Chinh 1968: 127).
7. Possible connections with Phùng-nguyên culture sites exist but comparisons remain to be made. See also DRV stone moulds, above.
8. Saurin (1968: 3) expresses doubt at these dates.
9. Could Hàng-gòn 5 be the pottery factory for the complex?
10. cf. Hàng-gòn ware with that of Dâu-giây (Saurin 1966: pl. 1, 16–17; also Fontaine 1971: pl. 11), although it is perhaps too early to argue close affinity.

11. C14 dates established at Gif-sur-Yvette by Mme G. Delibrias:
carbon deposits from jar 14: 2400 ±140 B.P. (c. 450 B.C.)
carbonized wood from jars 11 and 14: 2590 ±290 B.P. (c. 640 B.C.).

12. Examples are:

Fontaine 1972: pl. IV. 14 = Bâu-tró: Patte 1925: pl. V. 10; Phùng-nguyên: Nghia 1960: 31;

Fontaine 1972: pl. II. 6 reminiscent of Ðông-so'n;

Fontaine 1972: pl. III of Thiêu-du'o'ng = Lan 1963: pl. XXXIII; also in Fontaine 1972: a pl. III variant, also ibid., 409, fig. 5, occurs on a So'n-tây bronze dagger = Lan 1963: pl. XIV. 4;

Fontaine 1972: pl. VIII. 13 is found on a bronze battle-axe from Hà-đông = Lan 1963: pl. XVIII. 5;

Fontaine 1972: pl. IX. 15 is seen on a bronze *bình* from Viêt-khê = Tân 1968: fig. 2k.

ADDITIONAL REFERENCES

Chinh, Hoàng xuân, 1968. *Báo cáo khai-quật do't I di chi Lũng Hòa*. Hànôi, Ðôi khao cô, 201 pp. +30 plates.

Hu'o'ng, Lê, 1970. Nhũ'ng ngu'ò'i Viêt tiên phong trên bu'ó'c đu'ò'ng Nam Tiên tại Cao-lãnh–Kiên-phong. *Su'-dia* 19–20, 209–31.

Kinh, Phạm văn, 1969. Vài ý kiên vê môt nhóm di tích khao cô mó'i phát hiên đu'ọ'c o' miên Bắc Viêt-nam. *NCLS* 120 (3–1969), 53–60.

Lan, Lê văn, 1962a. Môt ít tài liêu vê nhũ'ng chiêc rìu cô cua ta. *NCLS* 36 (3–1962), 15–27.

—1963. (and Phạm văn Kinh, Nguyên Linh 1963). *Nhũ'ng vêt tích dâu tiên cua thò'i dại do dong thau o' Viêt-nam*. Hànôi, NXB Khoa học, 328 pp.

Lăng, Nguyễn bá, 1962. Phúc-Trình: Vê viêc đi tiêp nhũ'ng khâu súng cô và xem xét môt ngôi mô cô bằng đá o' tinh Long-khánh. *VNKCTS* 3, 270–1 and 274.

Lâm, Bà Tru'o'ng bu'u, 1962. Tò' Trình vê cuôc đi khao sát cua phái đoàn VKC đê quan sát các cô tích Chàm, kiêm điêm các cô vât tại viên Bao-tàng Chàm, Đà-nẵng, và nghiên cú'u cach tru'ng bày cô vât tại viên Bao-tàng Huê. *VNKCTS* 3, 255–65 and 266–70.

Linh, Nguyên, 1964. Di chi Gò Mun và vân đê thò'i đại đô đông thau o' Viêt-nam. *NCLS* 58 (1–1964), 29–40.

Nghia, Nguyên văn, 1960. Báo cáo vê công tác phát hiên và tham dò: Di chi tân thạch khí Cô-nhuê (Lâm-thao, Phú-thọ). *NCLS* 11 (1960), 27–34.

Ngọc, Huyên, 1965. Tin tú'c khoa học lịch su': Phát hiên đu'ọ'c khuôn rìu hình dao xén bằng đá. *NCLS* 72 (3–1965), 63–4.

So'n Nam. 1970. Viêc khân hoang vùng Rạch-gía. *Su'-dia* 19–20, 169–90.

Tân, Hà văn, 1968. Môt sô vân đê vê văn hóa Phùng-nguyên. *NCLS* 112 (7–1968), 51–9.

Thâm, Nghiêm, 1962. Phúc-Trình: Viêc đi tiêp nhân nhũ'ng tang đá châm tại Tru'ò'ng tiêu-học, Tam-hiêp, Quân Bên-tranh, Tinh Định-tu'ò'ng. *VNKCTS* 3, 275–6.

VKC. 1971. Nhũ'ng lu'õ'i búa đá thò'i tiên su' tại di-chi bên sông đông-nai gia-định. *VNKCTS* 8, 201–2.

Recent Data on the Cambodian Neolithic: The Problem of Cultural Continuity in Southern Indochina

J. P. CARBONNEL

PREHISTORIC Cambodia, almost unknown before 1965, has in these last years shown itself to be much more complex than previous studies could foresee. We shall extract from a recent synthesis (Carbonnel 1970 and 1973) the principal characteristics of the neolithic Cambodian sites known today and their radiocarbon datings (Table I).

TABLE I: Radiocarbon Dates from Cambodian Sites

Province	Sites	Authors (notes)	Date (B.P.)	Remains Analysed	Observations
Bas-Plateaux	Chamcar-Andong Chup-Thmar Pich	1, 2, 3	1150±100 2130±100	Vegetal temper of ceramic	Polished lithic industry, very varied ceramics
Kompong Chhnang	Samrong Sen	4, 1	3230±120	Shells	Date of layer 1 m. to 1·5 m.
Battambang	Loang Spean	5	6240±70 to 1120±50	Coal	Hoabinian industry
Kampot	Phnom Loang	1	4370±135	Shells	Bone industry; Bacsonian at this site
	Kbal Roméas	1	5370±140		Presence of ceramics but not industry
Mlu Prei	Mlu Prei	6	—	—	Bronze and iron

1. Carbonnel and Delibrias 1968.
2. Groslier 1966.
3. Malleret 1959.
4. Mansuy 1902, 1923.
5. C. and R. Mourer and Thommeret 1970.
6. Levy 1943.

This paper will consider only sites from the period 1000 B.C. to A.D. 1000. Two main places are particularly interesting: the sites of the 'Bas-Plateaux' region (Kompong Cham province) and of Loang Spean (Battambang province). In the first case we are faced with a homogeneous geographic zone which was inhabited at least from the second century B.C. to the eighth century A.D. On the other hand the Battambang site is a cave-habitat of 5,000 years proven occupation, from 4290 B.C. to A.D. 830.

The 'Bas-Plateaux' Neolithic Region

First discovered and described by Malleret (1959), the basaltic 'Bas-Plateaux' prehistoric sites are in the 'Terres Rouges' zone of Cambodia and South Viet-Nam. They are circular structures locally named 'forts moi' or 'forts cham'. Their morphological study and first chronological estimations have been recently published (Carbonnel 1970). Only one excavation has been carried out, by B. P. Groslier, who gave some brief preliminary indications of results (1966).

In Cambodia the sites can be divided into two groups in relation to the spatial organization of apparent structures:

(*a*) *Circular structures* (Mimot, Krek, Snoul region): These are circular artificial hillocks, with a centre more or less depressed, which contains the prehistoric layers. The peripheral excrescence, entirely without archaeological remains, can be considered a defensive protection; this protection looks like those of some existing villages of the Annamite chain. It is this kind of structure which was excavated by B. P. Groslier. Fourteen Late Neolithic layers were listed, with a succession of three polished adze types, and the name of 'Mimotian' has been given to this succession. The Mimotian has not so far been defined, either in time or in relation to other known South East Asian industries.

(*b*) *Tumuli*, grouped in more or less circular formation (Chup, Prek Krak, Chamcar Adong region). Here, it is the tumuli which contain the remains of human activity. We can compare them to *kjökkenmöddinger*. The 'village' is organized around a central place; the habitations, on piles, accumulate beneath them their own wastes. This is the same type of site as Samrong Sen (Mansuy 1923), but with a spatial organization which is also comparable with some present-day villages of Ratanakiri province (north-east Cambodia). The prehistoric remains found on the surface (no excavation has been carried out yet) comprise an important quantity of ceramics; small red clay balls with fingerprints on some of them; poorly made adzes; and allochthonous basaltic pieces of rocks (fire-stones?).

Two C14 dates were obtained on the vegetal temper of ceramics from two of these tumuli groups. These dates are 2130±100 B.P. (Chup-Thmar Pich, 12°00 N–105°37 E); and 1130±100 B.P. (Chamcar Andong, 12°22 N– 105°12 E). These two chronological references must be considered merely as provisional indications; they show the large temporal extension of human occupation of this zone by prehistoric people who had a type of culture related to the Late Neolithic. This culture extends at least down to the historic period (eleventh century).

Loang Spean Site

This is a cave-habitat, discovered and described by C. Mourer. The cave is situated at the summit of Phnon Teak Trang (altitude: 150 m.) located 40 km. west of Battambang. A precise stratigraphy has been elaborated and nine layers have been characterized in a total deposit 1·40 m. thick. The filling shows a nearly continuous human occupation over at least 5,000 years. In effect, six C14 dates on pieces of coal (C. Mourer *et al.*, 1970), coming from two vertical excavations, range from 6270±70 B.P. (between 30 and 50 cm.) to 1120±50 B.P. (surface). These dates refer to the upper part of the site, characterized by a poor industry, using large lithic pieces of Hoabinhian type (C. and R. Mourer 1970); pebbles with chips on one face only; and Sumatraliths (van Heekeren 1959: 69). The presence of a partly polished piece of schist indicates the knowledge of polishing 6,000 years ago.

Pottery manufacture was also known at this time. The ceramic ware is very similar to that of the Vietnamese neolithic, its ornaments use the same process: carvings, comb ornaments, and prints of tiny string seem to be the most important. The layers before 6,000 years ago do not show any Hoabinhian industry, but there are found pieces of silexite and local stones, without originality. A varied fauna is associated (Guerin and Mourer 1970; C. and R. Mourer 1970).

This ensemble, of which the earliest base is possibly already upper Paleolithic, is evidence of a continuity of occupation of the site and a constant type of industry, which is surprising. Such cultural isolation in an area so easily accessible, directly continuous with the Grand Lac Bassin (which, from the eighth century A.D., had an original civilization of its own) seems to be a constant in Cambodian history during the last 3,000 years.

Conclusions

The two neolithic regions which we have briefly described both have human occupation of long duration, without important cultural modification (certainly for Loang Spean; but we can say surely that the area of the Bas-Plateaux must be considered as a relatively homogeneously whole, in comparison with the two occupation structures of which we have evidence). These cultures had coexisted, in the manner of unchanging 'microclimates', with a kingdom in full cultural and economic expansion, exactly as if no influence reached them even during the tenth century.

The Upper Indochinese Neolithic, whose great extent and relative cultural homogeneity have given the Peninsular a truly autochthonous framework, was thus maintained for a long time with its own originality, and one can ask if some features of the landscape and cultural life of nowadays (ceramic art for example) are not direct evidence of it.

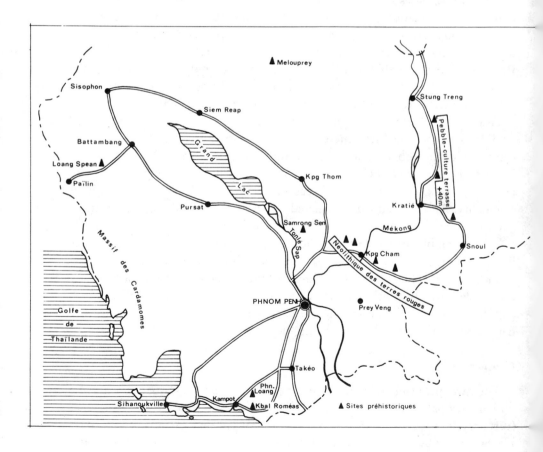

Cambodian prehistoric sites

The Philippines during the First Millennium B.C.

ROBERT B. FOX

Introduction

THE major factor influencing past social and cultural developments in the Philippines has been its insular isolation, the archipelago lying as it does on the Pacific margin of Asia. Its genesis is Asian but striking differences are seen when the cultural history of the Philippines is compared with countries of mainland South East Asia. Socketed bronze adzes and spears are excavated in sites of the Early Metal Age in the Philippines, *c.* 500–200 B.C., but there was *no* Bronze Age or Copper-Bronze Age in the Philippines as Beyer (1948) has reasoned. Early Indian influences are seen in the religions and languages of the traditional cultures but no monumental structures of stone have been dis-→ covered in the Philippines, such as the temples of Indonesia, Thailand, or Cambodia. The dissimilarities in the archaeological record of the Philippines when compared with mainland Asia may be explained by the differential selection during prehistoric times of influences and traits from Asia which were adaptable to the sea and riverine-oriented lives of the early Filipinos, as well as traits which were consonant with their levels of technological development (Fox 1958: 2–4). The elaboration of selected external influences, plus local developments and specializations, have thus formed the cultural heritage of the Filipino people; an heritage which evidences basic relationships with the culture area described as 'South East Asia' but which maintains a distinctive Filipino ethos.

Close ties are seen with Borneo and Indonesia—with 'Island South East Asia' as contrasted with 'Mainland South East Asia'—but the term 'Malay' if used to describe the prehistoric cultures as peoples of the Philippines is misleading, as is the term 'Indonesian'. The writer is impressed, for example, with data from recent excavations on Palawan Island which would suggest that the basic external influences which reached this area during the first millennium B.C.—the Late Neolithic and the Early Metal Age—came from northern Indochina and south China with people who moved either directly by boat from the south mainland of Asia (Beyer 1947, 1948) or by movements around the margin of the South China Sea basin (Fox 1970). During the Neolithic and early phases of the Metal Age, at least, affinities with Malaysia and Indonesia proper are less readily apparent in the archaeological record.

A non-political term is needed for describing the cultural substratum which reached the Philippines from the south mainland of Asia during the Neolithic and Metal Age.[1]

Influences from the south—Indonesia and Malaysia—certainly had a strong impact upon the cultures of the southern Philippines during the later Developed Metal Age and the subsequent Age of Contacts and Trade with the East, beginning in about the first millennium A.D. There is no support for the theory, however, that the Philippine Islands were associated politically with the Sri-Vijayan or Madjapahit Empires of Indonesia, as Hassel (1953) has pointed out, and no evidence of any earlier direct 'Further Indian' influences. The Indian influences seen in the indigenous religions of the mountain peoples in the southern Philippines were probably mediated through Indonesia at a relatively late date.

Monumental stone structures, as noted, are totally lacking in the Philippines and even a megalithic expression except as found among the rice terracers of northern Luzon who maintain relatively permanent villages. Certainly the earliest terraces in Luzon were built after metals had appeared in the Philippines and the spread of terracing in northern Luzon occurred during Spanish times in some areas. The general absence of stone structures in the Philippines may be attributed to the widespread practice in the past of swidden cultivation associated with impermanent communities (Fox 1962: 382–3). In addition, political organization was weakly developed in the islands prior to the appearance of Islam in the southern Philippines during the fifteenth century A.D., hardly the setting for religious and politically motivated monument-building. There is no evidence, despite the writings of some historians of the emergence of a body-politic—a state—in the Philippines in pre-Spanish times. Islam, incidentally, was later to spread northward in the Philippines but was terminated by the appearance of the Spaniards and Christianity in the sixteenth century. Thus, although Asian by birth and geographical setting, the Filipinos developed after the sixteenth century within a strong Western and Christian matrix.

Although the Philippines was linked with the cultural history of South East Asia, there was clearly a time lag in cultural developments within the archipelago, due again to its marginal position. Ancient tool traditions, such as the Palaeolithic flake industries, persisted in some areas of the islands up until relatively recent times, coexisting in fact with Neolithic industries. The view that cultural developments occurred in orderly stages coeval with developments on mainland Asia has no place in Philippine prehistory. The writer and his co-workers have also been concerned with the effect of adaptive developments on Philippine cultures rather than the attitude, as found in past publications, that all social and cultural changes in the islands were a product of successive 'waves of migrations' from Mainland Asia (or elsewhere). The expanding archaeological record for the Philippines is establishing many distinctive cultural developments which would be expected in this relatively isolated maritime area. There is, nevertheless, an internal homogenity in the archaeological record of the Philippines which may be seen when one island or area is compared with another. This may be explained, in part, by a basic coastal and riverine oriented population which moved with ease by boat on relatively protected seas. Sub-cultures developed among the more isolated mountain peoples of northern Luzon and Mindanao.

Horizons in Philippine Prehistory[2]

It is necessary to briefly describe at this time the archaeological background of prehistoric developments in the Philippines prior to the first millennium B.C.

The Palaeolithic. Excavations by the writer and the staff of the National Museum since 1962 have revealed widespread Palaeolithic hunting and gathering cultures in the Philippines with predominant flake industries—the Tabonian Flake Tradition of Palawan (and elsewhere) and the Liwanian Flake Tradition of Cagayan Valley, northern Luzon (Fox, n.). Professor von Koenigswald (1958) has reported pebble tools in Cagayan Valley which he described as the Cabalwanian Industry. This unifacial pebble (or cobble) tool industry shows relationships with the Chopper-Chopping Tool Tradition proposed by Movius (1948) but the pebble tools in Cagayan form only a relatively small percentage of the Palaeolithic artefacts recovered.

In Tabon Cave, Palawan, occupied from about 50,000 to 9,000 years ago, the Upper Palaeolithic assemblages were comprised almost entirely of flake artefacts which formed a single Tabonian Tradition, the pebble or core arteacts constituting only a fraction of one per cent of the artefacts excavated in the six assemblages which have been tentatively identified. Likewise in Cagayan Valley, northern Luzon, where Palaeolithic sites have been surveyed and three partially excavated, von Koenigswald's Cabalwanian pebble tool industry formed not more than 15% of the tools recovered in any one site. The characteristic artefacts in Cagayan Valley are utilized and retouched flakes, including small 'Horsehoof' scrapers with step trimming which are identical to those found in Australia. We are describing these tools as the Liwanian Flake Industry (Fox, n.d.).

The Liwanian tools are recovered in association with extinct Pleistocene fauna, including the elephant and stegodont. All are eroding from tuffaceous deposits which are described as the 'Awiden Mesa Formation' (Lopez, n.d.) and dated by geologists to the Middle Pleistocene or Late Middle Pleistocene (Fox and Peralta, n.d.). It is now certain that Palaeolithic Man trickled into the Philippines by then existing land connections along with *Stegodon* spp.,

Elephas spp., including dwarf forms of both which evolved in the islands, *Rhinoceros* spp., *Bubalus* spp., and others. Two excavations in Cagayan Valley (Fox and Peralta, n.d.) have demonstrated that Early Man hunted or trapped and butchered the extinct proboscis; and probably, as noted, during (Late) Middle Pleistocene times. The extinct fauna may have survived in the Philippines however, to a relatively late date. This is suggested by the recovery in Cagayan of one unique bifacial tool which had been flaked from the ivory of a proboscis. This tool is not completely fossilized. Distributional evidence would suggest too that the biomass of the Pleistocene mammals, as well as Early Man (no pre-*Homo sapiens* fossils have been found), was extremely small, probably due again to the marginal and insular position of the Philippine archipelago.

A recent attempt to rework South East Asian prehistory (Solheim 1970: 137) which distinguishes a Lithic 'stage' with a Chopper-Chopping Tool Tradition in the Lower Palaeolithic (and Middle?) from subsequent Lignic and Crystallitic 'stages' which feature 'unnamed flake traditions' is not consistent with the Palaeolithic record from the Philippines and possibly Island South East Asia generally. The earliest assemblage of tools used by Man in the Philippines, as in Cagayan Valley, included flake tools and a few unifacial pebble implements. The large pebble (or cobble) tools, often more than a kilogram in weight, were uncommon and probably had specialized functions associated with hunting and butchering large mammals (Fox, n.d.).

Flake industries formed not only the basic tools of Palaeolithic Man in the Philippines but persisted among hunter-gatherers (or perhaps more appropriately described as 'gatherer-hunters' for the tropical environments of Island South East Asia provided numerous useful and edible wild plants) until Holocene times. Guri Cave in Palawan yielded a Tabonian flake assemblage which dated to only 4,000 years ago (Fox 1970). In other areas of the Philippines, such as in Sulu, Mindanao, and Samar, flake industries have been found in apparent association with pottery. In 1971, the writer photographed a flake tool being utilized by the Tasaday gatherers who live in caves in the high forest of South Cotabato province, Mindanao (Fox 1973). It is highly probable that in island South East Asia flake tools have constituted an ancient and widespread tradition which was perhaps distinct from the coexisting industries of mainland South East Asia, at least as described in the literature. This flake tradition appears to have survived in Australia until modern times, the archaic industries in Australia probably having their prototypes in Island South East Asia.

The Early Neolithic. The first major movements of man into the Philippines did not occur until after the land connections had disappeared and when, beginning about 7,000 to 6,000 years ago (possibly earlier), the sea-faring

Neolithic peoples from Asia began to settle along the coastal areas of the many islands in the Philippines. *Early Neolithic developments on mainland South East Asia were apparently equivalent in time with persisting Upper Palaeolithic flake industries in the Philippines.* There is no evidence of a 'Mesolithic period' in the Philippines with distinctive tool traditions. Nor is this European term useful, it would appear, for any area of South East Asia.

The modern archaeological record for the Early Neolithic in the Philippines, as available to the writer, is confined to only three burial sites found on Palawan Island where a related assemblage of shell (*Tridacna gigas*) and stone adzes-axes, as well as shell ornaments, have been excavated (Fox 1970). One of the Early Neolithic cave sites with *Tridacna* adzes-axes—Duyong Cave—yielded two C14 determinations from associated charcoal of 5680±80 B.P., and 4630±250 B.P.[3] No pottery was found with these Early Neolithic graves. Thousands of Neolithic tools were recovered by Professor Beyer, nevertheless, as surface collections during his extensive surveys of central Luzon, the earliest of which he dates to '. . . about 6000 to 4000 B.C. or later' (Beyer 1948: 81). Harrisson (1959: 1) dates edge ground tools in Borneo as appearing in stratigraphic context about 7000 B.C. The recovery of shell adzes in Palawan, Sulu, and Mindanao—all islands in the extreme southern Philippines—suggests that this area may have played a significant rôle in the movements of people into the south-western Pacific and the Pacific World. The shell adzes will certainly appear elsewhere in the southern Philippines.

Cave sites of the Early Neolithic are apparently extremely rare in the Philippines, at least they have not appeared during the extensive surveys undertaken by the staff of the National Museum. And the three Early Neolithic cave sites which were found in Palawan are burial sites. It is presumed that the Early Neolithic people were inhabiting open sites and more often burying their dead near their residences. It must be emphasized, in addition, that no systematic excavation has been accomplished in the Philippines of an open Neolithic habitation site (except for the brief work of Warren Peterson in north-eastern Luzon, which has not yet been published). Nor have the specific locations of Early Neolithic habitation sites been established, probably reflecting a very small population of Early Neolithic peoples and a pattern of scattered residences as found today among the swidden farmers. Preliminary excavations by the staff of the National Museum in many large shell middens containing ground stone tools and pottery were made at Lal-lo, Cagayan Valley, near the banks of the Cagayan River. Mr. Yogi Aoyagi, a student of archaeology assigned with the National Museum, has reported two C14 determinations from Lal-lo which date to the second millennium B.C. (Aoyagi: 1973), but whether these were permanent habitation sites or sites frequented periodically has not been established.

No attempt has been made in this paper to summarize the pioneer efforts of the late Professor H. Otley Beyer, the Dean of Philippine archaeology, specifically as his views are related to an 'Early,' 'Middle,' and 'Late' Neolithic of the Philippines (see Evangelista 1967). Beyer's opinions as to close relationships between the stone tools of south China and the Philippines have been widely quoted and generally accepted. Insofar as the writer knows, however, Beyer was not able to systematically excavate even one stratified Neolithic site. His publications (Beyer 1947; 1948) were based upon typological analyses of tens-of-thousands of ground and polished Neolithic artefacts, obtained largely from central Luzon. These stone tools were then arranged into time and cultural sequences following Heine-Geldern's (1932) classic formulation of the characteristics of the Austronesian cultures in South East Asia. But it must also be remembered that while Professor Beyer was working with thousands of Neolithic tools recovered in the Philippines during the late 1920s and 1930s, other scholars abroad were continuing to publish statements that the Philippines was without a Stone Age. Beyer's pioneer efforts were a major contribution to Philippine prehistory, although his views may be modified in the future in considerable detail.

Duff (1970) has reviewed and criticized Beyer's earlier views as to the relationships of the Philippine Neolithic with mainland South East Asia and the Pacific World. But Duff too utilizes Philippine data without sufficient evidence of their archaeological contexts, arranging the stone tools chronologically on the basis of typological and distributional evidences. In order to accommodate the growing body of archaeological data from the Philippines based upon excavated materials, the writer, like Evangelista (1967), is simply using a twofold division of the Neolithic—the 'Early Neolithic' and the 'Late Neolithic' (see Suggs 1960). When justified by the archaeological record, as based upon stratified sequences or absolute dating, these two broad divisions of the Neolithic have been divided into local phases.

The First Millennium B.C.

The archaeological record from the Philippines (and Palawan Island) would indicate that the period of approximately the first millennium B.C. was one of (a) new and more extensive movements of people from mainland South East Asia into the Philippines, (b) increased mobility of people within the archipelago, (c) some changes in the technological milieu correlated with the first appearance of metals, and (d) continued adaptive developments which were to eventually distinguish this insular area from other South East Asian countries. The main area of stimulus, the writer believes, was generally that of Indochina and south China, although obviously influences were received from many other regions—Indonesia, Malaysia, and Taiwan. And cultural developments in the Philippines were also shared with neighbouring areas of Asia and the Pacific.

The Late Neolithic. Despite Beyer's (1948) earlier view that pottery did not appear in the Philippines until the 'Iron Age', all of the sites of the Late Neolithic excavated by the staff of the National Museum contained pottery; and during the latest phase of the Late Neolithic, jar burial. Manunggul Cave in Palawan yielded a highly sophisticated assemblage of earthenware burial jars, including the now famous Manunggul Jar which features a ship-of-the-dead on the jar cover, dated by associated charcoal (at the University of California at Los Angeles) to 710 B.C. and 890 B.C. It is probable that two other sites in Palawan which are not typical jar-burial sites—Ngipe't Duldug Cave and Leta Leta Cave—were earlier than Manunggul Cave, although no C14 determinations have been obtained. Thus, at least two phases of the Late Neolithic in Palawan (and elsewhere) may be tentatively recognized: (1) the *Late Neolithic: Early Pottery Phase*, and (2) the *Late Neolithic: Jar Burial Phase* (Fox 1970). The appearance of pottery may be the trait which distinguished the Late Neolithic in the Philippines from earlier Neolithic assemblages, although the first Austronesian speakers (Early Neolithic people?) would appear to have had pottery in their tool-kit (Dyen, personal comm.).

The Tabon Pottery Complex of the Late Neolithic in Palawan includes both cord-marking and carved paddle impressions as a significant element of surface treatment. It was the absence of cord-marking in the early pottery of the northern Philippines which led Beyer (1948) to deny the presence of a Neolithic pottery in the Philippines. He knew that cord-marked pottery was associated with the Neolithic on the south mainland of Asia and if the Philippines had a Neolithic pottery, cord-marking should be present. Cord-marked pottery is present, at least in Palawan, Mindanao, and possibly Sulu.

Solheim (1959; 1964) has argued with considerable conviction that a pottery tradition which had developed in Indochina diffused into the Philippines and island South East Asia by at least the first millennium B.C. or much earlier— the Sa-huỳnh-Kalanay Pottery Tradition. The designation of this tradition as Sa-huỳnh-Kalanay is unfortunate, however; for both type sites are Metal Age and the Kalanay pottery in the Philippines does not include cord-marking, even paddle impressions, as a feature (Solheim 1959). In the Philippines, the Kalanay pottery is found in Metal Age sites. For area workers too, the continued emphasis on pottery traditions and broad relationships tends to disguise the highly complex local ceramic development, as is found in the Philippines, where local pottery complexes may or may not have recognizable genetic ties with a single pottery tradition. The Tabon Pottery Complex from Palawan, for example, shows some relationships to Solheim's Sa-huỳnh-Kalanay Pottery

Tradition; but the Neolithic pottery in the Palawan sites includes cord-marking and carved paddle impressions, as well as distinctive features of form, which are absent in the Sa-huỳnh-Kalanay Pottery Tradition as presently described.

Similar confusion is found in Kurjack's and Sheldon's (1970) recent description of the urn burial caves found in the mountains of South Cotabato province, Mindanao, Philippines. These caves contain unique and beautiful stone urns carved from a relatively soft limestone, often with striking anthropomorphic covers, as well as earthenware burial jars. One cave has an associated human bone collagen determination of A.D. 585 with a standard deviation of eighty-five years (Kurjack and Sheldon 1970: 18). The location of the burial caves and the use of stone urns have suggestive Indonesian affinities (Soejono: 1969) and the sites would apparently date well into the Developed Metal Age.

The pottery found with the urns shows many distinct features which would be expected, as the complex of limestone urns itself is unique in the Philippines. The pottery associated with the urn burial includes, moreover, both cord-marked and paddle impressed surface treatment, which are distributed in Palawan—the Tabon Pottery Complex—and in Sulu(?) and Mindanao; and the pottery dates from a similar time period, the Developed Metal Age when iron was present. As the Palawan data were not available to Kurjack and Sheldon, they saw similarities with the 'Bau-Malay Pottery Complex' of Borneo, which based upon '. . . Solheim's interpretation of the distribution of this ceramic complex in time and space . . . did not reach Mindanao until A.D. 1000' (Kurjack and Sheldon 1970: 18). Thus it is extremely important that generalizations concerning time and space developments in South East Asia—of pottery or of bronze drums—be based upon clearly datable archaeological contexts; that 'historical typologies' be established for South East Asia as Suggs (1961) has suggested.

It is now apparent that cord and paddle impressed surface treatment was widespread in the extreme southern Philippines but absent or rare in the central and northern Philippines. These traits were also present at Niah in Borneo. The Niah Pottery Complex shows intimate similarities with the Tabon Pottery Complex of Palawan. Cord-marking was a basic feature of Neolithic surface treatment on the mainland of Asia. The distribution of cord-marked pottery in South East Asia would suggest that it came into the Philippines from the south through movements of people around the margin of the South China Sea basin. It is significant that cord-marking faded out in the Tabon Pottery Complex during the Developed Metal Age; that is, during the first millennium A.D., which may in part explain its absence in the central and northern Philippines, if the Tabon Pottery Complex moved northward.

Burials in large earthenware jars, either primary or secondary or both, are a diagnostic feature of the terminal phase of the Late Neolithic in the Philippines. These are generally found in limestone caves near the coast; caves the mouths of which overlook the sea. Neolithic jar burials, however, have been found by Alfred Evangelista in interior open sites of central Luzon, in Nueva Ecija province. Comparative data would suggest that the practice of jar burial was more highly developed in the Philippines than elsewhere in South East Asia; an example of area specialization which was related to the treatment of the dead and a highly developed cult-of-the-dead (Fox 1970: 166).

Beyer (1948*b*) attributed the appearance of jar burial in the Philippines to the migration of a 'Jar Burial People' from the north during the 'Iron Age'. It was present in Palawan, however, during the Neolithic, and the 'trunconical' jar covers show striking relationships to identical jar covers found at Sa-huỳnh, Indochina (Janse 1959). Similarities in the pottery, as well as distinctive types of ornaments and tools, as will be seen, would suggest that the jar burial tradition recovered in Palawan was introduced into Palawan through the actual movements of people from northern Indochina and south China around the margins of the South China Sea basin. The great variation in the practice of jar burial in the Philippines from Late Neolithic times to the present, as well as its association with very different pottery complexes and other artefacts, would indicate that jar burial came into the Philippines from different directions and at different times, as both Solheim and Fox have pointed out. The origin of the jar burial tradition, however, was certainly the south mainland of Asia, the differences in this tradition as found in the Philippines being an expression of local developments and specializations.

The data on the Late Neolithic in the Philippines have been derived almost entirely from jar burial sites. No definitive excavation has been made in any habitation site of the Late Neolithic people, and the associated artefacts with the exception of ornaments provide relatively limited data. The ground stone tools which have been excavated in Late Neolithic jar burial sites are generally the types which were first described by Heine-Geldern (1945) as typical of the 'Quadrangular Adze Culture' and elaborated upon by Professor Beyer (1948) —relatively small, highly ground and polished adzes-axes of fine-grained stones, including *local* nephrite, which were rectangular or trapezoidal in cross-section with sharply bevelled edges. The inventory of tool types includes adzes, axes, gouges, chisel-gouges, and tools which are presumed to have been used in working wood—a craft highly developed among Philippine groups in prehistoric times, as at present among the Ifugao, the Tagalog, and the Kapampangan. Characteristically, the Late Neolithic adzes have fully developed stepped butts. Both sawing and drilling of stone was a diagnostic feature of Late Neolithic craftsmanship. Significantly, the 'Fully Shouldered Adze' distributed in Thailand, Malaya, Burma, and Indochina, as pointed out by Duff (1970: 127), which reached its peak in development during the Late

Fig. 1. Jade ear-pendants from Palawan Island

Neolithic, has not been recovered in Philippine sites of this period. The stone tools in the Philippines generally show closer relationships with the coastal areas of south China (Beyer 1948).

Flake tools continued to be used in Neolithic times, although rarely recognized, and a developed blade tradition appears in Late Neolithic sites of southern Luzon (Fox and Evangelista 1957; 1958) and probably will be found elsewhere. Regardless of earlier statements (Fox 1970), blade tools struck from a prepared core are *not* an attribute of the Tabonian Flake Tradition in Palawan, although blade-like flakes appear. A small flake-and-blade tradition is found in Duyong Cave, Palawan, which dates to 7,000 years ago (Fox 1970); and small blades with use-gloss—the Buadian Industry—have been recovered in Samar (Scheans, Hutterer, Cherry 1970) in a probable preground tool assemblage. It would appear at present that large, parallel-sided blades are found only in Neolithic sites, although the tradition may stem from Upper Palaeolithic industries.

A wide range of stone and shell beads and bracelets have been recovered in

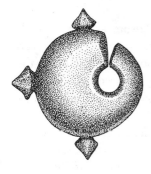

identical to types found in northern Indo-China

all of the Late Neolithic jar burial sites, as well as some stone, bone, and shell pendants. Rare gem-quality nephrite beads which were probably imported have also been excavated in Late Neolithic sites. A local nephrite was also worked, it would appear, by the Late Neolithic inhabitants of the Philippines.

The Early Metal Age. One suspects that the basic transition in the Philippines was from the use of stone tools to iron tools, although a number of sites have been excavated in Palawan which would indicate that there was a brief period—about 200 to 300 years—when the use of copper, bronze, and gold predated the appearance of iron (but these sites too have possible iron associations). Without question, there is no evidence of a Philippine 'Bronze Age', as Beyer (1948) has reasoned. To paraphrase Tom Harrisson (1959), the appearance of bronze did not distinguish a major period of technological development in Borneo and, the writer would add, the Philippines. Nor is the term 'Chalcolithic', as previously used by the writer (Fox 1967), necessary.

Jar burial sites have been excavated which include in the assemblage of artefacts both socketed bronze adzes, small trapezoidal or quadrangular stone adzes, and possibly iron. The still questionable association of iron in the early sites which contained bronze and copper has led the writer to speak of a 'Metal Age' rather than an 'Iron Age', although recognizing that the techno-logical transition was basically from stone to iron. Thus, the writer has tenta-tively recognized two phases of the Metal Age in the Philippines: (1) an 'Early Metal Age' of extremely short duration when only bronze, copper, and gold may have been present and (2) a 'Developed Metal Age' when iron imple-ments were a characteristic feature. Moulds for casting bronze adzes have been recovered in the Early Metal Age sites of Palawan (Fox 1970). The bronze tools also show their closest relationships with forms found on the south main-land of Asia. As tin has not been mined in the Philippines, it is apparent that imported bronze was reworked in the islands.

Charcoal from Manunggul Cave (Chamber B), Palawan, associated with thirty fragments of iron objects, yielded a C14 determination of 2140±100 B.P. or 190 B.C. This date is remarkably close to Professor Beyer's estimate for the appearance of iron in the Philippines: '. . . probably between 100 B.C. and A.D. 100' (Beyer 1949: 6). But there were undoubtedly areas within the Philip-pines which did not receive metals until well into the Christian era. It is probable too that the early metals were 'drift' materials, for even in historic times, the Spaniards noted, iron was difficult for the Filipinos to obtain. The writer is familiar with only one area in the Philippines which possibly pro-duced iron in pre-Spanish times—near Angat, Bulacan province—and it is likely that iron was obtained in trade during the proto-historic period from Santubong, Sarawak, where large iron-workings have been found (Harrisson and O'Connor 1969), as well as from China.

In 1971, edge ground tools and flake implements were still being used by the Tasaday of South Cotabato province, Mindanao, although they also pos-sessed one bladed tool when their material culture was first inventoried by the writer (Fox 1973). This tool, possibly one other, was obtained by them from Dafal, a hunter of the neighbouring Manubo Blit who first contacted the Tasaday a few years earlier. The manner in which the Tasaday possessed and used both stone and metal tools is also reflected in the transitional Early Metal Age sites of Palawan where both stone tools and socketed bronze adzes were excavated.

The early metals—bronze and copper—found in the Palawan caves, which date to the first millennium B.C., probably beginning about 500 B.C. or slightly later, were also associated with the first appearance of a unique series of nephrite ornaments: probably ear-pendants (Fig. 1a), which the writer (fol-lowing Beyer 1948) has described as 'lingling-o', an Ifugao term, for this mountain group casts similar metal ear-pendants today. Absolutely identical types of these jade ornaments are found in northern Indochina, south China, and the Hongkong area (Fox 1970). A glass ear-pendant of 'lingling-o' form was also recovered in Rito-Fabian Cave, Palawan, an Early Metal Age site containing iron. Bracelets made of nephrite are common in the Early Metal Age sites of Palawan (Fox 1970), but disappear generally when iron is present.

One ear-pendant which features two horse heads carved from jade (Fig. 1*b*) was recovered in Duyong Cave, Palawan, another Early Metal Age site. According to J. H. C. S. Davidson, University of London, identical types of zoomorphic ear-pendants have been recovered at Hàng-gòn and Phú-hoà (South Viet-Nam), of approximately the same date (cf. *supra*, p. 217).

The 'lingling-o' types of jade ornaments have been found in the central Philippines and in Luzon, but in extremely limited numbers when compared with Palawan, and it has been reasoned that these pendants faded out in numbers as they were being carried from the south into the central and northern Philippines during the Early Metal Age (Fox 1970). The distribution of these jade ornaments in the Philippines and mainland Asia provides additional evidence that movements around the margins of the South China Sea, which entered the southern Philippines by way of Palawan (and the Sulu Archipelago) during the first millennium B.C., had a significant impact upon developments in the southern Philippines and possibly upon the entire archipelago.

Utilizing archaeological evidence from Palawan, the Early Metal Age is also correlated with the appearance of the first ancient glass in the Philippines—beads, bracelets, and pendants. There is no evidence, as Beyer (1948) has written, that blue and green glass was manufactured in the Philippines, although possibly imported cullet was reworked. Beads of semi-precious stones with cylindrical drill holes also appear in quantity for the first time during the Metal Age. One large green glass bead from Uyaw Cave, Palawan, a type site of the Early Metal Age, is of marked interest. The form of this bead is like that of a cicada with folded wings, similar in design to ear-pendants carved from jade recovered in Palawan in the same sites (Fox 1970). Cicada glass beads of Han times have been recovered in south China, which include the element barium in the composition of the glass. The Palawan cicada bead does not contain barium; but glass which did not contain barium was also made by the Chinese. It is highly probable that this glass bead was manufactured in China, its form copying carvings in jade. Other types of early glass beads found in Palawan, however, were undoubtedly manufactured in the Near East and first traded into China and Indochina, from where they reached the Philippines.

The beads of semi-precious stones—carnelian, banded onyx, jasper, agate—are most numerous in the early phase of the Developed Metal Age when iron was present. Caustic etched beads of carnelian and black flint do appear, however, in the earliest Metal Age sites. The caustic etched beads were certainly made in South Asia, and probably India, where they appear by at least the beginning of the first millennium B.C. Identical types of carnelian beads are also found at Sa-huỳnh, and they may have first been traded into Indochina and south China before being carried into the Philippines (Janse 1959).

Prehistorians have suggested that iron came into the Philippines from India rather than China, which would appear to be supported by the early Indian-type beads found in the Metal Age sites of Palawan which contained iron. Carnelian beads are not found in Neolithic sites. But these beads probably appeared on the south mainland of Asia prior to their reaching the Philippines. An exhaustive study is now being made of the types of glass and stone beads which reached the Philippines in prehistoric times, for these were one of the highly valued items most easily carried by man during his early movements. And a study of the distribution of bead types may mirror the actual movements of people into the Philippines. Many types of glass beads made in the Near East or Europe reached the Philippines before the Europeans. A formal trade of glass beads throughout South East Asia appears to be far earlier than has been previously believed.

Sites of the Metal Age are far more numerous than Late Neolithic sites, which cannot be attributed simply to an expansion of the local population; for there is no evidence of a basic change at this time in agricultural practices, such as from swidden farming to wet rice agriculture, which would have supported a marked population growth. Abrupt changes in the artefactual record during Early Metal Age times, as well as the greater number of sites, would indicate that extensive movements of people into the Philippines occurred during the second half of the first millennium B.C. Movements into the Philippines at this time were, it would appear, stimulated by developments among the civlizations of northern Indochina and south China (Chang 1962).

The view that the civilizations of south China and Indochina had a strong impact upon Philippines during the first millennium B.C., a view implicit in the writings of Professor Beyer and many others, must be qualified however; for Filipino heritage has been shaped by many diverse influences in earlier and at later times. It is probable too that most of the basic features of prehistoric Philippine cultures—patterns of agriculture, residence, social and political organization—had been shaped during the earlier Neolithic period, and even then external influences from the south mainland of Asia may be seen in the stone tool technology. And, at all times, external influences which were minimal at best were reshaped as they were adapted to the insular and tropical environment in which the Filipino people lived, as well as being modified by the then existing prehistoric cultures.

NOTES

1. Perhaps the construct *Marasian* from the Latin term for sea, *mare*, might be useful, for this term emphasizes that these migrants were from mainland Asia and were sea-oriented groups who settled in coastal areas.

2. The writer has continued to use traditional categories for describing periods of Philippine prehistory—the 'Late Neolithic', the 'Metal Age', and so forth—categories which stress technological developments and the types of tools recovered in Philippine sites. Jocano (1967) has proposed a far more satisfactory multilinear and developmental description of Philippine culture history. The present archaeological record for the Philippines, however, is wholly inadequate for an effective developmental analysis. We know, for example, that the Neolithic peoples used a vastly improved technology of ground and polished tools but we have little archaeological evidence about their residential patterns or the plants which they cultivated. Nor, in fact, do we have even adequate descriptions of their tools and how they were used. A new scheme at this time will not produce new archaeological data; only a continuation of carefully controlled excavations and exhaustive analyses of the materials and evidences recovered.

3. All Radiocarbon-14 determinations were obtained through the courtesy of Dr. W. F. Libby of the Institute of Geophysics, University of California at Los Angeles.

The question of megaliths figures prominently in earlier studies of ancient South East Asia, but their study is surrounded by controversy. Two quite different approaches to them were represented in the proceedings of the London Colloquy, and the conflict between them will be apparent from the paper and comment which follow.

Editors.

The Megalithic Problem in South East Asia

A. H. CHRISTIE

WHEN Atkinson came to write, in *Stonehenge*, his sixth chapter 'The meaning of Stonehenge', he stated:

> This chapter is concerned with the final question: *Why?* Why was anything built at Stonehenge at all? Why, once built, was it rebuilt no less than four times? Why were the various structures built in these particular ways? What does it all *mean*? To all these questions beginning 'Why'? there is one short, simple and perfectly correct answer: We do not know, and we shall probable never know (1956: 166).

He went on to argue, following Hawkes, that there are four kinds of archaeological evidence: technological, economic, socio-political 'and evidence for those non-material aspects of life subsumed under the term "religion"'. Pointing out that the four types are arranged in decreasing order of reliability, he went on to say that when the archaeologist came to

> matters of faith and religion, he is usually inclined to take refuge altogether in silence, on the ground that archaeology can deal only with the results of human actions, not with human motives.
>
> This attitude is natural enough. One has only to think how difficult would be the task of future archaeologists if they had to reconstruct the ritual, dogma and doctrine of the Christian Churches from the ruins of the church buildings alone, *without the aid of any written record or inscription* (1956: 167).

Nonetheless, he went on to give an account of the monument's four phases in terms of the religious practices and beliefs of which it was the scene and the expression, stressing that he was 'indulging in speculation upon subjects about whicn there is no possibility of greater certainty' (168). He had in an earlier chapter shown cogent reasons why Lockyer's astronomical analysis of the monument in 1901 was unacceptable, but within a few years of his own study, work by Thom and Hawkins had made it seem more than likely that the alignments of Carnac, Brittany, and Stonehenge itself were, in effect, calendrical computers of great sophistication and complexity. If, as I believe, Hawkins has succeeded in 'decoding' Stonehenge, then one very substantial answer to its 'Why?' has been provided, though it must be assumed that such a structure had other, additional socio-economic and religious functions, if, indeed, it is even proper to separate these in the cultural period (*c.* 1900– *c.* 1400 B.C.) to which the monument belongs.

When we turn to the question of megaliths in South East Asia, the problems which confront us are essentially those to which Atkinson set out to provide answers. What are they? When were they built? How were they built? Who did it? And why? The answer to the second question—when?—is rather more complicated than in western Europe, for while we have no absolute dates (e.g. from C14) for any of the prehistoric monuments, we are dealing with a region in which megaliths are still being erected, albeit far less frequently than even a century ago, so that there is a body of ethnographic material, of very varying value, regarding all the questions which Atkinson posed. But this very material raises a number of problems which are germane to any study of the megalithic cultures with which we are concerned. It is therefore tempting, and quite natural, to turn to this evidence in order to interpret the relics of earlier periods in the region's history, and by extension, those of other areas where similar monuments are to be found. The justification for this is to be found in a passage from Chadwick, aptly cited by Wales (1957: 2) who has made a sustained study of the history of South East Asian religion and its development (1951; 1953; 1957).

> It is part of the value of the oral traditions and culture of the communities on the outer edge of the world that they have preserved for us, not the primitive experiments of early man, but reflections of the long forgotten spiritual life and art of the great civilizations of the past (1942: xv).

One of the hazards in the procedure which appears to be implied in this passage has been clearly set out by Wales himself:

> The premature fancies of Elliot Smith and Perry undertaken before even the existence of a Bronze Age in South-East Asia was known, are enough to show that no analysis of the anthropological data could have been productive before prehistory had provided us with an elementary archaeological framework (1957: 3).

It may be noted in passing that Heine-Geldern, who described Perry's main thesis as 'unacceptable and . . . indeed, in complete contradiction to well established archaeological facts', continued:

> his books contain many valuable and stimulating observations. It might prove a worthwhile task for a future critic, who is both patient and unbiased, to extricate these valuable sections from the maze of arbitrary and phantastic interpretations and unfounded assertions in which they are imbedded (1945: 149).

Heine-Geldern's own view of the megalithic cultures of South East Asia were set out in his paper of 1928 where his principal concern was with surviving megalithic users, but it inevitably involved him in the consideration of the origins of the practices which he found in the various anthropological field reports which he examined. Twenty years later he found little reason to alter his main conclusions, or the opinion that the forms of monuments and the beliefs connected with them had 'a common origin, probably somewhere in the Mediterranean region'. At that time he left open the question of dating.

> Further research convinced me, however, that it must have been brought by the same ethnic wave which introduced the neolithic Quadrangular Adze Culture (Heine-Geldern 1932: 594; 1934: 5; 1936: 35–6). If this proves correct, its first appearance in Indonesia would probably have to be dated between 2500 and 1500 B.C. (1947: 149).

The concatenation seems, on the present evidence, to be acceptable; the dates suggested are probably conservative.

The culture which Heine-Geldern was discussing is characterized by menhirs, both single and in groups, and dolmens, stone seats, terraces, and pyramidal structures, 'megalithic assembly places' (Heine-Geldern's somewhat imprecise phrase: I take it to mean areas enclosed by menhirs), and 'various types of stone tombs' (Heine-Geldern 1945: 151). This last item is again imprecise and does not seem to accord with the review of the evidence by van Heekeren who talks of

> burying the dead near the dwellings so that in death they may remain linked with the ground on which they lived (1958: 45).

He goes on to dispute the linking of this megalithic culture with the Quadrangular Adze culture on the grounds that

> up to now no megalith of a neolithic age has been found either in Indochina or in Indonesia.

This is not really a very compelling objection since in most cases there is singularly little evidence for dating South East Asian megaliths and there is not *a priori* reason for denying some of them a neolithic dating (whatever absolute chronology may be assigned to the term 'neolithic'). It may be, indeed, that in arguing thus, van Heekeren was subconsciously constructing a relative chronology of consequential phases in which, by definition, 'neolithic' would precede 'megalithic', even though the opening paragraph of his book makes the real position for Indonesia, and elsewhere in the region, perfectly clear:

> In Indonesia the Neolithic came to an end at dates that were widely different for various regions of the territory. In the Island of Enggano, for instance, an Early Neolithic Civilisation was still in existence in the 18th century; the Neolithic colony of Kalumpang in West Central Celebes has been dated at 1000 A.D. by the author, and it is general knowledge that even today in the interior of New Guinea there are Papuan tribes living in conditions of the Neolithic proper (1958: 1).

But while disputing Heine-Geldern's association of certain megalithic traits with the Quadrangular Adze Culture, he retains the former's distinction between two megalithic cultures which he characterized as Older and Younger, though van Heekeren more cautiously places the terms within quotation marks (1958: 44–5). For Heine-Geldern, on the other hand the epithets were certainly temporal as well as culturally distinctive:

> On the basis of van der Hoop's results in South Sumatra and of metal finds in the megalithic graves of the Malay Peninsula and of Java, I had to revise my chronology of megalithic cultures. I came to the conclusion that we had to distinguish at least two, and possibly more megalithic waves which reached Indonesia at different times. The older one (in reality probably a series of ethnic and cultural waves) came in the neolithic period. . . . The younger megalithic wave (again probably a series of migrations rather than a single one) came during the period of the Dongson Culture and the Early Iron Age . . . (1945: 151).

The typological distinction, following on the researches in south Sumatra, was, according to him, the occurrence in the Younger Megalithic of stone cist graves, dolmen-like slab graves, stone sarcophagi, and stone vats. In his extended account of the prehistoric background to the art of colonial India (1934: 5–40), he argued that while the older culture had been very widespread, the younger was much more restricted and had wholly disappeared. But he revised this opinion and by 1945 was of the view that:

> the younger megalithic complex still survives among the Batek of Sumatra and in Soemba and, to a certain extent, strongly mixed with elements of the older complex, in the island of Nias (1945: 151).

Although he does not mention them in his recapitulation of the Younger

Megalithic typology, Heine-Geldern was also at pains to emphasize the importance of the famous carved stones in the Pasemah region with their 'strongly dynamic, agitated style' (1945: 149). [In marked contrast, it should be noted, to the large statue from Pakauman (van Heekeren 1958: 50; pl. 19) and similar figures from Sukasari, Kamal, and Kalianjar. Equally to be distinguished are the figures reported by Kaudern from Sulawesi of which at least thirty-six are known (1938: *passim*).] It was the presence of apparent bronze drums on some of the Pasemah carvings which led Heine-Geldern, following van der Hoop to assign the Pasemah group to the Dong-son cultural phase, but the typology of the sites investigated by van der Hoop is not wholly consistent with Heine-Geldern's own differentiations, and it seems to most desirable that a reanalysis of the sorting criteria should be undertaken. In any event, the finds from Phùngnguyên (Davidson, *supra*), must bring into question the problem of dating on the mainland and this may well affect our view of the Pasemah material. That there was some connection between the Dong-son culture and the makers of megalithis has been proposed by a number of writers. A properly careful statement of the probability is that by Groslier:

Along the edge of the highlands [of Indochina] from Tran-ninh to the Moi tableland overlooking the Mekong delta in the south, and as far as the Roi Et plateau in the west, we find a chain of probably inter-related megalithic monuments. These, in their turn, form but part of a vast megalithic complex stretching from India to Sumatra, by way of Malaya (Perak especially).

Another series of ancient works has also been observed in the same area. They are generally round and consist of an earth wall surrounded by a ditch. They have only been counted from the air, and no systematic excavations have been undertaken to determine their function or date. Some may have been fortified settlements. Others, with roads radiating away from them in all directions, may well have been burial places.

The megalithic monuments proper; the urns, dolmens and menhirs of Laos, Annam and Malaya, were certainly funerary in purpose. The same is true of the curious cist found at Xuan-loc, Bien-hoa in Cochin-China. Of these the urns are the best known for they have been found in thousands in huge cemeteries, especially in Tran Ninh and Xieng Khouang (Laos). Made of white sandstone, they were three to ten feet high, and often covered with a round lid. They served as tombs; human ashes were placed inside, or, more often, in earthenware vessels at their feet and surrounded by all manner of funeral furniture. Some of the urns were decorated, for instance with the carved shape of some crawling feline animal.

Unfortunately we know nothing about the peoples who erected these monuments, nor about the succeeding stages of their civilisation. Simply because of their geographical distribution it is tempting to connect megaliths and earthworks, and to regard the former as tombs, and the latter as dwelling places, of agricultural people inhabiting the edges of the deltas and the valleys. This inland culture peculiar to the western side of Indochina and the axis of the Mekong, would then correspond to the area occupied by the Mon-Khmer peoples. This however, can only be put forward as a working hypothesis which must be treated with caution.

Moreover it would seem unlikely that this cultural complex could develop so near the brilliant Dong-son civilisation of the coastal strip without coming into contact with it. We have already mentioned that Samrong Sen, which probably shared in the origin of this megalithic civilisation and Sa-huynh, which was not far removed from it, both show the influence of Dong-son. The two cultures must therefore have been closely linked, and this gives us a clue to the date of the urns in the fields in Tran-ninh, if the analogy with Dong-son holds, and it is somewhere between the 5th and 1st centuries B.C.

Available evidence does not allow us to carry the arguments further. One point, however, is worth stressing. These urns are among the first examples of anything that can strictly be called art, that is to say the plastic expression of the beliefs and ways of life of a society (1962: 30–1).

The links proposed are somewhat tenuous, it is clear, and there are other considerations which we should take into account.

The methods of disposal of the dead seem to require to be distinguished. If we are looking for an analogy in a bronze-using culture, then the neighbouring sites of Shih-chai-shan do not, to my knowledge, provide any evidence for urn-burials, either of skeletons or of ashes. Both these have extended burials in shallow graves with grave goods. On the other hand, there is considerable evidence for an association between urns and megaliths in South East Asia, as indeed elsewhere in Eurasia. (There are, of course, other megalithic burial methods, both in single graves of stone of different types or rock-cut graves, nor do all urn burials appear to link with megaliths. This is discussed, for Indonesia, by van Heekeren (1958: 80–9). It is interesting to speculate on the Pyu stone urns as a survival of the apparently 'big man' stone urns from earlier periods in South East Asia.) The practice of surrounding a stone urn by others in earthenware, to which Groslier draws attention, is reminiscent of the western Eurasiatic barrows with a primary burial to which other urns have been added. At Bada in the vicinity of one of the largest of the Sulawesi stone figures Kaudern reported:

West of the large image a valley has been formed by the small tributary we had crossed. Its western side is gently sloping, its eastern a steep cliff. Between the gigantic stone man and this steep cliff the ground is covered with small hills, suggesting mounds. Besides, there are several circular or oval pits. It does not seem impossible that this could be a large old grave-field (1938: 96).

Similarly at Gintu he reported 'small hills, about one metre high, often more or less ranged in rows. Possibly this is a graveyard' (1938: 108). Neither of these sites has been investigated further.

The implication that the association with Dong-son can provide a dating for the Tran-ninh and related megalithic remains does not, in fact, rest upon any very secure base but if we accept it in general terms, we are no longer, as has already been remarked, bound to the previously received dating for the former. The Phùngnguyên material is particularly important here because of Groslier's postulated case for Sa-huỳnh as a linking site. Once the limiting date of 500 B.C. is removed, then the temporal distinction between the Older and Younger Megalithic begins to look considerably less significant, though at the same time it also removes the nearest thing to date that we have for any large prehistoric megalithic complex in South East Asia. *When?* remains enigmatic.

Groslier's 'working hypothesis which must be treated with caution' that the area of the megaliths coincides with that occupied by the Mon-Khmer people seems to me to raise as many problems as solutions. It appears to separate this group of monuments from others which are typologically similar in areas where there is no trace of Mon-Khmers. On the other hand, there is evidence for Indonesian languages in the area, though there is the problem of their date there: they may be the result of a later intrusion, rather than a relict from an earlier Indonesian presence. The suggestion clearly requires much more study. Wales argued in *The Mountain of God* that the Mon-Khmer were associated with the shouldered adze and thus, in his view with the Older Megalithic (1953: 135–42). In a lengthy footnote in *Prehistory and Religion in South-East Asia*, where he reiterates this view, he nonetheless draws attention to a paper by Coedès which pointed to a dynasty with Cham affinities on the middle Mekong in the fifth century A.D. (1957: 128–9). Wales is not prepared to admit the presence of anything more than a Cham occupation of an area with a basically Khmer population, though he seems to qualify this opinion in the concluding sentences of the note:

But even if we were to suppose that some Cham tribes had been in part occupation of the Middle Mekong region since Neolithic times, being remote from the coast they would not have received the full Dongsonian acculturation as did the coastal Chams. They would have maintained their basic Older Megalithic culture and would in fact have been part of the Malayo-Polynesians of Quadrangular Adze culture who intermingled with, and imparted their Older Megalithic culture to, the Mon-Khmers of Shouldered Adze culture (129).

From an earlier passage it is clear that he believes that 'the erecting of megaliths, and a complex of religious beliefs associated with them' was 'among the features imparted to the Shouldered Adze culture'. It may be noted, in passing, that Fürer-Haimendorf associated the megalithic culture of north-east India with speakers of Austro-Asiatic languages, that is with the westernmost outliers of the Mon-Khmer (1943: 177). Wales quotes, with approval, a passage from another paper by Fürer-Haimendorf which summarizes the complex of beliefs which he holds to be attributable to the practitioners of the megalithic cultures:

> the belief in an intimate relation between the living and the dead, and particularly in the powerful influence which the departed exert on the fertility of man and crops, and the conviction that the beneficial 'virtue' of a deceased kinsman can be concentrated in a stone, which is set up in his honour and becomes his seat and symbol (Fürer-Haimendorf 1945: 74).

Wales does, however, add a reservation:

> This picture, however, is an anthropological not a historical one, and so it does not tell the whole story (1957: 25)

since, in his view:

> What we have before us today represents essentially a return to primitive animism and ancestor worship, as a result of a loss of culture after the advanced influences [of previously existing more complex religious concepts—A.H.C.] had ceased to operate.

These more complex religious concepts are to be found in the 'Old Asiatic religion', expounded in *The Mountain of God*, and derive from his view of the significance of Heine-Geldern's postulated origin of the Older Megalithic in the eastern Mediterranean in the third millennium B.C.

The most convenient summary of Heine-Geldern's hypothesis, which was originally developed in 1928, is to be found in his paper of 1945:

> With very few and unimportant exceptions, the megaliths are concerned with special notions concerning life after death; that the majority are erected in the course of rites destined to protect the soul from the dangers believed to threaten it in the underworld or on its way there, and to assure eternal life either to the persons who erect the monuments as their own memorials while alive, or to those to whom they are erected after their

death; that at the same time the megaliths are destined to serve as a link between the living and the dead and to enable the former to participate in the wisdom of the dead; that they are thought to perpetuate the magic qualities of the persons who had erected them or to whom they had been erected, thereby furthering the fertility of men, livestock and crops and promoting the wealth of future generations. I compared the forms of monuments and the beliefs connected with them with similar ones in Oceania, Central Asia, India, ancient Palestine and Europe and found that they were everywhere essentially identical, or, at the very least, closely related, thereby indicating a common origin, probably somewhere in the Mediterranean region (1945: 149).

Wales accepts the general statement, but finds it rather surprising that Heine-Geldern did not suspect that the Older Megalithic 'might not have altogether escaped the influence of the higher religions developed in the urban centres of Mesopotamia and quickly diffused therefrom' (1957: 26). It was as a result of this that the bearers of this culture acquired among other things the concept of the artificial mountain, the ziggurat, which was to figure in China as *le dieu du sol* studied by Chavannes, as the *kithucie* of the Angami Nagas, the *sindibor* of the Bondos of Orissa and is also to be seen in the *kut* of the Chams as analyzed by Mus (1933: 367–410). The various pyramidal monuments of the South East Asian megalithic (e.g. Lebak Sibedug, West Java), presumably Candi Sukuh, and certainly the *foho* of the Timorese Belu (Vroklage 1953) all belong in this same series. We must, I suppose, assume, that those cultures which otherwise exhibit Older Megalithic characteristics, but lack pyramids have suffered 'a loss of culture after the advanced influences had ceased to operate' (Wales 1957: 25).

Stated thus baldly, the proposition sounds like one of the lucubrations of the original Diffusionists, but the hypothesis must, in my opinion, be treated seriously, though I do not subscribe to Wales's view that the cult is fundamentally ethnic. I think that we must pay far more attention to the possibility that some at least of the menhirs/dolmens were intended for astronomical-calendrical purposes. Hawkins (and his computer) have shown that with no more than the rudimentary structure of Stonehenge I its users were able to determine the most important twelve sun-moon-rise-set points. I have not yet been able to determine experimentally whether any of the South East Asian groupings of menhirs in rectangular arrangement enable us to make similar calculations in that region, but it is perhaps significant that both Macdonald in the case of Tibet (1953) and Maringer in the case of Mongolia (1955) have drawn attention to the cosmic implications of megaliths in those areas. Wales, while admitting the possibilities, persists in stressing the primary importance of the fertility rôle of the megaliths. In so doing, he appears to overlook the fact that one function of calendrical observations is precisely in connection with the agricultural cycle (1957: 28–9, 46–7). There are, admittedly, problems in connection with such observations in the equatorial and sub-tropical zones, but I believe that study of the possibilities are called for. A greater difficulty may be the fact that we still have no real idea of the date of the structures which may be relevant.

This brings us back to the fundamental problems which confront us in the study of the megalithic cultures of South East Asia. What are the megaliths? When were they built? By whom and why? It has been conventional since Heine-Geldern's studies to accept the concept of two cultures, Older and Younger, but the evidence from Viet-Nam is beginning to throw doubt on the temporal distinction. If we need to maintain the distinction, should we perhaps adopt some less time-tied epithets? Does the link Quadrangular Adze culture/Megalithic correspond to our present knowledge of the prehistoric archaeology of neolithic South East Asia? Can we properly link cultures, defined by type tools, with linguistic groups, and then, by a chain process, associate the introduction of megalithic cultures with the speakers of Austronesian languages? Was the function of the megaliths solely to promote fertility and to express ideas about the life after death, the two functions being linked by the facility they provided for drawing upon the wisdom of the dead ancestors? Or were they, in part, intended to serve cosmological ends, a function which is not unconnected with fertility, since it can not only provide a calendar, but also, through the power this creates, as well as the power to predict astronomical phenomena, enhance the influence of the 'big men' (for whom menhirs are erected) and thus make them more potent sources of prosperity for the group? Is there any evidence that these calendrical potentials were forgotten, at least on the periphery of South East Asia, and did they still survive at the time when the classical Khmer were constructing temple complexes with manifest cosmological implications? To what extent can the surviving megalithic cultures be used in the interpretation of monuments of much earlier date? A re-examination of the known sites, in itself a formidable enough task, may provide the answer to some of these questions. Further field-work is obviously an essential, especially to resolve the problems of dating. A re-analysis of the anthropoligical literature with new questions in the analysts minds is also required. With Atkinson, I do not believe that

> the archaeologist who offers his wares to the public has any right to take refuge in a smug nescience, by appeal to the strict canons of archaeological evidence, when faced with perfectly legitimate questions of this kind (1956: 167).

ADDITIONAL REFERENCES

Atkinson, R. J. C. 1956. *Stonehenge*. London, Hamish Hamilton.
Chadwick, N. K. 1942. *Poetry and prophesy*. London, CUP.
Hawkins, G. 1970. *Stonehenge decoded*. London, Fontana.

Comment on 'Megaliths' in South East Asia

I. C. GLOVER, B. BRONSON, D. T. BAYARD

THE words 'megalith' and 'megalithic' are useful for archaeologists in South East Asia only as descriptive terms for certain structures employing rather large rocks. There are certainly many such monuments in the region, comprising, as mentioned by Christie, 'menhirs, both single and in groups, dolmens, stone seats, terraces, and pyramidal structures, . . . assembly places or areas enclosed by menhirs, and various sorts of stone tombs.' The latter category we might profitably break down into slab-built cist graves (south Sumatra and Malaya), massive stone sarcophagi (Java and Bali), stone-lined chambers (south Sumatra and central Java), stone vats or urns (Laos, Mindanao, Minahasa, and central Sulawesi), and rectangular stone-built platforms (Flores, Sumba, Timor). We should also add large stone sculptures (south Sumatra, Java, and central Sulawesi), and the very specialized stone structures of Nias and Samosir.

Do these megaliths have any common features which enable the archaeologist to discuss them as a single class of phenomena, let alone to speak of 'megalithic culture' as has so often been done in the past? Throughout South East Asia as a whole, we believe that there is no such unity other than the fact that megaliths are built of large stones and have survived for us to see and record, whereas the majority of monuments which were structurally and functionally similar were almost certainly built of wood and are not readily discovered. Within limited areas, however, south Sumatra, the Plain of Jars in Laos, central Sulawesi, and Bali, to mention only the most obvious examples, groups of monuments survive which have, within each area, a degree of a structural and stylistic unity. Although none of these groupings has been investigated systematically, some appear sufficiently uniform to allow us to guess that they belong to a single cultural tradition, or perhaps even to a single cultural phase.

But the antiquity of none of these groups of monuments is adequately known, although it is clear that some have a considerable antiquity (2,000 years or more), whereas others have been made in the recent past and still play a rôle in the living cultures of many of the hill-peoples of South East Asia.

The purpose of these monuments is seldom precisely known but it is reasonable to suggest, on the basis of a little direct evidence, and numerous analogies with other regions, that they were usually commemorative or funerary. The hypothesis put forward by Christie, that some of the menhirs and dolmens were intended for astronomical-calendrical purposes, is new for South East Asia, and ought to be taken seriously, although as yet there seems to be no directly supporting evidence. Certainly some Indonesian peoples associate seasonal changes with the location of the rising and setting of certain stars, and use these occasions to initiate various phases of agricultural activity. As an example, we can quote the Tetum-speakers of the south coast of Portuguese Timor who initiate the different stages of rice agriculture according to the movement of the Pleiades in the sky. Thus the need for astronomical calculations is present in parts of South East Asia, despite the low latitudes and the relative lack of seasonal climatic variation.

In Polynesia and Micronesia, where we know a little more about the purposes of large stone structures (Lewis 1973), it appears that they served the purposes of nautical astronomy, as sailing-course-sighing-stones, as navigational training instruments, and for predicting the position of sunrise at the solstices.

A last subject that needs comment is the relationship between South East Asian megaliths and similar complexes of large stones from other regions. Such relationships have often been hypothesized. Indeed, the global distribution of megalithic monuments has served as the foundation for several of the more notably extreme reconstructions of human history, involving vast migrations of 'Megalithic Builders' from Europe and Africa to South East Asia and South America. One suspects that the traditional emphasis on megaliths owes much to a lingering fascination with hypotheses like this. But the hypotheses receive little empirical support. If there is no intra-regional unity of megaliths within South East Asia, still less is there convincing evidence for inter-regional unity. The south Indian megalithic monuments do not significantly resemble their counterparts in South East Asia. Even the associated artefacts are quite different. No data exist which might validate the assumption of a cultural connection between the megaliths of South East Asia and those of south India, the Mediterranean, the Pacific Islands, or Peru. To the extent that 'Megalithic' continues to connote such connections, the use of that term will be misleading and unproductive.

In summary, we can say that the label 'megalithic culture' cannot reasonably be applied to any of the phases or levels of social integration recognizable in the recent or prehistoric past of South East Asia. And given the very wide distribution in space and time, and the functional and morphological diversity of large stone structure within the region, the term has no meaning even within the restricted sense of 'culture' as used by archaeologists. In consequence, although there are many megaliths in South East Asia, a 'megalithic problem' as such does not exist.

PART II

SOUTH EAST ASIA IN THE FIRST MILLENNIUM A.D.

Protohistory and the Early Historical Kingdoms: *Introduction*

I

THE period from the ninth to the thirteenth centuries might be called the 'high middle ages' of South East Asian history, if one can be forgiven for borrowing a term originally used to refer to a chronologically parallel period in the history of Europe. Once we reach that period, we are dealing with a recognizable pattern of political and social life which can be identified, at least in outline, across the whole region. There are still many unanswered questions and much research remains to be done, but it is possible in principle to write a continuous history of South East Asia from that time onwards. When we go back beyond about 800, we enter a period whose outlines are much less clear, and where even the patterns which seemed to have been worked out by pioneer historians like Coedès are now beginning to be challenged.

If one pursues the analogy with European history, one might be tempted to adopt the term 'dark ages' to describe the centuries before the emergence of the temple-building states of Cambodia and Java and the Buddhist kingdoms of Thailand and Sumatra. But the very suggestion highlights a significant difference between South East Asia and Europe. For Europeans are able to look back across the 'dark ages' to a time when large parts of their region were ruled from Rome, and to feel a sense of broken continuity with an imperial past. In South East Asia there was never any comparable period. The Chinese conquered what is now northern Viet-Nam, but their rule did not extend farther south; whilst Indian cultural influence reached South East Asia by other means than that of political conquest. It is necessary to consider the origins of South East Asian civilization in terms of the protohistory, and the prehistory, of the area itself: it was never merely an appanage of India or of China. But in attempting to define those origins we must recognize that we are embarking upon an extraordinarily difficult task.

The tendency of much previous historical writing about early South East Asia has been to identify an important change in the region as a whole at about the middle of the second century A.D. That was the period when the first recorded relationships are found between the southern Chinese state of Wu and a number of countries in the Nan-hai, notably Lin-i and Fu-nan. The Funanese kings known to the Chinese as Fan Shih-man and Fan Chan, together with the (possibly Cham) leader who established Lin-i in 192, must count as the earliest South East Asian rulers whom we can know by name; whilst K'ang T'ai, who visited Fu-nan about 250, was the first Chinese visitor to the region to record his direct impressions. The earliest archaeological evidence of Chinese presence in South East Asia (south of Nam-Viet and Giao-chi) is probably the Han pottery mentioned by B. Bronson as having been discovered near the southern tip of Sumatra (*infra*, p. 333).

It may be mentioned too that at both Oc-eo (southern Viet-Nam) and P'ong Tuk (Kanchanaburi, Thailand), evidence has been found of contact with second- or third-century Rome. The impression of change in this period is completed by the fact that the first known Sanskrit inscription from South East Asia, found at Vo-canh (Nha-trang, Viet-Nam), would now appear also to date from the third century A.D.

There can be no doubt that all this evidence has great significance for the development of maritime contacts between South East Asian societies and other parts of the world, both to east and to west. In particular, the contacts with China represent the first step towards what became the 'tributary system', which was to last until the nineteenth century. But we have already seen (Part I) that by the latter part of the first millennium B.C. there was an observable distinction between maritime and hinterland societies in several parts of South East Asia, and it may well be the case that the first exchanges of missions between China and South East Asia represent a more significant change on the Chinese side than in South East Asia itself. We might be wise not to attach too great an importance to the events of the third century, merely because they were responsible for our first written source materials relating to South East Asia. More significant changes would appear to have come both earlier and later.

As with the prehistory of the region, so also in relation to the protohistoric period, the established view has been challenged most effectively by the results of recent excavations. Two of these are in central Thailand: U Thong, where a site called Tha Muang was dug by W. Watson with H. H. E. Loofs in 1965–6; and Chansen (Nakorn Sawan province), dug by B. Bronson and G. F. Dales in 1968–9. Both are 'Dvāravatī' sites, whose upper levels belong to the seventh century and later, but their deeper levels go back much earlier; in both cases to the third or second centuries B.C. and at Chansen probably even farther in time. It is perhaps of some significance that these sites show continuity with later periods, whereas major prehistoric sites such as Ban Kao, Non Nok Tha and Ban Chieng, though they continued into the 'iron age', were all abandoned before the rise of 'Dvāravatī'. A third site with continuity between the end of the first millennium B.C. and the second half of the first millennium A.D. is that of Phimai, also discussed in Part I (*supra*, p. 63). We have already seen that the evidence concerning the first use of iron in this area is still inconclusive, but the material from Chansen—and also from Lopburi (Artillery Centre)—suggests if nothing else that central Thailand was an important area in the early development of iron metallurgy in South East Asia. It is very likely that the consequence was an expansion of both settlement and population in certain lowland areas, though it may have been less rapid here than it was in India. It is to this development that we should look if we are seeking the first signs of that stage in South East Asian history which was later to produce Angkor and Borobudur.

Two other excavations have been important for the development of our understanding of the first half of the first millennium A.D.: at Oc-eo, and at Beikthano in Burma. Although it can be criticized on strict archaeological grounds, the excavation undertaken by L. Malleret at Oc-eo between 1940 and 1945 produced important evidence of a large rectangular site which appears to have been a major port during the third to sixth centuries. Its people had wide trading contacts with areas outside South East Asia, and the site has produced early evidence of both Hinduism and Buddhism. There are interesting parallels between Hindu finds from this region and some from peninsular Thailand. And it should also be mentioned that a number of wooden Buddha images dug out of the wet ground of Thap-muoi and other places in the Mekong delta and Transbassac have been dated by radiocarbon to the period between the second and seventh centuries.

At Beikthano, a site long believed to have been important in the Pyu period was excavated by U Aung Thaw and U Myint Aung in 1959–63 (Aung Thaw 1968). That settlement too had a long history, yielding four radiocarbon dates in the first to fourth centuries A.D., and had early contacts with India. Cultural affinities between this site and the central Thailand sites just mentioned, as well as between the latter and the Oc-Eo, are suggested by B. Bronson and H. H. E. Loofs in their papers (*infra*). Loofs suggests that we might indeed postulate a cultural zone stretching from lower Burma to lower Cambodia, as the context of this earliest period of 'Indianization'. Mainly Mon-Khmer and Pyu in its ethnic character, at that period, it may not be without significance that such a zone would also correspond to the area which was to be most receptive to Theravāda Buddhism in the thirteenth to fifteenth centuries.

It is in this archaeological context that we should view the debate, initiated by Boisselier, about the location of 'Fu-nan'. Since it was seen by Pelliot and Coedès as the predecessor of Chen-la, it was natural that they should place it in lower Cambodia. Boisselier suggests that its centre might have been closer to U Thong. But perhaps a more important question than that of its precise location is that of the whole character of political organization in South East Asia at the relevant period. Unfortunately the archaeological evidence throws little or no light upon that problem, but in writing about the fifth and sixth centuries (*infra*), C. Jacques warns against too ready a willingness to assume later historical patterns of statehood in dealing with early Cambodia.

The suggestion of a cultural axis linking Oc-eo to U Thong, Chansen, and Beikthano (and perhaps also to peninsular Thailand) must be considered in relation to the older conception of an 'Indonesian' cultural 'axis' linking central Viet-Nam (Lin-i, and later Champa) not only to Fu-nan but also to Java. This theme is covered in a paper by A. H. Christie (*infra*), and he suggests in passing that the 'Murunda' kingdom with which the Funanese had contacts in the mid-third century may well have been in Java. The subsequent relationship between Cambodia and Java is indicated by their Hindu-Buddhist temples of the seventh or eighth centuries onwards, and by evidence showing direct historical contacts around the year 800. It is not inconceivable that Oc-eo owed its early importance as an urban and commercial centre to a position where these two cultural 'axes' crossed one another. In his paper dealing with the origins of the state in South East Asia, Bronson argues that the most important impetus towards the growth of more elaborate political structures came with an expansion of external trade: trade, that is, involving contacts over an area well beyond the initial reach of the lowland societies which had begun to develop during the first millennium B.C. The theory is inevitably still somewhat speculative, but it fits in with such evidence as we have so far. It implies that we should place the first evidence of contacts with India and China into a context which also included significant developments within the lowland societies of South East Asia during the centuries between about 200 B.C. and A.D. 500. Other aspects of these developments are considered in papers by R. C. Y. Ng and P. Wheatley, dealing with the agricultural environment and with the origins of the city in mainland South East Asia.

When we come to the second half of the first millennium A.D. we are dealing with a period whose outlines are more familiar, and where arguments about change can at least be measured against a growing body of written source materials. Nevertheless, the papers which follow indicate that there is often room for a new approach to old evidence, and that the established picture of even this period must now be revised. Several of the papers examine new ideas or new evidence, or both, in a number of different fields of research. J. G. de Casparis examines the palaeographical aspect of the early inscriptions, with special reference to Indonesia; whilst H. L. Shorto considers some problems and suggestions arising from the study of the languages of mainland South East Asia. The sculptural and other artistic evidence of the early Indianizing period is considered in two papers relating to the development of Dvāravatī art, by M. C. Subhadradis Diskul and E. Lyons. In that field too, Thailand is an area where some interesting discoveries have been made which reflect the spread of Hinduism and Buddhism, without the building of large temples. The problem of periodization in relation to temples is discussed in a paper by

Soekmono, dealing with Java. It is not yet possible to balance this with a reinterpretation of the temple-chronology of pre-Angkorian Cambodia which is now badly needed, but it is clear that we must look more carefully at the period of the seventh and eighth centuries if we are to understand the eventual emergence of the much vaster temples of the era of Borobudur and Angkor Wat.

The political and social development of several lowland areas of South East Asia during the seventh to tenth centuries is considered in a number of papers. That by R. B. Smith argues for a fundamental change in the central areas of the Indochinese peninsula during the seventh and eighth centuries and considers the historical problems—and possible interpretations—arising from a re-examination of the record of South East Asian tribute missions to China between 600 and 800. It also notes that this was perhaps the period in which a sharp contrast developed between western and eastern areas of the region: the former characterized by Buddhism and stupas, and also (in Thailand) fortified settlements; the latter by temple-building and perhaps more highly organized societies. The problem of Srīvijaya is considered briefly from an archaeological point of view, in a paper by Bronson on Sumatra.

Three papers deal specifically with Cambodia. C. Jacques criticizes the old approach to early Cambodia, which assumed a monolithic Chen-la taking the place of a monolithic Fu-nan sometime during the sixth century: he presents a picture rather of small states amongst which the hegemony might move around from one period to another. It is in this context that O. W. Wolters examines the problem of Hinduism in seventh-century Cambodia, emphasizing the reception of those aspects of the religion which seem to have fitted in best with the needs of a society of warriors and small principalities: and in particular the concept of *bhakti*. The problem of the lower levels of agrarian society in Cambodia (before 800) is discussed by J. M. Jacob in a paper that examines certain aspects of the contents of the Khmer inscriptions, which have so far not been thoroughly examined for the light they throw on the character of a temple-building, temple-endowing society. Between them these three papers show how much can still be done towards the political and social analysis of the area which, by the ninth century, was undoubtedly the most 'advanced' part of South East Asia. The only other area for which there is a comparable opportunity is Java, and for that we have a paper by Boechari which discusses not only the problem of the shift from central to east Java in the tenth or eleventh century, but also several other aspects of the Javanese society indicated by the inscriptions of those times.

The Geographical Habitat of Historical Settlement in Mainland South East Asia

RONALD C. Y. NG

THE geographical extent of settlements is a function of the ability of the inhabitants to overcome some of the restrictions imposed by the environment. There are very few, if any, ecological niches in both historical and modern times that provide all the necessities for sustaining human life without the application of ingenuity and technology and of manual effort. Habitats, whether congenial or harsh, are the combined result of the relevant sets of environmental constraints. However, these environmental controls and limitations are and must be related intimately to the level of technological achievement of the historical time period and of the inhabitants concerned. This relationship between environment and technology is a dynamic one, and with every increase in technological skill there is a corresponding decline in the control and limitation of the particular environment. Through this process, the milieu of any set of settlers can be seen to be always evolving. The pace of this evolution can be said to be regulated by a myriad of internal and external factors which are subject matters for the historians, archaeologists and related professional specialists.

In situations where agricultural activities, particularly crop husbandry, form the basis of life and livelihood, as has been the case in mainland South East Asia since the first known settlements were established, this intimate relationship between environment and technology becomes even more significant than in other types of culture. Even in the present day, at localities within earshot of a bustling regional urban city, a seasoned field anthropologist could still be very much impressed by this intimate relationship which determines the survival of the individual, and his family and progeny.

> I was . . . impressed with how much particular bits of knowledge and understanding of local environment, rice farmers use in the course of a year. They understand a very great deal about how local soils, depths of water, seeds, animals etc., operate. If they tend to feel that they have very limited resources to do anything else beyond what they are doing, it does not follow that they understand only a little . . . (J. Ingersoll: 1972).

From the agronomic point of view, Grist concludes that 'there is probably no important cereal crop that is more influenced by environment than paddy' (1959: 63).

The dominant culture of mainland South East Asia has been of the lowland type. The constraints in lowland tracts are not altitude but the angle of slope of the land. Just over half of the land area of Thailand, Laos, Cambodia, and southern Viet-Nam has an angle of slope of less than twenty degrees, and could therefore be terraced for rice cultivation without too much difficulty even when the work had to be done with simple implements and predominantly manual labour. Most of these lowlands are in the deltaic areas, in the river valleys and on the inland plateaux. Following the regional scheme adopted by the ECAFE Committee for the Co-ordination for the Investigation of the Lower Mekong Basin (Mekong Committee), there are eight major topographical tracts in the basin and adjacent areas. The first of these is the Cambodian lowlands and the Mekong delta, where practically all the land area could be classified as lowland. The second tract is the Annamite Highlands, comprising the mountains of Laos and Viet-Nam north of the Mekong delta. The lowlands of this region include the Plateau de Khammouane, Plateau des Bolovens, Plateau du Kontom, Cao-Nguyen Dar-Lac, Plateau du Mnong, Cao-Nguyen Di-Linh, and the coastal lowlands of Hue, Da-Nang, Quang-Ngai, Qui-Nhon, Nha-Trang, and Ninh-Thuan. The Korat plateau forms the third region, where low relief predominates with the exception of the Phu Phan Hills, the Dang Rek Range, and the western hills of Phetchabun. The fourth region is the northern Laos mountains and hills where the Luang Prabang valley and the Plateau de Xieng Khong are the only extensive lowland areas. The mountains of northern Thailand and Phetchabun form the fifth region. Here the lowlands are found in the small intermontaine plains and the basin of Chiang Rai, Payao, Chiang Mai, Lamphun, Lampang, Nan, Phrae, and Sayabouri. The Chao Phya valley and its delta constitute the sixth region which is almost entirely lowlying. The Western Thai hills mark the border with Burma and form the seventh region and here there are virtually no lowlands of any extent. The eighth and last region in this schema is the Western Cambodia hills, where the only lowlands are found on the coast. These include the coastal plains of Rayong, Chanthaburi, Trad, Kampong Som, and Kampot. It is interesting to observe that many of the historical boundaries and limits of spheres of influence of the ancient kingdoms follow these topographical regional divides more closely than those of the present-day political boundaries in the region.

The relevant environmental conditions and technology for a consideration of historical settlement in mainland South East Asia in the post-Christian era are no doubt those related to lowland rice cultivation. Rice cultivation in its various primative forms is of great antiquity in the region. From the large number of wild species found here, it has been suggested that South East Asia might well be one of the original homes of the *oryza* (Vavilov 1926). Recent work (Solheim 1972: 36) suggests that the post-Hoabinhian peoples in northern

Thailand had known domesticated rice as early as 5000 B.C. Rice cultivation, albeit in its rudimentary form, has been established as part of the Dongsonian culture (Bronze and Iron Ages) in Tonkin by the work of Goloubew (1929). However, the prehistory of South East Asia, and particularly the rôle of rice cultivation in its various overlapping cultures, is still shrouded in controversy; and the fragmentary evidence from various parts of this vast tract of land mass of sub-continental dimension does not yield any conclusive proofs one way or the other.

The rôle of rice cultivation in society was much clearer when South East Asia felt the earliest impact of Indian culture. According to Coedès (1968: 12) the cultivation of irrigated paddy and the domestication of oxen and buffaloes were known to the people inhabiting the region. It seems that for several ensuing centuries, the practices of rice cultivation have changed relatively little. The success of rice planting, then as now, depended to a large degree on the ability of the farmer to ensure an optimal supply of water, coming mainly from natural rainfall and supplemented to a varying degree by various forms of irrigation, ranging from crude weirs on the stream bed and retention ponds for flood water, to the substantial modern irrigation dam and canal systems.

The rainfall regime however, in terms of the annual total amount and its distribution, presents much greater variations from place to place. Generally speaking, the climate of South East Asia can be described as a monsoonal one, characterized by the annual reversal of the prevailing wind directions separated by the two transitional periods. The rainfall totals of most areas are in excess of 1500 mm and can reach as high as 2500 mm in more exposed locations and mountainous areas. This amount is considered sufficient to support many of the known major staple food crops like rice and maize, especially when it is concentrated in most places during five to seven months of the year. However, such concentration has meant that under a low technological level of rainfed cultivation, only one crop could be grown annually. In some sheltered spots, the rainfall totals are much lower and cannot normally be sufficient for the range of staple crops that are known to the inhabitants, without some form of irrigation facilities. A dominant characteristic of the monsoonal rainfall regime is that it is associated with a marked degree of variation both in the timing and duration of the rainy season and in the total amounts received every year. At a primitive level, that is before the introduction of irrigation technology, the minimum threshold of total rainfall needs to be much higher than that expected in areas supporting people of higher technological achievement, in order to assure a sufficient harvest from the area which they could possibly manage to plant for their subsistence needs. Although the various measurements of the precipitation cycle could not be viewed as totally deterministic in defining the extent of the habitable milieu at various historical stages of settlement, it is logical to assume that the nearer the annual rainfall total to the minimum threshold and the greater the annual variations in the total amount, the greater will be the corresponding danger of crop failures with attendant threats of deprivation and hunger. Such areas could at best be marginal and peripheral areas appending to major social, cultural and political centres—marchlands in short. However, one must remember that the minimum rainfall threshold is not a static one and it could be and has been successively lowered with every stage of technological advance.

All the fundamental rubrics of irrigated rice cultivation, which replaced the earlier rainfed agriculture, were present even in the early centuries of the post-Christian era. Subsequent stages of technological evolution were more concerned with state organization of irrigation systems over the areas they ruled. The first stage of communally organized irrigation in mainland South East Asia was almost certainly the organization, by groups of inhabitants, of the construction and maintenance of crude weirs across the shallower and narrower stream beds in order to divert the river water into dug irrigation channels serving all the land cultivated by the people who contributed the labour. Such practices can still be seen in the northern valleys of present-day Thailand.

The flourishing Khmer Empire could be said to have been based on the development of an ingenious system of large-scale irrigation and water control. The extensive lakeshore tract of the Tonle Sap, on which Angkor Wat was constructed, is one of the most inherently fertile areas in South East Asia. But this tract is only exposed for cultivation during a short space of time every year and this coincides with the dry season when the water level is at its lowest. The natural rainfall at this time of the year is normally insufficient to support the rice crops. The essence of the Angkor system is the storage of part of the flood water in the Tonle Sap for regulated release during the planting season of rice.

In the area of the Red River Delta, the strength and prosperity of the Annamite Kingdom was very much due to success in harnessing the water of the Song Koi and Song Noi, which enabled the inhabitants there to produce a crop of rice during the dry season after the first main season crop. Because of the cultural heritage and the industry of the people, the stages of development followed one another in rapid succession. On a lesser scale one can see that the rise of the Kingdom of Sukothai, which eventually forced the northern kingdom of Chiang Saen, Chiangmai and Chiangrai into relative eclipse and final collapse, was due in no small measure to the successful introduction of a rudimentary state-organised irrigation system as described in the stone inscription of Ramkhamhaeng.

In present-day Thailand, the vast tract of land in the Chao Phya delta to the south of Ayuthia was not developed to any great extent before the Ratanakhosin period. The settlement of the Rangsit, Chachongsao and

Nakhon Nayoke areas had to await the introduction of modern irrigation engineering skills from a foreign, Western source in the 1920s; almost 150 years after the fall of Ayuthia. It could be said that with the prevalent technological skills of the day, Ayuthia had actually reached the end of the road in the expansion of its productive milieu soon after the consolidation of the Kingdom.

This delicate balance of agriculture and water control has been described in much detail elsewhere, and has been termed a 'hydraulic society' by Wittfogel. The point of departure here is that this balance can at best be a temporary equilibrium and at any single stage, including the present day, the perfect adjustment of the system is more often the exception than the rule. Marginal areas have been settled, albeit sparsely, and crop failures still occur from time to time even in this modern technological age. These failures are very much the result of applying inappropriate or inadequate irrigation techniques for the areas in question. Large areas with millions of inhabitants still await the introduction of modern irrigation facilities as envisaged by the efforts of the Mekong Development Scheme to rid them of the difficulties of periodic food shortages and lack of parity in the level of agricultural income compared with their fellow countrymen living in more favourable environs.

Water control does not merely imply manipulation of water for paddy cultivation to supplement natural supplies, but also the ability to remove excess water when it is not needed. It is customary in many countries to drain the land at certain times in the rice cultivation cycle, such as for weeding and fertilizing. It has also been proposed that frequent draining of the rice soils has a beneficial effect on soil aeration and on root penetration (Grist, 32). In areas that are subject to deep annual flooding and have not been regulated to any extent, only the floating variety of rice can be grown. In historical times, such areas included the lower Chao Phya valley, the lakeshore of Tonle Sap and parts of the Mekong Delta in southern Vietnam. Floating rice generally produces much lower yields than transplanted rice on irrigated paddies, and cannot produce the necessary surplus for the evolution of a culture that contains social classes like artisans and warriors, not directly involved in food production. Until quite recently, such environs which allow only floating rice to be grown were still sparsely settled in spite of mounting population pressure in other areas where water control could be more easily achieved.

Although it has often been said that even the poorest soils would support a crop of rice provided sufficient water is available (Pendleton, 1957), and that paddy apparently makes no special demand regarding soil, the influence of soil characteristics must still be of some importance (Grist, 12). The texture of the soil has an important bearing on the water supply, in that clayey and clayey loam soils are more retentive of water and lessen the demand for irrigation water. The inherent natural fertility finds reflection in the yield of the crop, other factors being equal. Alluvial soils on river banks and flood plains, where the soil nutrients are frequently replenished by fresh silt, generally produce larger quantities of paddy for the same effort, both human and animal, than is the case with sandy and skeletal soil.

The most preferred soil series for rice cultivation in mainland South East Asia is that of the poorly drained alluvium, which is characterized by high water retentivity and high natural fertility. These two factors combine to make possible rather high yields of paddy, even under rather primitive methods of water control and cultural practices. Such soils are found located in the following areas: on the coastal lowlands on the Vietnam coast, from Quang-Tri to Hue, Da-Nang, Quang-Ngai, Binh-Dinh, Quang-Nam, Khanh-Hoa, Nha-Trang and Phan-Thiet; in the Deltaic area of the Mekong extending into Cambodia and up along the Mekong River to southern Laos; in the valleys of the Mekong tributaries of the Chi and the Mun in north-east Thailand; on the Vientiane plain; in the coastal area at the head of the Gulf of Thailand; and along the valley of the Menam Chao Phya and in isolated pockets of the Ping, Yom and Nan in northern Thailand (Map 1).

Whereas water control technology is spatially transferable, inherent soil suitability is location-specific. Thus one can envisage that the water control technology possessed by the early peoples of South East Asia was applied to areas where the soil was found to be capable of producing a good crop with some form of irrigation. It can be said that the quality of the soil could be improved by such practices as the application of natural fertilizers in the form of animal manure. But unlike say, India, mainland South East Asia has never had a tradition of extensive animal husbandry. Even in the present day animals are domesticated mainly for the purpose of providing for the needs of farming. It is therefore unlikely that throughout the present millennium much conscious effort has been exerted on improving the soil. Besides, when the population density was rather low and so much good land was still awaiting human settlement, there was little need for settling in less favourable locales. The settlement of marginal areas in terms of paddy cultivation has been but a recent phenomenon (Ng, 1969).

Humic gley soils are another series that is also capable of giving a high return for effort devoted to paddy cultivation. These soils are more freely drained and have slightly lower inherent fertility than the alluvials. Such soils are found on the southern border of the Tonle Sap, in the Chao Phya valley, in Phetchabun and some valleys of northern Thailand and Laos. This slightly inferior land is invariably located on the periphery of the large tracts of alluvial land and probably represents areas in which settlement was later extended from the heartland of the alluvial tracts. Water supply on the humic gley soils is slightly more difficult to achieve than on the poorly drained alluvials and requires a more sophisticated technique for water control. A later date for settlement than the alluvials can therefore be inferred.

Map 1 Areas highly suitable for paddy

● Major centres
(for identification see Map 3)

Lacastrian soils as found on the lakeshore of Tonle Sap are basically fertile, but these low-lying soils would be waterlogged for the greater part of the year, particularly during the rice planting season. The yield of paddy would generally be much lower in spite of the inherent fertility. The proper handling of lacastrian soils for successful rice cultivation depends on a mastery of drainage which even from today's experience is more problematic than water supply and requires a higher degree of technological achievement.

In a monsoonal climate characterized by the existence of a prolonged dry season and variable annual rainfall, the availability of potable water from ground water sources must also be considered as an important determinant for human settlement. Potable water supply in the dry season is still a problem in many marginal areas which are more recently settled. In about a third of

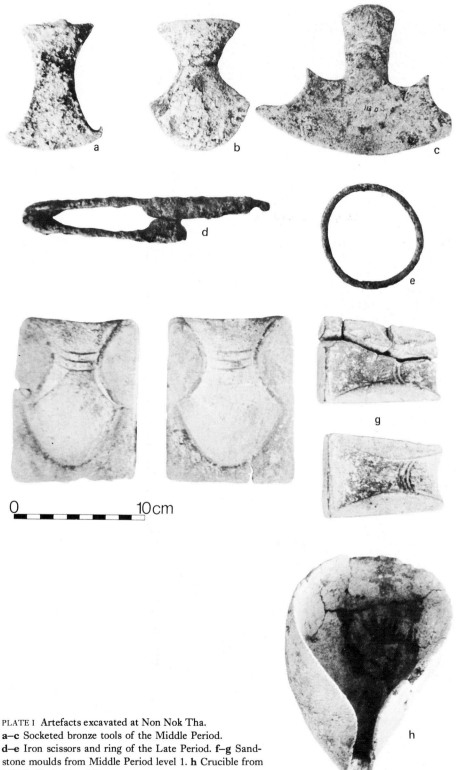

PLATE I Artefacts excavated at Non Nok Tha.
a–c Socketed bronze tools of the Middle Period.
d–e Iron scissors and ring of the Late Period. f–g Sandstone moulds from Middle Period level 1. h Crucible from
Middle Period level 5.

PLATE II Excavations at Ban Chieng. The painted urn at lower right was found in Pit B. Ch. 1/73.

PLATE III Pottery excavated at Kok
Charoen. **a** Kok Charoen I. Sub-spherical
urn with cord impressions. **b** Kok
Charoen I. Pedestal bowl with burnished,
haematite-red surface. **c** Kok Charoen II.
Pedestal bowl on fluted stem. **d** Kok
Charoen II. Pedestal bowl with pricked
decoration. Height: IIIa 13.5 cm; the
others 15–18 cm.

PLATE IV Incised and impressed jar from bottom layer at Non Nok Tha, North eastern Thailand; **b** Red on tan painted jar from Non Nok Tha; **c** Incised and impressed jar of prepainted level of Ban Chiang pottery (Jar in National Museum, Bangkok); **d** Painted jar said to be from Ban Chiang (*collection of Princess Chumbhot, Bangkok*).

PLATE V Phimai black pottery: **a** Shallow
bowl with straight rim and angle; **b** Shallow
bowl lenticular design on inside bottom; **c**
Globular pot with horizontal, parallel lines on
shoulder; **d** Large globular jar with three rows
of impressed circles on shoulder and widely
spaced polishing marks on body below
shoulder.

PLATE VI Bronzes from the Tien
necropolis at Shih-chai-shan (Shi-zhai-
shan), Yünnan: **a, b, c** Decorated drums;
d, e Models of houses (respectively M12-
26, M13-2, M20-1, M6-22, M3-64).

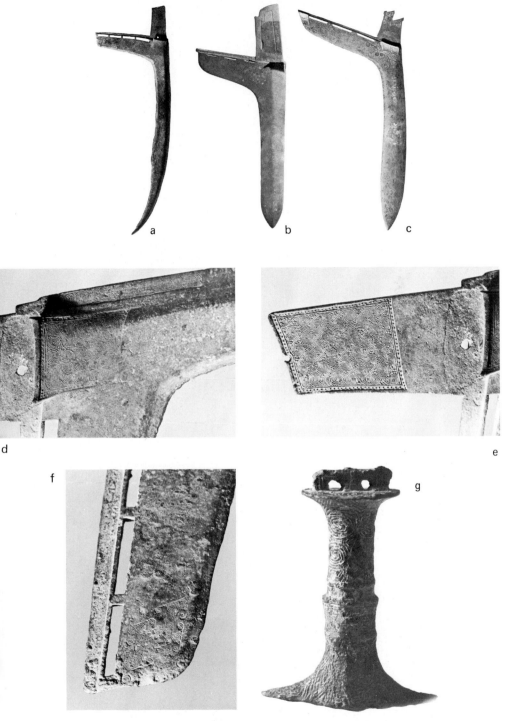

PLATE VII **a** Ko dagger-axe; 1. 72.5 cm. Udorn, N. Thailand. **b** Ko dagger-axe;
1. 21 cm. Provenance unknown, NW Thailand. **e** Ko dagger-axe; 1. 35 cm. Nan
Mu'ong, NW-Thailand. **d, c, f** Details of type A1; decoration on tang, wings and
shank. **g** Dagger-hilt; l. (without top figure) 8 cm. Uttaradit.

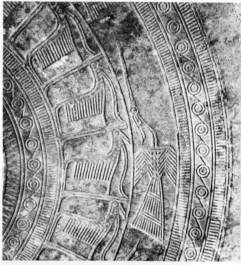

PLATE VIII Bronze drums from West Malaysia. **a** Drum found at Kampong Sungai Lang, Selangor. **b** Detail of the tympanum. **c** Detail of the tympanum of the second drum found at Kampong Sungai Lang, Selangor. **d** Fragment of a damaged drum found at Kuala Terengganu.

a

b

PLATE IX **a** Bronze bell from Klang, West Malaysia. **b** Burial exacavated at Sab Champa, Central Thailand. Flexed burial, S.P. II, with head towards the East.

a

b

c

d

e

PLATE X **a** Bronze Buddha from P'ong Tuk, h. 23 cm.
b Bronze Buddha from Nakorn Pathom, h. 20.5 cm.
c, d, e Three sculptures of Buddha on Banaspati.

a

b

PLATE XI **a** Toilet tray from Nakorn Pathom, 250.5 cm × 350.5 cm. **b** Seal from Nakorn Pathon l. 4 cm.

PLATE XII **a** Standing Buddha. Stone. National Museum, Bangkok. h. 59.3 cm. **b** Buddha seated under a Nāga. Stone. Found at Muang Fai, North East Thailand. h. 1.05 m. **c** Meditating Buddha. Stone. Found in a cave at U Thŏng, Central Thailand. U Thŏng National Museum. h. 1.59 m. **d** Standing Buddha. Stone. Found at Dong Si Mahapot, Prachinburi. **e** Standing Buddha. Bronze. Excavated at Muang Fai, North East Thailand. h. 1.20 m. **f** Meditating Buddha. Stone. Lopburi National Museum.

PLATE XIII **a, b, c** Fragments of silver plates from Kantarawichai, North East Thailand. **d** Stucco head of a dvārapāla from Khubua, Ratburi, South Thailand. **e** *Ubosoth* building excavated at Kantarawichai, North East Thailand. **f** Carved *sima* stone from North East Thailand.

b

a

PLATE XIV Khmer Temples of the Pre-Angkorian Period (7th–8th centuries). **a** Ashram Maha Rossei, Phnom Da (Angkor Borei), Cambodia. 'Funan style', 7th century. **b** Prasat Preah Srei, Cambodia. So-called 'Mixed style', transitional between 'Prei Khmeng' and 'Kompong Preah'

PLATE XV Javanese Temples of the Central Javanese Period (7th–8th centuries). **a** Candi Arjuno, Diëng, 'Old Diëng' style, late 7th–early 8th century. **b** Candi Bimo, Diëng, 'New Diëng' style, 8th century.

b

PLATE XVI Javanese Temples of the Central Javanese Period. **a** Candi Mendut, Magelang. 9th century. **b** Candi Kalasan (III), Prambanan. 9th century (?).

the land area of mainland South East Asia, there are small to moderate quantities of potable water located only a few metres below ground level which could fairly readily be reached by shallow open wells. Larger than average quantities could be found in areas with sandy alluvium and poorly consolidated rocks.

Map 2 Areas with access to potable water

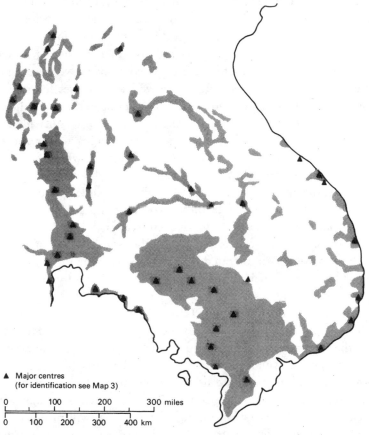

▲ Major centres
(for identification see Map 3)

0   100   200   300 miles

0   100   200   300   400 km

Areas where potable water could be obtained for the greater part of the year are shown on Map 2. It can be seen that the most extensive of such areas is in the Cambodian Lowlands. The Chao Phya basin in Thailand is also favourably endowed. More scattered areas could be found in northern Thailand, Central and Southern Laos, in north-east Thailand and coastal areas of Vietnam. Luang Prabang is situated on one such aquifers; which, combined with other factors of the environment, has made it suitable for early settlement.

Having considered the various environmental controls for settlement and paddy cultivation in the context of mainland South East Asia, and the geographical extent of the favourable tracts by each criterion, one might determine the location and the extent of each suitable tract for habitation by inhabitants cultivating irrigated paddy, at a time when the population pressure was such that suitable land could still be found and marginal land need not be settled.

The various environmental factors which are relevant to the understanding of the extent of the favourable habitat can be considered, as it were, as a set of filters which differentiate the area into suitable and unsatisfactory tracts. For example, the topographical limitations, relative to the existing agricultural technological level and settlement preference, could be viewed as a relief filter that, when applied, rules out all such areas which are either too steep or too high in elevation for rice cultivation at the time. Considering only those tracts which satisfy this particular condition, the inherent soil fertility filter is then applied, which in turn reduces the area somewhat to leave only those tracts that satisfy both conditions. Onto the resultant pattern, which highlights the suitable agricultural tracts, may be superimposed the settlement filter, as expressed in terms of the availability of easily accessible sources of potable water. This has the effect of farther restricting the habitable milieu, by excluding from areas favourable to rice cultivation all such locales where domestic water could be a serious problem in the establishment of settlements. The resultant pattern, as illustrated by Map 3, shows the location and extent of tracts of territory which have suitable relief, inherently fertile soil and convenient potable water supply.

There is of course an element of arbitration in the selection of the environmental filters, and different sets will yield different patterns. However, the choice of the filters can be determined by either induction from case studies or deduction from known locations of historic settlements. The same processes will suggest also the appropriate limits to be imposed on each filter. Here again, different conditions set up on each of the environmental factors to distinguish favourable tracts from unfavourable ones, will produce different results. The most convincing pattern can only derive from a series of trial and error reiterations. Naturally this would be a very time-consuming process, but modern mechanical and electronic facilities can help to relieve the arduous toil considerably.

Pondering over Map 3, showing the geographical distribution and extent of the various ecological niches suitable for the cultivation of irrigated rice, one feels that the pattern of the human habitats tallies well with the known historical facts of mainland South East Asia. Areas where civilizations flowered, and centres which held sway over extensive areas, seem to be located almost without exception on the larger and uninterrupted segments

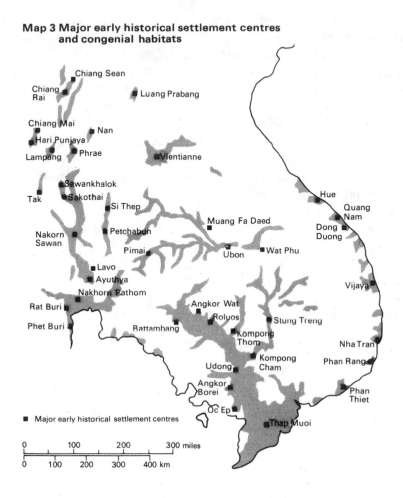

Map 3 Major early historical settlement centres and congenial habitats

Chiang Sean

Chiang Rai

Luang Prabang

Chiang Mai

Nan

Hari Punjaya

Lampang   Phrae

Vientianne

Sawankhalok

Tak   Sakothai

Si Thep

Hue

Quang Nam

Muang Fa Daed

Nakorn Sawan

Petchabun

Dong Duong

Pimai

Ubon

Wat Phu

Lavo

Ayuthya

Nakhorn Pathom

Vijaya

Rat Buri

Angkor Wat

Roluos

Phet Buri

Battamhang

Stung Treng

Kompong Thom

Nha Tran

Kompong Cham

Phan Rang

Udong

Angkor Borei

Phan Thiet

Oc Ep

■ Major early historical settlement centres

Thap Muoi

```
0        100        200        300 miles
|    |    |    |    |    |    |
0   100   200   300   400 km
```

of the most favoured habitats. The most extensive of these habitats, the Cambodian Lowlands, provides the stage for much of the dominant stream of South East Asian history—the rise and fall, in succession, of several of the most important civilizations and centres of political power, such as Funan, Chenla, Champa and finally Angkor. It can also be seen that once the migrant Thai began to settle and organize the western tract, extending from Sukothai to Ayuthia, the way to the south and their potential as a dominant power was opened for them. It is perhaps significant that the last stronghold of the Mons, the Nakhorn Pathom-Ratburi-Phetburi habitat, was separated from the Thai domain by the then intractable environment of the lower Chao Phya Basin, just south of Ayuthia. Further to the north, the more extensive Vientiane

Plain gave the rulers there an unrivalled advantage in overtaking their kinsmen in the older but rather limited centres of Luang Prabang. Similarly the earlier kingdoms of Nan and Kampengphet, of Chiangmai, Phayao, Lumphun and Lampang, faded away eventually under the impact of the southern powers, which had finally organized their extensive habitats for irrigated agriculture and were capable of producing an increasing surplus of grain for supporting armies and artisans.

It is not possible in a short paper to do more than merely to point the way towards viewing some of the historical facts of almost an entire millenium, in the light of geographical and environmental reality. It suffices as a conclusion to say that the pattern of the habitats fits that of the known centres of civilization and of political influence of the Christian era on mainland South East Asia (Map 3). One expects that there will be a number of discrepancies arising from considering only a few environmental factors, (topography, soil and potable water), from covering such a broad and imprecise historical extent of several centuries, and from analysing the sub-continent on such a large geographical scale. However, one is equally convinced that further work on refining the techniques of environmental filters could bring considerable rewards in the understanding of the historical past of the rice-growing world of South East Asia.

The Linguistic Protohistory of Mainland South East Asia

H. L. SHORTO

THE contributions which language studies can bring to protohistory are of two kinds, which unfortunately do not make a whole. There is, first, the evidence to be drawn from the emergence of inscriptions: not from their content, which is sufficiently accessible and exploited, but from their date, geographical location, and general character. This (in conjunction with the even earlier Chinese references, which are discussed in other pages in this volume) furnishes an incipit for the historical period itself, beyond which ethnographic and cultural outlines can be traced with relative certainty. The second kind of evidence is that derived by inference from the distribution of languages within the historical period and from studies of their structural affinity. It is of a far more indirect and conjectural sort and can at best, perhaps, be used to furnish hypotheses or suggest lines of archaeological inquiry. That is, however, an insufficient reason for failing to examine it.

Inscriptions

Inscriptions, in Sanskrit and the vernaculars, appear around the middle of the first millennium A.D. They are found about this date in a number of areas all readily accessible from the sea and prominent among those in which the beginnings of Indianized urbanism are to be sought. From Champa we have inscriptions of Bhadravarman in Sanskrit and Cham found at Tra-kieu and dating from the early fifth century. To the same century belong Sanskrit inscriptions from the region of Ligor at the southern end of the Kra isthmus, and around its end others from Fu-nan which continue into the succeeding century. They are, as near as can be determined, contemporary with the first Mon inscriptions of Dvāravati from Nakhon Pathom and (a recent discovery) near Lopburi. The earliest inscriptions in Khmer, from Sambor Prei Kuk, date from the beginning of the seventh century and reflect the spread of this politico-cultural movement inland. All these epigraphs are engraved in a script which appears to be derived from the Brahmi of southern India and is, at this early date, pretty well homogeneous; local differentiation only comes later. It is the ancestor of all modern non-Roman scripts on the mainland.

Burma shares this chronology, but clearly marked as a separate province. Śri Kṣetra at the head of the Irrawaddy delta yields in the seventh and eighth centuries the laconic funeral inscriptions of the Pyu kings in a wholly distinct script of possibly Kadamba affinities. It continued in use for Pyu alone down to the 'Myazedi' quadrilingual of 1112 and then became extinct. It can be traced back, however, to the oldest written document known from Burma, a set of gold plates inscribed with Pali texts now in the British Museum. These plates from Maunggan near Śri Kṣetra have been dated *c.* A.D. 500.

The chorological weight of this evidence is impressive, but care must be taken in drawing more general conclusions. First, writing may be presumed to have preceded the monumental act of setting up stone inscriptions, though not necessarily by long. It would be dangerous to equate the beginning of the epigraphic record with that of Indian settlement, as distinct from political 'Indianization'. We may note that some of the inscribed seals found at Oc-Eo may antedate the earliest Fu-nan inscriptions by as much as three centuries. Palaeographically, most local traditions show a more or less rapid development from script forms taken over from other writing media to forms better adapted to cutting on stone, suggesting the re-creation and not the trans-plantation of a technique. Linguistically, the phonological system deducible from vernacular inscriptions may show development from that for which the transcription must have been devised, a point deserving of more widespread investigation. Certainly in later history we can demonstrate continuity of the writing tradition over long periods when no stone inscriptions occur and other documents have not survived. Indeed, over the whole historical period epigraphy can in many places be only described as sporadic, an atypical product of the energy and literary ambition of some few particular rulers. The phenomena of the middle of the first millennium argue to me a competitive contagion and a fair degree of commerce between the states concerned.

To these implicit limitations must be added those of subject-matter, which is overwhelmingly religious. Political and social information has generally to be gleaned from the preambles of dedications and slave-rolls, so that a further constraint—that of economic surplus—has to be added to those controlling the output of texts. Eulogistic *praśasti* of the kind associated with Kyanzittha in Burma is exceptional. The subsequent stages of epigraphy provide rather a means of intermittently assessing the reliability of other sources such as chronicles than any accurate chart of political developments or ethnic movements. Where other sources are lacking, their effect ranges from indica-tive to tantalizing; as in the recent discovery of a Dvāravati inscription of uncertain date (7th-8th century?) 39 miles north of Vientiane. It contains a Mon place-name in a non-Mon form, suggesting a colonial occupation of some duration, and inviting a re-interpretation of the Dvāravati sites at Muang Fa Daed and elsewhere on the Korat plateau.

Not till after A.D. 1000 have we inscriptions from Pagan, Thaton or Haribhuñjaya. Pagan was founded in 850, but had small importance for the next two centuries. Thaton inscriptions come just after the end of our period, Haribhuñjayan ones two hundred years later, but by whatever percentage we discount tradition both states must have flourished well within the first millennium, though only Thaton was near the sea, and the other two were frontier principalities. With these exceptions, epigraphy provides a point of contact with all the early political centres of the mainland and with those ethnic groups which dominated them. These are, however, only a minority of the ethnic groups of the region; and estimates of their numerical importance at the time should not be projected from the dominant groups of much larger modern states, grown by linguistic and cultural absorption of their neighbours. To fill in the gaps in the account with, at any rate, intelligent conjecture we must turn to the evidence of linguistic classification; reflecting that, as discoveries accrue in other fields, intelligent conjecture is likely to need frequent revision.

Language families

The languages currently spoken in mainland South East Asia are repre-sentative of five families: Indonesian, Mon-Khmer, Tibeto-Burman, Tai and Miao-Yao. Of these, the Tai languages were brought in by groups whose arrival in the twelfth and thirteenth centuries is part of the historical record, while the Miao-Yao ones are confined even now to the northern fringe. Neither, therefore, immediately concerns us here, except to observe that the Tai wedge driven down the centre of South East Asia has (like the Slav intrusion into the Balkans) had the effect of sundering areas of cognate speech and interrupting a formerly constant communication between them.

The Indonesian languages of the mainland ('Chamic') form a coherent group extending from Phan-rang in the south-eastern corner of the peninsula northwards to Pleiku in the central Highlands, within the area of ancient Champa, plus some Cham-speaking colonies in Cambodia. The Cham remnant alone possesses a literary tradition (and the Muslim religion), the other groups being pagans and largely dry cultivators. Chamic appears as an isolated pocket of the Austronesian family which extends from Madagascar through the East Indies to New Zealand, and includes the aboriginal languages of Formosa. It has received less attention as a mainland curiosity than it would have done had it been located in Indonesia itself.

The Mon-Khmer languages may be regarded as the characteristic speech family of the mainland from the Menam basin eastwards. Their position in Burma was probably at all times marginal, even though once in the eighteenth century the Mons came close to seizing power throughout the country. They have, however, outliers across the northern highlands as far as the Khasi Hills south of the Assam valley, in the Nicobar Islands, and in the aboriginal languages of Malaya ('Aslian'). Any ethnic protohistory must take account of their relationship with the Munda languages of eastern India, which together with them constitute Austroasiatic. A remoter relationship between Austro-asiatic and Austronesian has been proposed and is accepted by the present writer, though it is not universally accepted. Three Mon-Khmer languages have longstanding literary traditions: Mon, Khmer, and Vietnamese.

The Tibeto-Burman languages of South East Asia are at the limit, in that direction, of a family extending from Tibet across Nepal and Assam through the hills of the Indo-Pakistan border region to Burma, where they pre-dominate, and in pockets across northern Thailand to Laos. They are now held to include the Karen languages, spoken characteristically throughout the hills between the Sittang and Menam basins. Within South East Asia only Burmese and the extinct Pyu have literary traditions older than the nineteenth century.

We must assume that languages belonging to none of these families have at times in the past been spoken in the area. They have left no identifiable traces. I. H. N. Evans once asserted that common elements can be found in all the Asian negrito languages, but unfortunately quoted no examples.

The relationships within the Mon-Khmer family are clearly crucial to any reconstruction of ethno-history. Early attempts at classification were based largely on geographical distribution and such structural arguments as could be extracted from generally inadequate material. Within the past decade or so more serious attempts have been made; but we are still some distance from a comprehensive ordering of the whole group. It is clear, first of all, that Khasi and the languages of the Shan Plateau from Palaung to Lawa stand in a close relationship and bear witness to one migratory current, while similarities between Shan Plateau languages and Khmu of northern Laos can be attributed to recent geographical contiguity. There is historical as well as traditional evidence that at the eastern limit of this group the Lawas were known to the Mons of Thaton. Second, descriptions now becoming available suggest that Aslian and Nicobarese stand nearer than other Mon-Khmer languages to Munda in their overall structural pattern; how this should be interpreted is obscure, but a special relationship between the two Mon-Khmer groups is not unlikely. Thirdly, Vietnamese, an undoubted Mon-Khmer language showing the effects of long contact with Chinese both in its vocabulary and in its phonological progress to monosyllabism, appears to have separated fairly early and to be peripheral in the technical linguistic as well as in the modern geographical sense.

A classification of the languages of the southern Annamite chain on lexico-statistic grounds has been made by members of the Summer Institute of Linguistics and shows a general correlation with geographical distribution. The most interesting question it raises derives from the probability of a close

relationship between the languages to the north and south of Chamic, implying that the inland part of that area is an intrusion and not a residuum.

Most intriguing is the position of Mon and of Khmer. Mon shows no
obvious immediate relationship with any other language except for those of
two tribal groups in the hills on the edge of the plateau north and south of
Korat, who appear to be remnants of an original Dvāravati population. The
position of Khmer has been recently examined by Headley, using a variety of
phonological and grammatical criteria. His general conclusions differ somewhat from those outlined above, notably in grouping Mon, the Annamite chain
languages and Vietnamese together at the centre of the family. But again he
puts Khmer in an isolated position, giving no clues to the route by which the
Khmers may have reached the lower Mekong.

The present distribution of languages in mainland South East Asia is
extremely intricate, and lexical investigation is complicated not merely by the
presence in any language of numerous loanwords but by reborrowings and
borrowings back into the first donor language, making an encyclopaedic
memory and logical rigour equally necessary to the investigator. There is
reason to think that this state of affairs goes back to an early date. Austronesian
loans are clearly recognizable, once the phonological rules are known, in
Vietnamese, and this is not surprising given the finds at Dong-son. More surprising are words known from Austronesian and found, in Mon-Khmer, in
one or other northern language; can they be loans? Benedict has proposed an
'Austro-Thai' grouping of Austronesian and Thai (relegating Austroasiatic to
a 'substratum' in some Indonesian populations), which would be disposed of
if, after eliminating Austric words which entered Tai from Mon-Khmer, the
possibility of early borrowing was accepted. 'Tiger' and 'river' (*kiung*) are
well-known Austroasiatic loans in Chinese, and there are many in Tibeto-
Burman. A hypothesis which traced back migration routes to contiguous
Urheimats would be attractive on more than one ground.

Certain terms, indeed, have an areal distribution which cuts across language-
family boundaries, reviving speculations as to extinct languages. Thus for
'horse' Tai has carried the Chinese *ma* down to the Gulf of Siam, cutting in
two a northern zone where Tibeto-Burman and Mon-Khmer alike have
mrang and a southern one where Karen, Mon-Khmer and Cham have *aseh*.

Various theories have been propounded as to the original home of the
Austronesians. Dyen, one of the most authoritative Austronesian comparatists,
has proposed either New Guinea or Formosa. The former is incompatible
with the Austric hypothesis and must be rejected here, leaving Formosa. But
Dahl, in a recent study, has shown that Formosan must have separated early
from the remainder of the Austronesian languages; making an Urheimat on
the opposing mainland equally probable. We can envisage it as an extensive, if
thinly populated one, with the future Austroasiatics ranging north to the

Yangtse *kiang*. It is possible to suppose successive migrations, first of Austronesians and then of Austroasiatics. But, given what is known of the chronology of Polynesian migration, it is equally plausible to suppose simultaneous migration of both groups and attribute the greater dispersal of the Austronesians to their taking early to the sea. The Northern Mon-Khmers and Khasis are likely to have followed what became a Chinese trade route to India, as the Mundas may well have done before them. But there seems no overriding reason to trace routes for the Mons and Khmers, and other groups who occupied the river-plains, down the rivers from the hinterland rather than up them from the coast. Why should they then, with a technology adapted to highland regions, have descended into plains where it was useless?

It is tempting to regard the Chams as a residual island of the Dongsonian transients, but the evidence is inconclusive. There are remarkable structural parallels between the mainland Indonesian languages and Achinese on the north-western tip of Sumatra, beyond what could be accounted for by parallel exposure to Mon-Khmer contacts (of which in Achinese there is sufficient evidence). This, again, is difficult to interpret.

Applications of comparative linguistics of the kind employed in this paper have been out of favour for at least thirty years, partly in reaction against earlier excesses. Even more firmly discarded has been what used to be called 'linguistic palaeontology', the analysis of reconstructed vocabulary to draw conclusions as to habitat and technology. This is a field in which, with due precautions, something of extralinguistic value might be achieved; and French scholars have been making a beginning, notably in the field of agricultural origins. It is to be hoped that these lines will be pursued, and in awareness of the work of Vavilov and his successors; so that we may recognize that Mon-Khmer and Austronesian have their word for 'cotton' from India, even if India has 'rice' and 'plough' from South East Asia.

Comment
D. T. Bayard

The contributions of comparative linguistics towards understanding prehistory have been substantial indeed in other parts of the world, and are now beginning to appear (although in a still quite tentative form) in the field of South East Asian prehistory. However, there are several points relating to the overlap between the two disciplines which should be borne in mind, particularly as they relate to South East Asia.

First, during the past twenty years, the efforts of such linguists as Pawley, Biggs, Grace, Milke, and many others (and also the occasional adventurous prehistorian, e.g. Roger Green) have resulted in a correlation of Austronesian language classification and distribution with the data of prehistory, which most Oceanic prehistorians find extremely valuable as a semi-independent check on such data. However, I doubt whether such a neat and tidy portrait will eventuate for the South East Asian mainland. The hundreds of millennia of prehistory and the linguistic complexity present there form a depressing contrast with the island isolates and comparatively shallow time depth of eastern Oceania, where we can talk with some confidence about the proto-language spoken by the ancestors of a particular island population. Such is not the case on the mainland, as Leach's work in northern Burma has so amply demonstrated.

North-east Thailand, where most of my own research has been carried out, provides another example. Fifty years ago the areas north and east of Nakhon Ratchasima province up to and across the Mekong were almost wholly Lao-speaking, with very few people fluent in the closely related, but not mutually intelligible, language of central Thailand. At present almost all males under sixty can converse in central Thai in addition to their everyday Lao language, and most men under thirty can be considered bilingual. I would estimate that another generation or two will see Lao largely limited to enclaves, replaced by central Thai as the language of everyday intercourse over almost all of the area. The dialect of Nakhon Ratchasima proper (mutually intelligible with central Thai but not Lao) represents a parallel process which took place during the nineteenth century. An even more striking transformation must have taken place at a date considerably earlier, but one well within the historic period. The archaeological evidence and such physical anthropological data as we possess suggest strongly that the people and much of the material culture of north-east Thailand 1,500 to 1,000 years ago are directly ancestral to the present population and its artefacts. I feel there would be general agreement that the dominant language in the area prior to A.D. 1000 was not Thai or Lao, but rather some language related to Mon or Khmer (archaeological evidence suggests Mon in the case of the Khorat region and Khmer-related languages elsewhere).

This brings me to my second point: the question of explaining the present distribution of languages (and peoples) in South East Asia as being largely the result of migrations. The linguistic mutability illustrated by the examples above cannot be assumed to be merely a recent phenomenon. On the other hand, I would venture that the large splotches of colour representing speakers of Burmese, Thai, Khmer, Vietnamese, etc. on the ethnolinguistic map of the area are a comparatively recent development, and are by no means wholly or even largely the result of mass migrations. I can envisage the southward spread of Thai, for example, as being the result of a 'migration' into northern Thailand consisting only of a royal court and small standing army. Political expediency on the part of the natives, rather parallel to Leach's Kachin-Shan example, could well explain the rest. In this view, the transition taking place in north-east Thailand is simply a continuation of the process. The archaeological evidence at hand would indicate that the spread of these now-dominant languages over wide areas of the lowlands was a phenomenon which occurred only after the beginnings of political centralization on the alluvium during the first millennium B.C. Prior to that time we seem to have a large number of isolated regional cultures (cf. Bronson, p. 320ff.), each limited to a relatively small area and possibly speaking a distinct language or dialect (although perhaps changing this on occasion as expediency dictated). The linguistic map of the lowlands at that time may well have approached the highlands of the contemporary South East Asian mainland in its complexity. The spread of languages and of peoples might thus better be viewed as a very large number of small-scale, localized movements of small, sometimes related groups, as in the case of the contemporary Meo-Yao, in many different directions and over many different routes. In view of both the archaeological evidence and the contemporary ethnolinguistic distributions in mainland South East Asia, this would appear to be a more satisfactory reconstruction than the occurrence of only a limited number of mass migrations of Austronesians or Austroasiatics over broadly defined but essentially single routes.

Finally, I would like to add my enthusiastic support to that given by Professor Shorto for increased attention to 'the analysis of reconstructed vocabulary to draw conclusions as to habitat and technology'. Such studies may well have fallen out of favour in many areas of the world; however, they are very much alive and well in Oceania. The work of Biggs, Pawley, and others at the University of Auckland have resulted in the reconstruction of some 2,000 items of Proto-Polynesian lexicon and much of the grammatical system. This has allowed valuable inferences to be made regarding Polynesian prehistory and the nature of the Polynesian homeland. While the geographical make-up of Polynesia allows such studies to be undertaken with an ease and accuracy denied to those with interests in the South East Asian mainland, nonetheless recent work such as that of Friedrich on Indo-European tree terms indicates that 'linguistic paleontology' continues to be feasible and valuable on the western portion of the Eurasian landmass; there would appear to be no reason why similar research will not prove of equal value to those of us concerned with its south-eastern extremity. Research such as Benedict's controversial, inconclusive, but nonetheless stimulating 'Austro-Thai' hypothesis and the possibility of early cultural loans into Sinitic is only the beginning; comparative linguistics has probably yet to make its most salient contributions to the pre- and protohistory of the area.

Lin-i, Fu-nan, Java

A. H. CHRISTIE

DESPITE the amount of space (pp. 36–80) which 'The first Indian kingdoms', 'The second indianization' and 'The dismemberment of Funan' occupy in Coedès' *The Indianized States of Southeast Asia* (1968), the real state of our knowledge of this crucial period in the early history of the region remains in almost every respect what it was twenty-five years ago. Then, in the first edition of his book, Coedès wrote:

> Ces Etats n'ont laissé que peu de traces archéologiques ou épigraphiques antérieures au Ve siècle. De la plupart d'entre eux, on ne connaît guère, avant cette date, que les noms mentionnés par les Annales dynastiques chinoises, qui enregistrent avec soin les ambassades en provenance des pays des mers du Sud. Dans bien des cas, leur localisation est incertaine ou seulement approximative (1948: 67–8).

There have, of course, been notable contributions to the understanding of the Chinese texts which allowed him to sketch the history of these states: Stein's *Le Lin-yi* (1947), Wheatley's *The Golden Khersonese* (1961), Wolter's *Early Indonesian Commerce* (1967) may serve as examples, to say nothing of periodical articles dealing with points of detail. Further work has been done on the early inscriptions, by de Casparis, Damais, and Coedès himself. In the fields of archaeology and art history the situation may, at first sight, appear somewhat more encouraging. The years 1959–63 saw the publication of Malleret's *L'archéologie du delta du Mékong* which brought together for the first time the results of the Oc-Eo excavations, together with much other material, and it must be added confirmed the technical inadequacy of much of the work, admittedly conducted under difficult conditions. Dupont published monographs on Dvāravati (1959) and *La statuaire préangkorienne* (1955); Janse's long-awaited reports on the Harvard-Yenching researches in Indochina finally appeared. Boisselier, carrying on and amplifying the work of Stern and de Coral-Rémusat, has made comprehensive attempts to set in order the statuary of the Khmers (1955) and of Champa (1963). Further attempts have been made to determine, by art historical methods, the precise areas in the Indian sub-continent from which influences reached South East Asia and the rôle of Ceylon in this process (e.g. Dupont 1959; de Casparis 1961; O'Connor 1972). In general these cannot be said to have been successful: the reasons for the failure are probably to be found in the difficulty of appreciating properly the nature of South East Asian cultural development at the time of the region's first contacts with the sub-continent in historical times.

There has been an increasing awareness that a picture of unsophisticated village cultures, which depended upon the coming of Indian traders and religious teachers for any advance in their degree of sophistication, was unduly simplistic. The technical and artistic achievements of the Dong-son metalworkers testify to a remarkable level of attainment. The early Chinese texts, while demonstrating a characteristic unwillingness to admit any real degree of 'civilization' to southern barbarians, nonetheless bear witness to considerable political sophistication. There is also a body of evidence to suggest a developed marine technology. Our limited knowledge of South East Asian proto-history indicates the existence of distinctive sub-cultures within the region. The accumulated implications of all this lend support to Rawson's view that:

> The nuclei of Indianization were mere trading colonies, where an Indian way of life was practised and Indian forms of religion were observed. They were seen by the indigenous population to be good, so they were adopted. Intermarriage and cultural assimilation took place. Most interesting of all, there apparently existed a fairly advanced native artistic tradition in Cambodia and Cochin-China [as elsewhere in South East Asia: A.H.C.], probably in perishable materials. For when the earliest versions in stone of Indian prototypes were made there, they were far from being mere copies, or even transcriptions. The sculptures of Indian icons produced in Cambodia during the sixth to eighth centuries A.D. are masterpieces, monumental, subtle, highly sophisticated, mature in style and unrivalled for sheer beauty anywhere in India. It is obvious that their style is not purely Indian; there are elements in it which were never created by Indian sculptors in India, and which must only be called local. It is not possible to say whence this style sprang. It must have developed in the region. Attempts to identify it exactly with a specific local Indian style have failed, though certain characteristics suggest links with western rather than eastern India. It cannot have been imported, fully fledged, and there may yet be further discoveries about its evolution to be made (1967: 18).

To quote Stein:

> Seules des recherches sur le terrain (archéologiques et géographiques) trancheront la question (1947: 54).

Unfortunately, during the subsequent quarter-century, this field of research, so far as the earliest historical period is concerned, has been almost entirely unexplored.

One reason for this is obvious enough: the continuing war in Indochina. In the case of Indonesia the explanation is less obvious. It seems in fact to stem from the former Oudheidkundige Dienst in Nederlandsch-Indië which, except in the field of prehistory, had little or no tradition of excavation: its main preoccupations were with the recording of monuments and their restoration (during the course of which the technique of anastylosis was developed, which became the foundation for work by the Ecole Française d'Extrême-Orient also); and in epigraphy, a line of research which accorded well with the dominantly linguistic training (Sanskrit, Arabic, Javanese) of most of the service's officers. Not unnaturally the staff of the Dinas (now Lembaga) Purbakala, trained by these Netherlanders, some of whom remained in Indonesian service for a considerable period, tended to follow in the same tradition, the results of which have been summarized by the first Indonesian director:

> At first glance it might be said that Indonesian ancient history has left us with a not inconsiderable number of written documents in the form of inscriptions and literary works, but actually these have proved to be inadequate when it comes to writing that history consecutively and completely. The gaps are still too great and too many. On the other hand, ancient Indonesian history has left us a great many buildings, statues and household and religious utensils which are all unwritten documents. It is the glory and magnificence of these architectural products which testify to Indonesia's greatness during that period (Soekmono 1965: 57–8).

Unfortunately the very existence of these objects has tended to continue the preoccupation with visible remains, and very limited funds have been devoted, largely to maintenance of what can be seen to exist. And none of this can be assigned to the crucial centuries before A.D. 600.

For these reasons any survey of the present position regarding our knowledge of the formative period in South East Asian history is depressingly negative. In the case of Lin-i there is nothing archaeological to report, although my own investigation of an area near Hue in 1952—a surface study only, excavation being expressly forbidden—revealed interesting traces of possible early material. So far as Java is concerned, the position is the same. The investigation by Soejono of west Javanese megalithic sites in the general area of Taruma have not yet yielded anything to link these with the historical period, or to indicate the nature of the gap, if any, between the two phases. I believe this area to be of great importance for our investigation of the early history of South East Asia, not least because of my discovery of the toponym Murunda, to the east of Jakarta. The local inhabitants claim that the word is Portuguese, and many of them are of Portuguese Eurasian stock; but the name does not appear to be so. On the other hand the name is familiar to students of the history of Fu-nan in connection with the visit of a relative of Fan Chan to the Ganges valley. The fact that Yüeh-chih horses were also traded to Chia-ying (syn. Ko-ying), as reported by K'ang T'ai in the *Wu shih wai kuo chuan*, draws attention to the undoubted significance of the Indo-scythians in the formative period of South East Asian history yet again, and may indicate that the state's location, last discussed by Wolters (1967: 49–61), was in west Java rather than east Sumatra. (It may be, of course, that the Murunda toponym indicates a third Yüeh-chih horse-trading zone. It is also interesting to note that at the time of Tomé Pires, the Sunda-South Sumatra area was noted for a similar trade.)

It is only when we turn to Funan that the position shows any real improvement, and even here, reservations are necessary, since for various reasons, the excavations at Oc-Eo were not, as has already been noted, of a technically satisfactory standard. But the material is, at least, of known provenance. This, unfortunately is not the case with the bronze objects discussed by Malleret (*Art. Asiae*, xix, 308 sqq.) which show affinities with the Dong-son culture, though it should be noted that there are a few pieces from Oc-Eo itself which may have links with that culture, and one (Malleret 1960: 214) tentatively linked with Luristan which may well be more properly assigned to the Shih-chai shan culture. But in general, as in the case of Java, the precise relationship between the historical culture and its predecessors remains indeterminate. The importance of the Oc-Eo material is that it does provide, for the first time, archaeological evidence for the period, long known from Chinese texts, before the surviving buildings, images and Sanskrit inscriptions which, in Boisselier's view date from the sixth century (the last two) and the eighth century (the first) (1961: 32). The building remains do not advance our knowledge: they are, in Boisselier's phrase 'd'une attribution douteuse'; while the fragments of pile-dwellings, still undated despite their obvious suitability for C14 testing, are without any real significance. The objects in clay which may have served some architectural end are not, in my view, separable from other pieces which are certainly pre-Angkorian; while other ceramics, as Boisselier has pointed out (1966: 37), seem to be common to Oc-Eo and Angkor Borei, or even sites in the area of the western Barai at Siemreap itself. It is when we turn to the smaller objects that the picture becomes more clear; and, incidentally, the general reliability of the Chinese textual sources receives a considerable degree of confirmation.

One point should, however, be made clear at the outset. Many of the finds which seem to link Oc-Eo with the eastern Mediterranean and the Near and Middle East are of a highly portable character and it is quite impossible to tell how many hands they passed through before reaching the Mekong delta. There is, on the other hand, a total absence of the Arretine wares which have been adduced as evidence for actual Roman trading stations in India. But there is a certain consistency in the finds which seems to testify to more than a fortuitous presence. The pieces associated with Antoninus Pius (A.D. 152) and Marcus Aurelius, as well as a piece from My-tho from the early third century A.D., the dancer from Tra-vinh (Poseidon in the Lysippan manner, according to Picard), and the figurine (Malleret 1960: lxxxvii), seem to confirm that traders from the Roman Orient may well have reached the area; a presence which the Pong-tuk lamp does nothing to deny. Substantial quantities of 'Roman' beads, and a large number of intaglios with designs which can confidently be assigned to the second to fourth centuries A.D. in western Asia, fit well into this picture; but I share Boisselier's doubts about the contacts with Iran. Nothing in these finds would occasion any real surprise, since the same objects might well have been found on the land routes before their interruption; an interruption which seems, more than anything else, to have brought South East Asia to the knowledge of the Indian sub-continent and countries to the west.

When we turn to the finds of Indian provenance a slightly odd situation arises, and seems to me to call into question much of the assumption upon which Coedès' interpretation of the first Indian contacts rests.

> Sculs de petits objets attestent ces contacts mais leur importance est exceptionelle puisqu'ils sont les premiers témoins de l'indianisation du pays. Au vrai, ces témoinages restent limités à la zone la plus méridionale (spécialement Oc-èo) mais ce sont les seuls dont l'influence apparaisse à la fois immédiate et durable (Boisselier 1966: 33).

But it is surely the case that the objects found are on all fours with those from western Asia on which Boisselier, very properly, comments

> Rien de tout cela n'implique une occupation quelconque du sol dont aucune trace n'a été jusqu'à présent signaler.

I do not think that we can, with any propriety, employ the term 'Indianization' in this context. The admittedly important Gandharan Buddha head (Malleret 1960: lxxxiv) and the lamp with a *makara* ornament (ibid.: xc) are strictly comparable with the Pong-tuk lamp or the figurine of Poseidon. The large number of seals and pieces of jewelry, the decoration of which is clearly Indian, and the inscriptions on which names in the genitive or protective formulae in various scripts seem to belong to the third to fourth centuries, are of Indian origin and a wide range of provenances. They seem to fit well with the view that they are the property of traders and others from various parts of the sub-continent, but can scarcely be evidence for any real degree of Indianization. At best they point to the manner in which the connection with India was established, the base from which influences were later to make their presence permanent. In one respect alone was this influence apparently immediate: in the objects made from tin which are characteristic of the Oc-Eo site itself. Even here caution is necessary, for it does not appear that any of the finds were *in situ*: all are the product of surface collections, so that their dating is conjectural. But all the motifs, or at any rate the overwhelming proportion of them, are of Indian type. Only one piece is three-dimensional, a standing bull; there are no images of deities in any material. Boisselier makes the point that the earliest Chinese references to images in Fu-nan is in the last quarter of the fifth century (1966: 34). This fact alone makes the suggestion of significant Indian influence, as opposed to the presence of Indians, most improbable; while the facts of its absence until the end of about the end of the fourth century seem perfectly consonant with the evidence from other parts of South East Asia. The few finds of Chinese origin, mirror fragments of later Han type which persisted in use to the San Kuo period, can do no more than suggest some measure of Chinese presence. A small number of Buddhist fragments are of types known from pre-Angkorean sites also, and are evidence only of continuing contacts with the Mekong delta.

That Oc-Eo and, to a lesser extent, Ta Kev were the centres of a prosperous and important trading zone seems to be without question. Whether this was the Ptolemaic Kattigara is another problem: certainly the presence of objects, however few in number, from the Roman Orient adds some weight to the conjecture. The very extensive finds of jewelry, much of local manufacture as the presence of jewellers' tools confirms, testify to its prosperity; while its distinctive nature—it is clearly distinguishable from that of the pre-Angkorean and Angkorean periods—make it obvious that Fu-nan was a developed culture of considerable international affiliations, which had during the first few centuries of the Christian era achieved a fair degree of sophistication. The proper realization of this seems to me to be essential for the understanding of the nature of the cultures with which Indian influences were subsequently to interact. The extent of the Fun-nan empire, to the existence of which the Chinese texts bear witness, has still to be established archaeologically, but the evidence from Oc-Eo does confirm both the existence of considerable overseas connections and an economic base which could sustain such an enterprise.

In the case of Buddhist art it has been possible within recent years to establish prototypes for the earliest examples from South East Asia, which have their affinities with images from Sarnath, Amaravati, and Mathura. The last centre seems also to be the inspiration for the Viṣṇu from Jaiya, probably an important town in P'an-p'an from which Kaundinya came to change the laws of Fun-nan to conform to those of India. Now O'Connor has shown (1972: 19–40) that this image is to be dated ±A.D. 400 and has gone on to argue that the similar example from Oc-Eo (Malleret 1959: 363: the piece was bought, not excavated), is a copy of a Jaiyan original. Nothing in the evidence from Oc-Eo is against such a view, which fits very well with the material adumbrated above. All of this seems to me to argue for a thorough re-examination of the case for Coedès' 'First Indian kingdoms', including a close analysis of the dating of the various Chinese sources. I incline to the view that the two Kaundinyas are the product of Chinese dittography, and would argue that before the last part of the fourth century there had developed in South East Asia a number of kingdoms which, with the growth of maritime traffic through the region, largely as the result of interruptions on the land routes and the internal shifts in centres of power in China, achieved a considerable degree of economic development. Only after this did local rulers seriously begin to adopt the practices and beliefs of Indian origin which were to characterize South East Asia for the next thousand years. Confirmation of this view will only be possible when detailed archaeological investigation of the kingdoms of Lin-i, Fu-nan, and Tarnma can be undertaken: the answer, as Granet used to remark, will be provided by the trowel.

Urban Genesis in Mainland South East Asia

PAUL WHEATLEY

Introduction

URBAN genesis in ancient South East Asia subsumed two distinct and, for all analytical and most practical purposes, unrelated processes. In the Viet territories it took the form of urban imposition, the establishment of Chinese-style settlements in a colonial context. In the Indianized realms of South East Asia it signified initially a process of urban generation, an internally induced restructuring of society. Whereas the first of these transformations reflected the extension *into* South East Asia of symbolic and organizational patterns developed in south China, the latter signified a progressive differentiation of autonomous institutional spheres and the emergence of specialized collectivities and rôles as a response to societal pressures generated *within* South East Asia.

Urban imposition is a topic pertaining to such general themes of enquiry as the consolidation of political domain or the spread of settlement. It constitutes, in fact, a mode of urban diffusion that is virtually inseparable from the expansion of empire, and is usually accompanied by the establishment of an administrative organization designed to sustain the value system of the colonial power, the imposition of the legal definitions of property current in the colonist's homeland, and the introduction into the dependent territory of certain sectors of the metropolitan economy. From this point of view urban imposition is one manifestation of the *Uberlagerungslehre* beloved of an older generation of German social theorists.[1]

Urban generation, by contrast, is a mode of processual change subsumed within the more inclusive field of social differentiation and stratification. Whereas urban imposition clearly partakes of the nature of change in an open system, the notion of urban generation encompasses a somewhat broader spectrum of systemic changes. At one extreme are those situations in which cities have arisen when some particular conjunction of internal forces has induced spontaneous readjustments in institutional forms and relationships. In such circumstances the transition *ideally* may be conceived as the structural transformation of a closed system,[2] though it needs no emphasis that in the real world social systems are seldom, if ever, of the closed type. Even ancient Sumer, the region with an undisputed claim to historical priority in the initiation of the process of urbanization, was not totally immune to external influences during and immediately preceding the emergence of its earliest urban forms.[3] In fact, what entitles an evolving society at an appropriate level of complexity to be characterized as an instance of primary urban generation is not its degree of systemic closure so much as the fact that none of the external cultures able to influence its development are significantly more complex than the particular society under consideration. Although opinions may vary as to precisely which communities at one time or another have generated urban forms in this manner, there is a virtual consensus among scholars in the field that the Middle East was the first region to experience this quantum transformation of society. There might be a divergence of views, though, as to whether Mesopotamia and Egypt should be treated as manifestations of a single process or as discrete realms. Other realms of primary urban generation on which there would be very substantial agreement are the Indus valley, the North China Plain, Middle America (where again there might be a division of opinion as to whether two realms or one have been involved), the central Andes, and—the realm on which there would probably be least agreement—the Yoruba territories of south-western Nigeria.

On the peripheries of these core regions of primary urban generation, particularly in those sectors where political jurisdiction has lagged behind cultural imperialism, cities have often arisen as a result of a secondary diffusion of cultural traits that has stimulated the evolution of society towards an urban level of integration. In such circumstances the process has still been one of urban generation rather than of imposition, but it has been a generational process stimulated by the diffusion of cultural traits from already urbanized regions.[4] It must be emphasized that it has been the diffusion of individual traits that has effected this transformation, not the diffusion of the total set of functionally interrelated institutions that constitutes the city. In other words it is not the artefact of the *city* itself that has been diffused but *particular institutions in an urbanized society*.[5] Among the realms which have experienced this mode of secondary urban generation, the western, or so-called Indianized, territories of South East Asia constitute a rather special case, for they represent virtually the only major realm of either primary or secondary urban generation where the process is even partially *documented* in written records (as opposed to *archetyped* in literary tradition). Normally the societal changes of which both urbanism and writing (conventional, visible, phonetized signs) are born are not themselves chronicled in literary form, but in South East Asia alone the archaeological and epigraphic record can be supplemented by topographical accounts relating to the formative period of urban development.[6]

The Concept of Urbanism

'Urbanism' is a term of equivocal import customarily employed to denote sets of qualities possessed by the larger and more compact clusters of settlement features that at any particular moment in time represent centroids of continuous population movements. Although these sets of qualities are often associated with a distinctive manner of life characterized as 'urban', there is no compelling reason to assume that all the multifarious groupings of population both past and present to which that term has been applied are necessarily subsumable within a single logically coherent field; or, more forthrightly, that urban structural regularities will ultimately be found to extend through all time and space.

Faced with the enormous diversity of phenomena that at one time or another have been designated as urban, scholars have sought to order their data in terms of four conceptual frameworks, namely (i) an interactional model which emphasizes the growth and structure of specialized networks of social, economic, and political relationships focussed in cities; (ii) a normative model in which urbanism is viewed as a way of life; (iii) an economic model, concerned primarily with productive activities in a spatial context; and (iv) a demographic model which treats urban forms essentially as aggregations of population in restricted areas. Some authors have simplified matters by combining (i), (ii), and (iii) into a unitary conception of the city as an organizing principle, in John Friedmann's phrase (1961a: 92)[7] a creator of effective space. This view contrasts sharply with that which characterizes the city as a locale (of events) or, what is much the same thing, as a container (of people and institutions).[8] In the following pages, for the sake of expediency, we shall incline to the view of the city as an organizing principle. Urbanists, in their attempts to elucidate the rationale of the city in whichever manner they may have perceived it, have devised five conceptually distinct, though in practice, substantially overlapping approaches, broadly (1) reliance on ideal-type constructs; (2) formulation of ecological theories; (3) delineation of trait complexes; (4) conceptualization of the city as a centre of dominance; and (5) classification according to size (usually of the population).[9] Our present approach to the ancient South East Asian city will be based mainly on (4).

It should be made clear at this point that the process of urbanization is a complex nexus of functionally interrelated, parallel-trending changes involving the whole of a society. Except in highly anomalous circumstances the influence of urban institutions is not terminated by the city wall. On this view urban generation is properly conceived to have been the systemic transmutation of one qualitatively distinct level of sociocultural integration into another with a higher degree of complexity, which in turn enhanced its potentialities for adaptation (Adams 1966: 7 and *passim*; Wheatley 1971: 317). From a broadly cultural point of view the generalized integrative patterns involved in the transformation, wherever and whenever it occurred, were those of relatively egalitarian, ascriptive, kin-based societies at the simpler level and stratified, politically organized, territorially defined societies as the more complex resultants of the process. In ecological terms they were levels respectively of reciprocally integrated, Developed Village-Farming Efficiency[10] and of super-ordinate redistributive integration about a religio-political centre that usually took the form of an assemblage of public ceremonial structures (Wheatley 1971: 225–6, 316–30). Operationally centres of this type were instruments for the creation of political, social, economic, and sacred space, at the same time as they were symbols of cosmic, social, and moral order. Under the authority of corporate priestly organizations and divine monarchs, they raised the redistributive mode of economic integration to a position of institutionalized regional dominance, functioned as nodes in a web of administered trade (Polanyi 1957: 243–70; 1968: 139–74), served as foci of craft specialization, and often promoted some proto- and a good deal of pseudo-science. At the same time they embodied the aspirations of brittle, pyramidal societies in which, typically, a sacerdotal elite, controlling a corps of officials and perhaps a praetorian guard, ruled over a broad understratum of peasantry. In short, small, relatively homogeneous communities in which kinship was the basis of all groupings, in which production was geared to the specific needs of producers or to the discharge of kin obligations, and in which power was extremely diffuse, had been replaced by stratified societies within each of which power and authority were concentrated in a ceremonial city exercising political and economic control over territory that comprised both a specifically urban and a rural component. On the one hand there was the city dweller proper, the resident within the urban enclave; and on the other there was the urbanized countryman, the cultivator who lived in terms of the city but not in it, who was bound to the city in an asymmetrical structural relationship that required him to produce, in one form or another, a fund of rent, and who is often referred to by anthropologists as a peasant (Redfield 1953: 31, 53; 1956: *passim*; Wolf 1966: 9–10). Together urban residents and peasants constituted an urbanized society. Or, phrased differently, urbanized society was to be contrasted not with that of the surrounding countryside but with pre- or non-urbanized society, with what Nieuwenhuijze (1966: 75) has aptly called *le vide culturel*.[11] It follows from this systemic view of urban generation that no single morphological feature is likely to afford a satisfactory criterion of urban status. It is the sustained interaction of a nexus of institutions rather than the presence of specific architectural components that certifies the advent of urbanism into a region.[12]

If urban generation is viewed as a form of *systemic evolution*, then urban imposition is to be regarded as a case of *systems interaction*, in particular of compound systems interaction (Blalock and Blalock 1959: 84–8). By this I mean that three modes of interaction are involved simultaneously—or are at least are potentially involved. In the first mode each system, although itself comprising a complex compound set of relationships (Klir and Valach 1967), acts and responds as a unit. This type of interaction under certain circumstances might represent reasonably accurately, for example, the operation of political linkages between the colonizing power and its dependent territory; though Parsons and Shils (1952: 4, 39, 56, 101), by referring to social collectivities as actors, would seem to extend its applicability to analysis of a very much wider range of societal relationships. In the second mode of interaction it is the components of the discrete systems (rather than the systems themselves) that act directly on each other in a manner that would seem to represent fairly accurately the most widely held conception of the social system. The third mode of interaction, which is certainly less common in the colonial experience, operates when one system acts *as a unit* on one or more of the constituent *components* of another system. A representative example might be the founding by the central government of the metroplitan power (symbolizing one system in its entirety) of a fortified city (a component of the second system) for frontier defence in a colony.

It is during the initial phase of urban imposition that one of the anomalies mentioned above occurs. When it is first founded the colonial city is essentially a subsystem of the metropolitan system transferred to the dependent territory. Its links with its environing countryside are rudimentary, so that the influence of its institutions necessarily ceases at the city wall. Only with the passage of time does a combined process of political absorption and cultural diffusion, often with assistance from the socially consolidatory mechanisms of the market, lead to the development of a mutual interdependence between city and country. From that point onwards generated city and imposed city are structurally homologous, though, naturally, significant ethnic distinctions within their populations may persist for many subsequent generations.

Urban Imposition in the Sino-Viet Territories[13]

Three phases are discernible in the early urbanization process in the territory later known as Tongking, each correlated with a particular mode of political organization. At the close of the third century B.C., when the Lac tribes and chiefdoms of the region were brought into tributary relationships with the kingdom of Nan-yüeh, a quasi-autonomous realm ruled from P'an-yü in the neighbourhood of modern Canton, two commandery seats were established, one at Giao-chi and the other at Cuu-chân. There is no reason to think that either of these settlements was anything more than a fortified frontier post where a *sú-gia* received the tribute of Lac chieftains.

When, in 111 B.C., the Tongking lowland was absorbed into a protectorate of the Chinese Empire, conditions did not immediately change significantly.

Indirect rule by the Dragon Throne replaced tribute obligations to Nan-Yüeh, the seat of government was located at Ts'ang-wu within the boundaries of the Empire proper,[14] and Jih-nan was added as a third commandery to the two mentioned above. Local customs seem not to have been seriously interfered with, and Lac chieftains, in whose persons were institutionalized customary rights to land, were confirmed in their traditional authority, some of the more prominent being appointed to the office of subprefect. Nevertheless, it is possible to discern beneath these surficial continuities the beginnings of social change, stimulated both by the extension into the Sông Cai delta of channels of trade between north China and the Hsi valley, and by the arrival in the commandery of Giao-chi (MSC Chiao-chih) of a stream of immigrants, both voluntary and involuntary, from the northward. Chinese farmers and traders established themselves more or less permanently in the delta side by side with fugitives, renegades, and those banished from the soil of Han. After A.D. 9 these were joined by Confucian officials and literati who found the régime of Wang Mang uncongenial. As a group these later arrivals possessed a deeper awareness of their cultural heritage than had most of the earlier immigrants, and their arrival can hardly have been unconnected with the policy of purposive sinicization that was implemented by Chinese officials such as Hsi Kuang, Jen Yen, and Su Ting during the earlier decades of the first century A.D.[15] Chinese political influence was strongest on the alluvial plains where Lac tribal society was exposed to a fairly well integrated but hybrid culture comprising both Han and Yüeh elements, and it was from this time onwards that there began to develop the marked dichotomy between ecological adaptations in the tribal uplands and in the urbanized lowlands that has characterized subsequent Vietnamese cultural history.

The third phase in the urbanization process was initiated in A.D. 39 when, after the revolt of an emergent class of supra-village chieftains, Giao-chi was fully incorporated into the Chinese polity as the southernmost province of the empire, and a hierarchy of commanderies and prefectures established on the pattern current in Han China.[16] Once the Tongking basin had become an integral part of the Chinese Empire, the operation of a bureaucratic centralism that effectively prevented the functioning of a provincial administration in isolation, the presence of a cadre of officials with a deeply ingrained consciousness of their own ethnic superiority, and the dissemination of a traditionally sanctioned ethos that subordinated the individual to society to an extreme degree, combined to accelerate the rate of sinicization of the indigenous folk. An integral part of this process was the establishment of *hsien* (Viet. *huyen*) cities, the lowest level of the urban hierarchy through which the central government exercised direct authority. These cities were wholly Chinese creations, established primarily for the administrative and social convenience of officials. If they sent down economic roots into the alien Viet soil, that was fortuitous and, as far as we can tell, contingent upon forces beyond the consideration of their founders.

Available information about the *huyen* cities established in Tongking during this period is scanty, as the descriptive material preserved in both Chinese and Vietnamese annals relates only to the provincial capital. Under the new régime of direct rule the seat of government was maintained at Luy-lâu in the present-day *phu* of Thuận-thành in Bắc-ninh province (Madrolle 1937: 267–71), but the degree of urbanism represented by this settlement is uncertain. Although at its founding it could have been no more than an administrative enclave and residential site for an alien elite residing temporarily and reluctantly among barbarians, there is some evidence that by the end of the second century A.D. it was beginning to develop cultural and commercial functions. The former were sustained by scholar refugees who sought a retreat in the peaceful political backwater of Giao-chi during the troublous years that marked the dissolution of the Han dynasty (*Mou-tzŭ likan*, preface: in *Hung-Ming Chi*) and by Buddhist monks who introduced Mahayana doctrines into the capital (Trân Văn Giáp 1932). The commercial importance of the city derived from the fact that, from the second to the sixth century, when it yielded precedence to Canton, Giao-chi was the eastern terminus of the south Asian maritime trade route that linked the Middle East to China.[17] Space does not permit discussion of the urban pattern that emerged from these tentative and uncertain beginnings. Suffice it to say that a colonial hegemony that fostered urban life for a thousand years ensured that a substantial proportion of the cities established by the Chinese administration developed roots in the local society and regional economy. In fact the urban system as a whole survived the elimination of Chinese authority in 968, and, through the continuing interplay of agglomerative tendencies and accesibility factors, was ultimately elaborated into the mature urban hierarchy of the era of the Nguyễn dynasty.

Events in Jih-nan commandery merit a few additional remarks. Under the Later Han this narrow strip of coastal plain running from the Porte d'Annam to the Col des Nuages was controlled from a commandery capital at Hsi-Chüan, in the neighbourhood of present-day Ba-dôn, with *huyên* headquarters at Chu-wu, Pi-ching, Lu-yung, and Hsiang-lin standing as islands of governmental authority amid a sea of tribally constituted peoples.[18] These tribal groups were especially turbulent in Hsiang-lin, the southernmost prefecture, where, towards the close of the second century, a group known to the Chinese as the Lin-i (Viet. Lâm-âp; *Lįəm-.įəp) established an autonomous polity (Stein 1947). That at least the rulers of the Lin-i did not regard themselves as totally alien to Chinese culture is evident from the fact that in 433 one of them petitioned the Emperor of Liu Sung that he be appointed to the governorship of Giao-chi. In the event, his territory was considered to be too distant from the capital of the commandery, so that a Chinese was eventually appointed to the post.[19] For present purposes the interesting thing about the Lin-i tribal confederacy, which ultimately extended northwards to the Hoành mountains and southwards to include present-day Quảng-nam, is that its urban pattern developed not, as in Tongking, under increasingly pervasive Chinese rule but, from the beginning of the third century onwards, through an internally generated evolution reinforced by the voluntary adoption of selected Chinese culture traits. The process as it is portrayed in extant records has been archetyped as aetiological myth (Stein 1947: 1–107), but it may be significant that principles of urban design allegedly were among the earliest cultural borrowings from south China (*Shui-ching Chu*, 36: 25a; *Chin Shu*, 97: 15b). In the descriptions of the two chief cities of the Lin-i,[20] however, Chinese influence is not especially apparent, and where similarities between the two cultures do occur, it is not always clear whether they are indicative of Chinese influence or of a substratum of traits common to both cultures. The point to be emphasized is that, after its initial imposition by the Chinese, the urban system in the Lin-i territories pursued a course of independent development.

Urban Generation in the Indianized Territories

In the region that may be described broadly as western South East Asia— that is present-day Burma, Thailand, the succession states of French Indochina (with the exception of Tongking and the northern Lin-i territories), the Malay peninsula, and the western sectors of modern Indonesia—urban origins appear on present evidence to have been related indirectly to the process whereby certain facets of south Asian civilization were assimilated to the cultural matrix of South East Asia.[21] The available evidence is so meagre and ambiguous that several internally consistent hypotheses can be devised to account for it. What follows is one such interpretation that seems, given the inchoate state of the investigation, to offer a reasonably coherent, though inevitably partial, explanation.

During the early centuries of the Christian era the so-called process of 'brāhmanization',[22] which for a millennium had been diffusing eastward and southward from its hearth of origin in the north-western part of the Indian subcontinent, finally reached across the ocean into South East Asia. With it came the concept of divine kingship, a political device especially attractive to village chieftains in situations in which the egalitarian solidarity of tribal society was proving incapable of extending authority to validate the power required for the institutionalization of supra-village rule. Dysfunctional situations of this sort could have arisen within tribal societies for a variety of reasons: when, for instance, foreign traders dealing with South East Asian villages as corporate entities through the agency of their chiefs brought about expansion and diversification of the habituated means and goals of such chiefs; or, alternatively, when an improvement in agricultural technology, by differentiating in the productivity, and hence in the value, of land, both encouraged the emergence of social stratification, and, possibly, by stimulating competition for a scarce resource, nourished the rise of militarism.[23] Wherever such a sequence of events took place, it would have led to a situation in which a chieftain was likely to seek to validate his newly acquired power on the only pattern of adequate flexibility and authority known to him, namely an Indian political model structured about the institution of divine kingship. It is this stage of the acculturation process that seems to be reflected in the well-known instances of the Sanskritization of the styles, in successive generations, of apparently indigenous dynasties (Vogel 1918; Chatterjee 1933: 8–19 and 29–34; Chhabra 1945: 14–17 and 1937: 118–19; Kern 1917: 115–28). A prerequisite for kingship was consecration which, in its Indian context, was a jealously guarded prerogative of the brāhman *varṇa*, so it is not altogether surprising that, as early as the middle of the third century A.D., the presence of brāhmans was attested in South East Asia.[24]

The maintenance of a state appropriate to kingship required the ministrations of increasing numbers of craftsmen and artisans, the most skilled of whom were often accommodated within the royal enceinte. It also presupposed the labour of a peasantry who contributed the surplus produce of their fields as a tax in kind for the support of the court, and a band of armed retainers who acted as household guards, organized the peasantry as a militia in the skirmishes inseparable from emergent kingship, and generally enforced the authority of the ruler. Concomitantly there developed material defences such as walls and palisades encircling the royal demesne. In short there had evolved the city-state, the *nāgara*, focused on a new landscape feature, the ceremonial city, which was the outcome of a series of social and political transformations that replaced the tribal chieftain by a divine king, gerontocracy or patriarchalism by patrimonial domain, concensus by hereditary charismatic authority, shaman by brāhman, tribesman as warrior by a kṣatriya, and tribesman as cultivator by a peasant, at the same time as occupational specialization hardened into something approaching *jāti*, age-sets were transmuted into *āśrama*, the tribal meeting was formalized as an assembly on the model of the *sabhā*, and custom broadened into law within the framework of the Dharmaśāstras. Concurrently the gift was transposed into tribute or tax, and the old economic reciprocity that marched with segmentary distance (Sahlins 1968: 84) was encompassed within a framework of redistributive exchange. These changes were reflected morphologically in the conversion of the chief's hut into a palace, the spirit-house into a temple, the spirit-stone into the *liṅga* that was to become the palladium of the state, and the boundary spirits into the Lokapālas presiding over the cardinal directions. In other words, the village community had become the city-state, the whole process signifying a transformation from culture to civilization.

On the mainland of South East Asia these early ceremonial cities were restricted almost exclusively to the lowland tracts, mainly—from west to east —the Pyū country of central and upper Burma, the coastal plains of Arakan, the Mon lands around the lower courses of the Irawadi and Chao Phraya rivers, the pre- and proto-Khmer territories in the middle and lower Mekong valley, and the coastal plains of east-central Viet-Nam. The earliest literary intimation of some sort of supra-village authority in these realms relates to the lower reaches of the Mekong valley, where the putative founder of a dynasty that subsequently assumed an Indian style[25] is alleged by relatively late Chinese annals to have enfeoffed his son with seven *i*, a graph which from Han times had been used for the seat of a subprefecture but which here was unlikely to have connoted anything more than a large and probably palisaded village (*Liang Shu*, 54, 7a; *Nan Shih*, 78, 6b).[26] Possibly the consolidation of political power (and also, if Wolter's interpretation presented on pp. 426–41 of this volume is valid, religious authority), is reflected in later events that are reported in the same Chinese sources. Apparently a ruler somewhere on the plains of the lower Mekong established patrimonial domain over an unspecified number of *i*, which he then apportioned among his sons and grandsons as benefices. The final stage in this transformation from paramount chief to territorial sovereign was reached when the ruler, having subdued a series of neighbouring principalities, assumed the personal style of Great King, perhaps a Chinese envoy's rendering of the Indian *Mahārāja* or an indigenous equivalent (*Liang Shu*, 54, 7a). A vision of political entities unified by common cultural traditions had been superseded by the thrust to statehood, an expansionism deriving from a moral vision of extended community had been replaced by an aggrandizement 'engined by power' (Redfield's phrase, 1953: 79; Singer 1960: 254–7). Whether events of this type were unique to one particular part of the lower Mekong valley (as the Chinese sources have usually been held to infer), or whether they occurred contemporaneously in several tribal groups located on the plains of southern Indochina (as some recent authors have maintained) remains to be resolved.

A handful of cities from this period, including the capital Vyādhapura, are known by name, but archaeology and Chinese texts combined permit only the broadest of generalizations about them. Essentially they consisted of agglomerations of dwellings, of light construction and often raised on piles, clustered about monumental complexes of wood, brick, or granite that are presumed on strong grounds to have served religious purposes, the whole settlement being palisaded and moated. Integrated into this assemblage in a manner presently unknown to us was the palace of the ruler, customarily, it would seem, a double-storeyed wooden building (*Chin Shu*, 97: 16b; *Nan-Ch'i*

Shu, 58: 11b; *T'ai-p'ing Yü-lan*, 786: 8a; *Liang Shu*, 54: 7b; Malleret 1959–63, II: 291–2 and pl. xcix). The architectural dispositions of the only urban site from this period to have received more than cursory archaeological attention, that at Oc-Eo (Malleret 1959–63), are not in fundamental disagreement with the vague prescriptions of literary sources, although neither the extreme regularity of its rectilineal cellular design, nor its orientation with the longer axis running approximately from north-north-east to south-south-west, are reflected in either Chinese writings or later Khmer architectural traditions. If the city at Oc-Eo should ever be positively identified with the Ptolemaic Kattigara (a notion vigorously opposed by Malleret, the excavator of Oc-Eo: 1947: 108–23; cf. also Herrmann 1938), and if Stein's equation of Kattigara with Chü-tu-ch'ien/ *K'iuət-tuo-kuən, allegedly founded by emigrants from the Chinese commandery of Jih-nan in Han times (*Shui-ching Chu*, 36: 23a; *T'ai-p'ing Yü-lan*, 790: 9b), is sustained, then it might not be too unrealistic to seek the inspiration for the distinctive urban layout at Oc-Eo to the north in the Chinese culture realm, or possibly in the Viet territories. In any case, on Stein's interpretation Chü-tu-ch'ien/Kattigara was an imposed city owing its origin to primary diffusion, a circumstance not in conflict with the fact that the plan of the settlement at Oc-Eo is not readily matched elsewhere in early South East Asia.

Among the Indianized regions of continental South East Asia, it is in the Lower Mekong valley that the transformation from folk to urban society is best documented, but on present evidence the process appears to have followed an essentially similar course in several other territories. In what is now the Vietnamese province of Quảng-nam it manifested itself among a group of Hinduized Lin-i at the beginning of the fifth century, though the relationship of this emergent polity to the sinicized Lin-i of Jih-nan commandery is still obscure (Stein 1947: 71, 111–13).[27] On at least the northern tracts of the isthmus of the Malay peninsula the process appears to have been initiated almost, if not quite, as early as in the Mekong valley, for in the first quarter of the third century the ruler of a kingdom in the latter region was conquering political entities 'across the Chang Hai (South China Sea)' which Chinese annalists referred to as *kuo*, and some of which exhibited distinctly urban characteristics (*Liang Shu*, 54, 9a; *Nan Shih*, 78, 6b). The capital of one of these 'kingdoms', which in reality were probably city-states, had already developed commercial functions with ramifications extending as far as India and South West Asia on the west and Tongking on the east (*Liang Shu*, 54, 7a; Wheatley 1956; Shorto 1963: 583). In the deltas of the Mekong and Salween rivers and on the plains of the lower Chao Phraya, however, the sequence of events is less clear. Thus far archaeology has provided no firm evidence of indigenous urban traditions in these regions prior to the alleged expansion of the Mekong kingdom, although the Ptolemaic corpus does appear to locate several *poleis* and *emporia* in the general area. But the *Geography* as it now exists is a cumulative text, and the precise date of any particular piece of its information is not easily ascertained. To no inconsiderable extent the view taken of the urbanization process in these regions must depend on the limits ascribed to the Mekong polity. If either the Irawadi or Chao Phraya deltas, or both, were brought under its sway, then the basis of the urban hierarchy is likely to have been imposed in the manner described at the beginning of this paper (though this interpretation will itself depend on convincing identifications and locations of the political entities conquered by the Mekong ruler, as well as on a satisfactory elucidation of the implications of the word *kuo*). Otherwise urban generation seems a more plausible hypothesis. In central Burma Pyū urban forms are not an issue before the end of the fifth century at earliest, and in Arakan ceremonial centres cannot be discerned prior to the fourth century (Johnston 1944). It is interesting to note though that, whereas epigraphy and palaeography leave little doubt that northern Arakan owed its urban traditions to India through a process of secondary generation, there is a strong presumption that southern Arakan derived its city forms from already urbanized societies in the Irawadi, or even the Chao Phraya, valley, either through generation stimulated by secondary diffusion or by a process of imposition consequent on political expansion. The latter is perhaps the more likely in view of the statements in the T'ang histories that the western boundary of Dvāravatī lay on the ocean (*Chiu T'ang-Shu*, 197: 4b; *Hsin T'ang-Shu*, 222C: 6a).

The reconstitution of a folk community as an urban society was the most momentous and pervasive transformation that a traditional people could undergo. It was a metamorphosis that, however initiated, ultimately involved society in its totality, that restructured all its functional sub-systems, afforded opportunities for the concentration of power, wealth, and prestige, and provided a basis for the evolution of an urban-orientated Great Tradition. In South East Asia this climacteric change took two forms: urban imposition and urban generation, processes which were analytically distinguishable though not necessarily operationally discrete. Generally speaking, urban imposition predominated in the Sino-Viet territories as one manifestation of a prevailing mode of primary diffusion (but see note 13), while urban generation was the originating process in the Indianized realms. In neither of these two regions was the prevailing style of systemic change totally comprehensive and exclusive. In the first place, neither in the Viêt nor in the Indianized territories did urbanization extend into the uplands: it was essentially a lowland phenomenon. In the second place, both regions exhibited significant deviations from the dominant mode of urbanization. In Jih-nan commandery the skeletal urban system imposed by Chinese authority from the end of the second century asserted a dynamism of its own which persisted until its presumed absorption of the proto-urban Hindu ceremonial centres of Quảng-nam in the sixth century. So far as the alluvial lowlands of continental South East Asia are concerned, it is presently impossible to assess with confidence the urbanizing rôle of the earliest recorded state based on the lower Mekong valley, and it is still debatable whether it imposed urban systems on certain neighbouring territories or usurped control over urban hierarchies already existing there, or, indeed, if it controlled these lands at all. If not, then they too were realms of urban generation. But that urban imposition occurred even closer to the Mekong focus of urban generation not later than the beginning of the third century is attested by the founding of Chü-tu-ch'ien by Jih-nan emigrants. It will be a task of future research to discriminate and delimit with much greater precision than is attempted here nuclear regions of urban generation in South East Asia, as opposed to those in which cities arose through the imposition of organizational patterns developed elsewhere.

NOTES

1. The most elaborate exposition of this concept was put forward by Rüstow 1949: vol. 1, 95–104 and *passim*. In America the chief proponent of the idea has been Eberhard 1965: *passim* and 1967: 11.

2. Analogies from physical science—not to be pressed too far—might perhaps be expressed in terms of adiabatic change or positive change of entropy. The process corresponds to the phase of primary urbanization in Redfield and Singer's typology of societal transformations (1954: 60): 'Primary urbanization thus takes place almost entirely within the framework of a core culture that develops, as the local cultures become urbanized and transformed, into an indigenous civilization.'

3. cf. Murphey's (1963–4) thesis that the acculturative situation is not only empirically the condition of, but is also structurally necessary to, virtually all human societies.

4. It was presumably this type of diffusion that Bronislaw Malinowski (1944: 14–15) had in mind when he wrote that, 'Diffusion . . . is not an act, but a process closely akin in its working to the evolutionary process. For evolution deals above all with the influence of any type of "origins"; and origins do not differ fundamentally whether they occur by invention or by diffusion.' In a similar vein cf. Steward (1951: 4; 1955: 182) and White (1957: 218).

5. There is an extended evaluation of realms of primary and secondary urban generation in Wheatley (1971: 6–9, 226–57).

6. For a conspectus of the categories of sources available see Wheatley 1961: 104–17, 160–2, 204–9.

7. cf. also Friedmann (1961b); Miner (1967: 6–8); and the whole body of formulations that go under the name of Central-Place Theory: Berry and Pred 1965; Beckmann 1958; Webber 1971.

8. Demographers in general are inclined to regard the city in this way, but the most prominent exponent of this point of view is probably Mumford (1961: *passim*).

9. These four conceptualizations of the city and the five strategies for elucidating its mysteries are discussed by Wheatley (1972).

10. Braidwood's term (1952: 41; 1960: 149). The phrase (coined in a South West Asian context) is not especially appropriate in its implications to the South East Asian situation, but may serve as a sufficiently neutral rubric for the immediately pre-urban period until such time as the archaeological periodization of that region as been

stabilized. As I understand its reference, Solheim's (1969: 137) proposed term *Extensionistic* carries many of the implications of Braidwood's *Developed Village-Farming*. In New World archaeology the analogous terms are *Late Formative* and *Early Florescent*.

11. In language more familiar to anthropologists this was the domain of Redfield's (1947) folk societies.

12. This remark would be otiose were it not for the fact that archaeologists have sometimes ascribed urban status to a settlement on the basis of a particular architectural feature such as a wall or a palace: e.g. Kenyon 1957: 65–6.

13. Exigencies of space prevent this and the next section from being anything more than bare outlines of the urbanization process. In the case of Tongking there is an additional complication. In the relevant sections of this paper I have adopted what may be termed the conventional Western view of early Viet history as propounded primarily by scholars of the Ecole Française d'Extrême-Orient during the first half of the present century. Recently, however, archaeologists and historians of the Democratic Republic of Viet-Nam have equated the newly revealed Phùng-nguyên archaeological culture with the Kingdom of Văn-lang which, although figuring prominently in Viet histories, has hitherto been regarded by Western historians as archetyped mythology [Report and sources in Davidson's contribution to this volume]. The implication of this interpretation evidently is that Phùng-nguyên/Văn-lang was an urbanized culture/state. A formidable language barrier prevents me from evaluating at first hand the reports of the excavations of the score or so known Phùng-nguyên sites (which, incidentally, appear from Davidson's bibliography to be preliminary notices rather than comprehensive reports), but the little that I have been able to glean from conversation, translation, and secondhand summaries does not clearly substantiate the claim for a developed urban hierarchy. This is not to suggest that such a claim may not ultimately be vindicated, but merely that the evidence presently available to me does not seem to justify the ascription of an urban level of social integration to the Phùng-nguyên culture. While differing from Dr. Davidson on this point, I would like to express my thanks to him for numerous thoughtful and incisive comments on this paper.

14. Except for the first five years of the occupation when a Commissioner (lit. 'inciting notary': MSC *tz'ü-shih*; Viet. *thú-su*) with authority over the whole of the former kingdom of Nan-Yüeh was based at Luy-lâu in the heart of the Tongking delta.

15. *An-nam chí luoc*, 7.

16. According to *Ch'ien-Han Shu* (28C:6) the commandery (MSC *chün*; Viet. *quận*) of Giao-chi originally comprised the following *huyên*: Luy-lâu, An-định, Càu-lâu, Mi-linh, Khúc-cuong, Băc-đái, Kê-tù, Tày-vu, Long-biên, and Chu-diên.In A.D. 44 Tày-vu was subdivided into the two *huyên* of Phong-khê and Vọng-hai (*Tzŭ-chih T'ung-chien*, 43:5b).

17. cf., for example, *Hou-Han Shu*, 118: 10b; *Liang Shu*, 54: 7b; *Chiu T'ang-Shu*, 41: 33b.

18. *Ch'ien-Han Shu*, 28B: 6a; *Hou-Han Shu*, 33: 8a; *Chin Shu*, 15: 9a; *Shui-ching Chu*, 36: 18b; *An-nam Chí luoc*, 1: 3b; *Khâm-dinh Viêt-su Thông-giám Cuong-mục* tiên-biên 2: 5a, 27b.

19. *Sung Shu*, 5: 12b and 97: 48b; *Đại-Viêt Sú-kí*, ngoai ki 4: 17b; *Đại-Viet Su-kí Toàn-thu*, 4: 16b; *Cuong-mục*, tiên-biên 3: 26b–27a.

20. Namely the strategically situated frontier fortress of Ch'ü-su, close to and possibly on the site of, the old Chinese commandery seat of Hsi-chüan, and the capital of the Lin-i confederacy, probably in the neighbourhood of Văn-xá, a short distance north-east of Hué. Both cities are described, though somewhat ambiguously, in *Shui-ching Chu*, 36, with commentaries provided by Stein 1947: 1–108.

21. Possibly the most comprehensive interpretation of the process of Indianization is provided by Coedès 1953 and 1954; 1962: 54–60; 1964: 35–72. cf. also Bosch 1961: 3–22; and Christie 1970.

22. I use this term simply as a convenient way of referring to the interaction between representatives of the Great Tradition of India on the one hand and Dravidian (including sub-cultural variants) and South East Asian elements on the other. I am aware that 'brāhmaṇization', like its customary synonyms 'sanskritization' and 'āryanization', is a problematical term of limited applicability.

23. The sequence of changes that I have in mind is something similar to that reported by Linton and Kardiner (1952) for the Tanala of Madagascar when wet-padi cultivation was adopted by dry-padi farmers.

24. *T'ai-p'ing Yü-lan*, 788, 1b, citing the third-century *Nan-chou I-wu Chih*. The earliest extant epigraphic, as opposed to literary, references to brāhmaṇs ('the twice-born resembling fire') in South East Asia occur in *yūpa* inscriptions from the Kutai valley in eastern Kalimantan dated to the beginning of the fifth century.

25. Skt. *Parvatabhūpāla* or *Śailarāja*; O. Kh. *Kuruṅ Vnam*, whence the Chinese rubrication of the kingdom as **B'iumnậm* > MSC Fu-nan: but see also Cl. Jacques's paper in this volume. No one can write of this kingdom, whose true name is unknown but which is customarily cited as Fu-nan, without acknowledging his indebtedness to Pelliot (1903), whose collation of the relevant Chinese texts first rendered their implications apparent.

26. The validatory myth of the founding of the dynasty in question alludes to an *i* ruled by an indigenous queen at an even earlier, but undetermined, period (*T'ai-p'ing Yü-lan*, 347, 7b). I tend to regard this reference as a projection into the past from the later era of city-states when the myth was given shape.

27. The following works devote paragraphs to the Lin-i subsequent to the end of the sixth century, by which time the ethnikon appears to have denoted a polity that united both the Sinicized northern and the Hinduized southern groups: *Chin Shu*, 97; *Liang Shu*, 54; *Nan-Ch'i Shu*, 58; *Nan Shih*, 78; *Sui Shu*, 82; *T'ung Tien*, 188; *Wen-hsien T'ung-k'ao*, 331.

ADDITIONAL REFERENCES

Adams, R. McC. 1966. *The evolution of urban society: early Mesopotamia and Pre-historic Mexico*. Chicago, Aldine Publishing Company.

Beckmann, M. J. 1958. City hierarchies and the distribution of city size. *Economic Development and cultural change*, 6, 243–8.

Berry, B. J. L. and Pred, A. 1965. *Central place studies. A bibliography of theory and applications* (Regional Science Research Institute, Bibliography Series 1). Philadelphia, Regional Science Research Institute.

Blalock, H. M. and Blalock, A. B. 1959. Toward a clarification of system analysis in the social sciences. *Philosophy of Science*, 26, 84–92.

Braidwood, R. J. 1952. *The Near East and the foundations for civilization* (The Condon Lectures). Eugene, Oregon State System of Higher Education.

— 1960. Levels in prehistory. In *Evolution of the man after Darwin*, 2 (ed.) S. Tax. Chicago, University of Chicago Press.

Friedmann, J. 1961a. Cities in social transformation. *Comparative Studies in Society and History*, 4, 86–103.

— 1961b. L'influence de l'intégration du système social sur le développement économique. *Diogène*, 33, 80–104.

Kenyon, K. M. 1957. *Digging up Jericho: the results of the Jericho excavations 1952–1956*. New York, Frederick A. Praeger.

Klir, J. and Valach, M. 1967. *Cybernetic modelling*. London, Iliffe.

Linton, R. and Kardiner, A. 1952. The change from dry to wet rice cultivation in Tanala-Betsileo. In *Readings in Social Phychology*, (ed.) T. M. Newcomb and E. L. Hartley. New York, Henry Holt and Company.

Miner, H. (ed.). 1967. *The city in modern Africa*. New York, Frederick A. Praeger.

Mumford, L. 1961. *The city in history. Its origins, its transformations, and its prospects.* New York, Harcourt, Brace & World, Inc.

Murphey, R. F. 1963–4. Social change and acculturation. *Transactions of the New York Academy of Sciences*, ser. 11, 22, 845–54.

Parsons, T. and Shils, E. (eds.). 1952. *Toward a general theory of action.* Cambridge, Mass., Harvard University Press.

Polanyi, K. 1957. The economy as instituted process. In *Trade and market in the early empires. Economies in history and theory* (ed.) K. Polanyi, C. M. Arensberg, and H. W. Pearson. Glencoe, Illinois, The Free Press and the Falcon's Wing Press.

—1968. The economy as instituted process. In *Primitive, archaic and modern economies. Essays of Karl Polanyi*, (ed.) G. Dalton. Boston, Beacon Press.

Redfield, R. 1947. The folk society. *The American Journal of Sociology*, 52, 293–308.

— 1953. *The primitive world and its transformations.*

— 1956. *Peasant society and culture.* Chicago, University of Chicago Press.

Radfield, R. and Singer, M. B. 1954. The cultural role of cities. *Economic development and cultural change*, 3, 53–73.

Rüstow, A. 1950–7. *Ortsbestimmung der Gegenwart*, 3 vol. Zürich, Eugen Rentsch Verlag.

Sahlins, M. D. 1968. *Tribesmen.* Englewood Cliffs, N.J., Prentice-Hall, Inc.

Singer, M. 1960. The expansion of society and its cultural implications. In *City invincible* (ed.) C. H. Kraeling and R. M. Adams. Chicago, University of Chicago Press.

Steward, J. H. 1951. Cultural causality and law: a trial formulation of the development of early civilizations. *American Anthropologist*, 51, 1–27.

— 1955. *Theory of culture change.* Urbana, University of Illinois Press.

Van Nieuwenhuijze, C. A. O. 1966. *The nation and the ideal city. Three studies in social identity.* The Hague and Paris, Mouton & Co.

Webber, M. J. 1971. Empirical verification of classical central place theory. *Geographical Analysis*, 3, 15–28.

Wheatley, P. 1972. The concept of urbanism. In *Man, settlement and urbanism* (ed.) P. J. Ucko, R. Tringham, and G. W. Dimbleby. London, Gerald Duckworth & Co.

White, L. A. 1957. Evolution and diffusion. *Antiquity*, 31, 219–8.

Wolf, E. R. 1966. *Peasants.* Englewood Cliffs, N.J., Prentice-Hall, Inc.

Urban Genesis in Viet-Nam: a Comment

JEREMY H. C. S. DAVIDSON

THE theories of urban genesis, and the two aspects of its process, that of urban imposition and of urban generation, as outlined by Professor Paul Wheatley in his paper to this Colloquy,[1] are of great interest to anyone attempting to understand the situations of settlement that obtained in early South East Asia.

The transformation of a society from village-based autonomies linked largely by means of kinship alliances into a consolidated state founded on city-centred power bases and the concomitant development of a pattern of urban-rural interdependence is a momentous societal upheaval, yet it is little chronicled and even less researched.

In the case of the Vietnamese experience, specifically in what was to become North Viet-Nam and Champa, the urbanization process is usually held to have begun with the imposition of Chinese control (Nán-Yùe = Nam-Viet: 207–111 B.C.), to have developed gradually during the periods of Xī-Hàn and Xīn (111 B.C.–A.D. 25) domination, and to have received fresh stimulus after A.D. 43 with the incorporation of large tracts of present-day North Viet-Nam into the provincial administrative system of the metropolitan China of the Dōng-Hàn. This position was reasonably adopted in the light of Chinese documentation of the period and subsequent French studies which, by and large, may be considered as historical geography and which ceased with the Second World War. Post-Independence researches dealing with the historical development of cities have tended to concentrate on the late historical period, from the Hậu Lê (1428–1789), especially the sixteenth century, onwards. However, the wealth of archaeological evidence that has been brought to light over the last twenty years, incomplete and as yet inadequately studied though it is, does nonetheless furnish us with fresh material on which to base new appraisals of the problem of urban genesis in a Vietnamese context.[2] With the French period researches rendered contestible by virtue of this new evidence,[3] we might also reconsider the Chinese sources with regard to provenance,[4] and their realities of subject matter.[5]

To view the city as an organizing principle and a centre of dominance is the most fitting approach and most compatible with what we know of the Vietnamese and Cham examples. However, the ascription by Professor Wheatley (ibid., 292 ff.) of the urban imposition pattern to what he terms Sino-Viet territories and of the pattern of secondary urban generation (ibid., 294–5 and 298 ff.) to Cham territories raises several doubts.

From observations of the urban-rural interdependent[6] relationship in the late historical period, certain factors concerning the development and structuring of towns in Viet-Nam, although they are perhaps not uniquely Vietnamese, become apparent. The settlement that would develop into an important centre was strategically sited for offence and defence, for accessibility to the surrounding countryside by river and land routes which afforded ease of military manoeuvre, whence military supremacy, and for control over the flow of produce. Because of its commanding position this dominant settlement achieved an administrative function, and since it was central to the trade cycle of the region it became the market-town,[7] the focus for the exchange of produce which in Vietnamese terms included products that were the specialties of certain villages. These craft and produce specializations coming together at the central market-place probably aided the development of street-guilds and wards.[8] Since not all settlements were self-supporting, mining communities for example, the market-place as a redistribution point was essential to the continued existence of such dependent communities. The administration of the exchange of goods and the machinery for the maintenance of order necessary to the continuedly smooth operation of different sectors of society was naturally located at such favourable sites. The town as a political, social, and economic space was thus engendered, enabling city-dweller and peasant[9] to achieve a symbiotic relationship.

However, it now appears that most of these aspects of urbanism are observable in the period prior to Nam-Viet. The discoveries of the Phùng-nguyên culture complex (Lan 1968: 34; 1969: 58; 1970*b*: 76; Linh 1968*a*: 21-3) on what is traditionally Phong-châu territory (Trãi 1435: 30-9; Chú 1820: vol. 1, 97) argue strongly for the acceptance of Văn-lang and the Hùng-vu'o'ng (?-258 B.C.) as historically valid (Châu 1967: 35 ff., i.a.).[10] Their confederation, which might have been ruled by a gerontocratic oligarchy (Linh 1968*a*: 18 ff.; 1968*b*: 19 ff.) governing from a settlement in the Bạch-hạc region[11] of So'n-tây province, collapsed under the onslaught of Thục Phán who founded Âu-lạc (257-208 B.C.) in its place (*Cuong-muc*, 1884: Tb 1/8 = 57).[12]

The study of these two kingdoms—and even of their successor, Trieu Đà's (= Zhào Túo) Nam-Viet, since we know that he permitted government by local leadership to continue, and no great changes appear to have occurred (Tắc 1339: q. 4/57/21 = 92)—must be viewed as a continuity of already existing forms only slightly modified (Khải 1968: 51). No written evidence suggests that Thục Phán revolutionized the society over which he held sway, yet an argument *ex silentio* implies that he may have introduced bigger earth-ramparted towns (viz. Co-loa thành: Châu 1969: 27 ff.) or replaced palisaded settlements with them (cf. Tắc 1339: q. 1/24/21 ff. = 39-40).

The strategic, commanding nature of the sites of the capitals of Văn-lang and Âu-lạc—looking downriver to the sea—is self-evident. However, no trace of Văn-lang period dwellings of any sort has been discovered. Co-loa, on the other hand, was certainly a defensible town of imposing appearance, nine earthen rampart stages[13] giving the edifice its name[14] 'walled town in the shape of a snailshell',[15] considerable extent[16] and probably the site of a military arsenal or encampment.[17] Whether it was a market town is as yet unknown, but if Âu-lạc incorporated Văn-lang organization this seems likely.[18] The city walls apparently encompassed a hill whose peak might have been the place of the ruler's abode (Hòe 1966: 42), while the legend of advice from the Divine Golden Tortoise[19] on the building of the city implies a spiritual potency invested in the founder Thục Phán.

Archaeological discoveries at the Phùng-nguyên complex, the preparatory and early stages of the so-called Đông-so'n Bronze Age,[20] evince an organizational pattern that required some centrally located market as a redistribution centre for specialized craft goods produced at various 'factories',[21] some, like Đong-đậu, of considerable antiquity.[22] There is little or no evidence that these 'factories' were agricultural, self-supporting communities, so grain and other foods must have been produced in surplus to support them. Central market towns must therefore have existed at least in the late Hong Bàng period, and Co-loa of the Âu-lạc was probably just such an establishment. Given the high level of cultural achievement revealed by the excavations in the Văn-lang area (Lan 1970*b*: 76, i.a.) we may surmise an even earlier development of townships, a situation of urban generation which meets the spatial and symbolic requirements discussed by Professor Wheatley (ibid. 290 ff.).[23] The succeeding rules of Thuc Phán and Trieu Đà are not recorded as having altered the status quo.[24]

During the Xī-Hàn the situation that had prevailed under Nam-Viet continued although more direct Chinese governorship probably resulted in certain societal changes, especially in relation to trade. Documents are confused about which towns were built when by the Chinese in this period, but Luy-lâu[25] was the earliest, Long-biên (= Long-uyen)[26] a later central government seat. Provincial towns[27] were also built, perhaps on already existing settlements.[28]

The brief interregnum of Wáng Mǎng's ill-fated Xīn did not affect the situation in North Viet-Nam where Chinese governors remained loyal to the Hàn and continued the Xī-Hàn pattern of government until A.D. 34. Up to that date, Chinese governors had administered more or less in a *laissez-faire* manner, although certain of them had set out to educate the people. Much of what the Chinese records tell us of their introduction of techniques to improve the material culture of the indigenous population must be regarded with scepticism. What may be more readily accepted is the education of sections of the indigenous population in Confucian morality presumably something given new life by the influx of refugees from the chaotic conditions obtaining in China, first before effective reunification by Gūang-wudì (25–57), and again at the end of the Hòu Hàn. Purposive sinicization seems to have begun with the governorship of Su Dìng (To Định), to be enforced, following the suppression of the Tru'ng rebellion against it, by Mǎ Yúan in A.D. 43, with the incorporation of the area into the provincial administrative system of China proper.

The number of towns multiplied[29] to administer the new framework of districts and commanderies established in the wake of Mǎ Yúan's reorganization of the region. From this date it might be possible to consider urban imposition as a pattern affecting large areas of North Viet-Nam that were not previously involved to any great degree in the pervasive complexities of urbanism and of urban-rural interdependence. In the more developed regions that had been the heartland of Văn-lang and Âu-lạc, however, Chinese urban styles subsumed existing townships that had evolved independently, representatives of a process of urban generation.

Our knowledge concerning the inclusion of northern Línyì groups in the cultural florescence of the Đong-so'n Bronze Age is still tenuous.[30] Cham elements do certainly appear to have been represented and Cham support for the rebellion of the Tru'ng may be postulated. Cham involvement in the society prevailing before the imposition of extensive and effectual Chinese control in the middle of the first century A.D. remains undetermined, but their barbarousness (q.v. Wheatley, ibid. 294) is perhaps a Chinese view. Contact with Nam-Viet that is, sinicizing Đong-so'n, traditions is discernible in the third century A.D.,[31] yet the ascription of one or other aspect of urban genesis to Línyì groups is probably premature.

So, although scarcity of data as yet prevents us from being able to decide conclusively which aspects of urban genesis forms in North Viêt-Nam and Champa represent, we must, it seems, look to the pre-Nam-Viêt period for the beginnings, in Northern Viêt-Nam, of a type of urbanization that appears to comply with the requirements demanded for qualification as urban *generation* rather than urban *imposition*.

NOTES

1. Wheatley, op.cit., 288–303.

2. Several aspects of Gourou's (1936: 9) now classic description of the Vietnamese town do, as we shall see, still apply.

3. Briefly stated, French attitudes *vis-à-vis* the early history of Viêt-Nam are: that the period to 258 B.C. (= Văn-lang) is 'legendary', while the period 258–111 B.C. (=Âu-lạc and Nam-Viêt) is 'proto-historic'. History is deemed to begin with 111 B.C. and Chinese documentation and, although archaeology permits an antiquation via Dong-so'n to the fourth century B.C. (Karlgren's 1942: 28, dating), this culture is maintained to be culture of non-Vietnamese (Bezacier 1972: 226, i.a.).

4. Three classes of document in Chinese on Viêt-Nam can be readily discerned:
(1) that by a Chinese written about Viêt-Nam, hence Sinocentric, e.g. Gāo Xióng-zheng's *Ānnán zhìyúan*;
(2) that by a Vietnamese whose cultural affinities and or political affiliations are with China, hence selective of information, e.g. Lê Tăc's *Annam chí lu'o'c*;
(3) that by a Vietnamese who remains Vietnamese (*dân Viêt tô Hùng-vu'o'ng*), hence sometimes over zealous in the naturalization or antiquation of historical events, e.g. Ngô thò'i Sĩ's *Viêt su' tiêu án*.

5. One example is the supposed introduction of the buffalo-drawn plough to Cu'u-chân (= *Jiuzhen*) by Rén Yén (= Nhâm Diên: 5–67) during his governorship of the region, 29–33. (Tăc 1339: q.7/85/21 ff. = 139–40; Maspero 1918: 22–3; cf. Lan 1963: 56–9 and 317 ff.; n.b. Bezacier 1966/7: 551 ff.).

6. Gourou, loc. cit.

7. Such centrally located townships acted and act as the nuclei of the trade-produce cycle for the surrounding countryside thereby coming to possess permanent market-places (= *chéngshì: thành-thi: cho' thành*) and thus become market-towns (*ke cho'*) as opposed to country villages which might be the sites, in rotation, for *cho' phiên*, travelling market-fairs. Note that Hanoi went under the name of Ke chọ' in the late Hâu Lê period.

8. Compare the ward (*fang*) system of Táng Chángan with Hànoi's thirty-six *pho phu'ò'ng*.

9. Wheatley, ibid., 291; Gourou, loc. cit.

10. Davidson, *supra* pp. 125–36. Phùng-nguyên culture develops into Dông-so'n culture, the two stages representing a cultural evolution that incorporated the traditionally 'historic' kingdom of Văn-lang, cf. n. 3 above.

11. This area was one of continuous settlement. The Viêt-trì region, at the confluence of the Hông river system, has yielded rich Bronze Age sites (Lan 1963: 64 ff.); during the Xī-Hàn, the district town (*xiàncheng: huyên-thành*) of Mê-linh in present-day An-lăng, So'n-tây province (Duc 1909: *So'n-tây*, 91 = 127) was built here (Trãi 1435: 30/3 ff. = 39; Maspero 1918: 11–12; Aurousseau 1923: 242 ff.) to be elevated in rank by the Tru'ng Sisters, natives of the region, to serve as their capital during their briefly successful independence from the Chinese. (Sĩ, eighteenth century: 39; *Cu'o'ng-mục*, 1884: Tb2/9 ff. = 82 ff.). Also in An-lăng was the Hàn *huyên* of Châu-diên (Trãi 1435: 33/6 = 42), as well as the two *huyên-thành* founded by Mã Yuán (14 B.C.–A.D. 49) in 43, Kiên-giang thành in Phong-khê and Vọng-hải thành. (*Hoù Hànshu*: j. 113/21b3–4; Gao 1691: j. 2/110/3; also: j. 2/135/10–12 and j. 1/38/11–12; *Cu'o'ng-mục*, 1884: Tb2/14–15 = 86). Kiên-(= *viăn*) giang 'walled town shaped like a cocoon' (*Cu'o'ng-mục*, ibid.)—not *Ty* (= *xi*) giang, an honourable *graphus lapsus* perhaps suggestive of the town's prime status in the new province, found in Sĩ (ibid., 44)—is a slight variant renaming of Cô-loa thành 'walled town shaped like a snail(shell)', on whose site it was built (Liên 1479: 319, n. 10), something which poses difficulties for stratigraphic correlation, for the separation and dating of remains from the site (Anh 1964: 67; Châu 1969: 40).

The coiling, twining nature of the imagery of these two town names finds further expression in the dragon-associated foundation legend of Kiên-giang and Long-biên (q.v. n. 26 below). The equation Cô-loa = Kiên-giang because of site and name is thus extended to include Long-biên through an identical foundation legend and indirectly, too, by similarity of name. The equation of Long-biên with Luy-lâu, in part because of their association with Shì Xìe (= Sĩ Nhiêp: 186–226) and also the probable link by meaning of the names of Luy-lâu with Kiên-giang and Co-loa (q.v. n. 25 below) leads us to a connected series of names with various associations and cognate meanings and in turn suggests the proposition that all four are in fact the same.

12. Traditionally, the founders of Âu-lac are believed to have been a part of the Hùng-vu'o'ng confederation based in south-western China. The belief that they were

the Bă-Shŭ was already questioned by Vietnamese scholars of the nineteenth century (*Cu'o'ng-mục*, 1884: Tb1/8 = 57), and more recently it has been suggested that they were the Āiláo, centred on Yunnán (Davidson, op. cit., 112 ff. and n. 10), although certain folk stories link them with Cao-băng (Châu 1969: 27). Whatever may be finally established about their origins, it seems that the Thục were a non-Chinese, but historical, group.

13. Gāo 1691: j. 2/135/2 ff.; Anh 1964: 24–5; Hòe 1966: 39–40. However, the earthen ramparts of Chinese period sites may have been fillings for walls that were originally tiled. This is suggested by the abundance of pottery tiles of the same type and general location in relation to the earthworks found at various sites of similar date, like Quèn-cô and Đại-áng, Hà-tây. (Châu 1969: 27–9).

14. By the Táng dynasty, Co-loa, or Loa-thành, was also known as Tu'-long thành (Liên 1479: 64; Pháp 1492: 33 = 72; Gāo, ibid.; *Cu'o'ng-mục*, 1884: Tb1/9 = 57 ff.), a name reminiscent of Long-biên. *Tu'* becomes *hăc* in some texts. (Dục 1909: Băc-ninh, 47 = 36). The Chinese also called it *Shāgŭi Kūnlun* (= *Sát-quy Côn-lôn*) (Pháp, ibid.): *Shāgŭi* 'kill devil' because of the legend associated with its foundation, the exorcism on the advice of the Divine Golden Tortoise (*Kim Quy: Jin-Gui = rùa thân/vàng*) of the guardian spirit of Văn-lang (*Cu'o'ng-mục*, 1884: Tb1/17 = 62: cf. n. 26 below); *Kūnlún* because of the impressive dimensions of its walls (Sĩ, ibid., 17; *Cu'o'ng-mục*, ibid., = 58; Dục, loc. cit.). And further, according to Sĩ (ibid.) it was known as Trung Quy thành ('Loyal Tortoise'). The name Co-loa led Anh (1964: 24 ff.) to assemble much documentary evidence to elucidate the origins of the names for Loa-thành and to attempt to equate Cô-loa = Kha-lu with *Ke Loa* 'the important male individual Loa', an improbable solution refuted at length by Hòe (1966: 39–44). Although *loa* 'snail; univalve mollusc' stands as a significant in both Loa-thành and Cô-loa, it seems highly probable that Cô-loa is a Chinese attempt to transliterate a non-Chinese word for 'snail/tortoise'. Included in the transliteration are an element that carries the gross or approximate meaning, a conscious euphony in the transliteration characters chosen, and an approximation of the major phonetic elements of the word transliterated, all of which are in keeping with the general principles and practice of Chinese transliteration technique, and suggest an initial consonant cluster *kl-/+wâ final/ > *klwa = 'snail/tortoise' (q.v. Karlgren 1957: GSR 18c.).

Anh's argument that the fourteenth century Kha-lũ of Lê Tăc (1339: q.1/24/21 = 39) is a chronologically determined variant of Cô-loa is eminently acceptable. That Kha-lũ too is part of a transliteration seems likely. *luo* (= *la*) is also to be included, since it is probable that an error in writing the abbreviated form of *luo* led to the reading *Lí-lü* (= *La-lũ*) as the supposedly original form of the name Luy-lâu, in turn misread to become *Liên-thụ* (q.v. n. 25 below), on the authority of the *Hànzhì*, quoted by Nguyên Siêu in his *Phu'o'ng dình địa chí* (*Cu'o'ng-mục*, 1884: Tb2/5 = 79, n. 1). *lâu* and *lũ* are interchangeable and so do not pose a problem.

We are left with: *Kha/Cô: La* (= *Loa/Luy?*): *Lũ/Lâu* 'the place (*Lũ/Lâu*) of the "snail/tortoise" (*Kha/Cô: La* (= *Loa/Luy?*)', where *Cô-loa* probably comes from *kl[o]*? (= *klu*ᵃ); and *Kha-lũ* is either *Kha-(la)-lũ*, a minimal variant *Kha-la-(lũ)*, or a vocalic metathesis *Kh(ũ)-l(a)*. In all these latter cases one should note the similarities with Cham *kara*: 'tortoise', Jarai *krŏa*; proto-Indonesian *ku[l]aᶜ*. Note also proto-Austronesian *Kalah* = proto-Malayo-Polynesian *Karaq* 'mother-of-pearl shell/ clam' (q.v. n. 15).

15. Although most documentary evidence and modern research is in favour of *lúo = loa* 'snail', which appears to be a Thục emblem (see plastic representation on a *thô*, Lan 1963: pl. VIII. 2; stylized forms, ibid., pls. VIII. 1 and XIV. 4), and *lúo* being a univalve mollusc or shell (Karlgren 1957: 24, GSR 14; cf. series GSR 18, 577) excludes the possibility of mother-of-pearl (but see n. 14), it is possible that *lúo* stands for the earth-bound tabu substitute representation of the Kim Quy (qqv. nn. 14 and

19). Similarly, could the son of Kim Quy, Cao Lô (var. Cao Thông: Liên 1479: 65 and 314, n. 25; *Cu'o'ng mục*, 1884: Tb1/17 = 63), protector of Thục Phán and the city, stand as a tabu euphemism for Cô-loa, the spirit of the city? Metathesis of this sort is quite common in Vietnamese.

Professor H. L. Shorto has kindly furnished me with a note containing a wealth of linguistic detail of Mon-Khmer and Austroasiatic forms that appear to confirm the postulated Vietnamese initial consonant cluster *kl- (q.v. n. 14) and the conceptual links 'snail-tortoise-clam/mother-of-pearl'. Archaic Chinese *klwa*, Ancient *kwa*, paralleling Archaic *glwâ*, Ancient *luâ* 'snail' (q.v. Karlgren 1957: GSR 18c; note GSR 14, 577), may come from a Mon-Khmer root which Professor Shorto reconstructs as *kl[o]? 'snail, shell, shellfish', (note the transition from univalve to bivalve), e.g.:

> . . . Biat kl : 'sh.f.', kl : ko 'sn.' Bahnar k d kl u 'sn.', Central Sakai kalô 'sn.-sh.'; with infix Old Mon kinlo' 'sh.', Central Nicobarese kendu: 'clam', . . . Biat kl : is the obstacle to reconstructing *klu?, but might represent a variant *kluᵓ (suggestive *vis-à-vis* Chinese!) which would allow us to do so. Then 'snail' could be a variant of PMK *kluu? 'tortoise' > Mon klao 'large species of t.'; Kharia; 'kulu 't.' . . . I should also mention proto-Indonesian *ku[l]aᶜ 't.' because of the 'vowel-medial metathesis' forms in some mainland dialects: Jarai krŏa, Röglai kroa (but Cham kara:).

Although Professor Shorto no longer connects *kl[o]? with proto-Austronesian *kalah (= proto-Malayo-Polynesian *karaq 'Schale'), these forms introduce mother-of-pearl. (q.v. n. 14.)

16. Wide, thick walls 1000 *zhàng* (=*tru'o'ng*) in circumference (Pháp 1492: 33 =72; Gāo, ibid.; Sī, ibid.; *Cu'o'ng-mục*, 1884: Tb1/9 =57).

17. Suggested by the enormous cache of bronze arrowheads found there (Châu 1969: 39–41, i.a.).

18. Finds of bronze ploughshares (=hoes?) within the confines of the walls of Cô-loa (Lự'u 1963: 40; Chi 1964: 38 ff.; Khai 1968: 51; Châu 1969: 41) need imply no more than some agricultural activity within the walled area, but the presence of axes, too, suggests something more than that, some sort of commercial activity.

19. The spirit-tortoise is the guardian-spirit common to all Mu'ò'ng tribes, is the object of the strictest tabus, and is regarded as the adviser of the tribal ancestors on housebuilding. Its form is said to be the model for the Mu'ò'ng house (Cuisinier 1948: 81; Linh 1968b: 21). Co-loa was built in Yueshāng (= Viêt-thu'ò'ng) (Liên 1479: 64–5), from whence the earliest *rùa thân* recorded in Vietnamese history are said to have come, as a tribute gift to China in 2353 B.C. (*Cu'o'ng-mục*, 1884: Tb1/6 = 55). In passing, it is perhaps of interest that a particularly efficacious spirit-tortoise, highly valued for divination purposes, is the *wéngui*, so called after the special colours and markings on its carapace. Recall Văn-lang 'country of the tatooed'.

20. Davidson, op. cit., 99 ff., esp. 102 and n. 11.

21. Agricultural communities are well represented among archaeological sites (Lan 1963: 31 ff.; 1964: 63–4; Linh 1964: 39), as are 'factories' that specialized in various wares such as the stone 'factories' of Đông-khôi (Tân 1968: 53; Kinh 1969: 56) and Dâu-du'o'ng (ibid., 55 ff.), and the pottery 'factories' of Gò Bông, Gò Mun, and Thiêu-du'o'ng. The existence of bronze goods 'factories' remains to be established, yet the concentration of moulds at a site like Đông-đâu (Lan 1968: 43) hints at the possibility, which finds further support in the number and variety of goods in bronze.

22. Davidson, op. cit., 102 and n. 8: 1378 B.C. ± 100 years.

23. Perhaps illustrative of symbolic spiritual potencies and their auras (q.v. n. 19) is the human figurine found at Văn-điên (Dung 1966: 64) which, given modern ethnographic parallels, appears to be a symbol of fertility, veneration, and communal worship (Lan 1970a: 35 ff.). In addition, the large number of pottery and bronze models, especially of birds, may serve a similar purpose, if we accept Lan's (1963: 249 and 293) interpretation of their function.

24. Dating of these bronze pieces with decorations presumably representative of various aspects of the material culture and society of the Vietnamese Bronze Age is not sufficiently precise for one to claim that these elements remained virtually unchanged from the middle of the second millenium B.C. until the Hòu Hàn, hence unaltered during the foreign control of Thục Phán and Triêu Đà. One should nonetheless note that Viêt territories were coveted by the Qín (255–207) for their jade (*Cu'o'ng-mục*, 1884: Tb1/10 = 58) and that Triêu Đà proclaimed himself king of Nam-Viêt in 183 B.C. following the prohibition by Hàn Gāohòu (187–179) of the operation of mountain pass markets selling iron goods (Tăc 1339: q.1/16/8 = 23; q.4/57/4 = 91; *Cu'o'ng-mục*, 1884: Tb1/22 = 66). The presence of iron goods among finds made at Cô-loa has led to some debate on the date of the beginnings of iron-working in the Hong Delta (Châu 1969: 33; Davidson, op. cit., 112 and n. 52).

25. Established in 110 B.C. as the seat of government from which Shí Dài (Thạch Đái) administered Jiāozhi (Giao-chi), and abandoned as such when the Xī-Hàn moved the seat of the regional administration to Guǎngxìn (Quang-tín), Luy-lâu became a *huyên-thành* that was captured by the Tru'ng in A.D. 40 (Maspero 1918: 13) and was eventually re-established according to tradition (Gāo 1691: j. 1/39/2–3) as the principal centre of government of Jiaozhǐ by Shì Xiê. The controversial opinion that Luy-lâu and Long-biên are two sites (Li 814: j. 38/10a9; cf. Trãi 1435: 39/1 = 48; Pháp 1492: 41 = 101; Dục 1909: *Bac-ninh*, 37/4 = 48) was accepted by Madrolle (1937: 267 ff.), supplementing H. Wintrebert's original identification, itself based on late Vietnamese traditions (*Cu'o'ng-mục*, 1884: Tb2/7 = 80; Châu 1969: 36), of Luy-lâu with xã Lũng-khê, *huyên* Siêu-loại, in Bắc-ninh province, which incorporated both Hàn *huyên* of Long-biên and Luy-lâu (Dục, ibid., 8–9 = 12; 2 = 6). Madrolle's arguments in support of this identification can be refuted on documentary evidence. In addition, the texts containing relevant geographical information position the three towns—Cô-loa, Luy-lâu, and Long-biên—in relation to the rivers running through the region (*Hong-dú'c ban do*, 1490: maps 5/9/26–27, esp. grids D 4, 6, 8; E 5) and of locational importance in the division of the country between Triêu Đà, holding the territory from the Bình-giang northwards, and the Thục, holding the territory to its south (Trãi 1435: 58/3 ff. = 66; Liên 1479: 67–8; Pháp 1492: 34 = 73; and 75; *Cu'o'ng-mục*, 1884: Tb1/15–16 = 61–62; Dục, ibid., 39–40 = 39), where Co-loa was situated. Note that Shì Xiê built his town to the south of the Bình-giang, a river also known as the Thiên-dú'c giang or song Đong-ngan

The location arrived at supports Lǐ Jífǔ's (814: j. 38/10a8; q.v. also *Hoù Hànshú*, j. 113/21a9) '75 *li* west' rather than Madrolle's claim that 'west' is a mislection for 'east'.

Luy-lâu has been represented by a series of characters, many misunderstood (q.v. Karlgren 1957: GSR 14 and 816), some of which led Madrolle (1937: 281–2) to attach eponymous and chronological significance to variant graphs whose pronunciation gives us the various readings found in western works. While Madrolle's associative interpretations may have some point, and one could spend considerable space discussing the intricacies of the character series involved in the names Luy-lâu and Cô-loa, we actually possess an early note on the meaning of Luy-lâu, in Meng Kāng's *Hànshu yinyì*, the relevant section of which, preserved in the *Hànshu* (j.28c/11a1) states: (*Lei* = *Luy*) is pronounced *lián* (*liän); (*Lǒu* = *lâu*) is pronounced *shòu* (* u): (it means) 'earthen basket'.

Unfortunately, Maspero (in Madrolle 1937: 281, n. 1) misread this passage, considering *shòu* and *tǔ* to be *fǎnqiè* characters (= *źúo), whereas it is patently obvious that the passage is an example of *yinyùnxúe*. Yán Shīgǔ (581–645) gave us the *fanqiè*: (*Hànshu*, loc. cit.): '*Lǒu* (= *lâu*) and *lǒu* are both spelt *lái kǒu* (= *lǒu*)'.

If we accept Mèng Kāng's *l än *ʑi u = 'earthen basket' as both the local pronunciation and meaning of the name, a term descriptive of the city, certain possible Vietnamese equivalents are suggested, the most satisfactory, in my opinion being the first. We should here remember Nguyên Siêu's *Hànzhì* reading La-lũ, where La is an error for *lúo* (= *la*) 'net', which may, as in *goūlúo* 'to repair rents in a net; to stop up cracks' stand for *lúo* ('basket-sieve for cleansing rice'.).

1. *lián shòu*='basket earthen' (reading à la vietnamienne)
    = *nom* (a) *liên* > *lan* = (hand)basket (< ?*mblan*; cf. 2a, 3a)
        (b) *thó* = clay, earth (= *thô*)
2. *lián shòu* = 'earthen basket' (reading à la chinoise)
    = *nom* (a) *liên* = an extensive ridge of earth (cf. *liêp* = 'circles, or circular areas, of earth'; a cognate which, by extension, = 'bamboo lattice-work partition; basket-(weave)'.
        (b) *gio* , *ro* = *ro* , *rô* = *rá* , *ro* = various types of basket.

Note that there is a conceivable Cham parallel:
liñan (*ta*)*thauk* (MSCh; *liñan* (*ta*)*thǒ*) = lit. 'earthen terrace that is basket-like', which does not conform to the word order expected of Cham, but where *liñan* suggests *liên* (ladder-like; connected, continuous; cf. *lúo* series) (=? *lan*), and (*ta*)*thauk* suggests *thó*| > ?*gio*.

3. *lián shòu* metathesized to become *ź än l*( ) *u* = 'basket earthen' (reading à la vietnamienne)
        = *nôm* (a) *giân*; giành, sành = (earthen) winnowing basket (Note *lúo* above, and the imaginative member of the series: *sên* 'snail' (< *sênh*).).
        (b) *niêu* =earthen pot.

These, and the previous discussion of the descriptive imagery existing between the names Cô-loa (= Kiên-giang) and Luy-lâu, and the locations pointed to by the geographical information, especially Li Jífŭ's which would place Luy-lâu on the Cô-loa site, combine to suggest that it is at the latter place that we might seek the actual site of Luy-lâu.

26. The dragon-associated legend of the site and the subsequent founding of Long-uyên = Long biên (Tăc 1339: q.1/20/19 ff.=31; Pháp 1492: 34 = 72; *Cu'o'ng-mục*, 1884: Tb2/7 = 81) finds a parallel foundation legend in that for Kiên-giang (q.v. n. 11) (where native versus Chinese is expressed by: serpent = dragon; spirit-pole=bronze pillar, symbolic of the substitution of Chinese control of cosmic forces in the stead of area control by the local deity: water, i.e. river, the abode of the dragon = restrained by the earthen walls of the city, implying flood control (qqv. Kaltenmark 1948; Mlle Pirazzoli-t'Serstevens paper to this Colloquy), and irrigation works with dykes; which lead to the eviction of the dragon from his demesne, whence *Thang-long* 'the ascent of the dragon' = Hànôi).

The involvement of Ma Yuán in an origin legend of this sort is unsurprising, and the purpose of the appropriation and transformation by the Chinese of indigenous beliefs has been studied often (q.v. i.a. Mlle Pirazzoli-t'Serstevens paper to this Colloquy pp. 125–136). The impact of the Chinese presence personified by Mǎ Yuán is restated in the person, similar activity and purpose of Zhūge Liàng (181–234). Long-biên became the administrative capital of the region in A.D. 210 under Shì Xie who was enfeoffed first as Longdūtínghou (= Long-đo đình-hâu) in A.D. 207 (Xuyên 1329: 1(227)/16 = 42; Tăc 1339: q.7/89/5 ff. = 146; Sĩ, ibid., 47; *Cu'o'ng mục*, 1884: Tb2/30 = 96) and then Lóngbianhou (= Long-biên hâu) (*Saengúozhì: Wuzhì*, 4: j. 49/11a7; Xuyên 1329: 2(226)/1 = 42; Tăc, loc. cit.; Liên 1479: 98; Sĩ, ibid., 49; *Cu'o'ng-mục*, 1884: Tb3/1 = 98), actually governing from there according to some sources (Trãi 1435: 39/1 = 48; Pháp 1492: 41 = 101–102, i.a.; nb. Xuyên 1329: 1(227)/4 = 41 and 4(224)/13 = 46).

27. Distinctions were made between central administrative seats (*thành-thi*), district towns (*huyên-thành*) and sub-district level settlements that appear to have had an administrative significance (*xiànyì: huyên-ap*) (*Hòu Hànshu* j.113/21a8 ff., and 21b3–4; *Cu'o'ng-mục*, 1884: Tb1/20 = 64–65; Tb2/5 = 79; Tb2/14–15 = 86; cf. Maspero 1918: 13, n. 1).

28. Excavations have yielded numerous instances of Hàn or later Chinese period

settlements built directly on top of indigenous Bronze Age settlements (e.g. Lan 1963: 33 ff.). Đông-khô (Chinh 1962: 42) is an example of a smaller scale settlement whose site was adopted by the Chinese. See also nn. 11 and 13, above.

29. Each *huyên* had its *thành*. During the Xĩ-Hàn 22 *huyên* were established (*Hànshū*, j. 28c/10b9 ff.), subsuming Triêu Đà's administrative organization of the territory (*Cu'o'ng-mục*, 1884: Tb2/4–5 = 78–9), and although the early Đông-Hàn reorganization shifted boundaries, it did not affect the total number of districts (ibid., Tb1/20 = 64–5; *Hòu Hànshū*, loc. cit.; Gão 1691: j. 1/38/12). Documentation contemporary to the period 111 B.C.–A.D. 50 does not supply us with a definite number of towns constructed and in use during that period, nor does it inform us of the locations and identifications of the towns (e.g. Dục 1909: *So'n-tây*, 87 and 91). Nonetheless, Tắc (1339: q. 4/58/2 = 92; q. 15/148/13 = 240) sets the number of towns captured by the Tru'ng at 60, while Trãi (1435: 30/7 = 40) is more cautious, giving 56, and Liên (1479: 91) puts the number as high as 65. This last figure seems excessive since that would place the total number of towns of pre-Nam-Viêt date as well as those dating from the start of Chinese control (207 B.C.) somewhat higher. The figure suggests a copyist's error in all or some of the Vietnamese texts.

30. Davidson, op. cit., 115 and n. 63.

31. In the Cham support given to Triêu Âu *c.* A.D. 248 (*Cu'o'ng-mục*, 1884: Tb3/6–9 = 103–4.

ADDITIONAL REFERENCES

Anh, Đào duy, 1964. *Đât nuó'c Viêt-nam qua các dò'i*. Hànôi, NXB Khoa học.

Châu, Tru'o'ng hoàng, 1967. Nên văn hóa khao cô học duy nhât trong thò'i đại đông thau Viêt-nam và vân đê nu'ó'c Văn-lang cua Hùng-vu'o'ng. *NCLS* 105 (12–1967), 35–41.

Châu, Tru'o'ng hoàng, 1969. Chung quanh vân đê tòa thành đât cô trên đât Cô-loa. *NCLS* 129 (12–1969), 26–41.

Chi, Nguyên đông, 1964. Vê môt loại nông cụ bằng đông thau tìm thây trong các địa diêm khao cô Đông-so'n và Thiêu-du'o'ng. *NCLS* 61 (4–1964), 35–41.

Chinh, Hoàng xuân, 1962. Nhân đọc bài 'Mây ý kiên vê nên văn hóa Đông-so'n'. *NCLS* 44 (11–1962), 42 51.

Chú, Phan huy, 1820. *Lịch triêu hiên chu'o'ng loại chí*. Hànôi, NXB Su học, 1960–1, 4 vols.

Cu'o'ng-mục, 1884. Quôc su' quán, *Viêt-su' thông-giám cu'o'ng-mục. Tiên biên*. Tâp 1. Tô biên dịch Ban nghiên cú'u văn su địa biên dịch và chú giai. Hànôi, NXB Văn su' địa, 1957–.

Dục, Cao xuân, 1909. *Đại-Nam Nhât Thông Chí*. Sàigòn, Nha Văn Hóa, Văn-hóa tùng-thu', sô 1–, 1960–.

Dung, Ngọc, 1966. Tin tú'c khoa học lịch su': Môt pho tu'ọng đá mó'i tìm thây trong môt di chi đô đá. *NCLS* 87 (6–1966), 64.

Gão Xióngzheng, *c.* 1691. *Ān-nam chí-nguyên*. EFEO Collection de textes et documents sur l'Indochine, 1: *Ngan-nan tche yuan*. Hànoi, Imprimerie d'Extrême-Orient, 1932, 56+257 pp.

Hànshū. Bónàbĕn edition.

Hòe, Lê văn, 1966. 'Góp ý kiên vó'i ông Đào-duy-Anh vê vân đê Loa-thành'. *NCLS* 86 (5–1966), 39–44.

Hông-dú'c ban đô. c. 1490, copy of 1800–7 text, Tu sách Viên khao cô 111, Sàigòn, Bô Quôc-gia giáo-dục, 1962.

Hòu Hànshū. Bónàbĕn edition.

Kinh, Phạm văn and Lê văn Lan. 1968. Xu'o'ng chê tạo đô đá o' Dâu-du'o'ng (Tam-nông, Phú-thọ). *NCLS* 109 (4–1968), 55–60.

Khai, Đào tu', 1968. Vài ý kiên vê công tác nghiên cú'u thành Cô-loa và tìm hiêu xã hôi Âu-Lạc. *NCLS* 109 (4–1968), 51–4.

Lan, Lê văn, 1963. (and Phạm văn Kinh, Nguyên Linh. 1963). *Nhữ'ng vêt tích dâu tiên cua thờ'i dại dô dông thau o' Viêt-nam.* Hànôi, NXB Khoa học, 328 pp.

— 1964. Tin tú'c khoa học lịch su': Tìm đu'o'c no'i cât giâu di vât cua thờ'i dại dô dông thau o' núi Mai-dô (Nam-định). *NCLS* 61 (4–1964), 63–4.

— and Phạm văn Kinh 1968. Di tích khao cô trên dât Phong-châu địa bàn gôc cua các vua Hùng. *NCLS* 107 (2–1968), 34–46.

— 1969. Tài liêu khao cô học và viêc nghiên cú'u thờ'i dại vua Hùng. *NCLS* 124 (7–1969), 52–60.

— 1970*a*. Vê môt hình thú'c sinh hoạt văn hóa tinh thân o' thờ'i dại các vua Hùng. *NCLS* 130 (1/2–1970), 35–44.

— 1970*b*. Vê tục hoa táng o' thờ'i dại các vua Hùng. *NCLS* 132 (5/6–1970), 74–80.

Liên, Ngô sĩ, 1479(–1697). *Đại Viêt Su' Ky Toàn Thu'.* Hànôi, NXB Khoa học xa hôi, 1967, 4 vols.

Lǐ Jífǔ. *c.* 814. *Yuanhé jùnxiàn tǔzhi.* Daìnángé cōngshū edition, bĕn 21–30 of 1797.

Linh, Nguyên, 1964. Di chi Gò Mun và vân dê thờ'i dại dô dông thau o' Viêt-nam. *NCLS* 58 (1–1964), 29–40.

— and Hoàng Hu'ng. 1968*a*. Vân dê Hùng-vu'o'ng và khao cô học. *NCLS* 108 (3–1968), 18–23.

— 1968*b*. Su' thât lịch su' trong truyên thuyêt Hông Bàng: Vê sự' tôn tại cua nu'ó'c Văn-lang. *NCLS* 112 (7–1968), 19–32.

— 1969. Bàn vê nu'ó'c Thục cua Thục Phán. *NCLS,* 124 (7–1969), 33–51.

Lụ'u, Đô and Đoàn thê Khai 1963. Hai chiêc thạp dông mó'i đu'ọ'c phát hiên o' Phú-thọ. *NCLS* 47 (2–1963), –60.

Pháp, Trân thê, *c.* 1492. Vũ Qùynh (ed.), *Linh-Nam Trích Quái.* Sàigòn, NS Khai Trí, 1961; VN trans. Lê Hũ'u Mục.

Sānguozhì. Bónàben edition.

Sĩ, Ngô thờ'i, Eighteenth century. *Viêt su' tiêu án.* Sàigòn, Văn-hóa A-châu, 1960.

Tắc, Lê, *c.* 1339. *An-nam chí-lu'o'c.* Viên Đại-học Huê Uy-ban phiên-dịch su'-liêu Viêt-nam, Huê, 1961, 19 q.

Tân, Hà văn, 1968. Môt sô vân dê vê văn hóa Phùng-nguyên. *NCLS* 112 (7–1968), 51–9.

Tu', Trân văn, 1966. Đào khao cô Gò Mun lân thu' hai. *Môt sô bao cao vê khao cô học Viêt-nam.* Hànôi, Đôi khao cô, 231–8.

Trãi, Nguyên, 1435. *U'c-Trai Tu'o'ng-công di tâp: Du' dịa chí.* Sàigòn, Nha Văn Hóa, Văn-hoá tùng-thu' 30, 1966; VN trans. Trân Tuân Khai.

Xuyên, Ly Tê, 1329. *Viêt diên u-linh tâp.* Sàigòn, NS Khai Trí, 1961, VN trans. Lê Hũ'u Mục.

The Late Prehistory and Early History of Central Thailand with Special Reference to Chansen

BENNET BRONSON

Introduction

THIS paper is intended first as an overview of the progress of research into the late prehistory and protohistory of central Thailand, and second as a brief inquiry into the chronology of the rise of the South East Asian state. The subject is large and the existing evidence far from abundant; I propose therefore to reach no radically new conclusions. But the accelerating archaeological research of the past few years has brought to light certain new data which bear on the well-worn theme of the origins of the classic South East Asian empires. These data (as well as the intrinsic and theoretical interest of the state-building process, so successful and potentially so accessible by contrast with similar sequences of events in other regions) make the subject worth reopening once again. I have arbitrarily elected to limit attention to the 1,500-year period which begins with the apparent introduction of iron-using into South East Asia, at about the start of the first millennium B.C.,[1] and ends with the appearance of what can be archaeologically recognized as the first state in central Thailand (the so-called Dvāravatī 'kingdom') in the late sixth or early seventh century A.D. The initial stirrings toward state-like political organization may have occurred much earlier, as is suggested by the considerable diffusion and elaboration of the Early Metal Age assemblages at Non Nok Tha and Ban Chiang, whilst the final entrance of central Thailand into the fully-developed pattern of the autocratic, highly centralized, religiously-buttressed South East Asian state may not have occurred until the Khmer conquest of the eleventh century. But it seems safe to say that the crucial events in the development of regional state-like polities took place somewhere between the tenth century B.C. and the sixth century A.D. The following discussion will therefore focus upon that span of time.

In relation to the origins of the state itself, I have left aside several critically important aspects of what goes into ordinary definitions of the state. The evolution of specific governmental institutions is outside the area of this inquiry; the evidence of any given institution, even of kingship, is very thin in early central Thailand. Likewise we cannot hope to recover anything of early state ideologies, in the absence of inscriptions and of detailed observations by foreigners. Except for a scattering of rather doubtfully dated statues and one or two buildings assigned to early dates without stratigraphic or any other hard evidence, protohistoric central Thailand (and indeed most of the rest of protohistoric South East Asia) is surprisingly empty of works of 'ideological' art. We may suspect that the strategy of monumental self-validation was acquired by the region's rulers only after some centuries of experimentation with political devices, presumably at about the same time that those rulers adopted the time-tested Indian strategies of temple-founding, inscription-erecting, and support for brahmanical royal cults.

The evidence that remains is economic in nature. If one accepts that the functions and causes of the state are in part economic, then it follows that the development of states in places where none had existed before should have marked effects on productive modes and exchange institutions. Control over means of production might be difficult to demonstrate in the particular case where the archaeological record reveals no large irrigation canals or government warehouses. But alterations in the institutions of exchange should in theory be readily demonstrable by archaeological means, in places like South East Asia where abundant evidence exists for ancient trade and other modes of inter- and intra-societal movement of artefacts. The greater part of this paper will be devoted to working out this relatively simple theme: that increasing political centralization within a region should be accompanied by and hence can be identified through a corresponding increase in regional-level economic integration.

In all honesty, I should point out that such assumption has only moderate strength. South East Asia and the western Pacific are in fact a *locus classicus* for elaborate exchange networks which transmit large volumes of non-luxury goods over long distances between groups without political, and often without ethnic, affiliations. One would be foolhardy to postulate a casual sequence in South East Asia where stable non-state exchange systems are commonplace and where the earliest states seem to have arisen in deltaic and inland plains areas—that is, in places where environments are relatively uniform. To be sure, some of these plains areas later supported economies which are notable for elaborate refinements of the division of labour (like Tongking, as described by Gourou 1936). But such productive specializations as these must be at least partly independent of microenvironmental enforcement. On the other hand we are under no compulsion to postulate that economic integration is an inevitable cause or an invariable sign of increased political control. All that interests us at the moment is one particular set of events that took place in the late prehistoric and protohistoric periods in central Thailand, and here our central assumption seems quite safe.

The Chansen Sequence

The next few sections of this paper make frequent reference to the arte-factual sequence at Chansen, on the surface a minor Dvāravatī period site about 30 km. north of Lopburi which was excavated in 1968 and 1969 by a joint team from the National Museum of Thailand and the University of Pennsylvania Museum. Chansen is not an ideal site on which to base a discussion of state-building processes; for the most of its history it was small, unimportant, and perhaps remote from the centres where the great events of the age unrolled. But as of now Chansen is all we have. It is the only central Siamese site thus far discovered which bridges the protohistoric gap, providing a good, though not continuous, sequence from the mid-Late Metal Age down through the time of fully-developed states.

Brief descriptions of the site have already been published (Bronson and Dales 1970; 1972). However, since these descriptions were written the excavators have revised portions of the site's chronology, partly because several new thermoluminescence dates have become available (Bronson and Han 1972) and partly because a re-examination of the excavated artefacts has indicated the probable existence of a previously unrecognized cultural component, Phase 'I*b*.' The radiocarbon and thermoluminescence dates for Chansen are summarized in Fig. 1. On the basis of this and other evidence, the phases of the sequence are now considered to have the following dates and relationships:

Phase	*Date*	*Artefactual parallels at*
VI	850/950–1100/1200 A.D.	Many late Dvāravatī and early Lopburi period sites.
V	600/650–850/950 A.D.	Many early Dvāravatī sites.
IV	450/500–600/650 A.D.	'Funan'-related sites—U Thong, Oc-Eo, U Ta Phao/Chainat, etc.
III	200/250–450/500 A.D.	'Funan'-related sites.
II	1/50–200/250 A.D.	No parallels known.
I*b*	200 B.C.?–50 B.C.?	Phimai Blackware levels; lower Huai Duk.
I*a*	800 B.C.?–500 B.C.?	No parallels known.

The Phase IV–V boundary is the late limit for the period that concerns us; as will be shown below, state-like economic and political organization seems to have reached full development in central Thailand by that date. The period of state-building that immediately precedes this climax is well covered by the middle portion of the Chansen sequence, which breaks the first half of the first millennium into no fewer than three distinct but closely-related phases, so closely related that one is confident that this part of the sequence contains no chronological gaps. However, the earliest portion of the sequence is unfortunately less complete. Chansen was not continuously occupied during the Late Metal Age.

The Chansen sequence contains two components which appear to have a Late Metal Age (i.e. prehistoric) date. The first, called Phase I in earlier publications and now called Phase I*a*, is a well-established and in many ways typical assemblage of the period, characterized by the presence of iron and bronze, of woven textiles, of inhumation burials within residential areas, and of pottery which is at once highly distinctive, technically competent, and quite different from the pottery of any other known site. Since the great bulk of this Phase I*a* material derives from deep strata which are easily distinguished and free of intrusion from the super-imposed Phase II strata, the separate identity of Phase I*a* was never in doubt. The only surprise has been the relative antiquity of the two TL determinations (1340±200 B.C. and 650±200 B.C.) made on Phase I*a* pottery. Dr. Dales and I originally suggested a dating of 200–1 B.C. in view of the absence of stratigraphic indications (i.e. depositional unconformities or intervening sterile layers) of a chronological gap between Phases I*a* and II. Now, however, we are inclined to think that Phase I*a* began and ended rather earlier, partly because of the already-noted dissimilarity between I*a* and II (Bronson and Dales 1972: 26) but also because of the TL dates (which, be it noted, are too widely separated in time to inspire great confidence) and because of the discovery of Phase I*b*.

This Phase I*b* is not an impressive entity. It consists of a total of eighteen (out of several tens of thousands of) rimsherds divided into three groups, all of them found in strata that contain a mixture of Phase I*a* and Phase II artefacts. The reasons for thinking that Phase I*b* is a chronologically if not stratigraphically separate component may be summarized as follows. The sherds do not occur in either undisturbed Phase I*a* strata or in those higher Phase II strata which are relatively free from redeposited Phase I*a* material; thus they are later than I*a* and either earlier than or contemporary with early II. They do not resemble the vessels known to belong to either phase—most of them are distinctive and different enough to be clearly intrusive. And they bear strong resemblances to sherds from two other sites, one of which, due to the presence of numerous inhumation burials, is believed to date to the Late Metal Age. Two of the eighteen Phase I*b* sherds may well come from this cemetery site, Phimai in north-eastern Thailand, while the other sixteen have close analogues in the lower levels of Huai Duk, a Dvāravatī pottery-containing site near Phayuhakiri (Nakhon Sawan province), which was tested briefly by the National Museum-University of Pennsylvania team in 1968. Lower Huai Duk is also believed to be prehistoric. While the 4 sq. m. test-pit produced no inhumation burials, an early date for the pre-Dvāravatī material seems to be indicated by (*a*) the complete dissimilarity between these sherds and any known sherds of the protohistoric period (i.e. sherds contemporary with Chansen II–IV) and (*b*) the rumoured presence of inhumations at Ban Nai Chen, a related site several kilometres north-east of Huai Duk.

None of these data actually proves that Phase I*b* is earlier than the beginning of Phase II; it is not after all impossible that an apparently cremating and otherwise progressive community like Chansen II could be closely contemporary with an inhumating and non-Indianized site like Metal Age Phimai. But the odds seem to favour the idea that I*b* and II are temporally separate and that the former dates to the late prehistoric period. The I*b* sherds are too scarce to indicate more than a fleeting minor occupation of Chansen, yet if an early dating is accepted they have some importance. They seem to indicate that connections of some kind existed between several sites of the terminal Late Metal Age. During a period notable for intra-regional isolation, any indications of cultural connection are of interpretive interest.

In summary then, Chansen provides us with only part of the information we need, although it is more pertinent than any contemporary site yet excavated. For the protohistoric period the sequence is excellent. Chansen II, III, and IV provide a continuous record which extends back from the beginnings of Dvāravatī to a time which must be close to the first historically documentable Indian and Chinese contacts. The utility of this part of the sequence is limited only by the small size of the area excavated, the shortage of excavated sites of comparable date, and the fact that Chansen during most of its history remained a sociocultural backwater. However, before Phase II—back in the Late Metal Age—the Chansen sequence is much less useful. Phases I*a* and I*b* still float in time; a number of additional TL dates will be needed before either can be fixed to an absolute time scale. However, Phase I*a* also floats in sociocultural space. It has no known cultural relationship with any other site; further, it cannot be even tentatively placed in chronological relationship with such nearby iron- and inhumation-producing sites as Ban Dai, Lopburi Army Camp, Phong Tuk, and later Ban Kao. Developmental patterns are therefore difficult to discern. The remainder of this discussion will necessarily involve a certain amount of guesswork which may need revision when new sites of the Late Metal Age are excavated.

The Indigenous Substrate: The Late Metal Age

For most of the Late Metal Age, central Thailand presents a picture of subregional isolation and sociocultural stasis. True, the deltaic heart of the region may then have been recently settled, as Gorman (1973) and Higham (1973) suggest, but the sites thus far discovered do not have the air of pioneer settlements; they seem quite prosperous and stable in spite of the sparseness of sites and the continued survival, discussed below, of large tracts of uncleared forest. Conceivably this appearance of late, sparse settlement is to some extent an illusion, the product of difficulties of recognition and of a low survival rate of sites. We have just begun to learn how to discern Metal Age and proto-historic settlements beneath the mask of material left behind by the rather dense populations of the Dvāravatī period. Moreover, it may well be that numerous earlier sites within the Chao Phya Delta have been buried by flood deposits too deeply to be discovered. Even at the edge of the Delta where the seasonal floods are normally not extensive, the Chansen I*a* strata are a half-metre below the present level of the surrounding plain.

Several characteristics of the few Late Metal Age settlements which *have* been discovered seem worth emphasizing. First, the inhabitants of these settlements were by no means technologically backward. Chansen I*a*, Lopburi Army Camp, and late strata at Ban Kao[2] were all three possessed of a varied and—in the case of the pottery—handsome material culture which included bronze ornaments, iron tools, woven textiles (at Chansen and, I believe, at Lopburi), complexly-designed ceramics, and probably wet-rice agriculture as well.[3] The fact that almost all the Chansen I*a* pottery is mineral-tempered and that no source for such minerals is known to exist in the immediate vicinity of the site, may even indicate that some amount of short-distance trading took place. In terms of purely technological resources the Late Metal Age peoples were not noticeably inferior to Thai villagers of the early modern period.

Yet it is not easy to see these Late Metal Age societies as socially or econo-mically advanced. We cannot say how large their settlements became: Chansen I*a* and Lopburi Army Camp were certainly not large; Ban Kao, depending on how much of it dates to the Late Metal Age, may have attained a respectable size; nor how dense their populations may have been. But it already seems clear that local groups tended to be surprisingly isolated from one another. Perhaps the most striking single fact about the period is that no site resembles any other in terms of the artefacts it contains. The ceramic assemblages of the sites already mentioned, and of Ban Dai, Phimai, and Ban Tha Nen as well, could come from sites thousands of kilometres apart for all the relationship they show. The societal configuration is an unusual one: a set of not noticeably primitive 'mini-societies' existing side-by-side in a region without important geographical barriers, but in almost hermetic isolation from one another. Such a configuration would seem to preclude the existence of even the most ele-mentary supra-local political structures.

With regard to population density, it is worth pointing out that as late as Phase II at Chansen large numbers of wild animals were being killed in the northern part of the Chao Phya Delta. Wetherill (1971) reports the presence in Phase II deposits of four species of deer (*Cervus unicolor* Cuvier, *C. eldi siamensis* Lydekker, *Axis porcinus* Sundervall and *Muntiacus muntjak* Zimmerman) as well as rhinoceros, tiger, and elephant. Some of the deer species were killed in very substantial quantities, making up almost half of the total number of individual animals present. These data seem to argue strongly for the continuing existence of large forested areas during all of the Late Metal Age and into the early protohistoric period. If wet-rice agriculture was being practiced, the survival of wild land need not indicate a low absolute density of population; even in the twentieth century a fraction of the surface area of Thailand continues to support most of the nation's people. But one has difficulty imagining that this ancient population, whatever its absolute size, was growing rapidly, or moving its settlements frequently, or experimenting with new life-styles.

All in all, the Late Metal Age in central Thailand is a puzzling period, one of the more strikingly anomalous patterns in a region notable for patterns which fail to fit anyone's models for normal sociocultural development. By comparison with the intensive economic and political activity of other regions after they came into possession of metals and intensive agriculture, late prehistoric central Thailand is distinctly backward. It seems backward, in fact, when compared with the showy and expansive societies of the north-east some 2,000 years before.

The Post-contact Proto-states

Let us pass over for the moment the terminal Metal Age and the initial protohistoric period and go on to the time when solid evidence for the existence of state-like entities in central Thailand first begins to appear. Both historical and archaeological data fix the appearance of the evidence, though perhaps not of the proto-states themselves, at about A.D. 200.

The historical data can be dealt with quickly, since there is not much of it and since the writer is not competent to review the primary sources. For South East Asia as a whole, excluding northern Viet-Nam, the first documentary references that give useful political details date to the mid-third century. They are focused almost entirely on a political unit called by the Chinese chroniclers, 'Fu-nan'. That this Fu-nan was a true state cannot be doubted; it fought wars, dispatched ambassadors, possessed a king and had inhabitants who paid taxes (Pelliot 1903; Coedès 1968: 42). But some points about Fu-nan remain unclear. Where was it? Assuming it was not in central Thailand (the matter is discussed below), to what extent can its prior existence explain the rise of later states in the Chao Phya Delta? Is Fu-nan in fact the first of all South East Asian states, or is it merely the first that came to the attention of the Chinese? In any case the Fu-nan of the mid-third century had already reached a high level of political development; when did this development begin?

As for the location of Fu-nan, most specialists have long accepted the lower Mekong area. The southern coast of South Viet-Nam seems a logical place for a trade port on the India–China sea route, fits in well enough with the itineraries recorded by the chroniclers, and has produced a major archaeo-logical site—Oc-Eo (Malleret 1959–63)—which looks very like a port, if not a capital, of a mercantile kingdom of the early first millennium A.D. However, it has recently been suggested by Boisselier (1968a; 1968b) that this consensus should be questioned and that U Thong in central Thailand might be con-sidered as an alternative location. Boisselier's suggestion has considerable plausibility but is perhaps premature. In spite of its impressive size, U Thong is not nearly as large as Oc-Eo. Moreover, a substantial portion of the remains at U Thong post-date the florescence of the historic Fu-nan; judging by the very precise ceramic parallels between Chansen V and VI and the upper strata at U Thong, almost everything still visible on the surface of the latter site, probably including its earthwork fortifications, dates to the period 600–1100 and is associated with the kingdom of Dvāravatī. The lower strata at U Thong are indeed earlier, being contemporary with Oc-Eo and with Phases III and IV at Chansen, but it is not clear how extensive these strata are. Watson, Loofs, and Parker encountered a considerable depth of Chansen III- and IV-related material in the trenches they dug at Tha Muang in 1968 and 1969 (Watson 1968), while on the other hand Wales (1969: 6–7) states that his earlier soundings elsewhere in U Thong produced little ceramic material that was not Dvāravatī in date. Thus at present no proof exists that protohistoric (pre-seventh century) U Thong was large enough to be a convincing capital for a major empire. It is also significant that the pottery of the deeper strata at U Thong is rather different from that of third- and fourth-phase Chansen, sharing only vague generic resemblances as though the two sites—which are only about 100 km. apart—maintained quite separate artefactual traditions during the several hundred years of historically-documented Funanese supremacy. In view of the thorough-going artefactual uniformity imposed over the whole of central Thailand by the relatively minor kingdom of Dvāravatī, it might seem strange for the capital of the Fu-nan 'Empire' to exert so little influence over a site in its near neighbourhood. My own inclina-tion is to reserve final judgment in the matter of Fu-nan's location but to accept provisionally that it was located elsewhere than in central Thailand.

The question that follows from this is, what kind of influence did a remotely-located Fu-nan have on political development in central Thailand? The his-torical record is not very helpful here. The mid-third century Funanese king Fan Man is said to have conquered numerous 'kingdoms' in the West, which might be interpreted to mean that organized states already existed in Thailand

and Malaysia prior to the expansion of Fu-nan. However, the sources are not forthcoming with details about most of these. One of the conquered kingdoms, Tien-sun or Tun-sun, was definitely a state in later times but whether it had already reached this status during the third century depends on the original date of descriptions quoted in later sources. Coedès (1968: 51) and perhaps Wheatley (1961: 15) consider that these descriptions apply to a late stage in Tun-sun's career, somewhere between the fourth and sixth centuries. On the other hand, Wolters (1967: 45–8) and Wheatley in a more recent work (1964: 43) are of the opinion that a third-century date is justified. If they are correct then it becomes conceivable that the rise of Fu-nan and of Tun-sun are roughly synchronized and that neither polity is responsible for the appearance of state-like institutions in the other.

In any case, these data may not have relevance to the situation in central Thailand. Only one of the Funanese conquests, Chin-lin, is placed by most authorities (Wheatley 1961: 15) in the Chao Phya Delta, and this need not be considered a true state on the basis of what the Chinese chroniclers say; to them it is no more than a place name. The historical evidence is relevant to the chronology of the emergence of the central Siamese state in only two respects. It provides a late limit (about A.D. 250) for the appearance of at least one developed state somewhere in South East Asia. And it suggests that the central Siamese may have had intimate if not friendly contact with that state at about the time it appears in the Chinese records, raising the possibility that this contact was an important stimulus to the commencement of state-building processes in central Thailand. But that is as far as the historical evidence can take us. To go further we must turn to data derived from archaeology.

The archaeological evidence for Thailand-Funan contacts, assuming that Oc-Eo is somehow connected with Fu-nan, is actually quite abundant. Objects very similar to objects at Oc-Eo have been found at U Thong, Chansen, Nakhon Pathom, and (reportedly) U Ta Phao-Chainat. They include a distinctive type of torque-like ring in tin or gold called by Malleret *anneaux alourdis* (1962: 81–4); earthenware stamps which may have been used for printing designs on fabrics (Malleret's *tampons*, 1960: pl. 48, 49); small bronze bells decorated with filigree spirals (Malleret 1960: 221–3); gold jewellery of various kinds, stone bivalve moulds for making this jewellery; and a type of coin or medal decorated with a *trisula*-like design and known to archaeologists as 'Fu-nan' coins despite their probable Burmese origin (cf. Bronson 1971). U Thong has produced the full range of these artefacts, many of which are illustrated by Chira and Woodward (1966). Examples of all except the 'coins' were found in stratified Phase III–IV contexts at Chansen (cf. Bronson and Dales 1972, illustrations).

All this seems to indicate some kind of connection; the question is, what kind? Can we conclude that Chansen and U Thong were actual colonies settled by migrants from Oc-Eo? Clearly not, since most of the artefactual material from late protohistoric central Thailand is quite different from the artefacts at Oc-Eo. The ceramics of the two regions do share vague similarities, but almost all points of mutual resemblance (including the use of zigzag comb-incised patterns) can be shown to appear at Chansen during Phase II— that is, before the expansion and perhaps before the founding of 'Fu-nan'.[4] Alternatively, can we conclude that the *anneaux alourdis* and so forth are the possessions of a small Funanese upper class which was left behind to administrate the conquered territories? Again, surely not: only the gold objects are an elite sort of artefact, and one could more plausibly suppose that the diffusers of these, since they brought manufacturing apparatus with them (jewellery moulds as well as fabric stamps) were artisans rather than administrators. Perhaps the demand for such craft products was itself a diffused element, and this might be interpreted as showing that a status-conscious and to some extent foreign-oriented elite class was coming into being. But with this we reach the limits of what can be inferred from the artefacts common to Oc-Eo and central Thailand. These artefacts do not permit us to postulate a migration, or a continuing imperial control, or even a substantial raid by the Funanese into central Thailand. While it is possible that early political consolidation in the Chao Phya Delta may have been stimulated by emulation of Fu-nan or by the needs of regional defense against it, we may not conclude that this consolidation was actually imposed by it.

Let us set aside the problem of Funanese influence, then, and turn to a more general question. What evidence do we have that states or state-like politics of any kind existed in central Thailand prior to the rise of Dvāravatī? One possible approach to the problem concerns the appearance of artefacts; some of them imported, which might belong to an elite class. The abundant gold jewellery from U Thong (much of it presently in the collection of Montri Harnvichai) looks very much like a group of status-conferring artefacts of this kind, as do several groups of finds from Chansen III and IV: two greenish-brown glazed lids made of grey stoneware, almost certainly Chinese in provenence; one fine greyware sprinkler-neck with a shiny burnish, whose closest analogues are found in India and at Beikthano in Burma (Aung Thaw 1968: fig. 27); and a number of strikingly handsome bowls in a lustrous metallic grey fabric which are either actual imports or excellent imitations of imports from Ceylon, where seemingly identical vessels are found near Hambantota (Roland Silva, personal information—see Bronson and Dales 1972, fig. 9, second from top). In the absence of residences and graves it is not of course possible to show definitely that these objects were distributed unequally among the residents of ancient U Thong and Chansen. But such an interpretation seems highly probable, and it seems quite likely that the objects were distributed along the lines of unequal wealth and status. In this and in the hierarchically-organized society thus indicated, Chansen and U Thong both begin to look vaguely like states.

Such an impression is reinforced when we consider the number of objects in Chansen III and IV which seem to be actual imports from overseas. About one-seventh of one per cent of the site's surface was excavated; the objects were found widely distributed through numerous separate trenches whose locations were chosen randomly with respect to the protohistoric strata. Yet those strata produced two Chinese artefacts, one possibly Burmese artefact, several objects which might be from Oc-Eo, and no fewer than eight metallic blackware bowls, at least two of which are close enough in paste to the Hanbantota examples to have actually come from Ceylon. The indicated volume of extra-regional trade is very large for a site as undistinguished and remote as Chansen. One finds it difficult to believe that so much trade could occur in the absence of a moderately high level of economic and political organization within central Thailand. By Phase IV (fifth to sixth centuries), to which the majority of the imported artefacts belong, the region must have been under at least loose control by a small number of polities that much resembled states.

On the other hand the distribution of locally-produced ceramics indicates that economic integration at the regional level was still far from complete. Whilst most of the ceramics, and also non-ceramic artefacts, from Oc-Eo-related sites within the region share certain generic resemblances, these resemblances are rarely strong enough to demonstrate a common place of manufacture. As I said earlier, Chansen and U Thong can hardly have belonged to the same ceramic-trading networks; in fact it seems unlikely that the potters and consumers at the former site were even in frequent contact with their counterparts at the latter site. Chansen III and IV resemble each other much more closely than either resembles the assemblage from the lower strata at U Thong, showing perhaps that the prehistoric pattern of sub-regional idiosyncrasy was still alive. However, vague indications do exist that economic integration was beginning on a more spatially-restricted scale. Scattered examples of what appears to be the mineral-tempered 'Bh' ware of Chansen III have been found at Ban Moh about 15 km. south of Lopburi and at U Ta Phao near Chainat: that is, over an area some 60 km. in length. Chansen IV sherds have not yet been found elsewhere, but it is interesting to note that the fourth phase saw the introduction of at least four new groups of vessels, each with a different paste and temper but covering the same range of forms and presumed functions, which seem to have been traded into the site from the outside. During Phase III all vessels with this form-range had apparently been supplied by the same outside manufacturing centre, the source of the 'Bh' wares mentioned above. The proliferation of suppliers during Phase IV seems to indicate both the breaking of a monopoly and an increase in economic activity within the sub-region.

In summary, we cannot yet speak of extensive economic or political development on a regional scale. There is no evidence during the third through sixth centuries for the kind of massive artefactual uniformity and intensive development of intra-regional trade that characterizes the seventh through eleventh centuries, when essentially identical pottery was diffused from Ku Bua in the south almost to the Mekong river in the north-east. But, on the other hand, some amount of sub-regional integration does seem to exist and perhaps this, together with evidence for a developing elite, an increase in local economic activity, and a large volume of long-distance trade, adds up to a group of smallish states or proto-states in a formative stage of political development.

These state-like entities were clearly not the equals of Dvāravatī, Chen-la, or even of the historical Fu-nan. They appear to have lacked most of the ideological hardware, the temples, statues, and royal inscriptions, that are the hallmarks of the classical South East Asian state of traditional scholarship. But if we compare these emerging polities with more recent quasi-states in less Indianized regions—for instance with the Minangkabau kingdom of Sumatra (Tanner 1972: 26–7) and the Makassarese states of south Celebes (Chabot 1960)—we can conceive that this enthusiasm for monuments is not a truly essential attribute of effective South East Asian statehood. Minangkabau may be said to resemble early Fu-nan in its almost complete lack of archaeologically-recoverable architecture and art, as well as in its notable success. The more developed proto-states of central Thailand need not have been too different from either Fu-nan or Minangkabau. Like both, they were short on works of art and, as events of the late sixth and seventh centuries were to prove, high in potential for expansion. It is a defensible hypothesis that a built-in expansive tendency is the most important of all qualities pertaining to the definition of the state.

The Politics and Economics of the Transition

It will be seen that the two preceding sections present a striking contrast. During most of the first millennium B.C. the region was internally compartmentalized, technologically advanced but static in terms of socioeconomic development, and seemingly cut off from other regions. By the third century A.D., however, all this has changed. The internal and external partitions have been breached. Trade is in full flow. And a set of social and economic processes have been set into motion which will result, by the end of the sixth century if not before, in the establishment of a full-fledged state in central Thailand. The key to the problem of state origins would seem to lie in the transition between these two periods, in the last few centuries of the Metal Age and the first two centuries of the protohistoric period.

Only a few locations have yielded relevant evidence: for the terminal Metal Age, the sites of Phimai, Huai Duk, Chansen, and possibly Ban Dai; for the earliest protohistoric period, only Phase II at Chansen. All of the terminal Metal Age sites must provisionally be placed in the early stages of the transition, for none are known to have had contacts with the historic societies of other regions. Three of them, however, yield evidence of intra-regional contacts which may be interpreted as actual trade.

The contacts between Huai Duk and Chansen I*b* consist of a number of bowls: some basally carinated and medium-sized, some straight-sided and small, with dense mineral-tempered pastes and streakily-burnished surfaces. They are distinctively unlike other vessels in either the Phase I or Phase II assemblages and so seem clearly intrusive. The examples from the lower strata at Huai Duk are similar enough to these to suggest that the vessels have a common origin, perhaps at Huai Duk or elsewhere.

The Phimai-Chansen I*b* link comprises only two artefacts: two fragments of black chaff-tempered bowls with pattern-burnished decoration, which seem almost certainly to have been exported from north-east Thailand to Chansen. Like the streakily-burnished vessels, these blackware bowls are anomalous in terms of ordinary Chansen ceramic design; unlike the streakily-burnished examples, the blackware sherds are so similar to a numerically dominant ceramic at another site as to make actual importation from somewhere near that site seem highly probable. By themselves, these two sherds are very slight evidence for a significant level of economic activity. But it is also relevant that Phimai is, by ordinary Metal Age standards, a very impressive-looking site (cf. Solheim, *supra*, p. 66f). The blackware deposits measure at least a half-kilometre in length and have proved to be quite artefact-rich at all points where excavations have been made: by Solheim in 1964, Parker in 1966, Peacock in 1968, and a Silpakorn University team in the same year. Such a volume of debris seems to indicate that prehistoric Phimai was more than a simple village in its heyday, certainly a more important and central place than, for instance, Chansen. Under the Khmers in later times, Phimai owed its prominence partly to its strategic economic and military location, being situated astride the main trade route between the Korat Plateau and the Chao Phya Delta. It is not impossible that its location and evident prosperity indicate a similar function during the Late Metal Age.

These few data from Chansen I*b*, Huai Duk, and Phimai exhaust the extant evidence for societal or economic development during the terminal prehistoric period. The next assemblage to be considered, Chansen II, appears to belong to a later stage in the developmental process despite its closeness to its predecessors in time.[5] It differs from earlier assemblages in several crucial respects, whilst it has a significant degree of continuity with later phases. It contains no burials and would seem to have been at least in indirect contact with places outside South East Asia.

The evidence for continuity comes largely from Phase II ceramics, which are quite clearly related to later ceramics at Chansen and elsewhere. One major group of vessels, the so-called 'Rh' Fabric Group (Bronson and Dales 1972, fig. 6, second from top) are so close to vessels of Phases III and IV (the 'Bh' Fabric Group: ibid. fig. 8, top) that one cannot doubt they were made by craftsmen working in the same continuing tradition, using the same source of tempering materials, and probably dwelling in the same small area. Moreover, the place of manufacture was probably not Chansen, since the mineral grit used as temper is not known to be available within a 10-km. radius of the site. The continuity of Rh-Bh vessels thus demonstrates not only a persistence of design but a persistence of a local pattern of trade or exchange. A number of more precise details about this apparent exchange pattern can be induced. In Phases II, III, and IV the Rh-Bh potters seem to have concentrated on producing only a few kinds of vessels, chiefly carinated (cooking?) pots and large (storage?) jars; their products were made to rather precise specifications of size and form, rendering the vessels easy to type and suggesting a certain professionalism on the part of their manufacturers. The other common vessels of Phases II and III form a contrast with the Rh-Bh vessels in these respects. The utilitarian medium and large bowls (perhaps used for preparing and serving food) and medium high-necked jars (perhaps for carrying water) are highly variable in shape and dimension, rather casually finished and tempered with vegetable material, all of which suggests they were made locally and perhaps by part-time potters. Only the mineral-tempered wares are known from sites outside the immediate hinterland of Chansen. The indicated interpretation is that the contrast between the two groups of vessels reflects a contrasting economic rôle of two sets of potters who between them supplied the Chansen 'market' with utilitarian pottery: (1) a group of full-time professionals located at some distance from Chansen who maintained their share of the market by virtue of the superior quality and durability of their products, and (2) a group of part-time potters, probably residents of Chansen itself, who concentrated on the production of vessels which, perhaps because their function involved frequent breakage and did not demand the fire-proof qualities conferred by mineral tempering, did not have to be so carefully finished and made. This pattern is not completely established during Phase II, when similar vessel shapes appear in both vegetable- and mineral-tempered fabrics. However, it is dominant during Phase III, and only begins to break down with the already-mentioned introduction of carinated pots in other mineral-tempered fabrics during Phase IV.

I do not insist on the correctness of the details of this particular explanation.

But it would seem that almost any explanation would involve hypothesizing a moderately complex economic system and that some configuration within this system could be shown to persist from Phase II down to the end of the proto-historic period, when all earlier economic patterns were swept aside by the consolidation of the region-wide Dvāravatī economy. The case for continuity between Phase II and the pre-Dvāravatī proto-states thus appears quite strong. Since both styles and economic patterns seem to continue through phase boundaries, it seems justified to postulate a degree of persistence of social organization as well. The polity of which Chansen II formed a part may well have possessed some characteristics of a formative state, albeit on an as yet very restricted spatial scale.

Another contrast between Chansen II and the Late Metal Age assemblages is the probable absence from the former of the custom of burying rather than burning the dead. A sufficient area of Phase II strata were excavated to eliminate the possibility that the lack of burials is an error of sampling, assuming that hypothetical Phase II burials would be as densely-spaced as they are in almost all known Metal Age cemetery sites in Thailand. If the Phase II peoples buried their dead, they did so outside the residential area, itself a rather atypical practice by Metal Age standards. But the probabilities favour the idea that the Phase II peoples were cremators; no central Siamese site, after all, has yet produced burials in stratigraphic association with identifiably protohistoric (i.e. Indian- or Chinese-associated) artefacts. The question then arises, does the shift to cremation indicate that Indian cultural values had penetrated as far as Chansen at such an early date? This seems to be the explanation for the complete absence of inhumation graves at later sites of the Classical period; but I am inclined to reserve an answer to the question as far as Phase II at Chansen is concerned. Whilst many of the non-Indianized peoples of South East Asia are notable inhumators, some are cremators and may have preserved this custom from the remote past; it is not impossible that the prehistoric diffusion of cremation practices has an indigenous origin. But on the other hand, Chansen during its second phase was probably in at least indirect contact with India, and, moreover, with Buddhism. It is therefore also possible that a preference for cremation does derive from India, perhaps diffused to central Thailand initially as an isolated value or perhaps embedded in the context of an introduced religion or heterodox cult.

The third major distinction between the Late Metal Age and the proto-historic period is the presence, at sites of the latter period, of evidence for extra-regional commercial contacts. Such evidence as exists has already been described in an earlier paper (Bronson and Dales 1972: 28–30). It consists of (1) a subjective impression that the ceramic vessels of Chansen II are rather Indian in overall appearance, and (2) a single ivory comb whose appearance is very Indian indeed, being engraved with a pair of horses, a goose with an elaborately plumed tail, and a row of Buddhist symbols (ibid: fig. 7).

The Indian appearance of the pottery I am now inclined to play down, not because the vessels have begun to look un-Indian to me but because it has become increasingly apparent that we still have only the vaguest conception of the great range of pottery forms and decorations present in central Thailand during the Late Metal Age. It may be that local lineal ancestors of the Chansen II pottery will be uncovered within the next few years. However, there is also nothing improbable about the idea that ceramic forms, and even the ceramics themselves, might have been transmitted from India to South East Asia. A later example of such a transmission is the above-mentioned group of metallic-looking fineware bowls found at Chansen and at Hambantota in Ceylon. The only early example so far discovered is the well-known fineware sherd found at Bukit Tengku Lembu in Malaysia. Although this latter bowl has evoked a wide variety of speculations about its origin (see, e.g. Sieveking 1962; Williams-Hunt 1952; Peacock 1964), little doubt exists that it actually comes from south India or Ceylon and that it dates to the first or second century A.D. Apparently identical bowls form one of the less publicized types associated with Wheeler's Rouletted Ware complex; examples are known from Arikamedu (type 18c of Wheeler 1946), from the lower levels of Gedige at Anuradhapura (type 17ei of Deraniyagala 1973), and from strata of a similar date at Kantarodai in northern Ceylon.[6]

The importation of a single example of a conspicuously handsome luxury item does not, of course, show that a vigorous international trade in Indian ceramics existed during the first and second centuries A.D. But it does show that pottery was among the items carried from India to South East Asia at that date, and that the users of this pottery need not have been completely Indianized. Tengku Lembu is in most other respects a characteristically prohistoric site.

As for the ivory comb, its Indian derivation is not open to question. In all probability it was actually made in India and thus, together with the Tengku Lembu sherd and the rather doubtfully dated (Picard 1955) 'Roman' lamp from Phong Tuk, bids fair to be one of the earliest imports from the West to have yet been discovered in South East Asia. The problem is that the comb is difficult to date at the Indian end. No early combs with incised decoration are known from the Indian sub-continent, and the motifs produce mixed reactions from the art historians who have examined them, some suggesting Amaravati (a style which itself is poorly dated) and others suggesting dates as late as Late Gupta.

The dating at the South East Asian end is rather more precise. The comb was found in Stratum I of Trench D, a secure Phase II context. Two C14 determinations exist for this stratum. One, coming from a sample collected less than a metre from the find-spot of the comb, was calculated at A.D. 60±41; the other, from a sample collected from the same stratum but at a point 18 m. distant, yielded a date of A.D. 300±120. A third sample from a Phase II stratum in another trench was dated to A.D. 120±47. Thus, while the weight of probability seems to support a first- or second-century date for the comb, a third-century date remains possible and an early-fourth-century date conceivable. But at the early fourth century we encounter the ceiling set by the six very convincing radiocarbon dates for Phase III, all of which cluster between 355±52 and 459±47. If the comb is to be later than A.D. 300–350, we must assume it was intruded from a higher stratum into a Phase II context. Since no sign of such an intrusion was observed at the find-spot (which was within a baulk, making careful observation easy), I am inclined to resist the suggestion of any Indian origin later than early Gupta. If a late Gupta analogue should be produced, my own reaction would be to challenge the attribution of the analogue; the comb is in fact more securely dated than the great majority of early Indian art objects.

With the comb we come to the end of the existing data on early economic development in central Thailand. For the period 200 B.C.–A.D. 200, the data are very slight indeed; they are none too good even for the period A.D. 200–600. But perhaps several tentative conclusions can be reached. First, economic consolidation at a low level begins quite early; but not, as far as is now known, before the date represented by Chansen I*b* and the blackware horizon at Phimai. (Similar processes may have been under way in the north-east during the third and second millennia, but these seem not to be connected with later developments in the Chao Phya Delta.) Second, extra-regional economic and perhaps cultural contact first becomes evident in non-Vietnamese South East Asia during the first century B.C., and at Chansen during the first or second centuries A.D. Third, both intra-regional consolidation and extra-regional contact are relatively far advanced by A.D. 400, although it is not until about A.D. 600 that we can speak of a fully-integrated regional economy. Fourth, political consolidation can be assumed to have proceeded roughly in concert with economic advances. Complex proto-states, controlling areas of as yet modest size, are in existence in central Thailand by A.D. 400. Central Thailand may have lagged somewhat behind the Mekong Delta in this respect. Fifth, a significant part of this political and economic development took place during a time when specifically political influence from India appears to have been negligible. Once these conclusions are in hand, it becomes possible to consider the applicability of several alternative explanations for the origin of the South East Asian state.

Explanations of State Origins

We may probably reject the idea that the earliest South East Asian states were wholly or essentially imposed from the outside. While states founded *ab novo* by outside conquerors are not unknown to historians—some examples may exist in pre-colonial Africa (see, e.g. Mair 1964: 125–37)—they are not at all common. Davidson's paper in this colloquy shows that even the early Sinified states in northern Viet-Nam seem to have had roots in pre-existing advanced societies in the same area, and this may be taken as an instance of a general rule that successful conquest-states tend to be set up in precisely those places which have already undergone some degree of political unification. We cannot dismiss so easily the possibility that outsiders might have taken a hand in local politics during the protohistoric period. Foreign adventurers are a prominent feature of the South East Asian scene in later times. But there is no evidence that these putative early adventurers managed to impose any substantial part of the political patterns characteristic of their homelands. As already pointed out, political Indianization is not known to begin until the fourth or fifth century and identifiably Chinese sociopolitical institutions cannot be found outside northern and central Viet-Nam. It would seem that the initial contacts with the developed world involved transactions which were more commercial, and perhaps religious, than political.

The idea that Indian influence may have come in through the initiative of local rulers was originally suggested by van Leur (1954), and finds support both in the chronology of events during the first millennium A.D., when Indianization lagged well behind state development, and in general probabilities, since from a cross-cultural standpoint political institutions are highly diffusible entities. We can readily imagine that a chief or minor king of the year 400 might have felt himself in need of advanced management techniques, and that he might therefore have called in consultants from abroad. However, this should not lead us to believe that the initial movement toward political consolidation, was itself imported. And it is the factors behind this initial consolidation that we seek to explain.

Among other possible explanations of state origins are (a) the need to control conflict and to manage resources in a situation of rising population density, and (b) growth in domestic commerce stimulated by micro-environmental variability. Neither of these explanations seems applicable to ancient central Thailand. We find no evidence that ancient populations in state-containing areas were either large or dense in the early protohistoric period. In central Thailand, sites of that period may be actually scarce, judging by the difficulty one has in finding them and by the apparent survival down through the third century A.D. (Phase II at Chansen) of large tracts of forest. There are certainly far fewer sites than could be supported with relative ease through wet-rice farming, a subsistence régime which is thought to have come into use in South East Asia long before the time of initial state formation.[3]

As for the growth of internal trade, the microenvironments of this region

are not noticeably varied. Whilst there is some evidence of artefactual connections between central Siamese sites in the last two centuries B.C. the indicated
level of commercial activity is hardly great enough to plausibly constitute the
major stimulus for such a revolutionary social change. State formation and
economic integration can be expected to be roughly synchronized, enabling us
to use the latter as evidence of the former, but this says nothing about
causality. In the case of ancient central Thailand, we have no reason to think
that the growth of internal trade precedes or is a major cause of the growth of
states.

However, there is another possible explanation which, despite its venerable
antiquity among South East Asian specialists, still seems to stand up to the
test of evidence: that is, the growth of long-distance trade. Recent discoveries
have not upset the long-recognized synchrony between state formation and
the establishment of commercial links between South East Asia and the
developed regions to the north-east and West. Oc-Eo remains the first-known
commercial entrepôt as well as a probable part of the first historically-
documented state. The consolidation of proto-states in central Thailand during the third–sixth centuries is accompanied by a steady increase in the
quantity of goods brought in from abroad. The earliest extra-regional imports
—the Han ceramics in Java and Sumatra, the Tengku Lembu bowl and
perhaps the ivory comb from Chansen—appear in South East Asia at a date
just prior to the demonstrable inception of state-like political organization.
This chronology supports the idea that long-distance trade could be one of the
main precipitating causes of local state formation.

A highly developed inter-regional trade network seems empirically to be
often associated with the known states of the ancient world. It also has marked
theoretical advantages as a possible stimulus to state formation when that
subject is considered from the viewpoint of the decision-makers in pre-state
societies. One advantage is that imported objects, unlike local produce, are
inherently rare and correspondingly capable of conferring prestige even when
piled up in indefinitely large quantities. Imported objects are also intrinsically
monopolizable. Their purveyors—outside traders—are fewer, more easily
controlled, and more likely to deal with a small number of local persons than
are the suppliers of domestic produce. Moreover, these outside traders are
vulnerable and work with high profit margins, making them much more easily
taxable. A trader whose normal profit is a thousand units of goods on a hundred
units of investment will be relatively willing to relinquish a hundred-unit
custom duty, while that same one hundred units, collected from a hundred
farmers whose yearly profit or productive surplus is only two units, might
well provoke an insurrection. The presence of long-distance traders therefore gives a strong incentive to a chief to extend the power and size of his
chiefdom. It opens the way for accumulating large reserves of development

capital which can be used for public works or for maintaining a police and military establishment. It also makes territorial aggrandizement a profitable activity. Whereas formerly an expansion of the size of a chiefdom was unlikely to produce a corresponding expansion of income, now that long-distance trade exists in the vicinity, expansion to cover a complete coastline or the whole of a commodity-producing area can cause the chiefdom's income to increase many-fold. The group that controls half a coastline may obtain no entrepôt profit from passing traders, while the controllers of a complete coastline will get it all. And the chief who possesses only a portion of the area producing a commodity desired by long-distance traders is almost forced to seek a monopoly position, or at least an enforceable cartel agreement with his neighbours, if he is to avoid being cut out of the trade entirely.

Thus it seems reasonable to suppose that efforts to control inter-regional commerce could be one, and in some instances *the* primary, stimulus to state formation. It would be rash to insist that this model is universally applicable. Although a close correspondence seems generally to exist between advanced political organization and extensive inter-regional activity, we cannot always demonstrate that the activity precedes the organization. In some well-documented cases, as in West Africa during the eighteenth and nineteenth centuries, the priority and causal status of foreign trade seems well-established (e.g. in the Niger Delta—see Dike 1951). In other cases, as in the Chalcolithic and Bronze Age Middle East, we can only affirm that foreign trade was early and important, without assigning precedence to it or to the emerging states. But in South East Asia the issue seems clear cut. Not only does long-distance commerce have chronological priority but it can be assumed to have appeared for reasons largely independent of the existence of developed states in the region: the China–India sea route might well have existed even though the intervening lands were an uninhabited wilderness. Moreover, South East Asia remained conspicuously stateless for many centuries before this sea route was established, in spite of the fact that most of what are ordinarily thought to be the necessary conditions for statehood had long been present. Perhaps foreign trade is not itself an entirely sufficient condition. But the case for considering it as such in this particular case is, on present evidence, very strong.

NOTES

1. The only dates pertaining to prehistoric (first millennium B.C. or earlier) South East Asian iron-working which have been recovered thus far are a group of TL determinations published in Bronson and Han 1972. Two of these determinations came out earlier than 1000 B.C., which many will feel is less plausible than, say 500 B.C. However, several data argue for a considerable time depth for iron metallurgy in South East Asia. The first is the already-mentioned prevalence and variety of sites

where iron was used and inhumation practiced. The second is the early date of bronze in the region; it is in just such a context of sophisticated experimentation with non-ferrous metallurgical techniques that we would expect the knowledge of, though not necessarily the economic use of, iron to appear. A date of 1000 B.C. may seem somewhat more plausible if we consider that Soviet archaeologists are beginning to get early first millennium B.C. dates for sites (Pol'tso and Uril' Lake—Chard 1973: 11) in the Maritime province of Siberia. But on the other hand, we must also take into consideration the fact that the Han government was prohibiting the export of iron from China to hostile Nan Yueh as late as the early second century B.C. (Yu 1967: 119). Either the Han strategists were misinformed about the productive capabilities of the southern barbarians or iron was still scarce in South East Asia at that late date.

2. In this I am following Parker (1968) who maintains, only partly because of the presence of iron and bronze in some graves there, that much of the material at Ban Kao must date to the mid-first millennium B.C.

3. Wet rice, grown in flooded but not necessarily irrigated fields, may well be older than swidden-grown dry rice. Bartlett (1961) has argued this on historical and ecological grounds. Gorman (1973) points out that the only possible wild ancestors of *Oryza sativa* are all palustrine, marsh-adapted plants. The deep clay soils of many parts of South East Asia, including the Chao Phya Delta, are not suitable for many other crops; we may probably assume that the early inhabitants of such areas had wet rice (and perhaps taro and sago as well) at the time of initial settlement.

4. A number of South East Asianists (e.g. Levy 1954: pls. XXXVII, XL; Malleret 1960: 117–19, pls. LXXIII–LXXXIII; Stargardt 1973: 18–19) have taken notice of these comb-decorated potsherds and have suggested that they might be useful as indicators of temporal horizons or cultural connections. But comb-produced vessel decorations, composed of alternating horizontal bands of sinusoidal and straight lines, are very widespread in time and space. They occur on glazed ceramics of Han China and Angkorean Cambodia, on earthenware vessels throughout coastal and insular South East Asia, Melanesia, and—I believe—Africa, and on both Achaemenian and modern jars in Iran. Often they seem to have been produced by a suitable shell, perhaps a *Spondylus*. At Chansen, they are concentrated in strata of Phases II and III, but one or two appear in Phase I and others persist through Phase V or VI.

5. The one available radiocarbon date for the blackware strata at Phimai indicates that these strata may be as late as the first or second century A.D. (see Solheim's paper in this Colloquy). The Phimai iron-and-inhumation complex thus seems to overlap in time with the apparently cremating culture of Chansen II. The overlap may or may not be real. While it is entirely conceivable that inhumation could have survived in some parts of Thailand until well into the protohistoric period, I am inclined to favour a late limit of about A.D. 100 for it at Phimai. The site is located at a major inland communications nexus and should not have lagged too far behind a site like Chansen which is quite far from the coast, not far from Phimai, and not strategically located with respect to major routes.

6. Kantarodai, a presumed ancient seaport north of Jaffna in Sri Lanka, was partly excavated and reconstructed by the National Archaeological Survey in the late 1960s. In 1970 an archaeological team from the University of Pennsylvania Museum made two deep soundings there, recovering a sequence which ran from (1) an 'Iron Age' black-on-red ware phase, through (2) a phase characterized by the presence of Rouletted Ware and a single Roman intaglio seal, to (3) a phase of complexly-decorated pottery seemingly connected with mid-first millennium stupas found near by the Archaeological Survey. No radiocarbon dates are yet available, but the middle phase has many close connections with Arikamedu (Wheeler 1946) and so probably dates to the period 100 B.C.–A.D. 200. The members of the University of Pennsylvania team, Vimala Begley, Bennet Bronson, and Mohamed Mauroof, hope to have a preliminary report in press soon.

ADDITIONAL REFERENCES

Adams, R. M. 1966. *The Evolution of Urban Society*. Aldine, Chicago.

Fried, M. H. 1967. *The Evolution of Political Society*: An essay in political anthropology. Random House, New York.

Kradar, L. 1968. *Formation of the State*. Prentice-Hall, New Jersey.

Mair, L. 1964. *Primitive Government*. Penguin Books, Harmondsworth, Middlesex.

Mead, M. 1930. 'Melanesian middleman' in *Natural History 30*: 15–130.

— 1937. 'The Manus of the Admiralty Islands' in Mead ed., *Cooperation and Competition among Primitive Peoples*. McGraw-Hill, New York.

Sanders, W. T. 1956. 'The Central Mexican Symbiotic Region' in *Prehistoric Settlement Patterns in the New World*, ed. G. Willey. Viking Fund Publications in Anthropology 23. New York.

— and Price, B. J. 1968. *Mesoamerica: The Evolution of a Civilization*. Random House New York.

The Excavation at Sab Champa

VEERAPAN MALEIPAN

THE ancient city of Sab Champa is situated some 15 km. east of Chaibadal District, Lopburi province. Several years ago this area was part of a national forest, but now most of the area has been turned into farms. The area was visited only by hunters, prospectors, and slash-and-burn farmers, until a team from the Plant Pest and Disease Control Section of the Ministry of Agriculture visited it. The ancient city of Sab Champa was discovered by an agricultural officer, Mr. Rengchai Sootjarit, who went there to exterminate Patanga (*Pantanga succincta* Linn.), the destructive locust.

Our first expedition was in February 1970, when a team which included a curator of Lopburi Museum, an education officer of the sixth area and students from Silpakorn University, surveyed there for one week. We received a lot of help from the villagers, who collected some artefacts from the ancient city of Sab Champa and donated some of them to the Faculty's collection. These chance finds were: some ground stone adzes; a grinding stone; fragments of a limestone Buddha image; a red sandstone engraved with a design, possibly for printing on cloth; some iron tools and weapons; terra cotta figurines made from double moulds like those from the Chansen excavation and dated A.D. 600–800; part of a crouching deer made of red sandstone; and a fragment of a greenish sandstone Wheel of the Law. The most interesting find is a Buddha image, made of greenish sandstone standing on Banaspati, flanked on each side with a Bodhisattva. Stylistically speaking, the works of art belong to the early Dvāravatī school, dating about sixth–seventh century A.D. The general characteristic of the potsherds also pointed to the same period and can be compared to pottery from U Thong, the best-known Dvāravatī city in central Thailand. Part of an octagonal stone inscription had been acquired earlier by Air Vice-Marshal Prasit Sukarabaedya, Director of Air Force Finance. It is made of greenish sandstone and was inscribed in Pali in south-Indian style characters and concerns the Buddhist Law of Dharma.

The ancient city is a little to the north of the modern village. It was shaped like a heart, and its measurements (taken from an air-photograph) are 834 m. from north to south and 704 m. from east to west. The enclosing wall is made of compact earth and averages 10 m. high, with main entrances at the cardinal points of the compass. The wall is surrounded by a broad fortification moat which was cut into the limestone bed. We wonder how it was possible to dig this moat so broad and deep with the primitive tools available at the time.

Three artificial mounds were recognized in the ancient city. One might be the base of stupa of Dvāravatī style, judging from the building masonry which is similar to other stupas at U Thong, etc. The bricks are very large and thick with a very high percentage of rice-husks. The temperature of firing was very low and most of them are semi-baked bricks. The other two mounds seem to be round barrows and are covered with limestone rubble. At the south of the city, there is an earthwork very like a dyke. The suggestion that this might be a causeway was rejected after we had carefully examined the air-photograph and found that there is no more trace of this earthwork beyond 400 m. away from the city.

The source of the town's water supply is not yet clear as there is no large well or tank in that area. Nowadays, the villagers get water from an underground spring near the south-east of the city, and in the name of the city 'Sab' means a spring ('Champa' is a kind of wood). It was noticed that the land to the east of the city is much higher than that to the west. The water in the rainy season would thus flow past the city, through the moat, until some part of the city was washed away. The flowing water also cut through the city itself, like a canal.

North of the city, just across the moat, there is an earthwork similar to a round barrow, with a diameter of about 56 m. It is a very interesting site for prehistoric studies, as such round barrows are common in Thailand, and we expect to do more research on it in order to find out its relationship with the ancient people of Sab Champa.

There is another interesting burial site some 3 km. to the south of the ancient city. It is a small mound, where some skeletons, associated with potsherds and ground stone adzes, were accidentally unearthed by local people working on a charcoal-burning pit. Some pots are still in complete condition, but unfortunately some were broken when they were found. In any case, the pots have been restored to their original shapes in our laboratory and show strange designs that have not previously been found in this part of the world. The skeletons were all buried in an extended position, and the orientation was to the east. In this they are different from the Neolithic burials at Ban Kao, Kanchanaburi, and from the Bronze Age skeletons at the Artillery Centre, Lopburi. Another round earthwork is located about 1 km. to the east of this mound. It is very interesting that we found there a reasonable number of potsherds, rough and coarse, hand-made with cord-marked design.

The Excavation of the Ancient City

The excavation was undertaken between 4 April and 16 May 1971, after final surveys on the ground and from the air. Eighty students from the Faculty of Archaeology joined us in the field. Throughout the period in the field, Professor Sood Saengvichian, former Head of the Anatomy Department, Mahidol University, who participated in the Thai-Danish expedition's excavations at Ban Kao, Kanchanaburi, and who has done exhaustive research on prehistoric and protohistoric man in Thailand, helped us to dig up and classify the skeletons. He not only helped us in the field, but also classified the skeletons for the final report, and we should like to record our thanks to him here. I divided our team into two groups and the excavation was done at both sites simultaneously.

The excavation for that year had to be completed before the planting season when more of the topmost layer would be destroyed by tractors. Consequently we had to hurry, especially to dig up the bones before the rainy season. Before opening squares, the stratification of the site was studied by drill excavation at eight spots within the city. Afterwards we opened squares of 5 × 5 m. Three of them were laid on a small mound which was expected to be a graveyard. The rest were located on habitation sites to the east and north of the stupa. The ancient population seem to have built their houses with some kind of perishable material throughout the whole area inside the city. The population seemed to be more dense in the middle part of the city, and to decrease in density slightly in the north-west part. This is surmised from a study of the potsherds.

The earliest settlement may have started in late Neolithic times, according to the evidence from a reasonable number of ground stone adzes, shouldered adzes, or rubbing stones, etc. Their exact dating will be based on thermoluminescence or on a comparative study of all artefacts, especially the sherds. The people who lived there in Neolithic times seem to have passed suddenly into the Iron Age. One should not be much surprised by this, for we know from the historical background that some of the local people of central Thailand received a new culture from India by sea. The evidence for this consists of iron tools, accompanied by a few copper objects, associated with stone tools found in the same strata. We found various kinds of religious objects showing very strong Indian influence: for example, two terracotta plaques representing Gaja-Lakshami on one side and the figure of Kuvera on the other. This evidence can be compared to that from Chansen Phase V which has been dated to the early Dvāravatī period, round about A.D. 600.

Outside the city, about 200 m. to the north, we found fragments of a stone pillar with an inscription. It is octagonal in shape, made of greenish sandstone. The design on the pillar also can be identified as early Dvāravatī period. The inscription is Pali written in a south-Indian alphabet like the previous one. It is the best known chapter of the Buddhist law of Dharma which starts with the words 'YE DHAMMA[1]. . . .'

The excavation was continued until we reached the limestone bed, which averages 150 cm. deep. Although we found at least two living floors, the cultural change seems to be too difficult to distinguish, because the area of

excavation was limited and most of the top soil had been disturbed. Three skeletons were discovered in the city. Two were buried in extended position and
the other was in a kneeling position. The orientation was south-west and east.
Some grave goods were also found. All skeletons are now being studied in the
laboratory of Mahidol University, under the supervision of Professor Sood
Saengvichian.

The pottery includes both hand-made and wheel-thrown pieces. Some
carinated pots might be shaped by both techniques, the upper part of the
bodies being wheel-thrown and the rest then finished by beating, and the
whole burnt by domestic firing. A few pieces were painted with small red
bands; stamped pottery was also found. The designs are similar to Chansen
Phase V and VI, and some pieces have floral motifs similar to bas-reliefs on
stone pillars of Dvāravatī style. Ornaments were also found, for example, an
ear-ring made of lead, and one copper ring, accompanied by a skull. Few iron
tools were found among the burial goods but most of the iron objects are in
very poor condition.

A fragment of a human skeleton was found below the stupa's base in the
final phase of the excavation, showing that the earliest settlement at the ancient
site must have been much earlier than the early Dvāravatī period and could
have belonged to the transitional period from the Neolithic to the Metal Ages.

The Excavation at the Burial Site, South of the City

One trench of 3 × 15 m. was dug in the middle of the mound. Four layers
were discovered there, the top one being humus. The second layer was an
occupation floor of the Metal Age, according to the evidence of a large concentration of sherds and moulds for casting metal objects. Other artefacts and
animal bones were found in the upper part of this layer, which averages
60 cm. in depth. Remains of about sixteen individuals were recognized; but
some, in fragmentary condition, were confusing. There were both burnt and
unburnt skeletons. The orientation was varied but mostly eastwards. All were
in the extended position, except one which was a flexed burial. Such an
extraordinary case was also found at Ban Kao, Kanchanaburi, too. These
ancient people also believed in 'life after death', since funeral objects were laid
beside them. The grave goods were ground stone adzes, blades made of fresh
water shell, and pottery with and without decoration. The designs on the pots
were very strange including a kind of signeous or eliptical form of engraving
which was painted over. It seems to me that the ancient potters here had
invented a new technique (see Plate IXb).

A large piece of pottery covered with a bowl was unearthed at the lowest
level of this trench, which may be the largest piece of prehistoric pottery that
has ever been found in Thailand. At first it seemed to be a burial jar, but we

found only a few pieces of animal bones, all of them too small to be identified. A possible explanation is that the bones are the remains of food buried in the jar. Another suggestion is that the jar had not contained food when it was buried, but at some later time the covering bowl collapsed so that the jar was filled again naturally by the soil and animal bones. We surmise this from the condition of the jar *in situ* and from the section of soil inside the jar. More details about the objects inside this jar might become known after microscopic study in the laboratory. Close to this pot, we found an antler with cutting traces at one end. The same kind of antler-work had been found before at Ban Kao and might be a symbol of shamanism. Small beads made of animal bones, as in the Neolithic periods of Sam Liam Cave, Kanchanaburi, were also found. Some were discovered near the skull and some were still in their original condition. These kinds of beads were previously found at many sites along the River Kwai.

Conclusion

The first settlement at Sab Champa took place in the Neolithic period as shown by the evidence from the burial site near the ancient city. People who used both ground stone adzes and shouldered adzes seem to have lived in small groups around this area. They had their own culture characterized by the design on the engraved pottery. After that, another civilization expanded to the area and I think that probably the use of metal objects and Buddhist art reached there simultaneously. A city practising Theravāda Buddhism developed about the sixth to eighth centuries A.D. The dating, based on relative chronology, can be compared to other Dvāravatī sites, especially Chansen Phase V. Perhaps New Stone Age life in some parts of Thailand continued until the fifth century A.D. or even later. We do not know exactly why the ancient city of Sab Champa came to an end. I suppose that it ended before the tenth century A.D., because there is no evidence of the late Dvāravatī style there. I hope in the future to undertake further excavation there, and expect that absolute dating will be possible in the very near future.

NOTE

1. The dates of this inscription and of the one mentioned as having been found earlier, were discussed during the London Colloquy. One was thought to date from either the sixth or the seventh century, the other perhaps from the eighth century. *Editors.*

Problems of Continuity between the pre-Buddhist and Buddhist Periods in Central Thailand, with special reference to U-Thong

H. H. E. LOOFS

Chin-lin and Fu-nan

ALTHOUGH numerous finds of Buddhist objects (Buddha figures, votive tablets, and the like), as well as references in Chinese texts point to the implanatation of Buddhism in several parts of the Indo-Chinese peninsula prior to the sixth century, the earliest evidence of a thoroughly Buddhist society is still only that of the kingdom of Dvāravatī (sixth to eleventh century), centred on the lower Menam or Chao Phraya basin in what is now central Thailand. The discovery of the existence of this kingdom being a fairly recent one, much of the latter's history, political as well as cultural, remains to be elucidated. What is still more obscure, though, is the period preceding it.

In the most recent and most detailed study of Dvāravatī so far published, Dr. H. G. Quaritch Wales questions the validity of the hitherto widely held belief that prior to the coming into being of this kingdom the lower Menam basin was an integral part of the equally Indianized (though not Buddhist) kingdom of Fu-nan, and that it was the breaking-up of the latter, in the middle of the sixth century, which caused the independent kingdom of Dvāravatī to emerge, its culture being of course to a great extent based on that of Fu-nan (Wales 1969: 1–19). The similarity of objects found on the surface or at shallow depths at places like Ū-Thòng in western central Thailand (thought to have been the capital of Dvāravatī for some time) with those discovered at Oc-Eo in South Viet-Nam (thought to have been the main port of Fu-nan, near the country's capital), which was first pointed out by J. Boisselier several years ago (1965: 144) and was acknowledged by Quaritch Wales, seemed to confirm this belief. Instead, Quaritch Wales accepts the location of the 'kingdom' of Chin-lin in the lower Menam basin and credits it with having possessed an independent civilization at the time it was occupied by Fu-nan (early third century), much of which was then inherited by Dvāravatī after the break-up of Fu-nan and the end of Funanese rule over Chin-lin. Dvāravatī's real predecessor, in other words, is not Fu-nan, but Chin-lin. The main evidence on which this assumption is based seems to be of two kinds: (1) literary, and (2) archaeological.

His literary evidence is Wheatley's interpretation of a passage in the *Liang-shu* (Wheatley 1961: 117). This author makes clear, however, that his hypothesis of Chin-lin's location around the shores of the Bight of Bangkok is open to doubt, be it only because this area is not known to be a source of silver, one of the few pieces of information the Chinese text gives about Chin-lin; the silver, Wheatley thinks, may have come from the Shan States. Now this argument seems, one may be forgiven for saying, somewhat far-fetched, as it would mean that Chin-lin acquired its reputation of being a source of silver only because it received this metal from mines about 1,000 km. away and transported over a very difficult route; one would imagine the normal trade connections of the Shan States area to have been with the central Burmese lowlands or possibly along the Salween with the Martaban area, the latter having anyway been suggested by both Pelliot and Luce (1925: 153–4) as the most likely location of Chin-lin. Moreover, as the character *ch'u* used in the *T'ai p'ing yü lan* (Ch. 790, f. 23), translated by Luce (from Pelliot) as 'produces' (Luce 1925: 152) is more likely to really mean the producing, i.e. mining of silver than a mere trading of it, the obvious absence of silver mines in the area around the Bight of Bangkok can be seen as a weighty argument against placing Chin-lin there. Another one, connected with the same matter, is that it seems that the two known mentions of Chin-lin as being a silver-producing country come only from the seventh century or later: the mention in the *San tu fu* was added by a commentator of that century, and the mention in the *T'ai p'ing yü lan* (written 978–83), taken from the now lost *I wu chih*, is also unlikely to have then been older than three centuries. By that time, the lower Menam plain would already have been known by the name of *T'o lo po ti* (Dvāravatī) which was used for the first time in the middle of the seventh century by the Chinese pilgrim Hsüan-tsang (Julien 1858: 82).

It is generally agreed that the main territorial expansion of Fu-nan took place in the middle of the first half of the third century when Fan (Shih)-man conquered much of the coastal areas around the Gulf of Siam. The evidence for this is of course the almost contemporary report of the Chinese envoy K'ang T'ai who was sent to Fu-nan by the newly established state of Wu to reorganize commercial relations with the *Nan Yang*, interrupted since the beginning of the century after the collapse of the Han Dynasty. K'ang T'ai's original report is lost, but much of it is incorporated in later annals, notably in the *Liang-shu* (*Annals of the Liang Dynasty*, 502–57, compiled by Yao Ssu-lien who died in 637), from which the following crucial passage comes (translated by Wheatley 1961: 15, where this passage is also given in characters): 'Once more [Fan-man] used troops to attack and subdue the neighbouring kingdoms, which all acknowledged themselves his vassals. He himself adopted the style of Great King of *Fu-nan*. Then he ordered the construction of great ships and, crossing right over the *Chang-hai*, attacked more than ten kingdoms, including *Chü-tu-k'un*, *Chiu-chih*, and *Tien-sun*. He extended his territory for 5–6,000 *li*. Then he attacked the kingdom of *Chin-lin* [a country seemingly situated on the northern shores of the Gulf of Siam]'.

Apart from pointing out that the last phrase in square brackets is somewhat superfluous as it has no relation to the original text, and without wishing to become involved in controversies related to the localization of *Chü-tu-k'un*, *Chiu-chih*, and *Tien-sun*, there are a few points which warrant further explanation.

(a) Fan-man's first action (after he had himself declared Great King of Fu-nan) was to have great ships built to enable him to 'cross right over' the *Chang-hai*. This latter name has been interpreted in many ways (even as meaning the Gulf of Tonkin), but the arguments put forward by Wheatley (1961: 15) that it most probably means the Gulf of Siam are convincing enough to accept this interpretation. This being so, why then was this name preferred to that of 'the great bay of Chin-lin', which is used to describe the sea to be crossed if one sails from Fu-nan to the four kingdoms of *Pien-tou*, *Tu-k'un*, *Chu-li*, and *Pi-sung*, all seemingly situated on the Malay peninsula? (Luce 1925: 144). The conclusion seems to be warranted that Chin-lin was not situated at the Gulf of Siam, or at least not in such a prominent position that this Gulf should have been called after it, but elsewhere. As we are not concerned here with locating the unidentified kingdoms in K'ang-T'ai's report, but solely with examining what kind of civilization may have existed in the lower Menam plain prior to the emergence of Dvāravatī, the matter will not be pursued further.

(b) The word *ch'iung* is taken by Wheatley to mean 'to cross right over' ('transversing', according to Luce). In the context of this report it could then only signify that Fan man, from his point of departure somewhere near the southernmost tip of the Indochinese peninsula (e.g. Oc-Eo) 'crossed right over' in a westerly or south-westerly direction, to arrive somewhere at the eastern coast of the northern part of the Malay peninsula; from here, then, he would have worked his way through along this western side of the Gulf of Siam towards the north, conquering 'more than ten kingdoms' in the process, until he took Chin-lin, situated at the Bight of Bangkok. This is a possible interpretation of Fan-man's conquests—except for one detail: Chin-lin *was not conquered* by him! There is indeed no mention anywhere of Chin-lin being taken by Fu-nan. All the text says is that Fan-man *was about to* attack Chin-lin ('he wished to subdue the kingdom of Chin-lin'—Luce 1925: 142), when he fell ill and died. Nothing is said about his successors (Chin-shêng, Chan, Ch'ang, or Fan-hsün having executed the wish of Fan-man. We have thus to imagine Chin-lin as a kingdom just beyond the reach of Fu-nan (at least at that time); it becomes practically impossible then to locate it at the Bight of Bangkok. This location is also of course altogether impossible if one accepts Boisselier's theory (1968: 34–5, n.d. 13–16) that the lower Menam basin itself was the heartland of Fu-nan, whence Fan-man expanded his power towards both sides along the shores of the Gulf.

If another meaning of *ch'iung*, such as 'exhaust', 'follow out to the end', or simply 'explore' is adopted, things become much easier. Instead of crossing right over the Gulf of Siam (always assuming a starting point in southern Cambodia or present south-western South Viet-Nam), Fan-man could have followed the eastern coast of the Gulf to the end, i.e. to the Bight of Bangkok, whence he continued along the western coast of the same gulf towards the south, to conquer further kingdoms. As Fan-man died within sight of Chin-lin, this kingdom cannot be situated somewhere midway on his path of conquest but must necessarily mark its end.

(d) An oversight must have prevented Wheatley from realizing that, according to his own argumentation, the distance of Chin-lin from Fu-nan could in fact be much greater than assumed. In the *Fu-nan-chi* by Chu-chi, a work of the fifth century and thus two centuries nearer to K'ang T'ai's original report than the *Liang-shu*, and the author of which was moreover apparently an Indian (Wheatley 1961: 113; Pelliot 1903: 252, n. 4), who may well have known more about Fu-nan and its relations with other countries than Chinese envoys who spent only a short time in the area and had no background knowledge to speak of, it is said clearly that *Chin-ch'en* (and Wheatley himself proves that this can only mean *Chin-lin*) is 2,000 *li* overland distant not from Fu-nan, but from a Buddhist country called *Lin-yang* which in turn is (according to the *T'ai p'ing yü lan*) situated 7,000 *li* south or south-east of Fu-nan. Although not much reliance can be placed on the accuracy of distances given in *li* (and directions) in sources of that time, it seems nevertheless that the difference between 2,000 and 2,000 + 7,000 *li* also prohibits the location of Chin-lin in the lower Menam basin.

Archaeological Evidence from U-Thong

The main archaeological argument put forward by Quaritch Wales in support of his theory that Chin-lin was the predecessor of Dvāravatī is the absence of 'Funanese' objects (other than on the surface) in a trial trench dug in 1968 at Ū-Thòng, except for one sherd decorated with three wavy lines in the typical Oc-Eo manner, found at the *bottom* of the deposit (Wales 1969: 6–7. Emphasis mine), at a depth of 4 ft. 6 in. (i.e. *c.* 1·35 m.), while otherwise the trench was full of sherds which 'were of the plain carinated ware that we everywhere recognize as typically Dvāravatī'. This seems to imply that all layers in this trench, except the lowest one, should be ascribed to the Dvāravatī period, which would thus be sandwiched between 'Funanese' finds at the surface and at the bottom of the deposit (i.e. immediately above sterile soil)— an implication contradicting strongly the theory it is supposed to support.

However, during the last two seasons of excavations at Ū-Thòng by the Thai-British Archaeological Expedition (1969 and 1970) at Tha-Muang site, situated within the precincts of the old town of Ū-Thòng like Quaritch Wales' 1968 trench and barely 1 km. distant from the latter, a surprising amount of objects of clearly 'Funanese' character was found, down to considerable depths as well as on the surface. These include not only a number of decorated pot-sherds identical with Oc-Eo ones, here found throughout the deposit to well beyond 2 m. below the surface, but also other objects (or fragments thereof) common in Oc-Eo, such as saddle querns or associated rollers (down to 2·10 m. in undisturbed deposit); parts of what Malleret, the excavator of Oc-Eo, calls *fourneaux* (to 1·80 m.), *tampons* (to 1·60 m.), *chandeliers* (to 2 m.), and *anneaux interrompus* (to 2·30 m.) (Malleret 1960); typically shaped 'phallic' spouts of pottery vessels (to 0·70 m.); carved stones (for printing on material?) (to 1·20 m.), and so on.

A special case is that of iron objects of which Tha Muang yielded a fair number, from the surface to a depth of 2·20 m., while they were notably scarce in Oc-Eo. However, as the latter site's acid and swampy soil conditions are particularly unfavourable to the preservation of such objects, this disparity does not point to the improbability of a connection between the two sites. On the contrary, the presence of considerable amounts of iron slag in Tha Muang (to a depth of at least 1·10 m.) as well as Oc-Eo (to still greater depths) indicates a contemporary or partly contemporary local iron production in both places which is impossible to conceive as having developed independently.

The Tha Muang excavation results are still being studied with a view to publishing them in the near future (for the last provisional report see Loofs 1970). However, five provisional C14 dates have been obtained from charcoal samples selected from different layers so as to get a reasonable idea of the site's chronological sequence.

Three of the dates are as follows:

Layer (below surface)	Location (cutting)	C14 Lab. Code and No.	Age
0·60–0·70 m.	F5	ANU–1184	1880±80 B.P. (A.D. 70)
1·50–1·60 m.	F5	ANU–1185	2160±110 B.P. (210 B.C.)
2·60–2·70 m.	E10 (25 m. from F5)	ANU–1186	1790±70 B.P. (A.D. 160)

Both layers in F5 yielded 'typical Dvāravatī' as well as 'typical Funanese' objects. The sample from E10 represents the lowest point of the excavation in which charcoal was found in sufficient quantities for dating purposes.

Unfortunately, as they stand, these three dates seem to pose more problems than they solve: that from 1·50–1·60 m. below surface in F5 appears utterly incompatible with the one from a depth of 1 m. lower down in E10, the latter being, even if we assume the extreme case of the ± values being entirely plus on one and entirely minus on the other end of this range, still more than a century *later* than the former. In other words, we would have to think of a very rapid and unequal accumulation of soil, in the order of over a metre in a century in certain places (and in a much shorter time still if these extremes are not assumed). However, evidence from sites in India and Pakistan seems to show that such a rapid accumulation is not impossible under the climatic conditions prevailing in this part of Asia (Wheeler 1956: 44–5). A quite high rate of soil accumulation has to be assumed anyway if one accepts the two straightforward dates in one cutting (F5), three-quarters of a metre distant in depth and a little more than two centuries in time. Furthermore, as a certain sloping of archaeological layers can be observed (although these are not as clearly distinguishable as one could wish) which goes in the opposite direction to that of the present surface, and if one takes into account that in both cuttings practically identical finds were made at the indicated depths (1·50–1·60 m. in F5 and 2·60–2·70 m. in E10), it can be surmised that we are dealing here with basically the same occupation period; this would reduce the problem of soil accumulation to manageable dimensions. But obviously more research is needed to explain this matter fully.

Two more charcoal samples were selected in order to date the fragment of a glazed pot and lumps of glass which were found in two test cuttings a little way from the main excavation, at depths of 1·20 m. and 1·70 m. respectively (in undisturbed deposits), proving, it is suggested, local manufacture of glass and/or glazes. They produced the B.P. dates 1600 ± 100 (ANU–1187) and 1590 ± 100 (ANU–1188), both in the middle of the fourth century A.D.

In addition to being somewhat inconsistent, these five radiocarbon dates are also surprisingly early. As the charcoal samples submitted for dating were sufficient in weight and quality, and no pits or disturbances could be observed at the places they were collected from, and no contamination is suspected, these dates must however be taken into consideration. But provisional thermoluminescence dates obtained in the Australian National University[2] from potsherds from the same cutting (F5) the first two radiocarbon dates came from, do not support the latter. They are (taken to the nearest ten):

Layer (below surface)	C14 Date	Thermoluminescence Dates
0·60–0·70 m.	A.D. 70	
0·70–0·80 m.	—	A.D. 710
		A.D. 860

Layer	C14 Date	Thermoluminescence Dates
1·50–1·60 m.	210 B.C.	A.D. 400
		A.D. 800
1·80–1·90 m.	—	A.D. 660
		A.D. 710
		A.D. 980
2·10–2·20 m.	—	A.D. 590
		A.D. 960

While these dates are more in line with the traditional chronology of the area in pre- and early Dvāravatī times, it is difficult to accept them out of hand, mainly because of their internal inconsistency and the fact that no clear pattern emerges from them, for two dates from the lowest layers are the youngest of the entire series and the oldest date comes from much higher up in the same cutting. Further evidence is needed to clarify the chronology of this site. At present, for the reasons stated above, the possibility cannot be dismissed that the continuous and intensive occupation which produced this soil accumulation was mainly a pre-Dvāravatī one. Thus only the upper layers (1A, 1B, 2A, 2B, and possibly 3) are indubitably Dvāravatī and later, whilst the major part of the deposit, including the three 'zones of burning', or Phases 1 to 3, mentioned in the first preliminary report (Watson and Loofs 1967: 240), may be pre-Dvāravatī, beginning possibly as early as the third century B.C. As the archaeological record does not show any drastic changes from pre-Dvāravatī to Dvāravatī layers, a cultural continuity can be assumed throughout the site, and much of what was hitherto considered 'typically Dvāravatī, (including the carinated ware), does now seem to come in fact from pre-Dvāravatī times.

As I tried to demonstrate elsewhere (Loofs, n.d.), this carinated round-bottomed mostly cord-marked pottery found at Ū-Thòng may well have evolved from a Neolithic pottery tradition of the wider area (although there is insufficient evidence for this to be seen in Ū-Thòng itself), rather than being the result of some strong outside influence, be it connected or not with a migration or conquest. The nearest Neolithic or partly Neolithic sites to Ū-Thòng are Ban Kao in Kanchanaburi province (only about 70 km. distant from Ū-Thòng as the crow flies) and Khok Charoen, Lopburi province, on the other side of the Menam Plain (at a distance of about 150 km. from Ū-Thòng). They yielded, in addition to the earlier globular cord-marked bowls some with slight, and in Ban Kao more pronounced, carination. So much so that some of these pots are practically identical with those from Oc-Eo (compare, for instance, Ban Kao types 14 and 16, var. A and B, with Oc-Eo types 18, 19, and 21. Sørensen 1967: 80, 82; Malleret 1960: pl. XXIV); and others come very near to pre-Dvāravatī and Dvāravatī pottery as known from Ū-Thòng.

As no clearly Buddhist objects were discovered from the pre-Dvāravatī layers of the Tha Muang excavation, and in the absence of conclusive literary evidence, it is at present difficult to determine the date of the introduction of Buddhism in the lower Menam area. It could, however, be argued that the presence of the numerous bricks or brick fragments throughout this excavation, all showing 'typically Dvāravatī' characteristics such as rice-husk temper and standardized dimensions, can best be explained by assuming that they come from some undiscovered *chedi* in the neighbourhood, i.e. a Buddhist monument similar to the many *chedis* known from Dvāravatī times in this area. As there is no evidence for bricks having been used for non-religious structures, and no other religious structures are known or need be presumed here than Buddhist ones, one could go as far as to conclude that bricks must indicate Buddhism. Now, the layer dated (by carbon dating) to the third century B.C. contained many such brick fragments, as did also the layers dated to the first and second centuries A.D.

If this argument is accepted and these early dates are proved to be correct, we would have here the earliest archaeological traces of Buddhism in South East Asia. It would, if not confirm, at least support Prince Subhadradis Diskul's theory, based in turn on one formulated already by King Mongkut (though rejected by Coedès), that nearby Nakhom Pathom may well have been the *suvarṇabhūmi* to which the two Buddhist missionaries Soṇa and Uttara were sent by Aśoka, and that thus Buddhism was implanted in this area as early as the mid-third century B.C. (Diskul 1964: 6–8; Boisselier 1970: 57; Coedès 1932: 531).

Conclusions

Piecing together the above archaeological evidence (in a preliminary way only), three alternatives to Quaritch Wales' theory with regard to the lower Menam basin in pre-Dvāravatī times offer themselves, after the elimination of the possibility of Chin-lin having been located in the area:

(1) At the time of Fan Shih-man's conquest, this area was culturally 'underdeveloped', i.e. living in the Late Neolithic or Early Metal Age and possessing a pottery tradition similar to that of other parts of the Indochinese peninsula, but without having evolved a strong local cultural or political identity of its own. Apart from sporadic and superficial Indian influence, it was Funan, expanding from the lower Mekong which introduced civilization into the lower Menam basin, Chin-lin being situated elsewhere. The question of when and how Buddhism was introduced into the area is left open.

(2) This was the area in which Fu-nan itself emerged, its civilization developing out of the local Neolithic and Early Metal Age traditions, and influences coming from India. It was from here that Fan Shih-man conquered adjacent countries in the third century, 'exploring' the coastal areas of the Gulf of Siam (and of the Andaman Sea?) until he met his death while attempting to conquer the last kingdom in a series, Chin-lin. This intention to conquer Chin-lin may have been connected with the desire to secure a source of previous metals for Funan which were utterly lacking in the lower Menam basin. Here again, the implantation and development of Buddhism is unexplained, but the judicious arguments in favour of this theory put forward by Boisselier cannot be dismissed lightly. In particular, the evidence from the Tha Muang excavations supports one of them quite strongly, namely the obvious cultural continuity from Funanese to Dvāravatī times here, whilst such a continuity (from Funanese to post-Funanese times) is not easy to see in the lower Mekong area, traditionally taken as having been the heartland of Fun-nan. This would also agree with the findings of the Fine Arts Department, University of Pennsylvania Archaeological Expedition in Chansen, a site in the northern part of the lower Menam basin (not quite 200 km. north of Bangkok), where in Phases III and IV (dated A.D. 250–450 and A.D. 450–600 and labelled 'Early Fu-nan' and 'Late Fu-nan' respectively), many of the same Oc-Eo type objects as are known from Tha Muang have been found (Bronson and Dales 1970). This northern area would thus have come under Funanese influence at a relatively early date, a fact which is easier to reconcile with the assumption of the cradle of Funanese civilization having been nearby in the adjacent part of the lower Menam basin than far away on the southern tip of the Indochinese peninsula. However, acceptable as this theory looks on archaeological grounds, there seem to exist serious obstacles to its acceptance from the literary evidence (Colless, n.d.).

(3) Prior to the political conquest of Fu-nan there existed an as yet ill-defined Metal Age culture in the lower Menam basin which was sufficiently developed to be called a civilization in its own right, including very probably even already Buddhist elements. The Funanese conquest did not affect or alter this civilization in an appreciable way as the Funanese themselves were operating from the same cultural background. The marked similarities in the material culture of Tha Muang and Oc-Eo sites seem indeed to exist already at least a century before the Funanese expansion, although more exact dates on both sides are needed to confirm this. The assumption of the existence of such a local non- or little 'Indianized' civilization in this area (except for early Buddhist influence) would go well with Eveline Porée-Maspero's findings with regard to the beginnings of Fu-nan (1959: 790–800), and would also not clash with the literary evidence. But there is more. The above-mentioned similarity in material culture in the first centuries A.D. can also be observed in several

other sites, such as Chansen and even Beikthano in lower central Burma, where many objects were found which would look not at all out of place in Ū-Thòng or Oc-Eo (Thaw 1968 and 1972: 1–10; the excavator does not stress this fact, however) and some of which do indeed have their exact counterparts in these sites, although nobody ever seriously suggested that this area was conquered by Fu-nan.

The zone in which these sites are situated corresponds roughly to the extension, as far as it is known, of the Mon population at that time (assuming that the Funanese, too, were akin to the Mon). It is tempting to call this (still very hypothetical) civilization, stretching from the lower part of Burma through most of Thailand and Cambodia to the southernmost point of the Indochinese peninsula, that of the early Mon (or 'Proto-Mon'), who soon became the staunchest Buddhists in South East Asia and the creators of the first Buddhist kingdoms in the region. Needless to point out that this third possibility is the preferred 'working hypothesis' of the writer of these lines who is, however, of course aware of the urgent need for further research and for more corroborating evidence before it could be presented as a viable theory—if it can be done at all.

NOTES

1. This is the enlarged version of a preliminary note published under the title 'Funanese Cultural Elements in the Lower Menam Basin' in the *Journal of the Oriental Society of Australia*, vol. 8, Nos. 1 and 2 (Dec. 1971) (Commemorative Seminar in Honour of Professor F. H. van Naerssen), pp. 5–8. The writer thanks his colleague Dr. Kenneth Gardiner for advice on matters pertaining to Chinese philology and the writing of the Chinese characters in the manuscript.

2. Dates obtained by Mr. D. M. Price (Tests Nos. 124–32), under the supervision of Dr. A. J. Mortlock, Department of Physics, whose help is gratefully acknowledged. These dates are provisional in the sense that the potassium level could not be measured (it was assumed to be 1 per cent); now equipment is being installed in the Dating Laboratory, and this will make possible the exact measurement of the potassium level.

In an article by E. K. Ralph, H. N. Michael and M. C. Han, 'Radiocarbon Dates and Reality', *MASCA Newsletter* (Applied Science Center for Archaeology, University Museum, University of Pennsylvania), Vol. 9, No. 1 (August 1973), p. 9, table 2, the following corrections are given: A.D. 70 = A.D. 140 (MASCA), A.D. 160 = A.D. 220 (MASCA), 210 B.C. = 170–190 B.C.

Dvāravatī, a Consideration of its Formative Period*

ELIZABETH LYONS

HISTORIANS believe that the Dvāravatī empire covered a fairly large area of central Thailand between the seventh and the tenth or eleventh centuries, with an offshoot continuing in the north around Lampun until the late thirteenth. The existence of such a kingdom is corroborated by Hsuan-Tsang's mid-seventh century reference to the country of 'To-lo-po-ti' (Coedès 1968: 76), and by the discovery of three silver medals, two in Nakorn Pathom, one in U-Thong, inscribed 'Srī Dvāravatīsvara punya' (foundation-work of merit—of King of Dvāravatī) (Boeles 1964: 101). This is about as far as the facts go. We do not know when the kingdom of Dvāravatī was founded, or where exactly was its capital.

From the time of the *Periplus of the Erythrean Sea* to Hsuan-Tsang there were rumours and reports of countries in South East Asia with strange customs and exotic products. These sites are exceedingly difficult to identify with modern place-names and historians express strong differences of opinion. About the only belief held in common is that these ancient localities are all on the periphery of the Dvāravatī area, somewhere on the present Vietnamese coast, or in Cambodia, peninsular Thailand, Malaysia, Indonesia. The rich and fertile Menam Valley is largely ignored in the historical records of the first to seventh centuries and by modern historians of that period (Wheatley 1961; Wang Gungwu 1958, etc.). Anyone who studies the published material can easily receive the impression that nothing of any importance to the development of civilization in South East Asia was going on until Dvāravatī came into being. This brief paper aims at calling attention to the contradiction between archaeological facts and the conclusions hitherto drawn from the paucity of historical evidence. Central Thailand is the least known and least recorded area of South East Asia before the eighth century, and yet it seems to possess the greatest wealth of artefacts of that period.

Some of the background of this situation can be uncovered, but much more must be deduced, and one realizes that trying to materialize an image of history between the Prehistoric Age and the fully grown Dvāravatī kingdom of the eighth to ninth century is rather like attempting to solve a jigsaw puzzle which has most of the pieces missing. One must often depend on juxtaposition to suggest a design and by that indirect evidence to fill in a gap.

* See Plates X, XI.

Most probably the picture of the Dvāravatī civilization will always remain a patchy one, but the patient collection of clues must eventually reveal something of its development and historical importance.

The area of Dvāravatī that concerns us is defined as being loosely bounded by Chainat in the north, Ratburi in the south, Karnchanaburi to the west and Khon Kaen in the east although the discovery of Dvāravatī style artefacts is not entirely confined within these limits. To set the stage for the historical period we must go farther afield and also back in time. For several millennia before anything resembling a proto-historic state was established, there was a very extensive and vigorous prehistoric culture. The most important of the excavations, particularly in the north and the north-east are detailed in other papers, but there are a few facts which have some bearing on the later period. The number of sites now known and the extensive quantity of artefacts already recovered must mean that by the first century A.D. there was a sizable population contained in numerous communities. Many of the artefacts, especially the painted pottery of the Ban Chieng culture, show an extremely high level of technical and artistic skill, and metal had been in use by at least 1000 B.C. Although there are no mineral deposits within the Ban Chieng territory, these sites have produced a large quantity of bronze objects. One must presume that some system of trade existed with settlements lying in the mineral zones to the west.

Immediately to the west of Nongkai, through Loei province close to the Pasak river, and south to Lopburi there is a mineral zone shown on the modern map as having deposits of copper, iron, gold, and lead. Farther north and west, from Chiengrai to Tak there is another band of the same minerals, plus a smaller area near Maehongsorn in which a tin deposit is noted, and to the north and south of Karnchanaburi there is tin, iron, copper, and gold. Outside of the well-known tin ore in the peninsula, most of these metals do not now exist in sufficient quantity or in the form for modern commercial value, but their existence argues that there may have once been more easily extractable deposits in the vicinity.

The area of the pre-Dvāravatī states was favoured by a rich variety of natural resources; it had plenty of fertile, arable land, a network of waterways, and except for an occasional flood, an absence of disasters produced by earthquakes, volcanoes, typhoons. Each settlement must have been quite self-sufficient, and, by and large, on peaceful terms with its neighbours judging by the rarity of weapons found in prehistoric and proto-historic graves. Their lack is a striking contrast to the numerous deposits of spears, daggers, lance heads, etc. found in Late Chou and Han Chinese tombs.

Apparently these early communities felt no need of the outside world; it was east and west Asia that sought them out for their exotic and valuable products. Before the actual dates of contact are recorded by the Chinese, there is evidence from the Indian Jātaka stories, the *Rāmāyana*, the Tamil poem, *Paṭṭinappālai*, that voyages to the Land and the Island of Gold were fairly common in the early centuries A.D. (Wolters 1967). India's supply of gold was restricted after the barbarians cut the supply routes from the Siberian source, and the shortage was compounded in the late first century when Vespasian forbade the export of bullion.

The Indian literature is of little help beyond establishing that voyages did take place. The writers are story tellers rather than keepers of records; dates, ports of call, etc. are a minor consideration in tales of glory and spiritual inspiration. One would think that commercial interests were beneath them. Chinese records, on the other hand, picture the Chinese missions as strictly business affairs. They note all the points that would be useful to ship captains and traders on future trips to these strange countries. Although the presence of Buddha images among tribute gifts is recorded, only in the biographies of noted monks does one find evidence that trading groups were frequently joined by persons on a purely religious mission. As Soper points out more than once, Chinese lay historians (usually Confucian scholars) were biased against Buddhism and tended to ignore it.

It is most probable that in Thailand as in Han China there was some know-ledge of Buddhism before mass acceptance and the building of temples created the need for numerous images. The earliest Buddhist object to appear so far is an ivory comb engraved with Buddhist symbols. One face of the comb has a row of symbols: triratna, purnagata, umbrella, wheel, etc. above two running horses of Amarāvatī style. The other face has a hamsa done in the manner associated with a later Gupta style. The comb was excavated at Chansen, near Lopburi and comes from the Phase II level for which there are three C14 dates. The sample taken from within a metre of the comb dates A.D. 3 ± 42 and another from the same trench dates A.D. 65 ± 48 The same phase in another trench yields a sample dating A.D. 256 ± 87 A second-century date for the comb is reinforced by several C14 dates for the next, clearly defined, stratum which cannot begin later than A.D. 300 (Bronson, n.d.). In the same Chansen site there are shards of stamped pottery similar in technique and design motifs to the stamped pottery of Arikamedu (Wheeler 1946), Ahichchhatra (Ghosh 1946), and Sirkap (Ghosh 1947–8) in India of first to third century date and very close to the stamped shards from the second- to third-century site of Beikthano in Burma (Thaw 1968).

Chansen, and particularly U-Thong have yielded seals, jewellery, especially the *anneaux alourdis* and their moulds, identical with those found by Malleret at the early Funan site of Oc-Eo, a site which also contained seals, Roman coins or medals etc. of the second to third centuries carried from India (Malleret 1959–63). Malleret mentions two seals from Nakorn Pathom as being of the same age and category. Both are engraved on rock crystal, one with a slim figure he thinks may be Hellenistic (it is somewhat reminiscent of a figure on an Indo-Greek coin). The other seal depicts a fish and a water weed (Malleret 1963). A third seal from Nakorn Pathom has a masted, outrigger boat deeply engraved in stone (Guide 1970).

From U-Thong has come a rather large quantity of gold jewellery, and a smaller amount comes from Nakorn Pathom and other sites. Much of this jewellery is the Oc-Eo type, some appears to be related to examples from Taxila. These Thailand pieces were ploughed up by farmers or looted from mounds, and, with the exception of a few beads and insignificant bits, are in private collections. The writer has also seen ornaments of thin gold foil, and votives and Buddhist images embossed on heavier gold foil. They appear to be very early, but that statement cannot be supported without more opportunity for research.

To this probable first- to third-century material should be added the often published Alexandrine lamp decorated with Silenus mask and palmettes found in the early (1927) semi-scientific excavation at Pong Tuk (Picard 1955). The lamp, obviously of foreign manufacture, was probably not the only one of its type that came to Thailand as a locally made, crude variety of Roman lamp, a fairly common artefact in Dvāravatī sites. Coedès mentions the group of Greek or Roman entertainers who went from Burma to China in A.D. 120 and points out that Pong Tuk lies on the route that crosses into lower Burma at Three Pagodas Pass (Coedès 1428: 207). Such entertainers were evidently well known in India since one of the reliefs on a pillar at Sanchi (first century A.D.) is a good representation of a group of musicians with clearly non-Indian features. They are dressed in Greco-Roman costumes consisting of a short cloak tied around the neck, a kilt, and sandals with the straps criss-crossed to the knees and one of the group plays the Greek double flute, an instrument never adopted in India (Zimmer 1955, pl. 10). Quite probably some similar troupe sailed from the Indian coast with a trading party, landed at a peninsular port and slowly worked their way up to the pass. It has been calculated out that the Dvāravatī sites of Petburi, Ratburi, Pong Tuk, Ku Bua, Nakorn Pathom and so on in this area are a day's march apart.

From around the first century A.D. until its fall in the sixth century Funan is frequently mentioned in Chinese reports, but exactly what or how much territory it encompassed is a matter of speculation. The assumption that it included much of the pre-Dvāravatī territory rests merely on the similarity of a few objects from Oc-Eo with those from the U-Thong area. Perhaps the current went the other way. We know very little of the art of Funan; there is no sculpture attributed to it before the sixth century. When it does appear, its close stylistic affinities with Dvāravatī images or Indian monuments is apparent. It does not seem to go through a lengthy period of formation and experimentation such as we see in Dvāravatī.

In the third century, between A.D. 284–7, Funan and twenty other countries sent embassies to China to establish trade. The Chinese, through the centuries, have often complained at the cost of receiving foreign embassies and presenting them with state gifts in return for their tribute, and particularly during the time of trouble following the break-up of the Han empire, they must have felt that the arrival of some of the very minor entities of South East Asia was more of a burden than a benefit. Chinese officials would have preferred to deal with one or more leaders of more major states in what was essentially a commercial enterprise conducted with quasi-diplomatic flourishes. Funan would easily fit the picture as the leader of an economic confederation with several ports and trading marts to which products from the interior were brought, these products sometimes including religious images. In the mid-fifth century, Funan sent to China a seated Naga image in gold openwork (Soper 1959: 259). As far as we now know, the earliest South East Asian image of the Buddha seated under the Naga is found in Thailand. I think 'openwork' must mean a pierced base or halo or the flame-like radiance emanating from the Buddha's body. All of these characteristics are known in a few early bronzes from Pong Tuk and Nakorn Pathom.

It is not yet possible to set up an unassailable chronological sequence for Dvāravatī-style sculptures because we cannot tie in the known examples with C14 or thermoluminescence dates. It is obvious that most of the sculpture is strongly influenced by late Gupta and Pala style, and that by the seventh century the artistic canons and iconography were firmly established. There are, however, a number of images and objects which do not fit orthodox categories; they do not continue beyond the Dvāravatī age, nor are they found outside of Thailand. We believe they must belong to the period when Buddhism was being introduced by missionaries and pilgrims from different sects and different countries, no doubt all of them having stylistically different amulets, portable shrines or illustrated sutras which would both inspire and confuse the local artisan looking for a model to follow.

The earliest group of images are those closely modelled on imported examples of Amarāvatī or early Gupta style and found in Malaysia, Viet-Nam, and Indonesia as well as in Thailand. Two of the locally-made images, one from Nakorn Pathom and one from Pong Tuk wear a heavy, Gandhara type robe which moulds the legs and is crossed by a symmetrical, looping pattern of folds around the body. Their hands are extended at about the height of the waist (the right one of each is missing), the left hand with open palm is clearly not holding a corner of the robe as the Singhalese Amaravati, and their South East Asian copies do. Both of the Thai images, I believe, are intended to be small copies of the famous Sandalwood image, supposed to have been created by the order of King Udyāna of Kosambi before the Buddha's death. The story was depicted in Gandhara relief, it was known in third- and fourth-century China along with more than one statue said to be the original, and Fa Hsien found the cult flourishing in India in A.D. 400. The Sandalwood image is connected with the Sarvastivadin sect which existed in Thailand in the early Dvāravatī period. At any rate, the Pong Tuk and Nakorn Pathom images fit the scanty description as well as the two who are considered to have the best claim to resemblance, namely: the wooden Shaka of Seiryoji, Japan and the large, probably Central Asian bronze in the Metropolitan Museum, New York.

There is good reason to think that the distinctive series of stone reliefs known as the Banaspati stelae belong to the first period of Buddhism in the area. Each example, oval or shield shaped, shows the Buddha descending from heaven on the head of a composite animal, accompanied by two figures, usually identifiable as Indra and Brahma. The animal (Banaspati) with its garuda beak, horns, and wings is a combination of the vehicles of the Hindu gods. The earliest Banaspati stelae in the National Museum, Bangkok has the two attendant figures dressed in the Indian late Amaravati, early Gupta fashion of a short garment tied in the front, the ends of the girdle sash falling to the knees. The standing rather squat Buddha makes the double gesture, and the thick robe he wears falls from his wrists in a symmetrical U curve. In a somewhat later example, the attendant deities are dressed in long sarongs with a short girdle flap, the standing Buddha is of better proportion that the one in the previous example, and his robe is a simplified version of a fifth-century Gupta style. The sculpture is bordered with an ornament of blunt, comma-shaped motifs which appears in India in the fifth century.

A third and badly damaged example in this series has the Buddha framed in a niche and seated on a throne on the monster's head. This piece, the most skilfully done of the three is of mixed Amarāvatī, Ceylon, and late Gupta style. The throne back has two simple horizontal bars, the Buddha is seated with his legs crossed in the parayankasana fashion of Ceylon, the outer, irregular border of the stelae is ornamented with a strongly developed version of the blunt edged floral design, similar to the sixth-century ornament of Deogarh (Zimmer 1955, pl. 110), and found in later Cham design.

Not many of these objects are known and they have a limited range. They probably have originated during the time when both Buddhism and Hinduism were being introduced, and may have been either the result of a confused understanding of iconography, or were done with the intention to show the Buddha as the dominate and supreme being. They do not continue after the Dvāravatī period and are not found outside of Thailand.

Another series for which a chronology might be worked out is the stone Dhammachakra or Wheel of the Law. It appears very early in India, on a column of Asoka, on the pillars of Sanchi, and is frequently shown in Amaravati reliefs. The concept probably came to Thailand by way of a votive tablet having a representative of the wheel at a holy place, or by a small replica. A metal one, only 3½-in. high including its floral pedestal base was excavated along with Gupta artefacts at Rajbadidanga, ancient Raktamrittika, whose native son, the navigator Buddhagupta, is mentioned in a Malaysian inscription of the fifth century (Das 1968).

The Dhammachakra is associated with the deer as a symbol of the Deer Park in which the Buddha gave the first sermon and thereby set in motion the wheel of Buddhist law. The wheel can also be non-Buddhist, as one of the attributes of a Cakravartin or universal king. Apparently it can also represent the chariot of Surya, although the example in the National Museum, Bangkok, may be a unique one. Surya is seated cross-legged on a rectangular base and is flanked by two squatting yakshas who support the wheel on their backs and heads. The god wears a high crown, heavy ear-rings, a necklace, braclets, and a simple girdled kilt, and each hand raised to the shoulder holds a lotus. His head is framed in an oval halo, and the wheel rises behind him like the sun. The wheel-sun with its realistic hub, spokes braced against the inner rim with a block in the shape of an Ionic capital, and the side of the rim ornamented with a floral design between pearl bands is identical in type with the several known Dhammachakras in Thailand.

The other wheels, all Buddhist symbols, can be put into sequence by the design on their rims. The ornamental band which is most typical on Dvāravatī works is an alternate lozenge and floral rosette motif between pearl bands. An early form of it is found at Deogarh, c. A.D. 500, and the established design appears in Ajanta, Cave II, A.D. 600–42. Earlier Sanchi, Amarāvatī, and Sarnath monuments have bands and borders of a neatly ordered floral rinceau instead of the lozenge and rosette motif (Zimmer 1955, pls. 110, 156, 27, 30).

The National Museum has another interesting object which like the Surya wheel does not become part of a standard repertoire. It is a stone tray carved with various symbols and having a hollowed-out depression in the centre and each corner. The Museum also possesses a sizeable fragment of a similar tray. The symbols on the intact one are Gaja Laksmi, or Mahā Māyā flanked by elephants, two flywhisks, two conch shells, two garlands, two vajra, two goads, two umbrellas, two fans, two turtles, a fish, a banner, a bird carrying a crab, and a hamsa holding a lotus (Boeles 1964). It is most probably a mandala, a symbol of the four-cornered world with Mt. Meru in the centre, and the most likely use for it is as a ritual object in an investiture ceremony. We have assigned it a pre-seventh-century date for no better reason than the feeling its mixed iconography, and rather primitive workmanship belong to a formative period, and perhaps to a modest, not very royal, court.

Another group of objects that are found within a small area and have a limited period of production are the moulded terracotta figurines about 7 in. high of a boy with a monkey. The boy is nude except for bracelets, amulet, and a belt. In one hand he holds a rope fastened to a monkey clinging to his legs. There are two types, one skilfully done, the other somewhat more crude, but an example of each was found in a Phase V level at Chansen, dating between A.D. 600 and 800. Surface finds of the same types come from U-Thong and Sab Champa. It would have been far more satisfactory if these figurines had come from the Chansen Phase III level dating A.D. 250–400, as the only parallel, and a very close one, is with the figurines of a naked boy wearing the same amulet and belt, and holding a bird, from Satavatana sites in India of the second and third centuries (Lyons 1973).

Future researchers might also look into the early origins of some of the minor elements in Dvāravatī art, especially the elephant and the lion. We will only mention that the balustrade lions, and the relief profile of an elephant on the Phra Pathom chedi, Nakorn Pathom, have nearly identical counterparts on the Ruvanweli stūpa in Ceylon. This study does not take in the main body of Dvāravatī sculpture or the surviving foundations of Dvāravatī architecture. Most of that work has been analyzed by Dupont and others, and the major portion of it, by far, belongs to the period of Dvāravatī's full development, the seventh to ninth centuries (Dupont 1959).

This paper is a preliminary survey of a largely uncharted field. The number of clues however is growing as the increased archaeological activity in Thailand is rapidly turning up new material to study. If we cannot yet with certainty know the date when Buddhism became a force strong enough to unit the people of separate communities in a common spiritual cause, and to develop that inspiration into the Dvāravatī culture, we have evidence enough to believe that central Thailand had developed considerable religious and administrative cohesion before Hsuan-tsang gave notice that the state of 'To-lo-po-ti' existed.

ADDITIONAL REFERENCES

Charoenwongsa, Pisit. 1973. *Ban Chiang*, Bangkok, 1973.
Còedès, G. 1928. 'The Excavations at Pong Tuk and Their Importance for the Ancient History of Siam,' *JSS*, vol. XXI.
Maleipan, Veerapan. 1973. 'Sab Champa', *Archaeology*, vol. 3, no. 4 (Journal of Silpakorn University, Bangkok).
Thaw, Aung. 1968. *Report on the Excavations at Beikthano*, Rangoon, 1968.

The Development of Dvāravatī Sculpture and a Recent Find from North-east Thailand*

M. C. SUBHADRADIS DISKUL

I

IT is already known that Dvāravatī art in Thailand lasted from about the seventh to eleventh centuries A.D. in the central part of the country, and continued until the early thirteenth century in the kingdom of Haribhuñjaya in the north. Dvāravatī sculpture, mostly Buddhist, received its motivation from the Indian Gupta and post-Gupta styles (fourth to eighth centuries A.D.), but it also displays some reminiscence of the Indian Amarāvatī art which had arrived earlier.

Apart from small bronze Buddha images that usually show the typical characteristics of Indian Amarāvatī or early Singhalese styles, and might be imported from India or Ceylon, there is a small stone standing Buddha image 59·3 cm. high, of unknown provenance, which has been kept in the storeroom of the Bangkok National Museum for a long time (Plate XIIa). The Buddha is wearing a monastic dress in typical Indian Amarāvatī fashion, but no drapery folds exist; this latter characteristic is indicative of the Gupta tradition. The hands also follow the Amarāvatī attitude. The right one, although broken, was probably raised up to perform either the *abhaya* or *vitarka mudrā* as a scar on the right shoulder still testifies. The left hand, which is still intact, clutches firmly at the chest. The head is badly defaced, but one can still perceive large hair-curls and a broken round aureole behind the head. This image resembles strongly one discovered at Wat Crak in Cambodia, which is regarded by French archaeologists as the earliest Buddha image found in that country. Our effigy is probably even earlier, as the hands are still in the typical Amarāvatī style whereas those from Wat Crak thrust out more or less in the Gupta manner. This image in Thailand can therefore be dated about the fifth or sixth century A.D. and shows a connection between the Amarāvatī and Gupta influences.

A second image in the early Dvāravatī style is a stone Buddha seated under the Nāga, 1·05 m. high (Plate XIIb). The image was discovered at Muang Fai in Amphoe Lamplaimat (Buriram province, north-eastern Thailand) and is now kept in a Buddhist monastery at Amphoe Huai Thalaing in the province

* See Plates XII, XIII.

of Nakhon Ratchasima (Korat). The face of this image still evinces a strong Indian influence, with the hair-curls all curving towards the right and a small cranial protuberance without halo on top. The flap of cloth on the left shoulder of the Buddha is not present either. The legs are loosely crossed after the Indian Amarāvatī fashion, and the three coils of the snake are all of equal width, thus again testifying to its early age. The image is carved in high-relief and the faces of the Nāga already show the Dvāravatī style, being a rather simian type and having a projection on top of each head. These faces of the Nāga, however, if compared with other images of the same iconography in Dvāravatī style, are seen still to lack later ornamental developments, and therefore testify to the early age of this image. The statue might be dated around the seventh century.

A third image, also a stone Buddha in meditation, 1·57 m. high, was found in a cave at U-Thōng (Supanburi), central Thailand (Plate xiic). It is now preserved at the National Museum branch in that district. The peculiar characteristic of this image is that, although the Buddha is in the attitude of meditation, at the base one can still see the profile of a Wheel of the Law, and a crouching deer turning its face back towards the Wheel on each side, exactly after the Indian fashion. This is quite interesting in that, although the scene implies the First Sermon of the Buddha at the Deer Park near Benares in India, the Buddha sits in the attitude of meditation. The figure is again carved in high-relief, but unfortunately the image of the Buddha has badly deteriorated and is covered with gold-leaf, so one cannot very well study the effigy of the Teacher. This image might also be dated about the seventh century. It is probably not out of place to mention here that no Buddha image in the attitude of the First Preaching, in the real Indian sense, has so far been found in Thailand, Cambodia, or Laos.

Let us turn now to some terracotta figurines from Khubua, in the province of Ratburi, southern Thailand, which can be attributed to the same period. First of all, two beautiful standing and smiling figures should be described. Both of them are standing in a triple flexion (*tribhanga*) 94 cm. and 88 cm. high, and wear long hair in a chignon with the ends hanging down on both shoulders, after the Indian Gupta and post-Gupta modes. One of them can be identified as Avalokiteśvara Bodhisattva as he is wearing an antelope shawl diagonally across his body, and his right hand is holding a nectar bottle. Their dress is a long cloth draped like a *sarong* and tied with a cloth belt around the thigh. These figures display strong Indian influence and can therefore be dated back to about the seventh century. They also testify that during this period Mahāyāna Buddhism reached the Dvāravatī kingdom. Another piece of sculpture that supports this early date of the terracotta figurines at Khubua is a head, probably of a Dvārapāla (door-guardian) also found at the same *stūpa* (Plate xiiid). Apart from the serene and gentle expression of the face, the statue is also wearing a head-dress composed of many short-hanging floral pendants. This kind of decorative motif reminds one very much of the head-gear of Umā in the remarkable three faces of Maheśvaramūrti, in the large cave on Elephanta Island in front of Bombay in India. The latter sculpture is dated about the sixth century, so our Khubua terracotta head might belong to the seventh century.

At Khubua, some stucco figures were also discovered. They are mostly of inferior workmanship to the terracotta ones and probably belong to a later period, about the ninth to tenth century. This presumably is one of the pieces of evidence which led Professor Jean Boisselier to put forward the hypothesis that during the first phase of the Dvāravatī period the artists used terracotta as their medium, but in the second phase they turned to stucco. One type of terracotta figurine found at Khubua must, however, also be mentioned. It represents a group of standing strangers, 87 cm. high, holding a lamp in their hands, probably used to adorn the base of a *stūpa*. Could they be Phoenicians or Scythians? They are surely not Indians or Mons. This problem is still left open.

Some other early terracotta figurines at U-Thong should also be mentioned. One represents a flying figure on a large piece of brick, 36×32 cm. The flying posture resembles strongly the Indian Gupta and post-Gupta prototype, and this figure might also be attributed to about the seventh century. The other represents a horse-shoe arched window with a human face peeping through, 69×37 cm. The face belongs already to an ethnic Dvāravatī type as well as having a peculiar style of hair and the usual form of round ear-rings. So this second piece might belong to about the eighth century.

Can early Hindu images discovered in Thailand, and mostly at the same sites as the Dvāravatī Buddha images, be classified as the Hindu aspect of the Dvāravatī art? The writer is rather doubtful of this classification as their characteristics, especially the facial features, are totally different. Here let us look at a stone Hindu image of Gaṇeśa, the elephant-headed god, recently discovered in Muang Pra Roth, Dong Si Mahapot (Prachinburi), eastern Thailand, where also many Dvāravatī Buddha images have been unearthed. The seated statue is $1 \cdot 70$ m. high and shows the strong forceful nature of the god. Unfortunately it was found in many broken fragments which have been now assembled together and preserved in the Bangkok National Museum. Judging from its simplicity and unadornment, this image might date back to about the sixth to seventh centuries.

II

We have talked thus far about some principal statues of the first phase of the Dvāravatī period, about the seventh century A.D., which still display strong

Indian influences. Let us now turn to the second phase, from about the eighth century. From this period onward the original elements of the Dvāravatī style emerged and the facial features of the statues changed. Sometimes a small halo in the form of a lotus bud is added on top of the cranial protuberance. The two arched eyebrows have merged into one curved and connected line. The eyes are protruding, accompanied by a flat nose and thick lips. The Buddha is standing in a straight position and performs with both hands the *vitarka mudrā*. Thus total symmetry is observed, more so with a monastic dress covering both shoulders and falling in the same way on both sides of the body. Sometimes a base decorated with a double row of lotus petals will have stamen on top, showing the Pāla influence from India, as well as the hem of the robe continuing from the end of the cloth flap on the left shoulder of the Buddha down to the left wrist and the left thigh, especially for the seated Buddha figure.

For this second period, we may mention a large stone standing Buddha image, which might belong to the early phase about the eighth century and which was recently discovered at Dong Si Mahapot (Prachinburi) (Plate XII*d*); and also a bronze one 1·20 m. high, the largest bronze Buddha image ever found in Dvāravatī art (Plate XII*e*). This last was unearthed at Muang Fai, Amphoe Lamplaimat (Buriram), the same district where the early stone Buddha image under Nāga already mentioned was discovered. The facial features of the standing bronze Buddha still keep some of the characteristics of the Indian influence, such as the *ūrṇā*, which is quite rare in Dvāravatī art in general. It should also be indicated that this large standing bronze Buddha was found with two other important statues of the same material: a Maitreya Bodhisattva, 47 cm. high, and a figure which might belong to the same saint but is much taller, 1·37 m. high. These last two bronzes might be compared to the Khmer pre-Angkorian statues of the late seventh to eighth centuries, and this might be used to support the early chronology of the standing bronze Buddha.

For this second period, the writer would like to attribute an age between the eighth and tenth centuries A.D. The Śrīvijayan influence from southern Thailand also spread northwards during this period, as Professor Jean Boisselier has suggested. An oval face 34·7 cm. high, bearing a soft impression of Maitreya Bodhisattva, found in a cave of Thamorat Hill (Petchabun province), northern-central Thailand, may be cited as an example. The writer, however, does not think that the Śrīvijayan influence was very strong in Dvāravatī sculpture. On the other hand, it might be more so in architecture and its decorating motifs. This stone face might date back to about the eighth century.

For the third and last period, the eleventh century, the Khmer influence of the Baphuon style crept in. One good example is a stone seated Buddha image in meditation, 1·39 m. high, which was discovered in the town of Lopburi and is now preserved in the Lopburi National Museum (Plate xII*f*). The face of the Buddha has become square and a dimple exists on the middle of the chin. The end of the robe on the left shoulder extends down to the navel and terminates in a straight line. The Master is seated in a completely folded-leg fashion and the base is decorated with stylized lotus-petals.

III

So far we have discussed the development of Dvāravatī sculptures mostly in the central part of Thailand which is believed to be the site of the Dvāravatī kingdom. The artistic expression of Dvāravatī art did not however limit itself only to the central part of the country. It extended north with the Haribhuñ-jaya kingdom, expanded to the north-east, to the east and also down to the south. This artistic influence need not however have been accompanied by any political extension. It occurred probably only through cultural expansion with the spread of Theravāda Buddhism. For this expansion, the influence of Dvāravatī art in north-eastern Thailand is quite interesting because it encoun-tered native elements, as well as foreign influences from the Khmer kingdom and Champā. But Dvāravatī sites in central Thailand such as Nakhon Pathom, Khubua, U-Thong, and Lopburi must still be considered the cradle of Dvāravatī culture.

An interesting recent find in north-east Thailand is a series of sixty-six silver plaques unearthed at Amphoe Kantarawichai (Kandaravijaya) in the province of Mahasarakham (Plate xIIIe). They were discovered in 1972 in the ruins of an *ubosoth* (ordination hall) called Um Ya Khu inside the old town of Khantharawisai (Gandharavisaya), Tambon Khanthar, which is quite near the Amphoe Kantarawichai office, by the Seventh Branch of the Thai Fine Arts Department. Now a highway has cut through this ancient town, which is in an oval form surrounded by a moat in between two earthern ramparts. The moat is about 18 m. wide and the ramparts are about 2–3 m. high and 6 m. wide. The name 'Gandhāra' probably has nothing to do with Gandhāra in ancient India.

The structure excavated was probably a Buddhist ordination hall, as a broken middle fragment of a sacred boundary stone was found at the north-eastern corner. It is a rectangular structure 37 × 10·50 m. with the rather peculiar feature that its entrance, with steps, faces south instead of east. The base is composed of laterite as a foundation and then bricks on top; it is redented at the two front corners and has small projections at the three other sides. The laterite base of the main Buddha image is at the farther side of the north, opposite the entrance to the south. No traces of columns have been found, so they were probably made of wood and the superstructure might have been in wood and covered with terracotta tiles. Unfortunately the original level of the floor of the building has not yet been reached through the excavation and no terracotta tiles have been found. Some broken bits of bronze fragments and terracotta Dvāravatī potsherds have however been discovered. The important finds are now displayed in the Khonkaen National Museum.

One of the interesting finds from the excavation of this structure is a terracotta Buddhist votive tablet of 14 × 22·5 cm. representing the Buddha in meditation. He is seated with his eyes closed and his head leaning a little bit forward. His head is surrounded by a halo and there are some motifs around his body as if flames are jutting out. The way in which the Buddha has also a halo on his head, in the form of a lotus bud, and is seated in a complete crossed-leg fashion with the hem of the robe passing over his left wrist and left thigh and the stamen on the double lotus-petal seat, indicates an Indian Pāla influence which might have arrived via Burma. This votive tablet can be attributed to about the ninth to tenth century A.D. It was discovered at the north-western corner of the building.

The most remarkable find was a terracotta bowl 12·5 cm. high and 20 cm. wide at the mouth, containing sixty-six 'repoussé' silver plaques (Plates XIIIa, b, c). The bowl was discovered at the north-eastern corner of the laterite base of the main Buddha image inside the *ubosoth* on the north. It might have been originally enshrined underneath the base of the Buddha image.

The silver plaques are rectangular. Their sizes vary but they are mostly of 10 × 5 cm. They are made by the 'repoussé' method and represent Buddha images, divinity or royal figures, *stūpa*, and Wheels of the Law on columns. Most of them however represent seated Buddha images. These figurines can be classified into ten groups:

(1) Two seated Buddha images with the right hand in the *vitarka mudrā* (attitude of argumentation) and the left one lifted up as if to hold the end of the robe on the left wrist. One of them shows that the hair-curls are very much stylized. They both have a halo around the head and one of them has flames coming out from the halo as well. The seated posture in loose crossed-leg fashion and the folds on the monastic dress show that they still retain some lingering characteristics of the Indian Amarāvatī influence, though their date cannot be too early (Plate XIIIa).

(2) There is only one example of this type. The Buddha is seated in a loose crossed-leg posture on an octagonal base, and he is in the attitude of meditation. His hair-curls are much stylized and he has also a halo around his head. His monastic dress is thin, transparent and clinging to the body after the Indian Gupta and post-Gupta fashions.

(3) There are quite a number in this group. The Buddha is seated in a more or less loose crossed-leg fashion. He is performing the *vitarka mudrā* with his right hand and his left one is placed on the lap. The monastic dress has no folds and the hair-curls are much stylized. They have a cranial protuberance

without a halo on top and their heads are always surrounded with an aureole. Some of them have an *ūrṇā* on the forehead which is quite peculiar for Buddha images in Thailand. The hem of the robe curves like an S from the left shoulder down to the right side of the body, leaving the right shoulder bare. Some of them have also a halo around the body and floral or flame-like motifs on the background on both sides of the head. A rather peculiar characteristic is that for the most part they have no flap of cloth on the left shoulder; only very few of them have it.

(4) This group is also numerous. It represents the Buddha seated again in a loose crossed-leg fashion. His right hand performs the *vitarka mudrā* while his left one is raised as if to hold the end of the monastic dress. The robe is thin and transparent. The hair-curls are always stylized and some of the figures have rays represented by straight lines as decoration in their halo. The *ūrṇā* still exists on some figures as also do the floral designs on both sides of the head and a halo around the body. Some of them have also a lotus bud as a halo on top of the cranial protuberance (Plate XIIIb).

(5) There is a peculiar small plaque representing the seated Buddha with the right hand on the knee as if in the attitude of subduing Māra or calling the Earth to witness, but his left hand is raised up and is more or less in the attitude of *vitarka mudrā*. One can be sure that this image is not reversed during the repoussé method as the hem of the robe shows clearly that the Buddha's right shoulder is left bare and the left one is covered. The head and hair are very much stylized. The meaning of the attitude of this Buddha is still unclear.

(6) There is again another peculiar plaque representing the seated Buddha performing the *vitarka mudrā* with both hands. This attitude when performed by the standing Buddha is usually recognized in Thailand as the Buddha 'descending from Tavatimsa Heaven', as can be seen from a carved stone slab representing such a scene discovered at Muang Fa Daed Sung Yang, a Dvāravatī town in the province of Kalasin not very far from that of Maha-sarakham, and now preserved in the Bangkok National Museum. This Buddha is seated, so one cannot be very sure about the meaning of this attitude. The robe of the Buddha has folds and the halo behind the head is decorated with straight lines and a double rim. The body is also surrounded by a halo and a scroll exists on each side of the head.

(7) Now we come to two standing Buddha figures, both wearing a thin and transparent monastic dress covering both shoulders, and performing the *vitarka mudrā* with both hands. As has been mentioned, this attitude in Thailand for the standing Buddha is recognized as 'descending from Tavatimsa Heaven'. The first one has a round face, stylized hair-curls, a small halo (?) on the cranial protuberance, and the halo around the head which is decorated with straight lines from behind the latter. Two floral motifs can be seen on the plaque. The drapery belongs to the Dvāravatī fashion. The second figure

resembles the first both in attitude and drapery but the halo around the head has disappeared. The face has changed to square, which might indicate the Khmer influence from Cambodia. The floral motifs on the background are more numerous. Judging from the style the second one might be a little bit later than the first and might be attributed to the eleventh to twelfth century A.D. (Plate XIIIc).

FIG. 1. Repoussé silver plaque of a deity, from Kantarawichai

FIG. 2. Repoussé silver plaque of a king or prince, from Kantarawichai

(8) Some of the silver plaques represent divinities and royal personages. The former might be the guardians of the Earth who are at the same time attendants of the Buddha and the latter worshippers of the Master. Here four pieces will be described, two of which probably belong to the same plaque: they represent the head and a lower part of the body of a divinity. One can identify him as such because of a halo around his head; he has also floral motifs as decorations on the background (Fig. 1). The divinity is wearing a crown, a pair of ear-rings, a necklace, and a dress very much resembling those of a king or a prince carved on stone slabs found at Muang Fa Daed Sung Yang,

in the neighbouring Kalasin province, depicting various scenes from the life of the Buddha or his previous incarnations. The dress also reminds one of the costume of a Vishnu sculpture, the Vishnu from Da-nghi in the Tourane Museum, which is attributed by Professor Jean Boisselier to about the early eighth century A.D. Our silver plaques from many points of view, especially from the stylization of form and the confused *mudrā* of the Buddha, cannot be as early as that. It probably belongs to the local style as pointed out by Dr. H. G. Quaritch Wales in his recent book *Dvāravatī* (1969).

Of the two other plaques in this group, one represents a seated deity in adoration. He is wearing the same decorations as the last one, but here one can notice that he is also wearing a pair of large armlets and bracelets. The floral motifs are again used to decorate the background. (Here one may raise some doubts about the sketch, as to whether the headgear and armlets are correctly reproduced.) The other (Fig. 2) probably represents a seated king or a prince. He might hold an object in his right hand. The decorations of this one are very much stylized and one can again raise doubts about the sketch.

(9) Now we will talk about seven silver plaques that represent various *stūpa* types. They are so much deteriorated that it might be better to study them from the sketches of the Thai Fine Arts Department artist (Fig. 3). They are very much stylized and can be more or less classified into two types. The first one derives from a round *stūpa* very much like the one of Dvāravatī style discovered at Wat Candraram, Amphoe Chaibadal (Saraburi).[1] The other type resembles strongly the *stūpa* discovered at Nakhon Pathom, representing a low pedestal, the central part of the *stūpa* in the form of an inverted alms-bowl, and the finial composed of many superimposed rings crowned on top of a bulb.[2] Thus it can be seen that the Dvāravatī types of *stūpa* in the central part of Thailand had also come up to the north-east. We have however so far found only bases of these monuments.

(10) The last two silver plaques represent, on each of them, a Wheel of the Law placed on a column. The column is set up on a square pedestal. The lower part of the former is composed of a round pot (*kumbha*) and the capital resembles an Ionic order very much like the spokes of the stone Wheel of the Law itself. The Wheel of the Law on the silver plaques is however very much stylized. It should be mentioned here that so far only one Dvāravatī stone Wheel of the Law in the round has been discovered in the north-eastern part of Thailand, at Amphoe Sung Noen (Nakhon Ratchasima).

Thus it can be seen that these silver plaques belong to Dvāravatī art, which probably spread up with Theravāda Buddhism from the central part of Thailand to the north-east. They also display local elements of the area, which are quite distinctive from those of the central part of the country. As they show much stylization, both in the form and the confused *mudrā* of the Buddha, they should be attributed to the late Dvāravatī period, about the tenth to eleventh century A.D., though some of them still retain Indian Amarāvatī influences. They are not beautiful, but as they were discovered in the large number of sixty-six, they are important in themselves and testify to the importance of Theravāda Buddhism in the north-eastern part of Thailand during that period. Because they were discovered near the base of the main Buddha image in an ordination hall (?), they might have been originally enshrined underneath that base for an auspicious sign when the hall was constructed.

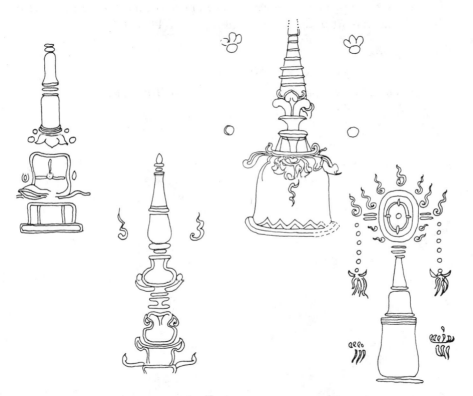

FIG. 3. Examples of *stūpas* found on the repoussé silver plaques from Kantarawichai

These plaques probably belong to Theravāda Buddhism, as no figures of Bodhisattvas of Mahāyāna Buddhism have been represented. The culture presumably belonged to the Mon race or was introduced by the Mon, as Mon inscriptions have also been found on four terracotta Buddhist votive tablets unearthed at Muang Fa Daed Sung Yang, in the neighbouring province of Kalasin. It has been mentioned that at that town many carved stone slabs have been found representing Buddhist scenes with the same kind of dress as our silver plaques. As for the Khmer influence from the eleventh century onward, it should not be surprising as many Khmer monuments from that century (some of them even earlier) abound in the north-eastern part of Thailand. Recently a Khmer small stone inscription 21 × 9 cm. containing fourteen lines of inscription was discovered at Sala Nang Khao, Tambon Nong Phai, King Amphoe Na Dun, Amphoe Vapipatum, also in the province of Mahasarakham. It relates a story of Vraḥ Pāda Kammraten Añ Śrī (Ja)yavarmmadeva who ordered Nāratasuvarṇṇapātra to offer an army to Kammraten Jagat (Lord of the World). It is not clear whether this (Ja)yavarmmadeva was Jayavarman VII. The characters date around the eleventh to twelfth century A.D.

Thus these silver plaques can be said to be one of the most important recent finds for Dvāravatī art in the north-eastern part of Thailand.

NOTES

1. Represented in my book *Arts of Thailand, a Brief History,* fig. 19.
2. Ibid. photograph no. 20.

'Funan', 'Zhenla': The Reality Concealed by these Chinese Views of Indochina[1]

CLAUDE JACQUES

ON glancing through the history of ancient Cambodia, it is evident that authors prefer, more often than not, to refer to the country during the so-called 'pre-Angkorean' period (that is before A.D. 802) by using Chinese names —Funan, Zhenla—rather than 'Cambodia' or one of the indigenous names (or more precisely, Sanskrit names which have become indigenous), even though some of them like Bhavapura, have long been well known. This could be just a question of vocabulary, and might have a certain interest if it was possible, for example, to explain these Chinese designations by Khmer facts, and thus throw additional light on the history of the country. But Zhenla has received so far no plausible explanation; and we shall see later that the existing explanation of Funan, perhaps satisfactory from the phonetic point of view,[2] nevertheless is not sure. Moreover, we can easily see that this method of giving a name to the country is the clearest indication of another fact: that the history of pre-Angkorean Cambodia was, to begin with, reconstructed much more on the basis of Chinese records than on that of inscriptions found in Cambodia itself. Later on, scholars attempted to fill in the gaps of the outline which had been created in that manner, by using new data supplied by inscriptions discovered from year to year. But this has all happened as if they preferred to adjust the newly discovered facts to the initial outline rather than to call the Chinese reports into question. In this way, some very basic historical mistakes have been made, mistakes which are nowadays more especially serious since they can be found printed in every handbook; and as we shall see, ones which are consequently very difficult to dismiss from our minds.

This apparently paradoxical method of elaborating the ancient history of the Khmer country could easily be explained at the very beginning of our century. There were not many epigraphical records, and the scholars who translated them did not think it possible to extract from them more than the names of kings; sometimes also the names of prominent figures, who, by the way, could not always be connected with the reign of a king; and finally some dates, very important indeed, but few in number. Moreover, the facts found in the Khmer parts of these texts added very little to knowledge of the history of events, to which attention was specially paid in those days. It was in that situation that Paul Pelliot, with his paper on Funan (1903) published one year after his translation of Zhou Daguan (1902), came and showed how much could be found in the Chinese reports: first of all, an antiquity appreciably more remote—at least two centuries were gained—and texts which were more explicit and gave comparatively more abundant and often precise dates. True, many gaps remained, and even obscurities, which P. Pelliot did not attempt to conceal; but some concordance could be observed between Chinese names transcripted from Sanskrit, used to refer to kings, and names found on Cambodian stones. It must be added that, regarding the most serious diffi-culty which arose, concerning the date at which Zhenla, a vassal country of Funan, conquered its suzerain state in the sixth to seventh centuries, and the method of the conquest, P. Pelliot had put forward his own hypothesis dis-playing quite remarkable carefulness. But the paper on Funan, as a whole, was done with such a strictness that the reserves of the great master were soon forgotten and his hypotheses were taken for well established facts.

In 1906, George Coedès, then a young student, made a fairly good publica-tion of the inscription of the Ta Prohm stele; the beginning of this long poem provides a genealogy of the King Jayavarman VII, going back on the one hand to the King Śrutavarman, and on the other hand to the King Bhavavarman; and it is for those kings that this part of the inscription concerns us here. In verse VIII (side A, l. 15–16), the name of a lady, Kambujarājalakṣmī, can be read: she was 'born in the maternal family of Śreṣṭhavarman'. The name of the King Bhavavarman follows immediately in stanza IX, and G. Coedès, per-plexed by the lady, supposed that she was the wife of the King Bhavavarman, although there was no clear indication. The hypothesis soon afterwards be-came certainty, because it allowed an admirable resolution of one of the problems set by the non-concordance of Chinese texts and Khmer epigraphy, whilst confirming furthermore one of P. Pelliot's hypotheses. In *Les Etats hindouisés d'Incochine et d'Indonésie*, G. Coedès felt justified in writing:

> Le roi du Tchen-la était alors dans la seconde moitié du VIe siècle Bhavavarman, petit-fils du monarque universel (*sārvabhauma*), c'est-à-dire du roi du Fou-nan. Un texte épigraphique, tardif il est vrai, mais dont on n'a pas de raison de révoquer le témoignage,[3] ajoute ce détail important qu'il était l'époux d'une princesse issue de la famille maternelle de Śreṣṭhavarman, la princesse Kambujarājalakṣmī, dont le nom signifie 'La Fortune des rois des Kambujas'.
>
> Bhavavarman, dont la résidence Bhavapura devait se trouver sur la rive septentrionale du Grand Lac, appartenait donc à la famille royale du Fou-nan et était devenu roi du Tchen-la par son mariage avec une princesse de ce pays (1964: 128).

As may be verified by reading the remainder of the chapter beginning with this assertion, this is the foundation, and the postulate too, which directs the whole of our knowledge on Pre-Angkorean Cambodia. Now unfortunately, it must be said that G. Coedès, though he may be excused because he was so young when he translated the inscription, made a mistake in interpreting the stele of Ta Prohm: he was not careful about the little word *tasyām* (st. XI, l. 22) which, connected as it must be with *Mahiṣyām*, can refer to none other than Kambujarājalakṣmī whose name is quoted three verses above. Therefore, without going into details, the facts which concern us in the genealogy of Jayavarman VII can be summed up in this manner:

st. VI: The King Śreṣṭhavarman was the son of the King Śrutavarman;
  VII: Śreṣṭhavarman, born in Jayādityapura, was the King of Śreṣṭhapura;
  VIII: Into the maternal family of Śreṣṭhavarman, was born Kambujarājalakṣmī;
  IX: From another side, Bhavavarman was the king of Bhavapura;
  X: Into the lineage of this king was born the King Harṣavarman;
  XI: Harsavarman obtained *from this queen* (that is, necessarily, from Kambujarājalakṣmī) a daughter, the Princess Jayarājacūḍāmaṇi.

Therefore, Kambujarājalakṣmī was the wife, not of Bhavavarman I, but of a king named Harsavarman; and they were both the maternal grandparents of the King Jayavarman VII, according to what is said in the stanzas which follow. Consequently it is certain that this princess does not belong to the pre-Angkorean period, and the clever hypothesis of G. Coedès must be re-examined. As a matter of fact, Bhavavarman—of whom it is impossible to say now whether he married a princess from Zhenla—was in any case grandson of the *sārvabhauma*, as stated in a famous line of other inscriptions.[4] But can the latter always be considered as the king of Funan, and more precisely as Rudravarman? We have no true evidence of it; even if we had, how, then, could it be stated that Bhavavarman I, king of Zhenla, conquered Funan? This solution had been propounded by P. Pelliot as a last resort, and by analogy with what is said by the Chinese about his brother Citrasena—Mahendravarman.[5] But in fact the hypothesis rests upon nothing well established. In addition, we must also transfer to another king the fact of the union of solar and lunar races, to which the inscription of Baksei Camkron makes reference.[6]

The name of the father of the kings Bhavavarman and Mahendravarman, that is Vīravarman, is known from several inscriptions. P. Pelliot, without quoting his sources, writes concerning this prince: 'Le nom en *varman* indique un grand seigneur, mais nous savons d'autre part que Vīravarman n'a pas régné' (1903: 300). It is possible that P. Pelliot, renouncing his usual carefulness, has made such a statement following Barth, who was however less categorical (1885: 29): Barth thought that Vīravarman had not reigned, because no trace could be found in the list of kings given by the inscription of

Kdei Ań (or Ang Chumnik), K. 53 (Barth 1885: 64). We have known for a long time now that this indication cannot be used as evidence, since, for example, the king Bhavavarman II cannot be found there either. To my knowledge, there is no document to show definitely that Vīravarman did not reign: on the contrary, I think that the prince was not so unimportant. His name is quoted more particularly, together with the *sārvabhauma* (whoever this king might be), and Bhavavarman and Citrasena-Mahendravarman, in the inscriptions refered to above.[7] The last king, in whose glory the inscription was written, is there compared to these others for his merits, and I cannot see why Vīravarman exclusively should not be a king, and even probably an important king (at least in the mind of the writer of the inscription). In my opinion, it is only a matter of chance that no inscriptions celebrating Vīravarman himself have been found so far; *argumentum a silentio*, here more than ever, is worthless. But on which throne was Vīravarman seated? Was it the throne of Funan, since it is believed that the *sārvabhauma*, who was probably his father, did so? Or on the throne of Zhenla, like Bhavavarman and Mahendravarman, his sons? Or else—how can we tell—on that of another kingdom? New data about this king, unfortunately still to be found, could possibly change appreciably our geographical and historical views of the old Khmer country.

Funan, as was said above, has been given an explanation that is reasonable on phonetic grounds. It was propounded by Louis Finot (1911) and accepted by, among others, G. Coedès. This name, which was anciently pronounced *b'iu-nâm*, according to B. Karlgren, should be the transcription of the old Khmer word *vnaṃ*, which means, as everybody knows, 'mountain'. Now, the opportunity of giving such a name to southern Cambodia may be questioned. P. Dupont gives a fairly good summary of the speculations which came to the fore following the discovery of the possible equivalence between *Funan* and *vnaṃ*:

> Si ch(inois) *fou-nan* est bien la transcription de v(ieux)-kh(mer) *bnaṃ* 'montagne', il autoriserait sans doute la restitution d'une titulature en vieux-khmer [*kuruṅ*] *bnaṃ*, ['roi de] la montagne' dont la contrepartie sanscrite, *parvatabhūpāla*, existe dans l'inscription de Han Cei au VIIe siècle . . . En ce cas, skr. *parvatabhūpāla* 'roi de la montagne' aurait sans doute été un titre dynastique que les Chinois ont confondu avec un nom de pays. On sait en outre que des rapprochements ont été faits avec un autre titre dynastique de même sens, celui de *Śailendra*, qui apparaît en péninsule malaise et à Java central à partir du VIIIe siècle (1955: 10).

And, taking up again a hypothesis already defined by P. Pelliot (1903: 302–3), P. Dupont then argues from ethnology, wondering if the inhabitants of the country called Funan by the Chinese in the third century were already

Khmer people, and therefore whether the name of the kingdom might be drawn from the old Khmer language. Presented in this manner, the problem seems to be not easy to solve, and anyway I have personally no ability to try to do it. My remarks then must rest on another ground. It must be insisted, in my opinion, that the terms *kurun vnaṃ* never occur in a Khmer inscription. As for the Sanskrit counterpart, it occurs, as a matter of fact, twice in the Han Cei door-pillars (K. 81, Barch 1885: 8),[8] but *it is found only in this inscription.* That inscription, it must be remembered, repeats, with some important differences which are not to be considered here, the same text on each door-pillar; and in fact, it could be said that *parvatabhūpāla* occurs only once, but twice repeated. Generally when we speak of Funan, a single realm is understood whose monarch would have borne this title of 'king of the mountain'. Now, it can be seen precisely in the Han Cei inscription that the word *parvatabhūpāla* occurs both times *in the plural*, and indicates kings defeated by a king Bhavavarman (first or second); we are obliged to conclude therefore, that *parvatabhūpāla* does not indicate *the king* of Funan, but several contemporary kings. As for the location of their kingdoms, the inscription does not give any indication allowing us to find it, unless we are to consider them simply as 'highland kings'!

To this indication of some of the problems arising from the utilization of Chinese documents as the principal source on ancient Khmer history, we might also make mention of the instance of the place Aninditapura, probably a city and certainly a realm, which was suggested by the present writer in a recent paper (1972). It was recorded there that, in spite of unquestionable evidence of the location of this kingdom in the Angkor area, afforded by an inscription which G. Coedès knew perfectly well, the great master of Khmer studies, by complying with Chinese sources and with the outline extracted from them, involved himself in speculations that were very ingenious indeed but which nevertheless led him into error.

It is not at all my intention to deny the great contribution of the Chinese annals to Khmer history. First of all, for the whole period which preceded the oldest inscriptions, they are our one and only source, and later on, they give some of the essential landmarks. Nevertheless, they do not seem to have been studied with a sufficiently critical mind, especially since the Khmer inscriptions at the disposal of research workers are comparatively numerous. However criticizable these sources of information might sometimes be, we are compelled to believe their genuineness and their considerable asset of being indigenous. On the whole, what did Funan represent for the Emperor of China? A remote country, which sent to him, from time to time, an ambassador and some tribute, by which he happened to be embarrassed;[9] so it was, most probably, with Zhenla. Some attendants summarized for the benefit of the Emperor, in a necessarily very schematic report, what they knew, directly or otherwise, about these countries. Of course, the larger the countries appeared, the greater was the honour received by the Emperor, when an ambassador of these remote countries happened to render homage to him; and temptation might be strong to magnify the importance of these 'vassals', who themselves could see in that only an advantage.[10] So perhaps the Chinese came to think that Funan was a large empire, and accordingly also Zhenla, which supplanted it. At the beginning of this century, European scholars followed them; and this, as I have tried to show, has on the whole hindered the advance of historical knowledge of those countries. Probably they would have granted them a more modest size, if they had attempted to place on a map of South East Asia side by side, all the countries described, for example, by Ma Duanlin. We must agree with Professor O. W. Wolters when he suggests that in Indochina, and even in the area assigned to them, there were doubtless many more realms than just Funan and Zhenla; some of them probably not unimportant. P. Dupont (1943) has demonstrated the actual multiplicity of Khmer realms in the eighth century, in relation to the 'Land Zhenla' and 'Water Zhenla' of the Chinese; and it has been generally thought that that state of division, sometimes called 'anarchistic' because it does not square with our western ideas which have led us to see in the preceding period a monolithic Funan or Zhenla, come crashing down on the country, for some unknown reason, after the death of the King Jayavarman I. It was forgotten that, if Charlemagne was in fact able to unite a part of Europe, he was something of an accident in the history of this part of the world. On the other hand, one may ask: did 'confusion' and 'anarchy' prevail in Germany more in the eighteenth century than at the beginning of the twentieth? The inscriptions give evidence in the Khmer country of a multitude of little realms and princedoms; those which the Chinese called Funan and Zhenla, on grounds unknown so far, were among them and may have been the most important. It seems that some princes managed, sometimes, to take the leadership of a more or less large group of realms; but this situation was to all appearances only temporary, lasting for the duration of their own reign, and in some lucky instances, that of their son's reign, but not beyond. It would be comparatively easy to show that, in the Angkorean period, things happened in the same way concerning the power of the kings.

Nevertheless, in these conditions there must have been a multitude of royal families. But when the lineage of the kings is known, it seems to converge every time on the famous couple Kauṇḍinya–Somā. That the *nagi* Somā was to some extent a mythical creation must indeed be accepted; but the authenticity of Kauṇḍinya, whose name is transcribed in the *Liang shu* as Jiao-chenru (Pelliot 1903: 269), can hardly be called in question. At the same time, to dispute the correctness of the genealogies provided by the inscriptions would be very dangerous; for then, what criterion would enable us to accept one genealogy whilst denying another? The logic of historians does not always coincide with the logic of history. But such experience as we have gained will permit us to state positively that the genealogies developed in the inscriptions, throughout Khmer history are remarkably coherent even though there are many breaks. In strict logic therefore, we ought to accept everything or to deny everything. But the latter solution, though it allows the historian's thoughts to run freely, seems rather radical! It is probably better to search for some other way: it has perhaps been too easily forgotten that succession to the crown was not governed by the same laws in ancient Indochina as in our countries; in particular, polygamy tended to multiply the numbers of possible heirs to the throne. After a comparatively short time, many men would undoubtedly have the possibility of claiming quite legitimately to be descendants of a single ancestor.

On the other hand, a passage in the *Liang shu* could help us to solve the problem:

> Houen-t'ien eut un fils et lui constitua à part un fief royal de sept villes. Un de ses successeurs, Houan-p'an-houang, à force de ruses, parvint à diviser les villes et à faire naître entre elles des sentiments de suspicion. Alors il leva des troupes, les attaqua et les soumit. Puis il envoya ses fils et petits-fils gouverner isolément chacune des villes; on les appelait *Petits-rois* (Pelliot 1903: 265).

At first, it must be noticed that there may be an element of legend in the facts as they are reported; certainly the personages mentioned belong to an indefinite period of Khmer history; but nothing is impossible to believe in this account. We should not forget that if Huntian and Hunpanhuang actually lived, it was probably long before the first inscriptions. However, it is possible that analogous events happened again later on. Without displaying unbridled imagination, the following hypothesis can be propounded: Kauṇḍinya—I mean the 'second' one—might have placed in the charge of his sons (or some of them) the government of various vassal realms, which were well attached to his crown during his life. But after his death, the question of the succession may have caused the collapse of his empire. Thus there would appear a number of petty kingdoms, which moreover, may have been independent before the reign of Kauṇḍinya. They would be ruled by 'royal families', all of them descended authentically from Kauṇḍinya; and, both in fact and in law, almost entitled to claim the throne of the Khmer 'supreme king of kings'. Of course, this outline is not intended to have any kind of rigidity, since we are reduced to pure hypothesis. It should be added also that ties of vassalage were characterized probably exclusively by the discharge of a tribute, as was the case until quite recent times; and therefore to break those ties was a comparatively easy task, being a negative one. In addition, the outline would call for the greatest possible care regarding the use of the word 'usurpation' in Khmer history.

The present writer is conscious of having posed many more problems than he has resolved, but Khmer history will advance only in so far as we first admit the deficiency of hypotheses which are improperly considered as well established. We shall not respect the great senior scholars merely by accepting without any discussion all their hypotheses, some of which they would have probably discarded if anyone had given them convincing arguments.

Bhavapura, Aninditapura, Vyādhapura, Śreṣṭhapura are well known and genuine names of ancient Khmer realms. One might add also the names of towns which perhaps constituted independent territories, when opportunity offered: Amoghapura, Cakrāṅkapura, Bhīmapura, Tāmrapura, Dhanvipura, Purandarapura, Liṅgapura, Ugrapura, Dhruvapura; all these names are attested in the pre-Angkorean period. The difficulty is often to place these names on a map, but we cannot deny them, nor set them aside. Such as they are, they certainly give a more accurate idea of the true geography of the ancient Khmer country than the names Funan or Zhenla, which are, in this form, words unknown in the Khmer language. Among the Sanskrit names quoted above, which one, or which group of them, corresponds to Funan or Zhenla? The disappearance of these words and of their by now traditional meaning, if not from the books then at least from the minds of historians, would appreciably contribute to clarifying the history of ancient Cambodia, allowing us to start again upon more realistic foundations, even if those foundations are, at least in the beginning, a source of some confusion.

NOTES

1. Transliteration used here is *pinyin*.

2. Provided however that one accepts that the restoration of ancient Chinese pronunciation propounded by B. Karlgren is correct; the present author is not a sinologist and therefore has no basis for taking sides.

3. That is, of course, the stele of Ta Prohm.

4. They are inscriptions K. 363, 496, 497, 508, which give the same poem; see Barth 1903; Coedès 1922.

5. G. Coedès proposed to see these two kings as first cousins and not as brothers, as was generally said (see *Inscriptions du Cambodge*, vii, 156–8); I have grounds for thinking that the documents used by G. Coedès, in any case partly destroyed, is not as clear as he says and may be give another interpretation; therefore, I continue to think that these kings were really brothers, as is stated by several inscriptions.

6. In stanza XI; see *Inscriptions du Cambodge*, iv, 95. G. Coedès alludes to this lineage-union in *Etats hindouisés* (1964: 128).

7. See n. 4, above.

8. See Barth 1885:8; *parvatabhūpāla* may be read on the northern pillar (A for Barth), in st. X, l. 10, and on the southern one (B for Barth), in st. V, l. 5.

9. See Pelliot 1903: 252–3 and 269.

10. Professor O. W. Wolters kindly told me that he could not agree with these assumptions; far better than I, he knows the Chinese people and is probably right. This was to me just a tentative explanation of the too great importance of Funan for the Chinese annalists.

Palaeography as an Auxiliary Discipline in Research on Early South East Asia

J. G. DE CASPARIS

COMPARED with other fields of South East Asian studies palaeography has been neglected both in mainland and in maritime South East Asia. As to the latter, the only existing study which is both detailed and comprehensive is one by K. F. Holle, published nearly a century ago.[1] In about the same period, viz. the two last decennia of the nineteenth century, a number of other detailed studies of early Indonesian script were published, especially by H. Kern and J. L. A. Brandes.[2] Since then until recent years there have been no detailed and scholarly studies, apart from a considerable number of *ad hoc* discussions of special problems and particular details arising mainly in connection with inscriptions.[3] In recent years, however, there are unmistakable signs of a revival of interest in Indonesian palaeography. As far as Java is concerned, Pigeaud's standard work on *Literature of Java*[4] includes the results of a judicious study of the script of Javanese manuscripts from the sixteenth century to the present time. For the relatively modern scripts of southern Sumatra a fairly recent study by M. A. Jaspan[5] is of great importance, while some of the scripts of the Philippines have even more recently been the subject of scholarly studies by Antoon Postma[6] and Juan Francisco.[7]

The importance of palaeography in historical research on ancient South East Asia has long been recognized. Palaeographic analysis has, in particular, proved invaluable for two reasons. In the first place it has been applied successfully in order to establish the approximate date of undated inscriptions, i.e. either those that bear no date or, much more frequently, those the date of which is lost (for instance, because part of the stone or copper plate on which the text is written was broken off) or has become wholly or partly illegible. In the second place, palaeographic analysis, in conjunction with the study of the language and style of a document, has been of great importance in arriving at a sound conclusion concerning the authenticity or otherwise of an inscription. Thus, if an epigraphic text is written in a type of script different from that usual in the period in which it purports to be dated it cannot be regarded as a completely authentic document. It is either a later, more or less correct, copy of an original charter or, in a few cases, a later falsification. The earliest example of the use of palaeography to demonstrate the inauthenticity of an inscription is an article by Brandes, dated 1896, in which it was convincingly demonstrated that an old Javanese copper-plate inscription bearing a date corresponding to A.D. 840 and mentioning Majapahit as the capital of the empire is a fourteenth-century fake or, at best, a complete renewal of an early inscription.[8]

Apart from these two basic methods of application of palaeographical methods to historical research it should be added that palaeography has sometimes been used in conjunction with other disciplines (such as archaeology and linguistics) in studies on the dating and place of origin of Indian influences in the early centuries of the Christian era.[9]

Unfortunately, most of the thorough and detailed research in this field, at least so far as Indonesia is concerned, was published long ago, in many cases more than half a century ago. Since that time much new material has come to light and, in addition, important palaeographic studies relating to India and Ceylon, as well as to mainland South East Asia, have appeared.[10] Finally, the remarkable progress achieved in our knowledge of the general historical background in South East Asia carries obvious advantages for palaeographic studies. It may therefore be of interest to re-examine the evidence available for the script of the earliest inscriptions of the area in the light of our present knowledge. As the use of writing is, more than any other single factor, characteristic of true history as opposed to the prehistoric and protohistoric age and is often regarded as the chief feature that distinguishes the historical period from earlier ages, there can be little doubt that an analysis of the earliest writing in South East Asia may contribute to a proper understanding of the beginnings of history in the area.

The survey which follows is divided into four sections. After a brief discussion of the earliest examples of writing in the area there follow two sections on the early and later 'Pallava' script and, finally, by way of comparison, a discussion of the early 'Nāgarī' type scripts in South East Asia.

The Earliest Scripts

The earliest examples of writing in South East Asia are a number of brief inscriptions on seals, entaglios, rings, and similar precious objects discovered at the ancient site of Oc-Eo, not far from Rach-gia near the west coast of the Ca-mao peninsula in southern Viet-Nam. As Oc-Eo was an important trading centre and most of the objects discovered there originate from elsewhere, often from the Indian subcontinent, there is no proof that the seals etc. were actually inscribed in South East Asia. For this reason it would not be justified to describe this script as South East Asian. On the other hand, the presence in South East Asia of these inscriptions must have a bearing on the history of writing in the area so that they cannot be ignored.[11]

All the known specimens show different examples of Indian *brāhmi* script datable, on the basis of a comparison with dated inscriptions in India, to the period from the second to the fifth century A.D. The earliest specimens are in a script that is strongly reminiscent of that of the Kuṣāṇa inscriptions of Kaniṣka and his successors, i.e. probably the last quarter of the first, and the second century A.D., while the apparently latest inscriptions are in a script which is very similar to the Gupta script of northern India. As regional differences were not yet clearly pronounced in India in the earlier part of this period it is not possible to relate the Oc-Eo script to any definite part of the subcontinent. Only for the samples in Gupta script it can be stated that they show some affinity with the Deccani style as represented e.g. by the Basim copper-plate inscription of Vindhyāśakti II (fourth century A.D.?) and the Rithpur copper-plate inscription of Prabhāvatī Guptā (middle fifth century A.D.).[12]

The earliest inscription of some length in South East Asia, the inscription of Vo-canh in the Nha-trang district of Viet-Nam, has been palaeographically analysed with great detail.[13] It can probably be dated back to the third century A.D. Despite some minor differences the script of the Vo-canh inscription shows the closest affinity with that of the inscriptions of the Ikṣvākus of Andhra Pradesh datable to the third century A.D.[14]

Early 'Pallava' Script

Apart from the Oc-Eo and Vo-canh inscriptions the other epigraphic texts in South East Asia before the middle of the eighth century are written in a script called 'Pallava' on account of its general similarity with the script used in the inscriptions of the Pallavas of Kāñcī. The name 'Pallava' has generally been applied to the script of these South East Asian inscriptions since Vogel's masterly study of the Kutai inscriptions published in 1918.[15] The use of this term has further been strengthened by an important study by B. Ch. Chhabra, *Expansion of Indo-Aryan Culture During Pallava Rule.*[16]

It has to be admitted that there is little *direct* evidence linking the Pallavas with the early inscriptions of South East Asia. In fact, the only inscription giving a direct reference to a Pallava ruler is the Takuapa inscription in southern Thailand, dated in the reign of the Pallava king Nandivarman III (*c.* 844–866).[17] The inscription, which is in the ancient Tamil language, is not written in Pallava *grantha*, the script used by the Pallavas in their Prakrit and Sanskrit inscriptions, but in early Tamil script. In addition, it belongs to a slightly later period, when 'Pallava' script had, in Java, already developed into 'Kawi' or 'Old Javanese' script. Whatever its interest for other aspects of South East Asian history (notably the evidence it supplies for the activities of a Tamil mercantile corporation) the Takuapa inscription cannot be used as evidence for Pallava influence in a period some four centuries earlier. It is, however, of considerable interest for quite a different reason. In contrast to

Pallava *grantha*, which was essentially a monumental script used to express pan-Indian languages such as Sanskrit and Prakrit, Tamil script was an everyday script confined to expressing the Tamil language. As these two kinds of writing could co-exist one may understand how the everyday script could occasionally be used for monumental purposes (thus, in an only slightly adapted form in the Takuapa inscription), whereas the *grantha* could occasionally be adapted to a cursive style of writing (thus, for instance, in the Mayidavolu copper-plate inscription of Śivaskandavarman).[18] The possibility of the co-existence of different styles of writing in the same period and in the same area has always to be taken into consideration.[19] But apart from emphasizing the complexity of the problems of palaeography the Takuapa inscription does not directly contribute to the understanding of the relationship between the early Pallavas of India and the early inscriptions of South East Asia.

In the absence of direct evidence for a particularly close relationship of this kind scholars have emphasized some arguments of indirect bearing on the problem. The most remarkable of these is the fact that there appears to be a chronological concordance between the inscriptions in 'Pallava' script in South East Asia and Pallava rule in south India. The earliest inscriptions in South East Asia (apart from the Oc-Eo and Vo-canh inscriptions) apparently date back to the end of the fourth or the early part of the fifth century A.D.,[20] which is just about the time when the Pallavas obtain control of Kāñcī and Toṇḍaimaṇḍalam. At the other end, the use of 'Pallava' script in South East Asia continues till about the middle or second half of the eighth century. The Plumpungan (Hampran) stone inscription of 750 and the Dinoyo stone inscription of 760 are the oldest known examples of texts written in so-called Kawi or Old Javanese script,[21] but 'Pallava' script still continued to be used in some areas in the second half of the eighth century, as appears from the 'Ligor' inscription of 775.[22]

Although there is a large measure of chronological concordance between the inscriptions in 'Pallava' script in South East Asia and the Pallava empire in south India, it should be emphasized that this concordance is by no means precise. Thus, the Pallavas continued to rule in south India as a major power till more than a century after the date of the Ligor inscription, in fact till *c.* 886, when the Pallava kingdom was annexed by the Cōḷas. It is true that their political power had somewhat declined from the middle of the eighth century, partly owing to mainly unsuccessful wars with the Rāṣṭrakūṭas of Mānyakheṭa, but this does not seem to have affected overseas activities, as appears from the Takuapa inscription.

There are also difficulties concerning the concordance between the beginnings of the Pallava empire and the earliest inscriptions of South East Asia, but these are not insuperable. Thus, we possess only copper-plate inscriptions of the early Pallava kings, but, on the contrary, only stone inscriptions of the early South East Asian kings (the earliest known copper-plate inscription of Java is dated A.D. 819).[23] Many of the Pallava inscriptions of the fourth and fifth century are written in a cursive style, as e.g. the above-mentioned Mayidavolu copper-plate inscription of Śivaskandavarman. Those that are written in a more ornate style of writing, such as the Mangalur grant, the Uruvapalli grant, and the Vilavatti grant, show a type of script which, though quite similar to the types found in the fifth-century inscriptions of South East Asia, differs from any of the latter in some important details. It is curious that some of the most striking similarities between South and South East Asian 'Pallava' are with some inscriptions in 'Pallava' script in Ceylon, as will appear from a comparison between the script of the Ruvanvälisäya Pillar Inscription of Buddhadāsa (A.D. 337–365) and the Tugu Rock Inscription of Pūrṇavarman. In both cases we find the same notched serifs, which are relatively uncommon, and also a broadening of the horizontal lines, which tend to become wavy at the base. Yet, even in this case the scripts are, despite their striking similarity, by no means identical; thus, the Ruvanvälisäya inscription has a curious *sa* in which the right-hand vertical does not rise to normal *akṣara* height.[24]

In this connection it should be emphasized that the views of scholars in this respect have been influenced by considerations other than purely palaeographic arguments. Thus, it has been pointed out that most of the early kings in South East Asia bore names ending in *-varman*, just as the Pallava kings did. Although this is correct it can hardly be regarded as a strong argument, as there were other dynasties in different parts of the Indian subcontinent in which the kings also had *-varman* names. Some examples are the kings of Daśapura (Mandasore), the Kadambas of Kuntala (northern Mysore), the Viṣṇukuṇḍins of Andhra Pradesh, and the kings of Kāmarūpa (Assam), and this list is not exhaustive. The prevalence of Śaivism both in the Pallava kingdom and in the early kingdoms of South East Asia does not necessarily constitute a valid argument, even if it is correct,[25] for Śaivism flourished in many other parts of India as well.

The arguments based on the history of art and architecture are of a subtle nature. The relations between the earliest art of South East Asia and Indian art are indeed most complicated. In a recent study of this relationship with reference to early Khmer art Mireille Bénisti concluded:

Si de nombreuses liaisons existent, certaines formant même des faisceaux privilégiés, ne se constate aucune transmission d'un *ensemble cohérent* de l'Inde en pays khmer. Quel que soit le niveau chronologique envisagé, jusqu'aux plus voisins du premier art khmer, aucun monument, aucune région, aucun style indien n'apporte le modèle, l'archétype du décor khmer. Il n'apparait pas qu'il y ait eu contiguité entre plastique khmère et plastique indienne. C'est dire que les exécutants qui élèverent et decorèrent les monuments religieux khmers ne devaient être, au moins de façon normale, ni des Indiens déplacés (temporairement ou définitivement) en pays khmer, ni des khmers qui seraient allés prendre une connaissance technique, et exacte, des monuments indiens.[26]

This conclusion, based on a detailed and convincing analysis of early Khmer art in comparison with the art of different parts of the Indian subcontinent, would give little support to any attempts at explaining the earliest scripts of South East Asia (after the Oc-Eo and Vo-canh inscriptions) as mere overseas branches of south Indian Pallava script.

On the other hand, we should be careful to avoid the other extreme, viz. that of underrating Pallava influence on the early South East Asian scripts for, as has been noted earlier, it would be impossible to ignore the general similarity both between the early South East Asian scripts themselves (at least before about the middle of the seventh century) and between these and the Pallava script of south India and (particularly?) Ceylon. Pallava script constitutes, in the precise terminology of Mireille Bénisti, a 'faisceau privilégié' to which other influences were grafted or added. The precise provenance of such influences is in many cases difficult to determine, but it may in a few instances be possible to suggest a possible place of origin. Thus, one peculiar feature of the script of the Kutai inscriptions of Mūlavarman, which generally corresponds fairly closely to the 'Pallava' type, is the curious method of expressing -*i* and -*ī* (i.e. medial short and long *i*). The former is expressed by an elegant curve, rising from the top of the *akṣaras* (or, in the case of wide *akṣaras*, from the right-hand part of the top line). The curve first rises straight ahead before bending to the left and terminating just above the left-hand end of the top line. As to -*ī*, this medial vowel is expressed by adding to the shape of the -*i* a smaller curve which rises from the left-hand end of the top line and bends to the right. These shapes of the -*i* and -*ī* are not, as far as known to me, attested in Pallava inscriptions but can be traced back to the inscriptions of the Īkṣvākus of Andhra Pradesh, in particular to the Nāgārjunakoṇḍa inscriptions of king Vīrapurisadatta, datable to the second half of the third century A.D.[27] Similar forms of the -*i* and -*ī* can also be seen in the Cho-dinh inscription of Bhadravarman, who can with some confidence be dated back to the end of the fourth century A.D.[28] The Ruvanvälisäya inscription of Buddhadāsa gives few examples of -*i* but these seem quite similar again, although the curves are much flatter than those of the Kutai inscriptions. In the contemporary Pallava inscriptions,[29] however, such as the Pīkira, Vilavatti and Uruvapalli grants of Siṃhavarman, the -*i* has its later form, viz. a little full circle on top of the *akṣara*, while the -*ī* is expressed as a small spiral turning clockwise. These forms, though not encountered in the Kutai inscriptions, became the normal

medial *i*s in the other, undoubtedly somewhat later, 'Pallava' inscriptions of
South East Asia, such as the Tārumā inscriptions of King Pūrṇavarman.

Until now no exact prototype of the script of the Kutai inscriptions has
been found in South Asia, and the same negative conclusion has to be drawn
with reference to the script of the other known early 'Pallava' inscriptions of
South East Asia. If one considers the large number of Pallava inscriptions, as
well as those of the contemporaries of the Pallavas, in South Asia datable to
the fourth and fifth centuries it is unlikely that the absence of precise prototypes is due to chance. I am therefore convinced that the views of Mireille
Bénisti would provide us with a satisfactory interpretation of the available
evidence.

As to the next problem, that of deciding how such different influences could
have come to South East Asia Mireille Bénisti considers three possibilities.
She excludes (at least as the normal course) the possibility of Indians transferring their activities, either on a temporary or on a permanent basis, to
South East Asia. On the other hand, she is also not convinced by the well
known and attractive theory of F. D. K. Bosch, who attributed the spread of
Indian ideas, motifs, and techniques to the activities of learned or skilled
South East Asian pilgrims who worked under the guidance of Indian *gurus* in
different parts of the Indian subcontinent and Ceylon, and subsequently
applied their newly-acquired skills and knowledge to the needs of the home
countries after their return.[30] Instead, she opts for a third possibility:

> L'hypothèse alors qui a pris consistance au fur et à mesure que nous
> poursuivions nos recherches et avancions dans nos analyses et com-
> paraisons, jusqu'à s'imposer enfin à notre esprit comme la plus plausible,
> est que les liens, indubitables mais disparates, qu'atteste la decoration
> des premiers monuments du premier art khmer, ont dû être indirects,
> discontinus, resultant non de contacts directs avec les édifices indiens,
> mais de l'importation d'objets mobiles indiens, décorés, pouvant être
> d'origine et de dates diverses.[31]

This interesting hypothesis, which can in some respects be seen as a renewal
of an old theory of F. D. K. Bosch (but later abandoned by him),[32] is subsequently tested by three different criteria, including especially the need to
demonstrate the possibility of the presence in South East Asia of the kind of
'objets mobiles', which constitute an essential link in the line of arguments. I
am convinced that Mireille Bénisti has fully succeeded in this demonstration,
mainly on the basis of the large number of decorated objects of all kinds which
have come to light in the Oc-Eo excavations. It would be interesting to
examine how far this last part of the hypothesis can be applied also to the
script. Here, however, there arises a serious difficulty in that, except for the
short inscriptions on rings etc., found at Oc-Eo, many of which may well have

been imported from India, and the Tamil inscription of Takuapa, no Indian inscriptions of the period under discussion have been found in South East Asia. Moreover, the script of the South East Asian inscriptions in 'Pallava' seems to bear no direct relationship to that of the Oc-Eo objects. As to the Takuapa Tamil inscription, this is written in a type of Tamil script which has, as far as is known, never been adapted to the needs of Indonesian or other South East Asian languages. Its use was confined to some groups of Tamil traders or settlers.[33] In addition, the hypothesis of Mireille Bénisti cannot well account for some remarkable agreements between a few among the different known 'Pallava' scripts outside India, such as that existing between e.g. the Ruvanvälisäya inscription in Ceylon, the Bukit Meriam stone inscription of *mahānāvika* Buddhagupta and the Tugu stone inscription of Pūrṇavarman.[34] Such agreements, which are never complete but nonetheless quite striking, would be consistent with Bosch' hypothesis if one assumes that the inscriptions concerned were written by scribes (or their pupils) who had worked under the same *guru* or in the same *āśrama*.[35] It is, of course, not impossible that the scribes responsible for these three inscriptions should have imitated the same Indian example (or different examples in almost the same script), but this would seem a rather unlikely coincidence, especially if one considers the numerous varieties of writing reflected in e.g. the different Oc-Eo samples. For these two reasons, especially the first, it would seem that, in general, the (second) hypothesis of Bosch offers a more satisfactory explanation than that of Mireille Bénisti. It should, however, be added that the two interpretations are not mutually exclusive, and in both cases the South East Asian scribes would have adapted the written shapes to their own requirements and aesthetic standards.

Later Pallava Script

It is not intended to present a full discussion of the later developments (i.e. after the fifth century) of 'Pallava' script in South East Asia, but attention may be drawn to one interesting aspect of its subsequent history. One may note a number of parallel or even identical developments in different parts of South East Asia, which in some cases also extend to south India and Ceylon. One striking detail is a curious form of the *akṣara la*, in which the rising vertical on the right-hand side is not terminated at the top but runs anti-clockwise around the remainder of the letter before terminating just in front of the letter. The result is a nearly elliptical shape. This *la* is found all over the area under consideration. Some typical examples are the Bangkok Museum Stone Inscription of Mahendravarman and, in Java, the Tuk Mas Rock Inscription.[36] In South East Asia this shape is merely a transitional phase leading everywhere to a tripartite form which can be described as an ascending, a descending, and again an ascending stroke. In south India and Ceylon, on the other hand, the 'elliptical' *la* has remained in use for centuries later, and the modern form of the *la* in Sinhalese script[37] is clearly derived from the *la* as found in the inscriptions all over the area at the end of the sixth and all through the seventh century A.D.

Such parallel developments are by no means limited to the *la*, but are hardly less pronounced for e.g. the *na* and the *ṇa*. The *na*, which in early Pallava script is similar to, not rarely hardly distinguishable from, the *ta*, has its loop flattened till it becomes quite small or even disappears (whereas the loop of the *ta* continues to grow). As to the *ṇa*, this letter everywhere develops into a quadripartite form, which can most conveniently be described as a *la* to which a fourth, descending, stroke has been added.

These parallel developments seem to come to a close by the end or in the second half of the eighth century, when the scripts begin to diverge and adopt separate regional forms. While this parallelism lasted, however, it was most striking and cannot be adequately explained as a mere coincidence. It strongly suggests the existence of some forms of contact between scribes in different parts of this vast area. At the present state of our knowledge of inter-state relations in South East Asia, as well as between South and South East Asia, it would be imprudent to suggest anything more than tentative explanations about the kinds of contact existing between scribes in South and South East Asia. Here again the theories of both Bosch and Mireille Bénisti may offer some clues. If scribes, like medieval clerks in the West, travelled about to centres of pilgrimage and monasteries or places of learning they would naturally come into contact with each other, learn from each other and from the teachers under whom they may have worked. Such an interpretation presupposes, however, a degree of mobility which is not impossible but cannot be assumed without further evidence. Perhaps the strongest argument in support of this interpretation is the continuous *va-et-vient* of scholars in seventh-century Śrīvijaya, as can be inferred from the accounts of I-tsing and others. On the other hand, inscribed objects and especially manuscripts, must have circulated in many important cultural centres of South East Asia. Not only Śrīvijaya, but also Ho-ling, probably identifiable with central Java,[38] was a centre where Buddhist Sanskrit texts were translated into Chinese.[39] In addition, the reliefs of Borobuḍur establish beyond doubt that texts such as the *Mahākarmavibhaṅga*, the *Lalitavistara*, and the *Gaṇḍavyūha* were known and studied in Java and must therefore have been available in copies of Indian manuscripts.[40] Like the script of other mobile objects that of manuscripts, especially those read by scholars from different areas in the great cultural centres, must have influenced the style of writing of local scribes. It could therefore have been a significant factor in certain innovations in writing over vast areas.

Early 'Nāgarī' Scripts in South East Asia

Finally, it may be of some interest to examine briefly another group of inscriptions which, though considerably later than those hitherto discussed, may throw light on some of the problems considered in the previous section. Here again one strongly feels the need for a comprehensive and detailed study which may well bring to light unsuspected data on relations between South East Asia and South Asia, as well as those between the different cultural centres in South East Asia themselves. In this context it is only possible to call attention to some of the problems.

As to the term Nāgarī, I am following Sivaramamurti and others in using this designation for the later types of *brāhmī* script which developed in northern India from about the seventh century A.D., in the inscriptions of the Pratihāras, Pālas, and other dynasties. Sivaramamurti has shown, more clearly than any scholars before him, how Nāgarī-type scripts expanded into the Deccan and south India, where they rarely replaced but often supplemented the local or regional scripts.[41] Only a detailed comparative study, which has never yet been undertaken, may reveal whether this is a kind of north Indian cultural influence limited to script (i.e. due to the migration or the mobility of scribes) or one that has important implications for other aspects of civilization. This expansion is not, however, limited to the Indian subcontinent but extends also to Ceylon,[42] and to parts of South East Asia. There is, however, one important difference in that the spread of Nāgarī in South East Asia, in contrast to what can be seen in India, is in most cases closely associated with Buddhism, especially in its Mahāyāna form. There are, however, some interesting exceptions, notably some inscriptions of Yaśovarman in Angkor, Cambodia,[43] and, in Indonesia, part of the Sanur inscription (Bali), probably dated A.D. 914 in the reign of Ugrasena.[44] All the other Nāgarī inscriptions are Buddhist. They comprise numerous short inscriptions on clay seals and on the pedestals of Buddhist images, as well as a group of four large stone inscriptions from central Java, dated in the last quarter of the eighth century. There are also some later (thirteenth- and fourteenth-century) Nāgarī inscriptions but these are not relevant to the present discussion.

The script of the four large stone inscriptions from central Java has been fully discussed by F. D. K. Bosch.[45] The script of these four inscriptions is closely related but not identical. That of the inscription of Kalasan (A.D. 778) and of that of Ratubaka (792) are nearly identical, whereas that of the inscriptions of Kelurak (782) and Plaosan (undated but clearly contemporary) differs considerably from the two others. Bosch has made a very detailed comparison between these two types and the script of more or less contemporary inscriptions of India. He concluded that the Javanese Nāgarī showed a close affinity with the script of the early Pāla inscriptions of Bengal and Bihar. The mention in one of the inscriptions of a *guru* from Bengal,[46] the evidence for close cultural relations between the Pālas and Indonesia in the Nālandā inscription of the thirty-ninth regnal year of Devapāla,[47] as well as the unmistakable influence of Nālandā on the Buddhist bronzes of central Java give strong support to the conclusion drawn for the script. Yet, Bosch also emphasized that, despite the similarity, it proved impossible to pinpoint precise prototypes for either of the two kinds of early Nāgarī found in Java. He also called attention to the curious phenomenon that one can find in Java a few examples of forms of *akṣaras* which seem to be 'in advance' of developments in Indian Nāgarī, viz. features found in the script of the eighth-century Javanese inscriptions which do not appear in India until considerably later. Although, theoretically, this could be taken to mean that the Indian scripts showing such innovations were influenced by South East Asia, this seems unlikely as it would go against the stream. The probable explanation, as suggested by Bosch,[48] is that early Javanese Nāgarī was not derived from one of the monumental styles of writing in India but was adapted from Nāgarī types used in Indian manuscripts. It is at the present state of knowledge impossible to decide whether it was adapted *directly* from Indian manuscripts or, as may seem slightly more likely, from Buddhist manuscripts copied from Indian manuscripts by Javanese scribes. There may even have been more intermediate stages, for the actual historical process was undoubtedly, as in the case of other cultural influences, much more complicated than would appear at first. But whatever the precise nature of the process, there can be little doubt that the special features of the Nāgarī script in central Java in approximately the last quarter of the eighth century can be satisfactorily explained by assuming that the Javanese scribes adapted the Nāgarī script, which they had studied from manuscripts (or other mobile objects), to their own requirements and aesthetic standards, either by introducing innovations or, more often, by choosing between different styles and variants. The special features of the Nāgarī script in the inscriptions of Yaśovarman in Cambodia could be satisfactorily explained by the same assumption. This script again agrees in most respects with that of the contemporary inscriptions of India and Ceylon, from which it differs, however, in some details, especially the regular use of typical headmarks consisting of two little curves bending right and left respectively. This detail, also found in 'normal' Khmer writing of that period, lends this script its typical local colour.

Conclusions

The above analysis of some aspects of the palaeography of the earliest inscriptions of South East Asia, which mark the threshold of a period rich in achievements of many kinds, clearly confirms the views of those modern scholars who have argued, from different angles, that the beginnings of higher and literate civilizations in the past can be satisfactorily explained only if one assumes that they came about as a result of conscious efforts by élites in different parts of South East Asia. Such élites, far from blindly imitating the cultures with which they became acquainted, in actual fact mainly those of India and Ceylon, consciously selected those elements of culture which could be expected to enrich their own cultures. Their activity was not, however, limited to selection but also included a process of adaptation which gradually transformed elements of foreign origin into integral parts of South East Asian cultures. This process is clearly illustrated by the early South East Asian scripts which, for this reason, deserve greater attention than they have enjoyed in the past.

NOTES

1. K. F. Holle, *Tabel van Oud- en Nieuw-Indische Alphabetten*, 1882 (the tables were actually printed in 1877).

2. The numerous contributions of H. Kern can be most easily consulted in Volume VIII of his *Verspreide Geschriften*, 1917, pp. 1–226. The articles were originally published between 1877 and 1815. The inscriptions are illustrated not by photographs but by facsimiles, which are not always reliable. Most of Brandes' work on inscriptions was not published during his lifetime. The transcriptions were posthumously edited by N. J. Krom as *Oud-Javaansche Oorkonden, Verh. Bat. Gen.*, lx, 1916. The transcriptions are preceded by brief introductions which normally include some observations concerning the palaeography of the text under consideration. There are, in addition, fourteen excellent illustrations of inscriptions (or parts of inscriptions), based on photographs of either the originals (mostly copper plates) or the estampages (mostly stone inscriptions).

3. In particular J. Ph. Vogel, N. J. Krom, F. D. K. Bosch, W. F. Stutterheim, G. Coedès, and R. Ng. Poerbatjaraka gave much attention to the particular features of the script of the inscriptions they published, in some cases amounting to detailed analyses. L.-C. Damais, in addition, composed a brief, but most interesting, survey with tables illustrating the evolution of five *apsaras* in 'Les écritures d'origine indienne en Indonésie et dans le Sud-Est Asiatique continental', *Bull. Et. Indoch.*, N.S., xxx, 1955, pp. 365–82. For the Early Nāgarī script of Java see F. D. K. Bosch, 'De inscriptie van Kěloerak', *Tijdschr. Bat. Gen.*, lxviii, 1928, pp. 1–64, four plates.

5. Th. Pigeaud, *Literature of Java*, iii, 1970.

5. M. A. Jaspan, *Redjang Ka-ga-nga Texts, Folk Literature of South Sumatra*, 1964.

6. Antoon Postma, S.V.D., 'Contemporary Mangyan Scripts', *Phil. Journ. Lingu.*, 1972, pp. 1–12; *Treasure of a Minority*, 1972.

7. Juan Francisco, 'Philippine Palaeography', *Phil. Journ. Lingu.*, Special Monograph Issue, No. 3, 1973.

8. J. L. A. Brandes, *Pararaton (Ken Arok), of het Boek der Koningen van Tumapel en van Majapahit*, 2nd edn by N. J. Krom with collaboration of J. C. G. Jonker, H. Kraemer, and R. Ng. Poerbatjaraka, *Verh. Bat. Gen.*, lxii, 1920, pp. 112–17. C.f. N. J. Krom, *Hindoe-Javaansche Geschiedenis*, 2nd edn, 1932, pp. 221–4.

9. Especially J. Ph. Vogel, 'The *yūpa* inscriptions of king Mūlavarman from Koetei (East Borneo)', *Bijdr. Kon. Inst.*, lxxiv, 1918, pp. 167–232, pls I–III; J. Ph. Vogel, The Earliest Sanskrit Inscriptions of Java', *Publ. Oudh. Dienst*, i, 1925, pp. 13–35, pls 27–35; B. Ch. Chhabra, *Expansion of Indo–Aryan Culture during Pallava Rule*, 2nd edn, 1965.

10. For the Indian subcontinent two works deserve special mention, viz. C. Sivaramamurti, 'Indian Epigraphy and South Indian Scripts', *Bull. Madras Mus.*,

N.S., G.S. iv, 1952; and A. H. Dani, *Indian Palaeography*, 1963. For Campa cf. R. C. Majumdar, 'La paléographie des inscriptions du Champa', *BEFEO*, xxxiii, 1932, pp. 127–39, and K. A. Nilakanta Sastri, 'L'origine de l'alphabet du Champa', *BEFEO*, xxxv, 1935, pp. 233–41.

11. For a full discussion cf. L. Malleret, 'L'Archéologie du Delta du Mekong. III. La Culture du Founan.', *Publ.EFEO*, xliii, 1962; 'Aperçu de la glyptique d'Oc-eo', *BEFEO*, xliv, 1963, pp. 189–99.

12. For the former cf. the photographs published by D. C. Sircar, *Select Inscriptions*, 2nd edn, pls LII–LIV; for the latter J. F. Fleet, *Corpus Inscr. Indic.*, iii, 1889, pp. 236 ff.

13. E. Gaspardone, 'La plus ancienne inscription de l'Indochine', *Journ. Asiat.*, 1953, pp. 477 ff.; Kamaleshwar Bhattacharya, 'Précisions sur la paléographie de l'inscription dite de Vô-cạnh', *Art. As.*, xxiv 3/4, 1961, pp. 219–24; J. Filliozat, 'L'Inscription dite "de Vô-cạnh" ', *BEFEO*, lv, 1969, pp. 107–16; pls VII–XI; Claude Jacques, 'Notes sur la Stèle de Vo-cạnh', ibid., pp. 117–24.

14. In other respects, however, the script of the Vo-canh inscriptions seems more closely related to that of Rudradāman's Girnar inscription of A.D. 150. No real prototype of the Vo-canh inscription (as is, as will be shown, the case with almost all other South East Asian inscriptions) has yet been found. The most accurate description is that by J. Filliozat, quoted in n. 13 above.

15. J. Ph. Vogel, 'The *yūpa* inscriptions of king Mūlavarman from Koetei (East Borneo)', *Bijdr. Kon. Inst.*, lxxiv, 1918, pp. 167 ff.

16. This important work does not, however, include any detailed discussion of Pallava script, either in or outside India, but calls attention to a number of other features of the Pallava empire, some of which provide a proper background to the cultural expansion which is the principal concern of the work.

17. K. A. Nilakanta Sastri, 'Takuapa and its Tamil Inscription', *Journ. Mal. Br. R.A.S.*, xxii, 1, 1949, pp. 25–30; Alastair Lamb, 'Miscellaneous Papers on Early Hindu and Buddhist Settlements', *Fed. Mus. Journ.*, N.S., vi, 1961, p. 67.

18. E. Hultzsch, *Epigr. Ind.*, vi, 1898, pp. 86 ff.; D. C. Sircar, *Select Inscriptions*, 2nd edn, 1965, pp. 457–61, pls LV–LIX.

19. Some characteristic examples illustrating the use of different types of script in the same period and in the same area can be seen in the Mamallapuram inscriptions of the time of Mahendravarman; there are examples of four different ornate types of writing, in addition to plainer forms of Pallava script, both of monumental and of cursive types, and occasionally (in contemporary inscriptions) even Nāgarī script, can be seen. In the Kaḍiri period in Java (*c*. A.D. 1100–1222) there was, besides the elegant type of script used in the large stone inscriptions, also a highly sophisticated script in use: the so-called Kaḍiri Quadrate Script (with all letters transformed into a kind of decorated square), mainly found in brief inscriptions on temples, in caves, etc. For other examples cf. also *infra* n. 43 and 44.

20. In particular the Kutai and Tārumā inscriptions, the dating of which is, however, based exclusively on palaeographic grounds. For these cf. the publications mentioned in n. 9 above.

21. J. G. de Casparis, *Prasasti Indonesia*, i, 1950, No. I, pp. 1–4; L.-C. Damais, *BEFEO*, xlvi, Fasc. 1, 1952, n. 5 to pp. 20 f.

22. G. Coedès, 'Le Royaume de Crivijaya', *BEFEO*, xviii, 1918, pp. 1–36, pl. II.

23. The Pĕngging Copper-Plate Inscription from Central Java, first published by Goris, *Oudh. Versl.*, 1928, p. 65, who read the date, however, as (Saka) 751. I now agree, however, with Damais' reading of 741 (op. cit., n. 1 to p. 26).

24. Chhabra, op. cit., pl. 1, fig. 2. Another curious letter is the *ha*, in which the second, rising, vertical bends to the right well below the top line, while the third, descending, vertical is not yet fully developed.

25. Apart from the name Vaprakeśvara, hardly a strong argument by itself, there is no clear suggestion of Śaivism in the Kutai inscriptions. The emphasis is clearly on the

more traditional type of Brahmanism. There is also no indication of Śaivism in the Tārumā inscriptions, rather a hint (if no more) of Vaiṣṇavism (the king's footprints are compared to Viṣṇu's). The fifth-century Kĕdah inscriptions are Buddhist.

26. Mireille Bénisti, 'Rapports entre le premier Art Khmer et l'Art Indien', *Publ. E.F.E.O., Mem. Arch.*, v, 1970, p. 101.

27. D. C. Sircar, *Select Inscriptions*, 2nd edn, pl. xxxix, l. 9 (*digha*).

28. J. Boisselier, 'La Statuaire du Champa', *Publ. EFEO*, liv, 1963, p. 18. The date is partly based on the identification of the king mentioned in the inscription (Bhadravarman) with Fan Fo of the Chinese Annals; cf. G. Coedès, *Etats Hindouisés*, 3rd edn, 1964, pp. 94 f.

29. The details of the script of these Pallava inscriptions can most easily be studied from Sivaramamurti's work mentioned in n. 10 above, in particular figs. 104 and 105 (pp. 200 ff.), where further references are given.

30. F. D. K. Bosch, 'The problem of Hindu colonisation of Indonesia', *Selected Studies in Indonesian Archaeology*, 1961, pp. 3–22.

31. Mireille Bénisti, op. cit., p. 101.

32. F. D. K. Bosch, 'Een hypothese omtrent den oorsprong der Hindoe-Javaansche Kunst', *Hand. Eerste Congr. T.L. & V. van Java*, 1919.

33. Apart from the Takuapa inscription we have a Tamil inscription from the Vat Mahath'at at Nakhon Sri Thammarat (tenth or eleventh century A.D.; cf. G. Coedès, *Recueil des Inscriptions du Siam*, ii, 2nd edn, 1961, pp. 49 and 57), one from Lobo's Tua, Barus, Tapanuli, North Sumatra, dated 1088 (cf. K. A. Nilakanta Sastri, 'A Tamil Merchant Guild in Sumatra', *Tijdschr. Bat. Gen.*, lxxii, 1932, pp. 314–29). one from Batu Bapahat near Suroaso, Batusangkar, Sumatra Tengah (not yet read but found by the side of an inscription of Ādityavarman of the middle or latter half of the fourteenth century) and one at Pagan of probably the thirteenth century (cf. E. Hultzsch, 'A Tamil Inscription from Myinkaba, Pagan', *Epigr. Ind.*, vii, 1902, pp. 197 f., and Gordon H. Luce, *Old Burma, Early Pagan*, i, 1969, pp. 218 f.). All the Tamil inscriptions of South East Asia that have been read are concerned with activities of South Indian mercantile guilds.

34. This is especially striking for the two last mentioned inscriptions, the script of which does not show any difference of substance.

35. It is true that the Bukit Mĕriam inscription of *mahānāvika* Buddhagupta is Buddhist, whereas the Tugu inscription of Pūrṇavarman is Hindu, perhaps Vaiṣṇava, but these details may not have any direct bearing on the religious affiliations of the scribes responsible for the drafting of the inscriptions. In any case, this would not necessarily militate against the assumption that their respective scribes—or their teachers—could have learnt the script in the same *āsrama*, or in *āsramas* following the same tradition of writing.

36. Cf. B. Ch. Chhabra, op. cit., pl. 19, and *Journ. Siam Soc.*, xlix, 2, 1961, p. 119; G. Coedès, *Inscriptions du Cambodge*, vii, 1964, p. 152. The inscription originates from Khau Sra Cheng, Ta P'raya, Aranyaprat'et, Thailand. For the Tuk Mas inscription, no photograph of which has been published, cf. the facsimile in H. Kern, *Verspreide Geschriften*, vi, 1917, pp. 119–204 (original article of 1911). Excellent photographs are available in the office of the Archaeological Institute (Lembaga Purbakala dan Peninggalan Lama) at Jakarta, Indonesia, as well as at the Kern Institute, Leiden.

37. This modern form of the *la* was already fully developed in or before the ninth century A.D. and underwent little change from that time.

38. L.-C. Damais, 'Etudes Sino-Indonésiennes', iii. La transcription chinoise Ho-ling comme désignation de Java', *BEFEO*, lii, Fasc. 1, 1964, pp. 93–141; Yutaka Iwamoto, 'On the Ho'ling kingdom', *IATR, Proc. of the 1st Conf. Sem.*, i, 1966, pp. 58–66.

39. E. Chavannes, *Mémoire composé a l'époque de la grande dynastie T'ang*, 1894, pp. 60–2; cf. also N. J. Krom, *Hindoe-Javaansche Geschiedenis*, 2nd edn, 1931, pp. 107–110.

40. It is, of course, not impossible that such texts had already at this very early time been translated into Old Javanese (or Old Malay), but there is no evidence to support such a contention.

41. C. Sivaramamurti, 'Indian Epigraphy and South Indian Scripts', *Bull. Madn'. Mus.*, N.S., G.S. iv, 1952, pp. 185–93.

42. Cf., for instance, the Jetavanārāma Inscription, edited by M. de Z. Wickrema-singhe, *Epigr. Zeyl.*, i, 1904–12, No. 1, pp. 1–9, pl. 1, who dates the inscription back to the first half of the ninth century. The script, though not very different from that of the Kalasan and Ratubaka inscriptions of Java (with which it has the pronounced nail-heads in common), is, however, clearly later than the Javanese inscriptions. It shows a clear *kutila* style with the long verticals bending to the right. The Abhayagiri Copper-Plate Inscription (ibid., No. 3, pp. 39 f., pl. II) shows a more rounded style with sometimes (e.g. in *ta*) hollow triangular head marks. The letters are also less elongated. Its script is, on the whole more similar to that of the (Nāgarī part of the) Sanur inscription of 914 (cf. n. 44 below) than to that of the Śailendra inscriptions. Wickremasinghe's dating in the latter half of the tenth century therefore seems quite plausible to me.

43. An interesting type of Nāgarī is used in a dozen digraphic Sanskrit inscriptions, all giving the same text in both Early Nāgarī and Early Khmer script, dealing with the foundation by Yaśovarman (c. 889–900) of hermitages all named Yaśodharāsrama. Cf. G. Coedès, 'Etudes Cambodgiennes, XXX.—A la recherche du Yaśodharāsrama', *BEFEO*, xxxii, 1932, pp. 84–112, and the excellent illustrations in Album IV of the *Inscriptions du Cambodge publiés sous les auspices de l'Académie des Inscriptions et Belles-Lettres*, 1928. This Cambodian Nāgarī, though essentially quite similar to the script of the eighth-century Javanese inscriptions, shows some peculiar stylistic features, notably the characteristical notched head marks. These are not found in this form in Indian Nāgarī, as far as known to me, but are actually identical with the head marks of the contemporary Khmer script. It is this feature, as well as the elongated style of the letters, that gives this Nāgarī writing its striking similarity with Khmer script, at least if seen from a distance. This may well suggest that the Nāgarī was written by scribes used to Khmer script.

44. W. F. Stutterheim, 'A Newly Discovered Pre-Nāgarī Inscription of Bali', *Acta Orientalia*, xii, 1924, pp. 126–32, 2 plates. The inscription, as a whole is, like the Yaśodharāśrama inscriptions, digraphic but, contrary to what might have been ex-pected, the Nāgarī part is in Old Balinese language, while the part written in Old Balinese script is partly in Sanskrit and partly in the Old Balinese language.

45. F. D. K. Bosch, 'De inscriptie van Kĕloerak', *Tijdschr. Bat. Gen.*, lxviii, 1928, pp. 1–64, pls I–IV. For a more recently discovered fragment of the Ratubaka inscription see J. G. de Casparis, 'New Evidence on Cultural Relations between Java and Ceylon in Ancient Times', *Art. Asiae*, xxiv, 1961, pp. 241–8 (with illustration).

46. The Kĕlurak inscription of 782 mentions in verse 7: *Gauḍi-dvipa-guru-krāmambuja-rajaḥ-pūtottamāṅgatmanā*, 'by him (viz. the king) whose head was purified by the dust of the lotus-feet of the *guru(s)* from Gauḍi-*dvipa*. Although Gauḍi (in-stead of Gauḍa) and 'island' (instead of *desa* or *bhūmi*) are unusual there can be no reasonable doubt that the term indicates the whole or part of present Bengal and Ban-gladesh, including perhaps some adjoining areas of Bihar, where e.g. Nālandā is situated.

47. Hirananda Sastri, 'The Nālandā copper-plate of Devapāladeva', *Epigr. Ind.*, xvii, 1909, pp. 318 ff.; F. D. K. Bosch, 'Een Oorkonde van het groote Klooster te Nalanda', *Tijdschr. Bat. Gen.*, lxv, 1925, pp. 509–88; Hirananda Sastri, 'Nālandā and its Epigraphic Material', *Mem. A.S.I.*, No. 66, 1942, pp. 92–102.

48. F. D. K. Bosch, 'De inscriptie van Kĕloerak', *Tijdschr. Bat. Gen.*, lxviii, 1968, pp. 8–16.

The Archaeology of Sumatra and the Problem of Srivijaya

BENNET BRONSON

Introduction

SUMATRA, in spite of its size and strategic position on ancient communication routes, has never witnessed an excavation by a trained professional archaeologist. The archaeological bibliography of the island is minuscule and in large part unavailable to researchers outside the Netherlands and Indonesia. The ideas presented below therefore do not pretend to be definitive or, indeed, more than informed guesses. They are based on a variety of colonial-period data of uneven reliability, supplemented (and to a fair extent checked) by first-hand observations made during visits of one month in 1971 and two months in 1973, for a project carried out by a joint team from the Archaeological Institute of Indonesia and the University Museum, University of Pennsylvania (Bronson *et al.* 1973). Data which are presented without bibliographical references should be understood to derive from these first-hand observations.

Let it be said at the outset that we do not yet possess the beginnings of a chronology for prehistoric Sumatra. The very concepts of prehistory and history have rather indistinct boundaries, since in Sumatra even more than in other parts of South East Asia the dawn of written records comes patchily and late. I have placed the end of the prehistoric period at the beginning of the Christian era and the end of the protohistoric period—technically, the time-span that separates the earliest contact with literate foreigners from the first indigenous inscriptions—at about A.D. 650. These dates are quite arbitrary. Thus far, no place-name mentioned in the earlier Chinese sources has been securely fixed in Sumatra and, as will shortly be pointed out, the island is peculiarly lacking in archaeological evidence for 'Indianization' or any other foreign contact during what is here called the protohistoric period. If we knew nothing about the past of the South East Asian mainland, we might well conclude that the end of prehistory coincided with the start of true history, squeezing out protohistory entirely. The first fairly definite outside reference to any society in Sumatra is that of I Ch'ing in A.D. 671 (Coedès 1964: 81); this precedes the first dateable inscription at Kedukan Bukit (ibid. 82) by only eleven years. Although an obvious point, it is also worth observing that this simple chronological scheme (prehistoric-protohistoric-historic) breaks down completely when the more isolated parts of Sumatra are considered.

The highlands and western coastal regions supported reasonably complex societies (Minangkabau, Batak, Niasan) which remained outside the ken of history until well after A.D. 1000, beyond the end of the time-span that concerns us here.

Prehistory

Even under the definition offered above, identifiably prehistoric sites in Sumatra remain quite scarce. Lithic assemblages composed of large core and flake tools have been recovered from several locations in the mountainous areas of southern Sumatra—from Bunga Mas (Dinas Purbakala 1955: 23–4), the Mungkup River (Houbolt 1940), and the Kedaton Rubber Estate (van Heekeren 1957: 59). These have sometimes been called palaeolithic in spite of the absence of extinct faunal remains or, indeed, of any other positive non-stylistic indicator of an early dating. The unifacial 'sumatraliths' of the north-eastern coast (Schurmann 1931; Kupper 1930) are traditionally considered the next oldest group of assemblages, being termed 'mesolithic' or 'hoabinhian.' Like the large core-and-flake industries, these are not known to be associated with metals or (most of them) with pottery and hence are thought to be relatively early.

The third group of sites traditionally accepted as prehistoric are those which produce obsidian flake-blades and withe-marked (see below) pottery in western Jambi province (e.g., on the upper Tianko River—Zwierzycki 1926; the southern end of Lake Kerinci—van der Hoop 1940; and the middle Merangin River—Bronson and Wisseman, *n.d.*; Dinas Purbakala 1955: 15) and a single location in North Sumatra province which produces pottery in surface association with flake-blades made of a siliceous conglomerate stone (an unpublished site, Kebon Sayur Bungara, reported by E. E. McKinnon in 1973). The fourth group comprises the large number of vaguely located central and southern Sumatran sites where polished stone or 'neolithic' adzes have been found. One of these, Lubak Layang in South Sumatra province (Dinas Purbakala 1955: 24; Bronson *et al.* 1973: 26–7), is an actual workshop site, littered with stone-working debris and roughed-out blanks which rather resemble Duff's (1970: 36) 'Indonesia Type 2-D' adzes. There is reason to think that assemblages of the third and fourth groups are in part contemporary. Two obsidian flake-blades were found among the 'neolithic' debitage at Lubuk Layang, and one of the major obsidian sites, Kebon Baru Lolo or Danau Gadang on Lake Kerinci, is the find-spot of a number of polished adzes (see, e.g., van der Hoop 1940: 199), as well as of a bronze kettledrum in Heger I style (ibid. 200). Since obsidians and withe-marked sherds are the only other artefacts present in the area where the kettledrum was found, one is led to suspect that some of the Sumatran lithic industries are late, lasting through the initial metal-using period down to, perhaps, the first few centuries A.D. How much earlier than this the above-mentioned industries began is still an open question. On present evidence, none of them, even the large core-flake industries, need have appeared before 10,000 B.C.

Other classes of prehistoric Sumatran artefacts are still less well-understood than are the stone tools. Potsherds cannot yet be distinguished as prehistoric with any consistency except when they occur in association with lithic material; none bear a close resemblance to early ceramics from neighbouring regions such as the Buni Complex of western Java (Sutayasa 1973) or the vessels of Gua Cha (Sieveking 1944) and Tengku Lembu (Sieveking 1962) in west Malaysia. The only semi-prehistoric ceramics that could be readily identified out of context are the Han Dynasty Chinese vessels said by several authorities (e.g. Orsoy de Flines 1972: 13–14; van der Hoop 1940: 204) to have been found in southern Sumatra during the 1920s and 1930s. As these authorities do not seem to have observed the Han material *in situ*, we should consider the possibility that the Sumatran provenence is a Jakarta art dealer's fabrication.

Prehistoric metal undoubtedly existed in Sumatra. In terms of accessible natural resources, which include numerous deposits of tin, iron, copper, and gold, the island is perhaps as favoured an area for early metallurgy as any other part of the world. Yet few obviously prehistoric specimens have been reported. The only exceptions are three or four bronze kettledrums from Kerinci, Benkulen, and Lampung (van Heekeren 1958: 21), some related bronzes from Kerinci (van der Hoop 1940: 202–3), a number of small objects from 'megalithic' cist graves in the Pasemah area (van der Hoop 1932), and a set of bronze figurines from Riau province (van Heekeren 1958: 36–7). Any of these could have been made in the first millennium B.C., although for some a pre-historic dating seems more probable.

The renowned megaliths of the Pasemah and other parts in southern Sumatra may not even be as old as that. While these have traditionally been considered prehistoric (e.g., by van der Hoop 1932, and Heine-Geldern 1935), there is little hard evidence for a B.C. date. Some megalithic monuments are clearly much later: at Pugung Raharjo in Lampung, for instance, a primitive stone circle can be seen which overlies the outer slope of an earthwork of the fifteenth or sixteenth centuries A.D. Over most of southern Sumatra, megaliths and Hindu-Buddhist remains are found in the same areas; this complementary distribution suggests contemporaneity. And the reported presence of not only bronze but also glass and iron (van der Hoop 1932; Hooijer 1969: 21) in the Pasemah graves indicates a less than prehistoric age for those particular features. Were it not for one or two boulder sculptures depicting what appear to be bronze kettledrums, we would have little reason to entertain the notion that any of the megaliths antedate the fully historic period. Perhaps the most satisfactory solution is to abandon the terms 'Megalithic Period' and 'Megalithic Culture' and simply to note that monuments were frequently made of large stones in those areas where such stones were abundant. The practice may have begun quite early. But the presence of megaliths is not itself an indication of age or, unless detailed similarities can be shown, of cultural affiliation. As several participants in the London Colloquy emphasized, the rubric 'Megalithic' may comprise a wide variety of cultural phenomena which are only distantly, if at all, related.

The Protohistoric or Pre-Śrīvijaya Period

The boundary between Sumatran prehistory and history is difficult to place, at least in part because the historic record and archaeological data are not in close conformity. Wolters (1967) has argued most convincingly for the presence of developed complex societies in Sumatra as early as the fourth century A.D. Virtually all specialists familiar with the Chinese textual evidence agree; some might even feel that this is still too late, arguing that the high development of quasi-urban centres on the mainland by A.D. 200 suggests that similar centres should have been appearing in Sumatra by that date. Yet hardly a shred of archaeological evidence exists. With the possible exception of the Han Dynasty ceramics mentioned above and one seemingly Chinese dagger-axe (van Heekeren 1958: 43), no foreign trade artefact and no inscription, statue, or temple has yet been found in Sumatra which can be dated earlier than the fifth or sixth century. Moreover, the supposed fifth- to sixth-century artefacts are not as securely dated as one could wish. The chief among these artefacts is the famous granite Buddha from Bukit Seguntang near Palembang which is considered by most authorities (e.g. Schnitger 1937: 2–3) to show early Indian influence but which, because it weighs several tons, is clearly not an actual import from India. While the dating of the Indian analogues (Amarāvatī? Anurādhapura?) may be accurate enough, one is not convinced that there need be a close synchrony between the development of new styles within India and their appearance in remote Sumatra. Stylistic considerations do not compel us to accept a fifth- or sixth-century dating for any Indian-influenced Sumatran artefact thus far found.

Only in the seventh century do objects begin to appear in the lower basins of the Musi and Batang Hari whose age is not open to serious doubt. These objects, briefly summarized in the next two sections, are contemporaneous with the first inscriptions of Śrīvijaya and with the first mentions of that kingdom in the Chinese chronicles. Before that we are in a dark age. As far as we know now, Śrīvijaya sprang fully formed within one or two decades from antecedents which, although perhaps progressive and complexly organized, are singularly hard to find.

One reason why these antecedents are elusive is because, in spite of considerable theorizing, no one has looked for them. We may suspect that they are none too impressive in terms of large durable artefacts; if they had been, they would surely have been stumbled on by one of the colonial period amateurs. But we may also be fairly sure that a pre-Śrīvijaya site would not contain impressive artefacts in any case. Sixth-century Indianized artwork is thin on the ground everywhere in South East Asia, and such material from the fifth, fourth, and third centuries A.D. is scarce to vanishing point. From discoveries at U-Thong and Chansen in central Thailand and at Oc-Eo in South Viet-Nam we now have some idea of what a major protohistoric—pre-Dvāravatī, pre-Chenla, 'Funan'-related—site can be expected to look like. It would contain large quantities of pottery, little if any of it glazed; some iron, tin, and bronze tools and ornaments; some seals, coin-like medals, and gold jewellery, perhaps the only fine art objects present; some small items imported from India, the Mediterranean, and China; and possibly some defensive earthworks. But it would have no permanent architecture, nor monumental inscriptions, nor large plastic art. Considering the strongly artistic and epigraphic orientation of the colonial period amateurs, the 'invisibility' of pre-Śrīvijaya should come as no surprise.

We need not, on the other hand, invert this epistemological argument and conclude that the island *did* contain states and cities in the protohistoric period. At the moment it still remains a tenable hypothesis that the founders of Śrīvijaya came in from elsewhere in South East Asia, importing *en bloc* its population, its ruling line, its ideology and institutions, and its markedly heterogeneous monumental art. Nothing we now know about the historical and archaeological Śrīvijaya of the late seventh century forces us to assume a long period of indigenous development. Yet still we may feel that a certain implausibility inheres in the idea that the development of states and civilization in Sumatra (and for that matter in Java and Borneo) lagged so far as this behind the same process on the South East Asian mainland. There *must* be an Oc-Eo somewhere in Sumatra. Finding it is a central problem for future Indonesian archaeological research.

Early Historic Period

A. *Inscriptions*

The last four centuries of the first millennium are historic in the sense that indigenous literacy can be shown to have existed in Sumatra from the early seventh century onward. Although the inscriptions which demonstrate this literacy are far from abundant, they make up a large proportion of the total number of Sumatran artefacts that can be securely dated to the early historic period.

Six inscriptions actually mention Śrīvijaya by name. Three were found in the immediate vicinity of Palembang, at Talang Tuwo (Coedès 1930: 38), Kedukan Bukit (Coedès ibid.), and Telaga Batu (de Casparis 1956: 15–16). The three others are located some distance to the north-west, north-east, and south-east: at Karang Berahi in western Jambi province (Coedès 1930), Kota Kapur on Bangka Island (Kern 1913), and Palas Pasemah in eastern Lampung province (unpublished; Boechari, personal comm.). All are in old Malay and are assigned to the decade 680–690, either by dates in the Saka era or by textual parallels with other inscriptions so dated. The Telaga Batu inscription of 683 is the earliest closely datable text from Sumatra but may be preceded somewhat by several of the thirty or so minor inscriptions found in Palembang, at Bukit Seguntang and Sabukingking-Telaga Batu; these are in old Malay or Sanskrit and are palaeographically dated to the seventh century (de Casparis 1956: 1–15). One further example which may be contemporary with these is the old Malay inscription cut into a cliffside on Karimun Besar Island in the Straits of Malacca (Schnitger 1937: 12). It is dated, again palaeographically, to the seventh or eighth century.

This completes the list of known seventh-century inscriptions, of which the great majority are in Palembang. Interestingly it also comes very near to completing the list of known first millennium inscriptions. Thus far no epigraphic material from the eighth or ninth centuries has been reported from Sumatra. Even the tenth century has produced only three (palaeographically dated) examples, those at Hujung Langit-Bawang (Damais 1955: 275), Batu Bedil (ibid.: 283), and Ulu Belu (ibid.: 289). Two of these are in old Javanese, all are in western Lampung province, and none have any apparent connections with Śrīvijaya.

The distribution of inscriptions is thus seen to be most uneven and perhaps rather surprising. We are led by the Chinese chroniclers and their interpreters to expect a substantial degree of literacy in Sumatra during the last part of the millennium, a time when the thalassocracy of Śrīvijaya was supposedly at its apogee. Yet the Śrīvijaya of epigraphy is a short-lived and seemingly isolated phenomenon. It appears and then vanishes again within a space of twenty-five years, leaving little more behind it than did the evanescent inscriptional traditions of Pūrnavarman in western Java and Mūlavarman in eastern Borneo. This apparent disjunction between the historical and epigraphic evidence will be taken up again in a later section.

B. *Fine arts*

The inscriptions do at least provide convincing proof that Śrīvijaya was at one time located in or near Sumatra; this is not true of the fine arts material known from that island. Finds of first millennium statuary and architecture show little uniformity of style, less connection with the comparatively uniform 'Śrīvijaya Style' of southern Thailand, and none of the concentration or abundance that usually characterizes the fine arts of major South East Asian political foci. The only part of Sumatra whose ancient art and architecture approach this degree of density is Padang Lawas in southern north Sumatra province. Although the Padang Lawas sites (Schnitger 1937, 1939) undoubtedly do demonstrate the existence of a moderately important (and historically unidentified) state of the twelfth to fifteenth centuries, they seem too late to be associated with the Śrīvijaya of I Ch'ing.

Most of the (stylistically-dated) first millennium statuary of Sumatra is found on the lower Musi and near the mouth of two of the main tributaries of that river, the Lematang and Komering—that is, in the hinterland of Palembang. The only exceptions are several statues found at Muara Jambi and later removed to the palace at Solok which, Schnitger (1937) says, belong to the seventh or eighth century. On the other hand, Schnitger seems to have known of between ten and fifteen pieces from the Palembang area: at least one from Bukit Seguntang, several from Kedukan Bukit, several from Tanah Abang, three from the lower Komering (see also Bernet Kempers 1959: 174–6), and three from Geding Suro. One major piece has been found in Palembang since Schnitger's day, a Bodhisattva now in a house called Sarang Waty in the eastern part of the city. This Bodhisattva shows an apparent kinship with the mitred Vishnus of southern Thailand and of Cibuaya (Bernet Kempers 1959: pl. 28) in western Java. Possible Siamese connections are also shown by two of the three standing Buddhas excavated by Westenenck at Geding Suro and now in the Palembang Museum; although I have been unable to find any published reference, to my non-specialist eye they appear closely to resemble some of the Dvāravatī statuary of central Thailand. Most of the other major and minor plastic art from first millennium Sumatra is in good central Javanese style. Only the Bukit Seguntang Buddha and the three bronzes from the Komering are sufficiently idiosyncratic to be considered the products of an independent local stylistic tradition.

The early architecture of Sumatra is still scarcer and less indigenous than the statuary. A total of three structures have been found which can reasonably be assigned to the first millennium; at Jepara on Lake Ranau (Schnitger 1937: 4), at Si Mangambat in north Sumatra (Schnitger 1936), and at Tanah Abang on the lower Lematang (Tombrinck 1870). All are said to be in the style of central Java; Si Mangambat, the only one I have seen, is quite orthodoxly Javanese with no discernible detail of decoration which might be ascribed to local Sumatran influence. Several other structures exist or are known to have existed which may have been built before A.D. 1000: at Modong near Tanah Abang, at Muara Jambi (five or six structures, probably but not certainly eleventh or twelfth century in date—Schnitger 1937: 57), and at

Bukit Seguntang (Schnitger knew of four structures on or near the Seguntang hill, and one more—a stupa—was discovered in 1960; all have since been destroyed). The rest of the known archaeological architecture on the island, the great bulk of which is at Padang Lawas, definitely belongs to the second millennium.

C. *Other artefacts*

With regard to artefacts other than statues and buildings, we are faced with a recognition problem which is at present unsurmountable. Prehistoric objects can be identified as prehistoric by comparing them with analogous artefacts found in other places. But this technique will not work in instances where, as in the case of historic period pottery from Java, those analogues themselves are very little known. I must therefore restrict myself to a few general observations.

Sites surrounded by defensive earthworks do exist in Sumatra, although they have received little attention in the literature. One of these, Bawang in Lampung, can be dated to the tenth century by the presence of an *in situ* inscription in its centre. We may thus expect that earlier, perhaps Śrīvijaya-related, fortified town sites will eventually be discovered and that this will help us identify related small-finds. But so far most such sites can be shown to be late, by the presence of Sung and usually Ming Dynasty ceramics: T'ang three-colour ware, which may prove to be an important horizon marker in central Javanese archaeology, has not yet been found in Sumatra. The same is true of the few datable kinds of earthenware and other non-artistic artefacts which might appear on Sumatran sites. The only known site which seems to contain a substantial number of first millennium small-finds is Geding Suro in Palembang, where several statues of the seventh to eighth centuries have been found and where there are extensive deposits of potsherds and other domestic refuse. However, defining an early assemblage at Geding Suro will have to wait for an actual excavation. The surface deposits there are heavily mixed with debris from a Majapahit-related occupation of the fourteenth to sixteenth centuries.

What is Śrīvijaya?

The reader familiar with writings on early South East Asian history may be surprised at the poverty of the hard archaeological evidence for Śrīvijaya, an entity which some have envisioned as one of the two great ancient empires of the region, the political and economic equal of Angkor. Archaeologically-oriented specialists have of course long been aware that Śrīvijaya was not Angkor's cultural equal and have ceased expecting that a vast monumental complex will some day be discovered in the jungles of Sumatra, Borneo, or wherever else Śrīvijaya is thought to have been. The empire was clearly run in such a way as to dispense with the statues, temples, and other permanent ceremonial constructions that are standard features of the ancient kingdoms of the rice-rich plains areas of South East Asia. Many specialists would prefer the analogy with trade-oriented coastal states like Malacca and Brunei, with physical bases which are relatively impermanent and with traditions which emphasize war and commerce more than population control and farming.

Yet for all that, it is at least unexpected that the archaeology of Śrīvijaya should be so poor. While the historians speak of a Śrīvijaya that endured for half a millennium, the Śrīvijaya known to Sumatran epigraphy cannot be shown to have lasted for more than twenty-five or fifty years. And while the art historians have ascribed to Śrīvijayan influence a whole complex of southern Siamese art styles, that empire seems to have possessed in its presumed Sumatran homeland almost no art which was distinctively its own. There is not in fact much material evidence of any kind. Were it not for the testimony of the Chinese (and Arabic?) chroniclers and the occasional appearance of its name in foreign inscriptions, one would think Śrīvijaya no more than another of the abortive early kingdoms of Indonesian history, a proto-state like those of Pūrṇavarman, Adityavarman, and Mūlavarman. The contradiction between the archaeologically and historically-derived evidence is thus a major one. How can it be solved?

One possibility is to conclude that the ancient sources are misleading and that their recent interpreters have been building castles in air. I Ch'ing is not an altogether disinterested witness when describing the splendour and doctrinal authority of the place where he received his training. And, while the 'Shih-li-fo-shih' of the seventh- and eighth- century diplomatic records is a phonetically acceptable transcription of the name Śrīvijaya, this is not so true of the 'San-fo-ch'ih' and 'Sribuza' that appear, after a 150-year gap (Coedès 1964: 131), in tenth to twelfth century Chinese and Arabic records. As far as the documentary sources go, Śrīvijaya might have been a minor kingdom that ceased to exist within a hundred years after its founding in A.D. 650.

The main objection to such a drastically sceptical solution is the existence of two later epigraphic mentions of the name Śrīvijaya, one on a late eighth-century inscription at Ligor in southern Thailand (Chhabra 1965: 26–34; Bosch 1941) and the other in the context of a Cola military expedition described on an inscription from Tanjore in southern India (Nilakanta Sastri 1949). However, even these two items cannot be regarded as decisive evidence for the lasting importance or even the post-750 survival of Śrīvijaya as a socio-cultural entity. We can readily imagine that the same name might have been borne by one or two later and equally short-lived 'Śrīvijayas' which need not have had a significantly close connection with the seventh- to eighth-century kingdom whose remains are concentrated around Palembang. Just as medieval

German and Turkish states eventually came to call themselves Rome, so later South East Asian states could have preserved the name of Śrīvijaya for the sake, perhaps, of historical prestige or dynastic validation. The survival of the name alone does not imply an actual continuity of location, sovereignty, ethnicity, or any other meaningful kind of identity.

An alternative solution to the apparent contraction between the archaeological and historical evidence is to come down on the side of the chroniclers and their interpreters and to suggest that exploration has simply been inadequate. One can conceive that major undiscovered cities do exist out there in the swamp forest or buried under the alluvium, perhaps rather deficient in sculpture and standing architecture but nonetheless large and rich enough to be credible as centres of a great empire. Such a possibility cannot be disproved in the present state of the archaeological art. However, enough research has been done to make several potential discoveries seem improbable. For one thing, the hypothetical later capitals of Śrīvijaya cannot have produced many monumental inscriptions, since these are the one class of ancient cultural material which have aroused general interest among Sumatrans and which therefore have been regularly reported to the authorities. It is almost inconceivable that a substantially-sized set of inscriptions, referring to a Śrīvijayan kingdom in Sumatra during the nineth to twelfth centuries, will ever be found. Moreover, these later Śrīvijayas cannot have been securely in control of a large and well-populated hinterland, for no part of Sumatra contains the density of village and small town remains that characterizes polities with highly developed agricultural and demographic bases. If the island does contain a ninth- or tenth- (or fourteenth-)century Śrīvijaya, that state should be of a size and kind to be largely provisioned, like Malacca during the fourteenth to sixteenth centuries, by a rural population in another part of South East Asia. And finally, it seems unlikely that this later Śrīvijaya would have been organized according to the sociopolitical models one tends to regard as normal for great empires. We should consider, for instance, the idea that the hegemony of the Sumatran coast was in constant flux, moving from one place to the next within a span of one or two decades and changing at each move with respect to the ability to concentrate wealth and power. The later history of coastal Sumatra, or for that matter of the Sulu archipelago, suggests that effective pan-regional organization can be achieved and lost again almost overnight and that this organization can be implemented by a variety of institutional forms of which only some can intelligibly be called empires or monarchies. Śrīvijaya could be real enough but could have existed essentially in a body of more or less coherent traditions, not necessarily embodied in a single dynastic line or any other continuing institution, which from time to time threw up short-lived political entities of great international importance. This body of traditions might have been a major force in early Indonesian and Malaysian history. But it need not have left a great deal behind it of the sort that archaeologists can dig from the ground.

All such speculation is of course premature and must wait for actual digging to resume again after a thirty-five-year delay. An appreciable possibility still exists that Śrīvijaya was much as the text-books depict it, a metropolis located somewhere on the Sumatran coast which for many centuries exercised its sway over a vast area reaching from the fringe of the Indochinese peninsula down to central Java. This depiction seemed quite probable when Śrīvijaya was first discovered in the 1910s and 1920s by Coedès (1918) and his fellow historians. But its probability has begun to diminish in recent years as supporting evidence has steadily failed to appear. What we need now is an expansion of archaeological exploration coupled with a critical re-appraisal of the textual evidence. We must prepare ourselves for the likelihood that Śrīvijaya, though not entirely a myth, will prove to have been quite different from the way we have imagined it.

ADDITIONAL REFERENCES

Bronson, B., Basoeki, Machi Soehadi, and Wisseman, J. 1973. *Laporan Penelitian Arkeologi di Sumatera.* Lembaga Purbakala dan Peninggalan Nasional/Jakarta

Dinas Purbakala. 1955. *Amerta Warna Warta Kepurbakalaan 3.* Dinas Purbakala Republik Indonesia.

Pre-Angkor Cambodia: Evidence from the Inscriptions in Khmer concerning the Common People and their Environment

J. M. JACOB

THIS paper is based on an examination of the texts of the pre-Angkor inscriptions in Khmer, of which virtually all legible material has been published by G. Coedès (1924, 1936, and 1937–66). The works of Aymonier (1900–3), Lunet de Lajonquière (1901), Parmentier (1927), Briggs (1951), Malleret (1962–9), and Groslier (1968) have been consulted too, in order to mark on the map (at end) the position of as many inscriptions as possible. It seemed that the geographical position of the inscriptions, seen in relation to the relief of the area, would be of interest and it was hoped that inscriptions of certain areas might show some features different from those of other areas. Inscriptions are referred to throughout by their inventory numbers, K.1, etc. In Appendix B the pre-Angkor inscriptions in Khmer are listed in numerical order with, for each inscription, a rough indication of the date and, where possible, a reference to a marked area on the map. The key indicating which dot on the map refers to which inscription(s) is also given in Appendix B.

The pre-Angkor inscriptions in Khmer were intended to record, for the benefit and instruction of the public, details of the religious foundations to which they were related. The maximum content of an inscription, in terms of items of information, is set out below in the order in which items usually appear:

  (i) the date or name of the reigning king;
 (ii) the title and names of donors;
(iii) the name of the god;
 (iv) names of the people from whom the donor obtained land to offer to the foundation;
  (v) details of the price paid to those who relinquished land for the foundation;
 (vi) the extent, location, and capacity of the donated ricefields;
(vii) the names of the donated slaves[1] with an indication of their duties;
(viii) details of the subsistence to be given to the religious personnel;

(ix) details of other land given to the foundation: orchards, market gardens, etc.;

(x) list of precious objects given to the foundation;

(xi) the statement that the revenues are to be combined with those of another foundation;

(xii) warning of punishment for anyone using or abusing the belongings of the foundation.

Few inscriptions have even half of these items. Many are broken or partly illegible so that the total original content is a matter of guesswork. Others, however, seem to be complete, with perhaps only a few illegible characters, and it is clear that the information was intended to be less. Such inscriptions usually mention the donor, the gift, and the god. They may lack the date simply because this was given in an accompanying Sanskrit inscription. One suspects that when they lack details of duties of slaves or of lands other than ricefields or lists of precious objects it is because the foundation was not so rich or flourishing as others. With regard to details concerning the capacity and location of the ricefields and prices paid, one may speculate as to the reason why some inscriptions have them and some do not. It was advantageous to the foundation to have a clear statement written up about land transactions and personnel belonging to the god but perhaps not every locality could provide the people capable of writing down and inscribing all the names and composing a passage about the organization?

In spite of the restricted subject-matter and the lacunae which place even more restrictions on them for us, the Khmer inscriptions offer a wealth of information if studied minutely. Certain aspects of life in ancient Cambodia, its religions (Bhattacarya 1955), its political organization (Sahai 1970), the legal position of its slaves (Bongert 1959), etc. have been studied using the inscriptions as the major source. The aim of this paper is to assemble the information given by the pre-Angkor Khmer inscriptions about the populace: the work they did, the land they inhabited, the products they knew, the objects they made, and the conditions in which they lived. The material is set out in three sections with some subsidiary paragraphs. Lists of relevant vocabulary are given in Appendix A.

1. *The Non-élite Free People*

The inscriptions chiefly present to us the dignitaries on the one hand and the slaves they donated on the other, while we are hardly permitted more than a glimpse of those who lived in freedom but insignificantly. They surely included humble peasants, craftsmen, and traders who had not had the misfortune to be carried off as slaves or bonded for debt or crime. They certainly included the religious personnel, the *paṁnos*, who are mentioned on the inscriptions, chiefly as receivers of provisions, and the families of officials, themselves owners of household slaves. There are two direct references to people who had humble titles but owned land. A certain Nāgavindu who sold a piece of land is referred to as *Va*, 'Mr.' (K.22, l. 26), while we know of the reservoir belonging to a *Ku* 'Miss/Mrs.' from K.561, l. 19. The secular public were the *ge* 'persons' at whom warnings of punishment were directed. K.90, piédroit nord, ll. 4–7, reads *ge ta dap gui, ge ta sak gui, ge cmer ājñā, ge daṇḍa* 'Anyone who causes any hindrance here, anyone who steals from here, any transgressors of the edict will be punished'. From more detailed warnings of this kind, particularly in K.904, K.259, K.426, and K.451, it is clear that the public were known to take things, ask for things, use temple slaves as their own, seize slaves, cattle, carts, and even build their homes on a grotto (K.724)! Much of the evidence which will be produced in connection with the slave population obviously applied also to the free: the features of their environment; the artefacts, precious and ordinary, with which they were familiar; the assessment of the value of slaves, objects, and land in terms of other goods.

2. *The Slaves*[1]

In the briefest inscriptions, no more is said about the slaves than that a gift of *kñum* was made to the god. More informative inscriptions give lists of names, men first, women and children second, each adult entry being preceded usually by a title (or kinship term serving as a title). Unusually, on K.137, the women are given titles and the men are not! After each name there is usually a stroke or, more rarely, a circle. This mark for each of the slaves or potential slaves (i.e. the young children) would make it easier to count the totals. The most detailed inscriptions indicate the duties of the slaves. The information about slaves will be presented in five paragraphs.

2.1. *Categories of slaves*

Sometimes the lists of slaves were preceded by the terms *kñuṁ ta si* or *ghoda* 'menfolk' and *kñuṁ ta kantai* or just *kantai* 'womenfolk'. Further classification is found in connection with the status of the children, involving the following four categories:

der Possibly to be connected with Mod. Khmer *sto:(r)* 'on the point of' and interpreted, like Mod. Mon *hɔmɔe (leaŋ)* as 'on the verge of (puberty)'. This interpretation arose from discussion of this and the next word with Professor Shorto.[2]

lāñ Perhaps 'having attained puberty'. cf. Mod. Mon *leaŋ* 'puberty' and Mod. Khmer *khlaŋ* 'strong'.

rat 'running, toddler'.

pau 'unweaned'.

The word *si* 'male' or *tai* 'female' follows this classification, e.g. K.149, l. 11, *Ku Cañhvāy 1 kon Ku der si 1 pau si 1* 'Ku Skein 1, Ku's child, male of *der* age 1, unweaned male 1.'

Two more words describing categories of slaves, occurring once each, are Skt. *kārmmāntika* 'workers' (K.41, l. 4) and *klamuṁ* 'maidens' (K.24, B, l. 12). List 1 in Appendix A includes all the pre-Angkor words denoting categories of slaves: such words are not followed by a personal name.

2.2. *Slave duties*

On the inscriptions which give information about individual duties, the lists of slaves are divided first into groups according to the duty carried out and secondly, within each such group, into the categories of age and sex etc., described in the last paragraph. Where information about duties is not given we may imagine that all personnel were commandeered to work in the rice-fields, orchards, plantations, or market gardens in accordance with local requirements and that special tasks such as cooking, weaving, dancing were performed by the more talented and fortunate. Such people would probably help with the farming at harvest-time. However that may be, our evidence is that a great variety of duties is recorded. Some of the vocabulary is not yet understood but, since the context makes it clear that a duty is being mentioned, all such vocabulary is entered in the list. Many of the activities may easily be imagined by those familiar with South East Asia and will have been observed in Cambodia in the twentieth century. They include grinding, spinning, grooming the king's elephant, moulding statues, singing, and playing musical instruments. Even *tmir slik* ones who sew leaves' seem recognizable through the modern makers of woven plates and other utensils for many occasions. Some roles are not so clear-cut. The position held by the *kñuṁ vrah* 'slave of the god' was probably privileged; usually only one or two slaves have this duty. Among tasks for which the vocabulary is less clear come 'heaters of water for ceremonial ablutions' (Coedès' interpretation of *ᵃmuh* as 'heater'); 'trappers' (*camdak*, cf. Mod. K. *teak* 'trap'?); slaves working inside either *pi le* 'for above' (i.e. on the floor, not under the building), or *kamluṅ vrah* 'in the interior of the temple'. Slave duties are listed in Appendix A.2.

2.3. *Slave titles*

The words given in list 3, Appendix A are classed as titles on the criterion that they are followed immediately either by a personal name or, as in a minority of cases, by a word such as the title of a master or a description of a duty, which served equally well as an identification of the slave. *Va* and *Ku* occur the most frequently. The translation 'male adult', 'female adult' given in the list sound extremely impersonal, even inhuman, but it seems to the

writer that the titles were not lacking in dignity. If the masters had been
contemptuous in their attitude to the slaves they could have had them
entered, as in fact they are on a few inscriptions, by name only, following the
category indication 'menfolk', 'womenfolk'. In the translations of citations *Va*
and *Ku* have been left because, although 'Mr.' is satisfactory as a translation
of *Va*, neither 'Mrs.' nor 'Miss' is suitable for *Ku*; only the cumbersome
'Miss/Mrs.' would be adequate.

Mān and *On̄*, which occur on K.46 and K.76 are not known through Mod.
Khmer and must be compared respectively with Old Mon *mān* '(young) man'
and possibly *uin, in*, onomastic prefix (Shorto 1971: 18 and 25). K.76, l. 2
makes it clear that in that inscription the male slaves with this title were Mons:
kñum̐ ramañ ta si, Mān . . . 'Mon slaves, males, Mān . . .'

2.4. *Kinship*

All the kinship terms which occur in pre-Angkor inscriptions, whether or
not they occur in connection with slaves, are given for the sake of completeness in list 4, Appendix A. The kinship terms occur in several kinds of context
in the slave lists, chiefly, however, in the lists of women and children. In some
inscriptions a kinship term is used in place of the title *Ku*, e.g. K.138, l. 7, *Me
Kralā 1*; l. 9, *Me Nan̄ā 1* 'Mother Kralā 1 . . . Mother Nan̄ā 1'. No dependent
children are listed with these mothers. Sometimes a statement of kinship is a
means of identification without a name being given, e.g. K.766, l. 4, *[a]me Va
Kandot 1* 'Mother of Va Kandot 1'.[3] That *[a]me* is only an alternative title for
Ku, where appropriate, is shown by K.451, ll. 6–7, *[a]me Man̄, kon Ku 4* 'Mother
Man̄ (and) her (Ku's) 4 children'.

Sometimes a kinship term follows a title, as on K.808, l. 1, *Ku [a]me Kandai 1*.
Then it is grammatically ambiguous. It could mean 'Adult female, Mother
Kandai 1' or, as seems to the writer far more likely, 'Adult female, mother of
Kandai'. The second way of interpreting the kinship term in such a context is
sometimes supported by the occurrence of the name elsewhere in the lists,
suggesting a reference to the child of that mother. In other cases the names of
both mother and child are given, e.g. K.127, l. 8, *Ku [a]nan̄ 1 kon Ku Va
Tlos* 'Ku Anan̄ 1; her child, Va Tlos 1'. The clearest statement of all occurs
on K.74, l. 9, *Ku Droṅ kon ku Droṅ Va Tanlāṅ* 'Ku Droṅ; child of Ku Droṅ,
Va Tanlāṅ.'

The record of the children is made in various ways some of which have just
been encountered. They may simply be entered as numbers but it is quite
common for details to be given of their age and sex as has been shown in
paragraph 2.1. Grandchildren are sometimes mentioned too e.g. K.562, l. 6,
Ku Uy, kon ku 7, cau 2, 'Ku Uy; her 7 children; 2 grandchildren'. Occasionally the order is reversed, e.g. K.134, l. 16, *[a]me Kañā 1, Kañā 1*,' 'Mother

of Kañjā 1, Kañjā 1'; but l. 23, *Kampaṅ 1, ᵃme Kampaṅ 1*, 'Kampaṅ 1, mother of Kampaṅ 1'. Perhaps in the first case the mother was elderly and dependent upon Kañjā but was mentioned first because it was customary—see section on categories—to proceed from eldest to youngest. On a few inscriptions a father is identified *via* his children rather than by his own name, e.g. K.357, l. 14, *Va ᵃta Sravāy* 'Va, father of Sravāy'. In l. 15 we find his daughter (?) Ku Sravāy. This may also be because he was a dependent relative needing to be placed with his daughter.

A case suggesting two dependent parents is recorded on K.904, A, l. 23, *ᵃme Kandan 1 ᵃtā Kandan 1 Ku Kandan 1*. We must not interpret Kandan as a family name but we may nevertheless feel reassured by this glimpse of a complete family, 'mother of Kandan 1 father of Kandan 1 Ku Kandan 1'. Another is found on the same inscription expressed differently: A, l. 23, *Va ᵃtā Krasop 1 Kantai Ku Kaṁvai 1 kon Vā Krasop 1* 'Va, father of Krasop 1; (his) wife, Ku Kaṁvai 1; (their) son, Va Krasop 1'. In K.140, l. 11, a male slave is identified by his own name and that of both parents, if the stroke at the end of the long phrase is to be trusted and the reference is to one person only: *Vā Kantoṅ Naṅ, kon Laṅkah Va Aras 1* 'Va Kantoṅ Naṅ, child of Ku Laṅkah (and) Va Aras 1'. A clear indication is given on K.388, C, l. 6, that, in spite of the enslaved status, a family was regarded as a unit. No names of wives and children are given but a group is recorded as follows: *kyuṁ* (*sic* for *kñuṁ*) *vrah: Vodhigana, kantai gui, kon pi* 'Slaves of the god: Vodhigana, his wife (and) three children'. The reader is reminded that normally the *Va* and *Ku* are listed separately. Similarly on K.657, ll. 2–3, two families are listed: *Vā Samudra ku Dhan kon 1 Vā Hitaṅkara Ku Sam-ap kon 1* 'Vā Samudra, Ku Dhana, one child; Vā Hitaṅkara, Ku Sam-ap, one child'.

Younger siblings are also mentioned, accompanying older brothers and sisters, e.g. K.480, l. 12, *Va Caṁkap 1 paon 2* 'Va Camkap 1, 2 younger siblings', and K.926, l. 8, *Ku Rahval 1, paon Ku 2* 'Ku Busy 1, her 2 younger siblings'. We may imagine the local people queuing up, men in one place, women and dependents in another, and giving their names, probably to be written down on palm-leaf pages before being inscribed. Perhaps in some areas the palm-leaf list was the only record of the personnel.

2.5. *Slave names*

Until the registration of births, deaths, and marriages which began during French rule, it was the practice in Cambodia for ordinary people to have one personal name and no family name. The personal name might be a proper name or the name of an object, a descriptive word of good or bad import or even a made-up word. The names of slaves in pre-Angkor Cambodia suggest just this kind of custom, as will be seen from a glance at list 5 in Appendix A.

Names reflected bad qualities more often than good. If this was to avert the evil eye, however, it seems strange that it was not still more common. Some names consisting of a phrase, e.g. *cap pi hau* (lit. 'catch so as to call') 'catch him if you want him' have a thoroughly individual flavour. Many names are recurrent, however, and are found in widely separated areas. Names of plants and animals were popular. Sanskrit names, which were the norm for the élite, were also common among all classes of slaves. Some musicians and dancers had very poetic Sanskrit names, e.g. Vasantamallikā 'Spring jasmine', K.557, est, l. 3. Some names suggest a non-Khmer origin.

2.6. *Slave conditions*

Slaves were treated as goods possessed by an owner. Of how they became slaves little is told. We know from their names that some were foreign and some were prisoners of war. K.1, ll. 1–2 tells of persons who *cap Va Kandos Ku Tai dau jvan ta Mratāṅ Kloñ* 'seized Va Kandos (and) Ku Tai (and) went to offer them to Mratāṅ Kloñ'. The owner could give them to a religious foundation. *kñuṁ aṁnoy . . .* 'slaves, the gift of . . .' occurs *passim*. In some cases, e.g. K.49, l. 13, it was stated that the god had the exclusive right, *prasiddha*, to their use. They could be priced, as on K.726, A, ll. 9–10, *sre . . . pañjāhv teṁ kāryya sampol stri* 'ricefield acquired for a capital sum representing a band of sampol women'. On K.493, l. 20, mention is made of two women slaves given in exchange for land: *sre . . . sare kanlah, jnāhv gui kñuṁ kantai 2* 'half a ricefield; the price for this: 2 women slaves'. The phrase *oy sre daṅ kñuṁ* (K.18, l. 1) suggests 'gives ricefields *complete with* slaves' rather than merely 'gives ricefields *and* slaves'. This could mean not just that the gift consisted of the number of slaves required to work the land but that these slaves were the slaves who normally lived and worked there for an owner. Such slaves would probably not find their lives greatly changed. They would live where they had always lived and do the work they had always done. This may have been the case with the five groups of people of different localities referred to in K.134. The first of these groups was given, l. 21, *nu sre nu pdai karoṁ nu daṁriṅ* 'and the ricefields, lowland and orchards', while the third and fourth groups were given, ll. 24 and 25, *nu sre nu pdai karoṁ* 'and the ricefields and lowland'. Perhaps in the pre-Angkor period as in the Angkor period slaves worked partly for the temple and partly for their private owners. On K.154, l. 6, the word *vera* 'take turn and turn about, help each other in turn' occurs in the phrase *vera kñuṁ* 'rota of slaves', suggesting that the slaves given to the temple were on duty there only part of the time. It could of course also mean that they were off duty when not serving the god!

A glimmer of hope for the slaves is discernible on K.493, ll. 21–2, where there is mention of a Poñ (official) 'originally a servant' who had *soṅ ktiṅ* 'paid a debt'. Could this be a slave for debt who had paid his way back to freedom? The word *kñuṁ* is not used with reference to him but the word which is used, *pamre*, occurs on K.129, l. 1, with reference to *kñuṁ: kñuṁ . . . ta pamre ta paṁnos* 'slaves . . . those who serve the religious personnel'. On K.1 also the redemption (*loḥ* 'to redeem') of two slaves is mentioned, l. 5. Cases of slaves being freed are recorded occasionally in the Angkor period and more frequently on the Middle Khmer inscriptions (sixteenth to eighteenth centuries).

3. *The Environment*

The map shows the location of 125 pre-Angkor inscriptions in Khmer. Six further inscriptions have been attributed to an area, although the exact position of their place of origin is not known to the writer. Eight more inscriptions could not be attributed even to an area since no one knows where they were found. It will be seen that, while the heaviest concentration of finds is in the centre, the area covered by inscriptions extends in the north-west as far as Korat, in the north-east almost as far as Pakse, in the south-east as far as Kampot and in the south-west to Phu-Vinh in Viet-Nam. It indicates deep penetration of the Mekong basin and general avoidance of the hills. An examination of the inscriptions in groups according to the areas from which they came yielded no striking differences of content or language, apart from diphthongization in the Angkor and Thap-Muoi areas. It may be mentioned here that a similar examination of the inscriptions in chronological order has led to no important conclusions.

3.1. *Natural and made-made features of the environment*

The extent of ricefields was often described by reference to landscape features such as woods, rivers, lakes, hills, paths, water-tanks, thickets of bamboo. Orchards, plantations, groves of mango, and market gardens were given to the temples. Some of the work other than rice-growing which was done by the people has been mentioned in connection with slave duties. Coconut palms, arecas, pepper plants, beans, ginger, salt, goats, buffalo, elephant, and oxen came under their care. Lists 6 and 7 in Appendix A contain vocabulary connected with outdoor work. Building construction is not mentioned in the pre-Angkor inscriptions in Khmer but it will be seen from list 8 that quite a few constructions of one sort or another are mentioned. Some, such as *tnal* 'main road' and *jaṁnan* 'causeway' occur as place-names. Silver and cloth will be mentioned in the next paragraph as being among the valuable objects given as barter. These and other metals and artefacts known to the pre-Angkor Khmers, though not necessarily recorded as being bartered, are given in 9 and 10.

3.2. *The ricefields*

Our information is concerned with the acquisition of ricefields for religious foundations. Texts vary very greatly as to the amount of information they give. Many simply mention that slaves, ricefields, or both are given by an elevated person to the god. K.18, for example, tells, l. 2, that Mratāñ Bhāskarapāla *oy sre dañ kñuṁ ta Vrah Kaṁmratāñ Añ* 'gives ricefields together with slaves to the god'. No further details of the gift are recorded. K.49, a very short, though virtually complete, inscription, gives more information; it emphasizes the terms concerning possession by the foundation. It gives no slave names but it clearly says, l. 12, 'all these slaves, oxen, buffalo, ricefields (and) orchards which the Pu Cah Añ gave to the god—plus slaves offered by persons joining in this foundation—are *exclusively* given to the god and are to be administered by Poñ Çubhakīrtti exclusively'.

Other inscriptions mention an exchange of goods given to the owner of the land which is given up for the god, e.g. K.910, l. 10, *sre man jauhv nu çañkha* 'ricefield exchanged for a conch'. One of the most informative inscriptions in connection with land-transactions is K.79. This records the gift to a religious foundation by a Mratāñ Içānapavitra of several ricefields. These were obtained by him from the various Poñ (less elevated officials) who either owned them or simply used them. The Mratāñ obtained the land by giving goods to these owners or occupiers. A variety of goods given in exchange for land are recorded in this and other inscriptions. They include cloth, paddy, silver, etc. The exact nature of the exchange was probably decided by the owner or occupier. One such person for example received a bust of his son (K.79, l. 18), a thoroughly personal reimbursement! All the 'prices' mentioned in K.79 were paid by the same Mratāñ and constituted his gift, *aṁnoy*. The word *aṁnoy* is used also, however, with reference to the various owners or occupiers who give up the land they have been using. It seems quite possible that many other inscriptions which are brief and mention only the gift of a Mratāñ were concerned with transactions of this kind, where the Mratāñ was not the land-owner but the rich and powerful personage who gained land for the foundation from lesser landowners by persuasion or even coercion. However, in at least one case, the foundation itself provided the goods for exchange. K.41 begins: *sre Vrah Kaṁmratāñ Añ Çri Piṅgaleçvara aṁnoy Poñ Çivabhāsaṇa man jo nu dravya Vrah Kaṁmratāñ Añ* 'Ricefield (for) the god, Çri Piṅgaleçvara, gift of Poñ Çivabhāsana, which was exchanged for goods of the god.'

One might be inclined to regard goods thus offered for the release of land for the temple as compensation. However, it is clear from K.124 that the exchange of goods is a normal method of buying. This inscription tells us, ll. 17–22, that 'honey is given to buy oil, cloth to buy syrup, . . . cotton to buy ginger conserve'. The word *duñ* 'buy' and not *jau/jahv/jo* 'exchange' is used here. Still other words occur on other inscriptions. Transactions may be described from the point of view of the Poñ or other person who relinquishes his land. In K.79, for example, l. 9, we read *dmār gui Poñ Çveta* 'the claimant (of the exchange goods) was Poñ Çveta'. Sometimes the transaction is described from the point of view of the person who pays the 'price'. Thus K.493 begins *Poñ Bhā Vinaya ktiṅ krapi canmat 1* 'Poñ Bhā Vinaya gives-up-as-exchange-price a milk buffalo'. An apparently different kind of exchange and an extra condition about the land are recorded on K.726, A, ll. 6–11. The exchange goods given for the land and other gifts is paddy but its value is expressed in terms of silver and cloth which thus appear to have almost a monetary value. Ll. 7–8 read *sre ai ñeṅ travaṅ Devaçila. jñahv gi srū mūlya prak taṁliṅ 5 yugala yau 1* 'A ricefield near the tank of Devaçila. The barter for it is paddy. The value of this is 5 ounces of silver and a *yau* of double cloth'. The text continues, ll. 8–9: *dep ge crip ti ple jon ta Vrah Kaṁmratāṅ Añ* 'The land is reserved; the produce is given to the god.'

Although the meanings are clear we are left with many unanswered questions arising from these different statements. Are we to think that it is usual for the owner still to keep the land or is K.726, just cited, a special case? Is a transaction like the one cited above (K.49), in which 'exclusive rights' are mentioned, the less usual one? Later, in the Angkor period, inscriptions mention slaves working land for half the month and others working it in the other half (see K.809, l. 14). Does the original owner retain some use of his land even when it is 'given' to the god, and, if so, does this happen in some or all cases? Are the owners to expect the land back at some future date?

One of two further points about the actual transfer of land are of interest. Quite often more than one owner is mentioned as receiving goods in exchange for one ricefield, e.g. K.493, l. 20: *sre Phalada man jāhv ta Kurāk Jmeṅ doṅ Poñ Vidyāçakti*. 'Phalada ricefield which was brought from Kurāk Jmeṅ and Poñ Vidyāçakti'. K.79 similarly tells us, ll. 9–13, that five Poñ receive paddy, cloth and a ricefield in exchange for ricefields! Perhaps in such instances a vast area of riceland was involved, comprising contiguous ricefields belonging to more than one owner.

3.3. *Land measurement*

The measurements of rice-growing land were often given simply by reference to local landmarks, particularly reservoirs, *travaṅ*. This practice gives us no idea of their size.[4] Sometimes numbers of ricefields, *sare/sanre* were given, e.g. K.557, l. 2, *sre sanre 2* (lit. riceland 2 ricefields) '2 ricefields'. This leaves us to imagine the size of a ricefield. In other cases, however, a capacity measurement is stated; this almost certainly indicated the quantity of seed needed to sow the field. E.g. K.79, l. 13, *sre . . . je 2*; l. 14, *sre . . . tloṅ 1* 'ricefield (needing)

1 je (cf. Mod. Khmer *kɔnceo*: '20 litre basket'?) (of seed); ricefield needing) 1 *tloṅ* (of seed)'. At first sight the variety of ways of stating the amounts of seed is confusing. On some inscriptions the word *mā* occurs followed by *je*, e.g. K.79, ll. 8–9, *sre . . . mā je 2* while on others the form *mās* is found with *je*, e.g. K.18, l. 5, sre . . . mās 1 *je* 1. However, when all pre-Angkor statements on land measurement were collected for comparison, it became clear that:

(a) the numeral 1 is often absent, e.g. K.41, ll. 3–4, *sre . . . tloṅ mā 3* 'ricefield (needing 1) tloṅ 3 mā (of seed)' and K.718 where both *sre . . . pāda 1* and *sre . . . pāda* occur, both meaning 'a piece of ricefield'.

(b) the terms *tloṅ*, *mās/mā* and *je* were capacity measurements of decreasing size while *pāda* 'a piece' is probably not an exact measurement at all, any more than *sanre/sare*. The maximum number of *je* encountered is three, suggesting that 4 *je* = 1 *mās/mā*. The number of *mās/mā* however is most often no more than three but is occasionally much higher; 11 and 12 have been found. The number of *mās* in 1 *tloṅ* is not certain therefore.

The exchange of goods for ricefields was discussed in the last paragraph. In all the pre-Angkor texts in Khmer we have only one, K.79, in which the capacity measurement of land is given with its price. Two items from this inscription are quoted here, although the evidence they produce adds to our confusion rather than to our enlightenment about ancient Khmer economics, since two pieces of land of identical capacity have different quantities of cloth as their prices! Presumably one was superior to the other in some respect which we are not to know: K.79, l. 13, *sre . . . je 2. jnāhv* (price) . . . *canlek amval* (double cloth) *yau 1 vlaḥ 1*. l. 21, *sre . . . je 2. jnāhv* (price) . . . *canlek amval* (double cloth) *vlaḥ* 1.

APPENDIX

Lists of vocabulary

1. Slave categories

kantai	womenfolk. K.904, l. 1, etc. Sometimes to be translated 'wife'.
kārmmāntika	workers. K.41, l. 4 only
kon	children. K.24, B, l. 3, etc.
kñuṁ	slaves, *passim*.
klamuṁ	maidens. K.24, B, l. 12 only.
gho	Short for *ghoda*. Occurs on K.134, 135, l. 24 and K.749, l. 13.
ghoda	menfolk. K. 560, l. 2, etc.
tai	female. K.24, A. l. 2.
der	on the verge of puberty(?). K.149, l. 23, etc.
pau	unweaned. K.8, l. 8, etc.
meṅ	children. K.134, l. 21. Seems to be equivalent to *kon* in this one inscription of the extreme north-east. Presumably related to Old Khmer *kanmeṅ* 'young'.
rat	running about. K.66, l. 18, etc.
laṅ	strong, full-grown, having attained the age of puberty(?). K.149, l. 21.
si	male, menfolk. *passim*.

2. Slave duties

kñuṁ vihāra	slave of the temple. K.755, l. 2.
kñuṁ vraḥ	slave of the divinity. K.8, l. 9, etc.
kñuṁ vraḥ rapaṁ	slave of the sacred dance. K.137, l. 8.
kñuṁ sre	slave of the ricefield. K.137, l. 26.
gandharva	musician (male). K.155, I, l. 7
gvāl	herdsman. K. 155, II, l. 11.
camdak	trapper (?). K.748, II, l. 9, etc.
camreṅ	singer. K.137, l. 9, etc.
cam-uk	? (all men). K.24, B, l. 10, etc.
cmap	one who catches. K.137, l. 21 only.
cmuh	secretary. K.129, l. 5, etc.
cmaṁ	guard. K. 939, l. 8, etc.
taṁpeḥ	(fruit)-picker(?). K.137, l. 17 only.
tmāñ	weaver. K.956, l. 2, etc.
tmir slik	one who sews leaves (Mod. Khmer *de:(r)*). K.137, l. 15.
tmiṅ	player of stringed musical instrument (played by plucking). K.557, est, l. 1.
tmon	? K.124, l. 9 only.
dnuk	? (all men). K.155, II, l. 20 only.
pamas	grinder (e.g. of perfume). K. 124, l. 7.
pi le	for work inside? (lit. 'so as to be above').. K.155, I, l. 6
pedanātaka rpam	dancers (female with Indian names). K.155, I, l. 9.
pramah	chief of women (?). K.137, l. 14.
mahānasa	cook. K.155, I, l. 18.
raṅhvai	one who spins thread. K.155, II, l. 10.
ramaṁ	dancer. K. 557, est, l. 1.

vari	? (all men). K.129, l. 1, etc.
vādya	musician. K. 129, l. 3 only.
samantagajapati	chief of the king's elephant. K.140, l. 3 only.
smon	one who moulds (statues?) (Mod. Khmer *so:n*). K.137, l. 21 only.
ārttai	? (all women). K.24, B, l. 13 only.
aṁrah	chief of slaves (all men). K.423, B, l. 2, etc.
ᵃmuh	heater (i.e. of water). K.127, l. 6, etc.

3. Slave titles

ku	female adult. *passim.*
māṅ	male adult (Mon). K.46, B, l. 6 foll. and K.76, l. 2 only.
ya	Precedes female names and is preceded by *ku.* cf. Mon *ya,* a female prefix. Cannot be held to refer to Mons since it occurs in the list of Prous in K. 137.
yi	Occurs in Prou list in K.137 preceded, like *ya,* by *ku. ya* occurs several times in the same list. cf. Mod. Khmer *ŋi:* (female)?
va, vā	male adult. *passim.*
oṅ	female adult (Mon). K.46, ll. 7–9.

4. Kinship terms

ge kule	members of the family. K.561, l. 22, etc.
ᵃji, ji	ancestor. K.451, nord, 4, etc.
kamton	on the grandmother's side; (?)grandmother. K.38, l. 13.
ᵃta, ta	father, K.357, l. 14, etc.
ᵃme, me	mother. K.138, l. 7, etc.
cpoṅ	elder sibling. K. 79, l. 10, etc.
paon	younger sibling. K.480, l. 12, etc.
kon	child. K.451, l. 7, etc.
kon prasā	son/daughter-in-law. K.51, l. 14.
kmoy, kanmoy	nephew/niece; *kanmoy kamton* great-nephew on the female side. K.38, l. 13.
cau	grandchild. K.562, l. 6, etc.
cau dvot	great-grandchild. K.124, l. 5.

5. Examples of slave names
Suggesting good qualities:

jā pi sralañ	made to be loved
tlai	valuable
paem	sweet
saap anyāya	hating injustice

Suggesting bad qualities:

kreṅ	afraid
cgoṅ	imperfect
vlac	forgetful
sa-ap	hating
sgih	sullen
slāṅ	pale
sa-uy	stinking

Suggesting activities:

campaṅ	warfare
jul	mend
tpāñ	weaving
reṅ	do basket-work
raṁnap	kill
smoṁ	beggar
hām	forbid

Describing physical characteristics:

kaṁput	having lost a limb
kmau	dark
kvak	blind
damṅan	weight
pdai	stomach
muk kraham	red-faced
sku	white-haired

Suggesting non-Khmer origin:

jloy	prisoner-of-war
ramañ	Mon
vrau	Prou
syām	Siamese(?)

Names of animals:

kantur	mouse
kcau	shellfish
ktām	crab
klā	tiger
cke	dog
cmā	cat
jleṅ	leech
taṅku	maggot
tmāt	vulture
bhe	otter
mon	silkworm
skār	weasel
srāṅ	wasp
svā kmau	black monkey
aṇḍaṅ	eel
anrok	ox (cf. Kuy *anrok*?)

Names of plants:

candana	sandalwood
pkā jhe	blossom
vñe	flower
vñe vrai	forest flower
smau	grass
svāy	mango
anlik	melon
aṁvau	sugar-cane

Names of inanimate things:

dik	water
dyoṅ	carbon
pkāy	star

Sanskrit names:

ksān	peaceful
gurudeva	divine teacher
daçami	tenth
dvadaçi	twelfth
dharmmadat	given by the Law
dharmmapāla	protector of the Law
dharmmaçakta	having power in Law
pañcami	fifth
lābha	luck
vañān	understanding
vidyā	learning
saptami	seventh
sudat	given
çivadāsa	slave of Civa
amṛta	immortal
utpala	*lotus*

6. Agricultural areas

karom	low ground. K.426, l. 4.
caṁkā	place prepared for planting by burning (Co/dès). K.426, l. 4.

camnya	pasture. K.341, nord, l. 9.
camnoṁ	enclosure for animals. K.44, B, l. 2.
cpar	garden. K.562, l. 21, etc.
daṁriṅ	orchard. K.426, l. 4, etc.
sre	ricefield. *passim.*— *praṅ* dry ricefield, K.79, l. 24.

7. Agricultural products

kalmon	wax. K.124, l. 12.
krapās	cotton. K.124, l. 10.
ksira	milk. K.689, B, l. 6.
gmuṁ	honey. K.124, l. 11.
ñarṅor	syrup. K.124, l. 18.
toṅ	coconut. K.416, I, l. 7, etc.
tvau	sorghum millet. K.124, l. 11.
danhuṁ	perfume. K.877, II, l. 13.
pareṅ	oil. K.451, nord, l. 7.
madhu	honey. K.421, l. 8.
madhucchista	wax. K.421, l. 8.
yava	grain. K.421, l. 4.
raṅko	husked rice. K.561, l. 8.—*so* white rice. K.127, l. 10.—*samrat* refined rice. K.30, l. 27.
lṅo	sesamum. K.124, l. 11.
vanli	ginger, K.561, l. 8.
santek	beans. K.689, B, l. 12.
sru, srū	paddy. K.424, l. 6.
çunthi	ginger. K.124, l. 12.
ampel	salt. K.30, l. 29.

8. Buildings and constructions

kadaṁ	hut. K.425, B, l. 5.
kamluṅ	interior. K.135, l. 10.
kralā	court, room. K.557, est, l. 2.
gūha	grotto. K.44, B, l. 1.
jamnan	causeway. K.561, C, l. 16.
tnal	roadway. K.560, l. 11.
travaṅ	reservoir. K.561, l. 15, etc.
thalā	paved open space. K.44, A, l. 11.
dok	boat. K.426, l. 9, etc.

praṇāla	gutter. *pnañ*—cover for gutter, K.910, l. 14. *karap—yau* 1 cloth to cover the gutter, K.124, l. 13.	*chāya*	object giving shade. K.877, II, l. 15.
prāsāda (name)	palace. K.557, est, l. 4.	*chat* (name)	umbrella. K.44, B, l. 7
āvāsa khñum	living quarters of the slaves. K.582, l. 7.	*jeñ den*	chandelier. K.388, B, 18.

9. Metals and stones

tampoñ cane, stick. K.44, A, l. 11.

tek	iron. K.388, B, l. 18.	*tañ*	handle. K.877, II, l. 13.
tmo	stone, gem. K.134, l. 18.	*tpāñ* (name)	weaving. K.66, B, l. 16.
prak	silver. K.79, l. 17.	*thās*	tray. K.505, l. 18.
mās	gold. K.21, l. 5.	*pṛthivī*	the world (held in the hand of a statue of Vishnu). K.21, l. 5.
langau	copper. K.560, l. 2.		
samrit	bronze. K.505, l. 18.		

10. Artefacts[5]

kañ jeñ mās	gold anklet. K.21, l. 5.	*pkā dmeḥ* or *pkā jmeḥ*	artificial flowers of some kind. K.21, l.5.
kaṅsa[ta]tāla	copper gong. K.424, B, l. 5.	*pnañ*	screen, cover (?). K.910, l. 14.
kañje (name)	basket. K.11, l. 1.	*bhājana*	vessel. K.877, II, l. 13.
kataka	bracelet. K.21, l. 3.	*makuta*	diadem. K.910, l. 15.
kamrāl (name)	rug. K.129, l. 2.	*rddeh*	cart. K.426, l. 9.
karap	cover. K.21, l. 4.	*valvel*	candlestick-holder. K.21, l. 6.
kalaça	flask. K.877, II, l. 12.		
kirita	diadem. K.21, l. 2.	*vnāk*	arrangement, set (of jewels, utensils). K.21, l. 13.
knop	belt. K.21, l. 4.		
klas	umbrella. K.560, l. 2.		
cakra	disc. K.21, l. 5.	*siṅhāsana*	throne with seated lion. K.877, II. l. 15.
candal	support. K.877, II, l. 17.	*svok*	tray. K.124, l. 9.
canlak	sculpted figure. K.79, l. 18.—*samruk* engraved in repoussé. K.21, l. 3.	*çaṅkha*	conch. K.877, II, l. 15.
		çarāvana	shallow dish or lid. K.877, II, l. 13.
canlek	cloth.—*yugala* double (double-threaded?) cloth.. K.79, l. 8. Other kinds of cloth: *kamvar, kāpata, jli, uladdha, ple, vagṛsa, pan-eñ*	*çrivatsa*	Exact translation cannot be given for this symbol of good fortune K.877, II, l. 15.
		añjul (name)	needle. K.137, l. 19.
		ardhacandra	half-moon. K.877, II, l. 17.
		āstharana	bed. K.388, B, l. 19.
canhoy	steamer. K.877, II, l. 14.	*ᵃhvek*	ladle. K.124, l. 10.
cnañ	cooking pot. K.124, l. 9.	*udaravandha*	decorative band worn round the waist. K.21, l. 5.

APPENDIX B

1. The pre-Angkor inscriptions in Khmer.

All the published inscriptions[6] are entered below, represented by their inventory numbers, in numerical order. They are placed in the appropriate column with regard to their date. An inscription which is dated or has a refer ence to a reign or is approximately dated by Coedès because of the orthography is placed in the first or second column accordingly.[7] An inscription which can be attributed only to the pre-Angkor period is placed in the third column. The letters A–Z refer to the areal groups on the map. A bar, —, indicates that it is no longer known where the inscription was found.

Pre-A.D. 700	Post-A.D. 700 to 802	Pre-Angkor	Pre-A.D. 700	Post-A.D. 700 to 802	Pre-Angkor
		1 Y		124 I	
		6 Z			126 I
	7 Z				
		8 Z	127 I		
			129 I		
9 Z			133 I		
		11 X		134 I	
	18 W			135 I	
22 X			137 —		
24 U			138 K		
		25 U	140 K		
28 U				145 K	
30 U				146 K	
		37 T	149 H		
38 U			154 R		
41 U					155 —
44 X			159 G		
		46 X			163 G
		48 V		259 D	
49 V			341 B		
51 V			357 E		
54 V					
66 Q					388 A
73 S					389 A
74 S					400 A
76 T			416 S		
78 O					421 Z
79 —			422 X		
80 R			423 X		
90 M		98 P	424 S		
		103 P	426 R		
		107 P	427 S		
		108 P		428 M	
109 P			430 L		
113 P			437 H		
115 M			438 H		
			447 F		

Pre- A.D. 700	Post- A.D. 700 to 802	Pre- Angkor	Pre- A.D. 700	Post- A.D. 700 to 802	Pre- Angkor
451 D			728 —		
		480 —			739＝560, q.v.
482 —					
493 Q			748 U		
502 J					749 D
505 C				753 D	
		518 V			755 U
548 U					757 K
557,					759 R
600 U					764 T
		559 U	765 T		
560 T					766 O
561 U					784 S
562 W					785 S
563 T					786 —
582 T					787 R
	590 F				788 R
600			790 —		
See 557					808 D
607 H					810 R
608 H					811 U
648 M					816 H
		657 E			818 G
		664 Q			877 S
		670 U			884 Z
	688 D				903 R
689 X				904 D	
709 U			910 R		
710 T					911 Y
711 S					922 D
712 S			926 L		
718 W				927 L	
719 W					939 U
		723 B			940 R
		724 A			956 V
726 N			1010 T		

NOTES

1. The term 'slave' which I have used throughout the paper caused a lively discussion at the Colloquy. This is summarized in a note at the end of the paper.
2. This interpretation, if correct, would explain why, while the order eldest to youngest is strictly maintained elsewhere, the classes *der* and *lāṅ* have no fixed order. The order *der* 'on the verge of . . .' and *lāṅ* 'having attained . . .' would be wrong from the human development angle but very understandable linguistically. The interpretation of *lāṅ* as 'full-grown' would fit in with the occurrence of the word as a category of ox on K.748, 1.15.
3. cf. teknonyms in Javanese (Damais 1970) and Pacoh (Watson 1969).
4. I am indebted to Mrs. Stargardt for the suggestion that some indication of the relative size of ricefields may be obtained, as in Indonesia, from the number of tanks required to irrigate them.
5. I am grateful to Monsieur A. le Bonheur for help with the translation of some Sanskrit terms in this list.
6. Including K.1010, published by Monsieur C. Jacques, *BEFEO*, lvi, 70.
7. The datings obtained by Monsieur R. Billard, who computerized the astrological information given on pre-Angkor inscriptions, were kindly made available to me by Monsieur C. Jacques. I have thus been able to ensure that the inscriptions are placed in the correct columns in accordance with the most reliable and up-to-date information.
8. The exact position of this inscription was communicated to me at the Colloquy by Monsieur C. Jacques.

Note on the discussion during the Colloquy concerning the translation of kñuṁ *as 'slave'*

Monsieur Jacques was firmly of the opinion that the personnel listed as *kñuṁ*, all of whom were working for the god in some capacity and were the property of the god, and many of whom actually worked in the temple, could not, consistently with this, be 'slaves', since slaves are persons of the most abject human condition. The term 'slave' would seem particularly unsuitable when it referred to those personnel with the duties of dancer, musician, cook (for the god), *kñuṁ vrah*, etc. but would, in his view, not be right even for those who performed more menial tasks. Monsieur le Bonheur supported this with the argument that in India the god and the temple could not possibly be associated with persons who might be described as 'déclassés'. Both these speakers also felt strongly that persons having Sanskrit names—a practice which was normal for the élite in Cambodia—could not be described as 'slaves'.

My own view was that people who are bought, sold, and given are not free and should therefore be termed 'slaves'. The translation 'serf' would possibly be appropriate for those who seemed tied to the land (see pp. 408–9) but would not cover the *kñuṁ* with other duties. I also felt that it should be borne in mind that classical Greece and Rome had slaves in temples and that, while such a practice might be unthinkable in India, we were not in fact discussing India! I do, however, appreciate that the word 'slave' is associated with

2. Key to the groups A–Z on the map.
For each group the positions marked on
the map are dealt with from north to
south (N–S) or from west to east (W–E).
Inscriptions are identified by means of
their inventory numbers. Where more
than one inscription was found at one
place the numbers are separated by a
comma. Semi-colons separate the details referring to separate map positions.

A (N–S) 400; 388, 389.
B (N–S) 723, 724; 341.
C 505.
D Near Puok, 451; at Angkor, 749,
753, 904, 922; at Siemreap, 259; at
Roluos, 688, 808.
E (N–S) 657; 357.
F 590; 447.
G (N–S) 818; 159; 163.
H (N–S) 816; 149, 437, 438, 607, 608.
I (N–S) 127; 129, 133; 124, 126;
134, 135.
J 502.
K (N–S) 146; 145; and (W–E) 138;
140, 757.
L (N–S) 430; 926, 927.
M (W–E) 648; 90, 428; 115.

N 726.
O 766; 78.
P (Three northerly sites, W–E) 113;
103; 109; and (W–E) 107, 108; 98.
Q (N–S) 66; 493; 664.
R (Four most northerly sites, W–E)
903, 910; 759; 940; 426; (remainder W–E) 788; 810; 787; 80, 154.[8]
S 427; 416; 424; 784, 785; 877; 74;
73. Exact position not known to the
writer: 711, 712.
T (N–S) 76; 764, 1010; 563; 560;
765, 37; 710. Exact position not
known to the writer: 582.
U (N–S) 811; 748; 41; 38; 755; 30;
28; at Angkor Borei, 24, 25, 548,
557, and 600, 939; 670. Exact position not known to the writer: 559,
561, 709.
V (Westerly sites, N–S) 956; 51; 54;
49; 48; (NE site) 518.
W (N–S) 562; 718; 719; 21, 18.
X (W–E) 423; 46; 44; 689; 11, 422;
22.
Y (N–S) 1; 911.
Z (N–S) 6, 7, 8, 421; 9; 884.

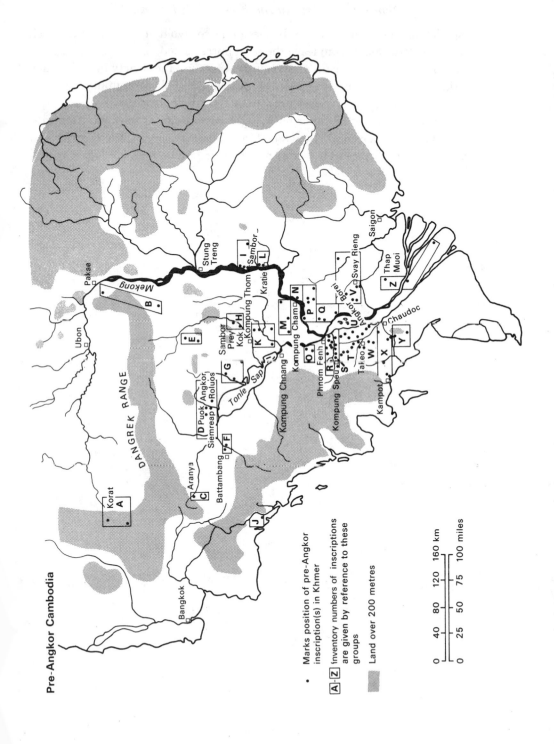

Pre-Angkor Cambodia

· Marks position of pre-Angkor inscription(s) in Khmer

Ⓐ-Ⓩ Inventory numbers of inscriptions are given by reference to these groups

Land over 200 metres

| 0 | 40 | 80 | 120 | 160 km |
| 0 | 25 | 50 | 75 | 100 miles |

degradation and that it might be desirable to avoid it. A solution which seemed to satisfy all was to leave the term untranslated.

In connection with the discussion of the *kñuṁ* and the society in which they worked, Mrs. J. Stargardt suggested to me that the whole community may have been conscripted, and therefore not strictly free, not only at the level of temple personnel, but also at all other levels right up to that of the highest officials. Mrs. Stargardt mentioned the case of craftsmen in ancient Burma, who had no choice but to take up the craft which their fathers had worked at before them.

Khmer 'Hinduism' in the Seventh Century*

O. W. WOLTERS

THIS essay is a historian's comment on Cambodian protohistory, and the seventh century is a time for taking stock of developments already under way. The scene is Cambodia because Cambodian protohistory is incomparably better served with relatively continuous Chinese and epigraphic evidence than any other part of South East Asia during the first centuries of the Christian era. Nearly 200 inscriptions in Sanskrit and also in Khmer have been attributed to the seventh century, and seventy-nine of them are dated or mention identifiable kings. These inscriptions supply the most important corpus of indigenous literary information so far available in the region before the end of the seventh century.

The intention in this essay is to discuss some social, political, and religious phenomena, especially visible in the seventh century, in order to enquire by way of hypothesis whether Khmers were construing what they had come to learn of Hinduism in terms intelligible to them because of their pre-Hindu experiences and beliefs. The assumption will be that, for the Khmers, Hinduism was essentially a religious phenomenon, to be examined later in the essay, and that we should think of it as coming to the Khmers originally in the form of news, travelling over trade routes. Men listen to news only when they can interpret it and can perceive that it has some meaning for them. We shall therefore be concerned with the possibility of Khmer 'Hinduism', which may be a concept as valid as, for example, Chinese 'Buddhism'. The Chinese were able to restate the Mahāyāna,[1] and the possibility that the Khmers did likewise in respect of Hinduism need not be entirely fanciful.

Consideration must first be given to the identity of those who appear in epigraphy in an apparently Hindu religious context. We shall refer to them as members of the Khmer élite, ruling as chiefs in independent territories which may be described as principalities. The Chinese records, though not throwing light on Khmer motivation during the protohistoric period, describe some fairly normal secular situations in which this élite found itself. These situations have been known to historians as long ago as 1903, when Pelliot published his study of 'Funan' (Pelliot 1903), but they will be briefly recapitulated because the extension of Hindu influences did little to modify them.

* See Plate XIV.

In the early centuries of the Christian era inter-territorial warfare seems to have been frequent. The location and social structure of the principalities cannot be accurately described, but one can suppose that 'Cambodia' comprised an unknown number of independent centres of territorial authority which correspond with the statement in the third century *Nan-chou i-wu chih* that 'all the vassal countries' of Funan 'have their own chiefs' (*TPYL*, 786, 3482b).[2] Certain chiefs could sometimes muster sufficient military power to impose a hegemony over their neighbours, but hegemonies were short-lived and followed by renewed warfare. A familiar event was what the Chinese regarded as an 'usurpation'. No matter how extensive had been a hegemon's supra-territorial authority, there was no assurance that his chosen successor would be unchallenged. Not many 'usurpations' are recorded in the Chinese texts, but we must remember that not every Khmer ruler was known to the Chinese government. One reason for believing that disturbed conditions persisted is that, as late as the seventh century, the conquering family of Bhavavarman I lost control before many decades had passed. Thereafter an interval of perhaps thirty years separated its hegemony from that of Jayavarman I. During most of the eighth century no hegemon appeared.[3]

The Chinese records reflect an important circumstance which accompanied this warfare during the protohistoric period. Marriage alliance enabled a would-be hegemon to bind other chiefs to his side. According to the *Liang-shu*, the great conqueror, **B'iwăm-*miwăn*, living about A.D. 200, had a sister who married someone sufficiently powerful that her son, **Tian*, 'who was the leader of two thousand men', could seize power from **B'iwăm-*miwăn*'s son.[4] But relatives by marriage were not disarmed. When the opportunity arose, they would mobilize their own allies and dependants in order to make or support a new bid for hegemony. And so **Tian* was later overthrown by another of **B'iwăm-*miwăn*'s sons, **D'iang*, 'who had lived among the people . . . and was able to collect good soldiers of the country'. These 'soldiers' would have included men from his mother's territory, where he must have taken refuge during the years of **Tian*'s power. But **D'iang* was subsequently overthrown by one of **Tian*'s generals, who would have been yet another chief, with his own manpower resources. The same circumstance of marriage alliance helps to explain Rudravarman's success in the first half of the sixth century. Rudravarman is described by the Chinese as a concubine's son and his father's intended heir as 'the son of the legal wife', but the Chinese, familiar with concubinage rather than with polygamy, misunderstood Rudravarman's status. He would have been the son of a woman from an important and independent princely family bound to his royal father by marriage alliance. Seventh-century epigraphy refers to the brother of Jayavarman I's mother, who, 'while not bearing the title of king, enjoyed a fortune worthy of a king' (*ISCC*, 71, v. 17). Perhaps Jayavarman had discharged a debt to his mother's family, incurred when the latter helped him in his campaigns. In the eighth and ninth centuries, the great Jayavarman II contracted at least seven marriages, two of which were of considerable political importance (Wolters 1973).

In this situation we can suppose with some confidence that would-be hegemons, after giving evidence of their ability, were acclaimed as overlords by their relatives and allies. And thus, again according to the *Liang-shu*, *B'iwăm-*miwăn* 'was promoted by the people of the country to be king', and similarly, perhaps, Kauṇḍinya II about A.D. 400 was summoned from the Malay Peninsula and 'established as king'.

The implication of this evidence is that the significant political event in the Khmer world was an overlordship, of temporary duration and made possible by a coalition of chiefs who recognized the capacity of the adventurer seeking the hegemony. Rewards would then be distributed, additional marriage alliances would be negotiated, and those who wished to be undisturbed in their local power would prudently hasten to have their authority confirmed by the new overlord.

The territories which were the scene of these king-making adventures cannot convincingly be described as a 'kingdom', possessing its own acknowledged and permanent identity. Only the Chinese, with their sense of 'dynasty', write of the existence of a 'kingdom of Funan', a term which they found convenient to retain until the early seventh century.[5] Their reason was simply that the chief of *B'iu-nam* (= 'Funan'), perhaps residing at his centre of Vyādhapura, happened to be the first Khmer chief with whom they established contact as long ago as the third century. Yet there is no certainty that an overlord always resided there. In the king-making process the practical significance of lineage probably lay in the means it provided for identifying family connections and therefore potential allies: lineage is unlikely to have compensated for an absence of the personal quality of leadership.[6] Moral stigma was not attached to what the Chinese regarded as 'usurpation', for an overlord's power was not protected by the concept of a 'dynasty' in a society with a plethora of half-brothers.[7] The political reality was a temporary overlordship based on this or that territorial centre. A ninth-century inscription, which mentions an eighth-century chief, Rājendravarman, states that he was descended on his mother's side from the overlords (*adhirāja*) of a particular centre, Vyādhapura (*ISCC*, 364, v. 3).

Because the chiefs did not understand the notion of a 'kingdom', with its supra-territorial demands on their loyalty, 'kingship' remained essentially a personal achievement. Those who acclaimed someone as 'king' realized that he was endowed with extraordinary qualities, which we shall call 'prowess'. The essential nature of his 'prowess' will be considered later in this essay. No more need be suggested here than that the adventurer was able to mobilize his coalition not because he could claim to be the descendant of an earlier overlord but because his supporters were able to perceive that he was distinguished by personal qualities of leadership and self-confidence, which guaranteed the success of his enterprise. Provided that he gave evidence of prowess, subordinate adventurers, living in a society which probably practised bilateral kinship as it does today and in which the establishment of new households was customary, would have been waiting in the wings for chances of bettering their fortunes. According to the *Sui-shu*, containing information brought to China during a mission in 616:

> When a man's marriage ceremonies are completed, he takes a share of his parents' property and leaves them in order to live elsewhere (*Sui-shu*, 82, 6b).

Enterprising men, not bound by parental ties, could therefore travel to seek their fortunes by putting themselves under the protection of chiefs of promise. The seventh-century inscriptions reflect this society in their references to brothers in control of separate territories and to pairs of brothers who made good in apparently independent careers (*ISCC*, 68–72; *IC*, I, 11; *IC*, IV, 31; *IC*, V, 37; *IC*, V, 43). When a man of prowess was perceived, families could mobilize their own independent resources and also those of their relatives in order to rally around him *en bloc*, as happened in the reign of Jayavarman II (Wolters 1973). The more relatives a supporter had, the greater would be his contribution to the royal adventurer's enterprise.[8]

We can now attempt a general comment on these aspects of Khmer protohistory. Part of the experience of the princely *élite* and their entourages was an awareness that society was composed of men with greatly different capacities for achievement. The overlordship was the symbol of the highest achievement, and what we would define as 'the kingdom' was no more than the territorial measurement of a particular overlord's prowess. Territories within an overlordship were defined not by geographical boundaries but by the behaviour of those who, for the time being, acknowledged the ruler's personal authority. The overlordship could not be won and the kingship seized until the would-be hegemon's fellow chiefs were able to recognize his prowess in the field of endeavour most familiar to them, which was warfare. Important changes in the *status quo* would therefore be bound to be accompanied by a sensation of *rapport* between leaders and supporters. In general, Khmer protohistory would have been the story of human inequality in terms of prowess but also of profitable dependent relationships at a time when the quickening of international trade through South East Asia was increasing the means and rewards of warfare.

These chiefs will now be considered as they appear in the epigraphy of Khmer protohistory and especially in seventh-century inscriptions. Their 'Hindu' professions will be seen to be by no means inconsistent with their behaviour as it is reflected in the fragmentary Chinese records, but their motivation now becomes explicit, though expressed by means of the Sanskrit vocabulary of Hinduism. Their modes of worship are, as Bosch insisted in a discussion of the Hinduisation of Indonesia, those of Śivaite devotionalism (Bosch 1961).

The influence of this doctrine is reflected in the definitions of Śiva's attributes, proclaimed by the invocations of the seventh-century inscriptions. He is 'the creator' (*IC*, I, 14, v. ii). He is 'omniscient' (*IC*, III, 172, v. i) and 'the first of the ascetics' (*IC*, II, 150, v. i). An inscription of 624, a statement of Śivaite doctrine, represents Śiva as a personal god of grace, with inherent qualities, and also as absolute *brahman* (*ISCC*, 36; Bhattacharya 1955; Bhattacharya 1961: 57–8).

The modes of worship, extolled in the inscriptions, are also those of Śivaite devotionalism. The worshipper is required to give 'undiverted' thought and devotion (*ISCC*, 70, v. 13; *IC*, I, 15, v. vii). Śiva is 'accessible to sages through meditation exclusively concentrated on him' (*IC*, V, 43, v. i). Sense control must be practised (*ISCC*, 70, v. 16; *IC*, I, 11, v. xv). One of Śiva's worshippers claims to be 'without pride' (*ISCC*, 70, v. 16). Asceticism in honour of Śiva, the first of the ascetics, is particularly emphasized. Ascetics are placed in charge of temples (*ISCC*, 19, v. 33; *IC*, IV, 32, v. viii). Land is granted to ascetics (*IC*, II, 12, v. iv). An ascetic, ablaze with Śiva's *śakti*, or divine energy, is in charge of a grotto for other ascetics (*IC*, V, 13).

Ascetics are referred to under several terms, including *muni* (*ISCC*, 50, v. 3), and among them are the Pāśupatas, mentioned on two occasions. The Pāśupatas were the ascetics *par excellence* in this period, and they were in the confidence of kings. Īśānavarman I entrusted one of them with the care of a temple (Finot 1928: 46, v. xii; *IC*, IV, 17–19), and Bhavavarman employed another as a poet; he practised asceticism according to the Śaiva rule (vidhi) (*IC*, I, 5, v. iv and viii).

The Pāśupatas are the only Śivaite sect known in the *Mahābhārata*, and they are mentioned in an inscription of Mathurā of the fourth century A.D. (Bhattacharya 1961: 43–4). Kauṇḍinya, who wrote a commentary on the *Pāśupata-sūtra*, is believed to have lived between the fourth and sixth centuries (Chakraborti 1970: 14). Hsüan-tsang observed Pāśupatas in several parts of India during the first half of the seventh century. He also saw them in Afghanistan, and they may have travelled as far east as Khotan in Turkestan (Chakraborti, 15; Beal 1969, under 'Pāśupata' and in Book II, 310–11, where a 'heretic covered with cinders' advises a king). Thus, they were to be found on or near the trans-Asian continental trade route, and their appearance in Cambodia near a trans-Asian maritime route is not altogether surprising.

We need not doubt that Śivaite devotionalism was established among the Khmer élite in the seventh century. By that time Khmer-language inscriptions

are using important Sanskrit terms as part of the vocabulary for honouring Śiva.[9] The antiquity and first origins of this situation will not be discussed
here, though we can note that the Buddhist Nāgasena had observed a royal
Śiva cult in Cambodia in 484 (Bhattacharya 1961: 12–13). The term *bhakti*,
albeit in the context of the worship of Viṣṇu by a king's son, appears in an
inscription of the second half of the fifth century (Coedès 1931: 7).

The feature of Hinduism in Cambodia by the seventh century which must
now be emphasized is that Śivaite devotionalism, implicitly individualist in
its goal of personal union with Śiva, was also practised within the social context of Khmer overlordship. Although many of the inscriptions make no
reference to the contemporary political situation, those in the names of kings
or the kings' followers reveal that devotionalism had taken into account the
distinction between a man of prowess and those over whom he had asserted
his hegemony. The hierarchy of temporal prowess, reflected in Chinese
evidence of king-making adventures against a background of independent
principalities, is complemented by a devotional hierarchy. The hierarchy is
maintained in spite of the circumstance that both overlords and their 'servants'
(*bhṛtya*) subscribe in their invocations to the same doctrinal beliefs concerning
Śiva. They respect ascetic practices, and they erect *liṅgas* or statues to Śiva.[10]

The overlord did not emerge in a social vacuum. He was only a territorial
chief, whose private military resources were never sufficient to enable him to
dispense with the need for allies, attracted to him by his abnormal powers of
leadership. Now, in a 'Hindu' guise, the overlord's superior prowess can be
measured. He is seen as one whose soul (*ātman*) had achieved the closest possible relationship with Śiva by virtue of his ascetic efforts in devotion to Śiva,
the first of ascetics. As a result, he enjoys Śiva's *śakti* and therefore spiritual
and physical power. Bhavavarman II is described as 'possessing unshakable
self-control as a result of his austerities (*tapas*)' (*IC*, II, 70, v. i). A king who
may be Bhavavarman I is 'able to conquer the six vices' (*ISCC*, 17, v. 4).[11]
Bhavavarman I had 'seized the kingship by means of his personal *śakti*', a
statement which epitomises the 'Hinduised' man with most prowess in Khmer
inter-territorial relations (*ISCC*, 69, v. 5). Īśānavarman I recalls Śiva as living
among the ascetics (*IC*, v, 31, v. i), and he himself 'took pleasure in the company of sages' (*IC*, v, 26, v. ii); his sages can be assumed to include ascetics.
Not surprisingly, Īśānavarman I is ascribed with *śakti* (*IC*, IV, 9, v. ix).
Jayavarman I, who came to the fore after some decades when overlordship
was in abeyance (Wolters 1974), is 'an incarnate portion (*aṃśa*) of the god, who
is Śiva, (*IC*, I, 10, v. iii). He, too, would have possessed *śakti*.

These kings apparently welcomed to their entourage religious ascetics,
including Pāśupatas. Other Śivaite ascetics as well as Pāśupatas would have
been represented, but they can be expected to have had much in common with
the Pāśupatas, differing only in ritual and religious practices (Gonda 1965:

237). Because the language of the invocations reflects Pāśupata doctrine as set forth in the *Pāśupata-sūtra's* commentary by Kauṇḍinya, Kauṇḍinya's text may throw some light on religious influences within Khmer royal courts, represented by the Pāśupatas.

These startling ascetics, covered with ashes, are bound to have made an impression. The commentary states that they share all Śiva's power with the exception of the power of creation (Chakraborti 1970: 28). They are, in fact, warned not to take too much delight in the attainment of miraculous power, placing them beyond Śiva's jurisdiction (ibid., 107). Even more impressive would have been their conception of the *guru's* status. The *guru* represents Śiva. 'There is no doubt that Śiva becomes worshipped by him who worships the teacher always in all circumstances' (ibid., 72). Or again, 'the disciple becomes powerful by (the power of) the *guru* . . .' (ibid., 89). The *guru* at court would have been the royal disciple's most accessible link with the god, who could link his disciple to god. The overlords therefore had opportunities and encouragement for cultivating their own close relationship with Śiva, bringing them limitless spiritual power and the temporal implications of such power.

The presence of Pāśupatas in the royal entourage tells us something more about Khmer 'Hinduism'. The Pāśupatas belonged to the religious élite in the sense that they were brahmans, but they were wayward brahmans who were not interested in Vedic sacrifices and believed that Śiva's grace prevailed over the law of *karma*. In India they turned their back on society and behaved as 'lunatics' for God's sake (Chakraborti, 140). Their willingness to cross the ocean may be another sign of their indifference to brahmanical conventions and of their zeal in incurring hardship for Śiva's sake. These Indian representatives of Hinduism in Cambodia are unlikely to have insisted that some form of brahmanical society should be reproduced there.

In Khmer 'Hinduism' the man of prowess, with his ascetic advisors, was now Śiva's foremost worshipper. What can be said of the 'Hinduism' of his 'servants', those who had come under his influence?

Their inscriptions are much less numerous than those of Śiva-worshippers who mention no overlord in their inscriptions and whose political relationships are not disclosed. On the other hand, a general consistency appears in the contents of the royal 'servants'' inscriptions; their inscriptions reveal the significance they attach to various kinds of royal gifts in the context of their devotion to Śiva, a devotion sometimes explicitly in support of their hope for a superior death status.

Four kinds of royal gifts are mentioned. The first kind comprises a wide range of posts with honourable responsibilities, including the posts of special counsellor, president of the royal council, governorships of towns, and head of the royal oarsmen. These posts are bestowed as signs of royal confidence in the recipients (*IC*, I, II, v. xvi, xx; *IC*, I, 15, v. vi; *IC*, III, 163, v. xiii; *ISCC*, 18–19, v. 22–4; *ISCC*, 71, v. 17), and they justify ascribing the office-holders with specific spiritual qualities (*IC*, II, 151, v. iii; *IC*, III, 163, v. xiii; *ISCC*, 18, v. 22; *ISCC*, 70, v. 16). Royal service is also seen as protecting the *dharma* (*ISCC*, 19, v. 30; *ISCC*, 25, v. 12; *ISCC*, 70, v. 14–15; *IC*, III, 163, v. xiii). The second type of gift is in the form of presents from the ruler (*ISCC*, 25, v. 6 and 9; *IC*, I, 15, v. vi). The third is the gift of titles of honour (*IC*, IV, 32, v. iv; *IC*, IV, 30).[12] Fourthly, the ruler confirms secular and religious privileges (*IC*, VI, 8, v. vi; *ISCC*, 71, v. 18).

The gift-recording inscriptions are undertaken when the recipient erects a *liṅga* or statue to demonstrate his devotion (*bhakti*) to Śiva (*IC*, II, 151, v. iv; *ISCC*, 19, v. 32). In one instance the royal gifts seem actually to be offered to the recipient's cult (*IC*, I, 15, v. viii–ix). Sometimes the intention in founding the cult is unambiguously expressed in the hope of a superior death status, described in conventional terms of a fortunate rebirth or entering Śiva's abode (*IC*, I, 12, v. xxiii; *IC*, II, 151, v. iv), and all these foundations can be assumed to be with this purpose in mind unless another intention is clearly stated.[13]

The overlord was evidently seen as a spiritual influence on his servants' lives and hopes of salvation. Not surprisingly, overlords attracted personal loyalty, described in one case as *bhakti* (*IC*, v, 29, v. xii). As gestures of homage, servants offer presents to the ruler's temple or erect statues of the god in the ruler's honour (*IC*, v, 29, v. xii; Coedès 1936: 9). But gifts to brahmans, not described as ascetics, are rare in the extant inscriptions (*IC*, IV, 61–3; *ISCC*, 47, v. 4). Brahmans would have benefited from their superintendence of the chiefs' temples, for which revenue was made available, but they do not seem to have been honoured because of the rituals which they performed in India on behalf of society. In inscriptions of the Gupta period the *Mahābhārata* is frequently quoted to emphasize the importance of gifts to brahmans, but not in the Khmer inscriptions. In Gupta times, brahmans, because of gifts specially made to them, were becoming wealthy landowners, but in Cambodia merit is earned by personal achievement and not by honouring brahmans.[14]

Khmer 'Hindu' practices are always on behalf of the worshipper, layman as well as ascetic, and those in royal service are seen as having most to offer their god. The secular and hierarchical structure of Khmer inter-territorial relationships is not modified by the presence of a brahman class on top of society. Instead, it is complemented by the hierarchical modes of Śivaite devotionalism. The members of the élite continue to perform their customary roles, and their secular performance on behalf of men of prowess enables them to earn additional merit and enhance their prospects after death.

The question may now be asked whether the Khmers were emphasizing certain features of available Hinduism to reflect pre-Hindu beliefs. Paul Mus has already proposed that Śiva's creative and fertilizing powers, cosmic in scale, permitted South East Asians to identify their stones in honour of gods of the soil with the Śiva-*linga* (Mus 1933).[15] Perhaps additional pre-Hindu beliefs are echoed in Khmer 'Hinduism'.

If Khmers were construing Hinduism in comprehensible terms, they may have instinctively accommodated two pre-Hindu assumptions. Gifts from above may already have been seen as possessing a religious quality, from which the recipient was believed to benefit. This assumption would explain the importance the 'servants' attached to symbols of royal favour in their death-wish inscriptions. Secondly, gifts may already have been regarded as spiritually efficacious only when the recipient had earned them by his own achievements. The overlord practised asceticism, and his servants exerted themselves by accepting and following royal leadership.

But these two assumptions would have been sustained by a further one, representing the essence of pre-Hindu religious experience. Society, seen as the scene for exhibiting various capacities for personal achievement with religious as well as secular significance, would also have been perceived as the scene of relationships between those with different capacities for achievement, enabling the man of superior prowess to provide those of lesser prowess with opportunities for achieving within their capacity.

Gupta and Pallava epigraphy, though a record of merit-earning and often in honour of Śiva, does not seem to articulate these assumptions as clearly and insistently as the Cambodian inscriptions of the seventh century do. In particular, the king-servant relationship, expressed in terms of honourable gifts, is not starkly elaborated. The social setting of religious beliefs in other cultures may resemble Khmer 'Hinduism' more closely.

For example, the inscriptions of bronze vessels in early Chou times 'advertise the honours conferred [by king or feudal prince] on the person responsible for the casting of the bronze' (Watson 1962: 76).[16] These bronzes were used in sacrifices to the recipients' ancestors, to be 'treasured perpetually' by their descendants (Watson 1966: 100), and Professor Watson has suggested that the religious and political purposes recorded in the inscriptions belong equally to the uninscribed bronzes buried in the tombs (Watson 1962: 68). Perhaps the Khmer death-wish inscriptions, also commemorating honours conferred by kings, are not dissimilar in religious intent: in both cultures gifts have significance in the after-life.

Another similarity may exist between Khmer 'Hinduism' and beliefs held in ancient China. The Chinese quality of *tê* has been understood to include the notion of potentiality, latent power, and the virtue inherent in things (Waley 1934: 31–2). *Tê* was a quality shared by the patricians, who had inherited it from the ancestors of their clans (Maspero 1955: 100). The Chinese king, like the Khmer overlord, was the first among the princes, and his *tê* had won him the favour of Heaven. But his *tê* also influenced others. As Granet puts it, 'the special genius (*tê*)' of the Chinese overlord was of a 'religious and magic nature. This genius rules and regulates all things by immediate action, the action of spirit upon spirit. It acts by contagion' (Granet 1930: 250–1). Or again, because of the princely virtue, 'le cœur des hommes va droit au devoir' (Granet 1951: 41).

This understanding of the nature of *tê* resembles, at least superficially, the Khmer 'Hindu' conception of the soul (*ātman*). The prowess of the overlord's soul, having won Śiva's favour in the form of *śakti*, creates conditions whereby his followers can perform roles on behalf of the *dharma*. Perhaps the coalitions on behalf of chiefs, recorded by the Chinese as early as in the third century of Cambodian protohistory, were motivated by the chiefs' belief that the souls of lesser men could respond beneficially to those of their leaders.

The possibility that a pre-Hindu system of beliefs enabled Khmers to interpret Śivaite devotionalism is not contradicted by what is known of the tribesmen in the highlands of mainland South East Asia. Professor Kirsch has attributed to the tribesmen a theory of 'unequal souls' (Kirsch 1973: 15). They seem to identify in themselves a quality similar to *mana*, expressed by the procedure of feast-giving. 'The successful feaster is actually demonstrating his "innate virtue", showing his "internal potency", and his control over external supernatural forces' (ibid., 15). We can interpret in this way the reverence paid to the Khmer overlord's gifts by his subordinates. The overlord has clearly displayed proof of his potency, and his association with 'external supernatural forces'. Again, we can note that among the Iu Mien-yao, for example, merit-making investments in the world of men ensure the individual's status in the spirit world (Kandre 1967: 596).[17]

Here, then, are some possibilities in support of the hypothesis that, when the Khmer élite began to hear of Hindu devotionalism, they brought to it as much as they took from it. Indeed, they may even have been recognizing some primitive notions in Hinduism which Hinduism shared with many peoples. The implication of the hypothesis is that Hindu ascetic practices tended to throw into sharper relief Khmer assumptions about an uneven distribution of prowess and the religious *rapport* that bound leaders and led.

Elsewhere in this volume references are made to graves known to have been occupied several millennia ago. These graves may one day be seen to yield evidence of the beliefs of those who occupy them. The time may not be premature for prehistorians to be asking themselves three questions. Are they in the presence of evidence which throws light on very early South East Asian conceptions of the after-life? Are there grounds for supposing that a connection was assumed between temporal achievement and a superior death status? To what extent does the evidence indicate that hierarchy was associated with religious attributes? In dealing with these questions the prehistorian has one advantage over the protohistorian. Those who have left evidence of themselves in prehistoric times are anonymous and can be studied without having to be classified as 'kings' or 'chiefs'. The protohistorian, on the other hand, has to avoid being misled by epigraphic distinctions of ranks. Hinduism was not something which only attracted would-be kings; it was essentially a religious experience of individuals in chieftain society. Moreover, if this experience were as much Khmer as 'Hindu', Hinduism would not inevitably have created a religious wedge between that society and the rest of the population. Śiva's procreative role, as Paul Mus foresaw, would have been understood not only by chiefs but by peasants in the monsoon-controlled lands of Cambodia.

But, if and when the day comes when indigenous elements in Khmer 'Hindu' evidence are more distinct, we must be careful not to react too strongly against the view that Hinduism swamped the Khmer outlook. Although Khmer 'Hinduism' has been discussed in this essay in terms of personal religion, feeding on circumstances of Khmer society and perhaps shaped by pre-Hindu beliefs, we shall suggest, by way of conclusion, that Śivaite devotionalism also brought in its train something which distinguishes protohistory from prehistory. The chiefs came to have a new perception of the environment in which their personal cults flourished. Continuing to perform their ancient roles, they, like the inhabitants of peninsular India, came to see themselves as living in a 'Hindu world'. They were not 'Hindus' only in their moments of worship.

By 'Hindu world' is meant less the actual world of the regional polities in India, visited by or described to Khmers, than the world of the gods and heroes as it is set forth in Indian sacred literature and perhaps, above all, in the *Mahābhārata*, known in parts of South East Asia from at least as early as the fifth century.

The Khmers would not have had much difficulty in identifying some prominent similarities between the 'Hindu world' and Cambodia. The assumption in Indian sacred literature is that all experience is an expression of universal truths, valid everywhere, and Khmers could verify the assumption from their own environment. For example, the *śāstras* assume that all space is organized in *maṇḍalas*, comprising warring polities sometimes brought under the influence of a 'king of kings', and the concept would have corresponded accurately with the Khmer tribal situation. Similarly, happenings in the past as recorded in the *Mahābhārata* would not have perplexed them. The epic does not describe the gradual expansion of a great 'kingdom'. Instead, it renders the past as a record of the continuous expansion and contraction of righteous living, when men beloved by the gods appear from time to time, and Khmers would have observed that heroic princes and warriors often practised asceticism to win divine support. The epic world would have been mirrored in Khmer tribal experience, with its series of overlordships and their collapses.

The feat of holding together a number of independent territories by the Khmer chief closest to Śiva could readily be seen as keeping the *dharma* intact. Again, Indian literature, extolling examples of excellent religious conduct, does not disguise the co-existence of 'barbarians'. Cambodia also had its population living beyond the chiefs' domains. There were 'horrible forests, the abode of savage men' (*IC*, I, II, v. xiv).

In other words, the world of the epic would not have made impossible demands on the Khmer imagination. The Khmer chiefs, hearing about other parts of the Hindu world, would not have felt that they were living in a greatly different environment. They, too, were in the lands of the monsoons. The Indian texts' lists of general categories of pheonomena, illustrated by examples classified under comprehensive headings, would more often than not have allowed Khmers to identify their own known facts within a framework of experience assumed in the texts to be universal. Hindu law acknowledged the importance of local customs. The Indians are likely to have had a Sanskrit word for most things familiar and important in Cambodia, enabling Khmer *literati* to invoke Indian texts, carrying great prestige, as ratifications of what they already knew to be true. Manu's seven constituents of government would have sounded as common sense.[18]

But a general comparability of experience does not necessarily mean that Khmers saw themselves as living in the Hindu world. Is there any evidence that they did in fact do so and by conviction? If so, why and how did they do so?

Two pieces of evidence indicate that they came to see themselves inside the Hindu world and not in its extension overseas. The first of these is that, when they observed certain stone mountain tops, they believed that they were seeing Śiva's natural *liṅgas* (*svāyambhuvaliṅgas*), fashioned in crude stone. These are the most prestigious of all *liṅgas*. Bhavavarman's Pāśupata poet, on a pilgrimage, visited mountains and, in a dream, Śiva brought him to a *liṅga*. When he woke up, he saw the *liṅga* on the top of a hill (*IC*, I, 5, v. vi–vii). A follower of Jayavarman I also venerated a natural *liṅga*; he, too, would have seen himself in the Hindu world (*IC*, I, 15, v. vii). Similarly, Tamils could apprehend these *liṅgas* in their own country.

The second piece of evidence concerns something which happened in the shadow of the natural *liṅga* at Vat Phu, and it shows not only that Cambodia could be seen as part of the Hindu world but also how this perception was possible.

A king Devānīka, perhaps a Cham conqueror, visited this region in the fifth century (Coedès 1956). He was installed in supreme power by 'the blessed Śrī Liṅgaparvata', the natural *liṅga* that dominated the region. He then resolved to found a *tīrtha* in the form of a tank. He gave his tank the name of 'Kurukṣetra', the name of the famous *tīrtha* in the region of Delhi and of the great civil war in the *Mahābhārata*. His tank's name therefore evokes the associations of a site which is in the very centre of the Hindu world as that world is portrayed in the epic. He undoubtedly had in mind the 'Kurukṣetra' of the epic, for verses from the epic concerning 'Kurukṣetra' are quoted in his inscription (Jacques 1962: 250–2). And so the inscription states: 'May the celestial fruit, proclaimed formerly in the Kurukṣetra and celebrated by the Devarṣi, find itself here in the new Kurukṣetra'; 'may the fruits obtained in the thousand *tīrtha* of Kurukṣetra find themselves present here and complete'.

Is Devānīka identifying the epic's tank in Cambodia in the sense of locating it there or is he merely transferring it? For him there could be only one 'Kurukṣetra', and it was the epic's tank, now to be found in Cambodia as a result of his pious intention. In the words of his inscription, he 'had created on earth the best of the *tīrtha*', and the reason why it was possible to execute such an intention tells us something about how he, and Khmer 'Hindus', could apprehend their environment as part of the world of the cosmic gods and therefore part of what we are calling 'the Hindu world'.

The *Tīrtha yātrā parvan*, the section of the epic which deals with Kurukṣetra and also the section quoted in the Vat Phu inscription, assures its reader or listener that 'he that is inspired with the desire of beholding all *tīrthas* should sojourn to them even in imagination . . . Men of piety and learning are able to visit these *tīrthas* by reason of their purified senses, their belief in Godhead, and their acquaintance with the Vedas' (*Tīrtha yātrā parvan*, 284). And of Kurukṣetra it is said: 'O foremost of warriors, the sins of one that desireth to repair to Kurukṣetra even mentally are all destroyed' (*Tīrtha yātrā parvan*, 250).

Devānīka was aware of the efficacy of travelling to Kurukṣetra in his mind. The reason need not necessarily be because he had obeyed the recommendation of the *Mahābhārata* concerning mental travel. Instead, he could have used the imaginative faculty which *gurus* were teaching their disciples as the means of strengthening an awareness of being in their god's presence. Devānīka states that he had just been installed in supreme power by the Śrī Liṅgaparvata, a manifestation of Śiva, and he, together with other Śiva-worshippers, may have been familiar with meditative techniques for willing states of mind which encouraged them to apprehend divinity in all its forms and everywhere. The world was Śiva's creation,[19] and his worshipper would wish to learn to see the world in this way. Moreover, at the beginning of his inscription, Devānīka invokes his many merits, and he probably considers himself qualified to perform what amounts to an 'Act of Truth (*satya*)', with the power to visit mentally all holy sites and therefore the one and only Kurukṣetra in the shape of the tank he has just built.[20] In this way he can invest the region with Kurukṣetra's sanctity. A holy site in the epic has, as a feat of pious volition, become part of Cambodian reality. By virtue of his own merits, the king can project and leave behind him a permanent mark of his privileged perception of the 'Hindu' world. Not surprisingly, this part of the Vat Phu region was still known as 'Kurukṣetra' at least as late as the eleventh century (*IC*, VI, 267).

Meditative techniques need not have been more difficult than remembering that even a criminal, pronouncing the god's name without knowing it, obtained salvation or at least forgiveness of his sins before the judge of the dead (Gonda 1965: II: 240). According to a seventh-century inscription, hearing Śiva's name destroyed all sins (*IC*, I, 11, v. xiii). Śiva could always be approached by speech. Listening to the recitation of the holy texts had particular efficacy; the listener earned merit and could, perhaps, identify himself with what was being recited. The *Mahābhārata*, *Purāṇa*, and *Rāmāyaṇa* were deposited in a seventh-century Khmer temple for the purpose of recitation (*ISCC*, 31, v. 4).

The *guru*'s techniques for teaching the worship of personal gods were therefore also those which enabled the worshipper to reinforce his quest for the omnipresent god by seeing around him a zone of holy sites, which he could himself enlarge as Devānīka had done. These holy sites were the landmarks of the Hindu world, and the centre of that world was always where the Hindu, be he Indian or Khmer, worshipped in the presence of his god.

But everything not connected with personal cults and the accompanying perception of zones of holiness had nothing to do with the Khmers' sense of being in the Hindu world.[21] The veneer of Indian literary allusions in their inscriptions is no more than a metaphorizing of their situations and heroes and a comment on the quality of their scribes' education. Kings are compared with Viṣṇu and Pṛthu, who was impregnated by Viṣṇu, but only to emphasize their courage. 'Viṣṇu' is the metaphor for describing the military qualities of an overlord and his spiritual and Śiva-like qualities which account for his heroism. Īśānavarman I is said to be 'like another Viṣṇu' (*IC*, I, 15, v. iv). Sometimes the royal metaphors are condensed into the single expression that the king is the 'compendium (*varṇamuṣṭi*) of the kings' in the sense of embodying all kingly qualities. Bhavavarman is such a person (*IC*, II, 70, v. I). Īśānavarman I is the *varṇamuṣṭi* 'of the kings of the first of the *yugas*' (Finot 1928: 45, v. iv).

The process of 'Hinduisation', as sketched above, can now be summarized. The process was one of empathy, and, because it was possible through the cultivation of mental aptitudes taught by devotional pedagogy, was essentially one of self-Hinduisation. It was a matter of imaginative intention, and the intention which supplied the underlying impulse was that of tapping cosmic power for personal ends. The process was a continuing one, in which generation after generation of local chiefs and those influenced by the chiefs' lifestyle willed their way ever more confidently into the universal reality in which their death wish could be most hopefully expressed. Perhaps times of king-making adventures were when there was a lively sense of achievement and therefore a sense of religious well-being.[22] But self-Hinduisation was always against a background of inter-territorial relations. As the centuries passed a more spacious measurement of the performance of royal prowess no doubt became available, but the consequence was never the establishment of the concept of a Khmer kingdom as something with its own identity. There was only a cult of kingship in the form of the personal cult of the man who had seized the kingship. Political allegiance, expressed by personal loyalty, was no more than the sum total of the personal religious concerns of the territorial chiefs who believed that an overlordship was providing them with additional means of earning merit and satisfying their death wishes. For them Cambodia was not a 'kingdom' but a holy land in the Hindu world, linked by networks of pilgrimage sites. Their past was lost in the origins of mankind and was adorned more recently by instances of devout warriors, performing great deeds. The present was always the time which mattered, when merit-earning achievement was possible. The future lay in the rewards beyond the tomb.

NOTES

1. See Arthur Wright, *Buddhism in Chinese History*. New York, 1968: ch. 3 and 4.

2. For a description of the urban status of the chiefs' settlements, see Wheatley 1971: 254.

3. Here I follow Professor Jacques' recent revision of Jayavarman II's chronology, which dates the king's rise to overlordship in the last decades of the eighth century: C. Jacques. 'Études d'épigraphie Cambodgienne: VIII. La carrière de Jayavarman II', *BEFEO*, lix, 1972: 205–20.

4. Karlgren's phonology has been followed for reconstructing the names of Khmer chiefs mentioned in the Chinese sources.

5. Elsewhere in this volume Professor Jacques has discussed epigraphic reasons for rejecting the conception of a 'kingdom of Funan'. The present author, in an article in *BSOAS*, xxxvii, 1974: 355–84, examines some Chinese preconceptions which required them to think in terms of a 'kingdom of Funan'.

6. I gratefully acknowledge my indebtedness to my colleague in anthropology, Professor A. Thomas Kirsch, for discussions on the phenomenon of alliance within the South East Asian social context.

7. The *Sui-shu* (82, 6*b*) records the Khmer practice of killing or mutilating brothers of a new king on the day of his accession.

8. The importance of relatives, albeit elsewhere in South East Asia and later in time, is well illustrated in the following passage in the Achinese *Hikatjat Malen Dagang*, brought to my attention by Professor James Siegel:

He has many relatives of both sides, there are many to help him as general.

He has many older and younger brothers, there are many to take his place as general (if he should be killed).

Counting all his relatives on both sides there are three hundred strong ones.

They are (willing to) follow, all (willing to) die . . .

9. *Pūjā* ('homage'): *IC*, ii, 11.

Pradāna ('donation'): *IC*, ii, 27. l. 16.

Satra ('offering'): *IC*, v, 57, l. 3; *IC*, v, 76 face B, l. 4.

Yajamāna ('he who offers gifts to a god'): *IC*, vii, 130, l. 1.

Punya ('merit'): *IC*, ii, 45, l. 2.

10. For example of a royal cult, *IC*, iv, 11. The servants are noted below.

11. Professor Jacques has suggested that certain inscriptions, conventionally attributed to Bhavavarman II, should be attributed to Bhavavarman I; *Annuaire, 1971–1972*) (École pratique des Hautes Études, IVe Section), 608.

12. *IC*, iv, 30, refers to an *ācārya*, who states that three successive kings had conferred on him the title of *Mratān An*.

13. For example, one's merits could be transferred to one's father; *ISCC*, 71, v. 22. See *IC*, iv, 25, v., vi for a queen's deathwish.

14. Nevertheless, the penalty for damaging a private cult is said to be equivalent to that for murdering a brahman; *IC*, ii, 125, face B, 12–14.

15. Śiva's fertilizing power explains the undecaying vegetation on his holy hill, reported by Nāgasena in 464; Pelliot 1903: 260. The hill is in Cambodia.

16. Sometimes the princes bestowed the bronze; Watson 1962: 78.

17. We need not suppose that the social setting of Khmer 'Hinduism' was only on the scale of overlordship. Some inscriptions suggest that a chief's cult could become a focus of homage in the neighbourhood. In 685 the Mratān Devaśvāmi performed a 'great cult ceremony' at which no less than twenty-two others are said to be present as witnesses; *IC*, ii, 124; Bhattacharya 1961: 149. In the same century twenty-five persons gave gifts to the god of the Lord of Tamandarapura, whose elder brother was the Lord of Rudrapurī; *IC*, v, 37–8. Ten contributed gifts to a tower built by Kṛṣṇamitra's grandson; *IC*, ii, 27–8. Gifts to cults were also made by wives and mothers-in-law; *ISCC*, 58, v. 3; *IC*, ii, 201. Kṛṣṇamitra's brother-in-law gave land to Kṛṣṇamitra's *liṅga*, which was for the sake of the 'family'; *IC*, ii, 27–8. The same inscription states that the grandson of these two chiefs, who had himself been the chief of a certain area since his youth, erected the tower on behalf of his two grandfathers. These scraps of information suggest that a considerable amount of inter-family alliance, reflected in cult worship, took place when families entered into marriage relationships. The network of alliances at regional level was a source of military power, available to a man of prowess with kingly ambitions.

18. i.e. king, capital, ministers, army, treasury, countryside, allies.

19. One of Iśānavarman I's inscriptions refers to the erection of a statue of Nṛtteśvara, the Śiva who dances the world into being; *IC*, iv, 11, v. xxxiii.

20. His reason for invoking the name 'Kurukṣetra' may be because he had just been consecrated as 'king of kings', with the appropriate rites to which his inscription refers. He would therefore have undergone the *rājasūya* ceremony, bathed with holy water no doubt from the *liṅga* mountain. The epic says that, 'by repairing to Kurukṣetra in a pious frame of mind, one obtaineth the fruits of the Rājasūya'.

21. The Khmers were not, of course, finding a place for themselves in a world dominated by 'India'. Their inscriptions show that they were aware only of regions in 'India'. They knew of Dakṣiṇapatha (*IC*, iv, 27, v. iii), Kāñcipura (*IC*, 10, v. iv), Madhyadeśa (*IC*, iv, 61, v. iii), Malava (*IC*, v, 39, v. ii).

22. In this context we can note the Chinese statement about Kauṇḍinya II, who was acclaimed about 400. He is said to have 'changed again the system and used Indian laws' (Pelliot 1903: 269). The alliance of kings and chiefs may have generated a mood of religious *rapport* in which everything could be seen in Hindu terms.

ADDITIONAL REFERENCES

Sui-shu. Po-na edition.

T'ai-p'ing yü-lan (Han fên lou facsimile of a Sung print). Chung-ha shu-chü edition. Peking, 1960.

Tirtha yatrā parvan. P. C. Roy's translation of the *Mahābhārata*, vol. 2. Calcutta, 1884.

Mainland South East Asia in the Seventh and Eighth Centuries

R. B. SMITH

Tribute Missions to China: the Changing Pattern

IN the long evolution of South East Asia, the two centuries immediately before *c.* 800 were of crucial importance. Their history has still to be written—if it ever proves possible to write it at all—but even a fairly cursory examination of the evidence suggests that they were a period of significant change, if not of regional 'crisis'. The present paper is an attempt to suggest some lines of enquiry which might one day lead towards a new interpretation of the period. There are still many difficult problems to be resolved in the detailed study of the evidence, both Chinese and 'Indian'. My concern here is no more than to suggest a perspective within which such problems might be reconsidered.

Among the most important kinds of information about South East Asia during this period are Chinese historical sources which record the occasions when representatives of 'states' or 'kingdoms' in the area were received in China. It was already the Chinese custom to refer to such relations in terms of tribute or submission, although they may well have had an underlying commercial character as in later centuries. Such information as we possess about the tribute missions suggests that there was a good deal of change during the seventh and eighth centuries: change, that is, either in South East Asia itself or in China's policy towards the area; or perhaps both. Table I summarizes the information collected by Professor Wang Gung-wu, in his well-known study of the Nanhai trade, together with a number of additional missions mentioned by Pelliot, and some indicated by Professor Wolters in a recent article on seventh-century Cambodia[1] (Pelliot 1904; Wang 1958; Wolters, 1974). Probably the list is not complete, but it seems unlikely that the pattern will be changed by anything short of the discovery of a whole new Chinese source.

Not all the places mentioned in the records as having sent tribute to China can be identified with confidence on the ground. Nor is it my intention to enter here into such controversies as whether Tan-tan was on the Malay peninsula, in Sumatra, or in Java; or where precisely we should place Ko-lo-shih-fen. These problems may one day be resolved, but the attempt is perhaps best left until more work on epigraphy has been completed. What is immediately obvious is the general statistical pattern which emerges. The difference between the first half of the seventh century and the second half of the eighth century is immediately striking.

Table I: South East Asian and Indian Missions to China, 600–850[2]

	600–50	650–700	700–50	750–800	800–50
South East Asian States:					
(not all effectively identified)					
LIN-YI	8	10	17	—	—
TAN-TAN	2	2	—	—	—
CH'IH-Y'U	3	—	—	—	—
CHIA-LO-SHIH	1	—	—	—	—
FU-NAN	1	—	—	—	—
CHEN-LA	5	3	4	—	2
TS'AN-PAN	1	—	—	—	—
T'OU-HO	1	—	—	—	—
P'O-LI	2	—	—	—	—
SU-NAI	1	—	—	—	—
TO-HO-LO	2	—	—	—	—
NOU-T'O-HUAN	2	—	—	—	—
=(T'O-YUAN)					
P'AN-P'AN	4	—	—	—	—
TO-P'O-TENG	1	—	—	—	—
SENG-KAO	1	—	—	—	—
WU-LING	1	—	—	—	—
CHIA-CHA	1	—	—	—	—
CHIU-MI	1	1	—	—	—
HO-LING	2	1	—	2?	3
MO-LO-YU	1	—	—	—	—
K'AN-PI	—	1	—	—	—
CHU-LU-MI	—	2	—	—	—
HSIU-LO-FEN	—	1	—	—	—
P'O-LO	—	1	—	—	—
HUAN-WANG	—	1	—	1	—
P'U-SHU	—	1	—	—	—
FU-NA	—	1	—	—	—
KO-LO-SHIH-FEN	—	2	—	?	—
P'O-AN	—	1	—	—	—
SHIH-LI-FO-SHIH	—	—	5	—	—
K'UN-LUN	—	—	1	—	—
WEN-TAN	—	—	2	3	—
SHE-P'O	—	—	—	—	2
Total number of missions from S.E. Asia	41	28	29	6?	6
Number of countries noted	20	14	5	3 or 4	3
India and Ceylon					
SHIH-TSE (Ceylon)	—	1	4	1	—
NAN-T'IEN-CHU	—	1	2	—	—
CHAN-PO	—	1	—	—	—
KAN-CHIH-FO	—	2	—	—	—
P'O-AN	—	1	—	—	—
MO-LO	—	1	—	—	—
Total number of missions from India-Ceylon	—	7	6	1	—

There are two possible explanations for the contrast, and also for the lesser contrast between the first and second halves of the eighth century itself. One is that the conditions of trade and political relationship changed during the interval, so that tribute was either less possible or less appropriate during the later period. The other is that the number of 'states' in South East Asia considerably diminished during the period under review. Let us consider the two possibilities in turn.

The evidence of the first half of the seventh century indicates a considerable revival of Chinese interest in receiving tribute from South East Asia. The fact that as many as twenty countries are mentioned suggests that some of them were small in size, and that both the interests and the renown of T'ang China reached far into the hinterland of mainland South East Asia, as well as to perhaps some of the more remote corners of the Nangyang. On the other hand, as many as twelve of the twenty-one countries sent tribute only once and are not heard of again. The same can be said of some of the countries appearing in the second half of the seventh century: at least five of the fourteen countries sending tribute in that period are not mentioned before or afterwards. These figures suggest a considerable discontinuity in China's relations with most 'states' in South East Asia, or else (equally remarkable) a discontinuity in the application of names to countries. But the degree of interest is clearly attested, and this continued through the second half of the century. The most significant feature of this second period in the table is that China began to receive tribute missions also from a number of states believed to be in India, six countries being mentioned there, and in addition from Ceylon (Shih-tse).

This was perhaps the period of China's greatest renown along the sea-routes to India until the expeditions of the early fifteenth century, and perhaps that goes some way towards explaining the importance of South East Asia itself, which lay along that route. The importance and regularity of missions from this general direction is reflected in a T'ang decree of 695, which laid down the appropriate sustenance to be offered to envoys from various countries for the return voyage: six months' supplies for those from India; five months' supplies for Shih-li-fo-shih (Srivijaya), Ho-ling (Java), Chen-la (Cambodia), etc.; and three months' for Lin-Yi (Champa) (Pelliot 1904: 334). This was also a period of great Chinese interest in Indian Buddhism, and one of the most celebrated of all travellers to India through South East Asia was the monk I-Ching. He left China first in 671, travelling by way of Fo-shih (Srivijaya) and Mo-lo-yu, and subsequently (in the period 685–95) spent several years studying in Srivijaya, which is believed to have had its 'capital' at Palembang at that time (Chavannes 1894).

During the first half of the eighth century, the contact with India was maintained: missions came from Nan-t'ien-chu in 710 and 720, and from Ceylon in 712, 742, 746, and 750 (with a last mission as late as 762). Contact was also maintained with Shih-li-fo-shih (Srivijaya), which lay on the route to Ceylon and beyond: it sent missions in 702, 716, 724, 728, and 742. Of the rest of the missions a further seventeen came from Lin-yi, which was also a port on the mainland of South East Asia. But that already accounts for as many as twenty-eight out of the thirty-five missions coming to China from the south between 700 and 750. Of the seven others mentioned in the sources so far used by writers on the period, one came from 'K'un-lun', a place whose identity is still unknown but which may well have been also in maritime South East Asia. The only tribute missions from inland South East Asian countries during these decades came from Chen-la and Wen-tan. In 711 and 717, the missions from these two countries came together.[3] Wen-tan is identified by one Chinese source as 'Land Chen-la'; the same source (the *Chiu T'ang-shu*) indicates that sometime after the year 706 'Chen-la', whatever its territorial significance, became divided into two parts. Wen-tan sent its first known missions in 711 and 717, and then nothing until after 750. The only conclusion one can draw is that by the middle of the eighth century the Chinese were no longer so interested in the hinterland of mainland South East Asia as they had been in the seventh century (Pelliot 1904: 211–12).

We do not of course know whether all the missions recorded from mainland countries in the seventh century were using the sea route. It is possible that, after restoring their control over Viet-Nam (Giao-chau, or An-nam) the Chinese of the Sui and early T'ang periods went farther inland towards the south-west and established land contacts with some parts of the Indochinese peninsula. They also appear, at some stage, to have been interested in Yunnan, although in 698 we find a memorial from the governor of Cheng-tu noticing that the Chinese presence in Yunnan had declined in recent years and that the barbarians of that region no longer sent tribute to the T'ang (Pelliot 1904: 151–2). What is clear is that these land relationships with South East Asia underwent something of a transformation during the first half of the eighth century. In 722 there was a rebellion in the southern part of the Vietnamese provinces, in the area now known as Nghe-tinh. We shall see later that there was an important route from that area towards Cambodia, over land; and it is not surprising therefore to find that the leader of the revolt (Mai Hac De) received some kind of assistance from the country called Wen-tan (Maspero 1918: 29). The revolt was suppressed, but it may for the time being have reduced the possibilities for the Chinese to explore or maintain any land route towards Cambodia. The second development came in Yunnan, where a 'king' called P'i-lo-ko established the foundations of the state of Nan-chao during the 730s. At first he was willing to co-operate with the Chinese and in the 740s he helped them to subdue the 'Tsuan' rebels. But the kingdom he had created was more powerful than anything that had existed in Yunnan in the previous century (perhaps since the ancient 'kingdom of Tien'), and in the 750s his successor Ko-lo-feng felt strong enough to resist China and to ally himself with the Tibetans.

In the second half of the eighth century, things changed yet again. Part of the explanation for this must be sought in China itself. The rebellion of An Lu-shan broke out in 755 and the civil war which followed lasted until 763, when it culminated in the sack of Chang-an. But even before that, the T'ang had suffered two notable defeats on their inner Asian frontiers: against the Arabs at Talas in 751 and against the forces of Nan-chao and the Tibetans in 754. The tide turned against the T'ang at this point, and the change was bound to be reflected in their capacity to command tribute from distant lands and to control trade routes far afield.

This change coincided, moreover, with the growing importance in the Nanyang of the Ta-shih traders (Muslim Persians or Arabs), who are sometimes mentioned in the same breath as the Po-ssu (non-Muslim Persians). Whatever the identity of these traders, they had established themselves as an important element in the Nanyang and in the ports of south China itself. In 758 they came and sacked Canton; but in 760 they fared rather less well in disturbances at Yang-chou, where they suffered losses of life and property at the hands of local people (Wang 1958: 79–80). These events suggest that already by 760 the 'Pax Sinica' of the earlier T'ang period had broken down. In the following decades, we get further evidence of piracy in the South China Sea. Pirates called 'Con-lon' and 'Cha-ba' made a serious attack on Giao-chau in 767, as a result of which the Chinese governor founded a new capital at La-thanh. Two inscriptions from southern Champa later in the eighth century record the restoration of major temples attacked and destroyed by pirates: at Nha-trang, where the Po-Nagar was attacked in 774, and at Phang-rang, where the attack came in 787 (Coedès 1964: 173).

It is hardly surprising in view of these developments that the pattern of tribute missions from the south changed yet again after about 750. The mission from Ceylon in 762 was the only one from beyond the Straits of Malacca during the second half of this century. Nor do we hear again of missions from Fo-shih after 742: Srivijaya reappears only in the tenth century. More remarkably, Lin-yi sent no missions after 749. Instead, we find references in the Chinese sources (though not always relating to tribute missions) to Ho-ling, in Java; and to a kingdom called Huan-wang, which appears to be southern Champa. The latter, which is mentioned as having sent tribute[4] in 793, was involved in attacks against Giao-chau in the early ninth century. Ho-ling is mentioned as having been approached by the Ta-shih about 760, but with what result is by no means clear. We know only that Ho-ling sent tribute to the T'ang at least once, possibly twice, in 767–8. But that completes the list of tribute missions from maritime South East Asia in the second half of the century: a mere two or three missions in all.

The only other country to send envoys from South East Asia in this period was Wen-tan: its tribute was received in 753-4, 771, and 799, and on the first of these occasions its envoy accompanied the Chinese army on the unsuccessful campaign against Nan-chao (Pelliot 1904: 212). But where *was* Wen-tan? The identification with 'Land Chen-la' is of only slight help, since we cannot be sure what 'Chen-la' meant by the end of the seventh century, and we know nothing of the details of the supposed 'partition'. Chinese sources make no further mention of Chen-la until the arrival of a tribute mission (presumably from Jayavarman II) in 813. Wen-tan itself is not mentioned again after 799. There is no necessary reason for assuming that Wen-tan lay within the boundaries of present-day Cambodia, or even that it was ethnically Khmer. Nor need we assume that all its tribute missions went to China by sea, through the mouth of the Mekong; it is possible that they went overland, via Giao-chau.

Probably the most important piece of evidence relating to Wen-tan is an itinerary recorded by the Chinese official Chia Tan, who is believed to have presented an account of three major routes between China and India in or about 800. The first of the three was the sea-route, by way of Srivijaya and the Strait of Chih (i.e. the Strait of Malacca). The second was the land-route through Yunnan and Upper Burma, entering India by way of Assam and Bengal, which we must come to in a moment. Thirdly, he described a route to and beyond Wen-tan, which linked up with the sea-route at a place called Lo-yüeh on the Malay peninsula. This third route started at Hoan-chau (the present-day Ha-tinh, in North Viet-Nam) and went south-westwards from there across the Annamite Chain. The way led past a series of remote sub-prefectures, technically regarded as dependencies of the Chinese empire, until it reached Hsuan-ts'ai which is described as a 'sub-prefecture' of Wen-tan. Before reaching the 'inner capital' of Wen-tan, the traveller came to its 'outer capital': the two places being one day's journey apart. Beyond the second of these cities or capitals the route led on to 'Water Chen-la', before reaching the 'small sea' (Gulf of Siam?) separating the latter from Lo-yüeh (Pelliot 1904: 210ff.). The itinerary gives precise indications of the time required for each stage of the journey, as far as Wen-tan. The whole journey from Hoan-chau to the 'inner capital' was said to take sixteen days: a period which, in view of the mountains that had to be crossed, can hardly have involved more than a distance of 1,000 *li*. This leads one to suppose that the centre of Wen-tan lay well to the north of present-day Cambodia, either in southern Laos or in north-east Thailand, depending on whether one interprets the account as including a passage across the Mekong. The most southerly possible candidate amongst known Hindu-Buddhist sites would seem to be Wat Phu, near Bassac, which had been a centre of some importance as early as the fifth century. Of course, it is not impossible that, even during the short period of its existence in the Chinese records, Wen-tan may have had different centres at different times.

What is clear is that Wen-tan was not on the coast. It was an inland centre, and its importance for the Chinese in this period seems to suggest that they were once more taking an interest in mainland South East Asia. Was this inland route perhaps a way of avoiding the unsettled conditions of the South China Sea? Was its use at this period also an element in the development of La-thanh (Hanoi), which became a more significant port than Canton during this half-century? An interpretation along these lines would fit in well enough with Chia Tan's interest in the other land route to India: the route which began at Hanoi and proceeded up the Red River into Yunnan, then by way of An-ning-ch'eng and Yun-nan-ch'eng to the Nan-chao capital of Ta-li (Pelliot 1904: 364ff.). Beyond Yung-chang-ch'eng the route forked, with one road leading directly across to Assam, whilst the other went through the country known as P'iao. This was the Pyu country of upper Burma, and it seems almost certain that this road went through Ha-lin before climbing across the Black Mountains towards Assam and Bengal. Nan-chao had, as we have seen, allied itself with the Tibetans during the 750s and had since proceeded along a path of complete independence from China. But in 791 the Nan-chao king I-mo-hsün changed sides, and three years later he helped the Chinese to defeat the Tibetans in a battle on the upper Yangtse. Thus by the time Chia Tan wrote it is very possible that the Yunnan routes to India were open. In the early years of the ninth century, the P'iao as well as Nan-chao sent tribute missions to the T'ang capital (Pelliot 1904: 156–7).

To complete this analysis of China's relations with South East Asia in these two centuries, it may be mentioned briefly that in spite of the small number of tribute missions there are just a few signs of a revival of Chinese power and interest in the area in the decades after 790. China's economy was perhaps stronger than at mid-century, following the tax reforms of Yang Yen (*c.* 780); and the Canton trade may have revived a little in the early ninth century. The arrival of Pyu embassies in 802 and 807 has already been alluded to. Huan-wang also sent an embassy in 793, and Wen-tan a final embassy in 799. From farther south, there was a mission from the 'new' Chen-la in 813; and Ho-ling reappears with three missions between 813 and 818. From 820, Ho-ling's place was apparently taken by She-p'o, which sent missions in that year and in 831.

But if the Nanyang seems more peaceful in the first half of the ninth than in the second half of the eighth century, the small number of tribute missions seems to argue in favour of some other explanation than a simple recovery of Chinese power in the area. Was it perhaps the case that after a period of conflict and development, with a good deal of piracy and disorder, South East Asia itself had now produced a new kind of political stability of its own?

Possible Changes in South East Asia

Let us turn now to the second possible explanation for the declining number of tribute missions: that there was a significant political and institutional change within South East Asia itself, with the result that a small number of major centres became dominant over the rest. Although we cannot always identify the precise location of the countries sending tribute in the seventh century, it is possible to relate the majority of them to broad areas of South East Asia, thanks to the detail given in the *T'ang-shu* and other sources, about distances and directions between various countries. Thus we can identify ten 'kingdoms' or 'states' in the area of the Lower Mekong and Menam basins (Luce 1925; Wolters, 1974):

  (i) Chen-la, which may well have been the same as Isanapura in the period 616–28, and should perhaps be located at Sambor Prei Kuk;

 (ii) Shu-chin, which sent tribute in 628 and is said to have been south of Huan-wang (possibly Phan-thiet?);

(iii) Ts'an-pan, which sent tribute in 625 and was situated either west or south-west of Chen-la;

(iv–vii) Seng-kao, Wu-ling, Chia-cha, and Chiu-mi, all thought by Professor Wolters to be in north-western Cambodia; they sent tribute in 638, and Chiu-mi also in 671;

(viii) Fu-na, which also sent tribute in 671 and is also thought to have been in the same part of Cambodia (not to be confused with Fu-nan);

 (ix) To-ho-lo, which sent tribute in 638 and 649, and is usually identified with I-Ching's To-ho-lo-po-ti, and so with Dvaravati; it was situated west of Chen-la, north of P'an-p'an (on the Thai peninsula), and south of Chia-lo-shih-fo;

  (x) T'o-yuan (or Nou To-yuan), which sent tribute in 644 and 647, but which is said by the *Hsin T'ang-shu* to have become a dependency of To-ho-lo; it was situated to the south-east of the latter and to the south-west of 'Champa'.

Of these, only Chen-la is found sending tribute after 700, and even it disappears between 717 and 813. Probably the five small 'kingdoms' in north-western Cambodia were absorbed by the expansion of Chen-la, whatever may have been the precise centre of the latter. We have an indication too that To-ho-lo expanded to subdue T'o-yuan; but To-ho-lo itself does not reappear as a tributary after 649. Was it perhaps in some way subjected to either Chen-la or Fo-shih (Srivijaya) by the end of the century? Or was it simply left on one side as a result of declining Chinese interest in the Indochinese mainland? These and other questions cannot be answered; but the evidence, such as it is, would fit in well enough with the thesis that a smaller number of kingdoms emerged to dominate mainland South East Asia. It would not be too far-fetched to suggest that already by the seventh and eighth centuries we have indications of the tendency towards gradual political integration which characterized the later history of the region. The same tendency is represented, in a period for which we have very full documentation, by the expansion of the kingdom of Ayuthya between 1350 and 1650, to embrace Sukhothai and its dependencies in the north and Nakorn Sri Thammarat in the south, and to claim tribute from Oudong in the east and Chieng Mai in the far north. The number of states in the seventh century was considerably greater than the number in the seventeenth century. But perhaps the rise of Chen-la and To-ho-lo represents the first step towards a new pattern of change.

One can find analogies in the maritime region of South East Asia. There too, a number of 'states' of the early period disappear after the middle of the seventh century, leaving two or three kingdoms to dominate Chinese relations with the region in the eighth and ninth centuries: Fo-shih (695–742), Ho-ling (768–818), and She-p'o (from 820). But as in the case of the mainland, we cannot hope to fill in the details of the political changes which seem to be implied by the statistics of tribute missions. Likewise, in the north of South East Asia we find an analogous tendency in the rise of Nan-chao. In the mid-seventh century there had been six *ch'ao* in the Ta-li region of Yun-nan, each with its own centre and ruler. But in the 730s the king of one of them, Pi-lo-ko of Meng-she, succeeded in subduing the other five and was recognized by the T'ang as the dominant figure in the area. He founded a new capital at T'ai-ho, near Ta-li, and it was his successor (Ko-lo-feng) who defeated the Chinese in 754. But if this pattern of development in Yunnan, involving the expansion and consolidation of a growing state, was characteristic of South East Asia in the eighth century, it must also be said that the Chinese were not able to control the process. From 754 to 791 Nan-chao cannot be regarded as in any sense a tributary of China, Moreover, in the ninth century, its expansion was threatening neighbours even farther afield. Its forces sacked the Pyu capital, probably Ha-lin, in 832 and captured Hanoi on more than one occasion between 846 and 866. The less clearly evidenced rise of Wen-tan in the eighth century, and of Jayavarman II's Chen-la after *c.* 770, were even farther beyond the limits of Chinese control.

Archaeological Evidence

What of other kinds of evidence about South East Asia in this period? As yet it is less easy to find any kind of pattern in the information of archaeology and epigraphy on their own, except to the extent that inscriptions enable us to trace the probable careers of individual kings such as Jayavarman II. However, there are several features of the archaeological evidence which would fit in with the suggestion that the seventh and eighth centuries saw a transformation of South East Asia and the emergence of new and more powerful kingdoms at certain points.

One of the most important indications is found in the development of temple-building in two key areas: Java and northern Cambodia. The dates of the temples of central Java are still not established with absolute certainty, but clearly a major development took place sometime between about 700 and about 850 (cf. Soekmono's paper, *infra*, pp. 471–72). Early on we find the temples of the Dieng Plateau, and at the end the culminating feat of the Borobudur. Leaving aside the question of the religious significance of the contrast, and avoiding completely the question how the temples are to be related to the epigraphic story, we can say with some confidence that the building of the Borobudur involved a much greater degree of organization than that of the small early temples. Whatever happened in the interval, some king or group of priests achieved sufficiently great a command over a labour force to be able to create a vast monument such as had never previously been possible for the Javanese. Was it perhaps the same development that enabled Ho-ling and then She-p'o to become great powers in the Nanyang, recognized as such by the Chinese, and also (*c.* 760) by the Ta-shih? By contrast, the previously powerful Srivijaya seems to have declined in this period. Palembang did not produce great temples, and this could well mean that its leaders were not able to bring about a comparable development in scale of organization. They presumably continued to depend on trade, and the apparent breakdown of direct Chinese trade with India may conceivably have reduced their resources after about 750. It fits in well with what we know about conditions in the South China Sea in the second half of the eighth century, to find a king of Srivijaya founding a temple in 775, not at Palembang but at Ligor on the Malay peninsula. But even then, it was merely a small *candi*.

Cambodia likewise saw a transformation in the art of temple-building between 700 and 850, which has corresponding implications for the scale of social organization. There are perhaps about a dozen temples in Cambodia belonging to the period before *c.* 800 (the 'pre-Angkorian' phase). They are mostly single-tower sanctuaries, some of them larger than others, and mostly of brick. Only at Sambor Prei Kuk (the Isanapura of the seventh century) do we find the beginnings of a tendency to put towers together in an arrangement where one primary sanctuary is at the centre of a square. But it is not until the ninth century, at Roluos, that we find in the Bakong a pyramid-temple whose dimensions imply a much greater measure of labour organization. From there the way lay directly to temples like Angkor Wat. We cannot in the nature of things have any direct evidence of the institutional arrangements which produced the towers, except for a few epigraphic indications of the division of labour as well as the development of status (cf. *supra*, pp. 407–13). But the size of the temples themselves indicates a kind of organization which was probably the product of changes in the eighth and early ninth centuries. The same factor of organization of labour must have been present in the development of irrigated agriculture. But to begin with, it is not necessary to assume that any group of labourers specialized in one activity or the other. For any wet-rice cultivation which did not yet involve major irrigation would leave the peasantry several months to devote time and energy to building, during the dry part of the year when rice could not in any case be grown.

There were other important centres on the South East Asian mainland, but by the mid-ninth century it must have already been clear that Angkor was capable of much more than the others. It was in fact the culmination of a long period of development in the region to the north and north-east of the Ton-le Sap, of which the sanctuaries at Sambor Prei Kuk are an early manifestation. Why should this area have developed into the predominant centre? Dr. Ng (*supra*, pp. 262–72) points out that one advantage enjoyed by Cambodia was that it had an extensive area congenial for habitation, with land suitable for wet-rice and with adequate supplies of potable water. It was an area, moreover, where expansion of settlement could be accompanied by the expansion of administrative or political control over territory; whereas in many other parts of the Indochinese peninsula the congenial habitats are separated from one another by various kinds of obstacle to continuous settlement and expansion. But another feature of the area also deserves to be taken into account. The region between the Ton-le Sap and the eastern part of the Dangrek mountains is an important one for metals, both copper and iron; indeed the Mekong Project's survey of mineral resources shows that it has an exceptional number of known deposits of iron, which must have been important in a period of expanding cultivation. Archaeological work has not yet been done on the early working of iron in Cambodia, though Professor Higham's recent investigations around Roi-Et have produced evidence of it in that area (Higham and Parker 1971). But looking at Cambodia and north-east Thailand in the longer perspective of prehistory and early history, it may not be without significance that the latter area has produced the earliest evidence so far for metallurgy in South East Asia. The relationship of early settlement patterns to the distribution of metal is something which deserves closer study.

The temples of Java and Cambodia, therefore, seem to belong to a new phase of political and social development in those areas in the eighth and ninth centuries. Other areas of South East Asia did not produce monuments of that kind. But the evidence of finds of sculpture and inscriptions, as well as of chedis on the ground, and in some places the remains of defensive enclosures, shows that there were a number of other political centres with a Hindu-Buddhist religious life. Not all this evidence has yet been assigned to a precise period, and consequently it is not easy to estimate its significance for the seventh and eighth centuries. Some of the remains are earlier in date, perhaps, whilst others—notably those assigned very generally to the 'Dvāravatī' period in Thailand—may well belong to the ninth, tenth, or even eleventh centuries. But it is clear that by the eighth century at least there was a sort of cultural continuum stretching from north to south, between central Thailand and southern Sumatra, or between 'Dvāravatī' and 'Srivijaya'. The detailed history of relationships between the various archaeological centres in that area will probably never be written with full confidence; nor is it possible yet to relate the archaeological remains to the Chinese names of kingdoms such as To-ho-lo, T'o-yuan, P'an-p'an, Lang-ya-hsiu, Chih-tu, Tan-tan, Lo-yueh, Ko-lo-shih-fen, Kan-to-li, and Fo-shih. But both here and along the Cham coast, one has the impression of a number of significant centres which may well have been continual rivals for the predominant position. It is in this context that we must consider the epigraphic references to Srivijaya, which occur in southern Sumatra in the later seventh century and at Ligor in 775. (In this context too we should observe the apparent decline of central Champa (Lin-yi) in the later eighth century, and the emergence into prominence of the more southerly Cham centres at Nha-trang and at Phan-thiet and Phan-rang during the period 750–850.)

Outside Cambodia and central Java, probably the most significant archaeological remains which may belong to the seventh, eighth, or ninth centuries are the fortified enclosures of central and north-east Thailand. They were by no means small in size, and even though they may well not have been very densely inhabited, their presence suggests some degree of organized political life. Interestingly, however, they are associated only with relatively small stupas and not with large-scale temples. Table II indicates the relative size of some of these enclosures, with corresponding information about other sites with which they might reasonably be compared.

Nakorn Pathom, whose enclosure has now been identified, was the largest of the sites. Although it may well be later in date than the ninth century, we know that the *chedi* at its centre, Chula Chedi Pathom, existed at that time. Professor Boisselier has identified three phases in its architectural history, stretching from the seventh to the tenth centuries (Boisselier 1970). He noted a 'Srivijayan influence' in the eighth or ninth century, which confirms the notion of a cultural continuum embracing both this area and at least the major centres of peninsular Thailand. Nakorn Pathom was no mean city, at least in its surface extent. It can be compared with Angkor Thom and also with Ayuthya, major centres of a later period. It was much larger than the actual fortified area at Pagan, though of course the latter has many square miles of temples outside its walls. It can also be compared with Oc-èo, which was rather smaller, and with a number of Chinese cities of the Warring States period which were not a great deal larger (Wheatley 1971).

Table II: Comparative Sizes of Ancient Sites

Place	Size	Notes
(a) *Dvaravati Sites:*		
NAKORN PATHOM	3,700 × 2,000 m.	Seventh–tenth century Chedi at centre
U-THONG	1,690 × 840 m.	Seventh century and earlier?
KU BUA	2,010 × 800 m.	Eight century? rectangular.
KAMPHENG SEN	775 × 730 m.	
DONG SI MAHA POT (Prachinburi)	1,500 × 800 m.	Important finds of Hindu–Buddhist sculpture.
SAB CHAMPA (Chaibadan)	834 × 704 m.	
CHANSEN	700 × 700 m.	
MUANG FA DAED	2,000 × 1,000 m.	Irregular shape; some sign of enlargement.
(b) *Other sites, for comparison:*		
OC-EO	3,000 × 1,500 m.	Probably second–fifth century 'Fu-nan' capital?
PAGAN	app. 1,190 m. square	Ninth–thirteenth century: temples cover wide area outside enclosure.
THATON	2,100 × 1,300 m.	Eleventh century?
ANGKOR THOM	app. 3,000 m. square	Twelfth–thirteenth century. Most of temples lay outside.
AYUTHYA	app. 4,000 × 2,000 m.	Area enclosed by river, seventeenth century.
LO-YANG (oldest city)	app. 3,000 m. square	The Han city was much larger.
HAN-TAN (Ho-pei)	app. 1,400 m. square	Capital of Chao in Chan-kuo period.
LIN-TZU (Shantung)	4,000 × 3,000 m.	Capital of Ch'i in Chan-kuo period.

(*Sources:* Boisselier 1970; Quaritch Wales 1969; Wheatley 1971; Luce 1969.)

Yet the fact that Nakorn Pathom was fortified at all suggests that it had to be defended. It does not seem unreasonable to suggest that the fortified enclosures of the 'Dvāravatī' area represent a social and political framework characterized by the continual likelihood of warfare between relatively equal centres rather than the complete dominance of a wide area by a single major centre with large temples. There may well have been, in the ninth and tenth centuries a marked contrast between the social pattern of the Menam basin and that of lower Cambodia. But the rise of fortified towns in the former area is as important a development in this period as the growth of the temple-building centres of Cambodia and Java. In considering the possible economic basis of the Menam Basin towns, it should be remembered that the richest soils of the central Thailand Plain could not be cultivated until a much later period, perhaps as late as the sixteenth or seventeenth century. We should not envisage at this early period a continuous band of settlement eastwards from Nakorn Pathom to Prachinburi, but rather a tract of uncultivated forest. Thus in spite of its size, Nakorn Pathom was not necessarily the same kind of centre as Ayuthya later became.

This pattern of society, characterized by fortified towns, might also be sought in north-eastern Thailand, where the largest enclosure was Muang Fa Daed. There too, we have no indication of date, and it is quite likely that the surviving enclosure was built as late as the eleventh century. But there are others in the region. Is it possible that 'Wen-tan' of the Chinese sources was a town of this kind, rather than a major centre of temple-building like 'Chen-la'? Alas, when it comes to questions of that kind the evidence peters out, and it is perhaps wise not to speculate too far.

NOTES

1. I have also incorporated into the table information and corrections supplied by J. H. C. S. Davidson, following the London Colloquy, for which I am duly grateful; any faults remaining in the table are, however, my own responsibility. In particular, the number of missions from countries in India and Ceylon is probably understated.

2. In this table and throughout the paper I have used the Wade-Giles transcription of names, since it will be the one most familiar to readers of existing English and French writings on the subject. The *pin-yin* transcriptions will be found in the Chinese character list, Appendix III.

3. I am indebted to Mr. Davidson also for this information. (*Ts'e-fu yüan-kuei*, ch. 971–2b2; 974/17b6).

4. Mr. Davidson points out that the mission of 793, said by some secondary sources to have come from Lin-yi, in fact came from Huan-wang. (*Ts'e-fu yüan-kuei*, ch. 972/4b6).

The Archaeology of Central Java before 800A. D.*

SOEKMONO

Introduction

IT is generally assumed that the ancient history of Indonesia starts in the middle of the seventh century A.D. and ends in the first decades of the sixteenth century. This so-called 'Hindu period' is further divided into two main periods: the central Javanese period from the seventh to the tenth century; and the east Javanese period from the tenth to the sixteenth century. Both periods witnessed such intense building activity that the study of the monuments has from the very beginning become the archaeology par excellence of Indonesia. Only later on did prehistory lay claim to recognition of its proper share.

The present paper deals exclusively with the historical monuments, limited to the area of central Java and to the period before A.D. 800. These restrictions may well define the objective to be dealt with, but do not make the study easier. The period concerned is at the start of Indonesian history in central Java, and consequently one cannot expect to be overwhelmed by documents and other material. On the contrary, it is the period of scantiest evidence with only a handful of written records, so that hypothesis after hypothesis will have the upper hand in any historical reconstruction.

The Central Javanese Monuments and their Chronological Order

Central Java boasts an extreme richness of historical monuments, which are popularly called *candi*. They are spread over a limited area, and topographically can be divided into three main groups: the Diëng and Gedong Songo group in the mountain regions in the very heart of Java; the Borobudur group in the southern Kedu plain; and the Prambanan group east of Jogjakarta.

It would be ideal if the topographical order from north to south could be associated with a linear development in time, so that it would correspond with the chronological order from the seventh to the tenth century. Indeed, the current opinion considers the Diëng temples to be the earliest products of architectural art in Indonesian history, whereas the Loro Jonggrang compound in the Prambanan plain marks the end of the central Javanese period.

* See Plates xv, xvi.

The Borobudur group, which is presumably dated around the year A.D. 800, would come in between, topographically as well as chronologically.

To a certain extent, this general outline is also suggested by de Casparis in his attempt to reconstruct the history of the Śailendras in central Java (de Casparis 1950). With regard to the monuments, he pointed out that the northern candis are to be ascribed to the Sañjaya dynasty, the Borobudur compound to the Śailendras; and the temples in the Prambanan plain to both the Sañjaya and the Śailendras, fused by an intermarriage (de Casparis 1950: 131). The religious aspects of the monuments are also in favour of such a reconstruction: the Diëng and Gedong Songo temples are purely Sivaite, the Borobudur–Pawon–Mendut trio is Mahāyāna–Buddhist, and the Loro Jonggrang compound shows clearly a syncretism between the two religions.

It was, however, not such a simple linear development that took place in central Java. The linga-foundation of A.D. 732 a few miles south of Borobudur is attributed to Sañjaya himself, whereas Candi Kalasan several miles east of Jogjakarta is a Tara-temple founded by a Śailendra prince in A.D. 778. These contradictory facts led de Casparis to the supposition that the Sañjaya, after having been co-operative in the foundation of Candi Kalasan, withdrew from the southern part of central Java to become sovereign only in the north, where the Diëng plateau and its surroundings remained the centre of Sivaism. In the meantime the Śailendras became mighty rulers over the Kedu and the Prambanan plains. It was not until the middle of the ninth century that Sañjayas and Śailendras became united by the marriage of the Śailendra princess Prāmodawardhanī to the Sañjaya prince Rakai Pikatan.

The existence of two different royal dynasties in central Java was refuted a few years later (Bosch 1952*a*, *b*; Poerbatjaraka 1958), but the new hypothesis does not affect the striking distinction between the northern and the southern monuments. A history which for the greater part is hypothetical cannot possibly serve as a firm basis for setting up a chronological order of the monuments, which in their turn are not dated either. And when it proves that any historical reconstruction may change every time a new hypothesis is attempted, the monuments cannot be dated merely on that basis. In this respect a comparative study of the stylistical features might well represent the proper approach.

Such a study has been undertaken by Volger, who made a thorough analysis of the *kala-makara* ornaments and on that basis attempted a sequence of the development and the dating of the monuments (Volger 1949, 1952, 1953). He distinguished five periods in the architectural art of central Java:[1]

First period (before *c.* 650), which is purely hypothetical, since no architectural evidences are found.

Second period (c. 650–c. 760), with presumably one building tradition only which is to be called the Old-Diëng style (no remains left).

Third (*or Śailendra*) *period* (c. 760–c. 812), with two centra:

    Northern circle with Candis Arjuno (Plate xva), Semar, Gatotkoco;

    Southern circle with Candis Borobudur, Pawon, Mendut in the Kedu area, and Kalasan, Sari, Lumbung, Sewu in the Prambanan plain.

Fourth period (c. 812–c. 928), to be subdivided into three phases:

    Phase 1 (c. 812–c. 838), with Candi Hgawen;

    Phase 2 (c. 838–c. 898), with Candis: Puntodewo, Gedong Songo C (1st circle), and Plaosan, Sajiwan (2nd circle);

    Phase 3 (c. 898–c. 928), with Candi Loro Jonggrang.

Fifth period (c. 928–end of Hindu period), for the greater part coincident with the east Javanese period, to be subdivided into three phases:

    Phase 1, with Candis: Sembodro, Ratna, Gunung Wukir, Pringapus;

    Phase 2, with Candis: Srikandi, Gedong Songo A, Gedong Songo B;

    Phase 3, without architectural remains.

Following in the footsteps of Vogler's chronological order the present paper will be confined to the first three periods. The first two can be dropped at the very outset, since no structural remains are left, but at the same time the question inevitably arises how it could be possible that blank periods were introduced in an attempt for setting up a chronological sequence. A hypothetical first period might be taken for granted, but a second period which is said to be represented by the Old-Diëng style is beyond expectation if it proves to be hypothetical also for lack of evidences.

It is a great pity that no satisfactory answer can be obtained from Vogler's treatises. His statement that the first period started with a colonization of Indians from the south-eastern part of India, either directly or via the west Javanese settlement in Taruma (Vogler 1949: 27) does not make much sense. Neither does his argumentation with regard to the second period, which would be introduced by a new influx of Saivas or of Sivaism from Kuñjara (Vogler 1949: 27, 220).

Apart from the regrettable fact that Vogler's view with regard to Indian colonization, as the source of the development of Indonesian art and architecture, is out of date (cf. the relevant articles on the subject by Bosch, Krom, Stutterheim, van Naerssen, and several other scholars), the inclusion of the blank periods may be meant to bring his scheme into line with the historical reconstruction. In fact, the period before 650 is only evidenced by a few undated inscriptions, which on palaeographical grounds are approximately dated to the middle of the seventh century; whereas Vogler's second period is only evidenced by the Canggal Charter of 732 and the inscription of Plumpungan dated 752.

Following Vogler consistently, only the monuments of the third period can be considered for our further study. They are the following *candi*:

(*a*) Arjuno, Semar, and Gatotkoco, on the Diëng plateau;
(*b*) Borobudur, Pawon, and Mendut, in the Kedu plain;
(*c*) Kalasan, Sari, Lumbung, and Sewu, in the Prambanan plain.

Monuments Related to Dated Inscriptions

Vogler's second period witnessed the reign of King Sañjaya, who was glorified by the Canggal Charter of 732. The charter also mentions that the king established a lingam on a mountain. This statement, according to the current interpretation, is identified with the foundation of Candi Gunung Wukir, which should be the 'holy and wonderful shrine dedicated to Siwa for the good of the world, set in the prosperous Kuñjarakuñjadesa and surrounded by Gangga and other holy rivers' (translation by Nilakanta Sastri 1949: 119). Vogler rejected the identification of King Sañjaya's linga sanctuary with Candi Gunung Wukir, and launched the theory that the present *candi* has nothing to do with the charter. Candi Gunung Wukir should belong to a much later date, and even to the very end of the central Javanese period (Vogler 1952; 1953).

Of all the monuments Vogler ascribed to the third period, only Candi Kalasan can be dated with certainty. The Kalasan Charter of 778 commemorates the establishment of a Tārābhavanam, or an abode for the Goddess Tārā, in the village of Kālasan. There is no doubt, therefore, that the charter refers to the present Candi Kalasan, which is actually called after the present name of the village of Kalasan. An archaeological investigation however, carried out in 1940, brought to light that inside our Candi Kalasan there are two more structures, one enclosed by the other (O.V. 1940: 20-1). The present monument is thus the third structure. It is a pity that of the first and the second buildings only the lower structures are left, so that no idea can be gained as to what the older temples looked like.

The discovery of three Candis Kalasan makes it most likely that the charter of 778 does not refer to the present monument, but rather to the first one. The text states explicitly that a temple was founded and not rebuilt. When Vogler ascribed Candi Kalasan to the third period, his argumentation was exclusively based on the analysis of the *kala-makara* ornaments. These ornaments, however, do not embellish the first but rather the third Candi Kalasan. Now that it proves that this structure must be dated to a much later period, we cannot any longer follow Vogler's hypothesis.

As a matter of fact, the dating of a monument on the basis of only one single ornamental design has too many weak points. It is inconceivable that we should neglect other features. Remarkably, it was Vogler himself who first admitted this shortcoming. When he dealt with Candi Sajiwan he found out that the *kala* head was not in agreement with the eventual dating of the temple. He came to the conclusion that *kala* and monument could not belong to each other, so that possibly the *kala* was a later product added to the edifice at a later date (Vogler 1952: 263, footnote). It is undeniable that the ornaments of a monument would be carved after the edifice was erected. An extreme case is offered by Candi Selogrio, north-west of Magelang. Structurally speaking, the monument was complete; the architect had finished his work. The sculptor, however, had apparently not yet started the carvings, so that we now have a *candi* with plain walls and rudimentary ornamental designs (*vide* Krom 1923, I: 404).

Keeping the case of Candi Selogrio in view, we inevitably have to look for other features in our attempt to ascribe an approximate dating to the monuments. The evidence revealed by the archaeological investigations at Candi Kalasan might pave the way for our purpose. The uncovering of the first Candi Kalasan brought to light the four corners of the temple foot and the middle parts of both the east and the west sides as well. Hence the original ground-plan can be reconstructed as having been square, without projecting parts on any of the four sides. The upright walls of the foot proved to have been kept plain, without any ornamentation, and even without the usual successive sections. A plinth at the very base is the only relief from the plainness

The lower structure of the second monument shows clearly the transition phase from the first to the third construction. The ground-plan resembles that of the present *candi*: a square with projecting parts on all four sides, with an additional square platform around the base. This platform is practically the same size as the present one. The only relief in the plainness of the upright walls is furnished by a plinth of considerable height.

The loss of the actual temple buildings, and of the upper structures of both the first and the second monuments, makes it impossible to know what the *kala-makara* ornaments looked like. On the one hand this excludes any attempt to follow in Vogler's footsteps; but on the other hand it obliges us to take quite different elements into consideration for the comparative study and for the eventual dating of other monuments.

The most striking feature revealed by Candi Kalasan is the plainness of the base, peculiar to both the first and the second constructions. Since an architectural peculiarity, particularly in religious architecture, is generally speaking not so liable to depend on the personal taste and freedom of the artist, as might be the case with ornamental designs, there is good reason to accept that what was found at Candi Kalasan is a demonstration of the current building practice of the period. Consequently this feature deserves a place in any comparative study to establish the chronological order of the monuments.

It turns out that the feature mentioned is also to be found at two other monuments, which are generally assumed to represent the oldest period: the

Candis Gunung Wukir and Badut. We have seen that Vogler rejected the association of Candi Gunung Wukir with the Canggal Charter. The finding-place of the inscription, 150 m. south of the compound, is not convincing as the only indication. He furthermore argued that the case of the Kalasan Charter should be a reminder of how careful one must be when identifying a charter with structural remains found at the same site (Vogler 1952: 315).

Vogler's warning against Stutterheim's identification of Candi Kalasan I with the Kalasan Charter is not quite clear. The information that the Canggal inscription was found 150 m. south of Candi Gunung Wukir was actually obtained from the villagers in 1937. It does not agree with older information, that the charter was found in 1879 at the entrance to the courtyard of the compound (Krom 1923, I: 166). Moreover, the missing part of the stone slab was found in 1937 at the very site of the excavated temple (O.V. 1938: 18), so that there is no longer any doubt that inscription and temple belong to one and the same site. And since the Canggal Charter in some way commemorates the establishment of a temple, it is inconceivable that it had nothing to do with the Gunung Wukir compound. On the contrary, the obvious conclusion to be drawn is that the Canggal Charter was intentionally set up at the very place where the temple was founded, so that we now have good reason to assume that Candi Gunung Wukir was founded in 732.

As mentioned above, this Candi Gunung Wukir shows the same architectural peculiarity as Candi Kalasan I, viz. that the base of the monument is an elevated terrace with plain walls. Moreover, both monuments have the same ground-plan, consisting of a square without projecting parts (except at the front side for the staircase). The similar architectural features at Candi Gunung Wukir and Candi Kalasan I may serve as a basis for further investigations. It is to be regretted that both monuments lack their upper structures, so that no more architectural elements can be included in the present study.

More evidence is to be found at Candi Badut. This monument, however, is located in east Java, so that it is in principle beyond our scope. Nevertheless its unquestionably central Javanese architectural order, and its association with the Dinoyo Charter of 760, might throw some light on the dark period with which we are concerned. Vogler rejected any relation between the inscription of Dinoyo and Candi Badut. He even ascribed this monument to the very end of the central Javanese period (Vogler 1952). Its finding-place, so far away from the *candi*, is indeed not so convincing. Moreover, in its vicinity were found several other remains, which have not yet been examined. One ruin however, Candi Besuki, has good reason to lay claim to the Dinoyo Charter as well.

In spite of all that, the purely square plan of Candi Badut, and its entirely plain base, are not comparable with any other specific features than those found at Candi Kalasan I and Candi Gunung Wukir. Therefore, if the year

760 is not applicable to the installation of the Agastya statue of Candi Badut, the middle of the eighth century can certainly be assumed as the period which witnessed the foundation of the monument. Thanks to the sufficient quantity of original stones of the monument, Candi Badut could be reconstructed (O.V. 1929). Striking features are the soberness of the ornamentation, the squat but vigorous look, the piled up architectural sections, and the emphasized distinction of the superimposed upper storeys. All the features mentioned are peculiar to the older central Javanese architecture.

In fact, the young architecture shows a tendency to strive for grandeur. On the one hand more stress is laid on the ornamentation by an abundance of elaborate carvings, and on the other hand the sharply defined horizontal sections are softened by gradual transitions. The storeys on top even give the impression of having grown together by the tight rows of bell-shaped turrets and antefixes. Furthermore, the vertical panels are flanked by upward-growing twines, as if to direct aloft the viewer's attention. All these elements of soaring monumentality are clearly displayed by the present Candi Kalasan (third building) (Plate xvi*b*) and Candi Loro Jonggrang, which can safely be dated after 800.

With respect to the unmoulded base as a standard for ascribing an early age to a monument, Stutterheim pointed out that Candi Pringapus is also supported by a plain base, so that he ranked this temple with Candi Gunung Wukir, Candi Badut, and Candi Kalasan I (O.V. 1940: 21). Krom, however, was inclined to associate it with the Perot inscription of 853 which was found in its immediate neighbourhood (Krom 1923, I: 210); whereas Vogler ascribed it to the fifth period in the early tenth century. Observing Candi Pringapus more closely, it now proves that the start of the walls of the actual temple building displays a set of mouldings consisting of an ogee and a rounded cornice. The superimposed arrangement of plinth–ogee–rounded cornice is generally called the classical central Javanese profile, and is associated with the Golden Age of the Śailendras from *c.* 750 until *c.* 860. This classical central Javanese profile is commonly found at the base of both the temple foot and the temple body. It is noteworthy, therefore, that this profile serves as the support of only the temple body at Candi Pringapus, whereas its combination with a plain temple foot may attract special attention.

Observing the details of Candi Badut once again, we are struck by the existence of the set of ogee and rounded cornice at the start of the walls, so that evidently the combination of a plain base and a classical central Javanese profile is not restricted to Candi Pringapus. The obvious conclusion is, of course, that both monuments belong to one and the same architectural order, of the second half of the eighth century. It is once more to be regretted that the lack of walls at Candi Kalasan I and II, and also at Candi Gunung Wukir, prevents us from verifying our conclusion.

There is, however, one more monument which might be included in the present study, and hopefully throw more light on the above matter. It is Candi Sewu in the Prambanan plain. The vast compound of Candi Sewu is generally assumed to have been founded in the ninth century, either at its beginning (Krom 1923, I: 283) or towards its end (Stutterheim 1929). Vogler, however, allotted it a place among the monuments of the southern circle of the third period (*c.* 760–*c.* 812). A stone inscription, found in 1960 at the site of the compound, proved to justify Vogler's opinion, since it is dated 792. It is a pity that several epigraphical difficulties have prevented its publication. Nevertheless, a few data with regard to the monument can be obtained. It mentions either the expansion or the enlargement[2] of the temple, called *Mañjusrigrha.*

The name *Mañjusrigrha* reminds us of the charter of Kelurak, dated 782, which is commonly associated with the compound of Candi Lumbung. The charter commemorates the installation of a Mañjusrī statue. It states further that Buddha, Dharma and Sangha are ever present in a hidden form in this visible jewel. The abundant praise of Mañjusrī may justify the identification of the temple with Candi Sewu rather than with Candi Lumbung (cf. Boechari 1972).

To what extent the expansion, or enlargement, of the temple was carried out still deserves thorough investigation. It is not easy to find out the precise changes; but that a reshaping of the main temple did take place is evident from many parts of the walls, and also from the narrowing of the passage around the central chamber. The main temple actually consists of a central building and, separated by the passage, 4 subbuildings at the four sides. Each of the buildings has its own roof, but the whole is erected on a common platform. It is noteworthy that the central building proves to have been constructed on a square, plain, base nearly one metre in height, whereas the walls start with a set of a plinth, an ogee and a rounded cornice in super-imposing order. Here again we see the combination we found at Candi Badut and Candi Pringapus. It is not too bold a presumption, therefore, to suggest the thesis that the combination of a plain base with the classical profile at the start of the walls is a specific feature of the architectural order before *c.* 800.

Monuments Associated with Undated Inscriptions

The Diëng temples have always been considered the oldest monuments, not only of central Java but of the entire architectural art of Indonesia. Krom stated this assumption as an established fact, and even took it as an axiom (Krom 1923, I: 170). Bernet Kempers thought it an honoured tradition to begin a survey of Hindu-Javanese art with the Diëng temples (Bernet

Kempers 1959: 32). Vogler, however, ascribed Candis Arjuno, Semar, and Gatotkoco to the third period (*c.* 760–*c.* 812), and Candi Puntodewo to the second phase of the fourth period (*c.* 838–*c.* 898). Candi Sembodro and Candi Srikandi would then belong to the fifth period (after *c.* 928), representing respectively the first phase and the second phase. Following Vogler's scheme, the monuments of Arjuno, Semar, Gatotkoco, and Puntodewo, would be founded during the Golden Age of the Śailendras. The classical profile, however, is quite lacking; instead, the moulding consists of an ogee and a set of small, plain, cornices.

In fact, the early age ascribed to the Diëng temples is based both on architectural features and on epigraphic evidence. The inscriptions found in the immediate vicinity of the monuments are not dated, except in one case. On the basis of palaeographical considerations, the oldest inscription represents the Pallava script of the middle of the seventh century; whereas the latest is a date inscribed on a rock, showing the Saka year 1132 (=A.D. 1210). There are thirteen more stone inscriptions which display the same script as the one dated A.D. 809, and an inscribed gold plate belonging to the temple deposit of one of the monuments shows a similar script (Krom 1923, I: 171).

It is evident that the Diëng plateau witnessed an apparently continuous religious activity for about five centuries. Consequently it is quite possible that the monuments are not to be ascribed to one and the same age. As a matter of fact, Candi Arjuno is differently shaped from Candi Puntodewo, and Candi Bimo displays yet another architectural order, to which no other monument can be ascribed. Candi Semar is again another type of building, which is to be associated with Candi Arjuno only thanks to the fact that the remains of an enclosing wall put both together.

In spite of the diversity in construction of the Diëng temples, there is good reason to distinguish two architectural orders only: an older type which is more squat and sober, and a later one which is more slender and elaborated. Since the earliest evidence with regard to the Diëng plateau as a centre of Sivaism date back to the middle of the seventh century, it is only reasonable to ascribe the older type of monuments to that same period. It does not mean, however, that the later order should belong to the thirteenth century. On the contrary, even the youngest temples like Candi Sembodro and Candi Srikandi, which Vogler ranked among the monuments of the tenth century, should be dated to a much earlier period.

Of all the Diëng temples, Candi Arjuno is the most likely to represent the earliest architecture. Its sober decoration, its practically cubic shape, its accentuated horizontality, its distinctly receding superstructure, in short all the architectural details, fully agree with the requirements for an early age. The base of Candi Arjuno is not plain, but is a moulded one displaying the set of small cornices with a flat ogee. Logically speaking, a moulded base is a later development of the plain one. Candi Arjuno, however, is difficult to ascribe to a later date than the more complicated Candi Badut. There is even good reason to consider it older than Candi Gunung Wukir. The idea of a linear development is, therefore, to be abandoned. In fact, Vogler distinguished a northern and a southern circle for the third period, respectively represented by the New Diëng style and the Śailendra style. Shifting Candi Arjuno now from the third to the second period, in conformity with the results of our study, there will no longer need to be a hypothetical Old Diëng style: our Candi Arjuno represents it.

With regard to Candi Srikandi, Vogler placed it in the fifth period, i.e. at the latest in the early tenth century. Observing its architectural composition however, this monument proves to be the one that most resembles Candi Arjuno. The obvious conclusion to be drawn is that this monument, together with Candi Arjuno and Candi Semar, represents the Old Diëng style. So also does Candi Gatotkoco. The New Diëng style then comprises the monuments of Puntodewo and Sembodro, both displaying the impression of striving for slenderness.

It was stated above that the Old Diëng style should most probably be ascribed to the earliest Diëng period, starting in the middle of the seventh century, and that the New Diëng style should be of a much earlier date than the tenth century. It is to be admitted that several Śailendra features are to be observed in the monuments of the later order (Krom 1931: 127); but their architectural affinities with the temples of the older order may at the most associate them with the early period of the Golden Age of the Śailendras in the second half of the eighth century. Consequently, the Diëng temples are entirely to be dated before 800.

Keeping in view the association of monuments with undated inscriptions, our attention is finally drawn to the famous Candi Borobudur. The inscriptions at the hidden foot led Krom to the belief that the monument dates back to the second half of the eighth century (Krom 1923, I: 335). Van Erp thought the middle of the eighth century more likely (Erp 1929, I: 128). Moens placed it at an even earlier date, ascribing it to around 700 (Moens 1937: 418). Vogler ranged himself on the side of Krom, but de Casparis has associated the temple with the inscriptions of Karangtengah and Sri Kahulunnan, which bear the dates 824 and 842 (A.D.) respectively (Casparis 1950). Stutterheim associated the system used in the construction of the monument with the religious system explained in the *Sang Hyang Kamahāyānikan*, a Javanese Buddhist treatise of the ninth century, and suggested the ninth century as the most probable date (Stutterheim 1929). Applying our newly-established standard for dating, whereby the moulding of the base as well as of the start of the walls proves to be of great significance, it turns out that the original, hidden, foot of Candi Borobudur displays a beautifully-shaped ogee and a fully developed rounded cornice. Subsequently the classical central Javanese profile is perfectly demonstrated.

It is to be noted that the obvious difference between the classical profile, shown by Candi Badut, Candi Pringapus, and Candi Sewu, and what is displayed by Candi Borobudur, is to be found in the stage of development of the rounded cornice. At the earlier mentioned monuments this cornice is actually a thin ribbon, or a flat list, of which the protruding end is rounded. Candi Sewu even shows the initial stage of such a rounded cornice at the moulding of the platform: a protruding bar, the angles of which are cut off, so that the end looks like a halved hexagon. Quite different is the rounded cornice of Borobudur, which is really a semi-circular cornice. It indicates a more advanced, if not the final, stage of the development of this kind of cornice. Hence we are inclined to ascribe Candi Borobudur to a period after 800, tallying quite well with the culmination of the greatness of the Śailendras. Consequently the Golden Age of the Śailendras can be divided into two parts: the Earlier and the Later Śailendra periods, coinciding respectively with *c.* 730–*c.* 800 and *c.* 800–*c.* 860.

In one and the same breath with Candi Borobudur are mentioned Candi Pawon and Candi Mendut (Plate xvia). In fact, the current opinion is that they belong to each other, being the manifestation of one conception. We have to keep in mind, however, that inside the present Candi Mendut there is an older structure (*vide* Krom 1923, I: 313–14). Judging from the photographs of the dismantled parts, the older temple is apparently constructed on a plain base, whereas the footing of the walls displays a rounded cornice. If this impression turns out to be true, it strengthens the argument for ascribing the present Candi Mendut to the Later Śailendra period, thus ranking it with Candi Borobudur, and Candi Pawon. And when the inscribed stone slab, found at the site of Candi Mendut, indicates that this temple is older than Candi Borobudur (R.O.C. 1902: 7), it is only reasonable to associate the inscription with the first Candi Mendut.

Finally, it is to be hoped that the forthcoming dismantling of Candi Borobudur, as the start of the restoration project, will reveal more architectural as well as historical evidence, so that at last the diverse attempts for the dating can be pulled together.

Other Monuments and Other Inscriptions

The monuments discussed in the previous sections are in some way related to dated or undated inscriptions. There are, however, many more temples that cannot be associated with any epigraphic material. In this case we have to seek support from other evidence.

The absence of a date in an inscription can be surmounted by applying the principles of palaeography, whereby the specific features of the characters serve the basis for a comparative study of the script. Hence, assisted by dated inscriptions, an approximate dating can be attempted. In a similar way the monuments which are not associated with a written document can also be approximately dated on the basis of the comparative study of the specific features peculiar to the structure. Reviewing the results of our investigations, thus far achieved, we can now distinguish between an older architectural style for the period before Sañjaya's installation of his lingam at Gunung Wukir, and a newer architectural order for the period from then until the remodelling of Candi Sewu. Both periods can roughly be fixed between A.D. *c.* 650 and A.D. *c.* 730, and between A.D. *c.* 730 and A.D. *c.* 800 respectively.

We have seen that the architectural art of the older period, which can safely be called the first period, is represented by the Old Diëng style. The second period proved to consist of three architectural orders, viz. the New Diëng style, represented by the younger Diëng temples; the Sañjaya style at Gunung Wukir; and the Śailendra style in the Prambanan plain. With regard to the second period it may be noted that Candi Gunung Wukir, in spite of the lack of architectural details, cannot be ranked otherwise than with the Śailendra monument of Candi Kalasan and Candi Sewu. The omission of a separate Sañjaya style can, therefore, be justified. As a matter of fact, if we follow Poerbatjaraka's historical reconstruction, the existence even of a Sañjaya dynasty should be denied, so that we cannot speak about a Sañjaya style in architecture (Poerbatjaraka 1958).

As mentioned above there are monuments in central Java which cannot be associated with any epigraphical material, though they are very likely to be ascribed to the period of our concern. On the other hand there are also inscriptions that do not refer to any of the monuments, but which can be approximately dated before 800.

It was not until 1966 that our epigraphical knowledge of the central Javanese period was enriched by the publication of the Sojomerto inscription, found near Pekalongan (Boechari 1966). Since then a few more inscriptions have been discovered in the Pekalongan region. Not far south of the village of Sojomerto, another inscribed stone slab was found recently; and north of it again another one came to light (Boechari 1971). All three inscriptions are undated, but Boechari thought it very likely that the first Sojomerto stone should be ascribed to the first half of the seventh century. On the same palaeographical grounds the second stone is to be dated to an earlier period, whereas the third one is still older and represents the Pallava script of the second half of the sixth century. The same script, of about 600, is also carved on the pedestal of a stone Nandi statue, found as far west from Sojomerto as Prupuk in the Tegal district.

It is noteworthy that the Sojomerto inscription mentions the name of a certain personage, called Dapūnta Selendra, together with the names of his wife, his father, and his mother (Boechari 1966: 243 ff.). The peculiar name led Boechari to the supposition that Dapūnta Selendra was the founder of the Śailendra dynasty. It is interesting to note that this same founder of the Buddhist dynasty of the Śailendras proved to be a Saivite himself. It was apparently not uncommon that members of one and the same dynasty embraced different religions. Proof of such a case in the middle of the eighth century is given by the inscription found very recently in the Sragen district, east of Surakarta. It mentions a king, called Sangkhara, who after the death of his father ceased to worship the Sivaitic god Sangkhara, and became an adherent of Buddhism. This fact agrees very well with Poerbatjaraka's historical reconstruction, which denied the existence of a Sañjaya dynasty and ascribed the change of faith from Sivaism to the Buddhism of the Śailendra dynasty to Rakai Panangkaran (Poerbatjaraka 1958). Boechari is inclined to identify this Rakai Panangkaran with King Sangkhara of the Sragen inscription, whose complete name should then be 'Rakai Panangkaran Dyah Sangkhara Srī Sanggramadhanañjaya' (Boechari 1972).

Apart from Boechari's further presumption that Buddhism was introduced into central Java through the ports at the southern coast of Jogjakarta, whereas Sivaism came from the north coast of Pekalongan, it must be admitted that the oldest Hinduized settlements in central Java are to be sought in the north. The rise of the Buddhist Śailendras in the south did not take place until the middle of the eighth century, when King Sangkhara abandoned Sivaism to embrace Buddhism. In the meantime Sivaism remained the only religion in the northern regions of central Java.

It is a great pity that none of the newly-found inscriptions can throw light on the northern monuments of central Java, but one thing can be fixed: whatever historical reconstruction may have been achieved thus far, we remain on firm ground in presuming that those northern monuments represent the oldest stage of Indonesian temple architecture. This fact may on the one hand once again confirm our earlier ascription of an early age to the Diëng temples, and on the other hand pave the way for the inclusion of other northern monuments in our discussion.

The monuments, commonly ranked with the Diëng temples, are the nine compounds of Candi Gedong Songo scattered over the southern slopes of Mount Ungaran. The greater part of the compounds are heaps of stones rather than monuments. Of the temples still erect, however, either in their original ruinous condition or as reconstructed buildings, sufficient material is available to permit a comparative study.

A striking peculiarity is that group II and group III display the closest affinity with Candi Arjuno, particularly in the sense that both are accompanied by a small, flat, rectangular building similar to Candi Semar. The lack of a rounded cornice in the moulding of the base, as well as at the start of the walls, might further suggest that we ascribe these Gedong Songo temples to the same period as Candi Arjuno; but other architectural and ornamental details indicate a later date. A ranking among the monuments of the New Diëng style may be the eventual conclusion.

A close affinity with Candi Gedong Songo, particularly with the reconstructed monuments of group I and II, is displayed by a Sivaitic compound of six very small structures, excavated in 1952–53 near Ungaran (south of Semarang). Its unexpected emergence from the ricefields was the reason why people called the compound 'Candi Muñcul'. The six temples of Candi Muñcul are practically of the same shape. The moulded base is composed of a set of plinth, ogee, and thin cornices, and the same composition serves as the footing of the walls. The distinctive vertical lines of the walls, the relatively high storeys of the top, and the spire-like summit of the monument, suggest a dating in the second period of our established scheme, though the extreme soberness and the primitive ornamentation might point to an earlier development.

A similar extreme soberness, both in the construction and in the ornamentation, is shown by a very small Sivaitic temple discovered in 1965 in the Sleman district, north of Jogjakarta. It was buried to a depth of 5 m. by volcanic sand, and was brought to light in practically a sound condition. Only the outer stones of the upper structure were missing. Very untypical in this Candi Batu Miring is the base, which is simply composed of three superimposing and gradually receding plinths, followed by a set of small flat cornices at the start of the walls. Both ogee and rounded cornice are completely lacking. The peculiarly shaped base might be due to the very small size of the monument ($2\frac{1}{2}$ m. square, against a height of less than 4 m.), rather than indicating an initial stage of architectural art. Several ornamental details like the distinctive vertical lines of the walls even suggest a date towards the end of our second period. It is very likely that the lack of the classical profile points to an intrusion (or a resurgeance) of the Diëng tradition.

Such a feature is more obvious at the Sivaitic compound discovered in 1966 in the Prambanan plain, a few miles east of Jogjakarta. After the name of the present village, it is called 'Candi Sambisari'. The excavations have been carried out at a snail's pace, and will go on in that way for many more years before the entire compound can be brought to light, because of the insurmountable difficulty in removing more than 5,000 cubic m. of sand and gravel. The site evidently belongs to the same flood area as the Sleman district, which buried the compound down to a depth of 5 m.

Thus far the excavations have dug out the main temple, which is for the greater part intact, and two sub-temples opposite it, of which only the lower structures are left. It is apparent that the main temple underwent a thorough change in construction, leaving the original base as it was earlier. Remarkably, this base proves to be simply an elevated platform on a square plan with plain walls. A plinth at the start of the base is the only element of an eventual mould-ing. The same peculiarity is also shown by the two sub-temples. The start of the walls displays a moulding that consists only of an ogee and a plain cornice. The combination of this with the plain base, and the total lack of the rounded cornice, might suggest a merger of northern and southern elements towards the end of the early Śailendra period.

Finally, remaining in the Prambanan plain whilst keeping in view the speci-fic features of the mouldings, two other monuments draw our attention with respect to the same merger. In the first place may be mentioned the solitary Candi Gebang, which lacks the rounded cornice and moreover shows a rudi-mental ogee, both at the base and at the start of the walls. The other monu-ment is the compound of Candi Lumbung, consisting of a main temple and sixteen sub-temples of the same shape. Striking is the presence of a rounded cornice that might be considered to be in its initial stage. It is a very small rounded protrusion in the middle of a plain bar, so that it is not a hazardous surmise to ascribe this peculiarity to some kind of compromise between the northern Diëng tradition and the southern order of the early Śailendra period.

Concluding remarks

Summarizing our achievements in dealing with the external features of the architectural sections of monuments, we have come to the following conclusions:

(1) Monuments referred to in dated inscriptions are characterized by a plain base and a classical profile of the early Śailendra period at the start of the walls. The tradition apparently started *c.* 730 and went on until the end of the eighth century.

(2) Monuments associated with undated inscriptions display two architec-tural orders: an Old Diëng style and a New Diëng style. Both styles coincide with the periods *c.* 650–*c.* 730 and *c.* 730–*c.* 800 respectively. The newer order was cultivated concurrently with the early Śailendra style: the former being found practically only in the north, and the latter mainly in the south.

(3) Monuments not related to any epigraphic evidence, but to be ranked among monuments before 800, represent the New Diëng style for the northern regions, and the early Śailendra style for the southern part of central Java.

Listing the monuments to be ascribed to the period of our concern, the follow-ing scheme can be drawn up, replacing Vogler's chronological order:

First period (*c.* 650–*c.* 730), represented by
>   the *Old Dieng style*, comprising the monuments of:
>   Arjuno, Semar, Srikandi, Gatotkoco.

Second period (±730–±800 A.D.), represented by
>   (*a*) the *New Dieng style*, comprising the monuments of:
>   >   Puntodewo, Sembodro, Bimo (Plate xv*b*), Gedong Songo, Muñcul;
>   (*b*) the *Early Śailendra style*, comprising the monuments of:
>   >   Gunung Wukir, Pringapus, Kalasan I and II, Sewu;
>   (*c*) the merger of (*a*) and (*b*), comprising the monuments of:
>   >   Batumiring, Sambisari, Gebang, Lumbung.

In drawing the above conclusions it should be borne in mind that our present study is not meant to be exhaustive. One very important and integral part of the temple architecture was not taken into account, namely the sculptural art which adorns the temples, with statues in the round as well as in relief. There are many architectural remains of which only a few loose stones are left, but on the other hand enrich our sculptural treasure in an amazing way. Candi Banon near Borobudur, for instance, is known only from its perfectly sculptured statues; even the site is very difficult to find. Iconographic study, therefore, is essential before Indonesian archaeology can pretend to completeness.

NOTES

1. The scheme presented here is derived from Vogler's latest study (1953). It is slightly different from the former ones (1949 and 1952), particularly with respect to the termination of the 3rd period (and subsequently the commencement of the 4th period).

2. The word *mawṛddhi* means both expansion and enlargement.

Some Considerations on the Problem of the Shift of Mataram's Centre of Government from Central to East Java in the 10th Century

BOECHARI

I

A remarkable fact in the ancient history of Indonesia is the shift of the centre of government from central to east Java in the first quarter of the tenth century. This fact was preceded by a gradual shift of the attention of the central Javanese rulers to east Java. Rakai Watakura Dyaḥ Balitung was the first of Matarām kings who left us inscriptions in east Java, viz. the inscription on the back of a Gaṇeśa image from Ketanen dated 826 *Śaka* (A.D. 904)[1] and the inscription of Kinwu dated 829 *Śaka* (A.D. 907), also on the back of a Gaṇeśa image (OJO, XXVI).[2] King Dakṣa also issued an inscription in east Java, the inscription of Sugih Manek dated 837 *Śaka* (A.D. 915: OJO, XXX), whereas King Rake Layang Dyaḥ Tuloḍong added his edict to the earlier inscription of Hariñjing (Stein Callenfels 1934). Of the three known inscriptions dating from the reign of Rakai Sumba (or Pangkaja) Dyaḥ Wawa two were found in east Java, viz. the stone inscription of Kinawa dated 849 *Śaka* (OJO, XXXII) and the stone inscription of Saṅguran dated 850 *Śaka* (OJO, XXXI).

Dr. N. J. Krom was of the opinion that it was King Pu Siṇḍok who defini- tively shifted the centre of government to east Java (Krom 1931: 206). He based his opinion on Poerbatjaraka's remark that in Siṇḍok's inscriptions we read in the imprecation formula '*kita prasiddha maṅraksa kaḍatuan rahyang ta i mḍangi bhūmi matarām i watugaluḥ*',[3] whereas in Dakṣa's and Wawa's inscriptions this part reads '*kita prasiddha maṅrakṣa kaḍatwan śrī mahārāja i mḍang i bhūmi matarām*'.[4] From these quotations it can be concluded that Pu Siṇḍok did not reside at the palace of Medang any more, because it is referred to in his inscriptions as the palace of his deified predecessors (*rahyang ta*). Siṇḍok's palace must thus be situated elsewhere, viz. in east Java.

As to the reasons of the shift, after scrutinizing several possibilities (e.g. a rebellion of an east Javanese vassal, the will of the gods through a volcanic explosion or an epidemic, and political considerations, i.e. the threat from the descendants of the Śailendras reigning in Śrīvijaya), Krom said: 'in our opinion we may not go further than formulating that around 928 A.D. the kingdom had to abandon its central Javanese part for pressing but unknown reasons. We do not know what had happened, even less why it had happened' (Krom 1931: 206–9).

More than twenty-five years after Krom had formulated his opinion two other scholars contributed their opinions on this problem, namely Dr. B. Schrieke (1957) and Dr. J. G. de Casparis (1958*a*). We will deal at length with their articles, and we will try to give our own conception, fully realizing that we will not be able to find definite evidence for the causes of the shift of the centre of Matarām's government from central to east Java.

II

The possibility of political considerations was put up again by Dr. J. G. de Casparis. According to him, as a consequence of the flourishing of Arab trade in the ninth century A.D. spices and sandalwood from eastern Indonesia were much in demand, east Javanese merchants went to eastern Indonesia, exchanging Javanese rice and other products with spices and sandalwood. They took it to Śrīvijaya, where they met foreign merchants, and exchanged their wares with foreign goods, such as gold, silk, and porcelain from China, robes from India, incense from Arabic countries, etc. This kind of trade made east Java prosperous. Śrīvijaya was filled with envy at east Java's good fortune. Their rulers were afraid that east Java would gradually monopolize this international trade by persuading foreign merchants to trade directly with east Java, bypassing Śrīvijaya. They became aware of the necessity to crush east Java before it was too late. This opened a phase in the history of relations between Śrīvijaya and Java, starting around 925, which lasted about a century.

In the first phase the initiative was in Śrīvijaya's hands. In 928–929 or one or two years later an army from Malayu, a vassal state of Śrīvijaya, landed in east Java. They advanced to near Ngañjuk, but were defeated by Pu Siṇḍok. This historical fact is attested by the inscription of Añjukladang dated 859 *Śaka* (A.D. 937: OJO, XLVI). According to de Casparis this fact clarifies two things. First, the position of Pu Siṇḍok. He was known to hold the function of *rakryān mapatih i halu* during Tuloḍong's reign, and of *rakryān mapatih i hino* during Wawa's reign. It was very unusual that a high minister succeeded to the throne, except for very extraordinary reasons. In this case it was because he had saved the country from the attack from Śrīvijaya. As an example he quoted an episode in India's history, viz. Candragupta Maurya, who succeeded King Nanda after he had defeated the Greeks. Secondly, it clarifies the shift of the centre of government to east Java. De Casparis proposed that in the first phase King Balitung, Dakṣa, Tuloḍong, and Wawa gave more and more attention to east Java because they were fully conscious of the importance of inter-insular trade at that time. In the second phase, when the Javanese rulers realized the threat from Śrīvijaya they decided to defend only east Java, leaving the area west of the Brantas delta, including central Java, to its own fate.

Dr. B. Schrieke connected the problem of why the centre of government shifted to east Java with the question of the reasons for the prosperity of east Java in the tenth century. He ascribed the latter to the flourishing of Arab trade during the heydey of the Abbasid caliphate. But it was not the only factor; there must have been a deeper cause. Quoting Th. van Erp's description of the Borobudur temple and measuring it with the supposed density of the population of central Java at that time, which he thought to be not more than one million people, and comparing the resulting picture with G. Groslier's calculations of the work and manpower involved in the building of Banteay Chmar in Cambodia, he expressed the opinion that during the two centuries of the heydey of central Java people bent under the excessive burden of corvée labour for the building of temples. The men were withdrawn from their work in the rice-fields and from other productive activities. The final conclusion is, according to Schrieke, that central Javanese royal culture was destroyed by its temples.

III

Before proceeding to discuss both theories we will first investigate the problem of when the shift to east Java took place. Afterwards we will deal with the social, economic, and religious background of ancient Javanese society, i.e. the structure of the ancient Javanese kingdom and its cosmogonic background, the relation between king and subject, the attitude towards the building of religious sanctuaries, and the nature of the ancient Javanese economy.

We know that Balitung was the first of the Matarām kings who left us inscriptions in east Java. On the evidence of the inscription of Kubukubu dated 827 *Śaka* (A.D. 905) we know that he had defeated Bantan. Damais is of the opinion that Bantan has to be identified with the island of Bali, on account of the occurrence of toponyms like Batwan, Burwan, Airlaṅga, and the term *kulapati*. But those evidences may also point to east Java, since *kulapati* and Batwan also occurred in some other east Javanese inscriptions.[5] And since we do not have any indications of Javanese occupation in Bali at the beginning of the tenth century A.D., I think it better to assume that it was east Java which was conquered by Balitung. No evidence, hoewver, was found to show the reasons why he sent an expedition against east Java.[6] But it did not necessarily mean that it was Balitung who moved the centre of government to east Java. The fact that most of his inscriptions were found in central Java might indicate that he still resided in this area.[7]

As is pointed out above, Krom relies on Poerbatjaraka's opinion that we have to attach more weight on the word *rahyang ta* in the invocation formula. I do not quite agree with him; in my opinion the solution of the problem is not as simple as that. If we translate the above-mentioned passage of the inscriptions of Sugihmanek and of Sanguran we have 'thou who perfectly (or successfully) protects the palace of his majesty the king at Meḍang in the kingdom of Matarām', and for the passage in the inscriptions of Añjuklaḍang and of Paraḍah we have 'thou who perfectly (or successfully) protected the palace of the deified [kings] of Medang in the kingdom of Matarām situated at Watugaluḥ'.

One important thing has been left out of consideration by Krom, the site of the palace. We have other references pertaining to the site of the palace of Meḍang, viz. in the inscription of Mantyāsih I dated 829 *Śaka* (A.D. 907: Stutterheim 1927) and in the inscription of Śivagṛha dated 778 *Śaka* (A.D. 856: de Casparis 1956). In the inscription of Mantyāsih I we find the imprecation formula, *kadi laṇḍap nyān paka śapatha kamu rahyang ta rumuhun ri mḍang ri poḥ pitu. rakai matarām sang ratu sañjaya . . .*: 'like the sharpness of the curse of thou, deified kings, who in the past resided in Meḍang at Poh Pitu, to wit Rakai Matarām Sang Ratu Sañjaya . . .'. In the inscription of Śivagṛha we find the information that Dyah Lokapāla was consecrated king in 778 *Śaka* in the palace of Medang at Mamratipura (*ginlar i mamratipurastha meḍang kaḍatwan*).

In our opinion the clue does not lie in the word *rahyang ta*, but in the site of the palace. Poh Pitu is the site of the palace of Balitung's predecessors. It is most likely that it was the palace built by Sañjaya after the destruction of Sanna's capital by an enemy, alluded to in the inscription of Cangal dated 654 *Śaka* (A.D. 732: see Poerbatjaraka 1958). Poh Pitu must consequently be located in central Java, since we know that Balitung's predecessors did not issue inscriptions in east Java. Mamratipura, Rakai Kayuwani's palace, must also be located in central Java, since Mamrati is mentioned in several central Javanese inscriptions, such as the inscription of Haliwangbang dated 799 *Śaka* (A.D. 877: unpublished), the inscription of Poh dated 827 *Śaka* (A.D. 905: Stutterheim 1941), the inscription of Sangsang dated 829 *Śaka* (Naerssen 1937), the inscription of Lintakan dated 841 *Śaka* (KO, 1), and the inscription of Wulakan dated 849 *Śaka* (Goris 1928).[8] Watugaluh is not attested in the already known central Javanese inscriptions. Worthy of closer examination is the reading Watuwalu in the inscription of Hariñjing A dated 726 *Śaka* (A.D. 804: Stein Callenfels 1934). If it can be shown that it is a misreading for Watugaluh, which is not impossible, then Watugaluh has to be located in east Java.[9] We still have at present a village called Watugaluh near Jombang in the Brantas delta.

But then it means that Siṇḍok's predecessors already resided in east Java, and we cannot possibly know who was the king who shifted the capital from central Java; it could be either Daksa, or Tulodong or Wawa. Unless we need not take the invocation formula in Sindok's inscriptions too literally, and have to interpret it as 'thou who perfectly (or successfully) protected the palace of the deified kings in the past [and the palace of his majesty the king] of Medang in the kingdom of Mataram, situated at Watugaluh'. That we frequently do not have to take phrases in inscriptions too literally is shown in note 8 above, because the phraseology in Old Javanese inscriptions tends to be made as concise as possible at the cost of clarity. And if that was actually what the scribe had meant then it must have been Pu Sindok who shifted the capital from central to east Java. One might ask why should Pu Sindok invoke the deities who protected an abandoned palace instead of his own.

From epigraphic evidence it can be deduced that during the ancient period there was no centralized government. Haji Wurawari who attacked Dharm-mawaṅśa Teguh in A.D. 1016 for other reasons (cf. Boechari 1965), and killed him in battle, must have been one of his vassal kings residing in central Java.[10] After Airlaṅga was crowned king in A.D. 1019 he had to cope with several local rulers, including Haji Wurawari, who would not recognize his suzerainty. His battles of unification were attested by *inter alia* the inscription of Baru dated 952 *Śaka* (A.D. 1030: OJO, LX) and the inscription of Pucanan dated 963 *Saka* (A.D. 1041: OJO, LX; Kern 1917; Poerbatjaraka 1941). The inscriptions of Cane dated 943 *Saka* (A.D. 1020: OJO, LVIII) and of Kakurugan dated 945 *Śaka* (A.D. 1023: KO, v) also allude to battles. In the inscription of Terep dated 954 *Śaka* (A.D. 1032: Damais 1955) we find the information that Airlaṅga was even ousted from his capital town of Watan Mās by an enemy.

We get thus the picture of a kingdom comprised of a number of autonomous areas governed by local rulers with the title of *haji*, *sāmya haji*, *bhra* or *bhaṭāra*. We are of the opinion that the situation during the central Javanese period was not different. We have a large number of persons with the title of *rakai*, *rakryān i* or *rakarayān i*, followed by a toponym. They were local rulers who might or might not be members of the royal family. The *mahārāja* himself had such a title. There were also 'clerical' functionaries with the title of *pamgat*, who apparently were allotted 'apanage' domains, too. They may be termed 'secular clergymen'.

The territories of the *rakai* and *pamgat* were denoted with the term *watak*. We have thus for instance *si kbel anak wanua i wuatan yai watak watuhumalang* in the inscription of Paṅgumulan dated 824 *Śaka* (A.D. 902: Bosch 1925), which means 'Si Kebel, inhabitant of the village of Wuatan Yai which is part of the territory of Watuhumalang'. The territory of Watuhumala is governed by Rakai Watuhumalang. Another example in the same inscription is *si parbwata anak wanua i limus watuk puluwatu*, meaning 'Si Parbwata, inhabitant of the village of Limus which is part of the territory of Puluwatu, a territory under the jurisdiction of Sang Pamagat Puluwatu Pu Kunir Sang Winīta'.[11]

The information in the *Hsin T'ang shu* about the kingdom of Ho-ling, that 'on different sides there are twenty-eight small countries and none of them do not acknowledge its supremacy' (Groeneveldt 1880; 1960: 13) may confirm our opinion that the kingdom of Matarām comprised autonomous principalities. We think it rather improbable that we have to interpret it as referring to countries outside central Java. Moreover the above-mentioned passage, plus the information that there are thirty-two high ministers, reflects the cosmogonic background underlying the idea of Javanese kingship. The numbers twenty-eight and thirty-two are certainly symbolical numbers. Twenty-eight is 4×7, which is an interpretation of the seven continents surrounding Jambudvīpa; we have thus seven countries on each of the four cardinal points of Ho-ling.[12] And the thirty-two high ministers are the thirty-two deities having their abodes on the Mahāmeru, on the summit of which is found the heaven of Indra, king of the gods (cf. von Heine Geldern 1943).

Although we already have a replica of the Mahāmeru in the royal palace, we think that the kingdom as a whole is not yet complete without the state temple, the *pura penataran* in Balinese terminology. For the central Javanese period it is very likely that the Caṇḍi Sewu, built around A.D. 782, the Caṇḍi Plaosan and the Caṇḍi Prambanan, both built around A.D. 850, were considered as the state temples. Their layout, viz. the main temple(s) in the central courtyard, surrounded by respectively two, three, and four rows of smaller buildings, is supposed to reflect the structure of the kingdom (Krom 1923; de Casparis 1958), and as such they were also reflections of the macrocosmos. Caṇḍi Borobudur, built around the end of the eighth century A.D., was a temple for the worship of the deified founder of the Śailendra dynasty (de Casparis 1950). We do not know for certain which temples were the state temples before the accession of Sañjaya to the throne in A.D. 717,[13] when the kingdom was still centred in the Pekalongan area and north Kedu. For the east Javanese period, at least from the Kaḍiri period onwards, the Caṇḍi Penataran was most likely the state temple; the name explains itself.

We do not know whether there was also an actual mountain which served as replica of the cosmic mountain, because no such reference is found in inscriptions up to now. But Mount Penanggungan in east Java with its very peculiar form, i.e. a nearly perfect conical peak surrounded by four minor tips at a lower level, and again by four more nearer the foot, which strongly recalls that of Mount Meru, might be the sacred mountain for the east Javanese period (Stutterheim 1926, 1937). Its sacred character is attested by the large number of archaeological remains found scattered along its slopes (Romondt 1951).

In another article we have tried to show that ancient Javanese kings were no despots. They were expected to reign according to the ideals of kingship as is

put down in *inter alia* the *aṣṭabrata*. They ought to be just, generous, and bene-
volent, rewarding the meritorious and punishing the evildoers. People had the
right to lodge their complaints to the king, and if they proved to be right the
king was always ready to make decisions to the advantage of the people. On
the other hand people were expected to show their unswerving faithfulness
and loyalty to the king. We can cite a large number of passages in inscriptions
showing the ideal of how a good servant (*sewaka*) should be (Boechari 1973).

The Chinese chronicles give us a glimpse of the wealth of the island of Java.
The *Hsin T'ang shu* gives the information that 'the land produces tortoise
shell, gold and silver, rhinoceros horns and ivory; the country is very rich . . .'
(Groeneveldt 1960: 13). The Sung annals give a more detailed description
(ibid., 16). Although the Sung period coincides with the east Javanese period,
we think that the situation in central Java during its heyday was not much
different. It is to be noted, however, that the description of the location of the
capital in the Sung annals gives the impression that it still refers to the central
Javanese period. It is said that the distance from the capital to the sea in the
east is one month, whereas to the west it is forty-five days. To the north the
distance to the sea is five days, whereas to the south it is three days. And it
seems that there were harbours in the east, in the north, and in the south.
Such information could not possibly refer to the Brantas delta, in which the
capital of the east Javanese kingdom was situated. It fits more to the Kedu and
Matarām plains.

The inscriptions also reflect the wealth of the population. When a piece of
land or a village or a number of villages was made a freehold, the grantee had
to offer *pasek pasek* to the king, the high court dignitaries, the village elders
from the neighbouring villages, and to all other people who were involved in
the ceremonies on the occasion of the foundation of the freehold. He also had
to pay for the offerings and the festivities. Stutterheim has calculated that in
the inscription of Poh dated 827 Śaka (A.D. 905), the *pasek pasek* to be offered
by the village elders of Poh, Rumasan, and Nyū amounted to 187 pieces of
kain, 2,023 kg. of gold, 4 buffaloes, 11 sheep, rice, and cooked rice with side
dishes, not to mention the amount of food and drinks consumed during the
festivities. To give an idea of the extravagance of these festivities we will cite
an example from the inscription of Taji (OJO, XXIII), viz. 57 bales of rice,
6 buffaloes, 100 chickens, and all kinds of salted fish and meat, and intoxicating
drinks.[14]

IV

We will now give some comments on the theories of J. G. de Casparis and
B. Schrieke. Both scholars agree that one of the reasons for the move from
central Java was the prosperity of east Java, due to the flourishing trade during

the heyday of the Abbasid caliphate. But did central Java not share the profit? Were there no merchants and no harbours in central Java? As we have shown above, these questions have to be answered in the negative. Pemalang, Kendal, and Japara were the harbours in the past, which still played an important role during the Muslim Matarām period (Schrieke 1957: 105–8). And even after the centre of government was shifted to east Java there was a flourishing international trade in central Java, as witnessed the abundance of Sung ceramics found there, from the north coast regions (de Flines 1947) to the Ratu Baka hills in the south.

It is true that there are no big rivers running from the interior to the north coast. The Kali Serang and the Kali Tuntang are perhaps too small and not navigable for big river boats. Moreover those rivers do not reach down to the fertile plains of Kedu and Matarām. But we think that it did not constitute a disadvantage for the trade from the interior to the coastal areas, because we still have the road system. In the inscription of Mantyāsih is mentioned a big road (*hawān*) which had to be protected by the *patihs* of Mantyāsih. In our opinion this was the road connecting the Kedu plains with the north coast via Parakan. A branch of this road runs via Wonosobo to the Diëng mountains and thence to the north-west in the neighbourhood of Pekalongan. We think that the road system known to the Dutch in the seventeenth century was the traditional one dating back to the ninth century A.D., or even earlier.

As for the theory that the struggle between Śrīvijaya and Java was another cause of the move to east Java, we think that de Casparis failed to give sufficiently convincing arguments. If it was true that around A.D. 928 an army from Malayu had landed in east Java, why should Pu Siṇḍok decide to defend only this region? Was it not rather proof that the Brantas delta could be more easily reached by an army from overseas? We may remind readers of the expedition of Kubhilai Khan which landed in east Java at the end of the thirteenth century, resulting in the downfall of Kaḍiri. In our opinion the interior of central Java was less vulnerable to attacks from outside Java than the Brantas delta. Seen in this light it is more likely that the rulers of Matarām would prefer to stay in central Java when facing the attack from Śrīvijaya.

Moreover de Casparis' theory has lost another argument, now that it is shown that Haji Wurawari who attacked Dharmmawangśa Teguh, judging from the whole context of the inscription of Pucanan, was his own vassal king from central Java (Schrieke 1957: 215; Boechari 1965: 71). There remains one piece of evidence pointing to the enmity between Matarām and Śrīvijaya, viz. the Chinese chronicles, which mention an attack from She-p'o against San-fo-ch'i around A.D. 992 (Groeneveldt 1960: 18, 65). But it does not necessarily mean that this was an action in a series of attacks and counter-attacks between the two countries. L. C. Damais saw in the inscription of Hujung Lañit, dated A.D. 997, found near Liwa in south Sumatra, a vestige of this expedition (Damais 1957, 1962). But since the stone inscription is too weathered to allow a satisfactory reading, and since in our opinion its site is too far to the south, we would rather be more careful in dealing with it, and not too rash in drawing any conclusions.

Now we come to Schrieke's theory that Javanese royal culture was destroyed by its temples. We have in fact a large number of ruins of temples, large and small, in central Java, the exact number of which is unknown since new remnants of temples are found nearly every year. They are found in the residences of Pekalongan, Kedu, Semarang, Surakarta, and the Sultanate of Jogyakarta; the residences of Banyumas and Pati only yield an insignificant number of archaeological remains.

If we adopt the opinion that She-p'o and Ho-ling in the Chinese chronicles always meant Java (Damais 1964), then the history of central Java covers a period of five centuries, from the fifth to the tenth century A.D. But up to now we do not have evidence of temples dating from before the eighth century. That is why Schrieke spoke of only two centuries of building activities in central Java (1957: 300).

It may be assumed that, like the situation in Bali, there were several kinds of temples in ancient Java. There were at least three territorial units: first the kingdom as a whole, ruled by the *mahārāja*; second, the regions governed by local rulers, princes, and state functionaries, the *watak*; and third, the villages or *wanua*. Each territorial unit must have had its own temples; notably temples for the worship of the deified ancestors; temples of the dead, to be compared with the *pura dalem* in Bali; and temples for the worship of the gods. There might have been other kinds of temples, such as temples for sacred places, and for special voluntary associations, to be compared with the *pura pemaksan* (Goris 1935, 1938).

In fact the inscriptions give us evidence of several kinds of sanctuaries, viz. *caitya*, *prāsāda*, *caṇḍi* (or *pacaṇḍyan*), *silunglung dharmma panasthūlān*, *parhyanan*, *kuṭi*, the exact meaning of which is still problematical. Of these *Caitya*, the *caṇḍi* (or *pacaṇḍyan*), *silunglung*, and *dharmma pañasthūlān* seem to denote burial temples. The meaning of *prāsāda* is uncertain. The inscription of Sugih Manek (OJO, xxx) mentions a *prāsāda kabikuan*. In the inscription of Mañjuśrīgṛha dated 714 *Śaka* (A.D. 792), the Caṇḍi Sewu is called a *prāsāda* (*prāsādeni kumang gap ya puṇya ṇḍa śrī nareśwara*). In the inscription of Kañcana (Buṅur) dated 782 *Śaka* (A.D. 860), copied in 1295 *Śaka*, there is mentioned a *sang hyang prāsāda. sthāna nira sang hyang arccha boddha prati-wimba* (Kern 1917), but we also find a *prāsāda silunglung sang siddha dewata rakryān bawang* in the inscription of Cunggrang dated 851 *Śaka* (A.D. 929), which certainly means a burial temple (Stutterheim 1925). *Parhyañan* may be interpreted as a sanctuary for the worship of the gods. According to the Nāgarakṛtāgama *parhyañan* falls into the category of *dharmma lpas*, i.e. free sanctuaries or other than royal sanctuaries (*sudharmma haji*), which is under the supervision of a Śivaite *adhyakṣa*. And *kuṭi*, according to the *Nāgarakṛtā-gama*, also falls into the category of *dharmma lpas*, but under the supervision of a Buddhist *adhyakṣa* (*Nāg.* 75, 2; cf. van Naerssen 1937).

From the inscriptions it can also be learned that some of the state functionaries had their own sanctuaries. In the inscrpition of Marsemu (KO, XIII) is mentioned a *dharmma rakryān i wka i pastika*, i.e. a sanctuary of the Rakryān i Wka, situated at Pastika. From other inscriptions, viz. the inscription of Pastika dated 803 *Śaka* (A.D. 881: Brandes 1886) and the inscription of Muṅgu Antan dated 808 *Śaka* (A.D. 836: OJO, XVIII) it can be deduced that the sanctuary of Rakryān i Wka is a burial temple of a deified king, presumably his own father or grandfather. In the inscriptions of Humanḍing dated 797 *Śaka* (A.D. 875), of Juruṅan dated 798 *Śaka* (A.D. 876), of Mamali dated 800 *Śaka* (A.D. 878, and of Taragal dated 802 *Śaka* (A.D. 880) all of them still unpublished, Rakryān i Sirikan pu Rakap founded freeholds on behalf of *his prāsāda* at Gunung Hyang (*sīmā ni prāsāda nira i gunung hyang*).

As we have said above, Caṇḍi Sewu, Caṇḍi Plaosan, and Caṇḍi Prambanan were most probably the state temples for the central Javanese period, which functioned as the replica of Mount Meru, whereas Caṇḍi Borobudur was a temple for the worship of the deified founder of the Śailendra dynasty (de Casparis 1950: 170–5). In our opinion it was only those four temples and the 'burial' temples of the kings[16] which were built by order of the *mahārāja*, whereas the tens or perhaps hundreds of smaller temples were built by the local rulers and the village community.

From the short inscriptions found at a large number of the accessory temples of Caṇḍi Plaosan Lor, it can be learned that this temple compound was built by Śrī Mahārāja Rakai Pikatan in collaboration with his state functionaries and local rulers. Each of them contributed one or more buildings, sometimes several functionaries together contributed one building (de Casparis 1958). Caṇḍi Prambanan was also built in the same manner, since we also find short inscriptions on several buildings and on parts of the main temple and the first surrounding wall. Unfortunately they were written with paint, red and white, so that most of them are obliterated and very difficult to read.[17] Caṇḍi Sewu has yielded five short inscriptions, and an Old Malay inscription dated 714 *Śaka* (A.D. 792) gives evidence of a *nāyaka*, a state functionary, contributing to the enlargement of the temple (*mawṛddhi ḍing wajrāsana mañjuśrīgṛha namaña*).

We can visualize the local rulers and the state functionaries sending their artisans and their workers who belonged to the *śudra* caste, and slaves (*Kawula*)[18] to the central government to contribute to the building of the state temples. This among other things is what is termed *buat haji* in the inscriptions. With this picture in mind we ask whether it is justified to speak (with Schrieke) about the burdensome corvée labour forcing people to move to other territories. In our opinion people belonging to the *vaiśya* caste who were engaged in agriculture, trade, and home industry were left to do their daily work, because they were not actively needed in the building of temples. It required *brāhmaṇas* to draw the layout of the temple, to determine the exact location of the sanctuary, the exact date to start with the building, and to carry out the ceremonies; sculptors to carve the statues and the reliefs; and slaves and *śudras* for the dirty work of carrying the stones from the quarries to the building site and for the preparatory chipping and shaping of the stones.

Moreover it is to be noted that most of the work in the rice-fields could be carried out by women. It was only the hoeing and the ploughing of the fields, and the regulation of the irrigation waters which were the men's business. The planting of the rice, the weeding, and later on the reaping of the harvest could be carried out by women. We even have evidence of a female *hulair* (*hulair anakbi*) in the inscription of Juruñan. The chasing away of the birds when the paddy is ripening was the work of the boys and girls (*raray laki laki wadwan*) of the village.

We see thus that the men could easily leave the village without harming rice production. If they were nevertheless needed in the building activities they left the village in times when their presence was not necessary. Perhaps we can compare the situation with that on the island of Bali during the so-called *ngayah*, i.e. a co-ordinated co-operative work by the whole village in cases which concern the interest of the village community, for instance the restoration and building of *puras*, of assembly halls, etc. On such occasions the entire population of the village, old and young, men and women, contribute their share, but the work is arranged in such a way that the individual's interest is not harmed (Soekmono 1965: 33). We are of the opinion that we also have that kind of institution in ancient Java, although perhaps in a somewhat different form, but with the same principle of not harming the individual's interest. Temples for the village community, which are usually of modest size, are most likely built in this manner.

We still have the problem of manpower, indeed. According to Schrieke, the total population of central Java in the ninth and tenth centuries could not exceed one million. We do not know on what basis he made his estimate. We are of the opinion that it is not so simple as that. We cannot simply take as a starting point a known number in a certain period, say, the estimate of the population of Java and Madura in 1800, or the result of the 1930 census, and then count back on the basis of a certain rate of population growth, because there is a total lack of data about the fluctuations of Java's population in certain periods. To illustrate our difficulty we may cite the information that the population of Java increased with an average of 2·17% a year between 1930 and 1961, whereas between 1961 and 1971 the rate was 1·94% (Hafid 1973:

53). J. M. van der Kroef believed that the period of most rapid growth was 1815–90, during which years the population multiplied 5·2 times (cited from Hollingsworth 1969: 76).

Here we enter the domain of historical demography; but since we are anything but an historical demographer we cannot give our own calculations. We can only mention some data which might help to give an idea of how to estimate the number of population in ancient times. We have in fact indications of the existence of a census. Several inscriptions: viz. the inscription of Kuṭi dated 762 *Śaka* (A.D. 840: KO, II), the inscription of Kañcana dated 782 *Śaka* (A.D. 860: Kern 1917), the inscription of Waharu dated 795 *Śaka* (A.D. 873: OJO, IX), the inscription of Kaladi dated 831 *Śaka* (A.D. 909: unpublished),[19] and the inscription of Barsahan (Stutterheim 1938) all mention a *wilang thāni* or *wilang wanua*, i.e. a functionary with the duty of counting the number of villages. We think that it was in the first place the number of the inhabitants which was their concern. They were mentioned among the *maṅilāla drawya haji*, up to now interpreted as tax collectors,[20] which is understandable, since the only frequent reason for counting people was for raising taxes (Hollingsworth 1969: 42). However, not a single vestige of their activities, no records of the number of population at a given period, no vital registration data, no fiscal documents, etc. have been recovered up to now.

We can also make an estimate by counting the number of *wanua* (villages) mentioned in all extant central Javanese inscriptions.[21] The number of inhabitants of a village can be estimated by the number of *rāma* (village elders), by assuming that each *rāma* had for his sustenance a certain number of households, the so-called *cacan* of later times. We may sometimes be fortunate in finding information like that in the inscription of Baru dating from the reign of Airlaṅga (OJO, LX), in which the names of all *karamān*, old and young, who received grants from the king, were mentioned. We have a total of around 400 *karamān* for the village of Baru and its dependencies.[22]

But we still have serious difficulties. In the first place we do not know, and will never know, what percentage of all issued inscriptions in the past have been recovered, and not all recovered inscriptions have been published. As to the number of *rāma* of a *wanua*, we are not certain whether the lists always denote all functioning *rāma*, because we have evidence of such varying numbers; there are villages with twenty to forty *rāma*, but there are also villages with fewer than ten *rāma*. And if a village is mentioned among the 'adjacent villages' (*wanua tpi siring*) which send witnesses to the ceremonies of the foundation of a freehold, usually only one *rāma* of that village is mentioned.

As to the information in the inscription of Baru, we do not know whether *karamān* means the total number of village elders or head of a family, or core villagers, to be compared with the Balinese *krama desa*. In either case we cannot know the exact number of the resident population of the village of

Baru, since we will never be in the position to know how many people did not receive grants from the king or how big the average Javanese family was in the past, or what percentage of the total householders constituted the core villagers. The Sung annals give the information that there were 30,000 soldiers (Groeneveldt 1960: 17). We might have been able to estimate the total population of central Java, if we knew that the *Sung-shu* mentioned the whole army which the *mahārāja* of Ho-ling could raise in times of war, including the army of the local rulers, since it might be assumed that the army constituted a certain percentage of the total population. But we are inclined to the belief that 30,000 was only the number of soldiers of the central government, excluding that of the local rulers.

The number of archaeological remains might also be used for estimating the population of central Java. In this case we might apply Cook's method of assessing the population of the Teotihuacan civilization at its height (Cook 1947). In Th. van Erp's architectural description of the Borobudur we find some figures regarding the quantity of stones used for the building of the temple, the total length and extent of the reliefs, the number of statues and other ornaments, etc. (van Erp 1931 : 39). If we compare these figures with that for Bantay Chmar, and with Groslier's estimate of how many workers and sculptors and how many years were needed for building it, then we will get some idea of the amount of work involved in the building of the Borobudur. In the same manner we can get an estimate of how many workers and sculptors and the number of years needed for the building of Caṇḍi Sewu, dating from the last quarter of the eighth century A.D., and for the building of Caṇḍi Plaosan and Caṇḍi Prambanan, both dating from the middle of the ninth century A.D. Adding the estimate for the numerous other temples, and by using Cook's method, we are of the opinion that the outcome will show that the total population of central Java in the eighth and ninth century A.D. was much more than Schrieke's estimate.

To summarize, we can say that the portrait of the ideal king, the structure of the ancient Javanese kingdom, the relation between king and subject, the attitude towards the building of religious sanctuaries and the nature of ancient Javanese economy, including the estimate of the density of the population of central Java, make the picture of a despotic ruler, forcing his subjects to build splendid edifices to his own glory, resulting in economic collapse, rather improbable. Maybe the very humorous scenes among the reliefs of Caṇḍi Borobudur and Caṇḍi Prambanan, improvisations of the Javanese sculptors, strengthen our conclusion. We may point to the picture of a dog carrying away food in the scene depicting the rape of Sītā, the picture of a frog, of playing monkeys and birds, etc. We cannot imagine that an oppressed spirit would produce such a great sense of humour. We would rather visualize the sculptors singing and chatting when carving those reliefs.

Another drawback for Schrieke's theory is the fact that Caṇḍi Prambanan, believed to be the latest temple in central Java, was already inaugurated in A.D. 856 (de Casparis 1956), but apparently it remains unfinished. If de Casparis' theory on the date of Caṇḍi Prambanan is correct, then more than half a century before the shift to east Java no building activities had been undertaken.

v

Now that we have shown that it is unlikely that the shift of Matarām's capital from central to east Java was due to strategic and economic considerations, or to a movement of the population to east Java because of the excessive burden laid upon them for the building of temples, what then were the causes of the shift?

In fact the shifting of capitals is a common feature in Javanese history. We have shown that Matarām's capital had been shifted at least twice during the central Javanese period, as was attested by the mention of Mamratipura and Poh Pitu as the site of the capital (*v. supra*, p. 476). We still have a number of villages called Medang scattered between Purwadadi-Grobegan and Blora in north central Java, but whether they were ever the site of Matarām's capital in ancient times cannot be made out. Perhaps archaeological excavations at those villages may reveal some evidence.

Airlaṅga's capital was also moved twice during his reign. His first capital, built after he was consecrated king after the destruction of Teguh's capital, was apparently located at Watan Mās, mentioned in the inscription of Cane dated 943 *Śaka* (A.D. 1021: OJO, LVIII). In the inscription of Kamalagyan, dated 959 *Śaka* (A.D. 1037: OJO, LXI) Kahuripan is mentioned as the location of the palace. It is to be supposed that the shift from Watan Mās to Kahuripan was due to the invasion by an enemy, attested by the inscription of Terep dated 954 *Śaka* (Damais 1955). It seems that the palace was again shifted to Dahaṇa(pura), indicated by the occurrence of the word *dahaṇa* carved in big square script in the fashion of a seal on the inscription of Pamwātan dated 964 *Śaka* (A.D. 1041).[23] No evidence of the reasons for this second shift has been found up to now.

From evidence concerning later periods, it can be learned that the shift of a capital was usually caused by the invasion of the palace by an enemy. This is conceivable, since in the Javanese belief such a palace is desecrated and has to be abandoned. However, in the seventeenth century the shifts to Karta by Sultan Agung, and from Karta to Plered by Amangkurat I, are not explained in this way. In our opinion it was the belief in cycles which was the cause of those shifts. Sultan Agung represented the fourth generation of kings after Ki Ageng Pemanahan, founder of the dynasty; whilst Amangkurat I was the fourth generation after Panembahan Senapati, the first ruler of Matarām. There is among the Javanese a belief that after three generations, or after a century, there will occur a catastrophe unless the next king moves to a new palace elsewhere.[24]

This belief in cycles must also have been known in ancient times. It is what Schrieke termed the *kaliyuga* concept in Javanese historiography (Schrieke 1957). The phrasing of the invasion of Sanna's capital by an enemy in the inscription of Caṅgal, the wording of the destruction of Teguh's palace in the inscription of Pucaṅan, and the description of the fall of Kertanagara in the *Nāgarakṛtāgama* certainly point to this belief in cycles (cf. Poerbatjaraka 1958). After those catastrophes a new palace was built.

It can also be seen that the shift of the capital was mostly limited to within the same area. We are of the opinion that we have to view this phenomenon against the cosmogonic background of ancient Indonesian kingship. To move to another area, viz. from central to east Java, means the creation of a new *maṇḍala*, accompanied by the adoption of a new sacred mountain and the building of a new state temple as replica of Mount Meru. Hence the shift from central to east Java is only understandable if it was caused by a tremendous happening, which in the belief of the Javanese must be seen as an omen of the gods that the present order had come to an end. This cannot be anything else but a cataclysmic explosion of a volcano or another form of natural catastrophes.

Dr. R. W. van Bemmelen thought he found indications of a catastrophic eruption of Mount Merapi in the past. Its western part collapsed, and slid down with such a tremendous force that the Gendol Hills were formed. This explosion was preceded by heavy earthquakes and accompanied by ash rains so that a large area around Mount Merapi was entirely destroyed and became a barren ash-covered desert. Van Bemmelen connected this explosion with the so-called *pralaya*, the destruction of Teguh's kingdom in A.D. 1016, mentioned in the inscription of Pucaṅan (Bemmelen 1949: 560–2). This is certainly wrong, because the palace was already shifted to the Brantas delta by that time, so that it cannot possibly have been much affected by the eruption.

We need thus a more exact dating of this catastrophe. If it can be shown that it occurred around the first quarter of the tenth century instead of the eleventh century A.D., we are certain that it was this explosion which was the cause of the shift of Matarām's capital from central to east Java around A.D. 925. We are thinking of the possibility of the capital town being destroyed by the earthquake or by the lava flow, or by both.

In another article we have tried to show that before the shift ancient Matarām was troubled by incessant wars of succession after the reign of Rakai Kayuwaṅi Pu Lokapāla (Boechari 1968b). To the people's belief this would provoke the wrath of the gods. And actually it came in the form of the catastrophe. A large number of the population, including members of the royal family, fled away trying to escape from the lava flow and the ash rains. The once fertile plains of Kedu and Matarām were abandoned because they became uninhabitable and unfit for agriculture for a long time.[25] This might be termed an economic factor, indeed, but in our opinion religious belief played a bigger role.

NOTES

1. This inscription is still unpublished. In this article we only mention the stone inscriptions, because they are less liable to being moved from central to east Java. We have in fact other east Javanese inscriptions issued by Dyah Balitung, viz. the copper-plate inscription of Taji (OJO, XXIII), the copper-plate inscription of Kubu Kubu (unpublished), the copper-plate inscription of Kaladi (unpublished), and the copper-plate inscriptions of Tulaṅan (OJO, XXVIII). The stone inscription of Mantyāsih (OJO, XXVII) is supposed to originate from east Java, but since it commemorates the establishment as a freehold, villages and wooded areas which are most likely to be situated in north Kedu, we doubt the correctness of the supposition (see Rouffaer, 1909, p. LXXX).

2. The last part of this inscription, written on a stone block has been discovered in the village of Klampok, Jiwut, regency of Blitar, about ten years ago.

3. We find this phrase in the inscription of Añjukladang (OJO, XLVI), and in the inscription of Paraḍah (OJO, XLVIII).

4. We find this phrase in the inscription of Sugih Manek (OJO, XXX) and in the inscription of Sangguran (OJO, XXXI).

5. Batwan is mentioned in the inscription of Kubu Kubu and in another unpublished inscription from Gunung Gaprang, in the village of Leran Kulon, regency of Tuban. *Kulapati* is mentioned in the inscriptions of Hariñjing, of Kubu Kubu, of Sugih Manek, of Piling Piling and of Sangguran. Damais also mentions *burwan*, which he considers as a toponym (Damais 1952; n. 2 on p. 46). It sounds indeed like the name of a Balinese village. But in his latest posthumous work he corrected his mistake, and rightly observed that it is part of the term *katuhaburwan*, a derivative form of *tuhaburu*, i.e. hunter or gamekeeper.

6. It is to be noted that there are no indications of the existence of a kingdom in east Java except for the inscription of Dinoyo dated 682 *Śaka*, which gives evidence of a kingdom called Kāñjuruhan in the region of the present Malang in the middle of the eight century A.D. (Bosch 1916; 1925; de Casparis 1941). No evidence has been found to show whether it was this Kāñjuruhan which flourished until the beginning of the tenth century and was defeated by Dyah Balitung.

7. From the thirty inscriptions dating from the reign of Dyah Balitung only five certainly originate from east Java. Of three other inscriptions the place of origin is uncertain (see Damais 1970: 50–2, from No. 117 to 147).

8. The evidence in the inscription of Śiwagṛha showing that Rakai Kayuwani's palace was situated at Mamratipura contradicts the evidence in the inscription of Manyāsih from which must be concluded that the palace of Balitung's predecessors, from the time of Sañjaya onwards, was situated at Poh Pitu. In our opinion the solution of this problem is not to take the latter too literally. The most likely explanation is that Poh Pitu was the location of the palace built by Sañjaya after he restored the kingdom of his predecessor. The fact that afterwards the palace was probably shifted from one place to another was too complicated to phrase in the invocation formula.

9. We do not have the time to verify the reading on the original stone which is now kept at the Jakarta Museum.

10. For the location of Wurawari in central Java, see Schrieke (1957: 211 ff.).

11. In the inscription of Sugih Manek the village of Limus is mentioned as part of the region of Kanuruhan. We are of the opinion that we are here dealing with another Limus to be located in east Java, because Kanuruhan is found solely in east Javanese inscriptions, except for its occurrence among the short inscriptions of Caṇḍi Prambanan. The number of homonyms in Javanese toponyms is legion; we have a Koripan in east as well as in central Java, a Bumi Jawa in central Java as well as in Lampung (south Sumatra), etc. According to de Casparis *kanuruhan* is derived from Kāñjuruhan. When in all probability the kingdom of Kāñjuruhan was defeated by Metarām, the ruling family retained authority over the territory as *sāmya haji* with the title of *rakryan kamuruhan* (de Casparis 1941). The occurrence of *kanuruhan* among the short inscriptions of Caṇḍi Prambanan may lead us to the conclusion that Kāñjuruhan had already lost its independence during the reign of Rakai Pitatan (cf. n. 6 above). It is also interesting to note here that Sang Pagmat Puluwatu does not live in his own territory, but in the village of Cukulan which is part of the region of Tilimpik (*sang pamagat puluwatu pu kunir sang winīta anak wanua i cukulan watak tilimpik*). Presumably Tilimpik is a region under the jurisdiction of a Samgat Tilimpik.

12. On the identification of Ho-ling with Java, see Damais (1964).

13. For this probable date of Sañjaya's accession to the throne, see Damais (1951). [*Editors note:* compare these dates with the revised chronology in the paper by Soekmono (p. 472).]

14. Quoting these instances, should not we speak of the extravagance of the people rather than of their wealth? In more recent times we frequently hear of people, usually influential people in a village, who give extravagant feasts on the occasion of, e.g. the marriage of their daughters, although to be able to finance the feasts they go into debt to Chinese or Arab usurers. Presumably the *kilalan* were also the usurers in ancient times. In this connection it is to be noted that we also have evidence of people giving their piece of land in lease to another, even a *sima*. Evidence of the latter is found in e.g. the inscription of Tija (Stutterheim 1925a) in which it is said that the grantee had the right to give in lease or even sell to another a *sima kawajwan*, i.e. a *sima* on behalf of an *awaju*, whatever this last term means. We are not certain whether *sang awaju* is an abbreviated form of *sang awaju haji*, a synonym of which is *sang akalambi haji*, a functionary who is mentioned in some inscriptions as the one who pronounces the curse. In Old Javanese law-books clauses are included on lend-lease matters.

15. We did not have the time to read the inscription of Añjukladang ourselves. There are indeed lacunae in the transcription of Brandes, but as far as we can make out of the published text there is no evidence of an attach from Malayu. We hope that Dr. de Casparis will soon publish his new and more complete transcription of this important inscription.

16. The existence of 'burial' temples can be deduced from inscriptional evidence. We find, e.g. *haji dewata lumāḥ ing satasrengga* in the inscription of Telang (Stutterheim 1934); *sang hyang caitya sang dewata sang lumāḥ ing pastika* in the inscription of Poh (Stutterheim 1940); *sang lumāḥ i layang* in the inscription of Panunggalan (KO, IX); *sang lumāḥ ri twak* in the inscription of Hbriñjing (Stein Callenfels 1934); *kryan ladheyan sang lumāḥ ring alas* in the inscription of Wulakan (Goris 1928); and a *rakarayān mapatiḥ sang lumāḥ ing bulai* in the inscription of Bulai (de Casparis 1956: 335); *sang dewata ing pacaṇḍyan i kwak* in the inscription of Laṇḍa (OJO, cvi).

17. De Casparis has collected around fifty inscriptions. They are very short, giving only the titles, such as, e.g. *pikatan, gurunwaṅi, hino, sirikan, kanuruhan, maḍaṇḍar, lablab*, etc. (cf. de Casparis 1956: 310/11 n. 112).

18. There were indeed slaves in Ancient Javanese society (*hulun, kawula, dāsa, dāsī*). The law-books include clauses about the social status of those slaves, and about the reasons why a person can be enslaved (Jonker 1885).

19. It is to be noted that all those inscriptions are late copies. The inscription of

Kañcana is certainly a copy dating from the Majapahit period (1295 *Śaka*). The question arises as to whether the *wilang* thāni existed in ancient Matarām, because this functionary is never mentioned in original central Javanese inscriptions.

20. Up to now this term is usually interpreted as tax collectors. But the fact that among the *maṅilāla drawya haji* were mentioned functionaries who were called *watak i jro* or *watak i dalem*, i.e. belonging to a group inside [the palace compound] like singers, washermen, king's servants, etc., makes us inclined to the belief that not all of the *maṅilāla drawya haji* were tax collectors who went to the villages to collect taxes directly from the tax payers. Part of them were to be compared with the *abdi dalem kraton* in later Javanese courts, i.e. lower court functionaries who did not get appanage domains, so that for their sustenance they had to be paid from the state treasury.

21. Unfortunately in Damais' 'Repertoire Onomastique' (Damais 1970) no separate list of *wanua* has been included. The quotation under *wanua* and *anak wanua* do not give the total number of villages in the extant central Javanese inscriptions because a greater number of villages are mentioned in the inscriptions without the preceding *wanau i* or *anak wanua i*.

22. There are four 'dependencies' of the village of Baru, i.e. the *duwān* of Punaśapadma (?), the *duwan* of Gunung Ḍarāt, the *duwān* of Depur and the *duwān* of Pekan. This reminds us of the so-called *pañatur desa*, the latter *mācāpat* organization, i.e. a territorial unit comprising five villages, a 'mother' village in the centre and four 'daughter' villages on its four cardinal points. But it appears that such a cluster of villages does not always comprise five villages. In the inscription of Kañcana is mentioned the *pañatur desa* of the freehold of Kañcana, but in fact there were mentioned villages situated on the eight points of the compass, bordering Kañcana. Other inscriptions mention five, seven, or even twelve dependencies of a village. In present day Bali we still have this cluster of villages; the 'mother' village is headed by a *perbekel*; the 'daughter' villages by a *bendesa* (Soekmono 1965).

23. This inscription is still unpublished. The word *dahaṇa* is omitted in the existing paper prints at the Archaeological Institute. This is perhaps the reason why preceding authors did not mention it.

24. Worthy to be noted in connection with the belief in cycles is the fact that if we assume that Dapūnta Selendra, founder of the Śailendra dynasty, appeared on the historical scene around the first quarter of the seventh century A.D. (Boechari 1966), then the shift from central to east Java occurred three centuries afterwards. Pu Siṇḍok who, judging from his position in the administrative hierarchy, was still a member of the Śailendra dynasty (Boechari 1968b), called himself Iśana, so that scholars often speak of a new dynasty, the Iśānawangśa. And three centuries later another dynasty emerged, viz. the Rājasawangśa, starting in A.D. 1222 with a new kingdom, Singhasāri. This new dynasty lasted three centuries, because it may be assumed that the kingdom of Majapahit disintegrated around the first quarter of the sixteenth century. And the turn of each century also witnessed radical changes. The first quarter of the eighth century witnessed the destruction of Sanna's capital by the invasion of an enemy; the first quarter of the tenth century the shift to east Java; the first quarter of the eleventh century the destruction of Teguh's capital by the invasion of an enemy; the first quarter of the thirteenth century the downfall of the kingdom of Kaḍiri. The next century witnessed the invasion of Majapahit's capital by the rebel Kuti; a century later we have the Paregreg, the war of succession which marked the beginning of the disintegration of the kingdom of Majapahit. The latter, which occurred around the first quarter of the sixteenth century, was the end of a chain of recurring facts which took place within the period of nine centuries, i.e. three times three centuries. We do not know yet what events at the first quarter of the ninth and twelfth century might be mentioned as parallel cases in this connection. Dr. M. C. Ricklefs also mentioned such recurring events after the sixteenth century in a seminar held at Leiden in 1972.

The question then arises whether the above mentioned dates and events were fabricated by the ancient historians with the cycle-concept in mind, or whether the belief in cycles was based on real historical facts. We hope to be able in the future to return to this subject in more detail, in connection with the problem of the nature of Javanese historiography.

25. For comparison we may mention the explosion of Gunung Agung on the island of Bali in 1964. A number of villages had to be abandoned, and its inhabitants had to migrate, even to the other islands.

Appendix I
A Check-list of Published Carbon-14 Datings from South East Asia (c. 5,000 B.C.-c. 1,000 A.D.)

R. B. SMITH

Introductory Note

RADIOCARBON dates are likely to be increasingly important in shaping our understanding of the prehistory of South East Asia, for two essential reasons. First, the presence of differential rates of technological development means that it is not very useful to employ—for dating purposes—a periodization defined according to 'ages' of stone, bronze, etc. It is clear that some parts of the area were 'still in the stone age' when others were already using bronze and iron. Moreover, we do not yet have any very sure knowledge of which parts of the area developed most quickly during prehistoric times. Secondly, the 'protohistory' of South East Asia is less firmly established than that of China or India, so that we have only very limited written evidence before c. 500, A.D. and none at all before c. 200. A.D.

The present check-list is designed to gather together all published C14 dates, without too much concern for critical judgement of individual cases. Some system of grouping seemed advisable, and by way of experiment the dates are presented in four series:

    I. Cave sites, c. 5000–c. 500 B.C.
    II. Lowland sites, c. 5000–c. 500 B.C.
    III. All sites, c. 500–c. 1 B.C.
    IV. First millennium A.D.

(Dates clearly relating to the millennia before c. 5000 B.C. are not included.)

So far as can be ascertained, all these dates are calculated according to the criteria used for *Radiocarbon*: they are based on a 'half-life' of 5,568 years ($\pm$30), using the year 1950 as 'present'. It may well be necessary to recalculate them all on the basis of 'half-life' of 5,730 years. The 'date-ranges' in the table are calculated according to a simple 'one sigma' variation, which is now regarded as possibly too narrow.

Appendix I

Laboratories

The following abbreviations are standard, with numbers indicating individual samples:

ANU:	Australian National University
BM:	British Museum
FSU:	Florida State University
GaK:	Gakushuin University, Tokyo
Gif:	Gif-sur-Yvette
GrN:	Groningen
GX:	Geochron Laboratories
I:	Isotopes, Inc., Westwood, N.J.
K:	Copenhagen
MC:	Monaco
P:	University of Pennsylvania, Philadelphia
Sa:	Saclay
TF:	Tata Institute, Bombay
UCLA:	University of California (Los Angeles)
Y:	Yale University

References

So far as possible, dates have been taken from the information given in *Radiocarbon*, the journal devoted entirely to C14 dates, first published in 1959 as a supplement to the *American Journal of Science*. Additional information comes from the following sources, as indicated in individual cases; or from books and articles included in the Bibliography (pp. 531 f. *infra*).

APAO:	*Archaeology and Physical Anthropology in Oceania*
Ant.:	*Antiquity*
BMJ:	*Brunei Museum Journal*
JMBRAS:	*Journal of the Malay Branch of the Royal Asiatic Society*
PPS:	*Proceedings of the Prehistoric Society*
SMJ:	*Sarawak Museum Journal*

Maps illustrating Appendix I will be found at the end of the book.

Series I. Cave Sites, c. 3000 B.C. to c. 500 B.C.

Place	Object and Context (for notes, see end)	Date-range	B.P.	Number	Submitted or Collected by	Reference
THAM ONGBAH Kanchanaburi, Thailand.	Charcoal.[1] Hall 4: layer 2, cont. burials said to be 'late metal age'.	2390–2190 B.C.	4240 (±100)	K–1298	P. Sørensen (1965)	*RC*, 1973, p. 111
,,	Charcoal.[1] Hall 4: layer 5, cont. traces of bronze.	2110–1910 B.C.	3960 (±100)	K–1299	P. Sørensen (1965)	,,
LAANG SPEAN Battambang, Cambodia.	Charcoal. Black layer (30–50 cm.); ass. with burnt bones, crude tools, a few potsherds.	4360–4220 B.C.	6240 (±70)	MC–273	R. and C. Mourer (1968)	*RC*, 1973, p. 342
,,	Charcoal. Red layer (12–30 cm.); ass. with pottery and crude Hoabinhian tools and flakes.	2140–1960 B.C.	4000 (±90)	MC–269	R. and C. Mourer (1968)	,,
,,	Charcoal. Lower red layer (below 30 cm.), at entrance.	2110–1930 B.C.	3970 (±90)	MC–274	R. and C. Mourer (1968)	,,
,,	Charcoal. Red layer (15–30 cm.) at entrance.	590–410 B.C.	2450 (±90)	MC–272	R. and C. Mourer (1968)	*RC*, 1973, p. 341
PHNOM KBAL ROMEAS Kampot, Cambodia.	Marine shells. From kitchen midden, in front of a rock-shelter; ass. with potsherds.	3560–3280 B.C.	5370 (±140)	Gif–872	J. P. Carbonnel (1967)	*RC*, 1972, p. 301
PHNOM LAANG Kampot, Cambodia.	Bone collagen. Bone tools from Cave no. 62 bis.	2660–2280 B.C.	4370 (±140)	Gif–1167	J. P. Carbonnel (1967)	*RC*, 1972, p. 300
GUA KECHIL Pahang, Malaysia.	Bone food-scraps. At depth of 14–16 in., marking the change from Period II (end Hoabinhian) to Period III (early typical Neolithic).	3650–2050 B.C.	4800 (±800)	GX–0418	F. L. Dunn (1963)	*PPS*, 1966, pp. 352–3
GUA HARIMAU CAVE Gunong Dayak, Perak,	Charcoal. Hearth, in cave; assoc. with	1650–1350 B.C.	3450 (±150)	BM–43	P. D. R. Williams Hunt	*RC*, 1960, p. 29

Plate	B.P.	Date-range	Object and Context (for notes, see end)	Number	Submitted or Collected by	Reference
Malaysia. DUYONG CAVE Palawan, Philippines.	7000 (±250)	5300–4800 B.C.	Neolithic cord-impressed pottery. Charcoal.	UCLA-286	(1951) R. B. Fox (1962)	RC, 1964, p. 336
"	5680 (±80)	3810–3650 B.C.	Flake-tool layer, assoc. with shell midden, at depth of 62–68 cm.: below a Neolithic burial. Assoc. with jar burials and Sa-Huyuh related pottery: depth of 30 cm.[2]	UCLA-994	R. B. Fox	RC, 1966, p. 479
"	4630 (±250)	2930–2430 B.C.	Charcoal. Assoc. with Neolithic burial, at depth of 48 cm.; overlain by a chalcolithic jar burial.	UCLA-287	R. B. Fox (1962)	RC, 1964, p. 336
GURI CAVE Lipuun Pt, Palawan, Philippines.	4070 (±100)	2220–2020 B.C.	Shells (Nevita). Assoc. with flake tools.[3]	UCLA-698	R. B. Fox	RC, 1966, p. 478
MANUNGGUL CAVE Palawan, Philippines.	2840 (±80)	970–810 B.C.	Charcoal. Chamber A: Late Neolithic jar burials, with Sa-Huyuh-related pottery.	UCLA-992A	R. B. Fox	RC, 1966, p. 479
"	2660 (±80)	790–630 B.C.	Charcoal. Chamber A: Late Neolithic jar burials.	UCLA-992B	R. B. Fox	"
NIAH GREAT CAVE Sarawak, Malaysia.	4040 (±70)	2160–2020 B.C.	? West mouth, depth of 12 in.	GrN-1960	T. & B. Harrisson (1958?)	SMJ, 1959, p. 137; and 1967, p. 96
"	3620 (±55)	1725–1615 B.C.	? West mouth(?): 'sub-surface'.	GrN-1962	T. & B. Harrisson (1958?)	SMJ, 1959, p. 137
"	3175 (±105)	1330–1120 B.C.	Burnt wood. Inside jar, with human remains; burial no. 159	Gx-1428	T. & B. Harrisson	SMJ, 1968, p. 64
"	2700 (±70)	820–680 B.C.	Charcoal.[4] Subsurface layer of main frequentation deposit, at west mouth: said to be 'Late Neolithic'.	GrN-1905	T. Harrisson	RC, 1964, p. 359

Place	B.P.	Date-range	Object and Context (for notes, see end)	Number	Submitted or Collected by	Reference
Malaysia—*cont.*	2695 (±65)	800–680 B.C.	Wood sample.[5] From tree-trunk coffin of extended burial, said to be latest Neolithic type from this site.	GrN-1907	T. Harrisson	,,
JEREGAN CAVE near Niah, Sarawak, Malaysia	4300 (±160)	2510–2190 B.C.	? From burial in cave.	?	T. Harrisson (?)	*SMJ*, 1967, p. 96
,,	3070 (±410)	1530–710 B.C.	? From burial in cave.	?	T. Harrisson (?)	,,
MAGALA CAVES near Niah, Sarawak, Malaysia.	3130 (±240)	1420–940 B.C.	? Neolithic phase of burial cave.	Gx-337	B. Harrisson (1964–65)	*JMBRAS*, 1966, p. 192
ULU LEANG CAVE South Sulawesi, Indonesia.	7170 (±650)	5870–4570 B.C.	Charcoal. Depth of 110 cm.	ANU-606	I. C. Glover (1969)	(I. C. Glover, private communication)
,,	5740 (±230)	4020–3650 B.C.	Charcoal. Depth of 50 cm.	ANU-394	I. C. Glover (1969)	*Ant.*, xlv, p. 32
LEANG-BURUNG CAVE South Sulawesi, Indonesia.	3420 (±400)	1870–1070 B.C.	Charcoal. From trench outside cave, at depth of 150 cm., assoc. with stone tools and pottery.	ANU-390	D. J. Mulvaney (1969)	*Ant.*, xlv, p. 31
,,	2820 (±210)	1080–660 B.C.	Charcoal(?). From trench inside cave, at depth of 270 cm.; assoc. with stone tools and pottery.	ANU-391	D. J. Mulvaney (1969)	,,
UAI BOBO CAVES Timor.	7010 (±125)	5185–4935 B.C.	Charcoal. Cave 2: hearth at depth of 260 cm., in Horizon IV.	ANU-328	I. C. Glover (1967)	Glover, 1972, p. 70
,,	5520 (±60)	4630–4510 B.C.	Charcoal. Cave 2: hearth in Horizon VIII, at depth of 160 cm.; assoc. with earliest pig bone at site. (Pre-pottery.)	ANU-187	I. C. Glover (1967)	*APAO*, 1969, p. 111
,,	3740 (±90)	1880–1700 B.C.	Charcoal.	ANU-239	I. C. Glover	,,

Place	B.P.	Date-range	Object and Context (for notes, see end)	Number	Submitted or Collected by	Reference
"	(±90)		Cave 2: hearth in Horizon IX, 100 cm. below surface; assoc. with decorated pottery.		(1967)	
	3470 (±110)	1630–1410 B.C.	Charcoal. Cave 1: at depth of 70 cm.	ANU–414	I. C. Glover (1967)	Glover, 1972, p. 70
Lie Siri Cave Timor.	7270 (±160)	5480–5160 B.C.	Charcoal. At depth of 100 cm. in cave.	ANU–236	I. C. Glover (1967)	*APAO*, 1969, p. 108
"	6635 (±140)	4825–4545 B.C.	Hearth at depth of 60 cm.; pre-dates appearance of pottery and domesticated fauna.	ANU–171	I. C. Glover (1967)	,,
"	3545 (±120)	1715–1475 B.C.	Charcoal. Scattered; depth of 10–20 cm. (Horizon VIb); assoc. with pottery occasionally decorated, in Kalanay tradition.	ANU–172	I. C. Glover	,,
"	3530 (±90)	1670–1490 B.C.	Charcoal. Hearth, 20 cm. below surface; related to samples in ANU–172–3.	ANU–235	I. C. Glover (1967)	,,
"	2660 (±110)	820–600 B.C.	Charcoal. Scattered, at depth of 10–15 cm. (Horizon VIb) (cf. ANU–172).	ANU–173	I. C. Glover (1967)	,,
Liang Toge near Ruteng, West Flores, Indonesia.	3550 (±525)	2125–1075 B.C.	Bone. Human ('proto-negrito') burial.	GX–209	Th. Verhoeven	Jacob, 1967
Pintu Cave north-east Luzon, Philippines.	3880 (±240)	2170–1690 B.C.	Charcoal. Layer 10, of rock shelter, 160 m. above sea level.	Gak–2943	W. Peterson	*APAO*, 1974, pp. 26–35
"	3290 (±230)	1270–1110 B.C.	Charcoal. Layer 6, same site.	Gak–2942	,,	*APAO*, 1974, pp. 26–35
Bolobok Cave Sanga-sanga Is. Tawi-tawi, Sulu archipelago,	7945 (±190)	6185–5805 B.C.	Charcoal. Layer 2, 120 cm. depth.	Gx–?	A. Spoer	Spoer, 1973

Place	B.P.	Date-range	Object and Context (for notes, see end)	Number	Submitted or Collected by	Reference
Philippines.						
"	6650 (±180)	5680–5520 B.C.	Charcoal. Layer 2, 85 cm. from surface.	Gx–?	"	"
Series II: Open Lowland Sites, c. 5000 B.C. to c. 500 B.C.						
BAN KAO Kanchanaburi, Thailand.	4370 (±100)	2520–2320 B.C.	Charcoal, possibly post of house. Lue site: dwelling-site below habitation layer 100 cm. thick; assoc. with Neolithic artefacts.[6]	K–1474	P. Sørensen (1962)	RC, 1973, p. 110
"	3720 (±140)	1910–1630 B.C.	Charcoal. Bang site 1: habitation layer with Neolithic pottery: earliest phase.	K–838	P. Sørensen (1962)	RC, 1973, p. 109
"	3520 (±120)	1690–1450 B.C.	Charcoal. Bang site 6: in habitation layer directly above 'Group II' graves.	K–1088	P. Sørensen (1962)	RC, 1973, p. 110
"	3440 (±120)	1610–1370 B.C.	Charcoal. Bang site 7: habitation layer, directly above graves of 'Group I'.	K–1089	P. Sørensen (1962)	"
.	3310 (±140)	1500–1220 B.C.	Charcoal.	K–842	P. Sørensen (1962)	RC, 1973, p. 109
BAN KAO Kanchanaburi, Thailand.	3290 (±120)	1460–1220 B.C.	Charcoal. Bang site 8: habitation layer above 'Group I' graves.	K–1090	P. Sørensen (1962)	RC, 1973, p. 110
"	3280 (±120)	1450–1210 B.C.	Charcoal. Bang site 5: habitation layer above 'Group II' graves.	K–1087	P. Sørensen (1962)	"
"	3260 (±120)	1430–1190 B.C.	Charcoal. Bang site 9: habitation layer with 'Group II' graves.	K–1091	P. Sørensen (1962)	"
"	3250 (±120)	1420–1180 B.C.	Charcoal. Bang site 10: habitation layer directly above 'Group II' graves. ?	K–1092	P. Sørensen (1962)	"
NON NOK THA Khon Khaen,	5370 (3±20)	3740–3100 B.C.	Layer 21: 'Early Period 3'.	GaK–1034	W. G. Solheim (1966)	Bayard, 1971

Place	B.P.	Date-range	Object and Context (for notes, see end)	Number	Submitted or Collected by	Reference
Thailand.						
"	4435 (±65)	2550–2420 B.C.	Carbonized wood. Layer 11, below all occupation: pre-'Early Period 1'.	FSU–340	D. T. Bayard (1968)	*RC*, 1971, p. 25
"	4155 (±200)	2405–2005 B.C.	Charcoal. Layer 19, at depth of 120 cm.; thought to be assoc. with evidence of bronze: 'Middle Period 3'.	TF–651	W. G. Solheim (1966)	*RC*, 1968, p. 138
"	4120 (±90)	2260–2080 B.C.	? Layer 19, 'Middle Period 3'.	GaK–956	W. G. Solheim (1966)	Bayard, 1971
"	3685 (±110)	1845–1625 B.C.	'Middle Period 4'.	GX–1611	D. T. Bayard (1968)	"
"	3560 (±65)	1675–1555 B.C.	Charcoal. Mound 125: Early Period 1.	FSU–345	D. T. Bayard (1968)	*RC*, 1971, p. 25
"	3170 (±200)	1420–1020 B.C.	Charcoal. Layer 20 (disturbed area): possibly really belongs to layer 17 or 18: 'Middle Period 4'.	Y–1851	W. G. Solheim (1966)	*RC*, 1969, p. 638
"	3055 (±65)	1170–1040 B.C.	Charcoal. Layer 8: 'Early Period 3'.	FSU–342	D. T. Bayard (1968)	*RC*, 1971, p. 25
"	2990 (±110)	1150–950 B.C.	? Layer 17 or '17–18': 'Middle Period 4 or 5'.	GaK–1033	W. G. Solheim (1966)	Bayard, 1971
"	2830 (±100)	980–780 B.C.	? Layer 17 or '17–18': 'Middle Period 4 or 5'.	GaK–1029	W. G. Solheim (1966)	"
"	2750 (±130)	930–670 B.C.	Pit: 'Early Period 1'.	GX–1612	D. T. Bayard (1968)	"
"	2560 (±100)	710–510 B.C.	Layer II: 'Late Period 1'.	GaK–1028	W. G. Solheim (1966)	"
"	2530 (±120)	700–460 B.C.	Layer 18: 'Middle Period 3'.	GaK–1031	W. G. Solheim (1966)	"
"	2470 (±70)	590–450 B.C.	Charcoal. Layer 7: 'Middle Period 1'.	FSU–341	D. T. Bayard (1968)	*RC*, 1971, p. 25

Place	B.P.	Date-range	Object and Context (for notes, see end)	Number	Submitted or Collected by	Reference
SAMRONG SEN Kompong Chhnang, Cambodia.	3230 (±120)	1400–1160 B.C.	River shells.[7] From kitchen midden, assoc. with potsherds of kind found with bronze by Mansuy (1923); depth of 150 cm.	GiF-1057	J. P. Carbonnel (1967)	*RC*, 1972, p. 30
HANG-GON near Xuan-Loc, Long Khanh, Viet-Nam.	3950 (±250)	2250–1750 B.C.	Charred greasy deposit from pot-sherds, containing 3% carbon. Vague but said to be assoc. with moulds for bronze axes.[8]	Sa-205	E. Saurin	*RC*, 1965, p. 238
MAGAPIT BRIDGE Cagayan Valley, Luzon, Philippines.	3550 (±110)	1710–1490 B.C.	Cardium. Assoc. with undecorated red pottery, polished stone tools, and mollusc shells.	GiF-1272	F. Delany (1968)	*RC*, 1972, p. 300
DIMOLIT Isabella province, north-east Luzon, Philippines.	3900 (±140)	2090–1810 B.C.	Charcoal. House-floor, layer 5 (coastal habitation site).	GaK-2937	W. Peterson	*APAO*, 1974, pp. 26–35
,,	5100 (±220)	3370–2930 B.C.	,, (inconsistent)	GaK-2938	,,	*APAO*, 1974, pp. 26–35
,,	3280 (±110)	1440–1220 B.C.	,,	GaK-2939	,,	*APAO*, 1974, pp. 26–35
Series III: All Sites, 500–1 B.C.						
UAI BOBO CAVES Timor.	2450 (±95)	595–405 B.C.	Charcoal. Cave 1: at depth of 60 cm.	ANU-326	I. C. Glover (1967)	Glover, 1972, p. 70
,,	2190 (±80)	320–160 B.C.	Charcoal concentration. Cave 1: at depth of 50 cm.; close to a copper ornament, and assoc. with flint tools, pottery, and bones of pig.[9]	ANU-237	I. C. Glover (1967)	*APAO*, 1969, p. 110
BATO CAVES Sorsogon province, Philippines.	2550 (±200)	690–290 B.C.	Sea shells.[9] Cave 2: small unstratified midden at mouth of cave.	M-728	R. B. Fox (1956)	*RC*, 1959, p. 196
,,	2280 (±250)	A.D. 370–130	Sea shells. Jar-burial cave, pre-iron culture (Cave 1).	M-727(A)	R. B. Fox (1956)	,,

Plate	B.P.	Date-range	Object and Context (for notes, see end)	Number	Submitted or Collected by	Reference
MANUNGGAL CAVE Palawan, Philippines.	2140 (±100)	290–90 B.C.	Charcoal. Chamber B: jar burials, assoc. with iron.	UCLA-992C	R. B. Fox	*RC*, 1966, p. 479
NIAH: PAINTED CAVE Sarawak, Malaysia.	2300 (±80)	430–270 B.C.	Wood. 'Deathship' coffin from burial.	?	B. Harrisson (1964?)	*SMJ*, 1967, p. 96
GUA SAMTI, NIAH Sarawak, Malaysia.	2115 (±150)	315–15 B.C.	Wood. 'Deathship' coffin from burial.	?	T. Harrisson (?)	"
THAM ONGBAH CAVE Kanchanaburi, Thailand.	2180 (±100)	330–130 B.C.	Charcoal. Partly buried wood coffin, under undisturbed layers in gallery of cave.	K-1300	P. Sørensen (1965)	*RC*, 1973, p. 111
CHANSEN Takli district, Thailand.	2145 (±36)	230–160 B.C.	Charcoal.[10] From small pit with burnt sherds at level 7 (operation C).	P-1543	G. F. Dales (1968)	*RC*, 1970, p. 587
NON NOK THA Khon Khaen, Thailand.	2480 (±80)	620–450 B.C.	? Layer 9: 'Late Period 2'.	GaK-1027	W. G. Solheim (1966)	Bayard, 1971
"	2220 (±110)	280–60 B.C.	? Layer 9: 'Late Period 2'.	GaK-958	W. G. Solheim (1966)	"
CHUP Kompong Cham province, Cambodia.	2130 (±100)	280–80 B.C.	Straw debris scraped from surface of pottery. Surface find at a site with groups of mounds.	Gif-1448	J. P. Carbonnel (1969)	*RC*, 1972, p. 301
HANG-GON, near Xuan-Loc, Long-Khanh, Viet-Nam.	2300 (±150)	500–200 B.C.	Charcoal. Around jars found in field of burial urns (cremation burial).	MC-62	E. Saurin (1963)	*RC*, 1966, p. 290
"	2190 (±150)	390–90 B.C.	Charcoal. From jar no. 1 in field of burial urns (cremation burial).	MC-61	E. Saurin (1963)	"
"	2100 (±150)	300–0 B.C.	Carbonized deposit on potsherds. Burial urns, related to Sa-Huyuh	Gif-?	E. Sariuin (1965)	*RC*, 1970, p. 440

Place	B.P.	Date-range	Object and Context (for notes, see end)	Number	Submitted or Collected by	Reference
Viet-Nam—*cont.*			culture: similar results from deposits outside and inside urns.			
KAMPONG SUNGAI-LANG Selangor, Malaya.	2435 (±95)	580–390 B.C.	Wood.	GX–280	B. A. V. Peacock (1964)	*RC*, 1967, pp. 25, 60
,,	2145 (±100)	295–95 B.C.	From mangrove-swamp site; assoc. with 'Dong-son' bronze drum.	ANU–27	B. A. V. Peacock (1964)	,, ,,
,,	1850 (±90)	A.D. 10–190	,, ,, ,,	GaK–684	B. A. V. Peacock (1964)	,, ,,
PINTU CAVE north-east Luzon, Philippines.	2260 (±150)	460–160 B.C.	Charcoal. Layer 4 of rock shelter, with first occurrence of pottery and glass beads at this site.	GaK–2940	W. Peterson	*APAO*, 1974, pp. 26–35
PHU-HOA (near Hang-gon) Long Khanh, South Viet-Nam.	2400 (±140)	590–310 B.C.	Wood charcoal pieces. Jars 11 and 13, of jar-burial site (jar 11 containing iron).	Gif–1996	H. Fontaine	*BESI*, 1972, p. 441 *RC*, 1974, p. 57
,,	2590 (±290)	930–350 B.C.	Carbonized pottery. Jar no. 8, same site.	Gif–1999	,,	,,
Series IV: First Millennium A.D.						
BEIKTHANO Magwe district, Burma.	1950 (±90)	90 B.C.–A.D. 90	Charcoal. Structural post in a brick structure, from mound site within old city. (Phase I of site 9.)	I–434	Aung Thaw (1961)	*RC*, 1963, p. 76
,,	1880 (±?)	(A.D. 70)	Charcoal. Phase II of site 9.	NZ–?	Aung Thaw	Aung Thaw, 1968, p. 62
,,	1725 (±?)	(A.D. 225)	Charcoal. Phase I, site II.	,,	,,	Aung Thaw, 1968, p. 62
,,	1650 (±?)	(A.D. 300)	Charcoal. Phase II, site II.	,,	,,	Aung Thaw, 1968, p. 62
CHANSEN Takli district,	1890 (±41)	A.D. 20–100	Charcoal. Level 9 (operation D): from midden	P–1512	G. F. Dales (1968)	*RC*, 1970, p. 588

Place	B.P.	Date-range	Object and Context (for notes, see end)	Number	Submitted or Collected by	Reference
Thailand.						
"	1830 (±47)	A.D. 73–167	deposit with smashed skull, ivory comb, etc. Charcoal. Level 9 (operation C), at depth of 220–230 cm.; sealed below layer of concretion.	P-1508	G. F. Dales (1968)	"
"	1644 (±85)	A.D. 220–390	Charcoal. Phase II: depth of 230 cm. (operation Dg), said to date end of 'pre-Funan' phase.	I-4370	G. F. Dales (1967)	RC, 1972, p. 137
"	1580 (±50)	A.D. 320–420	Charcoal. Level 8 (operation B), fifth stratum below surface, at depth of 145–164 cm. (disturbed by pot-hunting).	P-1507	G. F. Dales (1968)	RC, 1970, p. 587
"	1595 (±52)	A.D. 300–410	Charcoal. Level 7 (operation C).	P-1541	G. F. Dales (1968)	"
"	1573 (±35)	A.D. 342–412	Charcoal. Level 6 (operation C).	P-1540	G. F. Dales (1968)	"
"	1540 (±47)	A.D. 363–457	Charcoal and ash: three samples. Hearth, at level 7 (operation C): depth of 204–210 cm.	P-1509	G. F. Dales (1968)	"
"	1503 (±43)	A.D. 404–490	" "	P-1538	G. F. Dales (1968)	"
"	1491 (±47)	A.D. 412–506	" "	P-1539	G. F. Dales (1968)	"
"	1416 (±84)	A.D. 450–618	Charcoal. Phase IV: depth of 100 cm. (operation Dg).	I-4368	G. F. Dales (1969)	RC, 1972, p. 137
"	948 (±78)	A.D. 925–1080	Charcoal (bamboo or reed). Phase V: depth of 48–50 cm.; assoc. with 'Late Dvaravati' pot-sherds.	I-4369	G. F. Dales (1969)	"
MUANG PHET	1810	10 B.C.–A.D. 290	Charcoal.	BM-41	H. G. Q. Wales	RC, 1960, p. 29

Place	B.P.	Date-range	Object and Context (for notes, see end)	Number	Submitted or Collected by	Reference
Thailand.	(±150)		'Early historic' site: layer II, at depth of 4 ft.		(1955)	Bayard, 1971
NON NOK THA Khon Khaen, Thailand.	1860 (±140)	50 B.C.–A.D. 230	? Layer 21: 'Early Period 2'.	GaK–959	W. G. Solheim (1966)	,,
,,	1720 (±80)	A.D. 150–310	? Layer 13: 'Middle Period 3'.	GaK–957	W. G. Solheim (1966)	RC, 1964, pp. 245–6
THAP-MUÔI Kien-Phong, Viet-Nam.	1620 (±150)	A.D. 180–480	Sample of wood from carving of Buddha, in Saigon Museum: found at Thap-Muôi. (Supposedly fifth century A.D.).	Sa–20	L. Malleret (1956)	,,
PHONG-MY Viet-Nam.	1490 (±150)	A.D. 310–610	Sample of wood from carved statue of Buddha found there, supposedly seventh century.	Sa–21	L. Malleret (1956)	,,
DUC-HOA Hau-Nghia, Viet-Nam.	1490 (±150)	A.D. 310–610	Sample of wood from a Buddha statue, supposed to be sixth century.	Sa–23	L. Malleret (1956)	,,
,,	1350 (±150)	A.D. 450–750	Sample of wood from a Buddha statue, believed to be sixth century	Sa–24	L. Malleret (1956)	,,
DA-NOI Viet-Nam.	1360 (±150)	A.D. 440–740	Samples of wood from two (?) Buddhist statues, thought to be fifth century A.D.	Sa–22	L. Malleret (1956)	,,
,,	1375 (±150)	A.D. 425–725	,, ,,	Sa–25	L. Malleret (1956)	,,
CHAMCAR ANDONG Kampong Cham province Cambodia	1150 (±100)	A.D. 700–900	Straw debris scraped from pottery. Surface finds at site with group of mounds.	Gif–1447	Carbonnel (1969)	RC, 1972, p. 301
LAANG SPEAN CAVE Battambang, Cambodia.	1200 (±70)	A.D. 686–820	Charcoal. Upper red layer (2–15 cm.); assoc. with shaped stone flakes, etc.	MC–270	R. & C. Mourer (1968)	RC, 1973, p. 341
,,	1120 (±60)	A.D. 770–890	,, ,,	MC–271	R. & C. Mourer (1968)	,,
NIAH: PAINTED CAVE Sarawak,	1180 (±70)	A.D. 700–840	Wood. 'Deathship' coffin, assoc. with iron	NZ–?	B. Harrisson (1964)	SMJ, 1967, p. 96; JMBRAS, 1965,

Appendix I

Place	B.P.	Date-range	Object and Context (for notes, see end)	Number	Submitted or Collected by	Reference
Malaysia.			and pottery; possibly older than the burial itself.			p. 246
„	1045 (±75)	A.D. 830–980	Wood.	?	B. Harrisson (1964?)	SMJ, 1967, p. 96
Kota Batu, Brunei.	2045 (±110)	205 B.C.–A.D. 15	'Death ship' coffin from burial.	GX–1807	T. Harrisson (1953)	BMJ, 1971, p. 104
„	1355 (±95)	A.D. 500–690	Charcoal. Depth of 72–78 in.	GX–1802	T. Harrisson (1953)	„
„	1350 (±90)	A.D. 510–690	Wood and charcoal. Depth of 48–54 in.	GaK–3459	T. Harrisson (1953)	„
„	1345 (±125)	A.D. 480–730	Charred wood. Depth of 42–48 in.	GX–1806	T. Harrisson (1953)	BMJ, 1972, p. 209
„	1260 (±95)	A.D. 595–785	Charcoal. Depth of 66–72 in.	GX–1801	T. Harrisson (1953)	BMJ, 1971, p. 104
„	1145 (±90)	A.D. 715–895	Wood. Depth of 84–90 in.	GX–1799	T. Harrisson (1953)	„
„	1130 (±90)	A.D. 730–910	Wood. Depth of 66–72 in.	GX–1808	T. Harrisson (1953)	„
„	1130 (±90)	A.D. 730–910	Charcoal. Depth of 72–78 in.	GX–1808	T. Harrisson (1953)	„
„	1075 (±100)	A.D. 775–975	Charcoal. Depth of 72–78 in.	GX–1803	T. Harrisson (1953)	„
„	1010 (±100)	A.D. 860–1020	Wood and charcoal. Depth of 48–54 in.	GX–1798	T. Harrisson (1953)	„
„	1100 (±80)	A.D. 860–1040	Wood. Depth of 54–60 in.	GaK–3458	T. Harrisson (1953)	BMJ, 1972, p. 209
„	1100 (±90)	A.D. 900–1060	Charred wood. Depth of 36–42 in.	GaK–3456	T. Harrisson (1953)	„
„	1070 (±80)	A.D. 950–1110	Charcoal. Depth of 30–36 in.	GX–1806	T. Harrisson (1953)	„
„	920 (±80)	A.D. 950–1110	Wood and charcoal. Depth of 54–60 in.	GX–1806	T. Harrisson (1953)	BMJ, 1971, p. 104
Batu Edjaja Cave nr. Banta Eng, south Sulawesi, Indonesia.	920 (±275)	A.D. 755–1305	Charcoal. Depth of 75 cm., assoc. with pottery related to Kalanay tradition.	ANU–392	D. J. Mulvaney (1969)	Ant., xlv, pp. 30–1

Place	B.P.	Date-range	Object and Context (for notes, see end)	Number	Submitted or Collected by	Reference
SEMINHO CAVE Cotabato, Mindanao, Philippines.	1365 (±85)	A.D. 500–670	Collagen fraction, human bone. Stone urn burial (urn no. 67518), representing middle of burial sequence.	GX-1439		Kujack and Sheldon, 1970
PINTU CAVE north-east Luzon, Philippines.	1400 (±100)	A.D. 450–650	Charcoal layer (inconsistent with GaK 2940 and 2942).	GaK-2941	Peterson	*APAO*, 1974, pp. 26–35

NOTES

1. Expected to be 200 B.C.
2. Information concerning context corrected by R. B. Fox (pers. comm. to I. C. Glover).
3. A much earlier date was expected.
4. Previously reported as 2460 (±70) (c. 500 B.C.): T. Harrisson, *SMJ*, ix (1959), p. 137.
5. Previously reported as 2455 (±85) (c. 500 B.C.). *SMJ* (1959), p. 137.
6. Older than expected.
7. Expected date was c. 300 B.C.
8. Earlier than expected: cf. later dates from same site, from Monaco.
9. A parallel check on live shells suggests that actual date should be later, by up to 500 years.
10. See p. 504, for later dates at level 7. (Operation C.).

Appendix II
Check-list of 'Heger Type I' Bronze Drums from South East Asia
R. B. SMITH

Place	Number of drums	Context	Date found	Present whereabouts	References
DONG-SON Thanh-hoa (Viet-Nam).	20(?)	Excavations by Pajot.	1924–7		V. Goloubew 1929 J. Loewenstein 1956
,,	2	Two 'Indonesian' burials excavated by Janse.	1935	Musée Cernuschi, Paris (MC 8006; MC 8644)	O. R. T. Janse 1958
,, THIEU-DUONG Thanh-hoa.	5	Excavations?	1961–2		Le Van Lan 1963: 189
	2	Excavations?	1961–2		,,
NUI-NAP Thanh-hoa.	1	?	1961–2		,,
NUI-SOI Thanh-hoa.	1	?	1961–2		,,
MAT-SON Thanh-hoa.	1	In brick tomb of Han dynasty.	1959	Cultural Office, Thanh-hoa	,,
VINH-NINH (h. Vinh-loc), Thanh-hoa.	1	In brick tomb of Han dynasty.	1963	,,	,,
QUANG-XUONG Thanh-hoa.	2	?	1928–34	Hanoi Museum (I. 25,966 and 23,757)	*BEFEO*, 1936: 746 Le Van Lan 1963: 189 V. Goloubew 1940: 250
NONG-CONG Thanh-hoa.	1	?	1928–34	Hanoi Museum (I. 26,406)	,,
DONG-HIEU Nghe-on (Viet-Nam)	1	?	1959	Cultural Office, Nghe-on	Le Van Lan 1963: 191
COI-SON Nam-dinh (Viet-Nam).	3	Dug up.	c. 1910?	One survives, rediscovered in 1959; at Nam-dinh	,,
PHU-XUYEN Ha-dong (Viet-Nam).	1	Found in digging of a canal.	c. 1907	Stockholm (bought, 1934)	*BEFEO*, 1937: 607 B. Karlgren 1942: pls. 6–7
HOANG-HA Ha-dong.	4	Found in digging of a canal.	1937	One in Hanoi Museum (D. 163,206)	*BEFEO*, 1940: 383–409 Le Van Lan 1963: 190
PHU-DUY	1	At a depth of 1·8 m.	1959	Cultural Office, Ha-dong	Le Van Lan 1963: 190

Place	Number of drums	Context	Date found	Present whereabouts	References
Ha-dong. TUNG-LAM (huyen Chuong-My)	1	At depth of 50 cm.	1932	Hanoi Museum (I. 25,415)	,,
Ha-dong. THUONG-TIN	1	?	1961	Hanoi Museum (61: 3,563)	,,
MIEU-MON Ha-dong.	1	?	(pre-193-?)	Hanoi Museum (61: 3,564) Possibly same as drum said (1934) to be from Thuong-lam	BEFEO, 1934: 752 Le Van Lan 1963: 190
VAN-TRAI Ha-nam.	1	?	1937	Hanoi Museum	BEFEO, 1937: 603
NGOC-HA Hanoi province (Viet-Nam).	1	Depth of 2 m.	1924	?	BEFEO, 1932 Le Van Lan 1963: 190
HANOI	1	?	1956	Hanoi Museum (I. 19,995)	Le Van Lan 1963: 190
NGOC-LU Ha-nam (Viet-Nam).	2	That of 1903 was found in a temple.	1903 1936	Hanoi Museum (D. 621,421 and I. 26,391)	Parmentier 1918: 4 BEFEO, 1937: 607 Le Van Lan 1963: 190 B. Karlgren 1942: figs. 3–4
YEN-TAP Ha-nam.	1	Said to have been in village for 100 years.	?	Still in village	BEFEO, 1937: 607
GIAO-TAT Bac-ninh.	1	?	1918	Hanoi Museum (I. 3,347)	BEFEO, 1922: 360 Le Van Lan, 1963, p. 191
VIET-KHE Haiphong (Viet-Nam).	2	In a tomb.	1961	At Haiphong	Le Van Lan 1963: 190
HUU-CHUNG Hai-duong.	1	?	1961	Cultural Office, Hai-duong	Le Van Lan 1963: 191
DONG-VAN Cao-bang (Viet-Nam).	3	?	1938	Hanoi Museum (I. 27,951–3)	,,
?	1	?	1923	Saigon Museum	,,

Place	Number of drums	Context	Date found	Present whereabouts	References
Son-tay province (Viet-Nam).				(D. 163,167)	
Cho-Bo Hoa-binh (Viet-Nam).	1	On bank of River Da.	1928	Hanoi Museum (I. 23,696)	,,
Dao-Thinh Yen-bay (Viet-Nam).	1	?	1962	Yen-bay	,,
Ban-Lau Lao-kay (Viet-Nam).	1		1959	Lao-kay	,,
Muong country, Indochina: (prob. Hoa-binh province, Viet-Nam).	1	?	1889 (then lost, and rediscovered)	Musée Giumet, Paris. ('Moulié' drum)	Heger 1903: 20–5 J. Loewenstein 1956: 15 R. Heine-Geldern 1932: 520 B. Karlgren 1942: figs. 1–2
Shih-Chai-Shan (Yunnan).	15	Excavation of 50 tombs: some 'drums' used as cowry-containers.	1955–7	Various museums in China(?)	*Asian Perspectives*, 1960 E. Bunker 1972: *passim*. M. van Dewall 1972: *passim*.
Chin-Ning Liang-wang-shan (Yunnan)	2	Fragment of tympanum, and fragments of mantle.	1947?	British Museum, London	J. Loewenstein 1956: p. 19 M. van Dewell 1972: 342–4
Hsiang-Yun: To-Po-Na (Yunnan).	1	Inside bronze coffin.	1964	Prob. Yunnan Provincial Museum, Kunming	*Kaogu*, 1964: 607–14
K'ai-Hoa (Kweichon or Yunnan).	1	?	pre-1900	Vienna: Museum für Volkerkunde (bought 1907: Gillet I, 83–624)	Heger 1903: 25–7 J. Loewenstein 1956: 28
?	1	?	pre-1885	Victoria & Albert Museum, London. (Heger's 'No. 11') ('Nelson' drum)	Heger 1903: 37–8
?	1	?	pre-1932		Parmentier 1932: 172–3 J. Loewenstein 1956: 28–30 Le Van Lan 1963: 196
Dak Glao Kontum	1	?	1921	Hanoi Museum (I. 7,514)	*BEFEO*, 1922: 355 Le Van Lan 1963: 191

Place	Number of drums	Context	Date found	Present whereabouts	References
BINH-PHU Thu-Dau-Mot (Viet-Nam).	1	?	1924	Haiphong Museum (D. 163,170)	Le Van Lan 1963: 191
UBON (?north-east Thailand).	1	?	1924	?Hanoi Museum (I. 17,849 'Laos' drum)	Parmentier 1932: 172–3 Loewenstein 1956: 29–30 Le Van Lan 1963: 196
KHORAT area (Thailand).	1	?	?	?	J. Loewenstein 1956: 20
THNOM MONG RUSEI Battambang (Cambodia).	1	?	?	Phnom Penh Museum (E. 696)	H. Parmentier 1932: 176 J. Loewenstein 1956: 20
TOS-TAK, TANG-PLOCH Kompong Chhnang (Cambodia).	1	?	?	Phnom Penh Museum (E. 695)	H. Parmentier 1932: 176
BAN GAW Chieng Mai (Thailand).	?	?	?	?	P. Sørensen, this volume
THUNG-YANG Uttaradit (Thailand).	4	Also found: bronze axes, and some iron implements.	pre-1932	National Museum, Bangkok	J. Loewenstein 1956: 20
ONG-BAH CAVE Kanchanaburi (Thailand).	6	Possibly associated with coffin-burials and with a C14 date of 230 ± 100 B.C.	1957–62	?	P. Sørensen, this volume
NAKORN SI THAMMARAT (Thailand).	1	?	?	?	J. Loewenstein 1956: 20
KUALA TRENGGANU Trengganu (Malaysia).	2	In burial, associated with iron spearhead.	1965	?	B. A. V. Peacock 1966
BATU PASIR GARAM (Tembaling River), Pahang (Malaysia).	1	Found in river; fragment.	1926	Raffles Museum, Singapore	J. Loewenstein 1956: 15

Place	Number of drums	Context	Date found	Present whereabouts	References
KLANG Selangar (Malaysia)	1	Fragments.	1944	National Museum, Kuala Lumpur	J. Loewenstein 1956: 15–17
KG. SUNGAI LANG Selangor	2	Buried in clay mound, on a wood plank: C14 dates in range 485±95 B.C. to A.D. 100±90.	1964	?	B. A. V. Peacock 1965
DANAU GADANG (Lake Kerintji), Sumatra.	1	Excavated? Other bronze objects from	1936	?	van der Hoop 1938; J. Loewenstein 1956: 23
LAMPONGS Sumatra.	1	?	?	?	van Heekeren 1958: 21
BENKULEN Sumatra.	1	?	?	?	„
SUMBERJAJA Bandinagun (near Lake Ranau), South Sumatra.	1	Fragment found in course of road building.	1914	?	„
SEMARANG Java.	3	Different places in south of town.	1883	Two are in Jakarta Museum (nos. 1712, 1831)	Heger 1903: 46; van Heekeren 1958: 18
BANJUMENING Semarang province, Java.	1	?	?	Jakarta Museum (no. 1832)	J. Loewenstein 1956: 23
MERSI BANJUMAS Java	1	?	pre-1899	Jakarta Museum (no. 1830)	Heger 1903: 47; J. Loewenstein 1956: 23; van Heekeren 1958: fig. 8
KEDU (Dieng plateau), Java.	1	Excavated near temple of Punta Dewa.	?	Jakarta Museum (no. 4947)	van Heekeren 1958: 18
PEKALONGAN Java.	2	One found in river (fragment)—the other complete	?	Jakarta Museum (one—no. 3002)	J. Loewenstein 1956: 23; van Heekeren 1958: 19
TANUREJO Temanggung, Java.	1	?	?	?	van Heekeren 1958: 18

Place	Number of drums	Context	Date found	Present whereabouts	References
CIBADAK (near BOGOR), Java.	1	Miniature size: funeral gift.	?	?	van Heekeren 1958: 20
CIANJUR Priangan, Java.	1	?	?	?	van Heekeren 1958: 18
SALAJAR ISLAND (south-east of Sulawesi) Indonesia.	1	Still kept locally and revered by	?	in situ	Heger 1903: 27–9 van Heekeren 1958: 33 J. Loewenstein 1956: 39
SANGEANG ISLAND (Gunung Api) (off Sumbawa), Indonesia.	5		1937	(? one called 'Makalamau')	J. Loewenstein 1956: 39–41
ROTI ISLAND Indonesia.	1	?	1871	Jakarta Museum	Heger 1903: 29–30 van Heekeren 1958: 28–9
LUANG ISLAND (between Timor and Timor Laut), Indonesia.	1	Said to have been captured from a neighbouring island.	1730 1880	in situ	Heger 1903: 48 van Heekeren 1958: 29–30
LETI ISLAND Indonesia.	1	?	1890?	Jakarta Museum	Heger 1903: 48 van Heekeren 1958: 30–1
KAI ISLANDS Indonesia.	2	Found half buried in ground; known locally as 'man and woman'.	1890	„	van Heekeren 1958: 31–3

Appendix III
Check list of Chinese Characters
JEREMY H. C. S. DAVIDSON

Introductory Note

WITH certain exceptions, the following list includes all Chinese words, transliterations, and titles, to which reference is made in this volume. The exceptions are: Chinese sources cited in the bibliographies of certain papers; names of dynasties and the titles of Dynastic Histories; and the names of present-day Chinese provinces.

The list is arranged under the following headings:

A. *Place-Names:*
   1. China.
   2. Viet-Nam.
   3. South East Asia (and India).
B. *Proper Names, Titles, and Terms:*
   1. Proper names and titles.
   2. Terms.
C. *Titles of Books.*

Within each section, the items are given in alphabetical order of pronunciation, as indicated by the Pīnyīn transliteration. In addition, the third and fourth columns of the table indicate respectively the Wade-Giles form of Romanization, and (where relevant), the Sino-Vietnamese form. Cross-references are made where comparison is necessary, or of interest. Where a name is commonly written with variant characters of identical pronunciation tion (e.g. Section B.1: *Píluógé*), the alternative characters are included in parentheses.

A. *Place-Names*

1. China

Ānníngchéng	安 寧 城	An-ning ch'eng
Bànpōcūn	半 坡 村	Pan-p'o-ts'un
Cāngwú	蒼 梧	Ts'ang-wu
Chángān	長 安	Ch'ang-an

Chéngdū	成都	Ch'eng-tu
Dàlǐ	大理	Ta-li
Dàpōnà	大波那	Ta-p'o-na
Daìhé	大和	Tai-ho
Diān	滇	Tien
Diānchí	滇池	Tien-ch'ih (Lake Dian)
Ěrhaǐ	洱海	Erh-hai
Gānzī	甘孜	Kan-tzu (Kantze)
Gōngchéng	恭城	Kung-ch'eng
Guǎngxìn	廣信	Kuang-hsin (Quang-tin)
Haǐménkoǔ	海門口	Hai-men-k'ou
Hándān	邯鄲	Han-tan
Huái	淮	Huai
Jiànchūan	劍川	Chien-ch'uan
Jiāngchūan	江川	Chiang-ch'uan
Jìnníng	晉寧	Chin-ning
Jiǔsī shān	九絲山	Chiu-ssu shan
Kaīhuà	開化	K'ai-hua
Kūnmíng	昆明	Kunming
Lǐfān	理番	Li-fan
Lǐjiā shān	李家山	Li-chia shan
Liángwángshān	梁王山	Liang-wang shan
Línzī	臨淄	Lin-tzu
Lóngshān	龍山	Lung-shan
Luòyáng	洛陽	Lo-yang
Nánshān	南山	Nan-shan
Nánzhoū	南州	Nan-chou

Níngěr	寧 洱	Ning-erh
Níngxiāng	寧 鄉	Ning-hsiang
Pānyú	番 禺	P'an-yü
Píngbà	平 壩	P'ing-pa
Qiánzhoū	黔 州	Ch'ien-chou
Qīngyǔan	清 遠	Ch'ing-yüan
Qīngzhèn	清 鎮	Ch'ing-chen
Shízhaì shān	石 寨 山	Shih-chai-shan
Tàijí shān	太 极 山	T'ai-chi-shan
Wǔweī	武 威	Wu-wei
Xìaxi zhoū	下 溪 州	Hsia-hsi chou
Yǎngsháo	仰 韶	Yang-shao
Yángzhoū	揚 州	Yang-chou
Yǒngchāng chéng	永 昌 城	Yung-ch'ang ch'eng
Yǒngshùn xiàn	永 順 縣	Yung-shun hsien
Zhōngyuán	中 原	Chung-yüan

2. Viet-Nam

Ānnán	安 南	An-nan (An-nam)
Báihè	白 鶴	Pai-ho (Bach-hac)
Bǐjǐng	比 景	Pi-ching (?Bi-canh)
Chāolèi	超 類	Ch'ao-lei (Sieu-loai)
Fēngxī	封 谿	Feng-hsi (Phong-khe)
Fēngzhoū	峯 州	Feng-chou (Phong-chau)
Gǔluó	古 螺	Ku-lo (Co-loa)
Jiǎnjiāng	蠶 江	Chien-chiang (Kien-giang)
Jiāozhǐ	交 阯	Chiao-chih (Giao-chi)
Jiāozhoū	交 州	Chiao-chou (Giao-chau)

Jiǔzhēn	九 真	Chiu-chen (Cuu-chan)
Kělǔ	可 縷	K'o-lü (Kha-lu)
Léilǒu	贏 陵	Lei-lou (Luy-lau)
Lóngbiān	龍 編	Lung-pien (Long-bien)
Lǒngxi	隴 溪	Lung-hsi (Lung-khe)
Lóngyūan	龍 淵	Lung-yüan (Long-uyen)
Lúyóng	盧 容	Lu-yung (Lo-dung)
Lúochéng	羅 城	Lo-ch'eng (La-thanh)
Mílíng	麊 泠	Mi-ling (Me-linh)
Píngjiāng	平 江	P'ing-chiang (Binh-giang)
Qūsù	區 粟	Ch'ü-su (qv. Xīquán) (cf. Qūxū)
Qūxū	曲 胥	Ch'ü-hsü (cf. Qū-sù)
Rìnán	日 南	Jih-nan (Nhat-nam)
Shāgǔi Kūnlún	殺 鬼 崑 崙	Sha-kuei K'un-lun (Sat-quy Con-lon)
Shēnglóng	升 龍	Sheng-lung (Thang-long)
Sīlóng	思 龍	Ssu-lung (Tu-long)
Tiāndéjiāng	天 德, 江	T'ien-te chiang (Thien-duc giang)
Wànghǎi (chéng)	望 海 (城)	Wang-hai (Vong-hai)
Wénláng	文 郎	Wen-lang (Van-lang)
Xīquán[1]	西 捲 (卷)	Hsi-ch'üan (Tay-quyen) (qv. Qūsù)
Xiànglín	象 林	Hsiang-lin (Tuong-lam)
Yuèshāng	越 裳	Yüeh-shang (Viet-thuong)
Zhōnggūi	忠 龜	Chung-kuei (Trung-quy)
Zhūwú	朱 吾	Chu-wu (Chau-ngo)
Zhūyuān	朱 鳶	Chu-yüan (Chau-dien)

3. *South East Asia (and India)*

Bāndǒu	班 斗		Pan-tou (q.v. Biǎndǒu)
Bǐsōng	比 嵩		Pi-sung
Biǎndǒu	邊 斗		Pien-tou (q.v. Bāndǒu)
Bùshù	不 述		Pu-shu
Cānbàn	參 半		Ts'an-pan
Chìtǔ	赤 土		Ch'ih-t'u
Dāndān	單 單		Tan-tan
Diǎnsūn	典 孫		Tien-sun (q.v. Dùnsùn)
Dūkūn²	都 昆		Tu-k'un (cf. Jūdūkūn)
Dùnsùn	頓 遜		Tun-sun (q.v. Diǎnsūn)
Duòhélúo	墮 和 羅		To-ho-lo
Dùoluóbōdǐ	墮 羅 鉢 底		To-lo-po-ti
Duòpódēng	墮 婆 登		To-p'o-teng
Fùnà	富 那		Fu-na
Fúnán	扶 南		Fu-nan
Gānbī	甘 卑		Kan-pi
Gāntuólì	干 陀 利		Kan-t'o-li
Gānzhīfó	干 支 佛		Kan-chih-fo
Gēluóshěfēn³	哥 羅 舍 分		Ko-lo-she-fen
Gēyíng	歌 營		Ko-ying (q.v. Jiǎyíng)
Hēlíng	訶 陵		Ho-ling
Huánwáng	環 王		Huan-wang (q.v. Línyì)
Jiāluóshě³	迦 邏 舍 (弗)		Chia-lo-she
Jiǎyíng	加 營		Chia-ying (q.v. Gēyíng)
Jiāzhà	迦 咤		Chia-cha
Jīnchén	金 陳		Chin-ch'en (q.v. Jīnlín)

Jīnlín	金 隣	Chin-lin (q.v. Jīnchén)
Jiūmì	鳩 密	Chiu-mi
Jiǔzhì	九 稚	Chiu-chih
Jūdūkūn²	屈 都 昆	Chu-tu-k'un (q.v. Dūkūn)
Jūdūqián²	屈 都 乾	Chü-tu-ch'ien (nb. Jūdūkūn)
Jūlì	拘 利	Chü-li
Jūlóumì	拘 婁 密	Chü-lou-mi
Kūnlún	崑 崙	K'un-lun (Con-lon)
Lángyáxiū	狼 牙 脩	Lang-ya-hsiu
Línyáng	林 陽	Lin-yang
Línyì	林 邑	Lin-i (Lam-ap) (q.v. Huánwáng)
Lù Zhēnlà	陸 真 臘	Lu Chen-la (q.v. Wéndān)
Lúoyuè	羅 越	Lo-yüeh
Mólà	摩 臘	Mo-la
Móluóyóu	摩 羅 游	Mo-lo-yu
Nán Tiānzhú	南 天 竺	Nan-t'ien-chu
Noùtuóhuán	耨 陀 洹	Nou-t'o-huan (q.v. Tuóyuán)
Pánpán	盤 盤	P'an-p'an
Piào	驃	P'iao
Póàn	婆 岸	P'o-an
Pólì	婆 利	P'o-li
Póluó	婆 羅	P'o-lo
Sāndūfǔ	三 都 賦	San-tu-fu
Sānfóqí	三 佛 齊	San-fo-ch'i (q.v. Shìlìfóshì)
Sēnggāo	僧 高	Seng-kao
Shěpó	闍 婆	She-p'o

Shìlìfóshì	室 利 佛 逝	Shih-li-fo-shih (q.v. Sānfóqí)
Shīzǐ	獅 (師) 子	Shih-tzu
Shūjìn⁴	殊 禁	Shu-chin (q.v. Shūnài)
Shūnài⁴	殊 柰	Shu-nai (q.v. Shūjín)
Shuǐ Zhēnlà	水 真 臘	Shui Chen-la
Suàntái	算 臺	Suan-t'ai
Tóuhé	投 和	T'ou-ho
Tuóyuán	陀 洹	T'o-yüan (q.v. Noùtúohuán)
Wéndān	文 單	Wen-tan (q.v. Lù Zhēnlà)
Wǔlìng	武 令	Wu-ling
Xiūluófēn	修 羅 分	Hsiu-lo-fen
Yèláng	夜 郎	Yeh-lang
Zhànbó	瞻 博	Chan-po
Zhànghǎi	漲 海	Chang-hai
Zhēnlà	真 臘	Chen-la

B. Proper Names, Titles, and Terms

1. Proper names and titles

À Dà	阿 大	A-Ta
Āi Láo	哀 牢	Ai-lao (Ailao)
Ān Lùshān	安 祿 山	An Lu-shan
Bā Shǔ	巴 蜀	Pa-Shu (Ba-Thuc)
Bǎi Yuè	百 越	Pai-Yüeh
Bōsī	波 斯	Po-ssu
Bóyí	百 夷	Po-yi
Cháng	長	Ch'ang
Chǔ	楚	Ch'u
Dàshí	大 食	Ta-shih
Dōngxiè	東 謝	Tung-hsieh

Dūlǎo	都 老	Tu-lao
Fàn Màn	范 蔓	Fan Man (q.v. Fàn Shīmàn)
Fàn Shīmàn	范 師 蔓	Fan Shih-man (q.v. Fàn Màn)
Fàn Xún	范 尋	Fan Hsün
Gāo Xióngzhēng	高 熊 徵	Kao Hsiung-cheng
Géluófèng	閣 羅 鳳	Ko-lo-feng
Guāngwǔdì	光 武 帝	Kuang-wu-ti
Hàn Gāohòu	漢 高 后	Han Kao-hou (Han Cao Hau)
Hàn Wǔdì	漢 武 帝	Han Wu-ti
Heī Miáo	黑 苗	Hei Miao
Hóngpáng	鴻 厖	Hung-p'ang (Hong Bang)
Hòu Lí	後 黎	Hou Li (Hau Le)
Hùnpánhuàng	混 槃 況	Hun-p'an-huang
Hùntián	混 填	Hun-t'ien
Jiǎ Dàn	賈 耽	Chia Tan
Jiāngxijūn	江 西 軍	Chiang-hsi chün
Jiāochénrú	驕 陳 如	Chiao-ch'en-ju (q.v. Qiaóchénrú)
Jin-Guī	金 龜	Chin-Kuei (Kim Quy)
Jinshēng	金 生	Chin-sheng
Kāng Tài	康 泰	K'ang T'ai
Láo	牢 = 僚	Lao
Lǎo	僚 獠 甫	Lao
Lǐ Jífǔ	李 吉 甫	Li Chi-fu
Lí Zé	黎 剗	Li Tse (Le Tac)
Líu Xiǎn	劉 顯	Liu Hsien
Liú Xún	劉 恂	Liu Hsün
Lóngbiān hoú	龍 編 侯	Lung-pien hou (Long-bien hau)

Lóngdùtíng hoú	龍度亭候	Lung-tu-t'ing hou (Long-do dinh hau)
Lóngwěi	龍尾	Lung-wei
Mǎ Duānlín	馬端臨	Ma Tuan-lin
Mǎ Yuán	馬援	Ma Yüan
Mèng Kāng	孟康	Meng K'ang
Méngshě	蒙舍	Meng-she
Miáorén	苗人	Miao-jen
Miáo-Yáo	苗猺	Miao-Yao
Nánzhào	南詔	Nan-chao
Nán Mán	南蠻	Nan-Man
Nányáng	南洋	Nan-yang
Nán Yuè	南越	Nan-Yüeh (Nam-Viet)
Nóng	儂	Nung (Nung)
Ōulùo	歐駱	Ou-lo (Au-lac)
Píluógé	皮羅閣（閤）	P'i-lo-ko
Qí	齊	Ch'i
Qiaóchénrú	僑陳如	Ch'iao-ch'en-ju (Jiaōchénrú)
Rén Yán	任延	Jen Yen (Nham Dien)
Sānguó	三國	San-Kuo
Shāguǐ	殺鬼	Sha-Kuei (Sat-quy)
Shì Xiè	士燮	Shih Hsieh (Si Nhiep)
Shǔ Pàn	蜀泮	Shu P'an (Thuc Phan)
Sōngwàizhūmán	松外諸蠻	Sung-wai-chu-man
Sū Dìng	蘇定	Su Ting (To Dinh)
Tián	填	T'ien
Tián Sīqiān	田思遷	T'ien Ssu-ch'ien
Tuòhè	拓鶴	T'o-ho

Wànlì	萬 歷	Wan-li
Wáng Mǎng	王 莽	Wang Mang
Wōnī	寫 泥	Wo-ni
Xí Guāng	錫 光	Hsi Kuang (Tich Quang)
Xióngwǎng	雄 王	Hsiung-wang (Hung-vu'ong)
Xúanzàng	玄 藏	Hsüan-tsang
Yán Shīgǔ	顏 師 古	Yen Shih-ku
Yáng Yán	楊 炎	Yang Yen
Yáo Sīlián	姚 思 廉	Yao Ssu-lien
Yìmóuxún	異 牟 尋	I-mo-hsün
Yuèzhī	月 支	Yüeh-chih
Zēng Shěngwú	曾 省 吾	Tseng Sheng-wu
Zhān	旃	Chan
Zhànguó	戰 國	Chan-Kuo
Zhào	趙	Chao
Zhào Túo	趙 佗	Chao T'o (Trieu Da)
Zhào Yǔ	趙 嫗	Chao Yü (Trieu Au)
Zhēng	徵	Cheng (Trung)
Zhòngjiā	仲 家	Chung-chia
Zhoū Dàguān	周 大 觀	Chou Ta-kuan
Zhoū Zhuāngwáng	周 莊 王	Chou Chuang-wang
Zhú Zhī	竺 芝	Chu-chih
Zhūgě Liáng	諸 葛 亮	Chu-ko Liang
Zhuāng Qiáo	莊 蹻	Chuang Ch'iao
Zuàn	爨	Tsuan

2. Terms

Bànliǎngqián	半 兩 錢	Pan-liang-ch'ien
chánchú	蟾 蜍	ch'an-ch'u

chéngshì	城 市	ch'eng-shih (thanh-thi)	
chū	出	ch'u	
cìshǐ	刺 史	tz'u-shih (thu-su)	
dǎo	導	tao	
dào	道	tao	
dùi	碓	tui	
fǎnqiè	反 切	fan-ch'ieh	
fāng	坊	fang	
fǔ	府	fu (phu)	
gǎn	感	kan	
gē	戈	ko (qua)	
goūlúo	鈎 羅	kou-lo	
guā	蝸	kua (guǎlùo: cf. luó)	
guǐ	鬼	kuei	
gúo	國 （国）	kuo	
hè	鶴	ho (hac)	
heī	黑	hei (hac)	
hú	胡	hu	
Jiǎn	繭	Chien (Kien)	
jiāng	江	chiang	
jùn	郡	chün (quan)	
kǒu	口	k'ou	
kúi	夒	k'uei	
lái	來	lai	
lí	羅	li (la)	
lǐ	里	li	
lián	連	lien (lien)	
liáo	僚 橑 療	liao	

loǔ	簍		lou
lù	鷺		lu
lúo	篳 箏 蘿		lo (la)
lúo	羅 螺		lo (la)
lúo	螺 蠃		lo (loa)
mǎ	馬		ma
míng	鳴		ming
mínggǔ	鳴 鼓		ming-ku
neì	内		nei
pùfāng	鋪 坊		p'u-fang (pho phuong)
qián	錢		ch'ien
qióng	窮		ch'iung
shǐzhě	使 者		shih-che (su gia)
shòu	受		shou
shù	樹		shu (thu)
tǔ	土		t'u (tho)
wénguī	文 龜		wen-kuei
Wǔshú	五 銖		Wu-shu
Xǐ	璽		Hsi (Ty)
xiàn	縣		hsien (huyen)
xiànchéng	縣 城		hsien-ch'eng (huyen thanh)
xiànyì	縣 邑		hsien-i (huyen-ap)
xióng	雄		hsiung (hung)
yì	邑		i (ap)
yīnyùnxué	音 韻 學		yin-yün hsüeh
zhàng	丈		chang (truong)
zhào	詔		chao (q.v. Nánzhào)
Zhí	質		Chih

C. Titles of Books

Ānnán zhìluè	安南志略	An-nan chih-lüeh (An-nam chi-luoc)
Cí Haǐ	辭海	Tz'u Hai
Dūyúnxiàn zhìgaǒ	都勻縣志稿	Tu-yün-hsien chih-kao
Fāngtíng dìzhì	方亭地志	Fang-t'ing ti-chih (Phuong-dinh dia-chi)
Fúnán jì	扶南記	Fu-nan chi
Guǎngzhoū jì	廣州記	Kuang-chou chi
Gùiyáng fǔzhì	貴陽府志	Kuei-yang fu-chih
Guìzhoū tōngzhì	貴州通志	Kuei-chou t'ung-chih
Hànshū yīnyì	漢書音義	Han-shu yin-i
Hànzhì	漢志	Han-chih (Han-chi)
Hóngmíngjí: Móuzǐ Lǐhuòlùn	弘明集:牟子理惑論	Hung-ming chi: Mou-tzu Li-huo-lun
Hòuhànshū	後漢書	Hou Han-shu
Huāyáng gúozhì	華陽国志	Hua-yang kuo-chih
Jìnshū	晉書	Chin-shu
Jiù Tángshū	舊唐書	Chiu T'ang-shu
Kúichéng tújīng	夔城圖經	K'uei-ch'eng t'u-ching
Liángshū	梁書	Liang-shu
Lǐngbiǎo lùyì	嶺表錄異	Ling-piao lu-i
Mánshū	蠻書	Man-shu
Míngshǐ	明史	Ming-shih
Míngshǐ: Liú Xiǎn zhuàn	明史:劉顯傳	Ming-shih: Liu Hsien chuan
Nán-Qíshū	南齊書	Nan-Ch'i-shu
Nánshǐ	南史	Nan Shih
Nánzhoū yìwùzhì	南州異物志	Nan-chou i-wu-chih
Sāngúozhì	三国志	San-kuo-chih
Shuǐjīngzhù	水經註	Shui-ching-chu

Sòngshǐ: Mán-Yí zhuàn	宋史：蠻夷傳	Sung-shih: Man-I chuan
Sòngshū	宋書	Sung-shu
Súishū	隋書	Sui-shu
Taìpíngyùlǎn	太平御覽	T'ai-p'ing yü-lan
Wúshí waìguózhuàn	吳時外国傳	Wu-shih wai-kuo-chuan
Wúzhì	吳志	Wu-chih (q.v. Sānguózhì)
Xin Tángshū	新唐書	Hsin T'ang-shu
Xin Tángshū: Nán Mán zhuàn	新唐書：南蠻傳	Hsin T'ang-shu: Nan-Man chuan
XùYúnnán tōngzhì gǎo	續雲南通志稿	Hsü Yün-nan t'ung-chih kao
Yìwùzhì	異物志	Yi-wu-chih
Yuèshǐluè	越史略	Yüeh shih-lüeh (Viet-su luoc)
Yúnnán tōngzhì	雲南通志	Yün-nan t'ung-chih

NOTES

1. Read *quán*, not *juǎn*.
2. *Dūkūn* is probably an abbreviation of *Jūdūkūn*, and *Jūdūqián* may be a further variant. The tentative equation of *Jūdūqián* with Kattigara would be phonetically more acceptable if *qián* were read *gān*.
3. *Jiāluóshě* and *Gēluóshěfēn* may be variants of the same name. Cf. *Jiāyíng* and *Gěyíng*.
4. *Shūjìn* and *Shūnài* are probably two names for the same country which came to be considered as two separate countries as the result of a copyist's error *jìn* for *nài*, or vice versa.

Bibliography

Note:
The following list includes all works in Western languages cited in the papers, dealing with South East Asia and adjacent regions. A number of titles have been added, to provide a comprehensive bibliography of works concerning the first millennia B.C. and A.D. Works in Asian languages, together with any general works cited which do not relate specifically to South East Asia, are included in the bibliographies of individual papers.

For ease of reference, the list is arranged alphabetically by authors, with three supplementary sections at the end:

A. Unpublished theses.
B. Articles and books still in press.
C. Papers presented at Conferences whose proceedings are not yet published.

List of Abbreviations:

AP	*Asian Perspectives.* Honolulu.
APAO	*Archaeology and Physical Anthropology in Oceania.* Univ. of Sydney.
BAVH	*Bulletin des Amis du Vieux Hue.* Hue.
BEFEO	*Bulletin de l'École Française d'Extrême-Orient.* Hanoi, Paris.
BKI	*Bijdragen Tot de Taal-, Lauden Volkenkunde uitgegeven door het Koninklink Institut.* The Hague.
BMFEA	*Bulletin, Museum of Far Eastern Antiquities.* Stockholm.
BRM	*Bulletin of the Raffles Museum.* Singapore.
BSEI	*Bulletin de la Société des Études Indochinoises.* Saigon.
FMJ	*Federation Museums Journal.* Kuala Lumpur.
JBRS	*Journal of the Burma Research Society.* Rangoon.
JFMSM	*Journal of the Federated Malay States Museum.* Kuala Lumpur.
JMBRAS	*Journal of the Malay Branch of the Royal Asiatic Society.* Singapore.
JSS	*Journal of the Siam Society.* Bangkok.
RC	*Radiocarbon:* published by *American Journal of Science.* Hew Haven, Yale.
SMJ	*Sarawak Museum Journal.* Kuching.
TBG	*Tijdschrift voor Indisch Taal-, Lauder Volkenkunde: Koninklijk Bataviaasch Genootschap van Kunsten en Wetenschappen.* Jakarta (formerly Batavia).
TNAG	*Tijdschrift van het Koninklijk Nederlandsch Aardrijks kundig Genootschap.*
VBG	*Verhandelingen van het Bataviaasch Genootschap van Kunsten en Wetenschappen.* Jakarta (Batavia).

Allchin, B. and Allchin, R. 1968. *The Birth of Indian Civilisation.* Harmondsworth, Penguin Books.

Arasaratnam, S. 1972. *Pre-Modern Commerce and Society in Southern Asia.* Inaugural lecture, Univ. of Malaya, Kuala Lumpur.

Aung Thaw. 1968. *Report on the Excavations at Beitkthano.* Rangoon, Government of Burma.

— 1969. The 'Neolithic' Culture of the Padah-lin Caves, *JBRS,* lii (1), 9–23.

— 1972. *Historical Sites in Burma.* Rangoon, Government of Burma.

Aurousseau, L. 1923. La première conquète chinoise des pays annamites (IIIe siècle avant notre ère), *BEFEO*, xxiii, 137–262.

Aymonier, E. 1900–3. *Le Cambodge*. 3 vols. Paris.

Barnard, N. 1967. The Special Character of Metallurgy in Ancient China, in *The Application of Science in the Examination of Works of Art*, (ed.) W. J. Young, 184–204. Boston Arts Mus., Boston.

— 1972. *Early Chinese Art and its Possible Influence in the Pacific Basin* (Symposium at Columbia Univ., 1967). 3 vols. New York, Intercultural Arts Press.

Barth, A. 1902. Stèle de Vat Phou, près de Bassac, Laos. *BEFEO*, ii (3), 233–40.

— 1903. Inscription sanscrite de Phou Lokhon (Laos), *BEFEO*, iii, 248–303.

— and Bergaigne, A. 1885. *Inscriptions sanscrites du Cambodge et de Champa*. Paris.

Barthère, F. 1911. Sur quelques gisements de la Province de Biên-Hoá, Notes pour servir à l'étude du Préhistoire Indochinois. *Mém. Soc. Archéol. Provence*, xi, suppl. 1.

Basham, A. L. 1954, 1959. *The Wonder that was India: a Survey of the Culture of the Indian Sub-Continent before the coming of the Muslims*. London, Sidgwick and Jackson. (American edition, New York, 1959.)

Bayard, D. T. 1970. Excavations at Non Nok Tha, Northeastern Thailand, 1968: An Interim Report, *AP*, xiii, 109–43.

— 1971. *Non Nok Tha: the 1968 excavation. Procedure, stratigraphy and a summary of the evidence*. Dunedin, Univ. of Otago, Studies in Prehistoric Anthropology, no. iv.

— 1972. Early Thai Bronze: Analysis and New Dates, *Science*, clxxvi, 1411–12.

Beal, S. 1969. *Buddhist Records of the Western World*. Reprinted. Delhi.

Beauclair, I. de. 1956. Culture traits of non-Chinese tribes in Kweichow Province, Southwest China, *Sinologica*, v, 1, 20–35.

— 1973. Jar Burial on Botel Tobago Island, *AP*, xv (2), 167–76.

Bemmelen, R. W. van. 1949. *The Geology of Indonesia*. 2 vols. The Hague, Government Printing Office.

Bénisti, Mireille. 1970. *Rapports entre le premier Art khmer et l'Art indien*. 2 vols. Paris, EFEO.

Beyer, H. Otley. 1947. Outline Review of Philippine Archaeology by islands and provinces, *Philippine Journal of Science*, lxxvii. (also Supplementary Illustrations, privately printed. Manila, 1949).

— 1948. Philippine and East Asian Archaeology and its relation to the origin of the Pacific Islands population, *Bull. of National Research Council, Philippines*, xxix.

Bezacier, L. 1953. Notice sur l'Archéologie du Vietnam, *BSEI*, n.s. xxviii, 73–6.

— 1954. *L'Art Vietnamien*. Paris, Éditions de L'Union Française.

— 1958. L'Archéologie au Viet-Nam d'après les Travaux de l'École Francaise d'Extrême-Orient, *France-Asie*, xv (nos. 149–50), 513–34.

— 1966–7. Sur la datation d'une representation primitive de la charrue, *BEFEO*, liii, 551–6.

— 1972. *Le Viêt-Nam*. (*Man. d'Archeologie d'Extrême-Orient*) *Premiere Partie: Asie du Sud-Est*, xi, (ed.) J. Boisselier). Paris.

Bhattacharya, K. 1961a. *Les Religions Brahmaniques dans l'Ancien Cambodge*. Paris, EFEO.

— 1961b. Précisions sur la paléographie de l'inscription dite de Vô-canh, *Artibus Asiae*, xxiv, 219–24.

— 1961c. La Secte des Pāśupata dans l'ancien Cambodge, *Journal Asiatique*, ccxliii, 479–90.

Boechari (Buchari). 1965. Epigraphy and Indonesian Historiography, in *Introduction to Indonesian Historiography*, (ed.) Soedjatmoko. Ithaca, Cornell Univ. Press.

— 1966. Preliminary report on the discovery of an Old-Malay inscription at Sodiomerto, *Madjalah Ilmu-ilmu Sastra Indonesia*, iii (2, 3).

— 1973. Epigraphic Evidence on Kingship in Ancient Java, *Madjalah Ilmu-ilmu Sastra Indonesia*, v (1), 119–26.

Boeles, J. J. 1964. The King of Sri Dvaravati and his Regalia, *JSS*, lii (1), 99–114.

Bongert, Y. 1959. Note sur l'esclavage en droit khmer, in *Études d'histoire du droit prive offertes à Pierre Petot*. Paris, Éditions Montchrestien.

Boisselier, J. 1955. *La statuaire khmère et son évolution*. 2 vols. Saigon, EFEO.

— 1963. *La Statuaire du Champs*. Paris, EFEO.

— 1965. Récentes Recherches Archéologiques en Thailande, *Arts Asiatiques*, xii.

— 1965. U T'ong et son importance pour l'histoire de Thailande, *Silpakon*, ix, 27–30.

— n.d. *U-Thong et Son Importance pour l'histoire de Thailande et Nouvelles Données sur l'Histoire ancienne de Thailande*. Bangkok, Fine Arts Department.

— 1966. *Le Cambodge. (Manuel d'Archeologie d'Extreme Orient, Asie du Sud-Est*, i.) Paris, Picard.

— 1968*a*. L'Art de Dvaravati, *Silpakon*, xi, 6, 34–56.

— 1968*b*. *Nouvelles Connaisances Archéologiques de la Ville d' U T'ong*. Bangkok.

— 1970. Récentes Recherches à Nakhon Pathom, *JSS*, lviii, (2).

— 1972. Travaux de la Mission Archéologique Française en Thailande, *Arts Asiatiques*, xxv, 27–90.

Boriskovsky, P. I. 1962. Exploration of ancient sites of the stone age in the Democratic Republic of Viêt-Nam, *Sovietskaya Archaeologia*, ii. (Russian)

— 1963. Archaeological Discoveries in Viet-Nam, *Herald of the Academy of Sciences of the USSR*, iv. (cf. *AP*, vi (1–2), 23–31.)

— 1966. *Peràobytnye proshloe Vietnama*. Moscow–Leningrad, Izdatelstvo, Akademia Nauka. (Russian)

— 1966. Basic Problems of the Prehistoric Archaeology of Viet-Nam, *AP*, ix, 83–5.

Bosch, F. D. K. 1916. De Inscriptie van Dinaja, *TBG*, lvii, 410–44.

— 1921. Een hypothese omtrent den oorsprong der Hindoe-Javaansche kunst, in *Hand. Eerste Congr. Taal-. Land-. en Volken-kunde van Java*, 93–169.

— 1928. De Inscriptie van Keloerak, *TBG*, lxviii, 1–64.

— 1941. De inscriptie van Ligor, *TBG*, lxxxi, 26–38.

— 1952*a*. Crivijaya, de Cailendra—en de Sanjayawamoa, *BKI*, cviii, 113–23.

— 1952*b*. Boekbespreking, *Prasasti Indonesia* I, *BKI*, cviii, 191–9.

— 1961. *Selected Studies in Indonesian Archaeology*. The Hague, M. Nijhoff.

Bouchot, J. 1927. Les Fouilles de Xuân-Lôc, *BSEI*, n.s., ii, 155–6; cf. additional note, iv, (1929), 114–24.

Braddell, R. 1947–9. Notes on Ancient Times in Malaya, *JMBRAS*, xx (1), 161–86; xx (2), 1–19; xxii (1), 1–25.

Brandes, J. L. A. 1918. Oud-Javaansche Oorkonden, *VBG*, lx (2).

Briggs, L. P. 1945. Dvaravati: the most Ancient Kingdom of Siam, *Journal of American Oriental Soc.*, lxv, 98–107.

— 1951. *The ancient Khmer empire*. Philadelphia, American Philosophical Society.

Brookfield, H. L. and Hart, D. 1971. *Melanesia—a geographical interpretation of an island World*. London, Methuen.

Bronson, B. 1971. Review of Aung Thaw, *Report on the Excavations of Beikthano*. *AP*, xii, 142–3.

— n.d. Excavations at Chansen, Thailand. (Report to Fine Arts Department, Bangkok).

— and Dales, G. F. An Excavation of the Dvaravati Period, *Silpakon*, xiii.

— 1973. Excavations at Chansen, Thailand: A Preliminary Report, *AP*, xv (1), 15–46.

— and Han, M. C. 1972. A Thermoluminescence Series from Thailand, *Antiquity*, xlvi, 322–6.

Bruyn, J. V. de. 1959. New archaeological finds at Lake Sentani, *Nieuw Guinea Studien*, iii, 1–8.

— 1962. New Bronze finds at Kwadeware, Lake Sentani, *Niew Guinea Studien*, vi, 61–2.

Bunker, E. C. 1972. The Tien Culture and Some Aspects of its Relationship to the Dong-Son Culture, in *Early Chinese Art and its Possible Influence in the Pacific Basin*. (ed.) N. Barnard. New York, Intercultural Arts Press.

Carbonnel, J. P. 1969. Les Études Française sur le Quaternaire en Asie: Quaternaire de la Péninsule Indochinoise, in *Études Françaises sur le Quaternaire*. (Eighth Congress of INQUA: Suppl. to *Bull de l'AFEQ*.) Paris.

— 1970 (1973). *Le Quaternaire cambodgien. Structure et stratigraphie*. (*Mém. de l'ORSTOM*, 1973.) Paris. (Originally thesis for Doctorat d'Etat, Univ. of Paris VI).

— and Delibrial, G. 1968. Premières Datations Absolues de Trois Gisementes Neolithiques Cambodgiens, *Comptes Rendues de l'Académie des Sciences*, Série D, 267: 1432–4.

— and Poupeau, G. 1969. Premiers éléments de datation absolue par traces de fission des basalyes de l'Indochine méridionale, *Earth and Planetary Science Letters*, vi, 26–30.

Chabot, R. T. 1950. *Verwantschap, Stand en Sexe in Zuid-Celebes*. Groningen and Djarkarta, J. B. Wolters.

Chakraborti, H. 1970. *Pasupata Sūtram with Panchārtha-bhāsya of Kaundinya*. Calcutta, Academic Publishers.

Chandran, J. 1973. The Cultural Significance of the Pengkalan Kempas Megaliths, *JMBRAS*, xlvi (1), 93–100.

Chang, K. C. 1958. Prehistoric Cultures in Thailand, in *Papers on Chinese and Thai Cultures*. Taipeh.

— 1962. Major Problems in the Culture History of S.E. Asia, *Bull. of Inst. of Ethnology, Academic Sinica*, xiii, 1–26.

— 1968. *The Archaeology of Ancient China: Revised and Enlarged Edition*. New Haven, Yale Univ. Press.

— 1970. The Beginnings of Agriculture in the Far East, *Antiquity*, xliv.

—, Grace, G. W., and Solheim, W. G. II. 1964. Movement of the Malayo–Polynesians, 1500 B.C. to A.D. 500, *Current Anthropology*, v (5), 359–406.

Chard, C. 1973. Northwest Asia: Report, *AP*, xiv, 1–28.

Chavannes, E. (trans.). 1894. *Mémoire sur les Religieux Eminents par I-Tsing*. Paris.

Cheng Te-Kun. 1969. *Archaeology in Sarawak*. Cambridge.

Chhabra, B. C. 1965. *Expansion of Indo–Aryan Culture during Pallava Rule*. 2nd edn. Delhi, Munshi Ram Monoharial.

Chira Chongkol and Woodward, H. 1966. *Guide to the U-Thong National Museum, Suphanburi*. Bangkok, Fine Arts Department.

Christie, A. H. 1961a. Some Western Writings on South East Asian Prehistory, in *Historians of South East Asia*, (ed.) D. G. E. Hall. London, Oxford Univ. Press.

— 1961b. The Sea-locked Lands: the diverse traditions of South East Asia, in *The Dawn of Civilization*, (ed.) S. Piggott, pp. 277–300. London, Thames and Hudson.

Clark, J. G. D. 1965. *World Prehistory: an Outline*. Cambridge Univ. Press.

— 1969. *World Prehistory: A New Outline*. Cambridge Univ. Press.

Clarke, D. L. 1973. Archaeology: The Loss of Innocence, *Antiquity*, xxxxvii (185), 6–18.

Coedès, G. 1906. La stèle de Ta Prohm, *BEFEO*, vi, 44–81.

— 1918. Le Royaume de Crivijaya, *BEFEO*, xviii, no. 6.

— 1922. *See* Seidenfaden, E., 1922.

— 1924. Études cambodgiennes XVIII. L'extension du Cambodge vers le sud-ouest au VIIe siècle (Nouvelles inscriptions de Chantaboun). *BEFEO*, xxiv, 352–8.

— 1926. *History of Thai Writing*. Bangkok.

— 1928. The Excavations at Pong Tuk and their importance for the ancient history of Siam, *JSS*, xxi, 195–209.

— 1930. Les Inscriptions malaises de Crivijaya, *BEFEO*, xxx, 29–80.

— 1931. Deux inscriptions sanskrites du Fou-nan, *BEFEO*, xxxi (1–2), 1–12.
— 1936. Études cambodgiennes, XXXI: A Propos du Tchen-la d'Eau: trois inscriptions de Cochinchine, *BEFEO*, xxxiv, 1–13.
— 1937–66. *Les Inscriptions du Cambodge*. 8 vols. Hanoi and Paris, EFEO.
— 1939. Les statuettes décapitées de Savankalok, *Bull. de l'Institut Indochinois pour l'Étude de l'Homme*, ii (2), 189–90.
— 1944. Une Nouvelle Inscription d'Ayuthya, *JSS*, xxxv, 73–6
— 1947. Fouilles en Cochinchine. Le site de Go Oc-Eo, Ancien Port du Royaume de Fou-nan, *Artibus Asiae*, x, 193–9.
— 1948. *Les États Hindouises d'Indochine et d'Indonésie*. 1st edn. Paris, Boccard.
— 1953. Le Substrat Autochthone et la Superstructure Indienne au Cambodge et à Java, *Cahiers d'Histoire Mondiale*, i, 368–77.
— 1956. Nouvelles données sur les origines du Royaume khmer: la stèle de Vat Luong Kau, près de Vat P'hu, *BEFEO*, xlviii (1), 209–20.
— 1959. L'Inscription de la Stèle de Ligor: état présent de son inscription, *Oriens Extremus*, vi (1), 42–8.
— 1964. *Les Etats Hinduisés d'Indochine et d'Indonésie*. 2nd edn. Paris, Boccard.
— 1966. *The Making of Southeast Asia*. (trans. H. M. Wright.) London, Routledge and Kegan Paul. (Translation of *Les Peuples de la Péninsule Indochinoise*. Paris, 1962.)
— 1968. *The Indianized States of Southeast Asia* (ed. W. F. Vella; trans. S. B. Chowning). Honolulu, East-West Center Press.
Colani, M. 1927. L'Age de la Pierre dans la Province de Hoa Binh, *Memoires, Service Géologique de l'Indochine*, xiv, fasc. i.
— 1929. Gravures primitives sur Pierre et sur Os (Stations hoabinhiennes et bacsoniennes), *BEFEO*, xxix, 273–87.
— 1930. Recherches sur le Préhistorique Indochinois, *BEFEO*, xxx, 299–422.
— 1932. Champs de Jarres mono-lithiques et de Pierres funéraires du Tran-ninh. *Praehistorica Asiae Orientalis*, i, 103–28. (Hanoi)
— 1935. *Megalithes du Haut Laos*. 2 vols. Paris, EFEO.
— 1936. Notes pré- et protohistoriques, province du Quang-Binh, *BAVH*, xxiii (1), 121–40.
— 1940a. Vestiges d'un culte solaire en Indochine, *Bull. de l'Institut Indochinois pour l'Étude de l'Homme*, iii (1/2), 37–41.
— 1940b. Emploi de la Pierre en des Temps Reculés: Annam, Indonesie, Assam, *BAVH*, xxvii.
Colless, B. E. 1972–3. The Ancient Bnam Empire: Fu-nan and Po-nan, *Journal of the Oriental Society of Australia*, ix (1–2), 21–31.
Collings, H. D. 1937. Recent finds of Iron Age sites in Southern Perak and Selangor, F.M.S.; and An Excavation at Bukit Chuping, Perlis, *BRM*, Ser. B, i (2), 75–120.
— 1949. An Iron Age find near Klang, *BRM*, Ser. B, i (4), 113–16.
Conklin, C. H. 1949. Bamboo Literacy on Mindoro, *Pacific Discovery*, ii (no. 4).
Coral-Rémusat, G. de. 1934. Art Cam: le probleme de la chronologie, in *Musée Guimet: Cat. des Collections Indochinoises* (ed.) P. Dupont, pp. 35–44. Paris Ministère de l'Education Nationale.
Cordier, H. 1908. Les Mo-sos, *T'oung Pao*, Sér. II, ix, 663–8.
Cuisinier, J. 1948. *Les Muong, Géographie humaine et Sociologie*. Paris, Institut d'Ethnologie.
Damais, L.-C. 1951. Études d'Épigraphie Indonésienne, I: Méthode de réduction des dates javanaises en dates européennes; II: La date des Inscriptions en ère de Sanjaya, *BEFEO*, xlv (1), 1–64.
— 1952. Études d'Épigraphie Indonésienne, III: Liste des principales inscriptions datées de l'Indonésie, *BEFEO*, xklvi (1), 1–106.

— 1953. Études d'Épigraphie Indonesienne III: datées Liste des Principales Inscriptions de l'Indonésie, *BEFEO*, xlvi (2), 1–107.

— 1955a. Études d'Épigraphie Indonesienne: IV: Discussion de la date des Inscriptions, *BEFEO*, xlvii (2), 7–290.

— 1955b. Les Écritures d'origine indienne en Indonesie et dans le Sud-Est Asiatique continental, *BSEI*, n.s., xxx, 365–82.

— 1957. Études javanaises, I: Les Tombes musulmanes datées de Tralaya, *BEFEO*, xlviii (2), 353–416.

— 1962. Études soumatranaises, I: La date de l'Inscription de Hujung Langit ('Bawang'); II: L'Inscription de Ulu Belu, *BEFEO*, 1 (2), 275–310.

— 1964. Études Sino-Indonésiennes, III: La transcription chinoise Ho-ling comme désignation de Java, *BEFEO*, lii (1), 93–142.

— 1970. *Répertoire onomastique de l'Epigraphie javanaise (jusqu'à Sindok Sri Tsanaivikrama Dharmmotungadewa)*. Paris, EFEO.

Das, S. R. 1968. Discovery of a Metal Dharmachakra, *Journal of the Asiatic Society*. (Calcutta), x, 77–8.

De Casparis, J. G. 1941. Nogmaals de inscriptie van Dinojo, *TBG*, lxxxi, 499–513.

— 1950. *Prasasti Indonesia I: Inscripties uit de Cailendra-tijd*. Bandoeng.

— 1956. *Prasasti Indonesia II: Selected inscriptions from the 7th to the 9th century*. Jakarta, Dinas Purbakala Republik Indonesia.

— 1958. Short inscriptions from Tjandi Plaosan-Lor, *Berita Dinas Purbakala, Rep. Indonesia*, iv.

— 1961. New evidence on Cultural Relations between Java and Ceylon in ancient times, *Artibus Asiae*, xxiv, 241–8.

Deraniyagala, S. 1972. The citadel of Anuradhapura 1969: Excavations in the Gedige area, *Ancient Ceylon*, ii, 48–169.

Devendra, D. T. 1958. *Classical Sinhalese Sculpture: c. 300 B.C. to A.D. 1000*. London, Tiranti.

Dewall, M. von. 1967a. The Tien Culture of South-West China, *Antiquity*, xxxxi (161), 8–21.

— 1967b. New Data on Early Chou Finds: their Relative Chronology in Historical Perspective, in *Symposium in Honor of Dr. Li Chi*, pp. 1–68. Taipeh, Tsing Hua Publ. Committee.

— 1972. Decorative Concepts and Stylistic Principles in the Bronze Art of Tien, *Early Chinese Art and its Possible Influence in the Pacific Basin*, (ed.) N. Barnard: ii, 329–72. New York, Intercultural Arts Press.

Dhanit Yupho. n.d. *Some Recently Discovered Sites of Dvāravati Period*. Bangkok, Fine Arts Department (English, Thai).

Drake, F. S. (ed.). 1967. *Symposium of Historical, Archaeological and Linguistic Studies on South China, South East Asia and the Hong Kong Region*. Hong Kong, Univ. Press.

Duff, R. 1970. Stone Adzes of Southeast Asia: an Illustrated Typology, *Canterbury Museum Bulletin* (New Zealand), no. iii.

Dunn, F. L. 1964. Excavations at Gua Kechil, Pahang, *JMBRAS*, xxxvii, (2), 87–124.

— 1966. Radio-carbon dating of the Malayan Neolithic, *Proc. Prehistoric Society*, xxxii.

Dupont, P. 1943. Etudes sur l'Indochine ancienne, I: La Dislocation du Tchen-la et la Formation du Cambodge Angkorien (VIIe–IXe siècle), *BEFEO*, xliii, 17–55.

— 1949. Le Sud-Indochinois aux VIe et VIIe siècles: Tchen-la et Panduranga, *BSEI* n.s., xxiv (1), 9–26.

— 1952. Etudes sur l'Indochine ancienne, II: Les Debuts de la Royauté Angkorienne, *BEFEO*, xlvi (1), 119–76.

— 1955. *La Statuaire pre-angkorienne*. Ascona: Editions *Artibus Asiae*.

— 1959. *L'Archéologie Mône de Dvāravati.* 2 vols. Paris: EFEO.

Durai Raja Singam, S. 1954. *India and Malaya through the Ages: A Pictorial Survey.* 3rd edn. Singapore.

Durand, M. 1953. Fonte d'une cloche a Tây-mo, *BSEI,* n.s., xxviii, 397–8.

Eberhard, W. 1942. *Kultur und Siedlung der Randvolker chinas* (suppl. to *T''oung Pao,* xxxvi). Leiden.

— 1965. *Conquerors and Rulers: Social forces in Medieval China.* 2nd edn. Leiden, E. J. Brill.

— 1967. *Settlement and Social Change in Asia.* Hong Kong Univ. Press.

Ellen, R. F. and Glover, I. C. 1973. Pottery manufacture and trade in the Central Moluccas, Indonesia: the modern situation and the historical implications, *Man,* n.s., ix, 353–79.

Elmberg, J. E. 1959. Further notes on the northern Majbrate (Vogelkop) Western New Guinea, *Ethnos,* xxiv, 70–80.

Erp, Th. van. 1929. De ommanteling van Baraboedoer's corsprankelijken voet, in *Feestbundel vitgegeven door het Konintlijk Bataviaasch Genootschap van Kunsten en Wetenschappen,* i, 120–60. Jakarta.

— 1931. *Barabudur Bouwkardige Beschrijring* (The Hague).

Evangelista, A. E. 1962. Philippine Archaeology to 1950, *Science Review,* iii, no. 9.

— 1965. The Indigenous Cultural Minorities of the Philippines, *Hemisphere,* ix.

— H. O. Beyer's Neolithic in the context of Postwar Discoveries in Local Archaeology, in *Studies in Philippine Anthropology,* (ed.) M. D. Zamora. Quezon City.

— 1969. Archaeology in the Philippines to 1950, *AP,* xii, 97–104.

Evans, I. H. N. 1920. Preliminary report on the exploration of a rock shelter in the Batu Kurau Parish, Perak, *JFMSM,* ix (1), 34–6.

— 1927. *Papers on the Ethnology and Archaeology of the Malay Peninsula.* Cambridge.

— 1928. On slab-built graves in Perak, *JFMSM,* xii (5), 111–19.

— 1929. Notes on the relationship between Philippine iron age antiquities and some from Perak, *JFMSM,* xii (7), 189–96.

— 1930. On a stone spearhead from Kelantan, *JFMSM,* xv (1), 1–2.

— 1931a. A search for antiquities in Kedah and Perlis, *JFMSM,* xv (2), 43–50.

— 1931b. A further slab-built grave at Sungkai, Perak, *JFMSM,* xv (2), 63–4.

— 1931c. A stone spearhead from Pahang, *JFMSM,* xv (2), 65–6.

— 1931d. Some pottery objects from Surat, *JSS,* xxiii (2), 207–9.

— 1931e. An attempted classification of Iron Age implements, *JFMSM,* xv (2), 71–6.

— 1932. Excavations at Tanjong Rawa, Kuala Selinsing, Perak, *JFMSM,* xv (3), 79–134.

Fernandez, M. F. 1970. Contributions à l'Étude du peuplement ancien du Lac Alactra, *Taloha,* iii, 3–54.

Ferrand, G. 1922. *L'Empire Sumatranois de Crivijaya.* Paris, P. Geuthner.

Filliozat, J. 1969. L'Inscription dite 'de Vo-Canh', *BEFEO,* lv, 107–16.

Finot, L. 1903. Notes d'Épigraphie, V: Panduranga (followed by note on Chinese texts by P. Pelliot), *BEFEO,* iii, 630–54.

— 1928. Nouvelles inscriptions du Cambodge, *BEFEO,* xxviii (1–2), 43–80.

Fisher, C. A. 1964. *Southeast Asia, a Social, Economic and Political Geography.* London, Methuen.

Fontaine, H. 1971. Renseignements nouveaux sur la céramique du champ de jarres funeraire de Dâu-Giây, *BSEI,* n.s., xlvi, 323–38.

— 1972. Nouveau champ de jarres dans la province de Long-khánh, *BSEI,* n.s., xlvii, 397–486.

Fox, R. B. 1959. *The Philippines in Prehistoric Times: a Handbook for the First Exhibition of Filipino Prehistory and Culture.* Manila, UNESCO National Commission of the Philippines.

— 1962. Ancient Filipino Communities, in *Proceedings of Symposium on the Impact of Man in Humid Tropics Vegetation*. Canberra, Government Printer.

— 1970. *The Tabon Caves: Archaeological Explorations and Excavations on Palawan Island, Philippines*. Manila, National Museum.

— 1973. The Tasaday: Stone Age Tribe of Mindanao, in *Britannia Yearbook of Science and the Future, 1973*.

— and Evangelista, A. 1957. The cave archaeology of Cagraray Island, Albay Province, Philippines, *Univ. of Manila Journal of East Asiatic Studies*, vi, pt. 1 (Univ. of Manila.)

— 1958. The Bato Caves, Sarsogon Province, Philippines: Preliminary Site Report of a Jar-burial-stone-tool Assemblage, *Nat. Research Council of Philippines Bulletin*, no. 42: Appendix E. (Quezon City)

Francisco, J. R. 1966. *Philippine Palaeography*. Quezon City, Univ. of Philippines (mimeo).

— 1971. *The Philippines and India: Essays in Ancient Cultural Relations*. Manila, National Book Store.

— 1973. Philippine Palaeography, *Philippine Journal of Linguistics*. (Special Monograph Issue, no. 3.) Manila.

Frédéric, L. 1965. *The Temples and Sculpture of Southeast Asia*. (Eng. trans.) London, Thames and Hudson.

Fürer-Haimendorf, C. von. 1943. Megalithic Ritual among the Gadabas and Bondos of Orissa, *Journ. Royal Asiatic Soc. Bengal, Letters*, ix, 149–78.

— 1945. The problem of megalithic cultures in Middle India, *Man in India*, xxv, 73–86.

Gait, E. A. 1898. Human sacrifices in Ancient Assam, *Journ. Asiatic Soc. Bengal*, lxvii, pt. iii (no. 1), 56–65.

Gaspardone, E. 1937. The Megalithic Tomb of Xuân-Lôc (Cochinchina), *Journal of Greater India Society*, iv, 26–35.

— 1953. La plus ancienne inscription de l'Indochine, *Journal Asiatique*, ccxli, 477–86.

Geertz, C. 1966. *Agricultural Involution—the process of ecological change in Indonesia*. Berkeley, Univ. of California Press.

Geertz, H. 1963. Indonesian cultures and communities, in *Indonesia*, (ed.) R. McVey, 24–96. New Haven, Yale Univ. Press.

Genet-Varcin, E. 1958–9. Les restes osseux des Cent-Rues (Sud Viet-Nam), *BEFEO*, xlix, 275–95.

Ghosh, A. and Panigrahi, K. C. 1946. Pottery of Ahichchhatra, *Ancient India*, i, 37–59.

— 1947. Taxila (Sirkap), 1944–5, *Ancient India*, iv, 41–84.

Gilhodes, P. C. 1909. La religion des Katchins, *Anthropos*, iv, 113–38, 702–25.

Giteau, M. 1965. *Khmer Sculpture and the Angkor Civilisation* (Eng. trans.). London, Thames and Hudson.

Glover, I. C. 1969. Radiocarbon Dates from Portuguese Timor, *APAO*, iv, 107–12.

— 1971. Prehistoric Research in Timor, in *Aboriginal Man and Environment in Australia*, (ed.) D. J. Mulvaney and J. Golson. Canberra.

— 1973a. Island Southeast Asia and the settlement of Australia, in *Archaeology, Theory and Practice*, (ed.) D. Strong, 105–29. London, Seminar Press.

— 1973b. Late Stone Age traditions in Southeast Asia, in *South Asian Archaeology*, 51–66. London, Duckworth.

Goloubew, V. 1929. L'Age du Bronze au Tonkin et dans le Nord Annam, *BEFEO*, xxix, 1–46.

— 1932. Sur l'origine et la diffusion des Tambours métalliques, *Praehistorica Asiae Orientalis*, i. Hanoi.

— 1937. *L'Archéologie du Tonkin et les Fouilles de Dong-son*. Hanoi.

— 1938. *Art et archéologie de l'Indochine*. Hanoi.

— 1941. La Tambour metallique de Hoang-ha, *BEFEO*, xl, 383–409.

Golson, J. 1972. Both sides of the Wallace Line: New Guinea, Australia, Island Melanesia and Asian prehistory, in *Early Chinese Art and its Possible Influence in the Pacific Basin*, (ed.) N. Barnard, iii, 533–96. New York, Intercultural Arts Press.

Gonda, J. 1965–6. *Les Religions de l'Inde*. Vols. ii–iii. Paris, Payot.

Goris, R. 1928, De Oud-Javaansche inscripties uit het Sriwedari-Museum le Soera-karta, Oudh. Versl., i–ii, pp. 63–70.

— 1938. Bali's tempelwezen, *Djǎwǎ*, xviii, 30–46.

Gorman, C. F. 1969. Hoabinhian: a pebble-tool complex with early plant associations in South East Asia, *Science*, no. 163, 671–3.

— 1970. Excavations at Spirit Cave: North Thailand, *AP*, iii, 79–107.

— 1971a. The Hoabinhian and After: subsistance patterns in Southeast Asia during the late Pleistocene and early Recent periods, *World Archaeology*, ii, 300–20.

— 1971b. *Guide to the National Museum, Bangkok*. 3rd edn. Bangkok, Fine Arts Department.

Gourou, P. 1936. *Les Paysans du Delta Tonkinois: Étude de géographie humaine*. Paris, Editions d'Art et d'Histoire.

Granet, M. 1930. *Chinese Civilisation*. London, Kegan Paul.

— 1951. *La Religion des Chinois*. Reprinted. Paris, Presses Universitaires de France.

Gray, B. 1949–50. China or Dong-son, *Oriental Art*, ii (3), 99–104.

Green, R. C. and Kelly, M. (eds.). 1971. *Studies of Oceanic Culture History*, vol. ii. (Pacific Anthropology Records, no. 12.) Honolulu, Bishop Museum.

Grist, D. H. 1959. *Rice*, 3rd edn. London, Longmans.

Groeneveldt, W. P. 1876 (1960). Notes on the Malay Archipelago and Malacca, com-piled from Chinese sources, *Verh. Kon. Bat. Gen.*, xxxix/v, 1876. Reprinted 1960.

Groslier, B. P. 1962. *Indochina: Art in the Melting-pot of Races*. London, Methuen.

— 1966. *Indochina* (trans. from French: 'Archaeologia Mundi' Series). London, F. Muller.

— 1973. Pour une géographie historique du Cambodge, *Cahiers d'Outre-Mer*, civ, 337–79.

— and Arthaud, J. 1966. *Angkor*. 2nd edn. London, Thames and Hudson.

Guehler, U. 1944. Studie Ueber Alte Metall-Trommeln, *Journal of the Thailand Research Society* (=*JSS*), xxxv (1), 17–71.

Guerin, C. and Mourer, C. 1970. Le *Rhinoceros sondiacus*, Desmaret du gisement néolithique de Loang Span, province de Battambang (Cambodge), *Ann. Fac. Sci. Phnom Penh*, 261–74.

Guthe, C. E. 1927. The University of Michigan Philippines Expedition, *American Anthropologist*, xxix.

Hall, D. G. E. 1968. *A History of South East Asia*. 3rd edn. London, Macmillan. (1st edn. 1955; 2nd edn. 1964.)

Harding, T. G. 1967. *Voyagers of the Vitiaz Strait* (American Ethnological Society Monographs, 44). Seattle, Univ. of Washington Press.

Harrisson, B. 1964. Recent Archaeological Discoveries in Malaysia, 1962–3: Borneo, *JMBRAS*, xxxvii, 192–200.

— 1967. A Classification of Stone Age Burials from Niah Great Cave, Sarawak, *SMJ*, n.s., xv, 126–200.

— and Harrisson, T. 1968. Magala: a series of Neolithic and Metal Age Burial Grottos at Sekaloh, Niah, Sarawak, *JMBRAS*, xli (2), 148–75.

Harrisson, T. 1957. The Great Cave of Niah: a preliminary report on Bornean Pre-history, *Man*, lvii, 161–6.

— 1958. The Great Cave, Sarawak, *The Archaeological Newsletter*, vi (9), 199–203.

— 1959. New Archaeological and Ethnological results from Niah Caves, Sarawak, *Man*, lix, 1–8.

— 1965. 'Turtle-Ware' from Borneo Caves, *SMJ*, n.s., xii, nos. 25–6, 63–8.

— 1966. Recent Archaeological Discoveries in Malaysia, 1965: East Malaysia and Brunei, *JMBRAS*, xxxix, 191–7.
— 1967*a*. Recent Archaeological Discoveries: East Malaysia and Brunei, *JMBRAS*, xl, 140–8.
— 1967*b*. Niah Caves: Progress Report to 1967, *SMJ*, n.s., xv, 95–6.
— 1968. Borneo's prehistoric 'turtle-ware' and 'Phallic-top' lidded pots, *AP*, xi.
— 1973. Megalithic Evidences in East Malaysia: an Introductory Summary; and Newly discovered Rock Carvings in Ulu Tomani, Sabah, *JMBRAS*, xlvi (1), 123–44.
— and O'Connor, S. J. 1969. *Excavations of the Prehistoric Iron Industry in West Borneo.* 2 vols. Ithaca, Cornell Univ.: S.E.A. Data Paper no. 72.
— 1970. *Gold and Megalithic Activity in Prehistoric and Recent West Borneo.* Ithaca, Cornell Univ.: S.E.A. Data Paper, no. 77.
Hassel, Elizabeth L. 1953. The Sri-Vijayan and Madjapahit Empires and the Theory of their Political Association with the Philippine Islands, *Philippine Social Sciences and Humanities Review*, xv (no. 1).
Heekeren, H. R. van. 1948. Prehistoric Discoveries in Siam, 1943–44, *Proc. of the Prehistoric Society*, xiv, 24–32.
— 1956*a*. Note on a proto-historic urn-burial site at Anjor, Java, *Anthropos*, li, 194–200.
— 1956*b*. The urn cemetery at Meblo, East Sumba (Indonesia), *Berita Dinas Purbakala*, iii, 194–200.
— 1958. *The Bronze–Iron Age of Indonesia.* The Hague, Nijhoff.
— 1972. *The Stone Age of Indonesia.* 2nd edn. The Hague, Koninklijk Institut voor Taal-Land, en Volkenkunde. (1st edn. 1957.)
— and Knuth, E. 1967. *Archaeological Excavations in Thailand, I: Sai-Yok, Stone-Age Settlements in Kanchanaburi Province.* Copenhagen, Munksgaard.
Heger, F. 1902. *Alte Metalltrommeln aus Südost-Asien.* 2 vols. Leipzig: K. von Hiersemann.
Heine-Geldern, R. 1928. Die Megalithen Sudostasiens und ihre Bedeutung fur die Klarung der Megalithenarage in Europa und Polynesien, *Anthropos*, xxiii, 276–315.
— 1932*a*. Urheimat und fruheste Wanderungen der Austronesier, *Anthropos*, xxvii, 543–619.
— 1932*b*. Bedeutung und Herkunft der altesten hinterindischen Metalltrommeln (Kesselgongs), *Asia Major*, viii, 519–37.
— 1932*c*. Uber Kris-Griffe und ihre mythischen Grundlagen, *Ostasiatische Zeitschrift*, n.f., viii, 256–92.
— 1934. Vorgesschichtliche Grundlagen der kolonialindischen Kunst, *Wiener Beiträge zur Kunst- und Kulturgeschichte Asiens*, viii, 5–40.
— 1935. The Archaeology and Art of Sumatra, in *Sumatra, Its History and People*, (ed.) E. M. Loeb, Vienna, Weiner Beitrage zur Kultur-Geschichte und Linguistik, vol. iii.
— 1936, Prehistoric Research in Indonesia, *Annual Bibliography of Indian Archaeology*, ix, 26–38.
— 1937. L'Art Prébouddhique de la Chine et de l'Asie du Sud-Est et son influence en Océanie, *Rev. des Arts Asiatiques*, xi.
— 1943. Conceptions of state and kingship in Southeast Asia, *Far Eastern Quarterly*, ii, 15–30.
— 1945. Prehistoric Research in the Netherlands Indies, in *Science and Scientists in the Netherlands Indies*, (eds.) Honig and F. Verdoorn. New York, Surinam, and Curacao.
— 1947. The Drum named Makalamau, *India Antiqua*, 1947, 167–79.
— 1966, Some Tribal Art Styles of Southeast Asia: an Experiment in Art History, in

The Many Faces of Primitive Art, (ed.) D. Fraser, 165–221. Englewood Cliffs, N.J.

Hervey de Saint-Denis, Marquis d' (trans.). 1876–83. *Ethnographie des peuples étrangers à la Chine de Ma Touan-lin*. 2 vols. Geneva.

Higham, C. F. W. 1972. Initial Model Formulation in *Terra Incognita*, in *Models in Archaeology*, (ed.) D. L. Clarke, pp. 453–76. London, Methuen.

— and Leach, B. F. 1971. An Early Center of Bovine Husbandry in Southeast Asia, *Science*, clxxii, 54–6.

— and Parker, R. H. 1971. *Prehistoric Investigations in North-East Thailand, 1969–70: a Preliminary Report*. Dunedin, Univ. of Otago.

Hirth, F. 1890. Uber hinterindische Bronzetrommeln, *T'oung Pao*, i, 137–42.

Ho Ping-ti. 1969. The Loess and the Origin of Chinese Agriculture, *American Historical Review*, lxxv, 1–36.

Ho, R. 1962. Physical Geography of the Indo–Australian Tropics, in *Symposium on the Impact of Man on Humid Tropics Vegetation*. Canberra.

Holle, K. F. 1882. *Tabel van Oud- en Nieuw-Indische Alphabetten*. n.p.

Hoop, A. N. J. Th. a Th. van der. 1932. *Megalithic Remains in South-Sumatra*. Zutphen, Thieme.

— 1940. A Prehistoric site near Lake Kerintji, Sumatra, in *Proc. of the Third Congress of Prehistorians of the Far East*, (eds.) F. N. Chasen and M. W. F. Tweedie. Singapore.

— 1941. *Catalogues der Prachistorische Verzamerling Bataviaasch Genootschaap*. Batavia.

Hooijer, C. R. 1969. Indonesian Prehistoric Tools: a catalogue of the Houbolt Collection, *South Asian Culture*, ii. Leiden, E. J. Brill.

Houbolt, J. II. 1940. Bijdrage tot de kennis van der verspreiding van palaeolithische artefacten in Nederlandsch-Indie, *TBG*, lxxx, 614–17.

Jacques, C. 1962. Notes sur l'inscription de la stèle de Vat Luong Kau, *Journal Asiatique*, ccl (2), 249–56.

— 1969. Etudes d'épigraphie cambodgienne III. Quatre fragments d'inscription récemment découverts au Cambodge. *BEFEO*, lvi, 70–3.

— 1969. Notes sur la stèle de Vo-canh, *BEFEO*, lv, 117–24.

— 1972. Sur l'emplacement du Royaume d'Aninditapura; and La Carière de Jayavarman II, *BEFEO*, lix, 193–205; 205–20.

Janse, O. R. T. 1931. Un groupe de bronzes anciens propres à l'Extrême-Asie méridionale, *BMFEA*, iii, 99–139.

— 1935. L'Empire des Steppes et les relations entre l'Europe et l'Extrême-Orient dans l'Antiquité, *Rev. Arts Asiatiques*, ix.

— 1941. An Archaeological expedition to Indo-China and the Philippines, *Harvard Journ. Asiatic Studies*, vi, 247–67.

— 1947, 1951. *Archaeological Research in Indo-China*, vols. i–ii. (Harvard-Yenching Institute Monographs, vii, x). Cambridge, Harvard Univ. Press.

— 1958. *Archaeological Research in Indo-China*, vol. iii. Bruges, St-Catherine Press.

— 1959. Some Notes on the Sa-Huynh Complex, *AP*, iii, 109–12.

— 1961. Vietnam, carrefour de peuples et de civilisations, *France–Asie*, xvii (no. 165), 1645–70.

— 1962, On the Origins of Traditional Vietnamese Music, *AP*, vi, 145–62.

Jaspan, M. A. 1964. *Folk Literature of South Sumatra: Redjang Ka-ga-nga Texts*. Canberra, Australian National Univ.

Jocano, F. L. 1967. Beyer's Theory on Filipino Prehistory and Culture: an alternative approach to the Problem, in *Studies in Philippine Anthropology*, (ed.) M. D. Zamora. Quezon City.

Jonker. 1885. *Een Oud-Javaarsch wetboek, vergeleken met Indische rechtsbronnen.*

Julien, S. (tr.). 1858. *Mémoires sur les contrées occidentales: II*. Paris.

Kaltenmark, M. 1948. Le dompteur des flots, *Han-hiue: Bull. du Centre d'Études Sinologiques de Pekin*, iii (1 et 2), 1–112.

Kandre, P. 1967. Autonomy and integration of social systems: the lu Mien ('Yao' or 'Man') Mountain Population and their Neighbours, in *Southeast Asian Tribes, Minorities and Nations*, (ed.) P. Kunstadter, ii, 583–638. Princeton, Univ. Press.

Karlgren, B. 1942. The Date of the Early Dong-Son Culture, *BMFEA*, xix, 1–28.

Kashkai, M. A. and Selimkhanov, I. R. 1954. On the chemical characteristics of some bronze objects from the jar burials of ancient Minguechaur, *Izvestia Akademii nauk Azerbaijanskoi SSR*, ii, 21–38 (in Russian).

Kaudern, W. 1938. *Megalithic Finds in Central Celebes*. Goteborg, privately.

Kauffmann, H. E. 1971. Stone Memorials of the Lawa (North West Thailand), *JSS*, lix, (i), 129–151.

Kempers, A. J. Bernet. 1959. *Ancient Indonesian Art*. Amsterdam, C. P. J. van der Peet; Cambridge, Harvard Univ. Press.

Kern, H. 1913. Inscriptie van Kota Kapoer, *BKI*, lxvii, 393–400.

— 1917. *Verspreide Geschriften, VII: Inscripties van den Indischen Archipel*. The Hague.

Kirsch, A. T. 1973. *Feasting and Social Oscillation: Religion and Society in Upland Southeast Asia*. Ithaca, Cornell Univ. S.E.A. Program.

Koenigswald, G. H. R. von. 1935. Das neolithicum der umgebung von Bandoeng, *TBG*, lxxv, 394–419.

— 1958. Preliminary Report on a newly-discovered Stone Age culture from Northern Luzon, Philippines, *AP*, ii (2).

Krom, N. J. 1923. *Inleiding tot de Hindoe-Javaansche Kunst*. 3 vols. The Hague, Martinus Nijhoff.

Kupper, H. 1930. Palaeolithische werktuigen uit Atjeh, *TNAG*, xlvii, 985–8.

Kurjack, B. and Sheldon, C. T. 1970. The Archaeology of Seminocho Cave in Lebak, Cotabato, *Silliman Journal*, xvii.

Kyuma, Kazutake. 1971. Climate of South and Southeast Asia according to Thornthwaite's Classification Scheme, *Tonan Ajia Kenkyu* (Kyoto), ix (no. 1), 136–58 (in English).

Lafont, P. B. 1956. Note sur un site néolithique de la Province de Pleiku, *BEFEO*, xlviii (1), 233–48.

Lamb, A. 1960. *Chandi Bukit Batu Pahat: a Report on the Excavation of an Ancient Temple in Kedah*. (Monographs on Southeast Asian Subjects, i.) Singapore, Eastern Univ. Press.

— 1961. Miscellaneous Papers on Early Hindu & Buddhist Settlement in Northern Malaya and Southern Thailand, *FMJ*, n.s., vi, 1–90.

— 1964. Early History, in *Malaysia, a Survey*, (ed.) Wang Gungwu, pp. 99–112. London, Pall Mall.

— 1965. Some Observations on Stone and Glass Beads in Early South-East Asia, *JMBRAS*, xxxviii (2), 87–124.

Leach, E. R. 1954, 1972. *Political Systems of Highland Burma*. London, Bell (French trans. 1972).

Leclère, A. 1904. Une campagne archéologique au Cambodge, *BEFEO*, iv, 737–49.

LeMay, R. S. 1954. *The Culture of South-East Asia: the Heritage of India*. London, Allen and Unwin.

Leur, J. C. van. 1967. *Indonesian Trade and Society: (Selected Studies on Indonesia*, i). 2nd edn. (Eng. trans. of writings in Dutch, 1934–47.) The Hague, Van Hoeve (1st edn. 1955).

Lévy, P. 1943. *Recherches Préhistorique dans la Région de Mlu Prei*. Hanoi, EFEO.

— 1948 Origine de la forme des tambours de bronze du Type I, *Dân Viêt-nam*, ii.

Lie Goan Liong. 1965. Palaeoanthropological results of the excavation at the coast of Lewoleba, Isle of Lomblen, *Anthropos*, lx, 609–24.

Linehan, W. 1928. Some discoveries on the Tembeling, *JMBRAS*, vi (4), 66–77.

— 1951. Traces of a Bronze Age culture associated with Iron Age implements in the regions of Klang and the Tembeling, Malaya, *JMBRAS*, xxiv (3), 1–59.

Ling Shun-sheng, 1955. New Interpretations of the Decorative Designs on the Bronze Drums of Southeast Asia, *Annals Academia Sinica* (Taipei), ii (pt. 1), 195–207.

Lingat, R. 1949. L'influence juridique de l'Inde au Champa et au Cambodge d'après l'épigraphie, *Journ. Asiatique*, ccxxxvii (2), 273–90.

Lo Hsiang-lin. 1967. The Tueh bronze drums, their manufacture and use, in *Symposium of Historical, Archaeological and Linguistic Studies on Southern China, South-East Asia and the Hong Kong Region*, (ed.) F. S. Drake, pp. 110–14. Hong Kong, Univ. Press.

Loewenstein, J. 1956 (1962). The Origin of the Malayan Metal Age, *JMBRAS*, xxix (2), 5–78.

Loofs, H. H. E. 1965. Some Remarks on 'Philippine Megaliths', *Asian Studies*, iii, (Manila) 393–402.

— 1970. A Brief Account of the Thai–British Archaeological Expedition, 1965–1970, *APAO*, v, 177–84.

— and Watson, W. 1970. The Thai–British Archaeological Expedition: a Preliminary Report on the work of the Second Season, 1967, *JSS*, lviii (2), 67–78.

Luce, G. H. 1925. Countries Neighbouring Burma, *JBRS*, xiv (2), 138–205.

— 1959. Introduction to the Comparative Study of Karen Languages, *JBRS*, xlii (1), 1–18.

— (trans.). 1961. *The Man Shu: Book of the Southern Barbarians*. Ithaca, Cornell Univ. (S.E.A. Program Data Paper, no. xliv.)

— 1969. *Old Burma—Early Pagan*. 3 vols. New York, Augustin.

Lunet de Lajonquière, E. 1901. *Atlas archéologique de l'Indo-Chine*. Paris, Leroux.

— 1902–11. *Inventaire Descriptif des Monuments du Cambodge*. 3 vols. Paris, Imp. Nat.

Lyons, E. 1973. Two Dvaravati Figurines, *JSS*, lxi (1), 193–201.

Ma Tuan-lin (Ma Duanlin). *See* Hervey de Saint-Denis, Marquis d'.

Macdonald, A. W. 1953. Une note sur les Mégalithes Tibetains, *Journal Asiatique*, ccxli, 63–76.

Majumdar, R. C. La Paléographie des Inscriptions du Champa, *BEFEO*, xxxii, 127–39.

Malleret, L. 1942. *Pour Comprendre la Sculpture Bouddhique et Brahmanique en Indochine*. Saigon, Portail.

— 1956. Objets de Bronze communs au Cambodge à la Malaisie et à l'Indonésie, *Artibus Asiae*, xix, pt. ii (in memory of P. Dupont), 308–27.

— 1957. A propos d'une poterie du British Museum, *Artibus Asiae*, xx, 50–4.

— 1959a. Ouvrages circulaires en terre dans l'Indochine méridionale, *BEFEO*, xlix (2), 409–34.

— 1959b. Quelques poteries de Sa-Huynh dans leurs rapports avec divers sites du Sud-Est de l'Asie, *AP*, iii, 113–120.

— 1959–63. *L'Archéologie du Delta du Mékong*. 4 vols: I: L'Exploration Archéologique et les Fouilles d'Oc-Eo; II: La Civilisation Materielle d'Oc-Eo; III: La Culture de Fou-nan; IV: Le Cisbassac. Paris, EFEO.

— 1963a. Aperçu de la glyptique d'Oe-co, *BEFEO*, xliv, 189–99.

— 1963b. Pierres gravées et cachets de divers pays du Sud-est d'Asie, *BEFEO*, li, 99–116.

— 1966. Une Nouvelle Statue préangkorienne de Sūrya dans le Bas-Mékong, in *Essays Offered to G. H. Luce*, ii, 109–20. Ascona, Artibus Asiae Press.

— 1969 (1971). Histoire abrégée de l'archéologie indochinoise jusqu'à 1950, *AP*, xii, 43–68.

Mansuy, H. 1902. *Stations Préhistorique de Samrong Sen et de Longprao*. Hanoi.

— 1923. Résultats de Nouvelles Recherches effectués sur le gisement préhistorique de Samrong Sen, *Mém. Soc. Géol. Indochine*, xi (1).

— 1931. *La Prehistoire en Indochine: Resumé de l'état de nos connaissances*. Macon, Protat Frères.

— and Colani, M. 1925. Contribution à l'étude de la préhistoire de l'Indochine, VII: Néolithic inférieur (Bacsonien) et Néolithique supérieur dans le Haut Tonkin, *Mém. Soc. Géol. Indochine*, xii (1).

Maringer, J. 1955. Graber und Steindenkmaler in der Mongolei, *Monumenta Serica*, xiv, 303–39.

— and Verhoeven, Th. 1970. Die Steinartefakte aus Stegodon-Fossilschicht von Mengeruda auf Flores, *Anthropos*, xlv, 229–47.

Marschall, W. 1968. Metallurgie und fruhe Besiedlungsge schichte Indonesiens, *Ethnologia*, n.f., iv, 31–263.

Marshall, H. I. 1922. *The Karen People of Burma, a study in Anthropology and Ethnology*. Ohio, Univ. of Columbus.

Maspero, G. 1928. *Le Royaume de Champa*. Paris, Brussels.

Maspéro, H. 1918. Études d'Histoire d'Annam: IV. Le Royaume de Van-Lang; VI. La Frontière de l'Annam et du Cambodge du VIIIe au XIVe siècle, *BEFEO*, xviii (3), 1–10, 29–36.

Matthews, J. M. 1966. A Review of 'Hoabinhian' in Indochina, *AP*, ix, 86–95.

Mead, M. 1930. Melanesian middlemen, *Natural History*, xxx, 115–30.

— 1937. The Manus of the Admiralty Islands, in *Cooperation and Competition among Primitive Peoples*, (ed.) M. Mead. New York, McGraw-Hill.

Mills, J. P. 1922. *The Lhota Nagas*. London.

Moens, J. L. 1937. Crivijaya, Yava en Kataha, *TBG*, lxxvii, 317–486.

Mohr, E. C. J. 1945. The relations between soil and population density in the Netherlands Indies, in *Science and Scientists in the Netherlands Indies*, (eds.) P. Honig and F. Verdoorn. New York, Board for the Netherlands Indies, Surinam and, Curacao.

Morris, T. C. 1935. The Prehistoric Stone Implements of Burma, *JBRS*, xxv (1), 1–39.

Mourer, C. and Mourer, R. 1970. The prehistoric industry of Laang Spean, Province of Battambang, Cambodia, *APAO*, v (2), 127–46.

— 1969. Note préliminaire sur la présence d'une industrie préhistorique dans la grotte de Laang Spean, Province de Battambang, Cambodge, *Proc. Eighth Congr. of Anthrop. and Ethn. Sci.*, iii, 141-2. (Tokyo)

— and Thommeret, Y. 1970. Premières datations absolues de l'habitat préhistorique de la grotte de Laang Spean, province de Battambang, Cambodge, *Comptes-Rendues, Acad. Sci.*, cclxx, 471–3.

Movius, H. L. 1948. The Lower Paleolithic Cultures of Southern and Eastern Asia, *American Philosophical Society Transactions*, n.s., xxxviiii (pt. 4), 329–420.

— 1954-5. Palaeolithic Archaeology in Southern and Eastern Asia, exclusive of India, *Cahiers d'Hist. Mondiale*, ii, 257–82.

Mulvaney, D. J. 1970. The Patjitanian Industry: Some Observations, *Mankind*, vii (no. 3).

— and Soejono, R. P. 1970a. Archaeology in Sulawesi, Indonesia, *Antiquity*, xlv, 26–33.

— 1970b. The Australian–Indonesian Archaeological Expedition to Sulawesi, *AP*, xiii, 163–77.

Mus, P. 1933. Cultes indiens et indigènes au Champa, *BEFEO*, xxxiii, 367–410.

Myint Aung. 1970. The Excavations at Halin, *JBRS*, liii (2), 55–64.

Naersson, F. H. van. 1937. Twee koperen oorkonden van Balitung in het Koloniaal Instituut de Amsterdam, *BKI*, xcv, 441–61.

Needham, J. 1964. *The Development of Iron and Steel Technology in China*. London: The Newcomen Society.

Nielsen, E. 1962. The Thai–Danish Prehistoric Expedition, 1960–62, *JSS*, l (1) 7–14.

Ng, R. 1968. Rice Cultivation and Rural Settlement Density in Northeast Thailand, *Tijdschrift voor Econ. en Soc. Geografie*, xxxv, 200–10.

O'Connor, S. J. 1966*a*. Ritual Deposit Boxes in Southeast Asian Sanctuaries, *Artibus Asiae*, xxviii, 53–60.

— 1966*b*. Satingphra: an expanded chronology, *JMBRAS*, xxxix (1), 137–44.

— 1968. Si Chan: an early settlement in Peninsular Thailand, *JSS*, lvi, 1–18.

— 1972. *Hindu Gods of Peninsular Siam*. Ascona, Artibus Asiae Press.

Ooi, J. B. 1963. *Land, People and Economy in Malaya*. London, Longmans.

Ormeling, F. J. 1955. *The Timor Problem*. Djarkarta and Groningen, J. B. Wolters.

Orsoy de Flines, E. W. van. 1972. *Guide to the Ceramic Collectoin*. 3rd edn. Jakarta, Mus. Pusat.

Parker, R. H. 1968. Review of P. Sørensen and T. Hatting: *Archaeological Excavations in Thailand*, ii, *Journal of the Polynesian Society*, lxxvii, 307–13.

Parmentier, H. 1909. *Inventaire descriptif des Monuments Cams de l'Annam*. 2 vols. Paris: EFEO.

— 1917. Ancien Tombeaux au Tonkin, *BEFEO*, xvii (no. 1), 1–32.

— 1918. Ancient Tambours de Bronze, *BEFEO*, xviii (no. 1), 1–30.

— 1922. *Sculptures cames du Musée de Tourane*. Paris: EFEO.

— 1923. Notes d'archéologie Indochoise, I–VI, *BEFEO*, xxiii, 267–300.

— 1924. Notes d'Archéologie Indochinoise, VII: Dépôts de Jarres à Sa-Huỳnh, Qu'ang-Ngái, *BEFEO*, xxiv, 325–43.

— 1927. *L'Art Khmer Primitif*. 2 vols. Paris: EFEO.

— 1928. Vestiges Mégalithiques à Xuân-Lôc, *BEFEO*, xxviii, 479–85.

— 1932. Notes d'Archéologie Indochinoise, IX: Nouveaux Tambours de Bronze, *BEFEO*, xxxii, 171–82.

Patte, E. 1925. 'Le kjökkenmödding néolithique du Bâu-Tro, Tam-Tòa, près de Dông-Hoi (Annam), *Bull. Serv. Géol. Indochine*, xiv.

— 1936. L'Indochine Préhistorique, *Rev. Anthropologique*, xlvi, 277–314.

— 1965. Les ossements du kjökkenmödding de Da-bút (province de Thanh Hoá), *BSEI*, n.s., xl, 5–201.

Peacock, B. A. V. 1959. A Short Description of Malayan Prehistoric Pottery, *AP*, iii, (2), 121–56.

— 1964*a*. The Kodiang pottery cones: tripod pottery in Malaya and Thailand, with a note on the Bukit Tengku Lembu Blackware, *FMJ*, xiii, 4–20.

— 1964*b*. Recent Archaeological Discoveries in Malaysia, 1962–63, *JMBRAS*, xxxvii (2), 201–6.

— 1965*a*. The drums at Kampong Sungai Lang, *Malaya in History*, x (1), 3–15.

— 1965*b*. A Preliminary Note on the Dong-son Bronze Drums from Kampong Sungai Lang, *FMJ*, n.s., ix, 1–3.

— 1965*c*. Recent Archaeological Discoveries in Malaysia, 1964, *JMBRAS*, xxxviii (1), 248–55.

— 1966. Recent Archaeological Discoveries in Malaysia, 1965, *JMBRAS*, xxxix (1), 198–201.

— 1967. Two Don-son drums from Kuala Trengganu, *Malaya in History*, x (2), 26–31.

— 1971. Early Cultural Development in South-East Asia with Special Reference to the Malay Peninsula, *APAO*, vi (2), 107–23.

— and Dunn, F. L. 1968. Recent Archaeological Discoveries in Malaysia, 1967: West Malaysia, *JMBRAS*, xli (1), 171–9.

Pearson, R. 1973. Radiocarbon dates from China, *Antiquity*, lxvii, 141–3.

Pelliot, R. 1902. Mémoires sur les coutumes du Cambodge, *BEFEO*, ii, 123–77.

— 1903. Le Fou-nan, *BEFEO*, iii, 248–303.

— 1904. Deux Itinéraires de Chine en Inde à la Fin du VIIIe Siècle, *BEFEO*, iv, 131–413.

Pelzer, K. J. 1963. Physical and human resource patterns, in *Indonesia* (ed.) R. McVey, pp. 1–23. New Haven, Yale Univ. Press.

Pendleton, R. L. 1943. Land Use in Northeastern Thailand, *Geog. Rev.* (A.G.S.), xxxiii, 15–41.

Picard, C. 1955. La lampe Alexandrine de P'ong Tuk, *Artibus Asiae*, xviii, 137–48.

— 1956. A Figurine of Lysipian type from the Far East: the Tra-Vinh Bronze 'Dancer', *Artibus Asiae*, xix, 342–52.

Pigeaud, Th. G. Th. 1967–70. *Literature of Java: Catalogue Raisonnée of Javanese Manuscripts in University of Leiden, etc.* 3 vols. The Hague: Nijhoff.

Piriya Krairiksh. 1973. Provisional Classification of Painted Pottery from Ban Chieng, *Artibus Asiae*, xxx (1/2), 145–50.

Pisit Charoenwongsa. 1973. *Ban Chieng*. Bangkok (in Thai and English).

Pittioni, R. 1969. 'Spektralanalytische Untersuchungen von Bronzen aus dem nordwestlichen Thailand, *Archaeologia Austriaca*, xlv, 77–9.

Playfair, A. 1909. *The Garos*. London, David Nutt.

Poerbatjaraka, R. M. N. 1940. 'Oorkonde van Krtarajāsa uit 1296 A.D. (Penang-grengan), *Inscripties van Ned.-Indie*, 33–49.

— 1958. Crivijaya, de Cailendra en de Sanjayavamca, *BKI*, cxiv, 254–64.

Porée-Maspero, E. 1962–9. *Étude sur les Rites agraiers des Cambodgeins.* 3 vols. Paris: Mouton.

Postma, A. 1970. *Treasure of a Minority: the Ambahan, a poetic expression of Southern Mindoro.* (n.p.)

— 1972. Contemporary Mangyan Scripts, *Philippines Journal of Linguistics*, 1972, 1–12.

Rao, T. A. Gopinatha. 1914–16. *Elements of Hindu Iconography.* 2 vols. Madras, Law Printing House.

Rawson, P. S. 1967. *The Art of Southeast Asia.* London, Thames and Hudson.

Romondt, V. R. van. 1951. *Peninggalan-peninggalan purbakala di Gunung Penanggungan.* Jakarta, Dinas Purbakala Republik Indonesia.

Rothpletz, W. 1951. Alte Siedlungsplatze bei Bandung (Java) und die Entdeckung Bronzezeitticher Gussformen, in *Sudseestudien*, pp. 79–126. Basel, Mus. fur Volkerkunde.

Rouffaer, G. P. 1909. Note in *Notulen Koninklijk Bataviaasch Genootschap*, 1909, p. lxxx.

Rudolph, R. C. 1960. Regional Reports VI. China Mainland: an Important Dong-son site in Yunnan, *AP*, iv, 41–9.

Sahai, Sachchidanand. 1970. *Les Institutions Politiques et l'Organisation Administrative du Cambodge Ancien VIe–XIIIe.* Paris, EFEO.

Sahlins, M. 1963. Poor man, rich man, big man, chief: political types in Melanesia and Polynesia, *Comparative Studies in Society and History*, v, 285–303.

— 1973. *Stone Age Economics.* Chicago and New York, Aldine-Atherton.

Sande, G. A. J. van der. 1907. Ethnography and Anthropology of New Guinea, *Nova Guinea*, iii, 225–6.

Sastri, K. A. Nilakanta. 1940. Sri Vijaya, *BEFEO*, xl (2), 239–314.

— 1949a. *History of Sri Vijaya.* (Sir William Meyer Lectures, 1946–7.) Madras, Univ. of Madras.

— 1949b. *South Indian Influences in the Far East.* Bombay, Hind Kitaba.

— 1949c. Takua Pa and its Tamil Inscription, *JMBRAS*, xxii (1), 25–30.

Saurin, E. 1940. Stations Préhistoriques du Qui Chàn et de Thuong Xuân: Nord-Annam, *Proc. of Third Congress of Prehistorians of the Far East, Singapore, 1938*, (ed.) F. N. Chasen and M. F. W. Tweedie. Singapore.

— 1957. 'Outillage hoabinhien à Giap Khâu, Port-Courbet (Nord Viêt-Nam), *BEFEO*, xlviii, 581–92.

— 1963. La Station Préhistorique de Hàng-Gòn, près de Xuân-Lôc, Viêt-Nam, *AP*, vi; and *BEFEO*, li, (2), 433–52.

— 1964. Nouveaux vestiges préhistoriques à Côn Son (Poulo-Condore), *BSEI*, n.s., xxxix, 7–13.

— 1966. Un site archéologique à Dâu-Giây, province de Long-Khanh, Sud Viêt-Nam, *Viêt-Nam Khao-Cô Tâp-San*, iv, 90–104.

— 1968. Nouvelles Observations Préhistoriques à l'Est de Saigon, *BSEI*, n.s., xliii, 1–17.

— 1969. Les Recherches Préhistoriques au Cambodge, Laos et Viet-Nam (1877–1966), *AP*, xii, 27–42.

— 1971. Le paléolithique des environs de Xuân-Lôc, *BSEI*, n.s., xlvi, 49–70.

Savina, F. M. 1930. *Histoire des Miao*. Hong Kong, Impr. de la Société des Missions Etrangères de Paris.

Scheans, D. J., Hutterer, K. L., and Cherry, R. L. 1970. A Newly Discovered Blade Tool Industry from the Central Philippines, *AP*, xiii, 179-81.

Schnitger, F. N. 1936. De tempel van Simangambat (Zuid Tapanoeli), *TBG*, lxxvi, 334–5.

— 1937. *The Archaeology of Hindoo Sumatra* (Supplement to *Internationales Archiv fur Ethnographie*, xxxv). Leiden.

— 1939. *Forgotten Kingdoms in Sumatra*. Leiden, E. J. Brill.

— 1939–42. Les terrasses Mégalithiques de Java, *Rev. Arts Asiatiques*, xiii.

Schrieke, B. J. O. 1957. *Indonesian Sociological Studies, Selected Writings, II: Ruler and Realm in Early Java*. The Hague, Van Hoeve.

Schurmann, H. M. E. 1931. Khokkenmoddinger und Palaeolithikum in Nord-Sumatra, *TNAG*, xlviii, 905–23.

Scott, J. G. 1900. *Gazetteer of Upper Burma and the Shan states*. 2 vols. Rangoon.

Seidenfaden, E. 1922. Complément à l'Inventaire déscriptif des Monuments du Cambodge pour les quatre provinces du Siam Occidental, *BEFEO*, xxii, 55–100. (With notes by G. Coedès.)

Shorto, H. L. 1971. *A dictionary of the Mon inscriptions from the sixth to the sixteenth centuries*. London, Oxford Univ. Press.

Sieveking, G. de G. 1955. Excavations at Gua Cha, Kelantan, 1954, *FMJ*, i–ii, 75–138.

— 1956. Recent Archaeological Discoveries in Malaya, 1955, *JMBRAS*, xxix (1), 200–11.

— 1956 (1962). The Iron Age Collections of Malaya, *JMBRAS*, xxix (2), 79–138.

— 1962. The Prehistoric Cemetery at Bukit Tengku Lembu, Perlis, *FMJ*, vii, 25–54.

Shutler, R. 1961. Peopling of the Pacific in the light of Radiocarbon Dating, *AP*, v (2), 207–12.

Sircar, D. C. (ed.). 1965. *Select Inscriptions bearing on Indian History and Civilization*, i. Calcutta Univ. Press.

Sivaramamurti, C. 1952. Indian Epigraphy and South Indian Scripts, *Bull. Madras Mus.*, n.s., g.s., iv.

Smith, J. 1961. Art and archaeology of Viêt-Nam in Washington, *France-Asie*, xvii (no. 165), 1789–93.

Soejono, R. P. 1962. Indonesia, 1959–61 (Regional Report), *AP*, vi, 34–43.

— 1969 (1971). The History of Prehistoric Research in Indonesia to 1950, *AP*, xii, 69–91.

— 1970. The study of Prehistory in Indonesia: retrospect and prospect, *AP*, xiii, 11–16.

Soekmono, R. 1965. Archaeology and Indonesian History, in *Introduction to Indonesian Historiography*, (ed.) Soedjatmoko. Ithaca, Cornell Univ. Press.

Solheim, W. G., II. 1954. The Makabog burial-jar site, *Philippines Journal of Science*, lxxxiii.

— 1958. The Kalanay Pottery complex in the Philippines. *Artibus Asiae*, xx, 279–88.
— 1959 (1961). Introduction to Sa-huynh; Sa-huynh-related pottery in Southeast Asia; and Further notes on the Kalanay Pottery Complex in the Philippines, *AP*, iii, 97–108, 157–65, 177–88.
— 1960. Jar Burial in the Babuyan and Batanes Islands and in the Central Philippines, *Philippines Journal of Science*, lxxxix, 115–48.
— 1963. Formosan Relationships with Southeast Asia, *AP*, vii, 251–60.
— 1964a. *Archaeology of the Central Philippines, a Study chiefly of the Iron Age and its Relationships*. Manila, National Institute of Science and Technology.
— 1964b. Further relationships of the Sa-huynh-Kalanay pottery tradition, *AP*, viii, 196–211.
— 1964c. Pottery Manufacture in Sting Mar and Bang Nong Sua Kin Ma, Thailand, *JSS*, lii (2), 151–61.
— 1964d. *See* Chang, K. C., Grace, G. W., and Solheim, W. G., II.
— 1965. A preliminary report on a new pottery complex in northeastern Thailand, in *Felicitation volumes of Southeast-Asian Studies*, ii, 249–54. Bangkok, Siam Society.
— 1966a. Prehistoric Archaeology in Thailand, *Antiquity*, xl, 8–16.
— 1966b. Thailand (Regional Report), *AP*, ix, 36–44.
— 1967a. The Sa-huynh-Kalanay Pottery Tradition, Past and Future Research, *Studies in Philippine Archaeology*, 151–74.
— 1967b. Southeast Asia and the West, *Science*, clvii, 896–902.
— 1967c. Notes on pottery manufacture near Luang Prabang, Laos, *JSS*, lv, 81–6.
— 1967d. Recent archaeological discoveries in Thailand, in *Archaeology at the Eleventh Pacific Science Congress*, (ed.) W. G. Solheim II, 47–54. Honolulu, Social Science Research Institute, Asian and Pacific Archaeology Series no. 1.
— 1967e. Molds for Bronze Casting found in N.E. Thailand, *JSS*, lv (1), 87–91.
— 1968. Early Bronze in Northeastern Thailand, *Current Anthropology*, ix (1), 59–62.
— 1969a. Reworking Southeast Asian Prehistory, *Paideuma*, 125–39. (Reprinted as *SSRI Reprints*, no. 34, Honolulu, 1970.)
— 1969b Review of *Archaeological Excavations in Thailand, II: Ban Kao, Part 1*, by P Sørensen and T. Hatting, *AP*, xii, 127–30.
— 1970a. Recent archaeological work in Thailand and the Philippines, *Boletin da Sociedade de Geografia de Lisboa*, xxxviii, 223–8.
— 1970b. Northern Thailand, Southeast Asia, and World Prehistory, *AP*, xiii, 45–57.
— 1972a. Prehistoric Pottery of Southeast Asia, in *Early Chinese Art and its Possible Influence in the Pacific Basin*, (ed.) N. Barnard, ii, 507–32. New York, Intercultural Arts Press.
— 1972b. An Earlier Agricultural Revolution, *Scientific American*, ccvi (4), 34–41.
— and Gorman, C. E. 1966. Archaeological Salvage Program: Northeastern Thailand: First Season, *JSS*, liv (2), 111–81.
— Harrisson, B., and Wall, L. 1961. Niah 'Three Colour Ware' and Related Pottery from Borneo, *AP*, iii (2), 167–76; also *SMJ*, x, 227–37.
— Parker, R. H., and Bayard, D. T. 1966. *Archaeological survey and excavations at Ban Nadi, Ban Sao Lao, Pimai No. 1*. Honolulu, Dept. of Anthropology, Univ. of Hawaii. (Mimeo)
— — — and Higham, C. F. W. To appear. *Prehistoric Excavations at Non Nok Tha, Northeastern Thailand, 1965–68*. Honolulu, Hawaii Univ. Press. (In preparation.)
Sood Sangvichien, et al. 1969. *Archaelogical Excavations in Thailand, III: Ban Kao, pt. 2: the Prehistoric Thai Skeletons*. Copenhagen, Munksgaard.
Soper, A. C. 1959. *Literary Eàidence for Early Buddhist Art in China*. Ascona, Artibus Asiae Press.
Sørensen, P. 1962. The Thai–Danish Prehistoric Expedition 1960–1962, *Folk*, iv, 28–45.
— 1964. Ban Kao, *JSS*, lii (1), 75–98.

— 1965. The Shaman's Grave, in *Felicitation Volumes of Southeast-Asian Studies*, ii, 303–18. Bangkok, Siam Society.

— 1972*a*. The Neolithic Cultures of Thailand (and North Malaysia) and their Lungshanoid Relationship, in *Early Chinese Art and its Possible Influence in the Pacific Basin*, (ed.) N. Barnard, vol. ii, 459–506. New York, Intercultural Arts Press.

— 1972*b*. The Rudder, *EAC News*, vol. xv, (6), 13–17.

— 1973. The Kettledrums from Ban Gaw, Chiang Mai, *Journal of the Northern Thai Society*, i.

— 1974. Prehistoric Iron Implements from Thailand, *AP*, xvi, 134–73.

— To appear. The Kettledrums from the Ongbah Cave, in *Archaeological Excavation in Thailand, IV*. Copenhagen. (In press.)

— and Hatting, T. 1967. *Archaeological Investigations in Thailand, II: Ban Kao, part 1: the Archaeological Materials from the Burials*. Copenhagen, Munksgaard.

Soulié, G. and Tchang Yi-tch'ou. 1908. Les barbares soumis du Yunnan, chapitre du Tien-hi, *BEFEO*, viii, 149–176, 333–79.

Stargardt, J. 1973. The Srivijayan Civilization in Southern Thailand, *Antiquity*, xlvii, 225–9.

Stein, R. A. 1942. A propos des sculptures de boeufs en métal, *BEFEO*, xlii, 135–8.

— 1947. Le Lin-yi, sa localisation, sa contribution à la Formation du Champa, et ses liens avec la Chine, *Han-hiue: Bull. du Centre d'Études Sinologiques de Pekin*, ii, 1–335.

Stein-Callenfels, P. V. van. 1932. Note préliminaire sur les Fouilles dans l'abri-sous-roche du Guwa Lawa à Sampung, in *Homage du Service Archéologique des Indes Nederlandaises au Premier Congrès des Préhistoriens d'Extrême-Orient à Hanoi, 1932*, pp. 16–29. Batavia.

— 1934. De inscriptie van Soekaboemi, *Med. Kon. Ak. Wet: Afd. Lett.*, lxxviii (4), 115–30.

— 1936. The Melanesoid Civilisation of Eastern Asia, *BRM*, Ser. B, i.

— 1937. The Age of Bronze Kettle Drums, *BRM*, Ser. B, i.

— 1951. Prehistoric Sites on the Karama River, *Journal of East Asiatic Studies*, i, 82–97.

Stern, P. 1942. *L'Art du Champa et Son Evolution*. Paris, Musée Guimet.

Stuart, A. B. Cohen. 1875. *Kawi Oorkonden in Facsimile*. 2 vols.

Stutterheim, W. F. 1925. Een oorkonde op koper uit het Singasarische, *TBG*, lxv, 208–28.

— 1929. De outerdom van Tjandi Sewu, *BKI*, lxxxv, 491–6.

— 1934. Een vrij overzetveer te Wanagiri (M.N.) in A.D. 903, *TBG*, lxxiv, 269–95.

— 1938. Note in *Jaarboek Batavie Gen.*, v, 119–21.

— 1940. Oorkonde van Balitung uit 905 A.D. (Rasdoesari I); Oorkonde van den Ācārya Monidra uit 885 A.D. (Rasdoesari II), *Inscripties van Ned. Indie*, i, 3–32.

— 1929 (1956). *Baraboedoer, Naam, verm en beteckenia*. Weltevredent, G. Kolff & Co. (English translation in *Studies in Indonesian Archaeology*. The Hague, Nijhoff. 1956.)

Subhadradis Diskul, M. C. 1956. Muang Fa Daed, an ancient town in North East Thailand, *Artibus Asiae*, xix, 362–7.

— 1971. *Art in Thailand, a Brief History*. 2nd edn. Bangkok.

Suggs, R. C. 1960. *The Island Civilisations of Polynesia*. New York, New American Library.

— 1961. The Archaeology of Naku, Marquesas Islands, French Polynesia, *Anthropological Papers of American Museum of Natural History*, xlix (pt. 1).

Sullivan, M. 1956. Archaeology in the Philippines, *Antiquity*, xxx, 68–79.

Supajanya, T. and Vallibhotama, S. 1972. The Need for an Inventory of Ancient Sites for Anthropological Research in Northeastern Thailand, *Southeast Asian Studies*, x (no. 2). (Japan)

Sutayasa, M. 1972. Notes on the Buni pottery complex, northwest Java, *Mankind*, viii, 182–4.

Tanner, N. 1972. Minangkabau, in *Ethnic Groups of Insular Southeast Asia*, (ed.) F. M. Lebar, et al. New Haven, Human Relations Area Files Press.

Tibbets, G. R. 1956. Pre-Islamic Arabia and South-East Asia, *JMBRAS*, xxix (3), 182–208.

Tichelman, G. L. 1963. Ethnographical bronze objects from Lake Sentani District, in *Sixth Int. Cong. Anthrop. and Ethnol. Sciences, 1960*, 645–51. Paris.

Tombrinck, E. P. 1870. Hindoe-monumenten in de Boven-Landen van Palenbang, *TBG*, xix, 1–45.

Trân vân Tôt, 1969. Introduction à l'art ancien du Viet-nam, *BSEI*, n.s., xliv, 1–104.

Treistman, J. M. 1972. *The Prehistory of China: an Archaeological Exploration.* Newton Abbot, David and Charles.

Trubner, H. 1959. A Bronze Dagger-axe, *Artibus Asiae*, xxii, 170–8.

Tweedie, M. W. F. 1953. *The Stone Age in Malaya. JMBRAS*, xxvi (2).

— 1965. *Prehistoric Malaya*. 3rd edn. Singapore, Eastern Univ. Press.

United Nations. 1968. *Atlas of Physical, Economic and Social Resources of the Lower Mekong Basin* (Prepared for a Committee of ECAFE). New York.

Vavilov, N. I. 1926. *Studies on the Origin of Cultivated Plants*. Leningrad, Inst. App. Bot. and Plant Breeding.

Veerapan Maleipan. 1973. 'Sab Champa', *Archaeology*, iii (no. 4). (Bangkok) (Thai with English summary.)

Verhoeven, Th. 1956. The Wan Wati (picture rock) of Flores, *Anthropos*, li, 1077–9

— 1968. Vorgeschichtliche Forschungen auf Flores, Timor and Sumba, *Anthropos*, xxi, 393–403.

Verhoeven, Th. and Heine Geldern, R. 1954. Bronzegerate auf Flores, *Anthropos*, xlix, 683–4.

Viekke, B. H. M. (1959 (1965). *Nusantara—a history of Indonesia*. Revised edn. (reprinted 1965). The Hague, Van Hoeve. (1st edn. Cambridge, Mass., 1944.)

Vogel, J. Ph. 1912. Prakrit Inscriptions from a Buddhist Site in Nagarjunakonda, *Epigr. Ind.*, xx, 16–26.

— 1918. The Yupa inscriptions of King Mulavarman from Koetei (East Borneo), *BKI*, lxxiv, 167–232.

— 1925. The Oldest Sanskrit Inscriptions of Java, *Publ. Oudh. Dienst*, i, 13–35.

Vogler, E. B. 1949. *De Monsterkop uit het omlijstingsormament van tempeldoorgaugen en nissen in de Hindoe-Javaanse Bouwkunst*. Leiden, E. J. Brill.

— 1952. De stichtingstojd van de tjandi's Gunung Wukir en Badut, *BKI*, cviii, 313–46.

— 1953.Ontwikkeling van de gewijde bouwkunst in het Hindoeistische Midden-Java, *BKI*, cix, 249–72.

Vroklage, B. A. G. 1953. *Ethnographie der Belu in Zentral-Timor*. 3 vols. Leiden, E. J. Brill.

Wagner, F. A. 1959. *Indonesia: the Art of an Island Group*. (Eng. trans.) London, Methuen.

Wales, H. G. Quaritch. 1935. A newly explored route of Ancient Indian Cultural Expansion, *Indian Arts and Letters*, ix, 1–31.

— 1936a. Further Excavations at P'ong Tuk, *Indian Arts and Letters*, x, 42–8.

— 1936b. The Exploration of Sri Deva, *Indian Arts and Letters*, x, 61–99.

— 1940. Archaeological Researches, *JMBRAS*, xviiii (1), 1–85.

— 1953. *The Mountain of God: a study in Early Religion and Kingship*. London, B. Quaritch.

— 1957a. *Prehistory and Religion in South East Asia*. London, B. Quaritch.

— 1957*b*. An Early Buddhist Civilisation in Eastern Siam, *JSS*, xlv, 42–60.
— 1961. *The making of Greater India*. London, B. Quaritch. (1st edn. 1951.)
— 1969. *Dvaravati: the Earliest Kingdom of Siam, 6th to 11th Century, A.D.* London, B. Quaritch.
Wall, L. 1962. Prehistoric Earthenwares: Pottery Common to Sarawak and Malaya, *SMJ*, x, 417–27.
Wang Gung-Wu, 1958. *The Nanhai Trade: a Study of the Early History of Chinese Trade in the South China Sea*. *JMBRAS*, xxxi, (2).
Watson, R. 1969. Pacoh names, in *Mon-Khmer Studies III* (Linguistic Circle of Saigon and the Summer Institute of Linguistics). Saigon.
Watson, W. 1962. *Ancient Chinese Bronzes*. London, Faber; Rutland: Tuttle.
— 1966. *Early Civilization in China*. London, Thames and Hudson.
— 1968. The Thai–British Expedition, *Antiquity*, xlii (168), 302–6.
— 1970. Dongson and the kingdom of Tien, in *Readings in Asian Topics*, (Scandinavian Institute of Asian Studies, Monograph Series, i), pp. 45–71. Lund.
— 1971. *Cultural Frontiers in Ancient East Asia*. (Rhind Lectures, 1965–6.) Edinburgh Univ. Press.
— and Loofs, H. H. E. 1967. The Thai–British Archaeological Expedition: a Preliminary Report on the work of the First Season, 1965–66, *JSS*, lv (2) 237-62.
Wheatley, P. 1961. *The Golden Khersonese: Studies in the Historical Geography of the Malay Peninsula to A.D. 1500*. Kuala Lumpur, Univ. of Malaya.
— 1964. *Impressions of the Malay Peninsula in Ancient Times*. Singapore, Eastern Univ. Press.
— 1971. *The Pivot of the Four Quarters: a Preliminary Enquiry into the Origins and Character of the Ancient Chinese City*. Edinburgh Univ. Press.
Weins, H. J. 1967. *Han Chinese Expansion in South China*. New Haven: Shoe String Press.
Wheeler, R. E. M., Ghosh, A., and Deva, K. 1946. Arikamedu: an Indo-Roman Trading Station on the East Coast of India, *Ancient India*, ii, 17–25.
White, J. P. 1972. *Ol Tumbuna. Archaeological Excavations in the Eastern Central Highlands, Papua New Guinea* (Terra Australis no. 2). Canberra, Australian National Univ.
Willems, W. J. A. 1940. Preliminary Report on the Excavation of an Urn-burial Ground at Sa'bang, near Palopo, Central Celebes, in *Proc. of Third Congress of Prehistorians of the Far East 1938*, (ed.) F. N. Chasen and M. W. F. Tweedie, pp. 207–8. Singapore.
Williams-Hunt, P. D. R. 1950. Irregular Earthworks in Eastern Siam: an air survey, *Antiquity*, xxiv (93), 30–6.
— 1952. Archaeological Discoveries in Malaya 1951, *JMBRAS*, xxv (1), 186–8.
Winstedt, R. O. 1941. Slab Graves and Iron Implements, *JMBRAS*, xix (1), 93–8.
Wolters, O. W. 1967. *Early Indonesian Commerce: A Study of the Origins of Srivijaya*. Ithaca, Cornell Univ. Press.
— 1973. Jayavarman II's military power: the territorial foundation of the Angkor empire, *JRAS*, (no. 1), 21–30.
— 1974. Northwestern Cambodia in the Seventh Century, *Bull. of School of Oriental and African Studies, London*, xxvvii, 2, 355–84
Worman, E. C., Jnr. 1949. Samrong Sen and the Reconstruction of Prehistory in Indochina, *Southwestern Journal of Anthropology*, v (4), 318–29.
Yu, Y. 1967. *Trade and Expansion in Han China*. Berkeley and Los Angeles, Univ. of California Press.
Zimmer, H. 1955. *The Art of Indian Asia*. New York, Bollinger.
Zaharah binti Haji Mahmud. 1970. The period and nature of 'traditional' settlement in the Malay Peninsula, *JMBRAS*, xliii (1), 81–113.
Zwierzycki, J. 1926. Een vondst uit de palaeolithische cultuurperiode in een grot in Boven-Djambi, *De Mijningenieur*, vii, 63–7.

SUPPLEMENT

A. Unpublished Theses

Alkire, K. n.d. *A Comparison of Pottery and Related Artifacts at Three Prehistoric Sites in Malaya.* M.A. Univ. of Malaya, Kuala Lumpur.

Bayard, D. T. n.d. *A Course Toward What? Evolution, Development and Change at Non Nok Tha, Northeastern Thailand.* Ph.D. Univ. of Hawaii, Honolulu.

Beirling, J. 1969. *Migration towards Melanesia: a Re-evaluation.* B.A. Dept. of Anthropology, Univ. of Sydney.

Buchan, R. A. n.d. *The Three-Dimensional Jig-Saw Puzzle: a Ceramic Sequence from Northeast Thailand.* M.A. Univ. of Otago, Dunedin.

Dunn, F. L. 1971. *Rain-Forest Collectors and Traders: a Study of Resource Utilization in Modern and Ancient Malaya.* Ph.D. Univ. of Malaya, Kuala Lumpur.

Glover, I. C. 1972. *Excavations in Timor: a study of economic change and culture continuity in prehistory.* Ph.D. Australian National Univ., Canberra.

Matthews, J. 1964. *The Hoabinhian in Southeast Asia and Elsewhere.* Ph.D. Australian National Univ., Canberra.

Wetherill, E. 1971. *The Fauna of Chansen.* M.A. Univ. of Pennsylvania, Philadelpia.

B. Articles and papers to appear

Bayard, D. T. Phu Wiang Pottery and the Prehistory of Northeastern Thailand, in *Readings in SEA Prehistory,* (ed.) I. C. Glover. London, Seminar Press.

Lewis, D. Voyaging Stars: aspects of Polynesian and Micronesian Navigation, *Phil. Trans. R. Soc. Lond.,* A 276. (In press.)

Macknight, C. C. The nature of early maritime trade: some points for analogy from the eastern part of the eastern Archipelago, *World Archaeology,* v (2). (In press.)

Saurin, E. and Carbonnel, J. P. Récents developpements de la Préhistoire indochinoise, *Paléorient,* forthcoming issue.

C. Papers presented to Conferences, not yet published

Bayard, T. D. appear. An Early Indigenous Bronze Technology in Northeast Thailand: Its Implications for the Prehistory of East Asia. Paper presented at 28 Int. Congress of Orientalists, Canberra, 8th Jan. 1971: to appear in *Proceedings,* in press.

Fox, B. The Philippine Palaeolithic: Ninth International Congress of Anthropological and Ethnological Sciences, Chicago, 1973.

Fox, R. B. and Peralta, J. T. Preliminary Report on the Palaeolithic Archaeology of Cagayan Valley, Philippines, and the Cabalwanian Industry: Seminar on Southeast Asian Prehistory and Archaeology, Manila, 1972.

Loofs, H. H. E. Diffusion of Early Pottery in Southeast Asia: Some Suggestions: Seminar on the Diffusion of Material Culture at the 28th International Congress of Orientalists, Canberra, 1971.

Lopez, S. M. Contributions to the Pleistocene Geology of Cagayan Valley, Philippines, I: Geology and Palaeontology of Liwan Plain: Seminar on Southeast Asian Prehistory and Archaeology, Manila, 1972.

Soejono, R. P. The distribution of types of bronze axes in Indonesia: Seminar on the Diffusion of Material Culture at the 28th International Congress of Orientalists, Canberra, 1971.

Solheim, W. G. II. Early pottery in northern Thailand and conjectures on its relationships: Seminar on the Diffusion of Material Culture at the 28th International Congress of Orientalists, Canberra, 1971.

Sutayasa, M. The study of prehistoric pottery in Indonesia: Paper presented at the 45th ANZAAS Congress, Section 25, Perth, 1973.

Vidya Intakosai. Painted pottery at Ban-Chiang, northeast Thailand: Seminar on Southeast Asian Prehistory and Archaeology, Manila, 1972.

Index

MINERAL DEPOSITS
IN SOUTH EAST ASIA

● Gold
○ Tin
△ Lead
▲ Copper
□ Iron

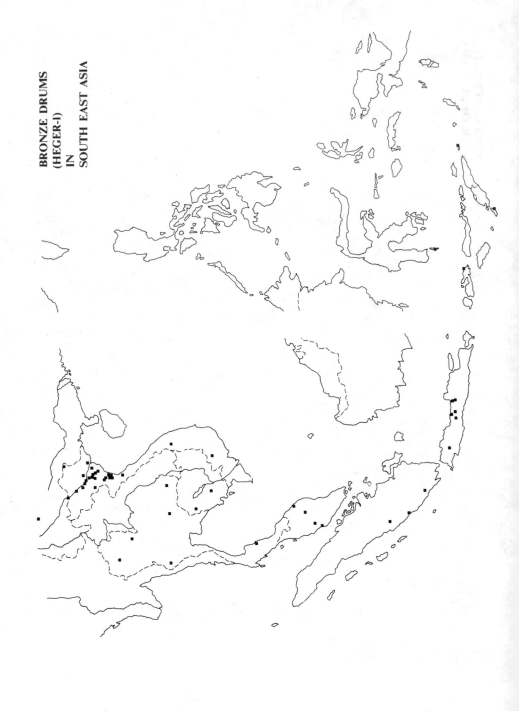

BRONZE DRUMS
(HEGER-I)
IN
SOUTH EAST ASIA

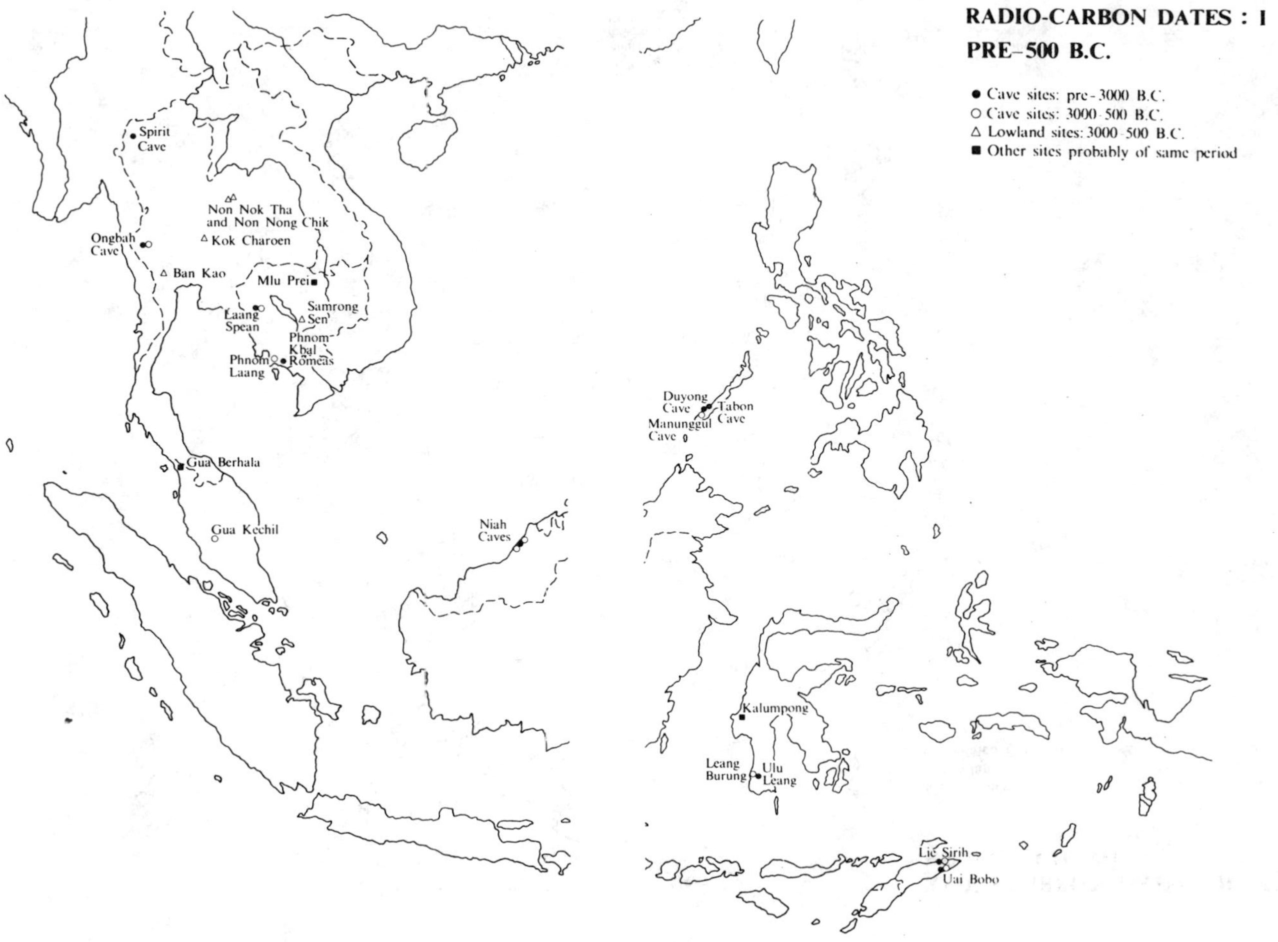

RADIO-CARBON DATES : 1
PRE–500 B.C.

● Cave sites: pre–3000 B.C.
○ Cave sites: 3000–500 B.C.
△ Lowland sites: 3000–500 B.C.
■ Other sites probably of same period

Spirit
Cave

Onghah
Cave

Non Nok Tha
and Non Nong Chik

△ Kok Charoen

△ Ban Kao

Mlu Prei

Sumrong
Sen △

Laang
Spean

Phnom
Khul
Phnom Romeas
Laang

Gua Berhala

Gua Kechil

Niah
Caves

Duyong
Cave   Tabon
Manunggul Cave
Cave ○

Kalumpang

Leang
Burung Leang

Ulu
Leang

Lie Siriti

Uai Bobo

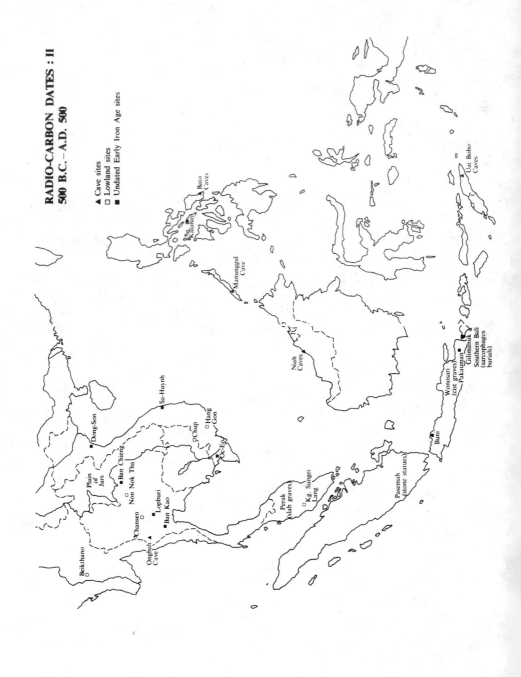

RADIO-CARBON DATES : II
500 B.C. – A.D. 500

▲ Cave sites
□ Lowland sites
■ Undated Early Iron Age sites

Beikthano

Plain of Jars

Dong-Son

Ban Chieng

Non Nok Tha

Chansen

Lopburi

Ban Kao

Onglah Cave

Sa-Huynh

Hang Gon

9Chup

Oc-Eo

Perak (slab graves)

Kg. Sungei Lang

Pasemah (stone statues)

Buni

Wonosari (cist graves)

Pakauman

Gilimanuk

Southern Bali (sarcophagus burials)

Niah Caves

Manunggul Cave

Kalanay

Tabon Caves

Ulai Bobo Caves

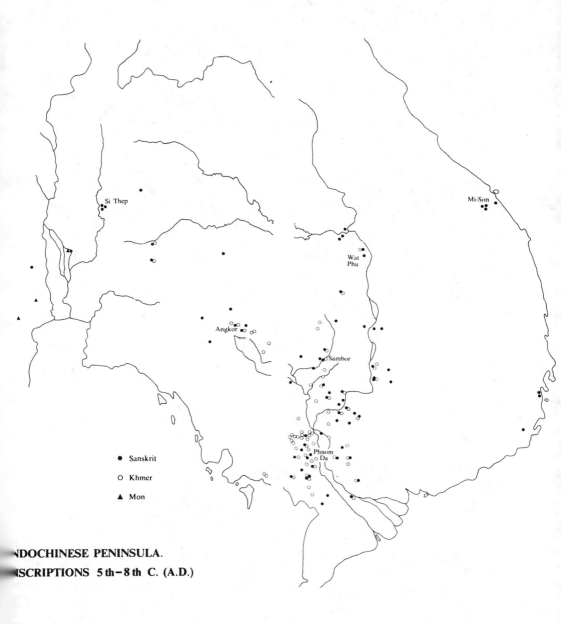

Si Thep

Mi-Son

Wat
Phu

Angkor

Sambor

Phnom
Da

● Sanskrit

○ Khmer

▲ Mon

NDOCHINESE PENINSULA.

ISCRIPTIONS 5th–8th C. (A.D.)